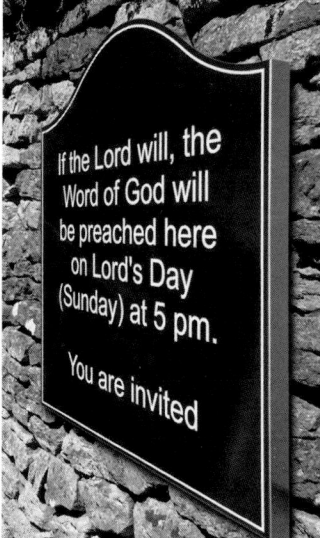

works through local partners in over 50 countries to eradicate poverty and promote justice. We do this through long term development work and campaigning as well as responding to natural and man-made natural disasters.

The Church of Scotland is committed to this work by sponsoring Christian Aid.

To become a committed giver:
ring 0131 220 1254 for details.

 We believe in life before death

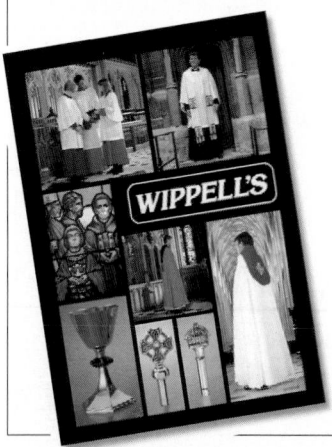

The Right Reverend Alan D. McDonald LLB BD MTh

MODERATOR

The Church of Scotland
YEAR BOOK
2006/2007

Editor
Rev. Ronald S. Blakey
MA BD MTh

Published on behalf of
THE CHURCH OF SCOTLAND
by SAINT ANDREW PRESS
121 George Street, Edinburgh EH2 4YN

THE OFFICES OF THE CHURCH

121 George Street	Tel: 0131-225 5722
Edinburgh EH2 4YN	Fax: 0131-220 3113
	Internet: http://www.churchofscotland.org.uk/

Office Hours:	Monday–Friday 9:00am–5:00pm
Office Manager:	Mrs Dorothy H. Woodhouse

MISSION AND DISCIPLESHIP COUNCIL

Glasgow Office	59 Elmbank Street, Glasgow G2 4PQ	0141-352 6946
Inverness Office	Main Street, North Kessock, Inverness IV1 3XN	01463 731712
Perth Office	Arran House, Arran Road, Perth PH1 3DZ	01738 630514

SOCIAL CARE COUNCIL

Charis House	47 Milton Road East, Edinburgh EH15 2SR	Tel: 0131-657 2000
	[E-mail: info@charis.org.uk]	Fax: 0131-657 5000

SCOTTISH CHARITY NUMBERS

The Church of Scotland	SCO11353
The Church of Scotland General Trustees	SCO14574
The Church of Scotland Investors Trust	SCO22884
The Church of Scotland Trust	SCO20269

QUICK DIRECTORY

A.C.T.S.	01259 216980
Bridgeton, St Francis-in-the-East Church House	0141-554 8045
Carberry	0131-665 3135/7604
Christian Aid London	020 7620 4444
Christian Aid Scotland	0131-220 1254
Church of Scotland Insurance Co. Ltd	0131-220 4119
Glasgow Lodging House Mission	0141-552 0285
Kirk Care	0131-225 7246
Netherbow	0131-556 9579/2647
Media Relations Unit (Press Office)	0131-240 2243
Safeguarding Office (item 36 in Assembly Committee list)	0131-240 2256
Scottish Churches Parliamentary Office	0131-558 8137
Year Book Editor	01899 229226

Pulpit Supply: Fees and Expenses
Details of the current fees and related expenses in respect of Pulpit Supply will be found as the last item in Section 1, number 3 (the Ministries Council) on page 9.

First published in 2006 by SAINT ANDREW PRESS, 121 George Street, Edinburgh EH2 4YN on behalf of the CHURCH of SCOTLAND

ISBN 0 86153 374 7

British Library Cataloguing in Publication Data
   A catalogue record for this book is available from the British Library.
Printed and bound by Bell and Bain Ltd, Glasgow

CONTENTS

All correspondence regarding the *Year Book* should be sent to
The Editor, *Church of Scotland Year Book*,
Saint Andrew Press, 121 George Street, Edinburgh EH2 4YN
Fax: 0131-220 3113
[E-mail: yearbookeditor@cofscotland.org.uk]

GENERAL ASSEMBLY OF 2007
The General Assembly of 2007 will convene on
Saturday, 19th May 2007

FROM THE MODERATOR

I confess I have quite a collection of *Church of Scotland Year Books*, dating back to the year when I was licensed to preach the Gospel. I have always found the *Year Book* to be a trusty companion and an invaluable assistance in ministry.

It is my privilege and pleasure this year to be able to thank the editor, Rev. Ronald S. Blakey, for all the hard work and painstaking detail that goes into producing this book. I cannot even begin to imagine how it is possible to edit a volume like this. However, I am encouraged by the knowledge that in our vocation we have all been given different gifts. It is the editor's attention to detail that is so particularly impressive in the pages of the red book.

Nobody is quite sure about the derivation of the phrase 'The devil is in the detail'. However, one thing is sure. As followers of the crucified and risen one, we don't believe that phrase to be true. On the contrary, we believe that God is in the detail. We believe in an incarnate God who is involved in all aspects of life and is passionately interested in every little thing. Furthermore, we are sure that the derivation of the phrase that enables us is taken from holy scripture, in the prologue to John's Gospel: 'The Word became flesh, and dwelt among us, full of grace and truth' (John 1:14). The Word lives among us – not only, for example, near Biggar, but, more precisely, in Broughton, Glenholm and Kilbucho (H) linked with Skirling linked with Stobo and Drumelzier linked with Tweedsmuir (H). Savour the detail.

Alan D. McDonald
July 2006

FROM THE EDITOR

In response to requests received, the current regulations in respect of Pulpit Supply fees and related expenses are included as the last item in Section 1, number 3, the Ministries Council.

Over the past twelve months, a number of correspondents have suggested that the *Year Book* would be rendered more user-friendly if the various Councils and Committees indicated in rather more detail than of late the particular responsibilities of named members of staff. It was felt that this would ensure that, where information was required, contact could at once be made with the right person. This comment was passed to Council and Committee Secretaries, and in many cases there has been a positive response.

The Assembly this year converted into a Standing Law of the Church the Overture anent Presbytery Membership. A few Presbyteries have already implemented some of its terms; most have not had time to do so. This does mean that, for this year, there will not be total consistency in regard to those who appear in section B of their Presbytery lists or further on in Sections 6-H and 6-I. The overriding aim of the *Year Book* was that no-one should be mislaid altogether.

There have been several amendments made in recent times to the Act dealing with 'Procedure in a Vacancy'. The new text is included in this volume. It is hoped that those required to implement this procedure will furnish themselves with the updated text and will not, as can happen, rely on whatever edition of the *Year Book* is nearest to hand at the time.

The school magazines which this writer still knows best are those that covered his school years in Glasgow. As befitted a school steeped in the classics, there was each year a 'Verb Sap' feature in which it was just about permitted to show members of staff warts and all, always provided that the words used came from the finest literary pens. (For any – surely none? – who ponder the meaning of 'verb sap', these seven letters stand for 'verbum sapienti', a word to the wise, or, as it might be in a modern translation, 'a nod is as good as a wink'.) So, for example, our raconteur art master was aptly outlined in words of Washington Irving: 'I am always at a loss to know how much to believe of my own stories'. A somewhat absent-minded science teacher was not unreasonably rewarded with words of Robert Louis Stevenson: 'I have a grand memory for forgetting'. The head of modern languages was wont to play his violin on almost any pretext; his skills had clearly not impressed everyone, as he was attached to this from Charles Dickens: 'in came a fiddle, tuned like fifty stomach-aches'. Our popular but rotund janitor was well captured in words of Keats: 'I cannot see what flowers are at my feet'.

Andrew Herron used to tell of a dinner at which he was to speak where the toast list employed the Verb Sap technique to highlight the guests. As the long-serving Presbytery Clerk of Glasgow, Andrew was compared to Tennyson's Brook: 'Men may come and men may go, but I go on for ever'. In fact, that was not too far wide of the mark a generation and more ago, when it did seem that Presbytery Clerks were as steadfast as they were immovable. Looking back only as far as the 1929 Union of the Churches, there would appear to have been some thirty clerks with periods in office in excess of twenty-five years. Two, indeed, truly went the second mile. The Rev. John T. Guthrie, ordained and inducted to Cullen Old in April 1937, became Clerk to the Presbytery of Fordyce in 1946 and held office through a number of Presbytery boundary and name changes until 1986. The Rev. David A. Williams, ordained and inducted to Stenness in Orkney in April 1944, was appointed Clerk to his Presbytery in 1949 and held that office until 1994.

This is the seventh *Year Book* for which this editor has been responsible. It perhaps says something about the increasing administrative, regulatory, legislative, pastoral and technical burdens that now go with the job of Clerk that, in that comparatively short time, no fewer than twenty-seven of today's forty-five Presbyteries have seen at least one change of Clerk.

Courteous attention has been drawn to the fact that, in last year's *Year Book*, the Lord High Commissioner was listed as one of the 'Officials of the General Assembly'. Clearly, this is incorrect, as the Lord High Commissioner is the Queen's representative at the Assembly. The Palace will be reassured to know that this error was reported by one of Her Majesty's Household in Scotland (Ecclesiastical). There is the added satisfaction that this confirms that members of that august body eschew the impulsive knee-jerk response to such a mistake, preferring rather to take time to establish that the error is no mere passing aberration. The entry in question had appeared in the *Year Book* each year since 1968.

With whatever truth, it has been said that Maurice Chevalier, the French film and vaudeville star who died in 1972, well nigh carved out a new career for himself in the number of final farewell performances that he gave. In last year's *Year Book*, the Editorial paid deserved tribute to the contribution that Sandy Gemmill had made to this publication over many years. It was worded as a final thank-you, since he had intimated that he was retiring imminently from the Church Offices. This writer is by no means alone in rejoicing that Sandy has been rather longer in going than had been threatened, so that in fact he again collated most of the statistics which appear towards the back of this book. It is not clear how many farewells Chevalier took of his fans; but it would be a considerable comfort to think that Sandy, for all that he received this year the Moderator's thanks in the Assembly, might yet decide to make a spirited attempt on that record.

In *Variations on a Philosopher*, written in 1950, Aldous Huxley ventures the thought that 'most human beings have an almost infinite capacity for taking things for granted'. Whether or not that is as generally true as he suggests, it is almost certainly correct in regard to editors who fondly imagine that all of their readers are fully familiar with each and every page of their publications, undertaking regular refresher courses to ensure that nothing escapes the memory. For some ten years, the *Year Book* has included in the Presbytery Lists, alongside qualifying churches, a variety of letters such as (H) or (L) or (GD). The key to these abbreviations has, over the same period, appeared in the preface to the Presbytery Lists. The assumption appears to have been that new users of the volume would know intuitively either what these abbreviations mean or, failing that, where the key was to be found. A recent enquiry to the editor's desk served as a reminder that this is not always so. In this instance, the letters (H) and (L) were proving a test of inventiveness. In fact, they record, respectively, where a church has installed a Hearing Aid Loop system and where a Chair Lift is available. It did, however, encourage the mind to speculate as to what a first-time reader, in a state of blissful ignorance, might imagine these letters indicated – High Church or Low Church; a church with heating that has a three-star rating for efficiency; a church with lighting that almost makes reading the pew Bibles easy; a preacher who is a hell-raiser or laid-back; a minister who is hard-working or . . .? Huxley is never to be underrated as a thinker; but perhaps the astute politician Benjamin Disraeli is nearer the practical truth. In a speech delivered on 5 October 1864, he said quite simply: 'Never take anything for granted'.

Ronald S. Blakey
July 2006

SECTION 1

Assembly Councils, Committees, Departments and Agencies

INDEX OF ASSEMBLY COUNCILS, COMMITTEES, DEPARTMENTS AND AGENCIES

[Note: Years, where given, indicate the year of appointment]

1. THE COUNCIL OF ASSEMBLY

Remit

1. To implement the plan of reorganisation and structural change of the Agencies of the General Assembly as formulated by the Assembly Council and approved by the General Assembly of 2004.

2. To monitor, evaluate and co-ordinate the work of the Agencies of the General Assembly, within the context of policy determined by the Assembly.

3. To advise the General Assembly on the relative importance of work being undertaken by its various Agencies.

4. To receive reports from, offer guidance to and issue instructions to Agencies of the General Assembly as required from time to time on matters of management, organisation and administration.

5. To bring recommendations to the General Assembly concerning the total amount of the Church's Co-ordinated Budget for the following financial year and the disposition thereof among Local Mission, Parish Staffing and the Mission and Renewal Fund.

6. To determine the allocation of the total budgets for the following financial year for Parish Staffing and the Mission and Renewal Fund among the relevant Agencies of the General Assembly and Ecumenical Bodies.

7. To prepare and present to the General Assembly an indicative Rolling Budget for the following five financial years.

8. To receive and distribute unrestricted legacies and donations among the Agencies of the General Assembly with power to specify the use to which the same are to be applied.

9. To consider and decide on proposals from Agencies of the General Assembly to purchase heritable property or any other asset (except investments) valued in excess of £50,000 or lease any heritable property where the annual rental exceeds £10,000 per annum, declaring that no Agency save those referred to in section 19 hereof shall proceed to purchase or lease such property without prior approval from the Council.

10. To consider and decide on proposals from Agencies of the General Assembly, save those referred to in section 19 hereof, to sell or lease for a period in excess of five years or otherwise dispose of any heritable property, or sell or otherwise dispose of any asset (except investments) valued in excess of £50,000, held by or on behalf of that Agency, with power to allocate all or part of the sale or lease proceeds to another Agency or Agencies in terms of section 11 hereof.

11. To reallocate following upon consultation with the Agency or Agencies affected unrestricted funds held by or on behalf of any of the Agencies of the General Assembly to another Agency or Agencies with power to specify the use to which the same are to be applied.

12. To determine staffing and resourcing requirements of Agencies of the General Assembly, including inter-Departmental sharing or transfer of staff, in accordance with policies drawn up by the Council of Assembly in line with priorities approved by the General Assembly, it being declared that the term 'staffing' shall not include those appointed or employed to serve either in particular Parishes or overseas.

13. To consult with the relative Councils and Agencies in their appointment of Council Secretaries to the Church and Society, Ministries, Mission and Discipleship, Social Care and World Mission Councils, to appoint the Ecumenical Officer, the Director of Stewardship, the Head of Media Relations and the Personnel Manager and to nominate individuals to the General Assembly for appointment to the offices of Principal Clerk of the General Assembly,

Depute Clerk of the General Assembly, General Treasurer of the Church and Solicitor of the Church.
14. To keep under review the central administration of the Church, with particular regard to resolving issues of duplication of resources.
15. To provide an Internal Audit function to the General Assembly Councils, Statutory Corporations and Committees (other than the Social Care Council).
16. To attend to the general interests of the Church in matters which are not covered by the remit of any other Agency.
17. To deal with urgent issues arising between meetings of the General Assembly, provided that:
    (a)   these do not fall within the jurisdiction of the Commission of Assembly or of any Presbytery or Kirk Session,
    (b)   they are not of a legislative or judicial nature and
    (c)   any action taken in terms of this clause shall be reported to the next General Assembly.
18. To encourage all Agencies of the General Assembly to work ecumenically wherever possible and to have regard to the international, evangelical and catholic nature of the Church.
19. For the avoidance of doubt, sections 9 and 10 shall not apply to the Church of Scotland General Trustees, the Church of Scotland Housing and Loan Fund for Retired Ministers and Widows and Widowers of Ministers and the New Charge Development Committee and its successor body, all of which may deal with heritable property and other assets without the approval of the Council.

Membership
(a)   Convener, Vice-Convener and eight members appointed by the General Assembly; the General Treasurer and the Solicitor of the Church; the Principal Clerk as Secretary to the Council; together with:
(b)   the Conveners of the Councils, namely Church and Society, Ministries, Mission and Discipleship, Social Care, Support and Services, and World Mission; the Secretaries of the following Councils, namely Church and Society, Ministries, Mission and Discipleship, Social Care and World Mission.

Convener: Mrs Helen McLeod MA (2004)
Vice-Convener: Rev. Gilbert Nisbet CA BD (2004)
Secretary: The Principal Clerk

2. THE CHURCH AND SOCIETY COUNCIL

Remit
The remit of the Church and Society Council is to facilitate the Church of Scotland's engagement with, and comment upon, national, political and social issues through:
•   the development of theological, ethical and spiritual perspectives in the formulation of policy on such issues;
•   the effective representation of the Church of Scotland in offering on its behalf appropriate and informed comment on political and social issues;
•   the building, establishing and maintaining of a series of networks and relationships with leaders and influence-shapers in civic society, and engaging long-term in dialogue and the exchange of ideas with them;

- the support of the local church in its mission and engagement by offering professional and accessible resources on contemporary issues;
- the conducting of an annual review of progress made in discharging the remit and the provision of a written report to the Council of Assembly.

Membership
Convener, Vice-Convener, 28 members appointed by the General Assembly, one of whom will also be appointed to the Ecumenical Relations Committee, and one member appointed from and by the Social Care Council and the Guild. The Nomination Committee will ensure that the Council membership contains at least five individuals with specific expertise in each of the areas of Education, Societal/Political, Science and Technology and Social/Ethical. This number may include the Convener and Vice-Convener of the Council.

Convener: Mrs Morag Mylne (2005)
Vice-Convener: Mr David Alexander (2005)
Secretary: Rev. Dr David I. Sinclair

3. THE MINISTRIES COUNCIL
Tel: 0131-225 5722; Fax: 0131-240 2201
E-mail: ministries@cofscotland.org.uk

Remit
The remit of the Ministries Council is recruitment, training and support of recognised ministries for the mission of the Church, and assessment of patterns of national deployment of parish ministries. In pursuance of this remit, the Council is charged with:
- developing patterns of ministry which allow the Church of Scotland to be effective in its missionary calling and faithful to the one ministry of Jesus Christ;
- recruiting individuals of the highest calibre collaboratively to lead the Church through its ordained ministries;
- providing the Church with a range of ministries including the ministry of word and sacrament, the diaconate, auxiliary ministers, readers and specialist workers;
- developing assessment processes which ensure that those who serve the Church in its various ministries do so in response to God's call on their life;
- providing education, initial training, in-service training and personal-development appraisal of the highest quality to ensure that all those engaged in the various ministries of the Church are equipped to engage in Christ's mission and make the Gospel relevant in a rapidly changing society;
- building good relationships with, and offering quality pastoral support and care to, all the ministries of the Church;
- assisting the whole Church in its responsibility to meet the gospel imperative of giving priority to the poorest and most marginalised in our society;
- undertaking all of its local planning and appraisal work in full co-operation with Presbyteries, local congregations and other denominations, in order to ensure that emerging patterns of church life are effective at a local level and are a viable use of the Church's resources;
- evaluating all developments in ministry in order to ensure their effectiveness and relevance to the life of the Church today;

- working transparently and in collaboration with the other Councils in order to ensure the most effective use of the Church's finance, property and human resources;
- conducting an annual review of progress made in discharging the remit and providing a written report to the Council of Assembly.

Membership

Convener, three Vice-Conveners, 34 members appointed by the General Assembly, one of whom will also be appointed to the Ecumenical Relations Committee, and one member appointed from and by the General Trustees, the Housing and Loan Fund, the Committee on Chaplains to Her Majesty's Forces and the Diaconate Council. For the avoidance of doubt, where a representative of these other bodies is a member of staff, he or she will have no right to vote.

Convener:	Rev. R. Douglas Cranston MA BD
Vice-Conveners:	Rev. David Clark MA BD
	Rev. James S. Dewar MA BD
	Rev. Graham S. Finch MA BD

Staff

Council Secretary:	Rev. Dr Martin Scott DipMusEd RSAM BD PhD (Tel: ext. 389; E-mail: mscott@cofscotland.org.uk)

Pastoral Adviser and
  Associate Secretary:
  (Ministries Development)
	Rev. John P. Chalmers BD
	(Tel: ext. 309; E-mail: jchalmers@cofscotland.org.uk)

Associate Secretary: (Planning and Deployment)	Mr John Jackson BSc (Tel: ext. 312; E-mail: jjackson@cofscotland.org.uk)
Associate Secretary: (VGET*)	Mrs Moira Whyte MA (Tel: ext. 266; E-mail: mwhyte@cofscotland.org.uk)
Priority Areas Support Worker:	Rev. Dr H. Martin J. Johnstone MA BD MTh PhD (Tel: 0141-423 3760; E-mail: priorityareas@ukuumail.com)
Ministries Support Officers:	Mrs Elizabeth Chalmers BA (Tel: ext. 348; E-mail: lchalmers@cofscotland.org.uk) Rev. Jane Denniston MA BD (Tel: ext. 204; E-mail: jdenniston@cofscotland.org.uk) Rev. Gavin J. Elliott MA BD (Tel: ext. 255; E-mail: gelliott@cofscotland.org.uk) Mr Garry Leach BD BSc (Tel: ext. 242; E-mail: gleach@cofscotland.org.uk) Rev. Angus R. Mathieson MA BD (Tel: ext. 315; E-mail: amathieson@cofscotland.org.uk) Mrs Suzie Stark (Tel: ext. 225; E-mail: sstark@cofscotland.org.uk) Mr John Thomson (Tel: ext. 248; E-mail: jthomson@cofscotland.org.uk)
Property and Safety Officer:	Mr Colin Wallace (Tel: ext. 352; E-mail: cwallace@cofscotland.org.uk)

* VGET – Vocational Guidance Education and Training

Ministries Council
Further information about the Council's work and services is obtainable through the Ministries Council at the Church Offices. Information is available on a wide range of matters including the Consolidated Stipend Fund, National Stipend Fund, endowment grants, travelling and other expenses, pulpit supply, study leave, ministry development conferences, pastoral care services (including occupational health), Enquiry and Assessment, Education and Training, Parish Appraisal, Priority Areas, New Charge Development, Area Team Ministry, Interim Ministry, Readership, Chaplaincies, the Diaconate, Parish Staffing, and all aspects of work connected with ministers and the ministry of word and sacrament.

Committees
The policy development and implementation of the work of the Ministries Council is managed under the following committees:

1.   Council Executive
Convener: Rev. R. Douglas Cranston MA BD
The Executive's function is to link the Council to the work of its Committees (listed below), to ensure the integrated implementation of the Council's strategy and, further, to ensure that the Council's work is contained within agreed budgets.
    The following Committees work in conjunction with the Executive:

1.1.   Assessment Scheme Committee
Convener: Rev. Lezley J. Kennedy BD ThM MTh
The Assessment Scheme Committee is responsible for overseeing and reviewing the Enquiry and Assessment Process for full-time and auxiliary ministers of word and sacrament, deacons and readers, together with the admission and readmission of ministers. The Committee has powers to make final recommendations on suitability for training, to undertake Committee reviews, recruit and train assessors and directors, and liaise with Presbyteries.

1.2   Candidate Supervision Committee
Convener: Rev. Donald Macleod BD LRAM DRSAM
The Candidate Supervision Committee is responsible for the supervision of those in training for the recognised ministries of the Church, and the production of training reports. It operates with powers to sustain placements, liaise with universities, recruit and train supervisors, arrange placements, deliver residential and conference programmes, liaise with Presbyteries, engage in review of candidature, and oversee the completion of other Church requirements in relation to recognised ministries.

1.3   Parish Appraisal Committee (see also separate entry at number 29)
Convener: Rev. David Clark MA BD
The Parish Appraisal Committee, in accordance with the overall policy of the Council, undertakes full responsibilities and rights in connection with the implementation of Act IV 1984, Act VII 2003, Act VIII 2003 and equivalent subsequent legislation. It is responsible for dealing with all matters coming from Presbytery regarding planning and vacancies, and deals with proposals for the staffing needs of parishes. It determines, in consultation with the Presbyteries concerned, and following detailed discussion with the Council, where new charges should be established, or where, as a result of significant change in an existing charge, an alternative location for the place of worship is deemed desirable. In addition, it is available, when requested, to assist and advise Presbyteries in regard to their own forward and readjustment planning.

1.4 Ministries Development Committee

Convener: Rev. Graham S. Finch MA BD

The Ministries Development Committee is responsible for implementing the Council's policies on pastoral care for all recognised ministries, including liaison with the Medical Panel, the integration of Occupational Health with ministries support services, and the oversight of the working of those Acts relating to Long-Term Illness of Ministers in Charge. It is responsible for the promotion of development opportunities for those engaged in recognised ministries, including study leave and accompanied review. It deals with the work of Interim Ministry, New Charge Development and Area Team Ministry, and with all aspects of chaplaincy work.

1.5 Ministries Finance Committee

Convener: Rev. Jeff A. McCormick BD

The Ministries Finance Committee operates with powers to deal with the Parish Ministries Fund, the National Stipend Scheme, Vacancy Schedules, Maintenance Allowances, Hardship Grants and Bursaries, Stipend Advances, management of investments, writing-off shortfalls and the granting of further endowments. It also maintains an oversight of the budgets for all recognised ministries.

1.6 Priority Areas Strategy Group

Convener: Rev. Ian F. Galloway BA BD

The Priority Areas Strategy Group implements the policy of the Council in developing, encouraging and overseeing strategy within priority areas parishes. It is empowered to develop resources to enable congregations to make appropriate responses to the needs of people living in poverty in their parishes, and to raise awareness of the effects of poverty on people's lives in Scotland. It also co-ordinates the strategy of the wider Church in its priority to Scotland's poorest parishes.

The Council also has several *ad hoc* Task Groups, which report to the Committees and implement specific policies of the Council, as follows:

Accompanied Review Task Group
Leader: Rev. Karen K. Watson BD MTh

Conference and Development Task Group
Leader: Miss Ann Lyall DCS

Interim Ministries Task Group
Leader: Rev. James Reid BD

Chaplaincies Task Group
Leader: Prof. Peter Howie

Communications Task Group
Leader: Rev. Malcolm I.G. Rooney DPE BEd BD

Curriculum Development Task Group
Leader: Rev. Peter White BVMS BD

Pastoral and Spiritual Care Task Group
Leader: Rev. Barry W. Dunsmore MA BD

Employment Issues Task Group
Leader: Mr Grant Gordon

New Charge Development Task Group
Leader: Rev. Norman Smith MA BD

Chaplains to HM Forces
See separate entry at number 10.

Housing and Loan Fund
See separate entry at number 21.

Pulpit Supply: Fee and Expenses
The General Assembly of 1995 approved new regulations governing the amount of Supply Fee and Expenses. These were effective from 1 July 1995 and are as follows:
1. In Charges where there is only one diet of worship, the Pulpit Supply Fee shall be a Standard Fee of £47 (or as from time to time agreed by the Ministries Council).
2. In Charges where there are additional diets of worship on a Sunday, the person fulfilling the Supply shall be paid £10 for each additional Service (or as from time to time agreed by the Ministries Council).
3. Where the person is unwilling to conduct more than one diet of worship on a given Sunday, he or she shall receive a pro-rata payment based on the total available Fee shared on the basis of the number of Services conducted.
4. The Fee thus calculated shall be payable in the case of all persons permitted to conduct Services under Act II 1986.
5. In all cases, Travelling Expenses shall be paid. Where there is no convenient public conveyance, the use of a private car shall be paid for at the Committee rate of Travelling Expenses. In exceptional circumstances, to be approved in advance, the cost of hiring a car may be met.
6. Where weekend board and lodging are agreed as necessary, these may be claimed for the weekend at a maximum rate of that allowed when attending the General Assembly. The Fee and Expenses should be paid to the person providing the Supply before he or she leaves on the Sunday.

---

4. THE MISSION AND DISCIPLESHIP COUNCIL

Remit
The remit of the Mission and Discipleship Council is:
* to take a lead role in developing and maintaining an overall focus for mission in Scotland, and to highlight its fundamental relationships with worship, service, doctrine, education and nurture;
* to take a lead role in developing strategies, resources and services in Christian education and nurture, recognising these as central to both mission and discipleship;
* to offer appropriate servicing and support nationally, regionally and locally in the promotion of nurturing, worshipping and witnessing communities of faith;
* to introduce policy on behalf of the Church in the following areas: adult education and

elder training, church art and architecture, congregational mission and development, doctrine, resourcing youth and children's work and worship;
- to establish and support the Mission Forum with representatives of relevant Councils;
- to encourage appropriate awareness of, and response to, the requirements of people with particular needs including physical, sensory and/or learning disabilities;
- to conduct an annual review of progress made in discharging the remit and provide a written report to the Council of Assembly.

Membership
Convener, three Vice-Conveners and 21 members appointed by the General Assembly, one of whom will also be appointed to the Ecumenical Relations Committee, the Director of Stewardship, one member appointed from and by the General Trustees, the Guild, the Parish Development Fund and the Scottish Churches Community Trust, and the Convener or Vice-Convener of the Committee on Church Art and Architecture as that Committee shall determine. The Nomination Committee will ensure that the Council membership contains at least three individuals with specific expertise in each of the areas of Education and Nurture, Mission and Evangelism and Worship and Doctrine.

Convener:	Rev. Angus Morrison MA BD PhD
Vice-Conveners:	Rev. Rosemary Frew (Mrs) MA BD
	Rev. Peter H. Donald MA PhD BD
	Rev. Jock Stein MA BD

Staff
Council Secretary:	Rev. Douglas A.O. Nicol MA BD
Associate Secretary: (Education and Nurture)	Mr Steve Mallon
Associate Secretary: (Mission and Evangelism)	Rev. Alex. M. Millar MA BD MBA
Associate Secretary: (Worship and Doctrine)	Rev. Nigel J. Robb FCP MA BD ThM MTh

Regional Development Officers
Regional Development Officers work with the Council and Associate Secretaries in developing and delivering quality resources for congregations. Based in Regional Offices in Inverness, Glasgow and Perth, the Officers appointed at the time of going to print are:

Rev. Andrew B. Campbell BD DPS MTh	Perth
Rev. David E.P. Currie BSc BD	Glasgow
Ms Fiona H. Fidgin BEd	Perth
Rev. Richard Gibbons BD	Inverness
Rev. Robin J. McAlpine BDS BD	Perth
Rev. Linda Pollock BD MTh	Inverness
Mrs Sheilah Steven	Glasgow
Mr Phil Wray BSc MSc	Glasgow

The Netherbow: Scottish Storytelling Centre: The integrated facilities of the **Netherbow Theatre** and the **John Knox House Museum**, together with the **Scottish Storytelling Centre**, are an important cultural and visitor centre on the Royal Mile in Edinburgh and provide advice and assistance nationally in the use of the arts in mission, education and worship. 'Story Source', 'Script Aid' and other resources are available. Contact the Director, The Netherbow: Scottish Storytelling Centre, 43–45 High Street, Edinburgh EH1 1SR (Tel: 0131-556 9579/2647; Website: www.storytellingcentre.org.uk).

The Well Asian Information and Advice Centre: The Council provides support and funding for the Presbytery of Glasgow's innovative project that serves the south side of Glasgow by assisting with welfare, housing, immigration, asylum and personal problems. The Well has a strong mission basis on the clear principles that sharing the love of Christ has to include accepting people for who they are and respecting the beliefs of others. A regular prayer letter is available. Contact The Well, 48–50 Albert Road, Glasgow G42 8DN (Tel: 0141-424 4523; Fax: 0141-422 1722; E-mail: the.well@btinternet.co.uk). See further under **Mission and Evangelism Task Group**.

Life and Work
(Tel: 0131-225 5722; Fax: 0131-240 2207; E-mail: magazine@lifeandwork.org)
Life and Work is the Church of Scotland's monthly magazine. Its purpose is to keep the Church informed about events in church life at home and abroad and to provide a forum for Christian opinion and debate on a variety of topics. It has an independent editorial policy. Contributions which are relevant to any aspect of the Christian faith are welcome.

The price of *Life and Work* this year is £1.60. With a circulation of around 38,000, it also offers advertisers a first-class opportunity to reach a discerning readership in all parts of Scotland. See further under **Publishing Committee**.

Saint Andrew Press
(Tel: 0131-240 2253; Fax: 0131-220 3113; E-mail: acrawford@cofscotland.org.uk)
Saint Andrew Press is the Church of Scotland's publishing house. In 2005, the Council of Assembly announced that the Church's two separate publishing operations, previously known as Saint Andrew Press and Scottish Christian Press, would be merged. The single new publishing house trades under the name of Saint Andrew Press. This is a very positive move for the Church's publishing house, enabling it to focus its creativity and harness combined resources to obtain maximum benefit for the Church and for its message of the Kingdom of God.

Saint Andrew Press produces a wide range of publications including Church of Scotland stationery and publications in the field of Christian education and parish resourcing. It publishes the series of New Testament commentaries, *The New Daily Study Bible* by the late Professor William Barclay, which has been read by many millions of people around the world. Best-sellers include *A Glasgow Bible* by Jamie Stuart, *Outside Verdict* by Harry Reid, *Iona* by Kenneth Steven and *Silent Heroes* by John Miller. Other popular titles include *Practical Caring* by Sheilah Steven, *Will You Follow Me?* by Leith Fisher, and *Common Order* and *Common Ground* from the Church of Scotland Panel on Worship. Up-to-date information can currently be found at www.churchofscotland.org.uk/standrewpress and www.scottishchristianpress.org.uk

All new proposals should be sent to the Head of Publishing in the form of a two-page description of the book and its readership, together with one sample chapter. Saint Andrew Press staff are always happy to offer professional help and advice. See further under **Publishing Committee**.

Committee on Church Art and Architecture
Membership
The Committee shall comprise a Convener, Vice-Convener and ten members appointed by the General Assembly.

Remit
This Committee replaces the Committee on Artistic Matters and will take forward that Committee's remit, which is in the following terms:

The Committee advises congregations and Presbyteries regarding the most appropriate way of carrying out renovations, alterations and reordering of interiors, having regard to the architectural quality of Church buildings. It also advises on the installation of stained glass, tapestries, memorials, furniture and furnishings, and keeps a list of accredited artists and craftsworkers.

Any alteration to the exterior or interior of a Church building which affects its appearance must be referred to the Committee for approval, which is given through the General Trustees. Congregations contemplating alterations are urged to consult the Committee at an early stage.

Members of the Committee are prepared, when necessary, to visit churches and meet office-bearers. The Committee's services are given free.

The Committee seeks the conservation of the nation's heritage as expressed in its Church buildings, while at the same time helping to ensure that these buildings continue to serve the worship and witness of the Church in the present day.

In recent years, the General Assembly has conferred these additional duties on the Committee:
1. preparation of reports on the architectural, historical and aesthetic merit of the buildings of congregations involved in questions of readjustment
2. verification of the propriety of repair and renovation work forming the basis of grant applications to public bodies
3. the offering of advice on the maintenance and installation of organs
4. facilitating the transfer of unwanted furnishings from one church to another through the quarterly *Exchange and Transfer*
5. the compilation of a Register of Churches
6. the processing of applications from congregations for permission to dispose of surplus communion plate, and the carrying out of an inventory of sacramental vessels held by congregations.

Education and Nurture Task Group
Individual Christians motivated and equipped for mission and service
This is the aim of the Task Group, and this ideal underpins all that we do. Our task is to create and to encourage learning opportunities in local churches and to provide national events and programmes alongside these that enhance what's going on in the local situation.

We work in the following areas:
*   Children's Ministry (Linda Pollock): lpollock@cofscotland.org.uk
*   Youth Ministry (Steve Mallon): smallon@cofscotland.org.uk
*   Adult Learning (Fiona Fidgin): ffidgin@cofscotland.org.uk
*   Elder Training (Sheilah Steven): ssteven@cofscotland.org.uk

In addition, we have the following key areas of concern for which we have established working groups:
*   Membership in the Church
*   Supporting people with learning difficulties
*   Adult learning and spirituality
*   Developing educational resources with Saint Andrew Press.

We also seek to continue to support Guild Educational Representatives in their vital role of providing and supporting learning at local Guild meetings around Scotland.

The Task Group is also responsible for the National Youth Assembly which meets each year in September, and supports the Youth Representatives who attend the General Assembly every May. In addition, we work alongside the BB for the Crossover children's and youth event every June.

New programmes coming on stream in 2006–7 will be:
*   Cosycoffeehouse – a kit for local churches to create an authentic coffee-house experience for younger teenagers
*   Digital Witness – new resources created by young people themselves

- Children's and Youth Ministry Trainers – local-resource people to encourage local workers
- Junior Youth Assembly – a forum for 'tweenagers' who want to get involved in the life of the Church of Scotland.

The Task Group is convened by the Rev. Jock Stein. Steve Mallon is the Associate Secretary for Education and Nurture.

Mission and Evangelism Task Group (METAG)
The Mission and Evangelism Task Group, within the Mission and Discipleship Council, operates with the following remit:
- *To encourage* local initiatives;
- *To offer* expertise, research, development and training;
- *To assist* local churches to be mission-focused;
- *To be alert to* new opportunities in today's Scotland; and lastly,
- *To identify* those shifts occurring in theological thinking and reflection that hint at something new, and to consider their appropriateness or otherwise in a Scottish context.

The Convener of the Task Group (Rev. Rosemary Frew) is a Vice-Convener of the Council; its Secretary (Rev. Alex. M. Millar) can be contacted by telephone at 0131-225 5722: ext. 307 or by e-mail at amillar@cofscotland.org.uk

The Task Group has the following priorities:
- **EMERGING CHURCH** (to explore the development of emerging patterns of church in the changing cultural scene that is contemporary Scotland);
- **RURAL CHURCH** (to support rural churches in outreach and community engagement);
- **CONFIDENCE IN SHARING AND SPEAKING ABOUT WHAT WE BELIEVE** (to seek to build confidence in personal witness and faith sharing through resources and training);
- **INTERFAITH** (to promote the development of interfaith relations, supported by The Well Asian Information and Advice Centre in Glasgow); and
- **IMPACT** (to sponsor and recommend the locally based children's and youth work that is undertaken through the programme and to develop it further).

Publishing Committee
Membership
Convener, Vice-Convener and eight members appointed by the General Assembly. The Head of Publishing shall act as Secretary to the Committee, and the Editor of *Life and Work* shall also be in attendance, both on a non-voting basis.

Remit
The remit of the Publishing Committee is:
- to oversee Saint Andrew Press, including the taking of all related commercial decisions, and to receive regular reports on the Press's operation from the Head of Publishing;
- to monitor pricing and delivery of published materials to Councils of the General Assembly and the use by such Councils of Saint Andrew Press;
- to monitor the cost of printing and related activities by Councils and Agencies and to make recommendations to the Council of Assembly's Budget Group on whether any or all of these activities should be outsourced;
- to oversee the publishing of *Life and Work* and to take all relevant commercial decisions affecting the magazine. For the avoidance of doubt, it is expressly declared that, in order to protect the magazine's editorial independence, the *Life and Work* Advisory Committee shall come within the aegis of the Council of Assembly through the Council's Communication Committee;

- to operate within a budget approved by the Council of Assembly and provided by the Mission and Renewal Fund, as augmented by surpluses generated by Saint Andrew Press, and to determine the balance between revenue-earning and subsidised activities within that budget;
- to report quarterly to the Council of Assembly's Budget Group.

Worship and Doctrine Task Group
The Worship and Doctrine Task Group, within the Mission and Discipleship Council, will have responsibility for the remits of the former Panels on Worship and on Doctrine.

The Panel on Worship existed to witness to the importance of worship as a primary function of the Church. In this, the Panel
- was concerned with the provision of worship materials for public use, being responsible for the production of *Common Order* and *Pray Now*;
- encouraged courses and retreats to promote spiritual growth;
- encouraged new developments in church music and the training of musicians;
- was engaged in providing materials for worship in Gaelic;
- was involved in the compilation of new hymn books and supplements;
- published occasional papers on aspects of the practice of public worship.

The Panel on Doctrine was required to:
- fulfil remits from the General Assembly on matters concerning doctrine;
- draw the attention of the Assembly to matters inside the Church of Scotland or elsewhere which might have significant doctrinal implications, with recommendations for action;
- be available for consultation by other Committees of the General Assembly on any matter which might be of doctrinal significance;
- communicate and consult in an ecumenical context on matters involving doctrine.

---

5. THE SOCIAL CARE COUNCIL
SOCIAL CARE (CrossReach)
Charis House, 47 Milton Road East, Edinburgh EH15 2SR
Tel: 0131-657 2000; Fax: 0131-657 2000
E-mail: info@crossreach.org.uk; Website: www.crossreach.org.uk

The Social Care Council, known as CrossReach, provides social-care services as part of the Christian witness of the Church to the people of Scotland.

Remit
The remit of the Social Care Council is:
- as part of the Church's mission, to offer services in Christ's name to people in need;
- to provide specialist resources to further the caring work of the Church;
- to identify existing and emerging areas of need, to guide the Church in pioneering new approaches to relevant problems and to make responses on issues arising within the area of the Council's concern through appropriate channels such as the Church's Church and Society Council, the Scottish Executive and the like;
- to conduct an annual review of progress made in discharging the remit and provide a written report to the Council of Assembly.

Membership
31 members; 28 appointed by the General Assembly, plus Convener and two Vice-Conveners. They attend meetings of the Council three times a year in February, June and October, and may be asked to serve on one of the two committees.

Convener: Rev. David L. Court (2005)
Vice-Conveners: Rev. David I. Souter (2006)
                      Mrs Elizabeth Millar (2006)

Staff
Director of Social Work: Mr Alan Staff
                           (E-mail: alan.staff@crossreach.org.uk)
Deputy Director: Mr James Maguire
                           (E-mail: james.maguire@crossreach.org.uk)

Management Structure
The management structure is service-based. There are six Heads of Service, each with specialist areas of responsibility. They are supported by Principal Officers who have lead roles for particular types of service and client groups.

Head of Service (Older People):   Marlene Smith (marlene.smith@crossreach.org.uk)
Principal Officers: Brenda Fraser (East)
                                   Allan Logan (West)

Head of Service (Children and
   Families, Criminal Justice and
   Learning Disabilities):   Paul Robinson (paul.robinson@crossreach.org.uk)
Principal Officers: David Clark
                                   George McNeilly

Head of Service (Addictions,
   Mental Health, Homelessness
   and Counselling):   Calum Murray (calum.murray@crossreach.org.uk)
Principal Officers: Flora Mackenzie
                                   Gerard Robson
                                   Dominic Gray (part-time)

Head of Service (Planning and
   Development):   Jeannette Deacon (jeannette.deacon@crossreach.org.uk)
Principal Officers: Greg Dougal
                                   Graham Lumb

Head of Service (Finance):   Robert Nelson (robert.nelson@crossreach.org.uk)
Principal Officers: Philip Chan
                                   Alastair Purves

Head of Service
   (Human Resources):   Peter Bailey (peter.bailey@crossreach.org.uk)
Principal Officers: Jane Allan
                                   Mari Rennie

| IT Manager: | Yvonne Farrant (yvonne.farrant@crossreach.org.uk) |

IT Manager: Yvonne Farrant (yvonne.farrant@crossreach.org.uk)

Estates Manager: David Reid (david.reid@crossreach.org.uk)

Fundraising, Marketing and
  Communications Manager: Pam Taylor (pam.taylor@crossreach.org.uk)

(Heads of Service can be contacted via Charis House on 0131-657 2000. Calum Murray is based at the Regional Office in Perth on 01738 783200.)

List of Services
CrossReach operates over 80 services across Scotland, and a list of these can be obtained from Charis House on 0131-657 2000, or from the CrossReach website: www.crossreach.org.uk

Fundraising, Marketing and Communications
Manager: Pam Taylor (pam.taylor@crossreach.org.uk)
Publicity, Marketing and Communications
  Officer: Hugh Brown (hugh.brown@crossreach.org.uk)
Volunteer Development Co-ordinator: Maggie Hunt (maggie.hunt@crossreach.org.uk)

The Fundraising, Marketing and Communications department encompasses the functions of fundraising, media and public relations, publicity, congregational liaison and volunteer development. Fundraising aims to increase income development for the Council's work to ensure the long-term sustainability of our valuable care services across Scotland. We want to inform people about our mission, and work with those who are the most needy in our society. We invite people to donate money to support all our work and to volunteer their time – either to fundraise or to help carry out essential tasks of all kinds. We also ask people to pray with us about our services; to help them do that, a free prayer letter is produced three times a year. You can also keep up to date with the latest news about CrossReach by receiving our free newspaper *Circle of Care*, which has a print run of 40,000 copies three times a year. If you would like to know more about any of the above work, or be added to our mailing list, please contact the FM&C team at Charis House on 0131-657 2000.

Congregational Contacts
Congregational Contacts are the link people between CrossReach and local churches. Each church should have an appointed Contact who receives mailings three times a year. There are currently over 1,000 Congregational Contacts. They undertake work in a variety of ways. They provide current, correct and appropriate information to their Church. They often act as distributors for the *Circle of Care* newspaper and act as agents for our calendar, Christmas card and merchandise. Church members are the most important part of the 'Circle of Care' provided by the Church of Scotland. It's the caring work in the communities of Scotland which is our largest area of service provision. Congregational Contacts provide the vital link between the formal services provided by CrossReach and the community work and prayers of the local churches, and we greatly appreciate the work done by these volunteer champions.

Speakers for Guilds and other Groups
Members of CrossReach staff will gladly visit congregations and other Church organisations to talk about our work. To request a speaker, please write to the FM&C team at Charis House, 47 Milton Road East, Edinburgh EH15 2SR.

6. THE SUPPORT AND SERVICES COUNCIL

Remit
The Support and Services Council will provide a network for its component Committees which report direct to the General Assembly. The remit of the Council is:
* to provide opportunities for consultation among its component committees with a view to identifying and eliminating areas of overlap and duplication of work and resources;
* to elect a Convener who will represent the Council on the Council of Assembly;
* to receive and consider annual reports from component committees on progress made in discharging their remits and transmit these to the Council of Assembly.

Membership
The Conveners and Vice-Conveners of the following Committees:
* Assembly Arrangements
* Central Services
* Ecumenical Relations
* Legal Questions
* Stewardship and Finance
* Safeguarding
together with (as non-voting members):
* The Principal Clerk
* The Depute Clerk
* The Solicitor of the Church
* The General Treasurer
* The Director of Stewardship
* The Ecumenical Officer
* The Head of the Safeguarding Office.

Staff
Minutes Secretary: Rev. Marjory A. MacLean LLB BD PhD
The Council shall meet annually within two weeks of the close of the General Assembly to elect a Convener who shall be one of the constituent committee conveners and a Vice-Convener who may be drawn from the convener or vice-convener members. Secretarial support will be provided by an appropriate member of administrative staff from within the area. The Convener may serve for up to a maximum of four years and the Vice-Convener for up to three years, both positions to be confirmed annually. Other meetings of the Council may be held as required.
Convener: Rev. William C. Hewitt BD DipPS
Vice-Convener: Mrs Vivienne A. Dickson CA

Assembly Arrangements Committee
See separate entry at number 8.

Central Services Committee
See separate entry at number 9.

Ecumenical Relations Committee
See separate entry at number 17.

General Treasurer's Department
See separate entry at number 19.

Human Resources Department
See separate entry at number 31.

Information Technology Department
See separate entry at number 22.

Law Department
See separate entry at number 23.

Legal Questions Committee
See separate entry at number 24.

Office Manager's Department
See separate entry at number 27.

Principal Clerk's Department
See separate entry at number 32.

Stewardship and Finance Committee
See separate entry at number 34.

---

7. THE WORLD MISSION COUNCIL
Tel: 0131-225 5722; Fax: 0131-226 6121
Answerphone: 0131-240 2231
E-mail: info@world-mission.org
Website: www.world-mission.org

Remit
The remit of the World Mission Council is:

- to give life to the Church of Scotland's understanding that it is part of Jesus Christ's Universal Church committed to the advance of the Kingdom of God throughout the world;
- to discern priorities and form policies to guide the Church of Scotland's ongoing worldwide participation in God's transforming mission, through the Gospel of Jesus Christ;
- to develop and maintain mutually enriching relationships with the Church of Scotland's partner churches overseas through consultation in the two-way sharing of human and material resources;
- to equip and encourage Church of Scotland members at local, Presbytery and national levels to become engaged in the life of the world Church;
- to help the people of Scotland to appreciate the worldwide nature of the Christian faith;
- to keep informed about the cultural, political, social, economic, religious and ecclesiastical issues of relevance to worldwide mission;
- to recruit, train and support paid staff and volunteers to work overseas;
- to direct the work of the Council's centres in Israel;
- to foster and facilitate local partnerships between congregations and Presbyteries and the partner churches;

- to undertake the responsibilities of the former Board of World Mission in regard to the Church's Overseas Charges and the Presbytery of Europe and its congregations as set out in the relevant Assembly legislation;
- to conduct an annual review of progress made in discharging the remit and provide a written report to the Council of Assembly.

Membership
Convener, two Vice-Conveners, 24 members appointed by the General Assembly, one of whom will also be appointed to the Ecumenical Relations Committee, and one member appointed by the Presbytery of Europe.

Convener: Rev. Colin Renwick BMus BD (2006)
Vice-Conveners: Dr Fiona Burnett BSc PhD (2005)
                       Mr Leon Marshall CA (2006)

Departmental Staff
Secretary: Rev. Prof. Kenneth R. Ross BA BD PhD
Associate Secretaries: Mr Walter Dunlop ARICS (Israel/Palestine and
                          Locally Supported Partnerships)
                       Mr Sandy Sneddon (Centrally Supported Partnerships)
                       Carol Finlay RGN RMN OIPCNE MSc (Local Development)

Finance: Mrs Anne Macintosh BA CA (General Treasurer's Department)

Personnel: Miss Sheila Ballantyne MA PgDipPm

Strategic Commitments: 2006–10
Mission in a New Mode – Local to Local
- **Evangelism** – working with partner churches on new initiatives in evangelism
- **Reconciliation** – working for justice, peace and reconciliation in situations of conflict or threat
- **The Scandal of Poverty** – resourcing the Church to set people free from the oppression of poverty.

Partnership Priorities
Following a consultation with partner churches held in St Andrews in September 1999, the then Board of World Mission identified the following priority areas for partnership in mission:
1. **Theological Education:** developing ministerial and lay training at appropriate levels in all our churches.
2. **Evangelism:** helping one another to create new models and launch new initiatives to take the Gospel to all people.
3. **Holistic Mission:** enabling one another to respond with Christian compassion to human needs in our rapidly changing societies.
4. **Mission in Pluralistic Societies:** strengthening Christian identity in our multi-religious and multi-cultural societies by supporting one another and sharing our experiences.
5. **Prophetic Ministry:** inspiring one another to discern and speak God's Word in relation to critical issues which arise in our times.
6. **Human and Material Resources:** finding new and imaginative ways of sharing our resources at all levels of Church life.

World Mission and World Resources
Sharing in the mission of God worldwide requires a continuing commitment to sharing the Church of Scotland's resources of people and money for mission in six continents as contemporary evidence that it is 'labouring for the advancement of the Kingdom of God throughout the world' (First Article Declaratory). Such resource-sharing remains an urgent matter because most of our overseas work is in the so-called 'Third World', or 'South', in nations where the effects of the widening gap between rich and poor is *the* major issue for the Church. Our partner churches in Africa, most of Asia, the Caribbean and South and Central America are desperately short of financial and technical resources, which we can to some extent meet with personnel and grants. However, they are more than willing to share the resources of their Christian faith with us, including things which the Church in the West often lacks: enthusiasm in worship, hospitality and evangelism, and a readiness to suffer and struggle for righteousness, and in many areas a readiness to sink denominational differences. Mutual sharing in the world Church witnesses to its international nature and has much to offer a divided world, not least in Scotland.

Vacancies Overseas
The Council welcomes enquiries from men and women interested in serving in the Church overseas. Vacancies for mission partner appointments in the Church's centrally supported partnerships, the World Exchange volunteer programme and opportunities with other organisations can all be considered. Those interested in more information are invited to write to the Personnel Manager in the first instance.

HIV/AIDS Project
On the Report of the Board of World Mission, the General Assembly of 2002 adopted an HIV/AIDS Project to run from 2002 to 2007. The 2006 General Assembly extended the Project to 2010. The Project aims to raise awareness in congregations about the impact of HIV/AIDS and seeks to channel urgently needed support to partner churches. For further information, contact the Co-ordinator, HIV/AIDS Project, 121 George Street, Edinburgh EH2 4YN.

Jubilee Scotland
The Council plays an active role in the coalition which works within Scotland for the cancellation of unpayable international debt. For further information, contact the Co-ordinator, Jubilee Scotland, 41 George IV Bridge, Edinburgh EH1 1EL (Tel: 0131-225 4321; Fax: 0131-225 8861; E-mail: mail@jubileescotland.org.uk).

Christian Aid Scotland
Christian Aid is an official relief development agency of churches in Britain and Ireland. Christian Aid's mandate is to challenge and enable us to fulfil our responsibilities to the poor of the world. Half a million volunteers and collectors and nearly 200 paid staff make this possible, with money given by millions of supporters. The Church of Scotland marks its commitment as a Church to this vital part of its mission through an annual grant from the Mission and Renewal Fund, transmitted through the World Mission Council which keeps in close touch with Christian Aid and its work.

Up-to-date information about projects and current emergency relief work can be obtained from:

- The National Secretary: Mr Gavin McLellan, Christian Aid Scotland, 41 George IV Bridge, Edinburgh EH1 1EL (Tel: 0131-220 1254)
- The four Area Co-ordinators:
  Edinburgh: Mrs Shirley Brown, 41 George IV Bridge, Edinburgh EH1 1EL (Tel: 0131-220 1254)

Glasgow: Ms Diane Green/Ms Eildon Dyer, 759A Argyle Street, Glasgow G3 8DS (Tel: 0141-221 7475)

Ayrshire: Mrs Ailsa Henderson, 10 Ferry Row, Fairlie, Largs KA29 0AJ (Tel: 01475 568585)

Perth: Miss Marjorie Clark, Perth Christian Centre, 28 Glasgow Road, Perth PH2 0NX (Tel: 01738 643982)

- The Director: Dr Daleep Mukarji, Christian Aid Office, PO Box 100, London SE1 7RT (Tel: 020 7620 4444)

Accommodation in Israel
The Church of Scotland has two Christian Residential Centres in Israel which provide comfortable accommodation for pilgrims and visitors to the Holy Land. Further information is available from:
(a)   St Andrew's Guest House, Jerusalem (PO Box 8619, Jerusalem)
       (Tel: 00 972 2 6732401; Fax: 00 972 2 6731711; E-mail: standjer@netvision.net.il)
(b)   The Scots Hotel, St Andrew's, Galilee, Tiberias (PO Box 104, Tiberias)
       (Tel: 00 972 4 6710710; Fax: 00 972 4 6710711; E-mail: scottie@netvision.net.il)

A list of Overseas Appointments will be found in List K in Section 6.

A *World Mission Year Book* is available with more details of our partner churches and of people currently serving abroad, including those with ecumenical bodies and para-church bodies.

A list of Retired Missionaries will be found in List L in Section 6.

---

8. Assembly Arrangements Committee

Membership
Convener, Vice-Convener and ten members appointed by the General Assembly on the Report of the Nomination Committee; the Convener and Vice-Convener also to serve as Convener and Vice-Convener of the General Assembly's Business Committee.

The Clerks are non-voting members of the Assembly Arrangements Committee, and the Moderator and Moderator Designate are members of the Committee.

Convener: Rev. William C. Hewitt BD DipPS
Vice-Convener: Rev. A. David K. Arnott MA BD
Secretary: The Principal Clerk

Remit
The Committee's remit is:
- to make all necessary arrangements for the General Assembly;
- to advise the Moderator on his or her official duties if so required;
- to be responsible to the General Assembly for the care and maintenance of the Assembly Hall and the Moderator's flat;
- to be responsible to the General Assembly for all arrangements in connection with the letting of the General Assembly Hall;
- to conduct an annual review of progress made in discharging the remit and provide a written report to the Support and Services Council.

9. Central Services Committee

Membership
(13 members: nine appointed by the General Assembly, and four *ex officiis* and non-voting, namely the Principal Clerk, the Solicitor of the Church, the General Treasurer and the Human Resources Manager)
Convener: Rev. Anne R. Lithgow MA BD (2005)
Vice-Conveners: Mrs Pauline E.D. Weibye MA DPA MCIPD (2006)
                     Rev. Douglas S. Paterson MA BD (2006)

Staff
Administrative Secretary: Mrs Pauline Wilson BA
                            (E-mail: pwilson@cofscotland.org.uk)

Remit
- To be responsible for the proper maintenance and insurance of the Church Offices at 117–123 George Street and 21 Young Street, Edinburgh ('the Church Offices');
- To be responsible for matters relating to Health and Safety within the Church Offices;
- To be responsible for matters relating to Data Protection within the Church Offices and with respect to the General Assembly Councils based elsewhere;
- To be responsible for the allocation of accommodation within the Church Offices and the annual determination of rental charges to the Councils and other parties accommodated therein;
- To oversee the delivery of central services to departments within the Church Offices, to Councils of the General Assembly and, where appropriate, to the Statutory Corporations, Presbyteries and Congregations, namely:
  1. Those facilities directly managed by the Office Manager;
  2. Information Technology (including the provision of support services to Presbytery Clerks);
  3. Insurance;
  4. Purchasing;
  5. Human Resources;
  6. Financial Services (as delivered by the General Treasurer's Department);
  7. Legal Services (as delivered by the Law Department and subject to such oversight not infringing principles of 'client/solicitor' confidentiality);
  8. Media Relations Services (as delivered by the Media Relations Unit);
  9. Design Services (as delivered by the Design Services Unit);
  10. Property Services.
- The Committee shall act as one of the employing agencies of the Church and shall, except in so far as specifically herein provided, assume and exercise the whole rights, functions and responsibilities of the former Personnel Committee;
- While the Committee shall *inter alia* have responsibility for determining the terms and conditions of the staff for whom it is the employing agency, any staff who are members of the Committee or who are appointed directly by the General Assembly shall not be present when matters solely relating to their own personal terms and conditions of employment/office are under consideration;
- To conduct an annual review of progress made in discharging this remit and provide a written report to the Support and Services Council.

10. Chaplains to HM Forces

Convener: Rev. James Gibson TD LTh LRAM
Vice-Convener: Rev. John Shedden CBE BD DipPSS
Secretary: Mr Douglas M. Hunter WS, Henderson Boyd Jackson, Exchange Tower,
                   19 Canning Street, Edinburgh EH3 8EH.

Recruitment
The Chaplains' Committee is entrusted with the task of recruitment of Chaplains for the Regular, Reserve and Auxiliary Forces. Vacancies occur periodically, and the Committee is happy to receive enquiries from all interested ministers.

Forces Registers
The Committee maintains a Register of all those who have been baptised and/or admitted to Communicant Membership by Service Chaplains.

At the present time, registers are being meticulously prepared and maintained. Parish Ministers are asked to take advantage of the facilities by applying for Certificates from the Secretary of the Committee.

Full information may be obtained from the Honorary Secretary, Mr Douglas M. Hunter, Henderson Boyd Jackson, Exchange Tower, 19 Canning Street, Edinburgh EH3 8EH (Tel: 0131-228 2400).

A list of Chaplains may be found in List B in Section 6.

---

11. Church of Scotland Guild

National Office-bearers and Executive Staff
Convener: Mrs Lesley McCorkindale MA
Vice-Convener: Mrs Ann Bowie
General Secretary: Mrs Alison Twaddle MA JP
                       (E-mail: atwaddle@cofscotland.org.uk)
Information Officer: Mrs Fiona J. Punton MCIPR
                       (Tel: 0131-225 5722 ext. 317; 0131-240 2217;
                       E-mail: fpunton@cofscotland.org.uk)

The Church of Scotland Guild is a movement within the Church of Scotland whose aim is '**to invite and encourage both women and men to commit their lives to Jesus Christ and to enable them to express their faith in worship, prayer and action**'. Membership of the Guild is open to all who subscribe to that aim.

Groups at congregational level are free to organise themselves under the authority of the Kirk Session, as best suits their own local needs and circumstances. Large groups with frequent meetings and activities continue to operate with a committee or leadership team, while other, smaller groups simply share whatever tasks need to be done among the membership as a whole. Similarly, at Presbyterial Council level, frequency and style of meetings vary according to local needs, as do leadership patterns. Each Council may nominate one person to serve at national level, where five main committees take forward the work of the Guild in accordance with the stated Aim.

These committees are:

- Executive
- Finance and General Purposes
- Projects and Topics
- Programmes and Resources
- Marketing and Publicity

Other sub-groups meet on an *ad hoc* basis to plan particular events and conferences. There has always been a close relationship between the Guild and other Departments of the Church, and members welcome the opportunity to contribute to the Church's wider mission through the Project Partnership Scheme and other joint ventures. The Guild is represented on both the Church and Society Council and the Mission and Discipleship Council.

The project scheme affords groups at congregational level the opportunity to select a project, or projects, from a range of up to six, selected from proposals submitted by a wide range of Church Departments and other Church-related bodies. A project partner in each group seeks ways of promoting the project locally, increasing awareness of the issues raised by it, and encouraging support of a financial and practical nature. Support is offered by the Project Co-ordinator at Council level and by the Information Officer based at the Guild Office.

The Guild is very aware of the importance of good communication in any large organisation, and regularly sends mailings to its groups to pass on information and resources to the members. In addition, the Newsletter, sent to members three times per session, is a useful communication tool, as is the website www.cos-guild.org.uk. These are means of sharing both local news and experiences, and of communicating something of the wider interest and influence of the Guild, which is represented on other national bodies such as the Network of Ecumenical Women in Scotland and the Scottish Women's Convention.

Each year, the Guild follows a Theme and produces a resources pack covering worship and study material. There is also a related Discussion Topic with supporting material and background information. The theme, topic and projects all relate to a common three-year strategy which, for 2006–9, is **'Let's Live: Body, Mind and Soul'**. Each of the six current projects reflects some aspect of fullness of life. The 2006–7 theme is **'Honouring the Body'**, and Guilds are invited to explore this in a variety of ways. The related discussion topic is **'Let's Talk about Body Image'**, which addresses the obsession with outward appearances which dominates so much of the media and, sadly, can dominate so many lives.

---

12. Church of Scotland Investors Trust

Membership
(Trustees are appointed by the General Assembly, on the nomination of the Investors Trust)
Chairman: Mr D.M. Simpson BA FFA
Vice-Chairman: Mrs I.J. Hunter MA
Treasurer: Mr I.W. Grimmond BAcc CA
Deputy Treasurer: Mr W.J. McKean BAcc CA
Secretary: Mr F.E. Marsh MCIBS

Remit

The Church of Scotland Investors Trust was established in 1994 by Act of Parliament and has Scottish Charity Number SCO22884. It offers to Councils, Committees and congregations of the Church a simple and economical medium for the investment of their funds. Investors are at liberty to invest in the Church of Scotland Investors Trust to an unlimited extent. The Church of Scotland Investors Trust provides three Funds for Church investors:

1.   **THE DEPOSIT FUND** is intended for short-term investment and aims to provide a high rate of interest. Deposits are repayable on demand. Interest is calculated quarterly in arrears and paid gross on 15 May and 15 November. The Fund is invested mainly in short-term loans to Banks, Building Societies and Licensed Deposit-Taking Institutions. The Deposit Fund is professionally managed by Noble Grossart Limited, Edinburgh.

2.   **THE GROWTH FUND** is very largely equity-based and is intended for long-term investment. The Fund is operated on a unitised basis and aims to provide capital growth. Units can be purchased or sold monthly. Income is distributed gross on 15 May and 15 November. The Growth Fund is professionally managed by Newton Investment Management Limited, London.

3.   **THE INCOME FUND** is intended for medium-term investment and aims to provide immediate high income. The Fund is invested predominantly in fixed-interest securities and is operated on a unitised basis. Units can be purchased or sold monthly. Income is distributed gross on 15 March and 15 September. The Income Fund is professionally managed by Baillie Gifford & Company, Edinburgh.

Application forms for investment and further information may be had by writing to the Secretary of the Church of Scotland Investors Trust, 121 George Street, Edinburgh EH2 4YN (E-mail: fmarsh@cofscotland.org.uk).

---

13. Church of Scotland Pension Trustees

Chairman: Mr D.D. Fotheringham FFA
Vice-Chairman: Mr W.J. McCafferty ACII ASFA CIP
Secretary: Mrs S. Dennison BA

Staff

Pensions Manager: Mrs S. Dennison BA
Assistant Pensions Administrators: Mrs M. Marshall
                                       Mr M. Hannam

Remit

The body acts as Trustees for the Church of Scotland's three Pension Schemes:
1.   The Church of Scotland Pension Scheme for Ministers and Overseas Missionaries
2.   The Church of Scotland Pension Scheme for Staff
3.   The Church of Scotland Pension Scheme for the Board of National Mission.
The Trustees have wide-ranging duties and powers detailed in the Trust Law, Pension Acts and other regulations, but in short the Trustees are responsible for the administration of the Pension

Schemes and for the investment of the Scheme Funds. Six Trustees are appointed by the General Assembly, and members nominate up to three Trustees for each Scheme.

The investment of the Funds is delegated to external Investment Managers under the guidelines and investment principles set by the Trustees: Baillie Gifford & Co., Newton Investment Management Ltd and Tilney Fund Management.

The benefits provided by the three Pension Schemes differ in detail, but all provide a pension to the Scheme member and dependants on death of the member, and a lump-sum death benefit on death in service. Scheme members also have the option to improve their benefits by paying additional voluntary contributions (AVCs) to arrangements set up by the Trustees with leading Insurance Companies.

Further information on any of the Church of Scotland Pension Schemes or on individual benefits can be obtained from the Pensions Manager, Mrs S. Dennison, at the Church of Scotland Offices, 121 George Street, Edinburgh EH2 4YN (Tel: 0131-225 5722 ext. 206; Fax: 0131-240 2220; E-mail: sdennison@cofscotland.org.uk).

14. Church of Scotland Trust

Membership
(Members are appointed by the General Assembly, on the nomination of the Trust)
Chairman: Mr Christopher N. Mackay WS
Vice-Chairman: Mr Robert Brodie CB WS
Treasurer: Mr Iain W. Grimmond BAcc CA
Secretary and Clerk: Mrs Jennifer M. Hamilton BA

Remit
The Church of Scotland Trust was established by Act of Parliament in 1932 and has Scottish Charity Number SCO20269. The Trust's function since 1 January 1995 has been to hold properties outwith Scotland and to act as Trustee in a number of third-party trusts.

Further information can be obtained from the Secretary and Clerk of the Church of Scotland Trust, 121 George Street, Edinburgh EH2 4YN (Tel: 0131-240 2222; E-mail: jhamilton@ cofscotland.org.uk).

15. Committee on Church Art and Architecture

See entry in full under **The Mission and Discipleship Council** (number 4).

16. Committee Planning the Church Without Walls Celebration
(now renamed as Church Without Walls Group)

This group now sits within the Mission and Discipleship Council. Rev. Albert O. Bogle serves as Convener.

17. Ecumenical Relations Committee

Remit

- to advise the General Assembly on matters of policy affecting ecumenical relations;
- to ensure that the members on the Committee serving on the other Councils are appropriately informed and resourced so as to be able to represent the ecumenical viewpoint on the Council on which they serve;
- to ensure appropriate support for the Ecumenical Officer's representative function in the event of his or her absence, whether through illness, holidays or other commitments;
- to nominate people from across the work of the Church of Scotland to represent the Church in Assemblies and Synods of other churches, ecumenical consultations and delegations to ecumenical assemblies and so on;
- to call for and receive reports from representatives of the Church of Scotland attending Assemblies and Synods of other churches and those ecumenical conferences and gatherings which are held from time to time;
- to ensure that appropriate parts of such reports are made available to relevant Councils;
- to ensure that information is channelled from and to ecumenical bodies of which the Church of Scotland is a member;
- to ensure that information is channelled from and to other churches in Scotland and beyond;
- to ensure the continued development of ecumenical relations by means of the Web and other publications;
- to ensure personal support for the Ecumenical Officer;
- to approve guidelines for the setting up and oversight of Local Ecumenical Partnerships;
- to conduct an annual review of progress made in discharging this remit and provide a written report to the Support and Services Council.

Membership

a) Five members appointed by the General Assembly, each to serve as a member of one of the five Councils of the Church (excluding the Support and Services Council, on which the Convener of the Committee will sit).

b) Convener who is not a member of any of the other Councils and who will act as a personal support for the Ecumenical Officer, and Vice-Convener, appointed by the General Assembly.

c) A representative of the Roman Catholic Church in Scotland appointed by the Bishops' Conference and one representative from each of three churches drawn from among the member churches of ACTS and the Baptist Union of Scotland, each to serve for a period of four years.

d) The Committee may co-opt, as a full voting member, one of the four Church of Scotland representatives on the Scottish Churches' Forum.

e) The Committee shall co-opt Church of Scotland members elected to the central bodies of Churches Together in Britain and Ireland (CTBI), the Conference of European Churches (CEC), the World Council of Churches (WCC), the World Alliance of Reformed Churches (WARC) and the Community of Protestant Churches in Europe (CPCE, formerly the Leuenberg Fellowship of Churches).

f) The General Secretary of ACTS shall be invited to attend as a corresponding member.

g) For the avoidance of doubt, while, for reasons of corporate governance, only Church of Scotland members of the Committee shall be entitled to vote, before any vote is taken the views of members representing other churches shall be ascertained.

Convener: Rev. William D. Brown BD CQSW (2005)
Vice-Convener: Rev. Valerie J. Ott BA BD (2002)

Secretary: Rev. Sheilagh M. Kesting BA BD
Administrative Officer: Miss Rosalind Milne

INTER-CHURCH ORGANISATIONS

World Council of Churches

The Church of Scotland is a founder member of the World Council of Churches, formed in 1948. As its basis declares, it is 'a fellowship of Churches which confess the Lord Jesus Christ as God and Saviour according to the Scriptures, and therefore seek to fulfil their common calling to the Glory of the one God, Father, Son and Holy Spirit'. Its member Churches, which number over 300, are drawn from all continents and include all the major traditions – Eastern and Oriental Orthodox, Reformed, Lutheran, Anglican, Baptist, Disciples, Methodist, Moravian, Friends, Pentecostalist and others. Although the Roman Catholic Church is not a member, there is very close co-operation with the departments in the Vatican.

The World Council holds its Assemblies every seven years. The last, held in Porto Alegre, Brazil in February 2006, had the theme 'God, in your grace, transform the world'. At that Assembly, Mr Graham McGeoch was elected to the new Executive and to the Central Committee of the Council.

The World Council is taking forward the discussion among the churches on global economic justice. In June 2005, it hosted the Conference on World Mission and Evangelism in Athens, Greece. Currently, two documents are with the churches for study: 'The nature and mission of the church' and 'Christian perspectives on theological anthropology'.

The General Secretary is Rev. Dr Sam Kobia, 150 route de Ferney, 1211 Geneva 2, Switzerland (Tel: 00 41 22 791 61 11; Fax: 00 41 22 791 03 61; E-mail: nan@wcc-coe.org; Website: www.wcc-coe.org).

World Alliance of Reformed Churches

The Church of Scotland is a founder member of the World Alliance of Reformed Churches, which began in 1875 as 'The Alliance of the Reformed Churches Throughout the World Holding the Presbyterian System' and which now includes also Churches of the Congregational tradition. Today it is composed of more than 200 Churches in nearly 100 countries, with an increasing number in Asia. It brings together, for mutual help and common action, large Churches which enjoy majority status and small minority Churches. It engages in theological dialogue with other Christian traditions – Orthodox, Roman Catholic, Lutheran, Methodist, Baptist and so on. It is organised in three main departments – Co-operation with Witness, Theology and Partnership. The twenty-fourth General Council was held in Accra, Ghana, from 30 July to 12 August 2004. The theme was 'That all may have life in fullness'. Rev. Sandy Horsburgh was elected to the Executive Committee.

The General Secretary is Rev. Dr Setri Nyomi, 150 route de Ferney, 1211 Geneva 2, Switzerland (Tel: 00 41 22 791 62 38; Fax: 00 41 22 791 65 05; E-mail: sn@warc.ch; Website: www.warc.ch).

Conference of European Churches

The Church of Scotland is a founder member of the Conference of European Churches, formed in 1959 and until recently the only body which involved in common membership representatives of every European country (except Albania) from the Atlantic to the Urals. More than 100 Churches, Orthodox and Protestant, are members. Although the Roman Catholic Church is not a member, there is very close co-operation with the Council of European Catholic Bishops' Conferences. With the removal of the long-standing political barriers in Europe, the Conference has now opportunities and responsibilities to assist the Church throughout the continent to offer united witness and service.

It is currently engaged with the Council of Bishops' Conferences in Europe (CCEE) in a process of consultation and involvement with churches towards the Third European Ecumenical Assembly to be held in Sibiu, Romania in September 2007 under the theme 'The light of Christ shines on all'.

Its General Secretary is Rev. Dr Keith Clements, 150 route de Ferney, 1211 Geneva 2, Switzerland (Tel: 00 41 22 791 61 11; Fax: 00 41 22 791 03 61; E-mail: cec@cec-kek.org; Website: www.cec-kek.org).

CEC: Church and Society Commission

The Church of Scotland was a founder member of the European Ecumenical Commission for Church and Society (EECCS). The Commission owed its origins to the Christian concern and vision of a group of ministers and European civil servants about the future of Europe. It was established in 1973 by Churches recognising the importance of this venture. Membership included Churches and ecumenical bodies from the European Union. The process of integration with CEC was completed in 2000, and the name, Church and Society Commission (CSC), established. In Brussels, CSC monitors Community activity, maintains contact with MEPs and promotes dialogue between the Churches and the institutions. It plays an educational role and encourages the Churches' social and ethical responsibility in European affairs. It has a General Secretary, a study secretary and an executive secretary in Brussels and a small office in Strasbourg.

The General Secretary is Rev. Rudiger Noll, Ecumenical Centre, 174 rue Joseph II, B-1000 Brussels, Belgium (Tel: 00 32 2 230 17 32; Fax: 00 32 2 231 14 13; E-mail: mo@cec-kek.be).

Churches Together in Britain and Ireland (CTBI)

In September 1990, Churches throughout Britain and Ireland solemnly committed themselves to one another, promising to one another to do everything possible together. To provide frameworks for this commitment to joint action, the Churches established CTBI for the United Kingdom and Ireland, and, for Scotland, ACTS, with sister organisations for Wales and for England.

In 2006, CTBI ceased being a separate ecumenical instrument and became an agency of the four national ecumenical bodies. It is governed by Trustees appointed by the national instruments, is managed by the General Secretaries, will have a Church Leaders' Meeting and will have a significant annual gathering around its AGM. It retains two Commissions on Racial Justice and Interfaith Relations. It has three core portfolios – study, church and society, and interfaith – together with a communication officer.

The General Secretary of CTBI is Rev. Canon Bob Fyfe, Third Floor, Bastille Court, 2 Paris Garden, London SE1 8ND (Tel: 020 7654 7254; Fax: 020 7654 7222). The General Secretariat can be contacted by telephoning 020 7654 7211 (E-mail: gensec@ctbi.org.uk; Website: www.ctbi.org.uk).

Action of Churches Together in Scotland (ACTS)

ACTS was restructured at the beginning of 2003. The new structure comprises the Scottish Churches' Forum (replacing the Central Council) composed of Church representatives from trustee member Churches. There are four Networks: Church Life, Faith Studies, Mission, and Church and Society. Contributing to the life of the Networks will be associated ecumenical groups. Such groups are expressions of the Churches' commitment to work together and to bring together key people in a defined field of interest or expertise. ACTS is an expression of the commitment of the Churches to one another.

ACTS is staffed by a General Secretary, an Assistant General Secretary and two Network Officers. Their offices are based in Alloa.

These structures facilitate regular consultation and intensive co-operation among those who frame the policies and deploy the resources of the Churches in Scotland and throughout Britain and Ireland. At the same time, they afford greater opportunity for a wide range of members of different Churches to meet in common prayer and study.

The General Secretary is Rev. Dr Kevin Franz, 7 Forrester Lodge, Inglewood House, Alloa FK10 2HU (Tel: 01259 216980; Fax: 01259 215964; E-mail: kevinfranz@acts-scotland.org; Website: www.acts-scotland.org).

18. Education and Nurture Task Group

See entry in full under **The Mission and Discipleship Council** (number 4).

19. General Treasurer's Department

Staff

General Treasurer:		Mr Iain W. Grimmond BAcc CA
Deputy Treasurer:		Mr William J. McKean BAcc CA
Assistant Treasurers:	Congregational Support	Mr John S. Steven CA
	World Mission	Mrs Anne F. Macintosh BA CA
	General Trustees	Mr Robert A. Allan CIMA CIPFA
	Ministries	Mrs Pauline E. Willder MA PgDipIS
	Mission and Discipleship	Miss Catherine E. Robertson BAcc CA
Accountants:	Congregational Contributions	Mr Derek W.C. Cant FCCA
	Payroll and VAT	Mr Ross W. Donaldson
	Mission and Discipleship	Mr Steven R. Lane MA MAAT
	Ministries	Mrs K.C. Hastie BSc CA

Responsibilities of the General Treasurer's Department include:
* payroll processing for the Ministries Council and the Support and Services Council;
* calculating congregational allocations;
* issuing to congregations their annual requirement figures for the Ministries and Mission Allocation;
* receiving payments from congregations towards their central requirements;
* making Gift Aid tax recoveries on behalf of Councils, Committees and Statutory Corporations;
* making VAT returns and tax recoveries on behalf of Councils, Committees and Statutory Corporations and providing support, training and advice on financial matters to congregational treasurers;
* receiving and discharging legacies and bequests on behalf of Councils, Committees and Statutory Corporations;
* providing banking arrangements and operating a central banking system for Councils, Committees and Statutory Corporations;
* providing accountancy systems and services for Councils, Committees and Statutory Corporations and the Trustees of the Church's Pension Schemes;
* providing accounting and financial support for the Councils, Committees and Statutory Corporations.

20. General Trustees

Membership
(New Trustees are appointed, as required, by the General Assembly, on the recommendation of the General Trustees)
Chairman: Rev. James H. Simpson BD LLB (2003)
Vice-Chairman: Mr W. Findlay Turner CA (2003)
Secretary and Clerk: Mr David D. Robertson LLB NP
Depute Secretary and Clerk: Mr T.R.W. Parker LLB

Committees:
Fabric Committee
Convener: Rev. James A.P. Jack BSc BArch BD DMin RIBA ARIAS
                                   (2004)

Chairman's Committee
Convener: Rev. James H. Simpson BD LLB (2003)

Glebes Committee
Convener: Rev. William Paterson BD (2003)

Finance Committee
Convener: Mr W. Findlay Turner CA (2004)

Audit Committee
Convener: Dr J. Kenneth Macaldowie LLD CA (2005)

Law Committee
Convener: Mr C. Noel Glen BL NP (2004)

Staff
Secretary and Clerk: Mr. David D. Robertson LLB NP
Depute Secretary and Clerk: Mr T.R.W. Parker LLB
Assistants: Mr Keith J. Fairweather LLB (Glebes)
                                   Mr Keith S. Mason LLB NP (Ecclesiastical Buildings)
Treasurer: Mr Iain W. Grimmond BAcc CA
Deputy Treasurer: Mr W.J. McKean BAcc CA
Assistant Treasurer: Mr Robert A. Allan ACMA CPFA

Remit
The General Trustees are a Property Corporation created and incorporated under the Church of Scotland (General Trustees) Order Confirmation Act 1921. They have Scottish Charity Number SCO14574. Their duties, powers and responsibilities were greatly extended by the Church of Scotland (Property & Endowments) Acts and Orders 1925 to 1995, and they are also charged with the administration of the Central Fabric Fund (see below) and the Consolidated Fabric Fund and the Consolidated Stipend Fund in which monies held centrally for the benefit of individual congregations are lodged.

The scope of the work of the Trustees is broad, covering all facets of property administration, but particular reference is made to the following matters:

1. **ECCLESIASTICAL BUILDINGS.** The Trustees' Fabric Committee considers proposals for work at buildings, regardless of how they are vested, and plans of new buildings. Details of all such projects should be submitted to the Committee before work is commenced. The Committee also deals with applications for the release of fabric monies held by the General Trustees for individual congregations, and considers applications for assistance from the Central Fabric Fund from which grants and/or loans may be given to assist congregations faced with expenditure on fabric. Application forms relating to consents for work and possible financial assistance from the Central Fabric Fund are available from the Secretary of the Trustees and require to be submitted through Presbytery with its approval. The Committee normally meets on the first or second Tuesday of each month, apart from July, when it meets on the last Tuesday, and August, when there is no meeting.

2. **SALE, PURCHASE AND LETTING OF PROPERTIES.** All sales or lets of properties vested in the General Trustees fall to be carried out by them in consultation with the Financial Board of the congregation concerned, and no steps should be taken towards any sale or let without prior consultation with the Secretary of the Trustees. Where property to be purchased is to be vested in the General Trustees, it is essential that contact be made at the earliest possible stage with the Solicitor to the Trustees, who is responsible for the lodging of offers for such properties and all subsequent legal procedure.

3. **GLEBES.** The Trustees are responsible for the administration of Glebes vested in their ownership. All lets fall to be granted by them in consultation with the minister concerned. It should be noted that neither ministers nor Kirk Sessions may grant lets of Glebe land vested in the General Trustees. As part of their Glebe administration, the Trustees review regularly all Glebe rents.

4. **INSURANCE.** Properties vested in the General Trustees must be insured with the Church of Scotland Insurance Co. Ltd, a company wholly owned by the Church of Scotland whose profits are applied for Church purposes. Insurance enquiries should be sent directly to the Company at 67 George Street, Edinburgh EH2 2JG (Tel: 0131-220 4119; Fax: 0131-220 4120; E-mail: enquiries@cosic.co.uk).

---

21. The Church of Scotland Housing and Loan Fund for Retired Ministers and Widows and Widowers of Ministers

Membership

The Trustees shall be a maximum of 11 in number, being:
1. four appointed by the General Assembly on the nomination of the Trustees, who, having served a term of three years, shall be eligible for reappointment;
2. three ministers and one member appointed by the Ministries Council;
3. three appointed by the Baird Trust.

Chairman: Mr William McVicar RD CA
Secretary: Miss Lin J. Macmillan MA

Staff

Property Manager: Miss Hilary J. Hardy
Property Assistant: Mr John Lunn

Remit
The Fund, as established by the General Assembly, facilitates the provision of housing accommodation for retired ministers and widows, widowers and separated or divorced spouses of Church of Scotland ministers. When provided, help may take the form of either a house to rent or a house-purchase loan.

The Trustees may grant tenancy of one of their existing houses or they may agree to purchase for rental occupation an appropriate house of an applicant's choosing. Leases are normally on very advantageous terms as regards rental levels. Alternatively, the Trustees may grant a housing loan of up to 70 per cent of a house-purchase price but with an upper limit. Favourable rates of interest are charged.

The Trustees are also prepared to consider assisting those who have managed to house themselves but are seeking to move to more suitable accommodation. Those with a mortgaged home on retirement may be granted a loan to enable them to repay such a mortgage and thereafter to enjoy the favourable rates of interest charged by the Fund.

Ministers making application within five years of retirement, upon their application being approved, will be given a fairly firm commitment that, in due course, either a house will be made available for renting or a house-purchase loan will be offered. Only within nine months of a minister's intended retiral date will the Trustees initiate steps to find a suitable house; only within one year of that date will a loan be advanced. Applications submitted about ten years prior to retirement have the benefit of initial review and, if approved, a place on the preliminary applications list for appropriate decision in due time.

Donations and legacies over the years have been significant in building up this Fund, and the backbone has been provided by congregational contributions.

The Board of Trustees is a completely independent body answerable to the General Assembly, and enquiries and applications are dealt with in the strictest confidence.

Further information can be obtained from the Secretary, Miss Lin J. Macmillan MA, at the Church of Scotland Offices, 121 George Street, Edinburgh EH2 4YN (Tel: 0131-225 5722 ext. 310; Fax: 0131-240 2264; E-mail: lmacmillan@cofscotland.org.uk; Website: www.churchofscotland.org.uk).

22. Information Technology Department

Staff
Information Technology Manager: Alastair Chalmers
Depute Information Technology Manager: Veronica Hay

The Department provides computer facilities to Councils and Departments within 121 George Street and to Presbytery Clerks and other groups within the new Councils. It is also responsible for the telephone service within 121 George Street and the provision of assistance and advice on this to other groups.

The facilities provided include:
- the provision and maintenance of data and voice networks
- the purchase and installation of hardware and software
- support for problems and guidance on the use of software
- development of in-house software
- maintenance of data within some central systems.

23. Law Department

Staff

Solicitor of the Church and of the General Trustees:	Mrs Janette S. Wilson LLB NP
Depute Solicitor:	Miss Mary E. Macleod LLB NP
Assistant Solicitors:	Mr Ian K. Johnstone MA LLB
	Mrs Elizabeth M. Kemp MA LLB
	Mrs Jennifer M. Hamilton BA NP
	Mrs Elspeth Annan LLB NP
	Miss Susan Killean LLB NP
	Miss Mairead MacBeath LLB NP

The Law Department of the Church was created in 1937/38. The Department acts in legal matters for the Church and all of its Courts, Councils, Committees, the Church of Scotland General Trustees, the Church of Scotland Trust and the Church of Scotland Investors Trust. It also acts for individual congregations and is available to give advice on any legal matter arising.

The Department is under the charge of the Solicitor of the Church, a post created at the same time as the formation of the Department and a post which is now customarily held along with the traditional posts of Law Agent of the General Assembly and the Custodier of former United Free Church titles (E-mail: lawdept@cofscotland.org.uk).

---

24. Legal Questions Committee

Membership

Convener, Vice-Convener and ten members appointed by the General Assembly on the Report of the Nomination Committee.

Convener:	Rev. Ann Inglis LLB BD
Vice-Convener:	Rev. Ian A. McLean BSc BD
Secretary:	The Depute Clerk

The Convener and Vice-Convener of the Assembly Arrangements Committee are also members of the Legal Questions Committee. The Assembly Clerks, Procurator and Solicitor of the Church are non-voting members of the Legal Questions Committee.

Remit

- to advise the General Assembly on questions of Church Law and of Constitutional Law affecting the relationship between Church and State;
- to advise and assist Agencies of the General Assembly in the preparation of proposed legislation and on questions of interpretation, including interpretation of and proposed changes to remits;
- to compile the statistics of the Church, except Youth and Finance; and to supervise on behalf of the General Assembly all arrangements for care of Church Records and for Presbytery visits;
- to conduct an annual review of progress made in discharging the remit and provide a written report to the Support and Services Council.

25. Mission and Evangelism Task Group

See entry in full under **The Mission and Discipleship Council** (number 4).

26. Nomination Committee

Membership
(44 members)
Convener: Rev. Iain D. Cunningham MA BD (2005)
Vice-Convener: Miss Moira Alexander MBA RGN SCM RNT (2005)
Secretary: The Principal Clerk

Remit
To bring before the General Assembly names of persons to serve on the Boards and Standing
Committees of the General Assembly.

27. Office Manager's Department

Staff
Office Manager: Mrs Dorothy Woodhouse
                                         (E-mail: dwoodhouse@cofscotland.org.uk)

The responsibilities of the Office Manager's Department include:
*   management of a maintenance budget for the upkeep of the Church Offices at 121 George
    Street, Edinburgh;
*   responsibility for all aspects of health and safety for staff, visitors and contractors working
    in the building;
*   managing a team of staff providing the Offices with security, reception, mail room, print
    room, switchboard, day-to-day maintenance services and Committee room bookings;
*   overseeing all sub-contracted services to include catering, cleaning, boiler-room maintenance,
    intruder alarm, fire alarms, lifts and water management;
*   maintaining building records in accordance with the requirements of statutory legislation;
*   overseeing all alterations to the building and ensuring, where applicable, that they meet DDR,
    Planning and Building Control regulations.

Design Services
Our designers offer a graphic-design service for full-colour promotional literature, display
materials and exhibitions to both Councils and organisations of the wider Church. For further
information, contact Peter Forrest (Tel: 0131-240 2224; E-mail: pforrest@churchofscotland.co.uk).

28. Panel on Review and Reform

Membership
(10 members appointed by the General Assembly)
Convener: Rev. David S. Cameron BD (2006)
Vice-Convener: Rev. Marion E. Dodd MA BD LRAM (2004)
(The Ecumenical Officer attends but without the right to vote or make a motion.)

Staff
Administrative Secretary: Valerie A. Smith MA
                                       (Tel: 0131-225 5722 ext. 336;
                                       E-mail: vsmith@cofscotland.org.uk)

Remit
The remit of the Panel on Review and Reform, as determined by the General Assembly of
2004, is as follows:
•   To listen to the voices of congregations, Presbyteries, Agencies and those beyond the
     Church of Scotland.
•   To present a vision of what a Church in need of continual renewal might become and to
     offer paths by which congregations, Presbyteries and Agencies might travel towards that
     vision.
•   To consider the changing needs, challenges and responsibilities of the Church.
•   To make recommendations to the Council of Assembly, and, through the report of that
     Council, to report to the General Assembly.
•   To have particular regard to the Gospel imperative of priority for the poor, needy and
     marginalised.

29. Parish Appraisal Committee

Due to the work currently involved in developing Presbytery and national plans, the Committee
on Parish Appraisal shall continue as a separate committee appointed by the General Assembly.
The Committee will be located within the Ministries Council, will be convened by a Vice-
Convener of the Council and will report through the Council to the General Assembly. These
arrangements will be reviewed no later than June 2008. The Committee will comprise nine
members appointed by the General Assembly and nine members appointed from the Ministries
Council, which will include a Convener and Vice-Convener. (See also under **The Ministries
Council.**)

30. Parish Development Fund Committee

Membership
(11 members appointed by the General Assembly. In addition, the Committee has powers to
co-opt up to six non-voting advisers with appropriate skills and knowledge.)

Convener: Rev. Dr Martin Fair (2006)
Vice-Convener: Mrs Mary Miller (2006)

Staff
Development Worker: Iain Johnston
                      (Tel: 0131-225 5722;
                      E-mail: parishdevelopment@uk.uumail.com)

Remit
The aim of the Parish Development Fund is to encourage local churches to work for the benefit of the whole community – and to take risks in living and sharing the Gospel in relevant ways.
   The Committee considers applications which are in the spirit of the above aim and the following principles:

* making a positive difference in the lives of people in greatest need in the community
* encouraging partnership work
* helping local people develop their gifts
* encouraging imagination and creativity.

The Committee meets four times each year, with main grant applications considered in April and October. Applications should be submitted by the end of February or the end of August.
   Further information on the types of projects supported by the Fund can be found in the Parish Development Fund section of the Church of Scotland website. Please contact the staff for informal discussion about grant-application enquiries and general advice on funding and project development.

---

31. Personnel Department
(now renamed as Human Resources Department)

Staff
Human Resources Manager: Mr Mike O'Donnell Chartered FCIPD
Deputy Human Resources Manager: Mrs Angela Ocak Chartered MCIPD
Human Resources Officer: Miss Maria Carena
Human Resources Assistant:

Remit
The Personnel Committee was set up in 1978 on the Report of the Advisory Board to determine salaries, length of service and conditions generally for Secretaries and Members of Office Staff. In 1991, and again in 1996, the General Assembly made certain minor adjustments to the remit, including a requirement that the Personnel Committee should conduct an annual salary review of those members of staff for which it is the employing agency.
   In recognition of the aim that the Personnel Committee may in time operate as the co-ordinating body for the Church in respect of the salaries and conditions of employment of all persons employed by the five employing agencies, the other four employing agencies are required to provide all information on such matters as requested by the Personnel Committee.
   As from 1 September 2001, this remit passed to the new Central Co-ordinating Committee, which has been renamed the Central Services Committee following the 2004 General Assembly.

32. Principal Clerk's Department

Staff

Principal Clerk:	Very Rev. Finlay A.J. Macdonald MA BD PhD DD
Depute Clerk:	Rev. Marjory A. MacLean LLB BD PhD
Personal Assistant to the Clerks of Assembly:	Mrs Linda Jamieson
Principal Administration Officer: (Assembly Arrangements and Moderatorial Support)	Mrs Alison Murray MA
Principal Administration Officer: (Council of Assembly, Central Services Committee and Nomination Committee)	Mrs Pauline Wilson BA

The Principal Clerk's Department has responsibility for the administration of the General Assembly and its Commissions, for supporting the Moderator in preparation for and during his or her year of office and for servicing the Council of Assembly, the Assembly Arrangements Committee, the Legal Questions Committee, the Committee to Nominate the Moderator, the Nomination Committee, the Committee on Overtures and Cases and the Committee on Classifying Returns to Overtures. The Clerks of Assembly are available for consultation on matters of Church law, practice and procedure.

Contact Details

Principal Clerk:	0131-240 2240
Depute Clerk:	0131-240 2232
Linda Jamieson:	0131-240 2240
Alison Murray:	0131-225 5722 (ext. 250)
Pauline Wilson:	0131-240 2229
Office fax number:	0131-240 2239
E-mail:	pcoffice@cofscotland.org.uk

33. Publishing Committee

See entry in full under **The Mission and Discipleship Council** (number 4).

34. Stewardship and Finance Committee

Remit

1. To teach, promote and encourage Christian Stewardship throughout the Church.
2. To provide programmes and training to assist congregations and their office-bearers in teaching, promoting and encouraging Christian Stewardship.
3. To be responsible with Presbyteries for allocating among congregations the expenditure

contained in the Co-ordinated Budget approved by the Council of Assembly, and for seeking to ensure that congregations meet their obligations thereto, by transmitting regularly throughout the year to the General Treasurer of the Church contributions towards their allocations.

4. To report annually to the General Assembly on the attestation of Presbytery and Congregational Accounts, and provide advice or arrange training for Congregational Treasurers and others administering congregational finances.

5. To issue annually to each congregation a Schedule of Congregational Financial Statistics, to be completed and returned by a date determined by the Committee.

6. To set standards of financial management and accounting procedures and to provide financial and accounting services for all Councils and Committees of the General Assembly (except for the Social Care Council).

7. To maintain and update such statistical and financial information as is deemed necessary.

8. To approve and submit annually to the General Assembly the Report and Financial Statements of the Unincorporated Councils and Committees of the General Assembly. In order to enable the Committee to fulfil this part of its remit, the Social Care Council shall provide regular financial reports and such other information as may be required by the Committee.

9. To appoint Auditors for the Financial Statements of the Unincorporated Councils and Committees of the General Assembly.

10. To consider Reports received from the Auditors of the Financial Statements of the Unincorporated Councils and Committees of the General Assembly.

11. To ensure that all funds belonging to Councils and Committees of the General Assembly, which are not contained within the Financial Statements submitted to the General Assembly, are audited or independently examined annually.

12. To exercise custody over funds and to provide bank arrangements.

13. To operate a central banking system for all Councils (except for the Social Care Council), Committees and Statutory Corporations.

14. To consider taxation matters affecting Councils, Committees and Statutory Corporations and congregations of the Church.

15. To determine the types and rates of expenses that may be claimed by members serving Councils, Committees and Statutory Corporations.

16. To carry out such other duties as may be referred to the Committee from time to time by the General Assembly.

17. To conduct an annual review of progress made in discharging the remit and provide a written report for the Support and Services Council.

Membership
The Committee shall consist of a Convener, Vice-Convener and 16 members all appointed by the General Assembly. The General Treasurer and the Director of Stewardship shall be *ex officiis* members of the Committee and of all its Sub-Committees but shall not have voting rights.

Convener: Mrs Vivienne A. Dickson CA (2005)
Vice-Convener: Mr Donald N. Carmichael BAcc CA (2005)
General Treasurer: Mr Iain W. Grimmond BAcc CA
Director of Stewardship: Rev. Gordon D. Jamieson MA BD
Administrative Secretary: Mr Fred Marsh MCIBS

Promoting Christian Giving
Stewardship and Finance staff are responsible for promoting Christian giving through stewardship programmes, conferences for office-bearers or members, wider use of Gift Aid, and legacies.

Contact the Church Offices to get in touch with the appropriate Stewardship Consultant or to obtain information about stewardship material produced by the Committee (Tel: 0131-225 5722 ext. 273; E-mail: stewardship@cofscotland.org.uk).

35. Worship and Doctrine Task Group

See entry in full under **The Mission and Discipleship Council** (number 4).

36. Safeguarding Office
Tel: 0131-240 2256; Fax: 0131-220 3113
E-mail: safeguarding@cofscotland.org.uk

(Reports through the Support and Services Council – see separate item, number 6)

Convener:	Rev. John Christie (2005)
Vice-Convener:	Anne Black (2005)

Staff

National Adviser in Safeguarding:	Jennifer McCreanor
Associate National Adviser:	Fiona MacKay
Training Officer:	Vacant

Remit

The Safeguarding Office, which developed from the Church's Child Protection Unit, plays a major part in the growing and ongoing work of child protection, training and assisting those who work in outreach with children.

The Safeguarding Office exists to:
* continue the development of the Church of Scotland's policy and procedure on child protection;
* coordinate the development of a system of national registration of voluntary workers;
* recruit, train and support a team of voluntary trainers in child protection across Scotland;
* facilitate, through the training network, training in child protection for volunteer workers and coordinators in congregations;
* develop resources relating to child protection;
* provide support, advice and guidance to congregations; and
* liaise with other church denominations, para-church bodies and other voluntary organisations.

SECTION 2

General Information

(1) OTHER CHURCHES IN THE UNITED KINGDOM

ASSOCIATED PRESBYTERIAN CHURCHES
Clerk of Presbytery: Rev. Archibald N. McPhail, APC Manse, Polvinister Road, Oban
PA34 5TN (Tel: 01631 567076).

THE REFORMED PRESBYTERIAN CHURCH OF SCOTLAND
Clerk of Presbytery: Rev. Andrew Quigley, Church Offices, 48 North Bridge Street, Airdrie
ML6 6NE (Tel: 01236 620107; E-mail: airdrierpcs@aol.com).

THE FREE CHURCH OF SCOTLAND
Principal Clerk: Rev. James MacIver, The Mound, Edinburgh EH1 2LS (Tel: 0131-226 5286;
E-mail: offices@freechurchofscotland.org.uk).

THE FREE PRESBYTERIAN CHURCH OF SCOTLAND
Clerk of Synod: Rev. John Macleod, 133 Woodlands Road, Glasgow G3 6LE (Tel: 0141-332 9283;
E-mail: jmac1265@aol.com).

THE UNITED FREE CHURCH OF SCOTLAND
General Secretary: Rev. John Fulton BSc BD, United Free Church Offices, 11 Newton Place,
Glasgow G3 7PR (Tel: 0141-332 3435; E-mail: office@ufcos.org.uk).

THE PRESBYTERIAN CHURCH IN IRELAND
Clerk of the General Assembly and General Secretary: Rev. Dr Donald J. Watts,
Church House, Fisherwick Place, Belfast BT1 6DW (Tel: 02890 322284; E-mail:
clerk@presbyterianireland.org).

THE PRESBYTERIAN CHURCHES OF WALES
General Secretary: Rev. Ifan R.H. Roberts, Tabernacle Chapel, 81 Merthyr Road, Whitchurch,
Cardiff CF14 1DD (Tel: 02920 627465; Fax: 02920 616188; E-mail:
swyddfa.office@ebcpcw.org.uk).

THE UNITED REFORMED CHURCH
General Secretary: Rev. Dr David Cornick, 86 Tavistock Place, London WC1H 9RT (Tel: 020 7916
2020; Fax: 020 7916 2021; E-mail: davidcornick@urc.org.uk).

UNITED REFORMED CHURCH SCOTLAND SYNOD
Synod Clerk: Dr James Merrilees, Church House, 340 Cathedral Street, Glasgow G1 2BQ
(Tel: 0141-332 7667; E-mail: scotland@urc.org.uk).

BAPTIST UNION OF SCOTLAND
General Director: Rev. William G. Slack, 14 Aytoun Road, Glasgow G41 5RT (Tel: 0141-423
6169; E-mail: mary@scottishbaptist.org.uk).

CONGREGATIONAL FEDERATION IN SCOTLAND
Rev. Alan Gibbon, 61 Fifth Avenue, Glasgow G12 0AR (Tel: 0141-334 1351; E-mail:
alan.gibbon2@ntlworld.com).

RELIGIOUS SOCIETY OF FRIENDS (QUAKERS)
Clerk to the General Meeting for Scotland: Pamala McDougall, Havana, 3 Teapot Lane, Inverkeillor,
Arbroath DD1 5RP (Tel: 01241 830238; E-mail: pamjames@havana.wanadoo.co.uk).

ROMAN CATHOLIC CHURCH
Rev. Paul Conroy, General Secretariat, Bishops' Conference of Scotland, 64 Aitken Street, Airdrie ML6 6LT (Tel: 01236 764061; Fax: 01236 762489; E-mail: gensec@bpsconfscot.com).

THE SALVATION ARMY
Scotland Secretary: Major Robert McIntyre, Scotland Secretariat, 12A Dryden Road, Loanhead EH20 9LZ (Tel: 0131-440 9101; E-mail: robert.mcintyre@salvationarmy.org.uk).

SCOTTISH EPISCOPAL CHURCH
General Secretary: Mr John F. Stuart, 21 Grosvenor Crescent, Edinburgh EH12 5EL (Tel: 0131-225 6357; E-mail: secgen@scotland.anglican.org).

THE SYNOD OF THE METHODIST CHURCH IN SCOTLAND
Secretary: Mrs Janet Murray, Methodist Church Office, Scottish Churches House, Kirk Street, Dunblane FK15 0AJ (Tel/Fax: 01786 820295; E-mail: meth@scottishchurcheshouse.org).

GENERAL SYNOD OF THE CHURCH OF ENGLAND
Secretary General: Mr William Fittall, Church House, Great Smith Street, London SW1P 3NZ (Tel: 020 7898 1000; E-mail: william.fittall@c-of-e.org.uk).

---

(2) OVERSEAS CHURCHES

PRESBYTERIAN CHURCH IN AMERICA
Stated Clerk: 1700 North Brown Road, Suite 105, Lawrenceville, GA 30043, USA (E-mail: ac@pcanet.org; Website: www.pcanet.org).

PRESBYTERIAN CHURCH IN CANADA
Clerk of Assembly: 50 Wynford Drive, Toronto, Ontario M3C 1J7, Canada (E-mail: pccadmin@presbycan.ca; Website: www.presbycan.ca).

UNITED CHURCH OF CANADA
General Secretary: Suite 300, 3250 Bloor Street West, Toronto, Ontario M8X 2Y4, Canada (E-mail: info@united-church.ca; Website: www.united-church.ca).

PRESBYTERIAN CHURCH (USA)
Stated Clerk: 100 Witherspoon Street, Louisville, KY 40202-1396, USA (E-mail: presbytel@pcusa.org; Website: www.pcusa.org).

REFORMED PRESBYTERIAN CHURCH OF NORTH AMERICA
Stated Clerk: 7408 Penn Avenue, Pittsburgh, PA 15208, USA (Website: www.reformedpresbyterian.org).

CUMBERLAND PRESBYTERIAN CHURCH
General Secretary: 1978 Union Avenue, Memphis, TN 38104, USA (E-mail: assembly@cumberland.org; Website: www.cumberland.org).

REFORMED CHURCH IN AMERICA
General Secretary: 475 Riverside Drive, NY 10115, USA (E-mail: rcamail@rca.org; Website: www.rca.org).

UNITED CHURCH OF CHRIST
General Minister: 700 Prospect Avenue, Cleveland, OH 44115, USA
(Website: www.ucc.org).

UNITING CHURCH IN AUSTRALIA
General Secretary: PO Box A2266, Sydney South, New South Wales 1235, Australia (E-mail: enquiries@nat.uca.org.au; Website: www.uca.org.au).

PRESBYTERIAN CHURCH OF AUSTRALIA
Clerk of Assembly: PO Box 2196, Strawberry Hills, NSW 2012; 168 Chalmers Street, Surry Hills, NSW 2010, Australia (E-mail: general@pcnsw.org.au; Website: www.presbyterian.org.au).

PRESBYTERIAN CHURCH OF AOTEAROA, NEW ZEALAND
Executive Secretary: PO Box 9049, 100 Tory Street, Wellington, New Zealand (E-mail: aes@presbyterian.org.nz; Website: www.presbyterian.org.nz).

EVANGELICAL PRESBYTERIAN CHURCH, GHANA
Synod Clerk: PO Box 18, Ho, Volta Region, Ghana.

PRESBYTERIAN CHURCH OF GHANA
Director of Ecumenical and Social Relations: PO Box 1800, Accra, Ghana.

PRESBYTERIAN CHURCH OF EAST AFRICA
Secretary General: PO Box 27573, 00506 Nairobi, Kenya.

CHURCH OF CENTRAL AFRICA PRESBYTERIAN
Secretary General, General Synod: PO Box 30398, Lilongwe 3, Malawi.
General Secretary, Blantyre Synod: PO Box 413, Blantyre, Malawi.
General Secretary, Livingstonia Synod: PO Box 112, Mzuzu, Malawi.
General Secretary, Nkhoma Synod: PO Box 45, Nkhoma, Malawi.

IGREJA EVANGELICA DE CRISTO EM MOÇAMBIQUE (EVANGELICAL CHURCH OF CHRIST IN MOZAMBIQUE)
(Nampula) General Secretary: Cx. Postale 284, Nampula 70100, Mozambique.
(Zambezia) Superintendente: Cx. Postale 280, Zambezia, Quelimane, Mozambique.

PRESBYTERIAN CHURCH OF NIGERIA
Principal Clerk: 26–29 Ehere Road, Ogbor Hill, PO Box 2635, Aba, Abia State, Nigeria.

UNITING PRESBYTERIAN CHURCH IN SOUTHERN AFRICA (SOUTH AFRICA)
General Secretary: PO Box 96188, Brixton 2019, South Africa.

UNITING PRESBYTERIAN CHURCH IN SOUTHERN AFRICA (ZIMBABWE)
Presbytery Clerk: PO Box CY224, Causeway, Harare, Zimbabwe.

PRESBYTERIAN CHURCH OF SUDAN (A)
Executive Secretary: PO Box 66168, Nairobi, Kenya.

PRESBYTERIAN CHURCH OF SUDAN (M)
General Secretary: PO Box 3421, Khartoum, Sudan.

UNITED CHURCH OF ZAMBIA
General Secretary: Nationalist Road at Burma Road, PO Box 50122, 15101 Ridgeway, Lusaka, Zambia.

CHURCH OF BANGLADESH
Moderator: Synod Office, 54 Johnson Road, Dhaka 1100, Bangladesh.

CHURCH OF NORTH INDIA
General Secretary: Synod Office, 16 Pandit Pant Marg, New Delhi 110 001, India.

CHURCH OF SOUTH INDIA
General Secretary: Synod Office, 5 White's Road, Royapettah, Chennai 600 114, India.

PRESBYTERIAN CHURCH OF KOREA
General Secretary: CPO Box 1125, Seoul 110 611, Korea.

PRESBYTERIAN CHURCH IN THE REPUBLIC OF KOREA
General Secretary: 1501 The Korean Ecumenical Building, 136–156 Yunchi-Dong, Chongno-Ku, Seoul, Korea.

THE UNITED MISSION TO NEPAL
Executive Director: PO Box 126, Kathmandu, Nepal.

CHURCH OF PAKISTAN
General Secretary: c/o St John's Cathedral School, 1 Sir Syed Road, Peshawar 25000, NWFP, Pakistan.

PRESBYTERY OF LANKA
Moderator: 127/1 D S Senanayake Veedyan, Kandy, Sri Lanka.

PRESBYTERIAN CHURCH IN TAIWAN
General Secretary: 3 Lane 269 Roosevelt Road, Sec. 3, Taipei, Taiwan 10763, ROC.

CHURCH OF CHRIST IN THAILAND
General Secretary: 109 CCT (13th Floor), Surawong Road, Khet Bangrak, Bangkok 10500, Thailand.

PRESBYTERY OF GUYANA
Moderator: 169 Thomas Street, Kitty, Georgetown, Guyana.

NATIONAL PRESBYTERIAN CHURCH OF GUATEMALA
Executive Secretary: Av. Simeon Canas 7–13, Zona 2, Aptdo 655, Guatemala City, Guatemala (E-mail: ienpg@terra.com.gt).

UNITED CHURCH IN JAMAICA AND THE CAYMAN ISLANDS
General Secretary: 12 Carlton Crescent, PO Box 359, Kingston 10, Jamaica (E-mail: unitedchurch@colis.com).

PRESBYTERIAN CHURCH IN TRINIDAD AND TOBAGO
General Secretary: Box 92, Paradise Hill, San Fernando, Trinidad (E-mail: pctt@tstt.net.tt).

UNITED PROTESTANT CHURCH OF BELGIUM
Rue de Champ de Mars 5, B-1050 Bruxelles, Belgium (E-mail: epub@epub.be; Website: www.protestanet.be/eput/index.htm).

REFORMED CHRISTIAN CHURCH IN CROATIA
Bishop's Office: Vladimira Nazora 31, HR-32100 Vinkovci, Croatia (E-mail: reformed.church.rcc@vk.htnet.hr).

EVANGELICAL CHURCH OF THE CZECH BRETHREN
Moderator: Jungmannova 9, PO Box 466, CZ-11121 Praha 1, Czech Republic (E-mail: ekumena@srcce.cz; Website: www.srcce.cz).

EGLISE REFORMEE DE FRANCE
General Secretary: 47 rue de Clichy, F-75311 Paris, France (E-mail: erf@unacerf.org; Website: www.eglise-reformee-fr.org).

HUNGARIAN REFORMED CHURCH
General Secretary: PF Box 5, H-1440 Budapest, Hungary (E-mail: zsinat.kulugy@zsinatiiroda.hu; Website: www.reformatus.hu).

WALDENSIAN CHURCH
Moderator: Via Firenze 38, 00184 Rome, Italy (E-mail: moderatore@chiesavaldese.org; Website: www.chiesavaldese.org).

NETHERLANDS REFORMED CHURCH
Landelijk Dienstcentrum Samen op Weg-Kerken, Postbus 8504, NL-3503 RM Utrecht (E-mail: ccs@ngk.nl; Website: www.ngk.nl).

REFORMED CHURCH IN ROMANIA
Bishop's Office: Str. IC Bratianu No. 51, R-3400 Cluj-Napoca, Romania (E-mail: office@reformatus.ro).

REFORMED CHRISTIAN CHURCH IN YUGOSLAVIA
Bishop's Office: Bratstva 26, YU-24323 Feketic, Yugoslavia.

SYNOD OF THE NILE OF THE EVANGELICAL CHURCH
General Secretary: Synod of the Nile of the Evangelical Church, PO Box 1248, Cairo, Egypt (E-mail: epcegypt@yahoo.com).

DIOCESE OF THE EPISCOPAL CHURCH IN JERUSALEM AND THE MIDDLE EAST
Bishop's Office: PO Box 19122, Jerusalem 91191, via Israel (E-mail: ediocese-jer@j-diocese.com; Website: www.jerusalem.anglican.org).

NATIONAL EVANGELICAL SYNOD OF SYRIA AND LEBANON
General Secretary: PO Box 70890, Antelias, Lebanon (E-mail: nessl@minero.net).

[Full information on Churches overseas may be obtained from the World Mission Council.]

(3) SCOTTISH DIVINITY FACULTIES

[* denotes a Minister of the Church of Scotland]
[(R) Reader   (SL) Senior Lecturer   (L) Lecturer]

ABERDEEN

(School of Divinity, History and Philosophy)
King's College, Old Aberdeen AB24 3UB
(Tel: 01224 272380; Fax: 01224 273750;
E-mail: divinity@abdn.ac.uk)

Master of Christ's College: Rev. J.H.A. Dick* MA MSc BD
(E-mail: christs-college@abdn.ac.uk)

Head of School: Professor Robert Frost MA PhD FRHistS

Deputy Head of School: Peter Williams MA MPhil PhD

Professors: Robert Segal BA MA PhD (Religious Studies)
Rev. John Swinton* BD PhD RNM RNMD (Practical Theology
and Pastoral Care)
Francis Watson MA DPhil LRAM (New Testament)
John Webster MA PhD DD (Systematic Theology)

Readers: Francesca Murphy BA MA PhD (Systematic Theology)
Joachim Schaper DipTheol PhD (Old Testament)

Senior Lecturers: Andrew Clarke BA MA PhD (New Testament)
Simon Gathercole BA MA PhD (New Testament)
Peter Williams MA MPhil PhD (New Testament)

Lecturers: Kenneth Aitken BD PhD (Hebrew Bible)
Brian Brock BS MA DipTheol DPhil (Moral and Practical
Theology)
Gabriele Maranci BA MA PhD (Religious Studies)
Martin Mills MA PhD (Religious Studies)
Nick Thompson BA MA MTh PhD (Church History)
Lena-Sofia Tiemeyer BA MA MPhil (Old Testament/Hebrew
Bible)
Will Tuladhar-Douglas BA MA MPhil (Religious Studies)
Donald Wood BA MA MPhil DPhil (Systematic Theology)
Philip Ziegler BA MA MDiv ThD (Systematic Theology)

ST ANDREWS
(University College of St Mary)
St Mary's College, St Andrews, Fife KY16 9JU
(Tel: 01334 462850/1; Fax: 01334 462852)

Principal, Dean and Head of School: T.A. Hart BA PhD

Chairs: R.J. Bauckham BA MA PhD FBA
                                            (New Testament Studies)
                                            P.F. Esler BA LLB LLM DPhil (Biblical Criticism)
                                            T.A. Hart BA PhD (Divinity)
                                            R.A. Piper BA BD PhD (Christian Origins)
                                            C.R. Seitz AB MTS MA MPhil PhD
                                            (Old Testament and Theological Studies)
                                            A.J. Torrance* MA BD DrTheol
                                            (Systematic Theology)

Readerships, Senior Lectureships, Lectureships:

M.I. Aguilar BA MA STB PhD (R) (Religion and Contextual Theology)
I.C. Bradley* BA MA BD DPhil (R) (Practical Theology)
J.R. Davila BA MA PhD (Early Jewish Studies)
M. Elliott BA BD PhD (Church History)
S.R. Holmes BA MA MTh PGDip PhD (Theology)
E.D. Reed BA PhD (SL) (Theology and Ethics)
N. MacDonald MA MPhil (Old Testament and Hebrew)

EDINBURGH
(School of Divinity and New College)
New College, Mound Place, Edinburgh EH1 2LX
(Tel: 0131-650 8900; Fax: 0131-650 7952; E-mail: divinity.faculty@ed.ac.uk)

Head of School: Rev. Professor David A.S. Fergusson* MA BD DPhil FRSE
Principal of New College: Rev. Professor A. Graeme Auld* MA BD PhD DLitt FSAScot
                               FRSE
Chairs: Rev. Professor A. Graeme Auld* MA BD PhD DLitt FSAScot
                               FRSE (Hebrew Bible)
                               Professor Hans Barstad DrTheol (Hebrew and Old Testament)
                               Professor Stewart J. Brown BA MA PhD FRHistS
                               (Ecclesiastical History)
                               Professor James L. Cox BA MDiv PhD (Religious Studies)
                               Rev. Professor David A.S. Fergusson* MA BD DPhil FRSE
                               (Divinity)
                               Professor Larry W. Hurtado BA MA PhD
                               (New Testament Language, Literature and Theology)

Professor Timothy Lim BA MPhil DPhil (Biblical Studies)
Rev. Professor Oliver O'Donovan MA DPhil (Christian Ethics)
Professor Marcella Althaus Reid BTh PhD
(Contextual Theology)

Readers, Senior Lecturers and Lecturers:

Biblical Studies:

David J. Reimer BTh BA MA MA (SL)
Graham Paul Foster PhD MSt BD
Helen K. Bond MTheol PhD (SL)

Theology and Ethics:

Jolyon Mitchell BA MA (SL)
Michael S. Northcott MA PhD (R)
Cecelia Clegg BD MSc PhD (L)
Rev. Ewan Kelly* MB ChB BD PhD (L) (part-time)
Nicholas S. Adams BA PhD (L)
John C. McDowell BD PhD (L)
Michael Purcell MA PhD PhL PhB (SL)
Sara Parvis BA PhD (L)

Ecclesiastical History:

Jane E.A. Dawson BA PhD DipEd (SL)
Jack Thompson BA PhD (SL)
Susan Hardman Moore MA PhD (L)

Religious Studies:

Jeanne Openshaw BA MA PhD (SL)
Elizabeth Kopping MA PhD DipSocSci MTh (L)
Steven Sutcliffe BA MPhil PhD
Hannah Holtschneider MPhil PhD (L)
Afeosemime U. Adogame BA MA PhD (L)

Fulton Lecturer in Speech and Communication:
Richard Ellis BSc MEd LGSM

Hope Trust Post-Doctoral Fellow:
Rev. Alison Jack* MA BD PhD

GLASGOW
(School of Divinity and Trinity College)
4 The Square, University of Glasgow, Glasgow G12 8QQ
(Tel: 0141-330 6526; Fax: 0141-330 4943; E-mail: divinity@arts.gla.ac.uk)

Head of School: Rev. Professor David Jasper
Head of Department: Dr Mona Siddiqui
Principal of Trinity College: Rev. Professor George M. Newlands*

Chairs: Rev. David Jasper MA PhD BD DD FRSE (Literature and Theology)
W. Ian P. Hazlett BA BD Dr theol DLitt (Ecclesiastical History)
Rev. Donald Macleod MA (Visiting Hon. Professor)
Rev. George M. Newlands* MA BD PhD DLitt FRSA (Divinity)
Rev. John K. Riches MA (Hon. Professor)
Perry Schmidt-Leukel Dipl theol MA Dr theol Dr theol habil
(Systematic Theology and Religious Studies)

Senior Lecturers and Lecturers: Theology and Religious Studies:
Julie P. Clague BSc PGCE PGDip MTh (L)
Rev. Alastair G. Hunter* MSc BD PhD (SL)
Sarah Nicholson MTheol PhD (L)
Lloyd V.J. Ridgeon BA MA PhD (SL)
Yvonne M. Sherwood BA PhD DipJS (SL)
Mona Siddiqui MA MLL PhD DLitt FRSE (SL)
Heather E. Walton BA MA(Econ) PhD (SL)
Douglas Gay MA BD PhD (L)

Centre for Study of Literature, Theology and the Arts:
Director: Dr Yvonne M. Sherwood
Assistant Director: Dr Heather E. Walton

Centre for Study of Islam:
Director: Dr Mona Siddiqui

HIGHLAND THEOLOGICAL COLLEGE
High Street, Dingwall IV15 9HA
(Tel: 01349 780000; Fax: 01349 780201;
E-mail: htc@uhi.ac.uk)

Principal of HTC: Rev. Professor Andrew McGowan* BD STM PhD
Vice-Principal of HTC: Rev. Hector Morrison BSc BD MTh ILTM

Lecturers: Hector Morrison BSc BD MTh ILTM (Old Testament and Hebrew)
Jamie Grant PhD MA LLB (Biblical Studies)
Michael Bird BMin BA PhD (New Testament)
Innes Visagie MA BTh BA PhD (Pastoral Theology)
Nick Needham BD PhD (Church History)
Robert Shillaker BSc BA PhD (Systematic Theology)

(4) SOCIETIES AND ASSOCIATIONS

The undernoted list shows the name of the Association, along with the name and address of the Secretary.

INTER-CHURCH ASSOCIATIONS

THE FELLOWSHIP OF ST ANDREW: The fellowship promotes dialogue between Churches of the east and the west in Scotland. Further information available from the Secretary, Rev. Robert Pickles, The Manse, 3 Perth Road, Milnathort, Kinross KY13 9XU (Tel: 01577 863461; E-mail: robert.pickles1@btopenworld.com).

THE FELLOWSHIP OF ST THOMAS: An ecumenical association formed to promote informed interest in and learn from the experience of Churches in South Asia (India, Pakistan, Bangladesh, Nepal, Sri Lanka). Secretary: Dr R.L. Robinson, 43 Underwood Road, Burnside, Rutherglen, Glasgow G73 3TE (Tel: 0141-643 0612; E-mail: robinson.burnside @surefish.co.uk).

THE SCOTTISH ORDER OF CHRISTIAN UNITY: Secretary: Rev. William D. Brown MA, 9/3 Craigend Park, Edinburgh EH16 5XY (Tel: 0131-672 2936; E-mail: wdbrown@ surefish.co.uk; Website: www.socu.org.uk).

CHURCH PASTORAL AID SOCIETY (CPAS): Consultant for Scotland: Rev. Richard W. Higginbottom, 2 Highfield Place, Bankfoot, Perth PH1 4AX (Tel: 01738 787429). A home mission agency working cross-denominationally through consultancy training and resources to encourage Churches in local evangelism: accredited officially to the Mission and Discipleship Council.

FRONTIER YOUTH TRUST: Encourages and resources those engaged in youth work, particularly with disadvantaged young people. Co-ordinator: Chris White, c/o 32 Hillview Street, Glasgow G32 7BQ (Tel: 07749 710552).

IONA COMMUNITY: Leader: Rev. Kathy Galloway, Fourth Floor, Savoy House, 140 Sauchiehall Street, Glasgow G2 3DH (Tel: 0141-332 6343; Fax: 0141-332 1090); Warden: Richard Sharples, Iona Abbey, Isle of Iona, Argyll PA76 6SN (Tel: 01681 700404; E-mail: ionacomm@gla.iona.org.uk; Website: www.iona.org.uk).

SCOTTISH CHURCHES HOUSING ACTION: Provides the Churches with information, education, advice and support concerning homelessness. Chief Executive: Alastair Cameron, 28 Albany Street, Edinburgh EH1 3QH (Tel: 0131-477 4500; Fax: 0131-477 2710; E-mail: scotchho@ednet.co.uk; Website: www.churches-housing.org).

WORLD EXCHANGE: Volunteers can help turn the world upside down, in Scotland and in the developing world. When it comes to making the world a better place, there are no limits to what's possible. Teachers, ministers, managers, accountants, joiners, engineers, musicians, artists and others are all invited to explore the possibility of working with World Exchange.
  • Consultancies and work camps (4–6 weeks)
  • Six-month 'gap' projects for school-leavers and younger volunteers
  • One-year programme (in Scotland or overseas)

Church-based community projects in Scotland, Africa, South Asia, Europe and the Caribbean (Tel: 0131-315 4444; Website: www.worldexchange.org.uk). Your potential is boundless. Now may be the time to unleash it.

ST COLM'S INTERNATIONAL HOUSE: Available for ministers and church conferences: an excellent place to stay and an opportunity to support an important ecumenical project. English-language and Capacity-Building Courses for community leaders from the developing world. A place to meet in the heart of the Capital on the perimeter of the Royal Botanic Gardens (Tel: 0131-315 4444).

FRIENDS OF ST COLM'S: An association for all from any denomination who have trained, studied or been resident in St Colm's or have an interest in its work and life. There is an annual retreat, an annual lecture and some local associations for more regular meetings. It offers support to St Colm's International House. Secretary: c/o St Colm's International House, 23 Inverleith Terrace, Edinburgh EH3 5NS (Tel: 0131-315 4444).

SCOTTISH JOINT COMMITTEE ON RELIGIOUS AND MORAL EDUCATION: Mr Rob Whiteman, 121 George Street, Edinburgh EH2 4YN (Tel: 0131-225 5722), and Mr Lachlan Bradley, 6 Clairmont Gardens, Glasgow G3 7LW (Tel: 0141-353 3595).

SCOTTISH NATIONAL COUNCIL OF YMCAs: National General Secretary: Mr Peter Crory, James Love House, 11 Rutland Street, Edinburgh EH1 2AE (Tel: 0131-228 1464; E-mail: info@ymcascotland.org; Website: www.ymcascotland.org).

INTERSERVE SCOTLAND: Part of Interserve International, an international, evangelical and interdenominational organisation with over 150 years of Christian service. Interserve internationally supports over 600 partners in cross-cultural ministry, and works in the Arab world and across Asia. Interserve's mission is to serve the Church and share Jesus Christ in all aspects of life, and Interserve workers are therefore involved in a wide range of work including children and youth, the environment, evangelism, Bible training, engineering, agriculture, business, development and so on. We rely on supporters in Scotland and throughout the UK to join us. Join the adventure with Interserve. Director: Grace Penney, 12 Elm Avenue, Lenzie, Glasgow G66 4HJ (Tel: 0141-578 0207; Fax: 0141-578 0208; E-mail: info@isscott.org; Website: www.interservescotland.org.uk).

SCRIPTURE UNION SCOTLAND: 70 Milton Street, Glasgow G4 0HR (Tel: 0141-332 1162; Fax: 0141-352 7600; E-mail: info@suscotland.org.uk; Website: www.suscotland.org.uk).

STUDENT CHRISTIAN MOVEMENT: Co-ordinator: Mr Liam Purcell, SCM Office, Unit 308F, The Big Peg, 120 Vyse Street, The Jewellery Quarter, Birmingham B18 6NF (Tel: 0121-200 3355; E-mail: scm@movement.org.uk; Website: www.movement.org.uk). See also Christian Action and Thought.

CHRISTIAN ACTION AND THOUGHT (Edinburgh SCM): Ms Amy Mormino, CAT, Chaplaincy Centre, 1 Bristo Square, Edinburgh EH8 9AL (E-mail: amymormino@hotmail.com; Website: www.eusa.ed.ac.uk/societies/euscm).

UNIVERSITIES AND COLLEGES CHRISTIAN FELLOWSHIP: Pod Bhogal, 38 De Montfort Street, Leicester LE1 7GP (Tel: 0116-255 1700; E-mail: pbhogal@uccf.org.uk).

WORLD DAY OF PRAYER: SCOTTISH COMMITTEE: Convener: Col. Ruth Flett, 25 South View, Wick KW1 4PL. Secretary: Mrs Morag Hannah MA, 8 Dovecote View,

Kirkintilloch, Glasgow G66 3HY (Tel: 0141-776 2432; E-mail: morag.hannah.wdp@ virgin.net; Website: www.wdpscotland.org.uk).

CHURCH OF SCOTLAND SOCIETIES

AROS (Association of Returned Overseas Staff of the Church of Scotland World Mission Council): Hon. Secretary: Rev. Kenneth J. Pattison, 2 Castle Way, St Madoes, Glencarse, Perth PH2 7NY (Tel: 01738 860340; E-mail: ken@thepattisons.fsnet.co.uk).

FORUM OF GENERAL ASSEMBLY AND PRESBYTERY CLERKS: Rev. David W. Lunan MA BD, 260 Bath Street, Glasgow G2 4JP (Tel: 0141-332 6606).

FORWARD TOGETHER: An organisation for evangelicals within the Church of Scotland. Secretary: Rev. Ian M. Watson LLB DipLP BD, The Manse, 2 Lanark Road, Kirkmuirhill, Lanark ML11 9RB (Tel: 01555 892409).

FRIENDS OF ST COLM'S: Secretary: c/o St Colm's International House, 23 Inverleith Terrace, Edinburgh EH3 5NS (Tel: 0131-315 4444).

SCOTTISH CHURCH SOCIETY: Secretary: Rev. W. Gerald Jones MA BD MTh, The Manse, Kirkmichael, Maybole KA19 7PJ (Tel: 01655 750286).

SCOTTISH CHURCH THEOLOGY SOCIETY: Rev. Gordon R. Mackenzie BSc(Agr) BD, The Manse of Dyke, Brodie, Forres IV36 2TD (Tel: 01309 641239; E-mail: rev.g.mackenzie@btopenworld.com). The Society encourages theological exploration and discussion of the main issues confronting the Church in the twenty-first century.

SOCIETY OF FRIENDS OF ST ANDREW'S JERUSALEM: Hon. Secretary: Major D.J. McMicking LVO, World Mission Council, 121 George Street, Edinburgh EH2 4YN. Hon. Treasurer: Mrs Anne Macintosh BA CA, Assistant Treasurer, The Church of Scotland, 121 George Street, Edinburgh EH2 4YN (Tel: 0131-225 5722).

THE CHURCH OF SCOTLAND CHAPLAINS' ASSOCIATION: Hon. Secretary: Rev. Donald M. Stephen TD MA BD ThM, 10 Hawkhead Crescent, Edinburgh EH16 6LR (Tel: 0131-658 1216).

THE CHURCH OF SCOTLAND RETIRED MINISTERS' ASSOCIATION: Hon. Secretary: Rev. Elspeth G. Dougall MA BD, 60B Craigmillar Park, Edinburgh EH16 5PU (Tel: 0131-668 1342).

THE CHURCH SERVICE SOCIETY: Secretary: Rev. Neil N. Gardner MA BD, The Manse of Canongate, Edinburgh EH8 8BR (Tel: 0131-556 3515).

THE IRISH MINISTERS' FRATERNAL: Secretary: Rev. Eric G. McKimmon BA BD MTh, The Manse, St Andrews Road, Ceres, Cupar KY15 5NQ (Tel: 01334 829466).

THE NATIONAL CHURCH ASSOCIATION: Secretary: Miss Margaret P. Milne, 10 Balfron Crescent, Hamilton ML3 9UH.

BIBLE SOCIETIES

THE SCOTTISH BIBLE SOCIETY: Director of Programmes: Mr Colin S. Hay, 7 Hampton Terrace, Edinburgh EH12 5XU (Tel: 0131-337 9701).

WEST OF SCOTLAND BIBLE SOCIETY: Secretary: Rev. Finlay MacKenzie, 51 Rowallan Gardens, Glasgow G11 7LH (Tel: 0141-563 5276; E-mail: f.c.mack51@ntlworld.com).

GENERAL

THE BOYS' BRIGADE: Scottish Headquarters, Carronvale House, Carronvale Road, Larbert FK5 3LH (Tel: 01324 562008; Fax: 01324 552323; E-mail: carronvale@boys-brigade.org.uk).

THE GIRLS' BRIGADE SCOTLAND: 11A Woodside Crescent, Glasgow G3 7UL (Tel: 0141-332 1765; E-mail: enquiries@girls-brigade-scotland.org.uk; Website: www.girls-brigade-scotland.org.uk).

GIRLGUIDING SCOTLAND: 16 Coates Crescent, Edinburgh EH3 7AH (Tel: 0131-226 4511; Fax: 0131-220 4828; E-mail: administrator@girlguiding-scot.org.uk).

THE SCOUT ASSOCIATION: Scottish Headquarters, Fordell Firs, Hillend, Dunfermline KY11 7HQ (Tel: 01383 419073; E-mail: shq@scouts-scotland.org.uk).

BOYS' AND GIRLS' CLUBS OF SCOTLAND: 88 Giles Street, Edinburgh EH6 6BZ (Tel: 0131-555 1729; E-mail: secretary@bgcs.co.uk).

YOUTH SCOTLAND: Balfour House, 19 Bonnington Grove, Edinburgh EH6 4BL (Tel: 0131-554 2561; Fax: 0131-454 3438; E-mail: office@youthscotland.org.uk).

CHRISTIAN AID SCOTLAND: National Secretary: Mr Gavin McLellan, 41 George IV Bridge, Edinburgh EH1 1EL (Tel: 0131-220 1254; Fax: 0131-225 8861; E-mail: edinburgh@christian-aid.org).

FEED THE MINDS: Scottish Secretary: Mr Stanley Bonthron, 41 George IV Bridge, Edinburgh EH1 1EL (Tel: 0131-226 5254; Fax: 0131-225 8861; Home Tel: 0131-663 1458; E-mail: stanleybonthron@btinternet.com).

LADIES' GAELIC SCHOOLS AND HIGHLAND BURSARY ASSOCIATION: Mr Donald J. Macdonald, 9 Hatton Place, Edinburgh EH9 1UD (Tel: 0131-667 1740).

COUPLE COUNSELLING SCOTLAND: Chief Executive: Mrs Hilary Campbell, 18 York Place, Edinburgh EH1 3EP (Tel: 0845 119 6088; Fax: 0845 119 6089; E-mail: enquiries@couplecounselling.org.uk; Website: www.couplecounselling.org).

RUTHERFORD HOUSE: Warden: Rev. Robert Fyall MA BD PhD, 17 Claremont Park, Edinburgh EH6 7PJ (Tel: 0131-554 1206; Fax: 0131-555 1002).

SCOTTISH CHURCH HISTORY SOCIETY: Rev. William D. Graham MA BD, 48 Corbiehill Crescent, Edinburgh EH4 5BD (Tel: 0131-336 4071; E-mail: w.d.graham@btinternet.com).

SCOTTISH EVANGELICAL THEOLOGY SOCIETY: Secretary: Rev. James K. Torrens MB ChB BD, 42 Melville Gardens, Bishopbriggs, Glasgow G64 3DE (Tel: 0141-562 6296; E-mail: james.torrens@ntlworld.com; Website: www.setsonline.org.uk).

CHRISTIAN ENDEAVOUR IN SCOTLAND: Winning, Teaching and Training Youngsters for Christ and the Church: The Murray Library, 8 Shore Street, Anstruther KY10 3EA (Tel:

01333 310345 Monday, Wednesday and Friday mornings; E-mail: christine@
ce-in-scotland.fsnet.co.uk).

TEARFUND: 100 Church Road, Teddington TW11 8QE (Tel: 0845 355 8355). Manager:
Peter Chirnside, Tearfund Scotland, Challenge House, 29 Canal Street, Glasgow G4 0AD
(Tel: 0141-332 3621; E-mail: scotland@tearfund.org; Website: www.tearfund.org).

THE LEPROSY MISSION: Suite 2, Earlsgate Lodge, Livilands Lane, Stirling FK8 2BG (Tel:
01786 449266; Fax: 01786 449766). National Director: Miss Linda Todd. Area
Co-ordinator, Scotland Central and South: Mr Stuart McAra. Area Co-ordinator: Scotland
North and Islands: Mr Jim Clark (Tel: 01343 843837; E-mail: contactus@tlmscotland.org.uk
and meetings@tlmscotland.org.uk; Website: www.tlmscotland.org.uk).

THE LORD'S DAY OBSERVANCE SOCIETY: Ryelands Road, Leominster, Herefordshire
HR6 8NZ (Tel: 01568 613740).

THE SCOTTISH REFORMATION SOCIETY: Secretary: Rev. A. Sinclair Horne, The Magdalen
Chapel, 41 Cowgate, Edinburgh EH1 1JR (Tel: 0131-220 1450; E-mail: ashbethany43@
hotmail.co.uk; Website: www.scottishreformation.co.uk).

THE SOCIETY IN SCOTLAND FOR PROPAGATING CHRISTIAN KNOWLEDGE:
J. Gordon Cunningham WS, Tods Murray LLP, Edinburgh Quay, 133 Fountainbridge,
Edinburgh EH3 9AG (Tel: 0131-656 2000).

THE WALDENSIAN MISSIONS AID SOCIETY FOR WORK IN ITALY: David A. Lamb
SSC, 36 Liberton Drive, Edinburgh EH16 6NN (Tel: 0131-664 3059; E-mail:
david@dlamb.co.uk).

YWCA SCOTLAND: Chief Executive: Elaine Samson, 7B Randolph Crescent, Edinburgh
EH3 7TH (Tel: 0131-225 7592; E-mail: info@ywcascotland.org; Website:
www.ywcascotland.org).

(5) TRUSTS AND FUNDS

THE SOCIETY FOR THE BENEFIT OF THE SONS AND DAUGHTERS
OF THE CLERGY OF THE CHURCH OF SCOTLAND
Chairman: Dr Douglas Grant
Secretary and Treasurer: R. Graeme Thom FCA
                               17 Melville Street
                               Edinburgh EH3 7PH (Tel: 0131-473 3500)

Annual grants are made to assist in the education of the children (normally between the ages of
12 and 25 years) of ministers of the Church of Scotland. The Society also gives grants to aged and
infirm daughters of ministers and ministers' unmarried daughters and sisters who are in need.
Applications are to be lodged by 31 May in each year.

THE GLASGOW SOCIETY OF THE SONS AND DAUGHTERS OF MINISTERS OF THE CHURCH OF SCOTLAND

President: Andrew T.F. Gibb LLB SSC
Secretary and Treasurer: R. Graeme Thom FCA
                                    17 Melville Street
                                    Edinburgh EH3 7PH (Tel: 0131-473 3500)

The Society's primary purpose is to grant financial assistance to children (no matter what age) of deceased ministers of the Church of Scotland. Applications are to be submitted by 1 February in each year. To the extent that funds are available, grants are also given for the children of ministers or retired ministers, although such grants are normally restricted to students. These latter grants are considered in conjunction with the Edinburgh-based Society. Limited funds are also available for individual application for special needs or projects. Applications are to be submitted by 31 May in each year. Emergency applications can be dealt with at any time when need arises. Application forms may be obtained from the Secretary.

HOLIDAYS FOR MINISTERS

The undernoted hotels provide special terms for ministers and their families. Fuller information may be obtained from the establishments:

CRIEFF HYDRO HOTEL and MURRAYPARK HOTEL: The William Meikle Trust Fund and Paton Fund make provision whereby active ministers and their spouses, members of the Diaconate and other full-time employees of the Church of Scotland may enjoy hotel and self-catering accommodation at certain times of the year. Crieff Hydro offers a wide range of leisure facilities such as the Lagoon swimming pool, in-house cinema, entertainment and over thirty-five activities both indoors and outside. Crieff Hydro has a registered children's club that provides expert childcare for children of 0 to 12 years of age. For reservations, please contact the Accommodation Sales Team (Crieff Hydro, Ferntower Road, Crieff PH7 3LQ) on 01764 651670 or by e-mail: enquiries@crieffhydro.com

THE CINTRA BEQUEST: The Trust provides financial assistance towards the cost of accommodation in Scotland for missionaries on leave, or for ministers on temporary holiday, or on rest. Applications should be made to Mrs J.S. Wilson, Solicitor, 121 George Street, Edinburgh EH2 4YN.

THE LYALL BEQUEST: Makes available the following benefits to ministers of the Church of Scotland:
1.   A grant towards the cost of holiday accommodation in or close to the town of St Andrews may be paid to any minister and to his or her spouse at the rate of £100 per week each for a stay of one week or longer. Grants for a stay of less than one week may also be paid, at the rate of £14 per day each. Due to the number of applications which the Trustees now receive, an applicant will not be considered to be eligible if he or she has received a grant from the Bequest during the three years prior to the holiday for which the application is made. Applications prior to the holiday should be made to the Secretaries. Retired ministers are not eligible for grants.
2.   Grants towards costs of sickness and convalescence so far as not covered by the National Health Service or otherwise may be available to applicants, who should apply to the Secretaries giving relevant details.
All communications should be addressed to Pagan Osborne, Solicitors, Secretaries to the Lyall Bequest, 106 South Street, St Andrews KY16 9QD (Tel: 01334 475001; E-mail: elcalderwood@pagan.co.uk).

MARGARET AND JOHN ROSS TRAVELLING FUND: Offers grants to ministers and their spouses for travelling and other expenses for trips to the Holy Land where the purpose is recuperation or relaxation. Applications should be made to the Secretary and Clerk, Church of Scotland Trust, 121 George Street, Edinburgh EH2 4YN (Tel: 0131-240 2222; E-mail: jhamilton@cofscotland.org.uk).

The undernoted represents a list of the more important trusts available for ministers, students and congregations. A brief indication is given of the trust purposes, but application should be made in each case to the person named for full particulars and forms of application.

THE ABERNETHY TRUST: Offers residential accommodation and outdoor activities for Youth Fellowships, Church family weekends, Bible Classes and so on at four outdoor centres in Scotland. Further details from the Executive Director, Abernethy Trust, Nethy Bridge PH25 3ED (Tel/Fax: 01479 821279; Website: www.abernethytrust.org.uk).

THE ARROL TRUST: The object of the Trust is 'to promote the benefit and advance the education of young people between the ages of 16 and 25 years who are physically or mentally disadvantaged or are in necessitous circumstances by assisting such persons to gain experience through education and training for their future careers through travel within or without the United Kingdom'. Further details and forms of application can be obtained from C.S. Kennedy WS, Lindsays WS, 11 Atholl Crescent, Edinburgh EH3 8HE (Tel: 0131-229 1212).

THE BAIRD TRUST: Assists in the building and repair of churches and halls, endows Parishes and generally assists the work of the Church of Scotland. Apply to Ronald D. Oakes CA ACMA, 182 Bath Street, Glasgow G2 4HG (Tel: 0141-332 0476; Fax: 0141-331 0874).

THE REV. ALEXANDER BARCLAY BEQUEST: Assists mother, daughter, sister or niece of deceased minister of the Church of Scotland who at the time of his death was acting as his housekeeper and who is in needy circumstances. Apply to Robert Hugh Allan LLB DipLP NP, Pomphreys, 79 Quarry Street, Hamilton ML3 7AG (Tel: 01698 891616).

BELLAHOUSTON BEQUEST FUND: Gives grants to Protestant evangelical denominations in the City of Glasgow and certain areas within five miles of the city boundary for building and repairing churches and halls and the promotion of religion. Apply to Mr John A.M. Cuthbert, Mitchells Roberton, 36 North Hanover Street, Glasgow G1 2AD.

BEQUEST FUND FOR MINISTERS: Assists ministers in outlying districts with manse furnishings, pastoral efficiency aids, educational or medical costs. Apply to A. Linda Parkhill CA, 60 Wellington Street, Glasgow G2 6HJ (Tel: 0141-226 4994).

CARNEGIE TRUST FOR THE UNIVERSITIES OF SCOTLAND: In cases of hardship, the Carnegie Trust is prepared to consider applications by students of Scottish birth or extraction (at least one parent born in Scotland), or who have had at least two years' education at a secondary school in Scotland, for financial assistance with the payment of their fees for a first degree at a Scottish university. For further details, students should apply to the Secretary, Carnegie Trust for the Universities of Scotland, Cameron House, Abbey Park Place, Dunfermline, Fife KY12 7PZ (Tel: 01383 622148; E-mail: jgray@carnegie-trust.org; Website: www.carnegie-trust.org).

CHURCH OF SCOTLAND INSURANCE CO. LTD: Undertakes insurance of Church property and pays surplus profits to Church schemes. It is authorised and regulated by the Financial Services Authority. The company can also arrange household insurance for members and adherents of the Church of Scotland. At 67 George Street, Edinburgh EH2 2JG (Tel: 0131-220 4119; Fax: 0131-220 4120; E-mail: enquiries@cosic.co.uk).

CHURCH OF SCOTLAND MINISTRY BENEVOLENT FUND: Makes grants to retired men and women who have been ordained or commissioned for the ministry of the Church of Scotland and to widows, widowers, orphans, spouses or children of such, who are in need. Apply to the Assistant Treasurer (Ministries), 121 George Street, Edinburgh EH2 4YN (Tel: 0131-225 5722).

CLARK BURSARY: Awarded to accepted candidate(s) for the ministry of the Church of Scotland whose studies for the ministry are pursued at the University of Aberdeen. Applications or recommendations for the Bursary to the Clerk to the Presbytery of Aberdeen, Mastrick Church, Greenfern Road, Aberdeen AB16 6TR by 16 October annually.

CRAIGCROOK MORTIFICATION:
Preses:	Michael J.R. Simpson
Clerk and Factor:	R. Graeme Thom FCA
	17 Melville Street
	Edinburgh EH3 7PH (Tel: 0131-473 3500)

Pensions are paid to poor men and women over 60 years old, born in Scotland or who have resided in Scotland for not less than ten years. At present, pensions amount to £600 p.a.
    Ministers are invited to notify the Clerk and Factor of deserving persons and should be prepared to act as a referee on the application form.

THE ALASTAIR CRERAR TRUST FOR SINGLE POOR: Provides churches, Christian organisations and individual Christians with grants to help single adults and groups of single people, who live on low incomes and have little capital, to improve their quality of life. Apply to the Secretary, Michael I.D. Sturrock, Garden Flat, 34 Mayfield Terrace, Edinburgh EH9 1RZ (Tel: 0131-668 3524; E-mail: actrust@uwclub.net).

CROMBIE SCHOLARSHIP: Provides grants annually on the nomination of the Deans of Faculty of Divinity of the Universities of St Andrews, Glasgow, Aberdeen and Edinburgh, who each nominate one matriculated student who has taken a University course in Greek (Classical or Hellenistic) and Hebrew. Award by recommendation only.

THE DRUMMOND TRUST: Makes grants towards the cost of publication of books of 'sound Christian doctrine and outreach'. The Trustees are also willing to receive grant requests towards the cost of audio-visual programme material, but not equipment. Requests for application forms should be made to the Secretaries, Hill and Robb, 3 Pitt Terrace, Stirling FK8 2EY (Tel: 01786 450985; E-mail: douglaswhyte@hillandrobb.co.uk). Manuscripts should *not* be sent.

THE DUNCAN TRUST: Makes grants annually to students for the ministry in the Faculties of Arts and Divinity. Preference is given to those born or educated within the bounds of the former Presbytery of Arbroath. Applications not later than 31 October to G.J.M. Dunlop, Brothockbank House, Arbroath DD11 1NE (Tel: 01241 872683).

ESDAILE TRUST:
Chairman: Dr Douglas Grant
Clerk and Treasurer: R. Graeme Thom FCA
                             17 Melville Street
                             Edinburgh EH3 7PH (Tel: 0131-473 3500)
Assists education and advancement of daughters of ministers, missionaries and widowed deaconesses of the Church of Scotland between 12 and 25 years of age. Applications are to be lodged by 31 May in each year.

FERGUSON BEQUEST FUND: For the maintenance and promotion of religious ordinances and education and missionary operations in the first instance in the Counties of Ayr, Kirkcudbright, Wigtown, Lanark, Renfrew and Dunbarton. Apply to Ronald D. Oakes CA ACMA, 182 Bath Street, Glasgow G2 4HG (Tel: 0141-332 0476; Fax: 0141-331 0874).

GEIKIE BEQUEST: Makes small grants to students for the ministry, including students studying for entry to the University, preference being given to those not eligible for SAAS awards. Apply to the Assistant Treasurer (Ministries), 121 George Street, Edinburgh EH2 4YN.

JAMES GILLAN'S BURSARY FUND: Bursaries are available for students for the ministry who were born or whose parents or parent have resided and had their home for not less than three years continually in the old counties (not Districts) of Moray or Nairn. Apply to R. and R. Urquhart, 121 High Street, Forres IV36 0AB.

HAMILTON BURSARY TRUST: Awarded, subject to the intention to serve overseas under the Church of Scotland World Mission Council or to serve with some other Overseas Mission Agency approved by the Council, to a student at the University of Aberdeen. Preference is given to a student born or residing in (1) Parish of Skene, (2) Parish of Echt, (3) the Presbytery of Aberdeen, Kincardine and Deeside, or Gordon; failing which to Accepted Candidate(s) for the Ministry of the Church of Scotland whose studies for the Ministry are pursued at Aberdeen University. Applications or recommendations for the Bursary to the Clerk to the Presbytery of Aberdeen by 16 October annually.

MARTIN HARCUS BEQUEST: Makes annual grants to candidates for the ministry resident within the City of Edinburgh. Applications to the Clerk to the Presbytery of Edinburgh, 10/1 Palmerston Place, Edinburgh EH12 5AA by 15 October (E-mail: akph50@uk.uumail.com).

THE HOPE TRUST: Gives some support to organisations involved in combating drink and drugs, and has as its main purpose the promotion of the Reformed Faith throughout the world. There is also a Scholarship programme for Postgraduate Theology Study in Scotland. Apply to Robert P. Miller SSC LLB, 31 Moray Place, Edinburgh EH3 6BY (Tel: 0131-226 5151).

GILLIAN MACLAINE BURSARY FUND: Open to candidates for the ministry of the Church of Scotland of Scottish or Canadian nationality. Preference is given to Gaelic-speakers. Information and terms of award from Rev. George G. Cringles BD, Depute Clerk of the Presbytery of Argyll, St Oran's Manse, Connel, Oban PA37 1PJ.

THE E. McLAREN FUND: The persons intended to be benefited are widows and unmarried ladies, preference being given to ladies above 40 years of age in the following order:
(a) Widows and daughters of Officers in the Highland Regiment, and
(b) Widows and daughters of Scotsmen.

Further details from the Secretary, The E. McLaren Fund, Apsley House, 29 Wellington Street, Glasgow G2 6JA (Tel: 0141-221 8004; Fax: 0141-221 2407; E-mail: rrs@bmkwilson.co.uk).

THE MISSES ANN AND MARGARET McMILLAN'S BEQUEST: Makes grants to ministers of the Free and United Free Churches, and of the Church of Scotland, in charges within the Synod of Argyll, with income not exceeding the minimum stipend of the Church of Scotland. Apply by 30 June in each year to Business Manager, Royal Bank of Scotland, 37 Victoria Street, Rothesay, Isle of Bute PA20 0AP.

MORGAN BURSARY FUND: Makes grants to candidates for the Church of Scotland ministry studying at the University of Glasgow. Apply to Rev. David W. Lunan MA BD, 260 Bath Street, Glasgow G2 4JP (Tel/Fax: 0141-332 6606).

NOVUM TRUST: Provides small short-term grants to initiate projects in Christian research and action which cannot readily be financed from other sources. Special consideration is given to proposals aimed at the welfare of young people, investment in training, and new ways of communicating the faith. The Trust cannot support large building projects, nor can it support individuals applying for maintenance during courses or training. Applications to Rev. Alex. M. Millar, 121 George Street, Edinburgh EH2 4YN (E-mail: amillar@cofscotland.org.uk).

PARK MEMORIAL BURSARY FUND: Provides grants for the benefit of candidates for the ministry of the Church of Scotland from the Presbytery of Glasgow under full-time training. Apply to Rev. David W. Lunan MA BD, Presbytery of Glasgow, 260 Bath Street, Glasgow G2 4JP (Tel: 0141-332 6606).

PATON TRUST: Assists ministers in ill health to have a recuperative holiday outwith, and free from the cares of, their parishes. Apply to Iain A.T. Mowat CA, Alexander Sloan, Chartered Accountants, 144 West George Street, Glasgow G2 2HG (Tel: 0141-354 0354; Fax: 0141-354 0355; E-mail iatm@alexandersloan.co.uk).

RENFIELD STREET TRUST: Assists in the building and repair of churches and halls. Apply to Ronald D. Oakes CA ACMA, 182 Bath Street, Glasgow G2 4HG (Tel: 0141-332 0476; Fax: 0141-331 0874).

SCOTTISH CHURCHES ARCHITECTURAL HERITAGE TRUST: Assists congregations of any denomination in the preservation of churches regularly used for public worship and of architectural value and historic interest. Apply to the Secretary, 15 North Bank Street, The Mound, Edinburgh EH1 2LP (Tel: 0131-225 8644; E-mail: info@scaht.org.uk).

SMIETON FUND: Makes small holiday grants to ministers. Administered at the discretion of the pastoral staff, who will give priority in cases of need. Applications to the Associate Secretary (Support and Development), Ministries Council, 121 George Street, Edinburgh EH2 4YN.

MARY DAVIDSON SMITH CLERICAL AND EDUCATIONAL FUND FOR ABERDEENSHIRE: Assists ministers who have been ordained for five years or over and are in full charge of a congregation in Aberdeen, Aberdeenshire and the north, to purchase books, or to travel for educational purposes, and assists their children with scholarships for further education or vocational training. Apply to Alan J. Innes MA LLB, 100 Union Street, Aberdeen AB10 1QR.

THE NAN STEVENSON CHARITABLE TRUST FOR RETIRED MINISTERS: Provides houses, or loans to purchase houses, for retired ministers or missionaries on similar terms to the Housing and Loan Fund, with preference given to those with a North Ayrshire connection. Secretary: Rev. Johnston R. McKay, Upper Burnfoot, 27 Stanlane Place, Largs KA30 8DD.

PRESBYTERY OF ARGYLL BURSARY FUND: Open to students who have been accepted as candidates for the ministry and the readership of the Church of Scotland. Preference is given to applicants who are natives of the bounds of the Presbytery, or are resident within the bounds of the Presbytery, or who have a strong connection with the bounds of the Presbytery. Information and terms of award from Rev. George G. Cringles BD, Depute Clerk of the Presbytery of Argyll, St Oran's Manse, Connel, Oban PA37 1PJ.

SYNOD OF GRAMPIAN CHILDREN OF THE CLERGY FUND: Makes annual grants to children of deceased ministers. Apply to Rev. Iain U. Thomson, Clerk and Treasurer, The Manse, Skene, Westhill AB32 6LX.

SYNOD OF GRAMPIAN WIDOWS FUND: Makes annual grants (currently £225 p.a.) to widows or widowers of deceased ministers who have served in a charge in the former Synod. Apply to Rev. Iain U. Thomson, Clerk and Treasurer, The Manse, Skene, Westhill AB32 6LX.

YOUNG MINISTERS' FURNISHING LOAN FUND: Makes loans (of £1,000) to ministers in their first charge to assist with furnishing the manse. Apply to the Assistant Treasurer (Ministries), 121 George Street, Edinburgh EH2 4YN.

---

(6) RECENT LORD HIGH COMMISSIONERS
TO THE GENERAL ASSEMBLY

1965/66	The Hon. Lord Birsay CBE QC TD
1967/68	The Rt Hon. Lord Reith of Stonehaven GCVO GBE CB TD
1969	Her Majesty the Queen attended in person
1970	The Rt Hon. Margaret Herbison PC
1971/72	The Rt Hon. Lord Clydesmuir of Braidwood CB MBE TD
1973/74	The Rt Hon. Lord Ballantrae of Auchairne and the Bay of Islands GCMG GCVO DSO OBE
1975/76	Sir Hector MacLennan KT FRCPGLAS FRCOG
1977	Francis David Charteris, Earl of Wemyss and March KT LLD
1978/79	The Rt Hon. William Ross MBE LLD
1980/81	Andrew Douglas Alexander Thomas Bruce, Earl of Elgin and Kincardine KT DL JP
1982/83	Colonel Sir John Edward Gilmour BT DSO TD
1984/85	Charles Hector Fitzroy Maclean, Baron Maclean of Duart and Morvern KT GCVO KBE
1986/87	John Campbell Arbuthnott, Viscount of Arbuthnott CBE DSC FRSE FRSA
1988/89	Sir Iain Mark Tennant KT FRSA
1990/91	The Rt Hon. Donald MacArthur Ross FRSE
1992/93	The Rt Hon. Lord Macfarlane of Bearsden

1994/95	Lady Marion Fraser
1996	Her Royal Highness the Princess Royal LG GCVO
1997	The Rt Hon. Lord Macfarlane of Bearsden
1998/99	The Rt Hon. Lord Hogg of Cumbernauld
2000	His Royal Highness the Prince Charles, Duke of Rothesay
2001/02	The Rt Hon. Viscount Younger of Leckie
2003/04	The Rt Hon. Lord Steel of Aikwood
2005/06	The Rt Hon. Lord Mackay of Clashfern KT

(7) RECENT MODERATORS
OF THE GENERAL ASSEMBLY

1965	Archibald Watt STM DD, Edzell and Lethnot
1966	R. Leonard Small OBE DD, Edinburgh: St Cuthbert's
1967	W. Roy Sanderson DD, Stenton with Whittingehame
1968	J.B. Longmuir TD DD, Principal Clerk of Assembly
1969	T.M. Murchison MA DD, Glasgow: St Columba Summertown
1970	Hugh O. Douglas CBE DD LLD, Dundee: St Mary's
1971	Andrew Herron MA BD LLB, Clerk to the Presbytery of Glasgow
1972	R.W.V. Selby Wright JP CVO TD DD FRSE, Edinburgh: Canongate
1973	George T.H. Reid MC MA BD DD, Aberdeen: Langstane
1974	David Steel MA BD DD, Linlithgow: St Michael's
1975	James G. Matheson MA BD DD, Portree
1976	Thomas F. Torrance MBE DLitt DD FRSE, University of Edinburgh
1977	John R. Gray VRD MA BD ThM, Dunblane: Cathedral
1978	Peter P. Brodie MA BD LLB DD, Alloa: St Mungo's
1979	Robert A.S. Barbour MA BD STM DD, University of Aberdeen
1980	William B. Johnston MA BD DD, Edinburgh: Colinton
1981	Andrew B. Doig BD STM DD, National Bible Society of Scotland
1982	John McIntyre CVO DD DLitt FRSE, University of Edinburgh
1983	J. Fraser McLuskey MC DD, London: St Columba's
1984	John M.K. Paterson MA ACII BD, Milngavie: St Paul's
1985	David M.B.A. Smith MA BD DUniv, Logie
1986	Robert Craig CBE DLitt LLD DD, Emeritus of Jerusalem
1987	Duncan Shaw Bundesverdienstkreuz PhD ThDr JP, Edinburgh: Craigentinny St Christopher's
1988	James A. Whyte MA LLD, University of St Andrews
1989	William J.G. McDonald MA BD DD, Edinburgh: Mayfield
1990	Robert Davidson MA BD DD FRSE, University of Glasgow
1991	William B.R. Macmillan MA BD LLD DD, Dundee: St Mary's
1992	Hugh R. Wyllie MA MCIBS DD, Hamilton: Old Parish Church
1993	James L. Weatherhead CBE MA LLB DD, Principal Clerk of Assembly
1994	James A. Simpson BSc BD STM DD, Dornoch Cathedral
1995	James Harkness CB OBE MA DD, Chaplain General (Emeritus)
1996	John H. McIndoe MA BD STM DD, London: St Columba's linked with Newcastle: St Andrew's

1997	Alexander Mcdonald BA CMIWSc DUniv, General Secretary, Department of Ministry
1998	Alan Main TD MA BD STM PhD, Professor of Practical Theology at Christ's College, University of Aberdeen
1999	John B. Cairns LTh LLB LLD DD, Dumbarton: Riverside
2000	Andrew R.C. McLellan MA BD STM DD, Edinburgh: St Andrew's and St George's
2001	John D. Miller BA BD DD, Glasgow: Castlemilk East
2002	Finlay A.J. Macdonald MA BD PhD DD, Principal Clerk of Assembly
2003	Iain R. Torrance TD MA BD DPhil DD, Professor of Patristics and Christian Ethics at the University of Aberdeen and Master of Christ's College
2004	Alison Elliot OBE MA MSc PhD LLD DD, Associate Director CTPI
2005	David W. Lacy BA BD DLitt, Kilmarnock: Henderson
2006	Alan D. McDonald LLB BD MTh, Cameron linked with St Andrews: St Leonard's

MATTER OF PRECEDENCE

The Lord High Commissioner to the General Assembly of the Church of Scotland (while the Assembly is sitting) ranks next to the Sovereign and the Duke of Edinburgh and before the rest of the Royal Family.

The Moderator of the General Assembly of the Church of Scotland ranks next to the Lord Chancellor of Great Britain and before the Prime Minister and the Dukes.

(8) HER MAJESTY'S HOUSEHOLD IN SCOTLAND
ECCLESIASTICAL

Dean of the Chapel Royal: Very Rev. John B. Cairns LTh LLB LLD DD
Dean of the Order of the Thistle: Very Rev. Gilleasbuig Macmillan CVO MA BD Drhc DD
Domestic Chaplain: Vacant

Chaplains in Ordinary: Very Rev. Gilleasbuig Macmillan CVO MA BD Drhc DD
Rev. Charles Robertson MA JP
Rev. Norman W. Drummond MA BD
Rev. John L. Paterson MA BD STM
Rev. Alastair H. Symington MA BD
Very Rev. Prof. Iain R. Torrance TD MA BD DPhil DD
Very Rev. Finlay A.J. Macdonald MA BD PhD DD
Rev. James M. Gibson TD LTh LRAM
Rev. Angus Morrison MA BD PhD

Extra Chaplains: Very Rev. W. Roy Sanderson DD
                                      Rev. H.W.M. Cant MA BD STM
                                      Rev. Kenneth MacVicar MBE DFC TD MA
                                      Very Rev. Prof. Robert A.S. Barbour
                                          KCVO MC BD STM DD
                                      Rev. Alwyn Macfarlane MA
                                      Rev. Mary I. Levison BA BD DD
                                      Very Rev. William J. Morris KCVO PhD LLD DD JP
                                      Rev. John MacLeod MA
                                      Rev. A. Stewart Todd MA BD DD
                                      Very Rev. James L. Weatherhead CBE MA LLB DD
                                      Rev. Maxwell D. Craig MA BD ThM
                                      Very Rev. James A. Simpson BSc BD STM DD
                                      Very Rev. James Harkness
                                          KCVO CB OBE MA DD

(9) LONG SERVICE CERTIFICATES

Long Service Certificates, signed by the Moderator, are available for presentation to elders and others in respect of not less than thirty years of service. It should be noted that the period is years of *service*, not (for example) years of ordination in the case of an elder.

In the case of Sunday School teachers and Bible Class leaders, the qualifying period is twenty-one years of service.

Certificates are not issued posthumously, nor is it possible to make exceptions to the rules, for example by recognising quality of service in order to reduce the qualifying period, or by reducing the qualifying period on compassionate grounds, such as serious illness.

A Certificate will be issued only once to any particular individual.

Applications for Long Service Certificates should be made in writing to the Principal Clerk at 121 George Street, Edinburgh EH2 4YN by the parish minister, or by the session clerk on behalf of the Kirk Session. Certificates are not issued from this office to the individual recipients, nor should individuals make application themselves.

(10) LIBRARIES OF THE CHURCH

GENERAL ASSEMBLY LIBRARY AND RECORD ROOM

Most of the books contained in the General Assembly Library have been transferred to the New College Library. Records of the General Assembly, Synods, Presbyteries and Kirk Sessions are now in HM Register House, Edinburgh.

CHURCH MUSIC

The Library of New College contains a selection of works on Church music.

(11) RECORDS OF THE CHURCH OF SCOTLAND

Church records more than fifty years old, unless still in use, should be sent or delivered to the Principal Clerk for onward transmission to the Scottish Record Office. Where ministers or session clerks are approached by a local repository seeking a transfer of their records, they should inform the Principal Clerk, who will take the matter up with the National Archives of Scotland.

Where a temporary retransmission of records is sought, it is extremely helpful if notice can be given three months in advance so that appropriate procedures can be carried out satisfactorily.

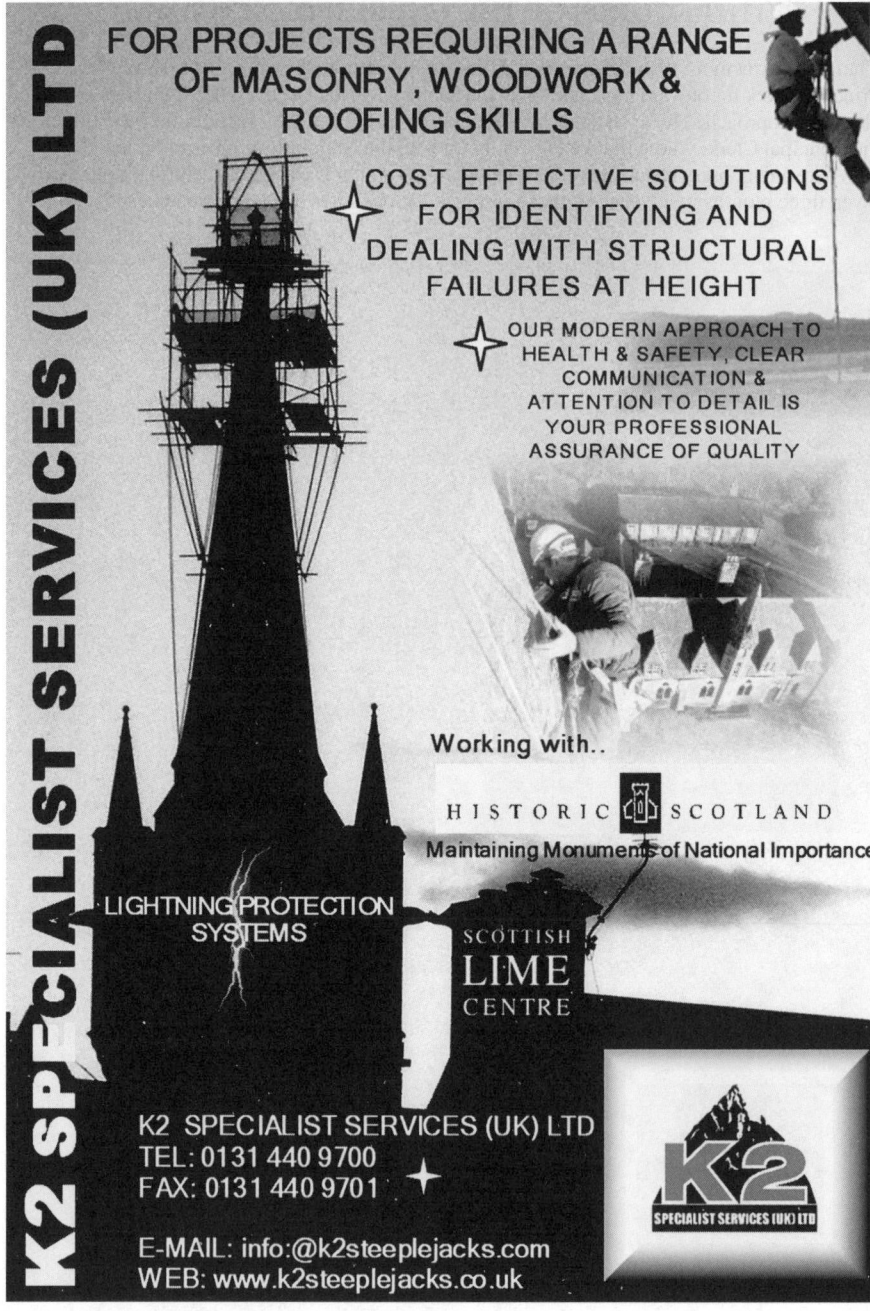

SECTION 3

Church Procedure

(1) THE MINISTER AND BAPTISM

The administration of Baptism to infants is governed by Act V 2000 as amended by Act IX 2003. A Statement and Exposition of the Doctrine of Baptism may be found at page 13/8 in the published volume of Reports to the General Assembly of 2003.

The Act itself is as follows:

3. Baptism signifies the action and love of God in Christ, through the Holy Spirit, and is a seal upon the gift of grace and the response of faith.
    (a) Baptism shall be administered in the name of the Father and of the Son and of the Holy Spirit, with water, by sprinkling, pouring, or immersion.
    (b) Baptism shall be administered to a person only once.
4. Baptism may be administered to a person upon profession of faith.
    (a) The minister and Kirk Session shall judge whether the person is of sufficient maturity to make personal profession of faith, where necessary in consultation with the parent(s) or legal guardian(s).
    (b) Baptism may be administered only after the person has received such instruction in its meaning as the minister and Kirk Session consider necessary, according to such basis of instruction as may be authorised by the General Assembly.
    (c) In cases of uncertainty as to whether a person has been baptised or validly baptised, baptism shall be administered conditionally.
5. Baptism may be administered to a person with learning difficulties who makes an appropriate profession of faith, where the minister and Kirk Session are satisfied that the person shall be nurtured within the life and worship of the Church.
6. Baptism may be administered to a child:
    (a) where at least one parent, or other family member (with parental consent), having been baptised and being on the communion roll of the congregation, will undertake the Christian upbringing of the child;
    (b) where at least one parent, or other family member (with parental consent), having been baptised but not on the communion roll of the congregation, satisfies the minister and Kirk Session that he or she is an adherent of the congregation and will undertake the Christian upbringing of the child;
    (c) where at least one parent, or other family member (with parental consent), having been baptised, professes the Christian faith, undertakes to ensure that the child grows up in the life and worship of the Church and expresses the desire to seek admission to the communion roll of the congregation;
    (d) where the child is under legal guardianship, and the minister and Kirk Session are satisfied that the child shall be nurtured within the life and worship of the congregation;
    and, in each of the above cases, only after the parent(s), or other family member, has received such instruction in its meaning as the minister and Kirk Session consider necessary, according to such basis of instruction as may be authorised by the General Assembly.
7. Baptism shall normally be administered during the public worship of the congregation in which the person makes profession of faith, or of which the parent or other family member is on the communion roll, or is an adherent. In exceptional circumstances, baptism may be administered elsewhere (e.g. at home or in hospital). Further, a minister may administer baptism to a person resident outwith the minister's parish, and who is not otherwise connected with the congregation, only with the consent of the minister of the parish in

which the person would normally reside, or of the Presbytery.

8.   In all cases, an entry shall be made in the Kirk Session's Baptismal Register and a Certificate of Baptism given by the minister. Where baptism is administered in a chaplaincy context, it shall be recorded in the Baptismal Register there, and, where possible, reported to the minister of the parish in which the person resides.

9.   Baptism shall normally be administered by an ordained minister. In situations of emergency,
(a)   a minister may, exceptionally, notwithstanding the preceding provisions of the Act, respond to a request for baptism in accordance with his or her pastoral judgement, and
(b)   baptism may be validly administered by a person who is not ordained, always providing that it is administered in the name of the Father and of the Son and of the Holy Spirit, with water.
In every occurrence of the latter case, of which a minister or chaplain becomes aware, an entry shall be made in the appropriate Baptismal Register and where possible reported to the Clerk of the Presbytery within which the baptism was administered.

10.   Each Presbytery shall form, or designate, a committee to which reference may be made in cases where there is a dispute as to the interpretation of this Act. Without the consent of the Presbytery, no minister may administer baptism in a case where to his or her knowledge another minister has declined to do so.

11.   The Church of Scotland, as part of the Universal Church, affirms the validity of the sacrament of baptism administered in the name of the Father and of the Son and of the Holy Spirit, with water, in accordance with the discipline of other members of the Universal Church.

(2) THE MINISTER AND MARRIAGE

1. BACKGROUND
Prior to 1939, every marriage in Scotland fell into one or other of two classes: regular or irregular. The former was marriage by a minister of religion after due notice of intention had been given; the latter could be effected in one of three ways: (1) declaration *de presenti*, (2) by promise *subsequente copula*, or (3) by habit and repute.

The Marriage (Scotland) Act of 1939 put an end to (1) and (2) and provided for a new classification of marriage as either religious or civil.

The law of marriage as it was thus established in 1939 had two important limitations to the celebration of marriage: (1) certain preliminaries had to be observed; and (2) in respect of religious marriage, the service had to be conducted according to the forms of either the Christian or the Jewish faith.

2. THE MARRIAGE (SCOTLAND) ACT 1977
These two conditions were radically altered by the Marriage (Scotland) Act 1977.

Since 1 January 1978, in conformity with the demands of a multi-racial society, the benefits of religious marriage have been extended to adherents of other faiths, the only requirements being the observance of monogamy and the satisfaction of the authorities with the forms of the vows imposed.

Since 1978, the calling of banns has also been discontinued. The couple themselves must each complete a Marriage Notice form and return this to the District Registrar for the area in which they are to be married, irrespective of where they live, at least fifteen days before the ceremony is due to take place. The form details the documents which require to be produced with it.

If everything is in order, the District Registrar will issue, not more than seven days before the date of the ceremony, a Marriage Schedule. This must be in the hands of the minister officiating at the marriage ceremony before the service begins. Under no circumstances must the minister deviate from this rule. To do so is an offence under the Act.

Ministers should note the advice given by the Procurator of the Church in 1962, that they should not officiate at any marriage until at least one day after the 16th birthday of the younger party.

3. THE MARRIAGE (SCOTLAND) ACT 2002

Although there have never been any limitations as to the place where a religious marriage can be celebrated, civil marriage can take place only in the Office of a Registrar. The Marriage (Scotland) Act 2002 permits the solemnisation of civil marriages at places approved by Local Authorities. Regulations are to be made to specify the kinds of place which may be 'approved' with a view to ensuring that the places approved will not compromise the solemnity and dignity of civil marriage and will have no recent or continuing connection with any religion so as to undermine the distinction between religious and civil ceremonies.

4. PROCLAMATION OF BANNS

Proclamation of banns is no longer required in Scotland; but, in the Church of England, marriage is governed by the provisions of the Marriage Act 1949, which requires that the parties' intention to marry has to have been proclaimed and which provides that in the case of a party residing in Scotland a Certificate of Proclamation given according to the law or custom prevailing in Scotland shall be sufficient for the purpose. In the event that a minister is asked to call banns for a person resident within the registration district where his or her church is situated, the proclamation needs only to be made on one Sunday if the parties are known to the minister. If they are not, it should be made on two Sundays. In all cases, the Minister should, of course, have no reason to believe that there is any impediment to the marriage.

Proclamation should be made at the principal service of worship in this form:

There is a purpose of marriage between AB (Bachelor/Widower/Divorced), residing at .... in this Registration District, and CD (Spinster/Widow/Divorced), residing at .... in the Registration District of ...., of which proclamation is hereby made for the first and only (second and last) time.

Immediately after the second reading, or not less than forty-eight hours after the first and only reading, a Certificate of Proclamation signed by either the minister or the Session Clerk should be issued in the following terms:

At .... the ...... day of ...... 20 ....
It is hereby certified that AB, residing at ...., and CD, residing at ...., have been duly proclaimed in order to marriage in the Church of .... according to the custom of the Church of Scotland, and that no objections have been offered.
Signed .... minister or
Signed .... Session Clerk

5. MARRIAGE OF FOREIGNERS

Marriages in Scotland of foreigners, or of foreigners with British subjects, are, if they satisfy the requirements of Scots Law, valid within the United Kingdom and the various British overseas territories; but they will not necessarily be valid in the country to which the foreigner belongs. This will be so only if the requirements of the law of his or her country have also been complied with. It is therefore most important that, before the marriage, steps should be taken to obtain from the Consul, or other diplomatic representative of the country concerned, a satisfactory assurance that the marriage will be accepted as valid in the country concerned.

6. REMARRIAGE OF DIVORCED PERSONS

By virtue of Act XXVI 1959, a minister of the Church of Scotland may lawfully solemnise the marriage of a person whose former marriage has been dissolved by divorce and whose former spouse is still alive. The minister, however, must carefully adhere to the requirements of the Act which, as slightly altered in 1985, are briefly as follows:

1. The minister should not accede as a matter of routine to a request to solemnise such a marriage. To enable a decision to be made, he or she should take all reasonable steps to obtain relevant information, which should normally include the following:
   (a) Adequate information concerning the life and character of the parties. The Act enjoins the greatest caution in cases where no pastoral relationship exists between the minister and either or both of the parties concerned.
   (b) The grounds and circumstances of the divorce case.
   (c) Facts bearing upon the future well-being of any children concerned.
   (d) Whether any other minister has declined to solemnise the proposed marriage.
   (e) The denomination to which the parties belong. The Act enjoins that special care should be taken where one or more parties belong to a denomination whose discipline in this matter may differ from that of the Church of Scotland.
2. The minister should consider whether there is danger of scandal arising if he or she should solemnise the remarriage, at the same time taking into careful consideration before refusing to do so the moral and spiritual effect of a refusal on the parties concerned.
3. As a determinative factor, the minister should do all he or she can to be assured that there has been sincere repentance where guilt has existed on the part of any divorced person seeking remarriage. He or she should also give instruction, where needed, in the nature and requirements of a Christian marriage.
4. A minister is not required to solemnise a remarriage against his or her conscience. Every Presbytery is required to appoint certain individuals with one of whom ministers in doubt as to the correct course of action may consult if they so desire. The final decision, however, rests with the minister who has been asked to officiate.

---

(3) CONDUCT OF MARRIAGE SERVICES
(CODE OF GOOD PRACTICE)

The code which follows was submitted to the General Assembly in 1997. It appears, on page 1/10, in the Volume of Assembly Reports for that year within the Report of the Board of Practice and Procedure.

1. *Marriage in the Church of Scotland is solemnised by an ordained minister in a religious ceremony wherein, before God, and in the presence of the minister and at least two competent witnesses, the parties covenant together to take each other as husband and wife as long as they both shall live, and the minister declares the parties to be husband and wife. Before solemnising a marriage, a minister must be assured that the necessary legal requirements are being complied with and that the parties know of no legal impediment to their marriage, and he or she must afterwards ensure that the Marriage Schedule is duly completed.* (Act I 1977)
2. Any ordained minister of the Church of Scotland who is a member of Presbytery or who holds a current Ministerial Certificate may officiate at a marriage service (see Act II 1987).
3. While the marriage service should normally take place in church, a minister may, at his or her discretion, officiate at a marriage service outwith church premises. Wherever conducted, the ceremony will be such as to reflect appropriately both the joy and the solemnity of the occasion. In particular, a minister shall ensure that nothing is done which would bring the Church and its teaching into disrepute.
4. A minister agreeing to conduct a wedding should endeavour to establish a pastoral relationship with the couple within which adequate pre-marriage preparation and subsequent pastoral care may be given.
5. 'A minister should not refuse to perform ministerial functions for a person who is resident in his or her parish without sufficient reason' (Cox, *Practice and Procedure in the Church of Scotland*, sixth edition, page 55). Where either party to the proposed marriage has been divorced and the former spouse is still alive, the minister invited to officiate may solemnise such a marriage, having regard to the guidelines in the Act anent the Remarriage of Divorced Persons (Act XXVI 1959 as amended by Act II 1985).
6. A minister is acting as an agent of the National Church which is committed to bringing the ordinances of religion to the people of Scotland through a territorial ministry. As such, he or she shall not be entitled to charge a fee or allow a fee to be charged for conducting a marriage service. When a gift is spontaneously offered to a minister as a token of appreciation, the above consideration should not be taken to mean that he or she should not accept such an unsolicited gift. The Financial Board of a congregation is at liberty to set fees to cover such costs as heat and light, and in addition Organists and Church Officers are entitled to a fee in respect of their services at weddings.
7. A minister should not allow his or her name to be associated with any commercial enterprise that provides facilities for weddings.
8. A minister is not at liberty to enter the bounds of another minister's parish to perform ministerial functions without the previous consent of the minister of that parish. In terms of Act VIII 1933, a minister may 'officiate at a marriage or funeral by private invitation', but, for the avoidance of doubt, an invitation conveyed through a commercial enterprise shall not be regarded as a 'private invitation' within the meaning of that Act.
9. A minister invited to officiate at a Marriage Service where neither party is a member of his or her congregation or is resident within his or her own parish or has any connection with the parish within which the service is to take place should observe the following courtesies:
    (a) he or she should ascertain from the parties whether either of them has a Church of Scotland connection or has approached the appropriate parish minister(s);
    (b) if it transpires that a ministerial colleague has declined to officiate, then he or she (the invited minister) should ascertain the reasons therefor and shall take these and all other relevant factors into account in deciding whether or not to officiate.

(4) THE MINISTER AND WILLS

The Requirements of Writing (Scotland) Act 1995, which came into force on 1 August 1995, has removed the power of a minister to execute wills notarially. Further clarification, if required, may be obtained from the Solicitor of the Church.

(5) PROCEDURE IN A VACANCY

Procedure in a vacancy is regulated by Act VIII 2003 as amended by Acts IX and X 2004, II 2005 and V 2006. The text of the most immediately relevant sections is given here for general information. Schedules of Intimation referred to are also included. The full text of the Act and subsequent amendments can be obtained from the Principal Clerk.

1. Vacancy Procedure Committee
(1)   Each Presbytery shall appoint a number of its members to be available to serve on Vacancy Procedure Committees and shall provide information and training as required for those so appointed.
(2)   As soon as the Presbytery Clerk is aware that a vacancy has arisen or is anticipated, he or she shall consult the Moderator of the Presbytery and they shall appoint a Vacancy Procedure Committee of five persons from among those appointed in terms of subsection (1), which Committee shall (a) include at least one minister and at least one elder and (b) exclude any communicant member or former minister of the vacant charge or of any constituent congregation thereof. The Vacancy Procedure Committee shall include a Convener and Clerk, the latter of whom need not be a member of the Committee but may be the Presbytery Clerk. The same Vacancy Procedure Committee may serve for more than one vacancy at a time.
(3)   The Vacancy Procedure Committee shall have a quorum of three for its meetings.
(4)   The Convener of the Vacancy Procedure Committee may, where he or she reasonably believes a matter to be non-contentious, consult members individually, provided that reasonable efforts are made to consult all members of the Committee. A meeting shall be held at the request of any member of the Committee.
(5)   Every decision made by the Vacancy Procedure Committee shall be reported to the next meeting of Presbytery, but may not be recalled by Presbytery where the decision was subject to the provisions of section 2 below.

2. Request for Consideration by Presbytery
Where in this Act any decision by the Vacancy Procedure Committee is subject to the provisions of this section, the following rules shall apply:
(1)   The Presbytery Clerk shall intimate to all members of the Presbytery by mailing or at a Presbytery meeting the course of action or permission proposed, and shall arrange for one Sunday's pulpit intimation of the same to be made to the congregation or congregations concerned, in terms of Schedule A. The intimation having been made, it shall be displayed as prominently as possible at the church building for seven days.
(2)   Any four individuals, being communicant members of the congregation or full members of

the Presbytery, may give written notice requesting that action be taken in terms of subsection (3) below, giving reasons for the request, within seven days after the pulpit intimation.

(3)   Upon receiving notice in terms of subsection (2), the Presbytery Clerk shall sist the process or permission referred to in subsection (1), which shall then require the approval of the Presbytery.

(4)   The Moderator of the Presbytery shall in such circumstances consider whether a meeting *pro re nata* of the Presbytery should be called in order to avoid prejudicial delay in the vacancy process.

(5)   The Presbytery Clerk shall cause to have served upon the congregation or congregations an edict in terms of Schedule B citing them to attend the meeting of Presbytery for their interest.

(6)   The consideration by Presbytery of any matter under this section shall not constitute an appeal or a Petition, and the decision of Presbytery shall be deemed to be a decision at first instance subject to the normal rights of appeal or dissent-and-complaint.

3. Causes of Vacancy

The causes of vacancy shall normally include:

(a)   the death of the minister of the charge;

(b)   the removal of status of the minister of the charge or the suspension of the minister in terms of section 20(2) of Act III 2001;

(c)   the dissolution of the pastoral tie in terms of Act I 1988 or Act XV 2002;

(d)   the demission of the charge and/or status of the minister of the charge;

(e)   the translation of the minister of the charge to another charge;

(f)   the termination of the tenure of the minister of the charge in terms of Act VI 1984.

4. Release of Departing Minister

The Presbytery Clerk shall be informed as soon as circumstances have occurred that cause a vacancy to arise or make it likely that a vacancy shall arise. Where the circumstances pertain to section 3(d) or (e) above, the Vacancy Procedure Committee shall

(1)   except in cases governed by subsection (2) below, decide whether to release the minister from his or her charge and, in any case involving translation to another charge or introduction to an appointment, instruct him or her to await the instructions of the Presbytery or another Presbytery;

(2)   in the case of a minister in the first five years of his or her first charge, decide whether there are exceptional circumstances to justify releasing him or her from his or her charge and proceeding in terms of subsection (1) above;

(3)   determine whether a vacancy has arisen or is anticipated and, as soon as possible, determine the date upon which the charge becomes actually vacant, and

(4)   inform the congregation or congregations by one Sunday's pulpit intimation as soon as convenient.

(5)   The provisions of section 2 above shall apply to the decisions of the Vacancy Procedure Committee in terms of subsections (1) and (2) above.

5. Demission of Charge

(1)   Subject to the provisions of subsection (2) below, when a vacancy has occurred in terms of section 3(c), (d) or (f) above, the Presbytery shall determine whether the minister is, in the circumstances, entitled to a seat in the Presbytery in terms of section 16 of Act III 2000 (as amended).

(2)   In the case where it is a condition of any basis of adjustment that a minister shall demit his or her charge to facilitate union or linking, and the minister has agreed in writing in terms

of the appropriate regulations governing adjustments, formal application shall not be made to the Presbytery for permission to demit. The minister concerned shall be regarded as retiring in the interest of adjustment, and he or she shall retain a seat in Presbytery unless in terms of Act III 2000 (as amended) he or she elects to resign it.

(3)   A minister who demits his or her charge without retaining a seat in the Presbytery shall, if he or she retains status as a minister, be subject to the provisions of sections 5 to 15 of Act II 2000 (as amended).

6. Appointment of Interim Moderator

At the same time as the Vacancy Procedure Committee makes a decision in terms of section 4 above, or where circumstances pertain to section 3(a), (b), (c) or (f) above, the Vacancy Procedure Committee shall appoint an Interim Moderator for the charge and make intimation thereof to the congregation subject to the provisions of section 2 above. The Interim Moderator shall be either a ministerial member of the Presbytery in terms of Act III 2000 or Act V 2001 or a member of the Presbytery selected from a list of those who have received such preparation for the task as the Ministries Council shall from time to time recommend or provide, and he or she shall not be a member in the vacant charge nor a member of the Vacancy Procedure Committee. The name of the Interim Moderator shall be forwarded to the Ministries Council.

7. Duties of Interim Moderator

(1)   It shall be the duty of the Interim Moderator to preside at all meetings of the Kirk Session (or of the Kirk Sessions in the case of a linked charge) and to preside at all congregational meetings in connection with the vacancy, or at which the minister would have presided had the charge been full. In the case of a congregational meeting called by the Presbytery in connection with adjustment, the Interim Moderator, having constituted the meeting, shall relinquish the chair in favour of the representative of the Presbytery, but he or she shall be at liberty to speak at such a meeting. In consultation with the Kirk Session and the Financial Court, he or she shall make arrangements for the supply of the vacant pulpit.

(2)   The Interim Moderator appointed in a prospective vacancy may call and preside at meetings of the Kirk Session and of the congregation for the transaction of business relating to the said prospective vacancy. He or she shall be associated with the minister until the date of the actual vacancy; after that date, he or she shall take full charge.

(3)   The Interim Moderator shall act as an assessor to the Nominating Committee, being available to offer guidance and advice. If the Committee so desire, he or she may act as their Convener, but in no case shall he or she have a vote.

(4)   In the event of the absence of the Interim Moderator, the Vacancy Procedure Committee shall appoint a member of the Presbytery who is not a member of the vacant congregation to fulfil any of the rights and duties of the Interim Moderator in terms of this section.

(5)   The Interim Moderator shall have the same duties and responsibilities towards all members of ministry teams referred to in section 16 of Act VII 2003 as if he or she were the parish minister, both in terms of this Act and in respect of the terms and conditions of such individuals.

8. Permission to Call

When the decision to release the minister from the charge has been made and the Interim Moderator appointed, the Vacancy Procedure Committee shall consider whether it may give permission to call a minister in terms of Act VII 2003, and may proceed subject to the provisions of section 2 above. The Vacancy Procedure Committee must refer the question of permission to call to the Presbytery if:

(a)   shortfalls exist which in the opinion of the Committee require consideration in terms of section 9 hereunder;

(b)   the Committee has reason to believe that the vacancy schedule referred to in section 10 below will not be approved;

(c)   the Committee has reason to believe that the Presbytery will, in terms of section 11 below, instruct work to be carried out on the manse before a call can be sustained, and judges that the likely extent of such work warrants a delay in the granting of permission to call, or

(d)   the Committee has reason to believe that the Presbytery may wish to delay or refuse the granting of permission for any reason.

Any decision by Presbytery to refuse permission to call shall be subject to appeal or dissent-and-complaint.

9. Shortfalls

(1)   As soon as possible after intimation of a vacancy or anticipated vacancy reaches the Presbytery Clerk, the Presbytery shall ascertain whether the charge has current or accumulated shortfalls in contributions to central funds, and shall determine whether and to what extent any shortfalls that exist are justified.

(2)   If the vacancy is in a charge in which the Presbytery has determined that shortfalls are to any extent unjustified, it shall not resolve to allow a call of any kind until:

(a)   the shortfalls have been met to the extent to which the Presbytery determined that they were unjustified, or

(b)   a scheme for the payment of the unjustified shortfall has been agreed between the congregation and the Presbytery and receives the concurrence of the Ministries Council and/or the Stewardship and Finance Committee for their respective interests, or

(c)   a fresh appraisal of the charge in terms of Act VII 2003 has been carried out, regardless of the status of the charge in the current Presbytery plan.

(i)   During such appraisal, no further steps may be taken in respect of filling the vacancy, and the Presbytery shall make final determination of what constitutes such steps.

(ii)   Following such appraisal and any consequent adjustment or deferred adjustment, the shortfalls shall be met or declared justifiable or a scheme shall be agreed in terms of subsection (b) above; the Presbytery shall inform the Ministries Council and the Stewardship and Finance Committee of its decisions in terms of this section; and the Presbytery shall remove the suspension-of-vacancy process referred to in sub-paragraph (i).

10. Vacancy Schedule

(1)   When in terms of sections 4 and 6 above the decision to release the minister from the charge has been made and the interim Moderator appointed, there shall be issued by the Ministries Council a Schedule or Schedules for completion by the responsible Financial Board(s) of the vacant congregation(s) in consultation with representatives of the Presbytery, setting forth the proposed arrangements for payment of ministerial expenses and for provision of a manse, showing the ministry requirements and details of any endowment income. The Schedule, along with an Extract Minute from each relevant Kirk Session containing a commitment fully and adequately to support the ministry, shall be forwarded to the Presbytery Clerk.

(2)   The Schedule shall be considered by the Vacancy Procedure Committee and, if approved,

transmitted to the Ministries Council by the Presbytery Clerk. The Vacancy Procedure Committee or Presbytery must not sustain an appointment and call until the Schedule has been approved by them and by the Ministries Council, which shall intimate its decision within six weeks of receiving the schedule from the Presbytery.

(3) The accuracy of the Vacancy Schedule shall be kept under review by the Vacancy Procedure Committee.

(4) The provisions of section 2 above shall apply to the decisions of the Vacancy Procedure Committee.

11. Manse

As soon as possible after the manse becomes vacant, the Presbytery Property Committee shall inspect the manse and come to a view on what work, if any, must be carried out to render it suitable for a new incumbent. The views of the Property Committee should then be communicated to the Presbytery, which should, subject to any modifications which might be agreed by that Court, instruct the Financial Board of the congregation to have the work carried out. No induction date shall be fixed until the Presbytery Property Committee has again inspected the manse and confirmed that the work has been undertaken satisfactorily.

12. Advisory Committee

(1) As soon as possible after intimation of a vacancy or anticipated vacancy reaches the Presbytery Clerk, the Vacancy Procedure Committee shall appoint an Advisory Committee of three, subject to the following conditions:

(a) at least one member shall be an elder and at least one shall be a minister;

(b) the Advisory Committee shall contain no more than two members of the Vacancy Procedure Committee;

(c) the Advisory Committee may contain individuals who are not members of the Presbytery;

(d) the appointment shall be subject to section 2 above.

(2) The Advisory Committee shall meet:

(a) before the election of the Nominating Committee, with the Kirk Session (or Kirk Sessions both separately and together) of the vacant charge, to consider together in the light of the whole circumstances of the parish or parishes (i) what kind of ministry would be best suited to their needs and (ii) which system of election of the Nominating Committee described in paragraph 14(2)(d) hereunder shall be used;

(b) with the Nominating Committee before it has taken any steps to fill the vacancy, to consider how it should proceed;

(c) with the Nominating Committee before it reports to the Kirk Session and Presbytery the identity of the nominee, to review the process followed and give any further advice it deems necessary;

(d) with the Nominating Committee at any other time by request of either the Nominating Committee or the Advisory Committee.

In the case of charges which are in the opinion of the Presbytery remote, it will be adequate if the Interim Moderator (accompanied if possible by a member of the Nominating Committee) meets with the Advisory Committee for the purposes listed in paragraphs (a) to (c) above.

13. Electoral Register

(1) It shall be the duty of the Kirk Session of a vacant congregation to proceed to make up the Electoral Register of the congregation. This shall contain (1) as communicants the names

of those persons (a) whose names are on the communion roll of the congregation as at the date on which it is made up and who are not under Church discipline, (b) whose names have been added or restored to the communion roll on revision by the Kirk Session subsequently to the occurrence of the vacancy, and (c) who have given in valid Certificates of Transference by the date specified in terms of Schedule C hereto; and (2) as adherents the names of those persons who, being parishioners or regular worshippers in the congregation at the date when the vacancy occurred, and not being members of any other congregation, have claimed (in writing in the form prescribed in Schedule D and within the time specified in Schedule C) to be placed on the Electoral Register, the Kirk Session being satisfied that they desire to be permanently connected with the congregation and knowing of no adequate reasons why they should not be admitted as communicants should they so apply.

(2)   At a meeting to be held not later than fourteen days after intimation has been made in terms of Schedule C hereto, the Kirk Session shall decide on the claims of persons to be placed on the Electoral Register, such claims to be sent to the Session Clerk before the meeting. At this meeting, the Kirk Session may hear parties claiming to have an interest. The Kirk Session shall thereupon prepare the lists of names and addresses of communicants and of adherents which it is proposed shall be the Electoral Register of the congregation, the names being arranged in alphabetical order and numbered consecutively throughout. The decision of the Kirk Session in respect of any matter affecting the preparation of the Electoral Register shall be final.

(3)   The proposed Electoral Register having been prepared, the Interim Moderator shall cause intimation to be made on the first convenient Sunday in terms of Schedule E hereto that on that day an opportunity will be given for inspecting the Register after service, and that it will lie for inspection at such times and such places as the Kirk Session shall have determined; and further shall specify a day when the Kirk Session will meet to hear parties claiming an interest and will finally revise and adjust the Register. At this meeting, the list, having been revised, numbered and adjusted, shall on the authority of the court be attested by the Interim Moderator and the Clerk as the Electoral Register of the congregation.

(4)   This Register, along with a duplicate copy, shall without delay be transmitted to the Presbytery Clerk, who, in name of the Presbytery, shall attest and return the principal copy, retaining the duplicate copy in his or her own possession. For all purposes connected with this Act, the congregation shall be deemed to be those persons whose names are on the Electoral Register, and no other.

(5)   If after the attestation of the Register any communicant is given a Certificate of Transference, the Session Clerk shall delete that person's name from the Register and initial the deletion. Such a Certificate shall be granted only when application for it has been made in writing, and the said written application shall be retained until the vacancy is ended.

(6)   When a period of more than six months has elapsed between the Electoral Register being attested and the congregation being given permission to call, the Kirk Session shall have power, if it so desires, to revise and update the Electoral Register. Intimation of this intention shall be given in terms of Schedule F hereto. Additional names shall be added to the Register in the form of an Addendum which shall also contain authority for the deletions which have been made; two copies of this Addendum, duly attested, shall be lodged with the Presbytery Clerk, who, in name of the Presbytery, shall attest and return the principal copy, retaining the duplicate copy in his or her own possession.

14. Appointment of Nominating Committee

(1)   When permission to call has been given and the Electoral Register has been attested, intimation in terms of Schedule G shall be made that a meeting of the congregation is to be

held to appoint a Committee of its own number for the purpose of nominating one person to the congregation with a view to the appointment of a minister.

(2) (a) The Interim Moderator shall preside at this meeting, and the Session Clerk, or in his or her absence a person appointed by the meeting, shall act as Clerk.

(b) The Interim Moderator shall remind the congregation of the number of members it is required to appoint in terms of this section and shall call for Nominations. To constitute a valid Nomination, the name of a person on the Electoral Register has to be proposed and seconded, and assurance given by the proposer that the person is prepared to act on the Committee. The Clerk shall take a note of all Nominations in the order in which they are made.

(c) When it appears to the Interim Moderator that the Nominations are complete, they shall be read to the congregation and an opportunity given for any withdrawals. If the number of persons nominated does not exceed the maximum fixed in terms of subsection (4) below, there is no need for a vote, and the Interim Moderator shall declare that these persons constitute a Nominating Committee.

(d) If the number exceeds the maximum, the election shall proceed by one of the following means, chosen in advance by the Kirk Session, and being either (i) the submission of the names by the Interim Moderator, one by one as they appear on the list, to the vote of the congregation, each member having the right to vote for up to the maximum number fixed for the Committee, and voting being by standing up, or (ii) a system of written ballot devised by the Kirk Session to suit the size of the congregation and approved by the Vacancy Procedure Committee or the Presbytery. In either case, in the event of a tie for the last place, a further vote shall be taken between or among those tying.

(e) The Interim Moderator shall, at the same meeting or as soon thereafter as the result of any ballot has been determined, announce the names of those thus elected to serve on the Nominating Committee, and intimate to them the time and place of their first meeting, which may be immediately after the congregational meeting provided that has been intimated along with the intimation of the congregational meeting.

(3) Where there is an agreement between the Presbytery and the congregation or congregations that the minister to be inducted shall serve either in a team ministry involving another congregation or congregations, or in a designated post such as a chaplaincy, it shall be competent for the agreement to specify that the Presbytery shall appoint up to two representatives to serve on the Nominating Committee.

(4) The Vacancy Procedure Committee shall, subject to the provisions of section 2 above, determine the number who will act on the Nominating Committee, being an odd number up to a maximum of thirteen.

(5) When the vacancy is in a linked charge, or when a union or linking of congregations has been agreed but not yet effected, or when there is agreement to a deferred union or a deferred linking, or where the appointment is to more than one post, the Vacancy Procedure Committee shall, subject to the provisions of section 2 above, determine how the number who will act on the Nominating Committee will be allocated among the congregations involved, unless provision for this has already been made in the Basis of Union or Basis of Linking as the case may be.

(6) The Nominating Committee shall not have power to co-opt additional members, but the relevant Kirk Session shall have power when necessary to appoint a replacement for any of its appointees who ceases, by death or resignation, to be a member of the Nominating Committee, or who, by falling ill or by moving away from the area, is unable to serve as a member of it.

15. Constitution of the Nominating Committee
It shall be the duty of the Interim Moderator to summon and preside at the first meeting of the Nominating Committee, which may be held at the close of the congregational meeting at which it is appointed and at which the Committee shall appoint a Convener and a Clerk. The Clerk, who need not be a member of the Committee, shall keep regular minutes of all proceedings. The Convener shall have a deliberative vote (if he or she is not the Interim Moderator) but shall in no case have a casting vote. If the Clerk is not a member of the Committee, he or she shall have no vote. At all meetings of the Committee, only those present shall be entitled to vote.

16. Task of the Nominating Committee
(1)   The Nominating Committee shall have the duty of nominating one person to the congregation with a view to the election and appointment of a minister. It shall proceed by a process of announcement in a monthly vacancy list, application and interview, and may also advertise, receive recommendations and pursue enquiries in other ways.
(2)   The Committee shall give due weight to any guidelines which may from time to time be issued by the Ministries Council or the General Assembly.
(3)   The Committee shall make themselves aware of the roles of the other members of any ministry team as described in section 16 of Act VII 2003 and may meet with them for this purpose, but shall not acquire responsibility or authority for the negotiation or alteration of their terms and conditions.

17. Eligibility for Election
The following categories of persons, and no others, are eligible to be nominated, elected and called as ministers of parishes in the Church of Scotland, but always subject, where appropriate, to the provisions of Act IX 2002:
(1)   A minister of a parish of the Church, a minister holding some other appointment that entitles him or her to a seat in Presbytery or a minister holding a current Practising Certificate in terms of Section 5 of Act II 2000 (as amended).
(2)   A minister of the Church of Scotland who has retired from a parish or appointment as above, provided he or she has not reached his or her 65th birthday.
(3)   (a)   A licentiate of the Church of Scotland who has satisfactorily completed, or has been granted exemption from, his or her period of probationary service.
     (b)   A graduate candidate in terms of section 22 of Act X 2004.
(4)   A minister, licentiate or graduate candidate of the Church of Scotland who, with the approval of the World Mission Council, has entered the courts of an overseas Church as a full member, provided he or she has ceased to be such a member.
(5)   A minister, licentiate or graduate candidate of the Church of Scotland who has neither relinquished nor been judicially deprived of the status he or she possessed and who has served, or is serving, furth of Scotland in any Church which is a member of the World Alliance of Reformed Churches.
(6)   The holder of a Certificate of Eligibility in terms of Act IX 2002.

18. Ministers of a Team
Ministers occupying positions within a team ministry in the charge, or larger area including the charge, and former holders of such positions, shall be eligible to apply and shall not by virtue of office be deemed to have exercised undue influence in securing the call. A *locum tenens* in the vacant charge shall not by virtue of office be deemed to have exercised undue influence in securing the call. Any Interim Moderator in the current vacancy shall not be eligible to apply.

19. Ministers of Other Churches
(1)   Where a minister of a church furth of Scotland, who holds a certificate of eligibility in terms of Act IX 2002, is nominated, the nominee, Kirk Session and Presbytery may agree that he or she shall be inducted for a period of three years only and shall retain status as a minister of his or her denomination of origin.
(2)   Upon induction, such a minister shall be accountable to the Presbytery for the exercise of his or her ministry and to his or her own church for matters of life and doctrine. He or she shall be awarded corresponding membership of the Presbytery.
(3)   With the concurrence of the Presbytery and the Ministries Council, and at the request of the congregation, the period may be extended for one further period of not more than three years.

20. Nomination
(1)   Before the candidate is asked to accept Nomination, the Interim Moderator shall ensure that the candidate is given an adequate opportunity to see the whole ecclesiastical buildings (including the manse) pertaining to the congregation, and to meet privately with all members of staff of the charge or of any wider ministry team, and shall be provided with a copy of the constitution of the congregation, a copy of the current Presbytery Plan and of any current Basis of Adjustment or Basis of Reviewable Tenure, and the most recent audited accounts and statement of funds, and the candidate shall acknowledge receipt in writing to the Interim Moderator.
(2)   Before any Nomination is intimated to the Kirk Session and Presbytery Clerk, the Clerk to the Nominating Committee shall secure the written consent thereto of the nominee.
(3)   Before reporting the Nomination to the Vacancy Procedure Committee, the Presbytery Clerk shall obtain from the nominee or Interim Moderator evidence of the eligibility of the nominee to be appointed to the charge.
(a)   In the case of a minister not being a member of any Presbytery of the Church of Scotland, this shall normally constitute an Exit Certificate in terms of Act X 2004, or evidence of status from the Ministries Council, or a current practising certificate, or certification from the Ministries Council of eligibility in terms of Act IX 2002.
(b)   In the case of a minister in the first five years of his or her first charge, this shall consist of an extract minute either from the Vacancy Procedure Committee of his or her current Presbytery, or from that Presbytery, exceptionally releasing the minister.

21. Preaching by Nominee
(1)   The Interim Moderator, on receiving notice of the Committee's Nomination, shall arrange that the nominee conduct public worship in the vacant church or churches, normally within four Sundays, and that the ballot take place immediately after each such service.
(2)   The Interim Moderator shall thereupon cause intimation to be made on two Sundays regarding the arrangements made in connection with the preaching by the nominee and the ballot thereafter, all in terms of Schedule H hereto.

22. Election of Minister
(1)   The Interim Moderator shall normally preside at all congregational meetings connected with the election, which shall be in all cases by ballot. The Interim Moderator shall be in charge of the ballot.
(2)   The Interim Moderator may invite one or more persons (not being persons whose names are on the Electoral Register of the vacant congregation) to assist him or her in the conduct of a ballot vote when he or she judges this desirable.
(3)   When a linking or a deferred union or deferred linking is involved, the Interim Moderator

shall consult and reach agreement with the minister or Interim Moderator of the other congregation regarding the arrangements for the conduct of public worship in these congregations by the nominee as in section 21(1) above. The Interim Moderator shall in writing appoint a member of Presbytery to take full charge of the ballot vote for the other congregation. In the case of a deferred union or deferred linking, the minister already inducted shall not be so appointed, nor shall he or she be in any way involved in the conduct of the election.

23. Ballot Procedure

(1) The Kirk Session shall arrange to have available at the time of election a sufficient supply of voting-papers printed in the form of Schedule I hereto, and these shall be put into the custody of the Interim Moderator who shall preside at the election, assisted as in section 22 above. He or she shall issue on request to any person whose name is on the Electoral Register a voting-paper, noting on the Register that this has been done. Facilities shall be provided whereby the voter may mark the paper in secrecy, and a ballot-box shall be available wherein the paper is to be deposited when marked. The Interim Moderator may assist any person who asks for help in respect of completing the voting-paper, but no other person whatever shall communicate with the voter at this stage. The Interim Moderator, or the deputy appointed by him or her, shall be responsible for the safe custody of ballot-box, papers and Electoral Register.

(2) As soon as practicable, and at latest within twenty-four hours after the close of the voting, the Interim Moderator shall constitute the Kirk Session, or the joint Kirk Sessions when more than one congregation is involved, and in presence of the Kirk Session shall proceed with the counting of the votes, in which he or she may be assisted as provided in section 22 above. When more than one ballot-box has been used and when the votes of more than one congregation are involved, all ballot-boxes shall be emptied and the voting-papers shall be mixed together before counting begins so that the preponderance of votes in one area or in one congregation shall not be disclosed.

(3) If the number voting For exceeds the number voting Against, the nominee shall be declared elected and the Nominating Committee shall be deemed to be discharged.

(4) If the number voting For is equal to or less than the number voting Against, the Interim Moderator shall declare that there has been failure to elect and that the Nominating Committee is deemed to have been discharged. He or she shall proceed in terms of section 26(b) without further reference to the Presbytery.

(5) After the counting has been completed, the Interim Moderator shall sign a declaration in one of the forms of Schedule J hereto, and this shall be recorded in the minute of the Kirk Session or of the Kirk Sessions. An extract shall be affixed to the notice-board of the church, or of each of the churches, concerned. In presence of the Kirk Session, the Interim Moderator shall then seal up the voting-papers along with the marked copy of the Electoral Register, and these shall be transmitted to the Presbytery Clerk in due course along with the other documents specified in section 27 below.

24. Withdrawal of Nominee

(1) Should a nominee intimate withdrawal before he or she has preached as nominee, the Nominating Committee shall continue its task and seek to nominate another nominee.

(2) Should a nominee intimate withdrawal after he or she has been elected, the Interim Moderator shall proceed in terms of sections 23(4) above and 26(b) below without further reference to the Presbytery.

25. The Call

(1)   The Interim Moderator shall, along with the intimation regarding the result of the voting, intimate the arrangements made for members of the congregation over a period of not less than eight days to subscribe the Call (Schedule K). Intimation shall be in the form of Schedule L hereto.

(2)   The Call may be subscribed on behalf of a member not present to sign in person, provided a mandate authorising such subscription is produced as in Schedule M. All such entries shall be initialled by the Interim Moderator or by the member of the Kirk Session appending them.

(3)   Those eligible to sign the call shall be all those whose names appear on the Electoral Register. A paper of concurrence in the Call may be signed by regular worshippers in the congregation and by adherents whose names have not been entered on the Electoral Register.

26. Failure to Nominate

The exercise by a congregation of its right to call a minister shall be subject to a time-limit of one year; this period shall be calculated from the date when intimation is given of the agreement to grant leave to call. If it appears that an appointment is not to be made within the allotted time (allowing one further calendar month for intimation to the Presbytery), the congregation may make application to the Presbytery for an extension, which will normally be for a further three months. In exceptional circumstances, and for clear cause shown, a further extension of three months may be granted. If no election has been made and intimated to the Presbytery by the expiry of that time, the permission to call shall be regarded as having lapsed. The Presbytery may thereupon look afresh at the question of adjustment. If the Presbytery is still satisfied that a minister should be appointed, it shall itself take steps to make such an appointment, proceeding in one of the following ways:

(a)   (i)   The Presbytery may discharge the Nominating Committee, strengthen the Advisory Committee which had been involved in the case by the appointment of an additional minister and elder, instruct that Committee to bring forward to a subsequent meeting the name of an eligible individual for appointment to the charge and intimate this instruction to the congregation. If satisfied with the recommendation brought by the Advisory Committee, the Presbytery shall thereupon make the appointment.

(ii)   The Presbytery Clerk shall thereupon intimate to the person concerned the fact of his or her appointment, shall request him or her to forward a letter of acceptance along with appropriate Certificates if these are required in terms of section 27 below, and shall arrange with him or her to conduct public worship in the vacant church or churches on an early Sunday.

(iii)   The Presbytery Clerk shall cause intimation to be made in the form of Schedule N that the person appointed will conduct public worship on the day specified and that a Call in the usual form will lie with the Session Clerk or other suitable person for not less than eight free days to receive the signatures of the congregation. The conditions governing the signing of the Call shall be as in section 25 above.

(iv)   At the expiry of the time allowed, the Call shall be transmitted by the Session Clerk to the Presbytery Clerk who shall lay it, along with the documents referred to in sub-paragraph (ii) above, before the Presbytery at its first ordinary meeting or at a meeting *in hunc effectum.*

(b)   Otherwise, the Presbytery shall instruct that a fresh Nominating Committee be elected in terms of section 14 above. The process shall then be followed in terms of this Act from the point of the election of the Nominating Committee.

27. Transmission of Documents

(1)   After an election has been made, the Interim Moderator shall secure from the person appointed a letter of acceptance of the appointment.

(2)   The Interim Moderator shall then without delay transmit the relevant documents to the Presbytery Clerk. These are: the minute of Nomination by the Nominating Committee, all intimations made to the congregation thereafter, the declaration of the election and appointment, the voting-papers, the marked copy of the Register and the letter of acceptance. He or she shall also inform the Clerk of the steps taken in connection with the signing of the Call, and shall arrange that, at the expiry of the period allowed for subscription, the Call shall be transmitted by the Session Clerk to the Presbytery Clerk.

(3)   After the person elected has been inducted to the charge, the Presbytery Clerk shall:

(a)   deliver to him or her the approved copy of the Vacancy Schedule referred to in section 10(2) above, and

(b)   destroy the intimations and voting-papers lodged with him or her in terms of subsection (2) above and ensure that confidential documents and correspondence held locally are destroyed.

28. Sustaining the Call

(1)   All of the documents listed in section 27 above shall be laid before the Vacancy Procedure Committee, which may resolve to sustain the call and determine arrangements for the induction of the new minister, subject to (a) a request for the release, if appropriate, of the minister from his or her current charge in terms of this Act and (b) the provisions of section 2 above. The Moderator of the Presbytery shall, if no ordinary meeting of the Presbytery falls before the proposed induction date, call a meeting *pro re nata* for the induction.

(2)   In the event that the matter comes before the Presbytery in terms of section 2 above, the procedure shall be as follows:

(a)   The Call and other relevant documents having been laid on the table, the Presbytery shall hear any person whom it considers to have an interest. In particular, the Advisory Committee shall be entitled to be heard if it so desires, or the Presbytery may ask for a report from it. The Presbytery shall then decide whether to sustain the appointment in terms of subsection (1) above, and in doing so shall give consideration to the number of signatures on the Call. It may delay reaching a decision and return the Call to the Kirk Session to give further opportunity for it to be subscribed.

(b)   If the Presbytery sustain an appointment and Call to a Graduate Candidate, and there be no appeal tendered in due form against its judgement, it shall appoint the day and hour and place at which the ordination and induction will take place.

(c)   If the Presbytery sustain an appointment and Call to a minister of the Church of Scotland not being a minister of a parish, or to a minister of another denomination, and there be no ecclesiastical impediment, the Presbytery shall appoint the day and hour and place at which the induction will take place.

(3)   In the event that the Call is not sustained, the Presbytery shall determine either (a) to give more time for it to be signed in terms of section 25 above or (b) to proceed in terms of subsection (a) or (b) of section 26 above.

29. Admission to a Charge

(1)   When the Presbytery has appointed a day for the ordination and induction of a Graduate Candidate, or for the induction of a minister already ordained, the Clerk shall arrange for an edict in the form of Schedule O to be read to the congregation on the two Sundays preceding the day appointed.

(2)   At the time and place named in the edict, the Presbytery having been constituted, the Moderator shall call for the return of the edict attested as having been duly served. If the minister is being translated from another Presbytery, the relevant minute of that Presbytery or of its Vacancy Procedure Committee agreeing to translation shall also be laid on the table. Any objection, to be valid at this stage, must have been intimated to the Presbytery Clerk at the objector's earliest opportunity, must be strictly directed to life or doctrine and must be substantiated immediately to the satisfaction of the Presbytery, in which case procedure shall be sisted and the Presbytery shall take appropriate steps to deal with the situation that has arisen. Otherwise, the Presbytery shall proceed with the ordination and induction, or with the induction, as hereunder.

(3)   The Presbytery shall proceed to the church where public worship shall be conducted by those appointed for the purpose. The Clerk shall read a brief narrative of the cause of the vacancy and of the steps taken for the settlement. The Moderator, having read the Preamble, shall, addressing him or her by name, put to the person to be inducted the questions prescribed (*see the Ordinal of the Church as authorised from time to time by the General Assembly*). Satisfactory answers having been given, the person to be inducted shall sign the Formula. If he or she has not already been ordained, the person to be inducted shall then kneel, and the Moderator by prayer and the imposition of hands, in which members of the Presbytery, appointed by the Presbytery for the purpose, and other ordained persons associated with it, if invited to share in such imposition of hands, shall join, shall ordain him or her to the office of the Holy Ministry. Prayer being ended, the Moderator shall say: 'I now declare you to have been ordained to the office of the Holy Ministry, and in name of the Lord Jesus Christ, the King and Head of the Church, and by authority of this Presbytery, I induct you to this charge, and in token thereof we give you the right hand of fellowship'. The Moderator with all other members of Presbytery present and those associated with it shall then give the right hand of fellowship. The Moderator shall then put the prescribed question to the members of the congregation. Suitable charges to the new minister and to the congregation shall then be given by the Moderator or by a minister appointed for the purpose.

(4)   When an ordained minister is being inducted to a charge, the act of ordination shall not be repeated, and the relevant words shall be omitted from the declaration. In other respects, the procedure shall be as in subsection (3) above.

(5)   When the appointment is for a limited or potentially limited period (including Reviewable Tenure, or an appointment in terms of section 19 above), the service shall proceed as in subsections (3) or (4) above, except that in the declaration the Moderator shall say: 'I induct you to this charge on the Basis of [specific Act and Section] and in terms of Minute of Presbytery of date . . .'.

(6)   After the service, the Presbytery shall resume its session, when the name of the new minister shall be added to the Roll of Presbytery, and the Clerk shall be instructed to send certified intimation of the induction to the Session Clerk to be engrossed in the minutes of the first meeting of Kirk Session thereafter, and, in the case of a translation from another Presbytery or where the minister was prior to the induction subject to the supervision of another Presbytery, to the Clerk of that Presbytery.

30. Service of Introduction

(1)   When a minister has been appointed to a linked charge, the Presbytery shall determine in which of the churches of the linking the induction is to take place. This shall be a service of induction to the charge, in consequence of which the person inducted shall become minister of each of the congregations embraced in the linking. The edict regarding the induction, which shall be in terms of Schedule O, shall be read in all of the churches

concerned. There shall be no other service of induction; but, if the churches are far distant from one another, or for other good reason, the Presbytery may appoint a service of introduction to be held in the other church or churches. Intimation shall be given of such service, but not in edictal form.

(2) In any case of deferred union or deferred linking, the minister elected and appointed shall be inducted 'to the vacant congregation of A in deferred union (or linking) with the congregation of B' and there shall be no need for any further act to establish his or her position as minister of the united congregation or of the linked congregation as the case may be. The Presbytery, however, shall in such a case arrange a service of introduction to the newly united congregation of AB or the newly linked congregation of B. Intimation shall be given of such service, but not in edictal form.

(3) When an appointment has been made to an extra-parochial office wholly or mainly under control of the Church (community ministry, full-time chaplaincy in hospital, industry, prison or university, full-time clerkship and so on), the Presbytery may deem it appropriate to arrange a service of introduction to take place in a church or chapel suitable to the occasion.

(4) When an appointment has been made to a parochial appointment other than that of an inducted minister, the Presbytery may arrange a service of introduction to take place within the parish. If ordination is involved, suitable arrangements shall be made and edictal intimation shall be given in terms of Schedule P.

(5) A service of introduction not involving ordination shall follow the lines of an induction except that, instead of putting the normal questions to the minister, the Moderator shall ask him or her to affirm the vows taken at his or her ordination. Where the service, in terms of subsection (3) or (4) above, includes the ordination of the minister, the vows shall be put in full. In either case, in the declaration, the Moderator in place of 'I induct you to . . .' shall say: 'I welcome you as . . .'.

31. Demission of Status
If a minister seeks to demit his or her status as a minister of the Church of Scotland, any accompanying demission of a charge will be dealt with by the Vacancy Procedure Committee in terms of section 4 of this Act without further delay, but the question of demission of status shall be considered by the Presbytery itself. The Moderator of Presbytery, or a deputy appointed by him or her, shall first confer with the minister regarding his or her reasons and shall report to the Presbytery if there appears to be any reason not to grant permission to demit status. Any decision to grant permission to demit status shall be immediately reported to the Ministries Council.

32. Miscellaneous
For the purposes of this Act, intimations to congregations may be made (a) verbally during every act of worship or (b) in written intimations distributed to the whole congregation provided that the congregation's attention is specifically drawn to the presence of an intimation there in terms of this Act.

For the purposes of this Act, attestation of all intimations to congregations shall consist of certification thereof by the Session Clerk as follows:

(a) Certification that all intimations received have been duly made on the correct number of Sundays shall be sent to the Presbytery Clerk before the service of induction or introduction.

(b) Certification that any particular intimation received has been duly made on the correct number of Sundays shall be furnished on demand to the Vacancy Procedure Committee or the Presbytery Clerk.

(c)   Intimation shall be made immediately to the Presbytery Clerk in the event that intimation has not been duly made on the appropriate Sunday.

SCHEDULES

A INTIMATION OF ACTION OR DECISION OF VACANCY PROCEDURE COMMITTEE – Section 2(1)

To be read on one Sunday

The Vacancy Procedure Committee of the Presbytery of .... proposes [here insert action or permission proposed]....... Any communicant member of the congregation(s) of A [and B] may submit to the Presbytery Clerk a request for this proposal to be considered at the next meeting of the Presbytery: where such requests are received from four individuals, being communicant members of the congregation(s) or full members of the Presbytery, the request shall be met. Such request should be submitted in writing to [name and postal address of Presbytery Clerk] by [date seven days after intimation].

A .... B ....   Presbytery Clerk

B EDICT CITING A CONGREGATION TO ATTEND – Section 2(5)

To be read on one Sunday

Intimation is hereby given that, in connection with the [anticipated] vacancy in this congregation, a valid request has been made for the matter of [here insert action or permission which had been proposed] to be considered by the Presbytery. [The proposed course of action] is in the meantime sisted.

Intimation is hereby further given that the Presbytery will meet to consider this matter at .... on .... the .... day of .... at .... o'clock and that the congregation are hereby cited to attend for their interests.

A .... B ....   Presbytery Clerk

C PREPARATION OF ELECTORAL REGISTER – Section 13(1) and (2)

To be read on two Sundays

Intimation is hereby given that in view of the [1]anticipated vacancy, the Kirk Session is about to make up an Electoral Register of this congregation. Any communicant whose name is not already on the Communion Roll as a member should hand in to the Session Clerk a Certificate of Transference, and anyone wishing his or her name added to the Register as an adherent should obtain from the Session Clerk, and complete and return to him or her, a Form of Adherent's Claim. All such papers should be in the hands of the Session Clerk not later than .... The Kirk Session will meet in .... on .... at .... to make up the Electoral Register, when anyone wishing to support his or her claim in person should attend.

C .... D ....   Interim Moderator

[1] This word to be included where appropriate – otherwise to be deleted

D FORM OF ADHERENT'S CLAIM – Section 13(1)

I, [1] .... of [2] ...., being a parishioner or regular worshipper in the Church of .... and not being a member of any other congregation in Scotland, claim to have my name put on the Electoral Register of the parish of .... as an adherent.

Date ....……..   (Signed)....................…….

[1] Here enter full name in block capitals
[2] Here enter address in full

E INSPECTION OF ELECTORAL REGISTER – Section 13(3)

To be read on one Sunday

Intimation is hereby given that the proposed Electoral Register of this congregation has now been prepared and that an opportunity of inspecting it will be given today in .... at the close of this service, and that it will be open for inspection at .... on .... between the hours of .... and .... each day. Any questions regarding entries in the Register should be brought to the notice of the Kirk Session which is to meet in .... on .... at .... o'clock, when it will finally make up the Electoral Register.

C .... D ....   Interim Moderator

F REVISION OF ELECTORAL REGISTER – Section 13(6)

To be read on two Sundays

Intimation is hereby given that, more than six months having elapsed since the Electoral Register of this congregation was finally made up, it is now proposed that it should be revised. An opportunity of inspecting the Register will be given in .... at the close of this service, and also at .... on .... between the hours of .... and .... each day. Anyone wishing his or her name added to the Electoral Register as a member should give in a Transference Certificate, or as an adherent should give in a Form of Adherent's Claim (copies of which may be had from the Session Clerk) not later than .... The Kirk Session will meet in .... on .... at .... o'clock, when it will finally make up the Revised Register.

C .... D ....   Interim Moderator

G INTIMATION OF ELECTION OF NOMINATING COMMITTEE – Section 14(1)

To be read on two Sundays

Intimation is hereby given that a meeting of this congregation will be held in the Church [or other arrangement may be given here] on Sunday .... at the close of morning worship for the purpose of appointing a Nominating Committee which will nominate one person to the congregation with a view to the appointment of a minister.

C .... D ....   Interim Moderator

H MINUTE OF NOMINATION BY NOMINATING COMMITTEE – Section 21

To be read on two Sundays

(1) The Committee chosen by this congregation to nominate a person with a view to the election and appointment of a minister, at a meeting held at .... on ...., resolved to name and propose [1] ...., and they accordingly do name and propose the said ....

Date ....

E .... F ....   Convener of Committee

[1] The name and designation of the person should at this point be entered in full

(2) Intimation is therefore hereby given that the Nominating Committee having, as by minute now read, named and proposed [Name], arrangements have been made whereby public worship will be conducted in this Church by him or her on Sunday the .... day of .... at .... o'clock; and that a vote will be taken by voting-papers immediately thereafter; and that electors may vote For or Against electing and appointing the said [Name] as minister of this vacant charge.

C .... D ....   Interim Moderator

I VOTING-PAPER – Section 23

FOR Electing [Name]
AGAINST Electing [Name]

Directions to Voters: If you are in favour of electing [Name], put a cross (x) on the upper space. If you are not in favour of electing [Name], put a cross (x) in the lower space. Do not put a tick or any other mark upon the paper; if you do, it will be regarded as spoilt and will not be counted.

Note: The Directions to Voters must be printed prominently on the face of the voting-paper

J DECLARATION OF ELECTION RESULT – Section 23(5)

First Form (Successful Election)

I hereby declare that the following are the results of the voting for the election and appointment of a minister to the vacant charge of [1] .... and that the said [Name] has accordingly been elected and appointed subject to the judgement of the courts of the Church.

Date ....   C .... D ....   Interim Moderator

[1] Here enter details

FOR Electing [Name]
AGAINST Electing [Name]

Second Form (Failure to Elect)

I hereby declare that the following are the results of the voting for the election and appointment of a minister to the vacant charge of [1] ……….. and that in consequence of this vote there has been a failure to elect, and the Nominating Committee is deemed to have been discharged. [Continue in terms of Schedule G if appropriate.]

Date ………………   C ………. D ……….   Interim Moderator

[1] Here enter details

FOR Electing [Name]
AGAINST Electing [Name]

K THE CALL – Section 25(1)

Form of Call

We, members of the Church of Scotland and of the congregation known as ………., being without a minister, address this Call to be our minister to you, ………., of whose gifts and qualities we have been assured, and we warmly invite you to accept this Call, promising that we shall devote ourselves with you to worship, witness, mission and service in this parish, and also to the furtherance of these in the world, to the glory of God and for the advancement of His Kingdom.

Paper of Concurrence

We, regular worshippers in the congregation of the Church of Scotland known as ………., concur in the Call addressed by that congregation to ………. to be their minister.

Note: The Call and Paper of Concurrence should be dated and attested by the Interim Moderator before they are transmitted to the Clerk of the Presbytery.

L SUBSCRIBING THE CALL – Section 25(1)

To be read on at least one Sunday

Intimation is hereby given that this congregation having elected [Name] to be their minister, a Call to the said [Name] has been prepared and will lie in ………. on ………. the ………. day of ………. between the hours of ………. and ………., when those whose names are on the Electoral Register of the congregation may sign in person or by means of mandates. Forms of mandate may be obtained from the Session Clerk.

A Paper of Concurrence will also be available for signature by persons who are connected with the congregation but whose names are not on the Electoral Register of the congregation.

C ………. D ……….   Interim Moderator

M MANDATE TO SIGN CALL – Section 25(2)

I, ………. of ………., being a person whose name is on the Electoral Register of the congregation, hereby authorise the Session Clerk, or other member of Session, to add my name to the Call addressed to [*Name*] to be our minister.

(Signed) ....……..

N CITATION IN CASE OF NOMINATION BY PRESBYTERY – Section 26(a)(iii)

To be read on one Sunday

Intimation is hereby given that [*Name*], whom the Presbytery has appointed to be minister of this congregation, will conduct public worship in the Church on Sunday the .... day of .... at .... o'clock.

Intimation is hereby further given that a Call addressed to the said [*Name*] will lie in .... on .... the .... day of .... between the hours of .... and .... during the day and between the hours of .... and .... in the evening, when members may sign in person or by means of mandates, forms of which may be had from the Session Clerk.

Intimation is hereby further given that the Presbytery will meet to deal with the appointment and Call at .... on .... the .... day of .... at .... o'clock and that the congregation are hereby cited to attend for their interests.

A .... B ....   Presbytery Clerk

O EDICTAL INTIMATION OF ADMISSION – Section 29(1)

To be read on two Sundays

*   Whereas the Presbytery of .... has received a Call from this congregation addressed to [*Name*] to be their minister, and the said Call has been sustained as a regular Call, and has been accepted by him/her[1];
*   And whereas the said Presbytery, having judged the said [*Name*] qualified[2] for the ministry of the Gospel and for this charge, has resolved to proceed to his or her[3] ordination and induction on .... the .... day of .... at .... o'clock unless something occur which may reasonably impede it:

Notice is hereby given to all concerned that if they, or any of them, have anything to object to in the life or doctrine of the said [*Name*], they may appear at the Presbytery which is to meet at .... on .... the .... day of .... at .... o'clock; with certification that if no relevant objection be then made and immediately substantiated, the Presbytery will proceed without further delay.

By order of the Presbytery

A .... B .... Presbytery Clerk

[1] add, where appropriate, 'and his or her translation has been agreed to by the Presbytery of ……....'
[2] omit 'for the ministry of the Gospel and' if the minister to be inducted has been ordained previously
[3] omit, where appropriate, 'ordination and'

P EDICTAL INTIMATION OF ORDINATION IN CASE OF INTRODUCTION –
Section 30(1)

To be read on two Sundays

*   Whereas [narrate circumstances requiring service of introduction]
*   And whereas the Presbytery, having found the said [*Name*] to have been regularly appointed and to be qualified for the ministry of the Gospel and for the said appointment, has resolved to proceed to his or her ordination to the Holy Ministry and to his or her introduction as [specify appointment] on .... the .... day of .... at .... o'clock unless something occur which may reasonably impede it:

Notice is hereby given to all concerned that if they, or any of them, have anything to object to in the life or doctrine of the said [*Name*], they may appear at the Presbytery which is to meet at .... on .... the .... day of .... at .... o'clock; with certification that if no relevant objection be then made and immediately substantiated, the Presbytery will proceed without further delay.

By order of the Presbytery

A .... B ....   Presbytery Clerk

SECTION 4

The
General Assembly
of 2006

(1) THE GENERAL ASSEMBLY

The Lord High Commissioner:	The Rt Hon. Lord Mackay of Clashfern KT
Moderator:	Right Rev. Alan D. McDonald LLB BD MTh
Chaplains to the Moderator:	Rev. G. Russell Barr BA BD MTh DMin Mrs Alison Twaddle MA JP
Principal Clerk:	Very Rev. Finlay A.J. Macdonald MA BD PhD DD
Depute Clerk:	Rev. Marjory A. MacLean LLB BD PhD
Procurator:	Miss Laura Dunlop QC
Law Agent:	Mrs Janette S. Wilson LLB NP
Convener of the Business Committee:	Rev. William C. Hewitt BD DipPS
Vice-Convener of the Business Committee:	Rev. A. David K. Arnott MA BD
Precentor:	Rev. Douglas Galbraith MA BD BMus MPhil ARSCM
Assembly Officer:	Mr David McColl
Assistant Assembly Officer:	Mr Craig Marshall

(2) THE MODERATOR

The Right Reverend Alan D. McDonald LLB BD MTh

Described by the *Press and Journal* following his nomination as Moderator as 'relaxed and welcoming, with a warm and engaging sense of energy and interest which puts visitors at ease', Alan McDonald brings to the role of Moderator not just the many gifts of his personality but also his wide range of experiences and insight.

From childhood and education in Glasgow to serving as a peace monitor in South Africa, from his legal training at Strathclyde University to his theological training at New College, including a year spent in Boston, USA, from his work as a solicitor in Glasgow with Biggart, Baillie and Gifford and the Edinburgh firm of Farquharson Craig to his work as a community minister in the Greater Pilton area of Edinburgh followed by parish ministry in both Aberdeen and St Andrews, there has been considerable breadth to Alan's life.

More importantly, there is considerable depth.

Both of us have been fortunate to know Alan for over thirty years. As well as his friendship, we have also appreciated his quiet authority and wisdom. Alan has a formidable intellect, and his insights into the life of the Church or the public life of the nation merit careful attention. Alan is someone who engages his brain before offering an opinion.

The General Assembly has already experienced his leadership during his time as Convener of the former Committee on Church and Nation. During his period of office, the Committee produced high-profile reports on sectarianism and on domestic abuse. He was also Convener during the attacks on America on 11 September 2001 and the war with Afghanistan. Critical of the war in Iraq, Alan addressed a large anti-war rally in Glasgow.

Mild-mannered though he may be, it was evident from his work with Church and Nation that Alan is passionate about the Biblical call to justice and the Gospel imperative to stand with the poor and the vulnerable. No matter how strongly held his opinions, however, Vivienne Dickson, the Session Clerk at St Leonard's in St Andrews, sees Alan's greatest attribute as his ability with people, especially his ability to be encouraging to those with whom he disagrees completely.

If that priceless ability has been of benefit to the life and work of his current congregation, we anticipate that it will be of equal benefit to the General Assembly and to the wider Church as Alan embarks on his term of office. His faith runs deep, has a strong Biblical and Gospel foundation, and is expressed in an integrity of life and work.

What we also know is that Alan likes to have fun.

He loves the music of Emmylou Harris and of Paul Simon, he can tell a joke with the comic timing of Eric Morecambe, and he enjoys a round of golf – although, as a slightly bruised lady from New York could testify, he can be a somewhat wayward golfer. He runs regularly along the west sands at St Andrews, ran a marathon in Aberdeen to raise funds for repairs to Holburn Central church, continues to follow the fortunes of Aberdeen Football Club and enjoys the view from the hill top.

What he can't stand is injustice or hypocrisy.

Blessed with happiness in marriage, family and congregational life, Alan is good news for the Church of Scotland, and we look forward to supporting him during his role as Moderator of the General Assembly, as an encourager of the faithful and as an ambassador to the nations.

Alison Twaddle and Russell Barr, Chaplains

---

(3) DIGEST OF ASSEMBLY DECISIONS

Over recent years, what has found its way into this section of the *Year Book* has been the editor's personal selection of those decisions of the most recent General Assembly which, in his view at the time of writing, seemed likely to be of most practical interest to those who might choose to read it.

In the main, this approach has seemed to find fairly general favour, or, if that is felt to be overly optimistic, it has not provoked serious discontent. As was recognised last year, there are always liable to be expressions of disappointment that some Council or Committee has either been totally ignored or not seen highlighted what might have been the choice of the Convener concerned. That will doubtless continue, so that it would be foolhardy to imagine that what follows will satisfy everyone. It will perhaps have served its purpose if it conveys tolerably accurately something of the flavour of the Assembly. The greater hope remains that it might move a significant number to explore for themselves parts of the published volume of Reports, copies of which are, as always, available from the office of the Principal Clerk.

If, as it is, that is the hope year by year, there is perhaps particular cause this year for underlining it. There were in the Assembly stimulating debates on a number of highly complex issues. This was particularly the case when the Assembly considered the Report of the Church and Society Council where, for example, stem-cell research and appropriate investment in Israel and Palestine focused Commissioners' minds on a range of questions to which future Assemblies will certainly wish to return. With the brief headline approach which this section of the *Year Book* mostly employs, it would be unwise to imagine that due justice could be done to such topics. The full reports would repay careful study.

REPORTS OF COUNCILS, COMMITTEES AND OTHER AGENCIES

Chaplains to HM Forces Committee:
Having received the Committee's Report which drew attention to the fact that there were at that time a number of vacancies for Chaplains in the Navy, the Army and the Air Force, the Assembly commended to eligible ministers and deacons of the Church the thought that they might consider offering for service in the Royal Navy, Naval Reserve or the chaplaincy service of the Sea Cadet Corps, Regular Army, Territorial Army or Army Cadet Force, Royal Air Force or Air Cadet Force.

Church and Society Council:
The Assembly commended the Council for its commitment to the production of resources for Religious Observance in schools and for its further commitment to training in the use of such resources to enable them to be effective and relevant to twenty-first-century young people. The Assembly called on the Scottish Executive to honour its previous commitment adequately to resource this work. (When, later in the week, the Assembly came to debate the Report of the Ministries Council, the Assembly instructed the Church and Society Council to consult with the Standing Committee on Education on revised methods of Religious Observance in schools.)

The Assembly regretted that Scottish Television and Grampian Television no longer broadcast church services on a Sunday morning. The Assembly encouraged both congregations and kirk sessions to look at ways of reaching out within their communities to help compensate for this loss of religious broadcasting.

The Assembly congratulated the Very Reverend Dr John and Mrs Mary Miller on the singular honour being accorded them in having a new school to be built in Glasgow's Castlemilk named 'Miller Primary School' in recognition of the more than thirty years' service that they have given to the parish and community.

Church of Scotland Guild:
The Assembly supported the joint initiative of the Guild and the World Mission Council in addressing the crime of human trafficking, and commended to the wider Church the report of the conference: 'Human Trafficking: today's slavery and our response'.

Council of Assembly:
The Assembly:
• encouraged the Council in its development of a co-ordinated communications strategy and instructed it in so doing to prepare guidelines for those who act as spokespersons for the Church, including the Moderator and Conveners;
• affirmed that statements and comments should be based on decisions of the General Assembly and, where there is no such decision, on the view of the relevant Assembly Council or Committee;
• instructed Councils and Committees to develop strategies for enabling Presbyteries to contribute timeously to the development of policy.

Ecumenical Relations Committee:
The Assembly approved the terms of a Covenant between the Church of Scotland and the United Free Church of Scotland and welcomed the proposed signing of the Covenant in Dunblane Cathedral on 16 September 2006.
Inter alia, the Covenant states:
Believing in one God, Father, Son and Holy Spirit, we affirm that:
• as churches in the one family of Reformed Churches, linked by our Presbyterian heritage, the time has come for us to put the divisions of the past behind us and to seek to journey onwards as companions on the way to ever closer unity;
• we share a common faith and calling, and that such differing emphases as may exist between our respective traditions are not sufficient to impede our progress on that journey.

In the belief that God is calling our two churches to a closer relationship with one another, we commit ourselves, *inter alia*:
• to encourage, where appropriate, local congregations to consider linking with neighbours in their own community rather than within their own denominations across community boundaries;
• to encourage local congregations to enter local covenants as a means of moving towards an ever deeper sharing of resources for mission and service to the community.

General Trustees:
In respect of manses,
• the Assembly urged congregations to take seriously the maintenance and modernisation of their manses and reminded them that they are required to inspect their manses annually;
• the Assembly invited the Trustees to include the Ministries Council in their deliberations on manses with a view to presenting a joint report on the future size, maintenance and upkeep of manses.

HIV/AIDS Project:
The Assembly:
• recognised that HIV stigma and discrimination continued to act as barriers to effective prevention and care within and furth of Scotland;
• confessed to people living with HIV that the Kirk had been involved in unwitting and unthinking stigmatisation of them;
• called on all Christians in Scotland to work to overcome ignorance and prejudice about people living with HIV wherever they might be.

Legal Questions Committee:
The Committee invited the Assembly to pass a Declaratory Act anent Civil Partnerships in terms as set out in an Appendix to the Committee's Report. Following debate, the Assembly resolved rather to cast the whole as an Overture under the Barrier Act.

Ministries Council:
In respect of candidates in training for the ministries of the Church, the Assembly:
• approved the Council's recommendation that the University of the Highlands and Islands Millennium Institute, UHI, be recognised as an appointed academic provider;
• instructed the Council to work with Highland Theological College, HTC, to ensure that the expectations listed in the Council's Report are realised;

- instructed the Council to conduct an interim review of the recognised status of HTC no later than January 2010 and to report to the General Assembly;
- noted the progress made in discussions between the International Christian College, Glasgow (ICC) and the Ministries Council in relation to the application by ICC for recognition as an approved academic provider for candidates in training for the ministries of the Church, and instructed the Council to bring a recommendation concerning such recognition to the General Assembly of 2007.

The Assembly instructed the Council to undertake research into issues of conflict and possible solutions to conflict within congregations and kirk sessions and to report to a future Assembly.

The Assembly noted the plans for a full reinstatement of a Study Leave Scheme to cover the full-time ministries of the Church and instructed the Council to implement this with effect from 1 June 2006.

Arising from the debate on an Overture from the Presbytery of Irvine and Kilmarnock, the Assembly instructed the Ministries Council to phase out the Voluntary Additional Payment Scheme.

Mission and Discipleship Council:
The Assembly invited members, elders and ministers to inform the Adult and Spirituality Group about their work in adult Christian education and to suggest ways in which the Church can encourage the growth of such education and nurture.

The Assembly instructed the Council, in consultation with the Ministries Council, to identify, and if necessary seek to establish, appropriate training courses for paid professional youth-work staff within local churches. The Council has to report on this to the General Assembly of 2007.

The Assembly instructed and encouraged the Council, in consultation with the Ministries Council, to develop and offer opportunities where study-leave funds will be available to assist ministers to become equipped to develop new and creative models of ministry for their local congregations.

Panel on Review and Reform:
The Assembly instructed the Panel, as it continued to take forward the Church Without Walls agenda, to liaise with the Mission and Discipleship Council in relation to issues arising from the Church of England's 'Emerging Church' programme.

Petition: A Voice for the Local Church:
The Assembly appointed a Commission of seven, under the Convenership of Lord Brodie, to identify and report to the General Assembly of 2008 on:

- the effect of changes to the structure and operation of the General Assembly, of central committees, of Boards and Councils of the Church, and of centrally held funds;
- the effect of changes resulting from recent amendments of or additions to Assembly regulations and guidelines upon the constitutional character of the Church and the respective powers of and relationship between the General Assembly, its Committees, Boards and Councils, the Presbyteries and the congregations of the Church.

The Commission was further instructed to investigate, comment upon and make recommendations to the General Assembly on matters referred to in the Petition or raised by Presbyteries in their responses and not otherwise covered in the crave.

Social Care Council:
The Assembly instructed the Council, in light of the current financial situation, to undertake a comprehensive review of counselling services as a matter of priority and, where possible, to maintain current services.

Stewardship and Finance Committee:
The Assembly affirmed the Biblical and theological principles of Christian stewardship, welcomed the production of new materials and encouraged congregations to make use of the resources provided by the Committee to make more of their giving potential.

World Mission Council:
The Assembly encouraged congregations and Presbyteries to consider seriously the development of local-to-local links with overseas partner churches.

SECTION 5

Presbytery Lists

SECTION 5 – PRESBYTERY LISTS

In each Presbytery list, the congregations are listed in alphabetical order. In a linked charge, the names appear under the first named congregation. Under the name of the congregation will be found the name of the minister and, where applicable, that of an associate minister, auxiliary minister and member of the Diaconate. The years indicated after a minister's name in the congregational section of each Presbytery list are the year of ordination (column 1) and the year of current appointment (column 2). Where only one date is given, it is both the year of ordination and the year of appointment.

In the second part of each Presbytery list, those named are listed alphabetically. The first date is the year of ordination, and the following date is the year of appointment or retirement. If the person concerned is retired, then the appointment last held will be shown in brackets.

KEY TO ABBREVIATIONS

(E)   Indicates a Church Extension charge. New Charge Developments are separately indicated.
(GD) Indicates a charge where it is desirable that the minister should have a knowledge of Gaelic.
(GE) Indicates a charge where public worship must be regularly conducted in Gaelic.
(H)   Indicates that a Hearing Aid Loop system has been installed. In Linked charges, the (H) is placed beside the appropriate building as far as possible.
(L)   Indicates that a Chair Lift has been installed.
(T)   Indicates that the minister has been appointed on the basis of Terminable Tenure.

PRESBYTERY NUMBERS

1	Edinburgh	18	Dumbarton
2	West Lothian	19	Argyll
3	Lothian	20	
4	Melrose and Peebles	21	
5	Duns	22	Falkirk
6	Jedburgh	23	Stirling
7	Annandale and Eskdale	24	Dunfermline
8	Dumfries and Kirkcudbright	25	Kirkcaldy
9	Wigtown and Stranraer	26	St Andrews
10	Ayr	27	Dunkeld and Meigle
11	Irvine and Kilmarnock	28	Perth
12	Ardrossan	29	Dundee
13	Lanark	30	Angus
14	Greenock and Paisley	31	Aberdeen
15		32	Kincardine and Deeside
16	Glasgow	33	Gordon
17	Hamilton	34	Buchan

35	Moray
36	Abernethy
37	Inverness
38	Lochaber
39	Ross
40	Sutherland
41	Caithness
42	Lochcarron–Skye
43	Uist
44	Lewis
45	Orkney
46	Shetland
47	England
48	Europe
49	Jerusalem

(1) EDINBURGH

Meets at Palmerston Place Church, Edinburgh, on the first Tuesday of October, November, December, February, March, April and May and on the second Tuesday in September and on the last Tuesday of June. When the first Tuesday of April falls in Holy Week, the meeting is on the second Tuesday.

Clerk:	REV. W. PETER GRAHAM MA BD		10/1 Palmerston Place, Edinburgh EH12 5AA [E-mail: akph50@uk.uumail.com]	0131-225 9137
1	**Edinburgh: Albany Deaf Church of Edinburgh (H)** Alistair F. Kelly BL (Locum)	1961	19 Avon Place, Edinburgh EH4 6RE	0131-317 9877
2	**Edinburgh: Balerno (H)** Jared W. Hay BA MTh DipMin DMin	1987	2001	3 Johnsburn Road, Balerno EH14 7DN [E-mail: jared.hay@blueyonder.co.uk]	0131-449 3830
	Charles W.H. Barrington MA BD (Assoc)	1997	502 Lanark Road, Edinburgh EH14 5DH [E-mail: charles.barrington@classicfm.net]	0131-453 4826
3	**Edinburgh: Barclay (0131-229 6810) (E-mail: admin@barclaychurch.org.uk)** Samuel A.R. Torrens BD	1995	2005	113 Meadowspot, Edinburgh EH10 5UY [E-mail: samtorrens@blueyonder.co.uk]	0131-478 2376
4	**Edinburgh: Blackhall St Columba (0131-332 4431) (E-mail: secretary@blackhallstcolumba.org.uk)** Alexander B. Douglas BD	1979	1991	5 Blinkbonny Crescent, Edinburgh EH4 3NB [E-mail: alexandjill@douglas.net]	0131-343 3708
5	**Edinburgh: Bristo Memorial Craigmillar** Vacant Agnes M. Rennie (Miss) DCS			72 Blackchapel Close, Edinburgh EH15 3SL 3/1 Craigmillar Court, Edinburgh EH16 4AD	0131-657 3266 0131-661 8475
6	**Edinburgh: Broughton St Mary's (H) (0131-556 4786)** Joanne C. Hood (Miss) MA BD		2003	103 East Claremont Street, Edinburgh EH7 4JA [E-mail: joanneclairehood@jch9.freeserve.co.uk]	0131-556 7313
7	**Edinburgh: Canongate (H)** Neil N. Gardner MA BD	1991	2006	Manse of Canongate, Edinburgh EH8 8BR [E-mail: nng@surfaid.org]	0131-556 3515
8	**Edinburgh: Carrick Knowe (H) (0131-334 1505) (E-mail: carrickknowechurch@btinternet.com)** Fiona M. Mathieson (Mrs) BEd BD	1988	2001	21 Traquair Park West, Edinburgh EH12 7AN [E-mail: fiona.mathieson@ukgateway.net]	0131-334 9774
9	**Edinburgh: Colinton (H) (0131-441 2232) (E-mail: church.office@colinton-parish.com)** George J. Whyte BSc BD DMin	1981	1992	The Manse, Colinton, Edinburgh EH13 0JR [E-mail: george.whyte@colinton-parish.com]	0131-441 2315

10 **Edinburgh: Colinton Mains (H)**
Ian A. McQuarrie BD   1993
17 Swanston Green, Edinburgh EH10 7EW
[E-mail: ian.mcquarrie1@btinternet.com]
0131-445 3451

11 **Edinburgh: Corstorphine Craigsbank (H) (0131-334 6365)**
Stewart M. McPherson BD CertMin   1991   2003
17 Craigs Bank, Edinburgh EH12 8HD
[E-mail: smcpherson@blueyonder.co.uk]
0131-467 6826
07814 901429 (Mbl)

12 **Edinburgh: Corstorphine Old (H) (0131-334 7864) (E-mail: corold@aol.com)**
Moira McDonald MA BD   1997   2005
23 Manse Road, Edinburgh EH12 7SW
[E-mail: moira.mc@tesco.net]
0131-476 5893

13 **Edinburgh: Corstorphine St Anne's (0131-316 4740) (E-mail: stannesoffice@surefish.co.uk)**
MaryAnn R. Rennie (Mrs) BD MTh   1998   2002
23 Belgrave Road, Edinburgh EH12 6NG
[E-mail: maryann.rennie@blueyonder.co.uk]
0131-334 3188

14 **Edinburgh: Corstorphine St Ninian's (H) (E-mail: st-ninians@corstorphine144.freeserve.co.uk)**
Alexander T. Stewart MA BD FSAScot   1975   1995
17 Templeland Road, Edinburgh EH12 8RZ
[E-mail: alextstewart@blueyonder.co.uk]
0131-334 2978

Margaret Gordon (Mrs) DCS
92 Lanark Road West, Currie EH14 5LA
0131-449 2554

15 **Edinburgh: Craigentinny St Christopher's**
Vacant
61 Milton Crescent, Edinburgh EH15 3PQ
0131-669 2429

16 **Edinburgh: Craiglockhart (H) (E-mail: craiglockhart_church@fsmail.net)**
Andrew Ritchie BD DipMin DMin   1984   1991
202 Colinton Road, Edinburgh EH14 1BP
[E-mail: andrewritchie@talk21.com]
0131-443 2020

17 **Edinburgh: Craigmillar Park (T) (H) (0131-667 5862)**
Sarah E.C. Nicol (Mrs) BSc BD   1985   1994
14 Hallhead Road, Edinburgh EH16 5QJ
0131-667 1623

18 **Edinburgh: Cramond (H) (E-mail: cramond.kirk@blueyonder.co.uk)**
G. Russell Barr BA BD MTh DMin   1979   1993
Manse of Cramond, Edinburgh EH4 6NS
[E-mail: rev.r.barr@blueyonder.co.uk]
0131-336 2036

19 **Edinburgh: Currie (H) (0131-451 5141) (E-mail: currie_kirk@btconnect.com)**
Keith W. Ross MA BD   1984   2000
43 Lanark Road West, Currie EH14 5JX
[E-mail: kirk.ross@blueyonder.co.uk]
0131-449 4719

20 **Edinburgh: Dalmeny**
Vacant

21 **Edinburgh: Davidson's Mains (H) (0131-312 6282) (E-mail: life@dmainschurch.plus.com)**
Jeremy R.H. Middleton LLB BD   1981   1988
1 Hillpark Terrace, Edinburgh EH4 7SX
[E-mail: life@dmainschurch.plus.com]
0131-336 3078

22	**Edinburgh: Dean (H)**		
	Mark M. Foster BSc BD	1998	1 Ravelston Terrace, Edinburgh EH4 3EF	0131-332 5736
			[E-mail: markmfoster@mac.com]	

23 Edinburgh: Drylaw (0131-343 6643)
Patricia Watson (Mrs) BD — 2005
15 House o'Hill Gardens, Edinburgh EH4 2AR
[E-mail: patricia@patriciawatson.wanadoo.co.uk]
0131-343 1441
07969 942627 (Mbl)

24 Edinburgh: Duddingston (H) (E-mail: dodinskirk@aol.com)
James A.P. Jack DMin BSc BArch BD — 1989 2001
Manse of Duddingston, Old Church Lane, Edinburgh EH15 3PX
[E-mail: jamesapjack@aol.com]
0131-661 4240

25 Edinburgh: Fairmilehead (H) (0131-445 2374) (E-mail: fairmilehead.p.c@btconnect.com)
John R. Munro BD — 1976 1992
6 Braid Crescent, Edinburgh EH10 6AU
[E-mail: revjohnmunro@hotmail.com]
0131-446 9363

26 Edinburgh: Gilmerton (New Charge Development)
Paul H. Beautyman MA BD — 1993 2002
43 Ravenscroft Street, Edinburgh EH17 8QJ
[E-mail: ncdgilmerton@uk.uumail.com]
0131-664 7538

27 Edinburgh: Gorgie (H) (0131-337 7936)
Peter I. Barber MA BD — 1984 1995
90 Myreside Road, Edinburgh EH10 5BZ
[E-mail: pibarber@supanet.com]
0131-337 2284

28 Edinburgh: Granton (H) (0131-552 3033)
Norman A. Smith MA BD — 1997 2005
8 Wardie Crescent, Edinburgh EH5 1AG
[E-mail: norm@smith1971.fsnet.co.uk]
0131-551 2159

Marilynn Steele (Mrs) DCS
2 Northfield Gardens, Prestonpans EH32 9LQ
[E-mail: marilynnsteele@aol.com]
01875 811497

29 Edinburgh: Greenbank (H) (0131-447 9969) (E-mail: greenbankchurch@btconnect.com)
Vacant
112 Greenbank Crescent, Edinburgh EH10 5SZ
0131-447 4032

30 Edinburgh: Greenside (H) (0131-556 5588)
Andrew F. Anderson MA BD — 1981
80 Pilrig Street, Edinburgh EH6 5AS
[E-mail: andrew@pilrig.fsnet.co.uk]
0131-554 3277 (Tel/Fax)

31 Edinburgh: Greyfriars Tolbooth and Highland Kirk (GE) (H) (0131-225 1900) (E-mail: enquiries@greyfriarskirk.com)
Richard E. Frazer BA BD DMin — 1986 2003
12 Tantallon Place, Edinburgh EH9 1NZ
[E-mail: tantallon@ukonline.co.uk]
0131-667 6610

32 Edinburgh: High (St Giles') (0131-225 4363) (E-mail: stgilescathedral@btconnect.com)
Gilleasbuig Macmillan
CVO MA BD Drhc DD — 1969 1973
St Giles' Cathedral, Edinburgh EH1 1RE
[E-mail: minister.stgiles@btconnect.com]
0131-225 4363

Hilary W. Smith (Miss)
BD DipMin MTh PhD (Assistant) — 1999 2003
11 South Lauder Road, Edinburgh EH9 2NB
0131-667 6539

No.	Charge / Minister	Ordained	Address	Appointed	Telephone
33	**Edinburgh: Holyrood Abbey (H) (0131-661 4883)**				
	Philip R. Hair BD	1980	100 Willowbrae Avenue, Edinburgh EH8 7HU [E-mail: phil@holyroodabbey.f2s.com]	1998	0131-652 0640
34	**Edinburgh: Holy Trinity (H) (0131-442 3304)**				
	Kenneth S. Borthwick MA BD	1983	16 Thorburn Road, Edinburgh EH13 0BQ [E-mail: kennysamuel@aol.com]	2005	0131-441 1403
	Ian MacDonald (Assoc)	2005	12 Sighthill Crescent, Edinburgh EH11 4QE		0131-453 6279
	Joyce Mitchell (Mrs) DCS	2005	16/4 Murrayburn Place, Edinburgh EH14 2RR		0131-453 6548
	Oliver M. Clegg BD (Youth Minister)	2003	256/5 Lanark Road, Edinburgh EH14 2LR		0131-443 0825
35	**Edinburgh: Inverleith (H)**				
	D. Hugh Davidson MA	1965	43 Inverleith Gardens, Edinburgh EH3 5PR [E-mail: hdavidson@freeuk.com]	1975	0131-552 3874
36	**Edinburgh: Juniper Green (H)**				
	James S. Dewar MA BD	1983	476 Lanark Road, Juniper Green, Edinburgh EH14 5BQ [E-mail: jim.dewar@blueyonder.co.uk]	2000	0131-453 3494
37	**Edinburgh: Kaimes Lockhart Memorial**				
	Iain D. Penman BD	1977	76 Lasswade Road, Edinburgh EH16 6SF [E-mail: iainpenmanklm@aol.com]	1995	0131-664 2287
38	**Edinburgh: Kirkliston**				
	Glenda J. Keating (Mrs) MTh	1996	43 Main Street, Kirkliston EH29 9AF [E-mail: kirkglen@aol.com]		0131-333 3298
39	**Edinburgh: Kirk o' Field (T) (H)**				
	Ian D. Maxwell MA BD PhD	1977	31 Hatton Place, Edinburgh EH9 1UA [E-mail: i.d.maxwell@quista.net]	1996	0131-667 7954
40	**Edinburgh: Leith North (H) (0131-553 7378)**				
	Kenneth S. Baird MSc PhD BD CEng MIMarEST	1998	6 Craighall Gardens, Edinburgh EH6 4RJ	2003	0131-552 4411
41	**Edinburgh: Leith St Andrew's (H)**				
	Elizabeth J.B. Youngson BD	1996	30 Lochend Road, Edinburgh EH6 8BS [E-mail: elizabeth.youngson@virgin.net]	2006	0131-554 7695
42	**Edinburgh: Leith St Serf's (T) (H)**				
	Sara R. Embleton (Mrs) BA BD MTh	1987	20 Wilton Road, Edinburgh EH16 5NX [E-mail: sara.embleton@blueyonder.co.uk]	1999	0131-478 1624
43	**Edinburgh: Leith St Thomas' Junction Road (T)**				
	George C. Shand MA BD	1981	107 Easter Warriston, Edinburgh EH7 4QZ [E-mail: georgeshand@blueyonder.co.uk]	2003	0131-467 7789

44	**Edinburgh: Leith South (H) (0131-554 2578) (E-mail: slpc@dial.pipex.com)**			
	Ian Y. Gilmour BD	1985	1995	37 Claremont Road, Edinburgh EH6 7NN [E-mail: IanYG@blueyonder.co.uk]	0131-554 3062
	Louise Duncan (Mrs) BD (Assoc)		2005	25 Elmwood Terrace, Edinburgh EH6 8DF	0131-538 0243
45	**Edinburgh: Leith Wardie (H) (0131-551 3847) (E-mail: admin@wardiechurch.freeserve.co.uk)**			
	Brian C. Hilsley LLB BD		1990	35 Lomond Road, Edinburgh EH5 3JN [E-mail: brian@wardie10.freeserve.co.uk]	0131-552 3328
46	**Edinburgh: Liberton (H)**			
	John N. Young MA BD PhD		1996	7 Kirk Park, Edinburgh EH16 6HZ [E-mail: LLLjyoung@btinternet.com]	0131-664 3067
47	**Edinburgh: Liberton Northfield (H) (0131-551 3847)**			
	John M. McPake LTh		2000	9 Claverhouse Drive, Edinburgh EH16 6BR [E-mail: john_mcpake9@yahoo.co.uk]	0131-658 1754
48	**Edinburgh: London Road (H) (0131-661 1149)**			
	Vacant			26 Inchview Terrace, Edinburgh EH7 6TQ	0131-669 5311
49	**Edinburgh: Marchmont St Giles' (H) (0131-447 4359)**			
	Karen K. Watson BD MTh	1997	2002	19 Hope Terrace, Edinburgh EH9 2AP [E-mail: theminister@marchmontstgiles.org.uk]	0131-447 2834
50	**Edinburgh: Mayfield Salisbury (0131-667 1522)**			
	Scott S. McKenna BA BD MTh	1994	2000	26 Seton Place, Edinburgh EH9 2JT [E-mail: scottsmckenna@aol.com]	0131-667 1286
51	**Edinburgh: Morningside (H) (0131-447 6745) (E-mail: office@morningsideparishchurch.net)**			
	Derek Browning MA BD DMin	1987	2003	20 Braidburn Crescent, Edinburgh EH10 6EN [E-mail: derek.browning@btinternet.com]	0131-447 1617 (Tel/Fax) 07050 133876 (Mbl)
52	**Edinburgh: Morningside United (H) (0131-447 3152)**			
	John R. Smith MA BD	1973	1998	1 Midmar Avenue, Edinburgh EH10 6BS [E-mail: ministermuc@blueyonder.co.uk]	0131-447 8724
53	**Edinburgh: Muirhouse St Andrew's (E)**			
	Continued Vacancy			35 Silverknowes Road, Edinburgh EH4 5LL	0131-336 4546
	Brenda Robson PhD (Auxiliary Minister)			Old School House, 2 Baird Road, Ratho, Newbridge EH28 8RA [E-mail: brendarobson@tiscali.co.uk]	0131-333 2746
54	**Edinburgh: Murrayfield (H) (0131-337 1091) (E-mail: mpchurch@btconnect.com)**			
	William D. Brown BD CQSW	1987	2001	45 Murrayfield Gardens, Edinburgh EH12 6DH [E-mail: wdb@fish.co.uk]	0131-337 5431
55	**Edinburgh: Newhaven (H)**			
	Vacant			158 Granton Road, Edinburgh EH5 3RF	0131-552 8906

56 **Edinburgh: New Restalrig (H) (0131-661 5676)**
David L. Court BSc BD   1989   2000   19 Abercorn Road, Edinburgh EH8 7DP   0131-661 4045
[E-mail: david@dlc.org.uk]

57 **Edinburgh: Old Kirk (H) (0131-332 4354) (E-mail: minister.oldkirk@btinternet.com)**
Vacant

58 **Edinburgh: Palmerston Place (H) (0131-220 1690) (E-mail: admin@palmerstonplacechurch.com)**
Colin A.M. Sinclair BA BD   1981   1996   30B Cluny Gardens, Edinburgh EH10 6BJ   0131-447 9598
[E-mail: colins.ppc@virgin.net]   0131-225 3312 (Fax)

59 **Edinburgh: Pilrig St Paul's (0131-553 1876)**
John M. Tait BSc BD   1985   1999   78 Pilrig Street, Edinburgh EH6 5AS   0131-554 1842
[E-mail: john.m.tait@btinternet.com]

60 **Edinburgh: Polwarth (H) (0131-346 2711) (E-mail: polwarthchurch@tiscali.co.uk)**
Linda J. Dunbar BSc BA BD PhD FRHS   2000   2005   88 Craiglockhart Road, Edinburgh EH14 1EP   0131-441 5335
[E-mail: polwarthminister@ouvip.com]

61 **Edinburgh: Portobello Old (H)**
Andrew R.M. Patterson MA BD   1985   2006   6 Hamilton Terrace, Edinburgh EH15 1NB   0131-669 5312

62 **Edinburgh: Portobello St James' (H)**
Peter Webster BD   1977   2002   34 Brighton Place, Edinburgh EH15 1LT   0131-669 1767
[E-mail: peterwebster101@hotmail.com]

63 **Edinburgh: Portobello St Philip's Joppa (H) (0131-669 3641)**
Stewart G. Weaver BA BD PhD   2003   6 St Mary's Place, Edinburgh EH15 2QF   0131-669 2410
[E-mail: stewartweaver@beeb.net]

64 **Edinburgh: Priestfield (H) (0131-667 5644)**
Thomas N. Johnston LTh   1972   1990   13 Lady Road, Edinburgh EH16 5PA   0131-668 1620
[E-mail: tomjohnston@blueyonder.co.uk]

65 **Edinburgh: Queensferry (H)**
John G. Carrie BSc BD   1971   1 Station Road, South Queensferry EH30 9HY   0131-331 1100
[E-mail: john.carrie@virgin.net]

66 **Edinburgh: Ratho**
Ian J. Wells BD   1999   2 Freelands Road, Ratho, Newbridge EH28 8NP   0131-333 1346
[E-mail: ianjwells@btinternet.com]

67 **Edinburgh: Reid Memorial (H) (0131-662 1203) (E-mail: reid.memorial@u.genie.co.uk)**
Brian M. Embleton BD   1976   1985   20 Wilton Road, Edinburgh EH16 5NX   0131-667 3981
[E-mail: brianembleton@btinternet.com]

68 **Edinburgh: Richmond Craigmillar (H) (0131-661 6561)**
Elizabeth M. Henderson (Miss)   1985   1997   13 Wisp Green, Edinburgh EH15 3QX   0131-669 1133
MA BD MTh   [E-mail: lizhende@aol.com]

69 **Edinburgh: St Andrew's and St George's (H) (0131-225 3847) (E-mail: standrewsandstgeorges@eh.quik.co.uk)**
Roderick D.M. Campbell TD BD FSAScot   1975   2003   25 Comely Bank, Edinburgh EH4 1AJ   0131-332 5324
[E-mail: rdmcampbell@aol.com]
Dorothy U. Anderson LLB DipLP BD   2006   5 West Castle Road, Edinburgh EH10 5AT   0131-229 5862
(Outreach Minister)

70 **Edinburgh: St Andrew's Clermiston**
Alistair H. Keil BD DipMin   1989   87 Drum Brae South, Edinburgh EH12 8TD   0131-339 4149
[E-mail: ahkeil@fish.co.uk]

71 **Edinburgh: St Catherine's Argyle (H) (0131-667 7220)**
Victor W.N. Laidlaw BD   1975   5 Palmerston Road, Edinburgh EH9 1TL   0131-667 9344
[E-mail: viclaid@aol.com]

72 **Edinburgh: St Colm's (T) (H)**
Douglas S. Paterson MA BD   1976   2005   6 Groathill Loan, Edinburgh EH4 2WL   0131-315 4541
[E-mail: dostpa@aol.com]

73 **Edinburgh: St Cuthbert's (H) (0131-229 1142) (E-mail: office@stcuthberts.net)**
Tom C. Cuthell MA BD MTh   1965   1976   34A Murrayfield Road, Edinburgh EH12 6ER   0131-337 6637
[E-mail: cuthbert@tccuthell.fsnet.co.uk]

74 **Edinburgh: St David's Broomhouse (H) (0131-443 9851)**
Robert A. Mackenzie LLB BD   1993   2005   33 Traquair Park West, Edinburgh EH12 7AN   0131-334 1730
[E-mail: rob.anne@blueyonder.co.uk]
Liz Crocker (Mrs) DipComEd DCS   77C Craigcrook Road, Edinburgh EH4 3PH   0131-332 0227

75 **Edinburgh: St George's West (H) (0131-225 7001) (E-mail: st-georges-west@btconnect.com)**
Peter J. Macdonald BD DipMin   1986   1998   6 Wardie Avenue, Edinburgh EH5 2AB   0131-552 4333
[E-mail: petermacdonald@blueyonder.co.uk]

76 **Edinburgh: St John's Oxgangs**
Gillean P. Maclean (Mrs) BD   1994   2003   2 Caiystane Terrace, Edinburgh EH10 6SR   0131-445 1688
[E-mail: gmaclean@fish.co.uk]

77 **Edinburgh: St Margaret's (H) (0131-554 7400) (E-mail: stm.parish@virgin.net)**
Carol H.M. Ford DSD RSAMD BD   2003   43 Moira Terrace, Edinburgh EH7 6TD   0131-669 7329
[E-mail: fordcar@fish.co.uk]

78 Edinburgh: St Martin's
Vacant — 5 Duddingston Crescent, Edinburgh EH15 3AS — 0131-657 9894

79 Edinburgh: St Michael's (H) (E-mail: office@stmichaels-kirk.co.uk)
James D. Aitken BD   2002 2005 — 9 Merchiston Gardens, Edinburgh EH10 5DD — 0131-346 1970
[E-mail: james.aitken2@btinternet.com]

80 Edinburgh: St Nicholas' Sighthill
Kenneth J. Mackay MA BD   1971 1976 — 122 Sighthill Loan, Edinburgh EH11 4NT — 0131-453 6921
[E-mail: revkenmackay@yahoo.co.uk]

81 Edinburgh: St Stephen's Comely Bank (0131-315 4616)
Vacant — 8 Blinkbonny Crescent, Edinburgh EH4 3NB — 0131-332 3364

82 Edinburgh: Slateford Longstone
Michael W. Frew BSc BD   1978 2005 — 50 Kingsknowe Road South, Edinburgh EH14 2JW — 0131-466 5308
[E-mail: mwfrew@blueyonder.co.uk]
Mary Gargrave (Mrs) DCS — 229/3 Calder Road, Edinburgh EH11 4RG — 0131-476 3493

83 Edinburgh: Stenhouse St Aidan's
Colin A. Strong BSc BD   1989 2001 — 65 Balgreen Road, Edinburgh EH12 5UA — 0131-337 7711
[E-mail: colinastrong@aol.com]
Mary Gargrave (Mrs) DCS — 229/3 Calder Road, Edinburgh EH11 4RG — 0131-476 3493

84 Edinburgh: Stockbridge (H) (0131-332 0122)
Anne T. Logan (Mrs) MA BD MTh DMin   1981 1993 — 19 Eildon Street, Edinburgh EH3 5JU — 0131-557 6052
[E-mail: annetlogan@blueyonder.co.uk]

85 Edinburgh: Tron Moredun
Vacant — 467 Gilmerton Road, Edinburgh EH17 7JG — 0131-666 2584

86 Edinburgh: Viewforth (T) (H) (0131-229 1917)
Anthony P. Thornthwaite MTh   1995 — 91 Morningside Drive, Edinburgh EH10 5NN — 0131-447 6684
[E-mail: tony.thornthwaite@blueyonder.co.uk]

Aitken, Alexander R. MA   1965 1997 (Newhaven)   36 King's Meadow, Edinburgh EH16 5JW   0131-667 1404

Anderson, Robert S. BD   1988 1997 Scottish Churches World Exchange   St Colm's International House, 23 Inverleith Terrace, Edinburgh EH3 5NS   0131-315 4444

Armitage, William L. BSc BD   1976 2006 (Edinburgh: London Road)   27 West Windygoul Gardens, Tranent EH33 2LB   01875 612047
[E-mail: bill@billarm.plus.com]

Auld, A. Graeme MA BD PhD DLitt FSAScot FRSE   1973 1973 University of Edinburgh   Nether Swanshiel, Hobkirk, Bonchester Bridge, Hawick TD9 8JU

Name	Years	Charge	Address	Tel
Baigrie, R.A. MA	1945 1985	(Kirkurd with Newlands)	32 Inchcolm Terrace, South Queensferry EH30 9NA	0131-331 4311
Baxter, Richard F. OBE MA BD	1954 1990	(Assistant at St Andrew's and St George's)		
Beckett, David M. BA BD	1964 2002	(Greyfriars, Tolbooth and Highland Kirk)	138 Braid Road, Edinburgh EH10 6JB	0131-447 7735
			1F1, 31 Sciennes Road, Edinburgh EH9 1NT [E-mail: davidbeckett3@aol.com]	0131-667 2672
Blakey, Ronald S. MA BD MTh	1962 2000	Editor: *The Year Book*	5 Moss Side Road, Biggar ML12 6GF	01899 229226
Booth, Jennifer (Mrs) BD	1996 2004	(Associate: Leith South)	39 Lilyhill Terrace, Edinburgh EH8 7DR	0131-661 3813
Brady, Ian D. BSc ARCST BD	1967 2001	(Edinburgh: Corstorphine Old)	28 Frankfield Crescent, Dalgety Bay, Dunfermline KY11 9LW [E-mail: pidb@dbay28.fsnet.co.uk]	01383 825104
Brown, William D. MA	1963 1989	(Wishaw: Thornlie)	9/3 Craigend Park, Edinburgh EH16 5XY [E-mail: wdbrown@surefish.co.uk]	0131-672 2936
Bruce, Lilian M. (Miss) BD MTh	1971 2001	(Daviot and Dunlichity with Moy, Dalarossie and Tomatin)	33 Falcon Court, Edinburgh EH10 4AF	
Cameron, G. Gordon MA BD STM	1957 1997	(Juniper Green)	4 Ladywell Grove, Clackmannan FK10 4JQ	01259 723769
Cameron, John W.M. MA BD	1957 1996	(Liberton)	10 Plewlands Gardens, Edinburgh EH10 5JP	0131-447 1277
Chalmers, John P. BD	1979 1995	Ministries Council	10 Liggars Place, Dunfermline KY12 7XZ	01383 739130
Chalmers, Murray MA	1965 1991	Hospital Chaplain: Royal Edinburgh and Astley Ainslie		
Clinkenbeard, William W. BSc BD STM	1966 2000	(Edinburgh: Carrick Knowe)	8 Easter Warriston, Edinburgh EH7 4QX	0131-552 4211
			4 Aline Court, Dalgety Bay, Dunfermline KY11 5GP [E-mail: bjclinks@compuserve.com]	01383 824011
Cook, John MA BD	1967 2005	(Edinburgh: Leith St Andrew's)	26 Silverknowes Court, Edinburgh EH4 5NR	0131-312 8447
Cook, John Weir MA BD	1962 2002	(Edinburgh: Portobello St Philip's Joppa)	74 Pinkie Road, Musselburgh EH21 7QT [E-mail: jwc@freeuk.com]	0131-653 0992
Crichton, Thomas JP ChStJ MA	1965 2004	(Hospital Chaplain)	18 Carlton Terrace, Edinburgh EH7 5DD	0131-557 0009
Cross, Brian F. MA	1961 1998	(Coalburn)	1474 High Road, Whetstone, London N20 9QD	0208 492 9313
Davidson, Ian M.P. MBE MA BD	1957 1994	(Stirling: Allan Park South with Church of the Holy Rude)	13/8 Craigend Park, Edinburgh EH16 5XX	0131-664 0074
Dawson, Michael S. BTech BD	1979 2005	(Associate: Edinburgh: Holy Trinity)	9 The Broich, Alva FK12 5NR [E-mail: mixpen.dawson@btinternet.com]	01259 769309
Dilbey, Mary D. (Miss) BD	1997 2002	(West Kirk of Calder)	41 Bonaly Rise, Edinburgh EH13 0QU	0131-441 9092
Dougall, Elspeth G. (Mrs) MA BD	1989 2001	(Edinburgh: Marchmont St Giles')	60B Craigmillar Park, Edinburgh EH16 5PU	0131-668 1342
Doyle, Ian B. MA BD PhD	1946 1991	(Department of National Mission)	21 Lygon Road, Edinburgh EH16 5QD	0131-667 2697
Drummond, Rhoda (Miss) DCS	1983 1998	(Deaconess)	Flat K, 23 Grange Loan, Edinburgh EH9 2ER	0131-668 3631
Dunn, W. Iain C. DA LTh	1976 2004	(Pilrig and Dalmeny Street)	10 Fox Covert Avenue, Edinburgh EH12 6UQ	0131-334 1665
Elliott, Gavin J. MA BD	1968 2000	Ministries Council	c/o 121 George Street, Edinburgh EH2 4YN	0131-225 5722
Faulds, Norman L. MA BD FSAScot		(Aberlady with Gullane)	10 West Fenton Court, West Fenton, North Berwick EH39 5AE	01620 842331
Fergusson, David A.S. MA BD DPhil FRSE	1984 2000	University of Edinburgh	23 Riselaw Crescent, Edinburgh EH10 6HN	0131-447 4022
Forrester, Duncan B. MA BD DPhil DD	1962 1978	(University of Edinburgh)	25 Kingsburgh Road, Edinburgh EH12 6DZ	0131-337 5646
Forrester, Margaret R. (Mrs) MA BD	1974 2003	(Edinburgh: St Michael's)	25 Kingsburgh Road, Edinburgh EH12 6DZ [E-mail: margaret@theforresters.fsnet.co.uk]	0131-337 5646
Fraser, Shirley A. (Miss) MA BD	1992 2001	Scottish Field Director: Friends International	30 Parkhead Avenue, Edinburgh EH11 4SG	0131-443 7268
Galbraith, Douglas MA BD BMus MPhil ARSCM	1965 2005	(Office for Worship, Doctrine and Artistic Matters)	c/o 121 George Street, Edinburgh EH2 4YN [E-mail: dgalbraith@cofscotland.org.uk]	0131-240 2233
Gardner, John V.	1997 2003	(Glamis, Inverarity and Kinnettles)	104 Comiston Drive, Edinburgh EH10 5QU [E-mail: jvg66@hotmail.com]	0131-447 6859

Name			Position	Address	Tel
Gibson, John C.L. MA BD DPhil	1959	1994	(University of Edinburgh)	Cairnbank, Morton Street South, Edinburgh EH15 2NB	0131-669 3635
Gordon, Tom MA BD	1974	1994	Chaplain: Fairmile Marie Curie Centre	22 Gosford Road, Port Seton, Prestonpans EH32 0HF	01875 812262
Graham, W. Peter MA BD	1967	1993	Presbytery Clerk	23/6 East Comiston, Edinburgh EH10 6RZ [E-mail: akph50@uk.uumail.com]	0131-445 5763
Harkness, James CB OBE QHC MA DD	1961	1995	(Chaplain General: Army)	13 Saxe Coburg Place, Edinburgh EH3 5BR	0131-343 1297
Hill, J. William BA BD	1967	2001	(Corstorphine St Anne's)	33/9 Murrayfield Road, Edinburgh EH12 6EP	0131-332 8020
Hutchison, Maureen (Mrs) DCS	1985	2005	(Deaconess)	23 Drylaw Crescent, Edinburgh EH4 2AU	0131-441 3384
Irving, William D. LTh	1974	2000	(Golspie)	122 Swanston Muir, Edinburgh EH10 7HY	01506 412020
Jamieson, Gordon D. MA BD	1954	1994	Director of Stewardship	41 Goldpark Place, Livingston EH54 6LW	0131-229 7815
Jeffrey, Eric W.S. JP MA	1953	1988	(Edinburgh Bristo Memorial)	18 Gillespie Crescent, Edinburgh EH10 4HT	0131-466 2607
Kant, Everard FVCM MTh	1994	2006	(Kinghorn)	10/1 Maxwell Street, Edinburgh EH10 5GZ	0131-551 7706
Kelly, Ewan R. MB ChB BD PhD	1963	1999	Chaplain: St Columba's Hospice	15 Boswall Road, Edinburgh EH5 3RW	0131-539 3311
Lawson, Kenneth C. MA BD	1965	2002	(Adviser in Adult Education)	56 Easter Drylaw View, Edinburgh EH4 2QP	0131-443 7640
Lyall, David BSc BD STM PhD	1952	1986	(University of Edinburgh)	1 North Meggetland, Edinburgh EH14 1XG	0131-449 5031
Lyon, D.H.S. MA BD STM	1971	1996	(Board of World Mission and Unity)	7 Marchbank Gardens, Balerno EH14 7ET	0131-225 5722
Macdonald, Finlay A.J. MA BD PhD DD	1976	1999	Principal Clerk	c/o 121 George Street, Edinburgh EH2 4YN	
Macdonald, William J. BD			(Board of National Mission: New Charge Development)	1/13 North Werber Park, Edinburgh EH4 1SY	0131-332 0254
McDonald, William J.G. DD			(Mayfield)	7 Blacket Place, Edinburgh EH9 1RN	0131-667 2100
McDowell, Brian BA BD	1953	1992	Chaplain: Fettes College	6 West Woods, Fettes College, Edinburgh EH4 1RA	0131-332 9510
McGillivray, A. Gordon MA BD STM	1999		(Presbytery Clerk)	7 Greenfield Crescent, Balerno EH14 7HD	0131-449 4747
MacGregor, Margaret S. (Miss) MA BD DipEd	1951	1993	(Calcutta)	16 Learmonth Court, Edinburgh EH4 1PB	0131-332 1089
McGregor, Alistair G.C. QC BD	1985	1994	(Edinburgh: Leith North)	22 Primrose Bank Road, Edinburgh EH5 3JG	0131-551 2802
McGregor, T. Stewart MBE MA BD	1987	2002	(Chaplain: Edinburgh Royal Infirmary)	19 Lonsdale Terrace, Edinburgh EH3 9HL [E-mail: cetsm@dircon.uk]	0131-229 5332
Maclean, Ailsa G. (Mrs) BD DipCE	1957	1998	Chaplain: George Heriot's School	28 Swan Spring Avenue, Edinburgh EH10 6NJ	0131-445 1320
MacLean, Marjory A. (Miss) LLB BD PhD	1979	1988	Depute Clerk: General Assembly	c/o 121 George Street, Edinburgh EH2 4YN	
McLeod, Roderick MA BD	1991	1998	(Lochwinnoch)	2 East Savile Road, Edinburgh EH16 5ND	0131-225 5722
MacMurchie, F. Lynne LLB BD	1951	1990	Health Care Chaplain	Edinburgh Community Mental Health Chaplaincy, 41 George IV Bridge, Edinburgh EH1 1EL	0131-667 1475
McPheat, Elspeth DCS	1998	2003	Deaconess: CrossReach	11/5 New Orchardfield, Edinburgh EH6 5ET	0131-220 5150
McPhee, Duncan C. MA BD	1953	1993	(Department of National Mission)	8 Belvedere Park, Edinburgh EH6 4LR	0131-554 4143
Macpherson, Allan S. MA	1967	1993	Merchiston Castle School	36 Craigmillar Castle Road, Edinburgh EH16 4AR	0131-552 6784
Macpherson, Colin C.R. MA BD	1958	1996	(Dunfermline St Margaret's)	7 Eva Place, Edinburgh EH9 3ET	0131-667 1456
Mathieson, Angus R. MA BD	1988	1998	Ministries Council	21 Traquair Park West, Edinburgh EH12 7AN	0131-334 9774
Middleton, Paul BMus BD ThM PhD	2000	2005	University of Wales: Lampeter	Department of Theology and Religious Studies, University of Wales, Lampeter SA48 7ED [E-mail: paul.middleton@totalise.co.uk]	
Moir, Ian A. MA BD	1962	2000	(Adviser for Urban Priority Areas)	28/6 Comely Bank Avenue, Edinburgh EH4 1EL	0131-332 2748
Monteith, W. Graham BD PhD	1974	1994	(Flotta and Fara with Hoy and Walls)	20/3 Grandfield, Edinburgh EH6 4TL	0131-552 2564
Morrice, William G. MA BD STM PhD	1957	1991	(St John's College Durham)	Flat 37, The Cedars, 2 Manse Road, Edinburgh EH12 7SN [E-mail: w.g.morrice@btinternet.com]	0131-316 4845

Name			Role	Address	Phone
Morrison, Mary B. (Mrs) MA BD DipEd	1978	2000	(Edinburgh: Stenhouse St Aidan's)	14 Eildon Terrace, Edinburgh EH3 5LU	0131-556 1962
Morton, Andrew R. MA BD DD	1956	1994	(Board of World Mission and Unity)	11 Oxford Terrace, Edinburgh EH4 1PX	0131-332 6592
Morton, R. Colin BA BD	1960	1998	(Jerusalem)	313 Lanark Road West, Currie EH14 5RS	0131-449 7359
Moyes, Sheila A. (Miss) DCS			(Deaconess)	158 Pilton Avenue, Edinburgh EH5 2JZ	0131-551 1731
Mulligan, Anne MA DCS			Deaconess: Hospital Chaplain	27A Craigour Avenue, Edinburgh EH17 1NH	0131-664 3426
Munro, George A.M.	1968	2000	(Edinburgh: Cluny)	108 Caiyside, Edinburgh EH10 7HR	0131-445 5829
Murison, William G.	1951	1990	(Department of World Mission and Unity)	21 Hailes Gardens, Edinburgh EH13 0JL	0131-441 2460
Murrie, John BD	1953	1996	(Kirkliston)	31 Nicol Road, The Whins, Broxburn EH52 6JJ	01506 852464
Musgrave, Clarence W. BA BD ThM	1966	2006	(Jerusalem: St Andrew's)	48 Bruntsfield Gardens, Edinburgh EH10 4DZ [E-mail: cwm_edinburgh@btopenworld.com]	0131-447 3573
Neilson, Peter MA BD MTh	1975	2003	(Mission Developments Facilitator)	12 Strathalmond Court, Edinburgh EH4 8AE	0131-339 4536
Nicol, Douglas A.O. MA BD	1974	1991	Mission and Discipleship Council	24 Corbiehill Avenue, Edinburgh EH4 5DR	0131-336 1965
Page, Ruth MA BD DPhil	1976	2000	(University of Edinburgh)	22/5 West Mill Bank, West Mill Road, Edinburgh EH13 0QT	0131-441 3740
Paterson, J.M.K. MA ACII BD DD	1964	1987	(Milngavie: St Paul's)	58 Orchard Drive, Edinburgh EH4 2DZ	0131-332 5876
Paterson, John M.	1976	1987	(Blackbraes and Shieldhill)	28/21 Roseburn Place, Edinburgh EH12 5NX	0131-337 0095
Philip, James MA	1948	1997	(Holyrood Abbey)	3 Ferguson Gardens, Musselburgh EH21 6XF	0131-653 2310
Philip, Connie (Miss) BD	1980	1995	(Arbuthnott with Bervie)	22/5 South Elixa Place, Baronscourt View, Edinburgh EH8 7PG	0131-661 3124
Plate, Maria A.G. (Miss) LTh BA	1983	2000	(South Ronaldsay and Burray)	Flat 29, 77 Barnton Park View, Edinburgh EH4 6EL	0131-339 8539
Potts, Jean (Miss) DCS			(Deaconess)	28B East Claremont Street, Edinburgh EH7 4JP	0131-557 2144
Rae, David L.	1955	1990	(Kolhapur)	29 Falcon Avenue, Edinburgh EH10 4AL	0131-447 3158
Reid, W. Scott BD MA DipPS PhD	1950	1990	(London Road)	14/37 Ethel Terrace, Edinburgh EH10 5NA	0131-447 7642
Renton, Ian P.	1958	1990	(St Colm's)	98 Homeross House, Strathearn Road, Edinburgh EH9 2QY	0131-447 0601
Ridland, Alistair K. MA BD	1982	2000	Chaplain: Western General Hospital	13 Stewart Place, Kirkliston EH29 0BQ	0131-333 2711
Robertson, Charles LVO MA	1965	2005	(Edinburgh: Canongate)	3 Ross Gardens, Edinburgh EH9 3BS	0131-662 9025
Ronald, Norma A. (Miss) MBE DCS			(Deaconess)	2B Saughton Road North, Edinburgh EH12 7HG	0131-334 8736
Ross, Andrew C. MA BD STM PhD	1958	1998	(University of Edinburgh)	20 Forbes Road, Edinburgh EH10 4ED	0131-228 8984
Ross, Kenneth R. BA BD PhD	1982	1999	World Mission Council	c/o 121 George Street, Edinburgh EH2 4YN	0131-225 5722
Schofield, Melville F. MA	1960	2000	(Chaplain: Western General Hospitals)	25 Rowantree Grove, Currie EH14 5AT	0131-449 4745
Scott, Ian G. BSc BD STM	1965	2006	(Edinburgh: Greenbank)	50 Forthview Walk, Tranent EH33 1FE [E-mail: iandascott@tiscali.co.uk]	01875 612907
Scott, Martin DipMusEd RSAM BD PhD	1986	2000	Ministries Council	18 Covenanters Rise, Dunfermline KY11 8QS	01383 722328
Shewan, Frederick D. MA BD	1970	2005	(Edinburgh: Muirhouse St Andrew's)	38 Tremayne Place, Dunfermline KY12 9YH	01383 734354
Sim, John G. MA	1946	1987	(Kirkcaldy Old)	7 Grosvenor Crescent, Edinburgh EH12 5EP	0131-226 3190
Skinner, Donald M. MBE JP FIES	1962	2000	(Edinburgh: Gilmerton)	12 Straid-a-Cnoc, Clynder, Helensburgh G84 0QX	01436 831795
Slorach, Alexander CA BD	1970	2002	(Kirk of Lammermuir with Langton and Polwarth)	61 Inverleith Row, Edinburgh EH3 5PX	
Stephen, Donald M. TD MA BD ThM	1962	2001	(Edinburgh: Marchmont St Giles')	10 Hawkhead Crescent, Edinburgh EH16 6LR	0131-658 1216
Stevenson, John MA BD PhD	1963	2001	(Department of Education)	12 Swanston Gardens, Edinburgh EH10 7DL	0131-445 3960
Stirling, A. Douglas BSc	1956	1994	(Rhu and Shandon)	162 Avontoun Park, Linlithgow EH49 6QH	01506 845021
Stiven, Iain K. MA BD	1960	1997	(Strachur and Strathlachlan)	7 Gloucester Place, Edinburgh EH3 6EE	0131-225 8177
Taylor, Howard G. BSc BD MTh	1971	1998	Chaplain: Heriot Watt University	The Chaplaincy, Heriot Watt University, Riccarton, Currie EH14 4AS	0131-449 5111 (ext 4508)
Taylor, William R. MA BD	1983	2003	Chaplaincy Co-ordinator: Scottish Prison Service	33 Kingsknowe Drive, Edinburgh EH14 2JY	
Teague, Yvonne (Mrs) DCS			(Board of Ministry)	46 Craigcrook Avenue, Edinburgh EH4 3PX	0131-336 3113
Telfer, Iain J.M. BD DPS	1978	2001	Chaplain: Royal Infirmary	Royal Infirmary of Edinburgh, 51 Little France Crescent, Edinburgh EH16 4SA	0131-242 1997

Thom, Helen (Miss) DCS — (Deaconess) — 84 Great King Street, Edinburgh EH3 6QU — 0131-556 5687

Torrance, Thomas F. MBE DLitt DD DSc DrTheol DrTheol FBA FRSE — 1940 1979

Walker, R.W. MB ChB — (University of Edinburgh) — 1941 1981 — 37 Braid Farm Road, Edinburgh EH10 6LE — 0131-667 0578

Whyte, Iain A. BA BD STM PhD — (Lesmahagow Abbeygreen) (Community Mental Health Chaplain) — 1968 2001 — 39/22 Blackford Avenue, Edinburgh EH9 3HN — 01383 410732
14 Carlingnose Point, North Queensferry, Inverkeithing KY11 1ER
[E-mail: iainisabel@whytes28.fsnet.co.uk]

Wigglesworth, J. Christopher MBE BSc PhD BD — (St Andrew's College, Selly Oak) — 1968 1999 — 12 Leven Terrace, Edinburgh EH3 9LW — 0131-228 6335

Wilkie, James L. MA BD — (Board of World Mission) — 1959 1998 — 7 Comely Bank Avenue, Edinburgh EH4 1EW — 0131-343 1552
[E-mail: jl.wilkie@btinternet.com]

Wilkinson, John BD MD FRCP DTM&H — (Kikuyu) — 1946 1975 — 70 Craigleith Hill Gardens, Edinburgh EH4 2JH — 0131-332 2994

Williams, Jenny M. (Miss) BSc CQSW BD — Christian Fellowship of Healing — 1996 1997 — 16 Blantyre Terrace, Edinburgh EH10 5AE — 0131-447 0050

Wilson, John M. MA — (Adviser in Religious Education) — 1964 1995 — 27 Belfield Street, Edinburgh EH15 2BR — 0131-669 5257

Young, Alexander W. BD DipMin — Chaplain: Royal Infirmary — 1988 1999 — Rosebank Villa, 68 Main Street, Newtongrange, Dalkeith EH22 4ND

EDINBURGH ADDRESSES

Albany	At Greenside
Balerno	Johnsburn Road, Balerno
Barclay	Barclay Place
Blackhall St Columba	Queensferry Road
Bristo Memorial	Peffermill Road, Craigmillar
Broughton St Mary's	Bellevue Crescent
Canongate	Canongate
Carrick Knowe	North Saughton Road
Colinton	Dell Road
Colinton Mains	Oxgangs Road North
Corstorphine	
Craigsbank	Craig's Crescent
Old	Kirk Loan
St Anne's	Kaimes Road
St Ninian's	St John's Road
Craigentinny	
St Christopher's	Craigentinny Road
Craiglockhart	Craiglockhart Avenue
Craigmillar Park	Craigmillar Park
Cramond	Cramond Glebe Road
Currie	Kirkgate, Currie
Davidson's Mains	Quality Street
Dean	Dean Path
Drylaw	Groathill Road North
Duddingston	Old Church Lane, Duddingston
Fairmilehead	Frogston Road West, Fairmilehead
Gilmerton	Ravenscroft Street
Gorgie	Gorgie Road
Granton	Boswall Parkway
Greenbank	Braidburn Terrace
Greenside	Royal Terrace
Greyfriars Tolbooth and Highland Kirk	Greyfriars Place
High (St Giles')	High Street
Holyrood Abbey	
Holy Trinity	Dalziel Place x London Road
Inverleith	Hailesland Place, Wester Hailes
Juniper Green	Inverleith Gardens
Kaimes Lockhart Memorial	Lanark Road, Juniper Green
Kirkliston	Gracemount Road
Kirk o' Field	The Square, Kirkliston
Leith	
North	Pleasance
St Andrew's	Madeira Street off Ferry Road
St Serf's	Easter Road
St Thomas' Junction Road	Ferry Road
South	Great Junction Street
Wardie	Kirkgate, Leith
Liberton	Primrosebank Road
Northfield	Kirkgate, Liberton
London Road	Gilmerton Road, Liberton
Marchmont St Giles'	London Road
Mayfield Salisbury	Kilgraston Road
Morningside	Mayfield Road x West Mayfield
Morningside United	Cluny Gardens
	Brunstfield Place x Chamberlain Road
Muirhouse St Andrew's	Pennywell Gardens
Murrayfield	Abinger Gardens
Newhaven	Craighall Road
New Restalrig	Willowbrae Road
Old Kirk	Pennywell Road
Palmerston Place	Palmerston Place
Pilrig St Paul's	Pilrig Street
Polwarth	Polwarth Terrace x Harrison Road
Portobello	
Old	Bellfield Street
St James'	Rosefield Place
St Philip's Joppa	Abercorn Terrace
Priestfield	Dalkeith Road x Marchhall Place
Queensferry	The Loan, South Queensferry
Ratho	Baird Road, Ratho
Reid Memorial	West Savile Terrace
Richmond Craigmillar	Niddrie Mains Road
St Andrew's and St George's	George Street
St Andrew's Clermiston	Clermiston View
St Catherine's Argyle	Grange Road x Chalmers Crescent
St Colm's	Dalry Road x Cathcart Place
St Cuthbert's	Lothian Road
St David's Broomhouse	Broomhouse Crescent
St George's West	Shandwick Place
St John's Oxgangs	Oxgangs Road
St Margaret's	Restalrig Road South
St Martin's	Magdalene Drive
St Michael's	Slateford Road
St Nicholas' Sighthill	Calder Road
St Stephen's Comely Bank	Comely Bank

| Slateford Longstone Stenhouse St Aidan's | Kingsknowe Road North Chesser Avenue | Stockbridge Tron Moredun | Saxe Coburg Street Fernieside Drive | Viewforth | Gilmore Place |

(2) WEST LOTHIAN

Meets in the church of the incoming Moderator on the first Tuesday of September and in St John's Church Hall, Bathgate, on the first Tuesday of every other month, except December, when the meeting is on the second Tuesday, and January, July and August, when there is no meeting.

Clerk: REV. DUNCAN SHAW BD MTh   St John's Manse, Mid Street, Bathgate EH48 1QD   **01506 653146**
[E-mail: akph78@uk.uumail.com]

Abercorn linked with Pardovan, Kingscavil and Winchburgh
A. Scott Marshall DipComm BD   1984   1998

Armadale (H)
Robert P. Sloan MA BD   1968   2006   70 Mount Pleasant, Armadale, Bathgate EH48 3HB   01501 730358
[E-mail: sloans1@btinternet.com]

Avonbridge linked with Torphichen
Clifford R. Acklam BD MTh   1997   2000   Manse Road, Torphichen, Bathgate EH48 4LT   01506 652794
[E-mail: cliff@torphichen.org]

Bathgate: Boghall (H)
Dennis S. Rose LTh   1996   2004   1 Manse Place, Ash Grove, Bathgate EH48 1NJ   01506 652940
[E-mail: dsrosekirk@aol.com]

Bathgate: High (H)
Ronald G. Greig MA BD   1987   1998   19 Hunter Grove, Bathgate EH48 1NN   01506 652654
[E-mail: rongreig@tiscali.co.uk]

Bathgate: St David's
Elliot G.S. Wardlaw BA BD DipMin   1984   70 Marjoribanks Street, Bathgate EH48 1AL   01506 653177
[E-mail: elliot@gswardlaw.freeserve.co.uk]

Bathgate: St John's (H)
Duncan Shaw BD MTh   1975   1978   St John's Manse, Mid Street, Bathgate EH48 1QD   01506 653146
[E-mail: duncanshaw@uk.uumail.com]

Blackburn and Seafield
Robert A. Anderson MA BD DPhil   1980   1998   The Manse, 5 MacDonald Gardens, Blackburn, Bathgate EH47 7RE   01506 652825
[E-mail: robertanderson307@btinternet.com]

(first entry address) The Manse, Winchburgh, Broxburn EH52 6TT   01506 890919
[E-mail: pkwla@aol.com]

Blackridge linked with Harthill: St Andrew's

Robert B. Gehrke BSc BD CEng MIEE	1994	2006	East Main Street, Harthill, Shotts ML7 5QW [E-mail: bob.gehrke@gmail.com]	01501 751239

Breich Valley

Thomas Preston BD	1978	2001	Stoneyburn, Bathgate EH47 8AU	01501 762018

Broxburn (H)

Terry Taylor BA MTh	2005		2 Church Street, Broxburn EH52 5EL [E-mail: revtaylor@tiscali.co.uk]	01506 852825

Fauldhouse: St Andrew's

Elizabeth Smith (Mrs) BD	1996	2000	7 Glebe Court, Fauldhouse, Bathgate EH47 9DX [E-mail: smithrevb@btinternet.com]	01501 771190

Harthill: St Andrew's See Blackridge

Kirknewton and East Calder

Ann M. Ballentine (Miss) MA BD	1981	1993	8 Manse Court, East Calder, Livingston EH53 0HF [E-mail: annballentine@hotmail.com]	01506 880802

Kirk of Calder (H)

John M. Povey MA BD	1981		19 Maryfield Park, Mid Calder, Livingston EH53 0SB [E-mail: revjpovey@aol.com]	01506 882495
Phyllis Thomson (Miss) DCS	2003		63 Caroline Park, Mid Calder, Livingston EH53 0SJ	01506 883207

Linlithgow: St Michael's (H) (E-mail: info@stmichaels-parish.org.uk)

D. Stewart Gillan BSc MDiv PhD	1985	2004	St Michael's Manse, Kirkgate, Linlithgow EH49 7AL [E-mail: stewart@stmichaels-parish.org.uk]	01506 842195
Mark R. Davidson MA BD STM (Assoc)	2005		Cross House, Linlithgow EH49 7AL [E-mail: markricdavidson@hotmail.com]	01506 842665
Thomas S. Riddell BSc (Aux)	1993	1994	4 The Maltings, Linlithgow EH49 6DS [E-mail: tsriddell@blueyonder.co.uk]	01506 843251

Linlithgow: St Ninian's Craigmailen (H)

W. Richard Houston BSc BD	1998	2004	29 Philip Avenue, Linlithgow EH49 7BH [E-mail: wrichardhouston@blueyonder.co.uk]	01506 202246

Livingston Ecumenical Parish
Incorporating the Worship Centres at:
Carmondean and Knightsridge

Suzanna Bates BTh			13 Eastcroft Court, Livingston EH54 7ET [E-mail: rev.suzanna@btinternet.com]	01506 464567

(*The Methodist Church*)
Craigshill (St Columba's) and Ladywell (St Paul's)

Colin R. Douglas MA BD STM	1969	1987	27 Heatherbank, Ladywell, Livingston EH54 6EE [E-mail: colin_douglas@tiscali.co.uk]	01506 432326

Dedridge and Murieston
Eileen Thompson BD MTh
(*Scottish Episcopal Church*)
53 Garry Walk, Craigshill, Livingston EH54 5AS
[E-mail: eileenthompson@blueyonder.co.uk]
01506 433451

Livingston: Old (H)
Graham W. Smith BA BD FSAScot   1995
Manse of Livingston, Charlesfield Lane, Livingston EH54 7AJ
[E-mail: gws@livoldpar.org.uk]
01506 420227

Pardovan, Kingscavil and Winchburgh   See Abercorn

Polbeth Harwood linked with West Kirk of Calder (H)
David A. Albon BA MCS   1991   2004
27 Learmonth Crescent, West Calder EH55 8AF
[E-mail: albon@onetel.com]
01506 870460

Strathbrock
David W. Black BSc BD   1968   1984
1 Manse Park, Uphall, Broxburn EH52 6NX
01506 852550

Torphichen   See Avonbridge

Uphall South (H)
Margaret Steele (Miss) BSc BD   2000
8 Fernlea, Uphall, Broxburn EH52 6DF
[E-mail: mdsteele@tiscali.co.uk]
01506 852788

West Kirk of Calder (H)   See Polbeth Harwood

Whitburn: Brucefield (H)
Richard J.G. Darroch BD MTh   1993   2003
Brucefield Manse, Whitburn, Bathgate EH47 8NU
[E-mail: richdarr@aol.com]
01501 740263

Whitburn: South (H)
Christine Houghton (Mrs) BD   1997   2004
5 Mansewood Crescent, Whitburn, Bathgate EH47 8HA
[E-mail: c.houghton1@btinternet.com]
01501 740333

Cameron, Ian MA BD	1953	1981	(Kilbrandon and Kilchattan)	Craigellen, West George Street, Blairgowrie PH10 6DZ	01250 872087
Dundas, Thomas B.S. LTh	1969	1996	(West Kirk of Calder)	35 Coolkill, Sandyford, Dublin 18, Republic of Ireland	00353 12953061
McMahon, John K.S. MA BD	1998	2004	Hospital Chaplain	Dunkeld, 46 Mallace Avenue, East Fells, Armadale, Bathgate EH48 2QE [E-mail: johnksmcmahon@btinternet.com]	01501 733583
MacRae, Norman I. LTh	1966	2003	(Inverness: Trinity)	144 Hope Park Gardens, Bathgate EH48 2QX	01506 635254
Manson, Robert L. MA DPS	1956	1991	(Chaplain: Royal Edinburgh Hospital)	4 Murieston Drive, Livingston EH54 9AU [E-mail: roy@manson25.freeserve.co.uk]	01506 434746
Moore, J.W. MA	1950	1983	(Daviot with Rayne)	31 Lennox Gardens, Linlithgow EH49 7PZ	01506 842534
Morrice, Charles S. MA BD PhD	1959	1997	(Kenya)	104 Baron's Hill Avenue, Linlithgow EH49 7JG [E-mail: cs.morrice@blueyonder.co.uk]	01506 847167

Morrison, Iain C. BA BD	1990 2003	(Linlithgow: St Ninian's Craigmailen)	Whaligoe, 53 Eastcroft Drive, Polmont, Falkirk FK2 0SU [E-mail: iain@kirkweb.org]	01324 713249
Murray, Ronald N.G. MA	1946 1986	(Pardovan and Kingscavil with Winchburgh)		
Nelson, Georgina (Mrs) MA BD PhD DipEd	1990 1995	Hospital Chaplain	6 Pentland Park, Craigshill, Livingston EH54 5NR	01506 434874
Nicol, Robert M.	1984 1996	(Jersey: St Columba's)	59 Kinloch View, Blackness Road, Linlithgow EH49 7HT	01506 670391
Russell, Archibald MA	1949 1991	(Duror with Glencoe)	4 Bonnytoun Avenue, Linlithgow EH49 7JS	01506 842530
Smith, W. Ewing BSc	1962 1994	(Livingston: Old)	8 Hardy Gardens, Bathgate EH48 1NH [E-mail: wesmith@hardygdns.freeserve.co.uk]	01506 652028
Trimble, Robert DCS		(Deacon)	5 Templar Rise, Dedridge, Livingston EH54 6PJ	01506 412504
Whitson, William S. MA	1959 1999	(Cumbernauld: St Mungo's)	2 Chapman's Brae, Bathgate EH48 4LH [E-mail: william_whitson@tiscali.co.uk]	01506 650027

(3) LOTHIAN

Meets at Musselburgh: St Andrew's High Parish Church on the last Thursday of January and June and the first Thursday of March, April, May, September, October, November and December. (Alternative arrangements are made to avoid meeting on Maundy Thursday. In 2007, what would otherwise be the April meeting will be held on 29 March.)

| Clerk: | MR JOHN D. McCULLOCH DL | | | Auchindinny House, Penicuik EH26 8PE [E-mail: akph65@uk.uumail.com] | 01968 676300 (Tel/Fax) |

Aberlady (H) linked with Gullane (H)

| John B. Cairns LTh LLB LLD DD | 1974 | 2001 | The Manse, Hummel Road, Gullane EH31 2BG [E-mail: johncairns@mail.com] | 01620 843192 |

Athelstaneford linked with Whitekirk and Tyninghame

| Kenneth D.F. Walker MA BD PhD | 1976 | The Manse, Athelstaneford, North Berwick EH39 5BE [E-mail: kandv-walker@connectfree.co.uk] | 01620 880378 |

Belhaven (H) linked with Spott

| Laurence H. Twaddle MA BD MTh | 1977 | 1978 | The Manse, Belhaven Road, Dunbar EH42 1NH [E-mail: revtwaddle@aol.com] | 01368 863098 |

Bilston linked with Glencorse (H) linked with Roslin (H)

| John R. Wells BD DipMin | 1991 | 2005 | 31A Manse Road, Roslin EH25 9LG [E-mail: wellsjr3@aol.com] | 0131-440 2012 |

Bolton and Saltoun linked with Humbie linked with Yester (H)

| Vacant | | The Manse, Tweeddale Avenue, Gifford, Haddington EH41 4QN | 01620 810515 |

Bonnyrigg (H)
John Mitchell LTh CMin   1991   9 Viewbank View, Bonnyrigg EH19 2HU   0131-663 8287 (Tel/Fax)
[E-mail: rev.jmitchell@tiscali.co.uk]

Borthwick (H) linked with Cranstoun, Crichton and Ford (H) linked with Fala and Soutra (H)
D. Graham Leitch MA BD   1974   2003   Cranstoun Cottage, Ford, Pathhead EH37 5RE   01875 320314
[E-mail: leitch@cranscott.fsnet.co.uk]

Cockenzie and Port Seton: Chalmers Memorial (H)
Robert L. Glover BMus BD MTh ARCO   1971   1997   Braemar Villa, 2 Links Road, Port Seton, Prestonpans EH32 0HA   01875 812481
[E-mail: rlglover@btinternet.com]

Cockenzie and Port Seton: Old (H)
Continued Vacancy   1 Links Road, Port Seton, Prestonpans EH32 0HA   01875 812310

Cockpen and Carrington (H) linked with Lasswade (H) linked with Rosewell (H)
Wendy F. Drake (Mrs) BD   1978   1992   11 Pendreich Terrace, Bonnyrigg EH19 2DT   0131-663 6884
[E-mail: drake@pendreich.fsnet.co.uk]

Cranstoun, Crichton and Ford (H) See Borthwick

Dalkeith: St John's and King's Park (H)
Keith L. Mack BD MTh DPS   2002   13 Weir Crescent, Dalkeith EH22 3JN   0131-454 0206
[E-mail: kthmacker@aol.com]

Dalkeith: St Nicholas' Buccleuch (H)
Alexander G. Horsburgh MA BD   1995   2004   116 Bonnyrigg Road, Dalkeith EH22 3HZ   0131-663 3036
[E-mail: alexanderhorsburgh@compuserve.com]

Dirleton (H) (E-mail: dirletonkirk@hotmail.com) linked with North Berwick: Abbey (H) (01620 890110) (E-mail: abbeychurch@hotmail.com)
David J. Graham BSc BD PhD   1982   1998   20 Westgate, North Berwick EH39 4AF   01620 890110
[E-mail: davidjohn@grahams.fsbusiness.co.uk]

Dunbar (H)
Eric W. Foggitt MA BSc BD   1991   2000   The Manse, Bayswell Road, Dunbar EH42 1AB   01368 863749 (Tel/Fax)
[E-mail: ericleric3@btopenworld.com]

Dunglass
Anne R. Lithgow (Mrs) MA BD   1992   1994   The Manse, Cockburnspath TD13 5XZ   01368 830713
[E-mail: anne.lithgow@btinternet.com]

Fala and Soutra See Borthwick

Garvald and Morham linked with Haddington: West (H)
Cameron Mackenzie BD   1997   15 West Road, Haddington EH41 3RD   01620 822213
[E-mail: mackenz550@aol.com]

Gladsmuir linked with Longniddry (H)
Robin E. Hill LLB BD PhD   2004   The Manse, Elcho Road, Longniddry EH32 0LB   01875 853195
[E-mail: robin.hill@homecall.co.uk]

Glencorse (H) See Bilston

Gorebridge (H)
Mark S. Nicholas MA BD   1999   100 Hunterfield Road, Gorebridge EH23 4TT   01875 820387
[E-mail: mark.nicholas@fish.co.uk]

Gullane See Aberlady

Haddington: St Mary's (H)
James M. Cowie BD   1977   21 Sidegate, Haddington EH41 4BZ   01620 823109
[E-mail: jim911@btinternet.com]

Haddington: West See Garvald and Morham

Howgate (H) linked with Penicuik: South (H)
Vacant   18 Broomhill Avenue, Penicuik EH26 9EG   01968 674692

Humbie See Bolton and Saltoun
Lasswade See Cockpen and Carrington

Loanhead
Graham L. Duffin BSc BD DipEd   1989   120 The Loan, Loanhead EH20 9AJ   0131-448 2459
[E-mail: gduffin@fish.co.uk]
Frances M. Henderson BA BD (Associate)   2006   14 (1F2) Viewforth Gardens, Edinburgh EH10 4EU   0131-478 1384
[E-mail: frances.henderson@blueyonder.co.uk]

Longniddry See Gladsmuir

Musselburgh: Northesk (H)
Alison P. McDonald MA BD   1991   16 New Street, Musselburgh EH21 6JP   0131-665 2128
[E-mail: alisonpmcdonald@btinternet.com]

Musselburgh: St Andrew's High (H) (0131-665 7239)
Yvonne E.S. Atkins (Mrs) BD   1997   8 Ferguson Drive, Musselburgh EH21 6XA   0131-665 1124
[E-mail: yesatkins@yahoo.co.uk]

Musselburgh: St Clement's and St Ninian's
Vacant   The Manse, Wallyford Loan Road, Wallyford, Musselburgh EH21 8BU   0131-653 6588

John Buchanan DCS | 2004 | 19 Gillespie Crescent, Edinburgh EH10 4HU | 0131-229 0794

Musselburgh: St Michael's Inveresk
Andrew B. Dick BD DipMin | 1986 1999 | 8 Hope Place, Musselburgh EH21 7QE [E-mail: dixbit@aol.com] | 0131-665 0545

Newbattle (H) (Website: http://freespace.virgin.net/newbattle.focus)
Monika R.W. Redman (Mrs) BA BD | 2003 | 70 Newbattle Abbey Crescent, Dalkeith EH22 3LW [E-mail: monika.walker@ukgateway.net] | 0131-663 3245
Gordon R. Steven BD DCS | 2004 | 51 Nantwich Drive, Edinburgh EH7 6RB [E-mail: grsteven@btinternet.com] | 0131-669 2054 / 07904 385256 (Mbl)

Newton
Vacant | | The Manse, Newton, Dalkeith EH22 1SR | 0131-663 3845

North Berwick: Abbey See Dirleton

North Berwick: St Andrew Blackadder (H) (E-mail: admin@standrewblackadder.org.uk) (Website: www.standrewblackadder.org.uk)
Neil J. Dougall BD | 1991 2003 | 7 Marine Parade, North Berwick EH39 4LD [E-mail: neil@standrewblackadder.org.uk] | 01620 892132

Ormiston linked with Pencaitland
Mark Malcolm MA BD | 1999 | The Manse, Pencaitland, Tranent EH34 5DL [E-mail: mark.minister@virgin.net] | 01875 340208

Pencaitland See Ormiston

Penicuik: North (H)
John W. Fraser MA BD | 1974 1982 | 93 John Street, Penicuik EH26 8AG [E-mail: john1946@fish.co.uk] | 01968 672213

Penicuik: St Mungo's (H)
Ronald W. Smith BA BEd BD | 1979 2004 | 31A Kirkhill Road, Penicuik EH26 8JB | 01968 672916

Penicuik: South See Howgate

Prestonpans: Prestongrange
Robert R. Simpson BA BD | 1994 | The Manse, East Loan, Prestonpans EH32 9ED [E-mail: robert@pansmanse.co.uk] | 01875 810308

Rosewell See Cockpen and Carrington
Roslin See Bilston
Spott See Belhaven

Tranent
Thomas M. Hogg BD | 1986 | 244 Church Street, Tranent EH33 1BW [E-mail: tom@hoggtran.freeserve.co.uk] | 01875 610210

Traprain
Howard J. Haslett BA BD   1972   2000   The Manse, Preston Road, East Linton EH40 3DS   01620 860227 (Tel/Fax)
[E-mail: howard.haslett@btopenworld.com]

Whitekirk and Tyninghame See Athelstaneford
Yester See Bolton and Saltoun

Name	Ord	Ind	(Previous charge)	Address	Tel
Andrews, J. Edward MA BD DipCG FSAScot	1985	2005	(Armadale)	1A Meadowpark, Haddington EH41 4DS [E-mail: edward.andrews@btinternet.com]	(Tel/Fax) 01620 829804 (Mbl) 07808 720708
Bayne, Angus L. LTh BEd MTh	1969	2005	(Edinburgh: Bristo Memorial Craigmillar)	14 Myredale, Bonnyrigg EH19 3NW [E-mail: angus@mccookies.com]	0131-663 6871
Black, A. Graham MA	1964	2003	(Gladsmuir with Longniddry)	26 Hamilton Crescent, Gullane EH31 2HR [E-mail: grablack@aol.com]	01620 843899
Brown, Ronald H.	1974	1998	(Musselburgh: Northesk)	6 Monktonhall Farm Cottages, Musselburgh EH21 6RZ	0131-653 2531
Brown, William BD	1972	1997	(Edinburgh: Polwarth)	13 Thornyhall, Dalkeith EH22 2ND [E-mail: william@brown1826.fsnet.co.uk]	0131-654 0929
Chalmers, William R. MA BD STM	1953	1992	(Dunbar)	18 Forest Road, Burghead, Elgin IV30 5XL	01343 835674
Donaldson, Colin V.	1982	1998	(Ormiston with Pencaitland)	3A Playfair Terrace, St Andrews KY16 9HX	01334 472889
Forbes, Iain M. BSc BD	1964	2005	(Aberdeen: Beechgrove)	6 Auld Orchard, Lothian Street, Bonnyrigg EH19 3BR [E-mail: panama.forbes@tiscali.co.uk]	0131-454 0717
Fraser, John W. BEM MA BD PhD	1950	1983	(Farnell)	The Elms Nursing Home, 148 Whitehouse Loan, Edinburgh EH9 2EZ	
Gilfillan, James LTh	1968	1997	(East Kilbride: Old)	15 Long Cram, Haddington EH41 4NS	
Hill, Arthur T.	1940	1981	(Ormiston with Prestonpans: Grange)	8A Hamilton Road, North Berwick EH39 4NA	01620 824843 01620 893961
Hutchison, Alan E.W.			(Deacon)	132 Lochbridge Road, North Berwick EH39 4DR	01620 894077
Jones, Anne M. (Mrs) BD	1998	2002	Hospital Chaplain	7 North Elphinstone Farm, Tranent EH33 2ND [E-mail: revamjones@aol.com]	01875 614442
Levison, L. David MA BD	1943	1982	(Ormiston with Pencaitland)	Westdene Conservatory Flat, 506 Perth Road, Dundee DD2 1LS	01382 630460
Macdonell, Alasdair W. MA BD	1955	1992	(Haddington: St Mary's)	St Andrews Cottage, Duns Road, Gifford, Haddington EH41 4QW	01620 810341
Macrae, Norman C. MA DipEd	1942	1985	(Loanhead)	49 Lixmount Avenue, Edinburgh EH5 3EW [E-mail: nandcmacrae@onetel.com]	0131-552 2428
Manson, James A. LTh	1981	2004	(Glencorse with Roslin)	31 Nursery Gardens, Kilmarnock KA1 3JA [E-mail: jamanson@supanet.com]	01563 535430
Pirie, Donald LTh	1975	2006	(Bolton and Saltoun with Humbie with Yester)	46 Caiystane Avenue, Edinburgh EH10 6SH	0131-445 2654
Ritchie, James McL. MA BD MPhil	1950	1985	(Coalsnaughton)	Flat 2/25, Croft-an-Righ, Edinburgh EH8 8EG [E-mail: jasritch_77@msn.com]	0131-557 1084
Robertson, James LTh	1970	2000	(Newton)	11 Southfield Square, Edinburgh EH15 1QS	
Sanderson, W. Roy DD	1933	1973	(Stenton with Whittingehame)	20 Craigleith View, Station Road, North Berwick EH39 4BF	01620 892780
Swan, Andrew F. BD	1983	2000	(Loanhead)	3 Mackenzie Gardens, Dolphinton, West Linton EH46 7HS	01968 682247
Thomson, William H.	1964	1999	(Edinburgh: Liberton Northfield)	3 Baird's Way, Bonnyrigg EH19 3NS [E-mail: wh.thomson@tiscali.co.uk]	0131-654 9799
Torrance, David W. MA BD	1955	1991	(Earlston)	38 Forth Street, North Berwick EH39 4JQ [E-mail: dwtmet@connectfree.co.uk]	(Tel/Fax) 01620 895109

Underwood, Florence A. (Mrs) BD	1992	2006	(Assistant: Gladsmuir with Longniddry)	The Shieling, Main Street, Stenton, Dunbar EH42 1TE [E-mail: geoffrey.underwood@homecall.co.uk]	01368 850629
Underwood, Geoffrey H. BD DipTh FPhS	1964	1992	(Cockenzie and Port Seton: Chalmers Memorial)	The Shieling, Main Street, Stenton, Dunbar EH42 1TE [E-mail: geoffrey.underwood@homecall.co.uk]	01368 850629
Whiteford, David H. CBE MA BD PhD	1943	1985	(Gullane)	3 Old Dean Road, Longniddry EH32 0QY	01875 852980

(4) MELROSE AND PEEBLES

Meets at Innerleithen on the first Tuesday of February, March, May, October, November and December, and on the fourth Tuesday of June, and in places to be appointed on the first Tuesday of September.

| Clerk: | MR JACK STEWART | | 3 St Cuthbert's Drive, St Boswells, Melrose TD6 0DF [E-mail: akph66@uk.uumail.com] | 01835 822600 |

Ashkirk linked with Selkirk (H)

| James W. Campbell BD | 1995 | | 1 Loanside, Selkirk TD7 4DJ [E-mail: revjimashkirk@aol.com] | 01750 22833 |

Bowden (H) linked with Newtown

| Joseph F. Crawford BA | 1970 | 2000 | The Manse, Newtown St Boswells, Melrose TD6 0PL [E-mail: joe@crawforda86.fsnet.co.uk] | 01835 822106 |

Broughton, Glenholm and Kilbucho (H) linked with Skirling linked with Stobo and Drumelzier linked with Tweedsmuir (H)

| Rachel J.W. Dobie (Mrs) LTh | 1991 | 1996 | The Manse, Broughton, Biggar ML12 6HQ [E-mail: revracheldobie@aol.com] | 01899 830331 |

Caddonfoot (H) linked with Galashiels: Trinity (H)

| Morag A. Dawson BD | 1999 | 2005 | 8 Mossilee Road, Galashiels TD1 1NF [E-mail: moragdawson@st-aidans.wanadoo.co.uk] | 01896 752420 |

Carlops linked with Kirkurd and Newlands (H) linked with West Linton: St Andrew's (H)

| Thomas W. Burt BD | 1982 | 1985 | The Manse, West Linton EH46 7EN [E-mail: tomburt@westlinton.com] | 01968 660221 |

Channelkirk and Lauder

| John M. Shields MBE LTh | 1972 | 1997 | Brownsmuir Park, Lauder TD2 6QD [E-mail: john.m.shields@btinternet.com] | 01578 722320 |

Earlston

| Michael D. Scouler MBE BSc BD | 1988 | 1992 | The Manse, High Street, Earlston TD4 6DE | 01896 849236 |

Eddleston (H) linked with Peebles: Old (H)

| Malcolm M. Macdougall BD | 1981 | 2001 | The Old Manse, Innerleithen Road, Peebles EH45 8BD [E-mail: calum.macdougall@btopenworld.com] | 01721 720568 |

Ettrick and Yarrow
Samuel Siroky BA MTh — 2003 — Yarrow Manse, Yarrow, Selkirk TD7 5LA [E-mail: sesiroky@onetel.com] — 01750 82336

Galashiels: Old and St Paul's (H) (Website: www.oldparishandstpauls.org.uk)
Leslie M. Steele MA BD — 1973 1988 — Barr Road, Galashiels TD1 3HX [E-mail: leslie@oldparishandstpauls.org.uk] — 01896 752320

Galashiels: St John's (H)
Vacant — Hawthorn Road, Galashiels TD1 2JZ — 01896 752573

Galashiels: Trinity (H) See Caddonfoot
(Charge formed by the union of Galashiels: St Aidan's and Galashiels: St Ninian's)

Innerleithen (H), Traquair and Walkerburn
Janice M. Faris (Mrs) BSc BD — 1991 2001 — The Manse, 1 Millwell Park, Innerleithen, Peebles EH44 6JF [E-mail: revjfaris@hotmail.com] — 01896 830309

Kirkurd and Newlands See Carlops

Lyne and Manor
Nancy M. Norman (Miss) BA MDiv MTh — 1988 1998 — 25 March Street, Peebles EH45 8EP [E-mail: nancy.norman@btopenworld.com] — 01721 721699

Maxton and Mertoun linked with St Boswells
Bruce F. Neill MA BD — 1966 1996 — St Modans Manse, Main Street, St Boswells, Melrose TD6 0BB [E-mail: bneill@fish.co.uk] — 01835 822255

Melrose (H)
Alistair G. Bennett BSc BD — 1978 1984 — Tweedmount Road, Melrose TD6 9ST [E-mail: agbennettmelrose@aol.com] — 01896 822217

Newtown See Bowden
Peebles: Old See Eddleston

Peebles: St Andrew's Leckie (H) (01721 723121)
James H. Wallace MA BD — 1973 1983 — Mansefield, Innerleithen Road, Peebles EH45 8BE [E-mail: jimwallace@freeola.com] — 01721 721749 (Tel/Fax)

St Boswells See Maxton and Mertoun
Selkirk See Ashkirk
Skirling See Broughton, Glenholm and Kilbucho
Stobo and Drumelzier See Broughton, Glenholm and Kilbucho

Stow: St Mary of Wedale and Heriot

Catherine A. Buchan (Mrs) MA MDiv	2002	The Manse, 209 Galashiels Road, Stow, Galashiels TD1 2RE [E-mail: buchan@alan-cath.freeserve.co.uk]	01578 730237

Tweedsmuir See Broughton, Glenholm and Kilbucho
West Linton: St Andrew's See Carlops

Bowie, Adam McC.	1976 1996	(Cavers and Kirkton with Hobkirk and Southdean)	Glenbield, Redpath, Earlston TD4 6AD	01896 848173
Brown, Robert BSc	1962 1997	(Kilbrandon and Kilchattan)	11 Thornfield Terrace, Selkirk TD7 4DU [E-mail: ruwcb@tiscali.co.uk]	01750 20311
Cashman, P. Hamilton BSc	1985 1998	(Dirleton with North Berwick: Abbey)	38 Abbotsford Road, Galashiels TD1 3HR [E-mail: mcashman@tiscali.co.uk]	01896 752711
Devenny, Robert P.	2002	Borders Health Board	Blakeburn Cottage, Westerhousebyres, Melrose TD6 9BW	01896 822350
Dick, J. Ronald BD	1973 1996	Hospital Chaplain	5 Georgefield Farm Cottages, Earlston TD4 6BH	01896 848956
Donald, Thomas W. LTh CA	1977 1987	(Bowden with Lilliesleaf)	The Quest, Huntly Road, Melrose TD6 9SB	01896 822345
Duncan, Charles A. MA	1956 1992	(Heriot with Stow: St Mary of Wedale)	10 Elm Grove, Galashiels TD1 3JA	01896 753261
Hardie, H. Warner BD	1979 2005	(Blackbridge with Harthill: St Andrew's)	Keswick Cottage, Kingsmuir Drive, Peebles EH45 9AA [E-mail: hardies@bigfoot.com]	01721 724003
Kellet, John M. MA	1962 1995	(Leith: South)	4 High Cottages, Walkerburn EH43 6AZ	01896 870351
Kennon, Stanley BA BD	1992 2000	Chaplain: Navy	1 Anson Way, Helston, Cornwall TR13 8BS	
Laing, William F. DSC VRD MA	1952 1986	(Selkirk: St Mary's West)	10 The Glebe, Selkirk TD7 5AB	01750 21210
McCann, George McD. BSc ATI	1994	Auxiliary Minister	Rosbeg, Parsonage Road, Galashiels TD1 3HS	01896 752055
MacFarlane, David C. MA	1957 1997	(Eddleston with Peebles: Old)	11 Station Bank, Peebles EH45 8EJ	01721 720639
Moore, W. Haisley MA	1966 1996	(Secretary: The Boys' Brigade)	26 Tweedbank Avenue, Tweedbank, Galashiels TD1 3SP	01896 668577
Rae, Andrew W.	1951 1987	(Annan: St Andrew's Greenknowe Erskine)	Roseneuk, Tweedside Road, Newtown St Boswells TD6 0PQ	01835 823783
Taverner, Glyn R. MA BD	1957 1995	(Maxton and Mertoun with St Boswells)	Woodcot Cottage, Waverley Road, Innerleithen EH44 6QW	01896 830156
Thomson, George F.M. MA	1956 1988	(Dollar Associate)	6 Abbotsford Terrace, Darnick, Melrose TD6 9AD	01896 823112

(5) DUNS

Meets at Duns, in the Old Parish Church Hall, normally on the first Tuesday of February, March, April, May, October, November, December, on the last Tuesday in June, and in places to be appointed on the first Tuesday of September.

Clerk:	MR PETER JOHNSON MBE MPhil	Todlaw, Duns TD11 3EJ [E-mail: akph49@uk.uumail.com]	01361 883724

Ayton (H) and Burnmouth linked with Grantshouse and Houndwood and Reston

Norman R. Whyte BD DipMin	1982	2006	The Manse, Beanburn, Ayton, Eyemouth TD14 5QY	01890 781333

Berwick-upon-Tweed: St Andrew's Wallace Green (H) and Lowick
Paul M.N. Sewell MA BD   1970   2003   3 Meadow Grange, Berwick-upon-Tweed TD15 1NW   01289 303304

Bonkyl and Preston linked with Chirnside (H) linked with Edrom: Allanton (H)
Duncan E. Murray BA BD   1970   2005   Parish Church Manse, The Glebe, Chirnside, Duns TD11 3XL   01890 819109
[E-mail: duncanemurray@tiscali.co.uk]

Chirnside See Bonkyl and Preston

Coldingham and St Abb's linked with Eyemouth
Daniel G. Lindsay BD   1978   1979   Victoria Road, Eyemouth TD14 5JD   01890 750327

Coldstream (H) linked with Eccles
James B. Watson BSc   1968   2004   36 Bennecourt Drive, Coldstream TD12 1BY   01890 883149
[E-mail: jimwatson007@hotmail.com]

Duns (H)
Andrew A. Morrice MA BD   1999   The Manse, Duns TD11 3DG   01361 883755
[E-mail: andrew@morrice5.wanadoo.co.uk]

Eccles See Coldstream
Edrom: Allanton See Bonkyl and Preston
Eyemouth See Coldingham and St Abb's

Fogo and Swinton linked with Ladykirk linked with Leitholm linked with Whitsome (H)
Alan C.D. Cartwright BSc BD   1976   Swinton, Duns TD11 3JJ   01890 860228

Foulden and Mordington linked with Hutton and Fishwick and Paxton
Geraldine H. Hope (Mrs) MA BD   1986   Hutton, Berwick-upon-Tweed TD15 1TS   01289 386396
[E-mail: geraldine.hope@virgin.net]

Gordon: St Michael's linked with Greenlaw (H) linked with Legerwood linked with Westruther
Thomas S. Nicholson BD DPS   1982   1995   The Manse, Todholes, Greenlaw, Duns TD10 6XD   01361 810316

Grantshouse and Houndwood and Reston See Ayton and Burnmouth
Greenlaw See Gordon: St Michael's
Hutton and Fishwick and Paxton See Foulden and Mordington

Kirk of Lammermuir linked with Langton and Polwarth
Ann Inglis (Mrs) LLB BD   1986   2003   The Manse, Cranshaws, Duns TD11 3SJ   01361 890289

Ladykirk See Fogo and Swinton
Langton and Polwarth See Kirk of Lammermuir
Legerwood See Gordon: St Michael's
Leitholm See Fogo and Swinton
Westruther See Gordon: St Michael's
Whitsome See Fogo and Swinton

Name	Years	Description	Address	Phone
Gaddes, Donald R.	1961 1994	(Kelso: North and Ednam)	35 Winterfield Gardens, Duns TD11 3EZ [E-mail: doruga@winterfield.fslife.co.uk]	01361 883172
Gale, Ronald A.A. LTh	1982 1995	(Dunoon: Old and St Cuthbert's)	55 Lennel Mount, Coldstream TD12 4NS	01890 883699
Hay, Bruce J.L.	1957 1997	(Makerstoun and Smailholm with Stichill, Hume and Nenthorn)	Tweed House, Tweed Street, Berwick-upon-Tweed TD15 1NG	01289 303171
Higham, Robert D. BD	1985 2002	(Tiree)	36 Low Greens, Berwick-upon-Tweed TD15 1LZ	01289 302392
Jackson, John MA	1958 1990	(Bonnybridge)	2 Milne Graden West, Coldstream TD12 4HE	01890 883435
Kerr, Andrew MA BLitt	1948 1991	(Kilbarchan: West)	Meikle Harelaw, Westruther, Gordon TD10 6XT	01578 740263
Landale, William S.	2004	Auxiliary Minister	Green Hope Guest House, Green Hope, Duns TD11	01361 890242
Ledgard, J. Christopher BA	1969 2004	(Ayton and Burnmouth with Grantshouse and Houndwood and Reston)	2 Northfield, St Abbs, Eyemouth TD14 5QF	01890 771833
Macleod, Allan M. MA	1945 1985	(Gordon: St Michael's with Legerwood with Westruther)	Silverlea, Machrihanish, Argyll PA28 6PZ	
Paterson, William BD	1977 2001	(Bonkyl and Preston with Chirnside with Edrom: Allanton)	Benachie, Gavinton, Duns TD11 3QT	01361 882727

(6) JEDBURGH

Meets at Jedburgh on the first Wednesday of February, March, May, October, November and December and on the last Wednesday of June. Meets in the Moderator's church on the first Wednesday of September.

Clerk	REV. W. FRANK CAMPBELL BA BD		22 The Glebe, Ancrum, Jedburgh TD8 6UX [E-mail: akph56@uk.uumail.com] [E-mail: jedburghpresbytery@uk.uumail.com]	01835 830318 (Tel) / 01835 830262 (Fax)

Ale and Teviot United (H)

W. Frank Campbell BA BD	1989 1991	22 The Glebe, Ancrum, Jedburgh TD8 6UX [E-mail: akph56@uk.uumail.com] [E-mail: jedburghpresbytery@uk.uumail.com]	01835 830318 (Tel) / 01835 830262 (Fax)

Cavers and Kirkton linked with Hawick: Trinity

E.P. Lindsay Thomson MA	1964 1972	Fenwick Park, Hawick TD9 9PA [E-mail: eplindsayt@aol.com]	01450 372705

Hawick: Burnfoot

Charles J. Finnie LTh DPS	1991 1997	29 Wilton Hill, Hawick TD9 8BA [E-mail: charles@finnierev.freeserve.co.uk]	01450 373181

Hawick: St Mary's and Old (H)

Vacant		Braid Road, Hawick TD9 9LZ	01450 377865

Hawick: Teviot (H) and Roberton
Neil R. Combe BSc MSc BD — 1984 — Teviot Manse, Buccleuch Road, Hawick TD9 0EL [E-mail: neil.combe@btinternet.com] — 01450 372150

Hawick: Trinity (H) See Cavers and Kirkton

Hawick: Wilton linked with Teviothead
Lisa-Jane Rankin (Miss) BD CPS — 2003 — 4 Wilton Hill Terrace, Hawick TD9 8BE [E-mail: lisajane20@tiscali.co.uk] — 01450 370744 (Tel/Fax)

Hobkirk and Southdean linked with Ruberslaw
Anthony M. Jones
BD DPS DipTheol CertMin FRSA — 1994 2003 — The Manse, Denholm, Hawick TD9 8NB [E-mail: revanthonymjones@amserve.com] — 01450 870268 (Tel/Fax)

Jedburgh: Old and Edgerston
Bruce McNicol JP BL BD — 1967 1992 — Honeyfield Drive, Jedburgh TD8 6LQ [E-mail: mcnicol195@btinternet.com] — 01835 863417

Jedburgh: Trinity
John A. Riddell MA BD — 1967 — 42 High Street, Jedburgh TD8 6DQ — 01835 863223

Kelso Country Churches
Vacant — The Manse, 1 The Meadow, Stichill, Kelso TD5 7TG — 01573 470607
(The name now of the united charge of Makerstoun, Smailholm, Roxburgh and Stichill, Hume and Nenthorn)

Kelso: North (H) and Ednam (H) (01573 224154) (E-mail: office@kelsonorthandednam.org.uk)
Tom McDonald BD — 1994 — 20 Forestfield, Kelso TD5 7BX [E-mail: revtom@20thepearlygates.co.uk] — 01573 224677

Kelso: Old (H) and Sprouston
Marion E. Dodd (Miss) MA BD LRAM — 1988 1989 — Glebe Lane, Kelso TD5 7AU [E-mail: mariondodd@btinternet.com] — 01573 226254

Linton, Morebattle, Hownam and Yetholm (H)
Robin D. McHaffie BD — 1979 1991 — The Manse, Main Street, Kirk Yetholm, Kelso TD5 8PF [E-mail: robinmchaffie@f2s.com] — 01573 420308

Oxnam
Continued Vacancy

Ruberslaw See Hobkirk and Southdean
Teviothead See Hawick: Wilton

Brown, Joseph MA	1954 1991	(Linton with Hownam and Morebattle with Yetholm)	The Orchard, Hermitage Lane, Shedden Park Road, Kelso TD5 7AN	01573 223481
Fox, G. Dudley A.	1972 1988	(Kelso Old)	14 Pinnacle Hill Farm, Kelso TD5 8HD	01573 223335
Hamilton, Robert MA BD	1938 1979	(Kelso Old)	Ridge Cottage, 391 Totnes Road, Collaton St Mary, Paignton TQ4 7PW	01803 526440
Longmuir, William LTh	1984 2001	(Bedrule with Denholm with Minto)	Viewfield, South Street, Gavinton, Duns TD11 3QT	01361 882728
McConnell, Robert	1959 1983	(Hawick: St Margaret's and Wilton: South with Roberton)	17 Kirk House, 110 Kings Road, Belfast BT5 7BX	02890 704867
Ritchie, Garden W.M.	1961 1995	(Ardersier with Petty)	23 Croft Road, Kelso TD5 7EP	01573 224419
Thompson, W.M.D. MA	1950 1997	(Crailing and Eckford with Oxnam with Roxburgh)	Beech House, Etal, Cornhill-on-Tweed TD12 4TL	01890 820621

HAWICK ADDRESSES

Burnfoot	Fraser Avenue		
St Mary's and Old	Kirk Wynd	Wilton	Princes Street
Teviot	off Buccleuch Road		
Trinity	Central Square		

(7) ANNANDALE AND ESKDALE

Meets on the first Tuesday of February, May, September and December, and the third Tuesday of March, June and October, in a venue to be determined by Presbytery.

Clerk: REV. C. BRYAN HASTON LTh   The Manse, Gretna Green, Gretna DG16 5DU
[E-mail: cbhaston@cofs.demon.co.uk]
[E-mail: cbhaston@uk.uumail.com]   **01461 338313 (Tel)**
08701 640119 (Fax)

Annan: Old (H)

Hugh D. Steele LTh DipMin	1994	2004	12 Plumdon Park Avenue, Annan DG12 6EY [E-mail: hugdebra@aol.com]	01461 201405

Annan: St Andrew's (H) linked with Brydekirk

George K. Lind BD MCIBS	1998	1 Annerley Road, Annan DG12 6HE [E-mail: gklind@onetel.com]	01461 202626

Applegarth, Sibbaldbie (H) and Johnstone linked with Lochmaben (H)

Jack M. Brown BSc BD	1977	2002	The Manse, Barrashead, Lochmaben, Lockerbie DG11 1QF [E-mail: jackmbrown@tiscali.co.uk]	01387 810066

Brydekirk   See Annan: St Andrew's

Canonbie United (H) linked with Liddesdale (H)
Alan D. Reid MA BD   1989   23 Langholm Street, Newcastleton TD9 0QX   01387 375242
                                       [E-mail: canonbie.liddesdale@talktalk.net]

Dalton linked with Hightae linked with St Mungo
Alexander C. Stoddart BD   2001   The Manse, Hightae, Lockerbie DG11 1JL   01387 811499
                                       [E-mail: sandystoddart@supanet.com]

Dornock
Ronald S. Seaman MA   1967   The Manse of Dornock, 5 The Ridge, Eastriggs, Annan DG12 6NR   01461 40268

Eskdalemuir linked with Hutton and Corrie linked with Tundergarth
Alan C. Ross CA BD   1988   2003   Yarra, Ettrickbridge, Selkirk TD7 5JN   01750 52324 (Tel/Fax)
                                       [E-mail: alkaross@aol.com]

Gretna: Old (H), Gretna: St Andrew's (H) and Half Morton and Kirkpatrick Fleming
C. Bryan Haston LTh   1975   The Manse, Gretna Green, Gretna DG16 5DU   01461 338313 (Tel)
                                       [E-mail: cbhaston@cofs.demon.co.uk]   08701 640119 (Fax)
                                                                                      01461 500412
Katherine A. Vivers (Aux)   2004   Blacket House, Eaglesfield, Lockerbie DG11 3AA
                                       [E-mail: katevivers@yahoo.co.uk]

Hightae See Dalton

Hoddam linked with Kirtle-Eaglesfield linked with Middlebie linked with Waterbeck
Trevor C. Williams LTh   1990   1999   The Manse, Kirtlebridge, Lockerbie DG11 3LY   01461 500378
                                       [E-mail: revwill@btopenworld.com]

Hutton and Corrie See Eskdalemuir

Kirkpatrick Juxta linked with Moffat: St Andrew's (H) linked with Wamphray
David M. McKay MA BD   1979   2001   The Manse, 1 Meadowbank, Moffat DG10 9LR   01683 220128
                                       [E-mail: demacmin@ukgateway.net]

Kirtle-Eaglesfield See Hoddam

Langholm, Ewes and Westerkirk
Robert B. Milne BTh   1999   1999   The Manse, Langholm DG13 0BL   01387 380252 (Tel)
                                       [E-mail: rbmilne@aol.com]   01387 381399 (Fax)

Liddesdale (H) See Canonbie United
Lochmaben See Applegarth, Sibbaldbie and Johnstone

Lockerbie: Dryfesdale
David M. Almond BD — 1996 — The Manse, 5 Carlisle Road, Lockerbie DG11 2DW — 01576 202361
[E-mail: rev.almond@btinternet.com]

Middlebie See Hoddam
Moffat: St Andrew's (H) See Kirkpatrick Juxta
St Mungo See Dalton

The Border Kirk
Vacant — 30 Dunmail Drive, Carlisle CA2 6DF — 01228 819832

Tundergarth See Eskdalemuir
Wamphray See Kirkpatrick Juxta
Waterbeck See Hoddam

Name			Charge	Address	Telephone
Annand, James M. MA BD	1955	1995	(Lockerbie: Dryfesdale)	48 Main Street, Newstead, Melrose TD6 9DX	
Beveridge, S. Edwin P. BA	1959	2004	(Brydekirk with Hoddam)	19 Rothesay Terrace, Edinburgh EH3 7RY	0131-225 3393
Byers, Alan J.	1959	1992	(Gamrie with King Edward)	Meadowbank, Plumdon Road, Annan DG12 6SJ	01461 206512
Byers, Mairi (Mrs) BTh CPS	1992	1998	(Jura)	Meadowbank, Plumdon Road, Annan DG12 6SJ	01461 206512
Fisher, D. Noel MA BD	1939	1979	(Glasgow: Sherbrooke St Gilbert's)	Sheraig Cottage, Killochries Fold, Kilmacolm PA13 4TE	
MacMillan, William M. LTh	1980	1998	(Kilmory with Lamlash)	Balskia, 61 Queen Street, Lochmaben DG11 1PP	01387 811528
Macpherson, Duncan J. BSc BD	1993	2002	Chaplain: Army	1 Bn The Black Watch, BFPO 38	
Rennie, John D. MA	1962	1996	(Broughton, Glenholm and Kilbucho with Skirling with Stobo and Drumelzier with Tweedsmuir)	Dundoran, Ballplay Road, Moffat DG10 9JX [E-mail: tworennies@talktalk.net]	01683 220223
Swinburne, Norman BA	1960	1993	(Sauchie)	Dameroschay, Birch Hill Lane, Kirkbride, Wigton CA7 5HZ	01697 351497

(8) DUMFRIES AND KIRKCUDBRIGHT

Meets at Dumfries, on the first Wednesday of February, March, April, May, September, October, November and December, and the fourth Wednesday of June.

Clerk: REV. GORDON M.A. SAVAGE MA BD — 11 Laurieknowe, Dumfries DG2 7AH — 01387 252929
[E-mail: akph44@uk.uumail.com]
Depute Clerk: REV. WILLIAM T. HOGG MA BD — The Manse, Glasgow Road, Sanquhar DG4 6BZ — 01659 50247
[E-mail: wthogg@yahoo.com]

Auchencairn and Rerrick linked with Buittle and Kelton
Alistair J. MacKichan MA BD — 1984 2005 — Auchencairn, Castle Douglas DG7 1QS — 01556 640041

Balmaclellan and Kells (H) linked with Carsphairn (H) linked with Dalry (H)
David S. Bartholomew BSc MSc PhD BD 1994 The Manse, Dalry, Castle Douglas DG7 3PJ 01644 430380
[E-mail: dhbart@care4free.net]

Balmaghie linked with Tarff and Twynholm (H)
Christopher Wallace BD DipMin 1988 Manse Road, Twynholm, Kirkcudbright DG6 4NY 01557 860381
[E-mail: cwallaceuk@hotmail.com]

Borgue linked with Gatehouse of Fleet
Valerie J. Ott (Mrs) BA BD 2002 The Manse, Planetree Park, Gatehouse of Fleet, Castle Douglas DG7 2EQ 01557 814233
[E-mail: dandvott@aol.com]

Buittle and Kelton See Auchencairn and Rerrick

Caerlaverock linked with Dumfries: St Mary's-Greyfriars
Jamie Milliken BD 2005 4 Georgetown Crescent, Dumfries DG1 4EQ 01387 257045
[E-mail: jamie@themillikens.co.uk]

Carsphairn See Balmaclellan and Kells

Castle Douglas (H)
Robert J. Malloch BD 1987 2001 1 Castle View, Castle Douglas DG7 1BG 01556 502171
[E-mail: robert@scotnish.freeserve.co.uk]

Closeburn linked with Durisdeer
James W. Scott MA CDA 1952 1953 The Manse, Durisdeer, Thornhill DG3 5BJ 01848 500231

Colvend, Southwick and Kirkbean
James F. Gatherer BD 1984 2003 The Manse, Colvend, Dalbeattie DG5 4QN 01556 630255
[E-mail: james@gatherer.net]

Corsock and Kirkpatrick Durham linked with Crossmichael and Parton
Sally Marsh BTh MTh 2006 Knockdrocket, Clarebrand, Castle Douglas DG7 3AH 01556 503645
[E-mail: rev.sal@btinternet.com]

Crossmichael and Parton See Corsock and Kirkpatrick Durham

Cummertrees linked with Mouswald linked with Ruthwell (H)
James Williamson BA BD 1986 1991 The Manse, Ruthwell, Dumfries DG1 4NP 01387 870217
[E-mail: jimwill@rcmkirk.fsnet.co.uk]

Dalbeattie (H) linked with Urr (H)
Norman M. Hutcheson MA BD 1973 1988 36 Mill Street, Dalbeattie DG5 4HE 01556 610029
[E-mail: norman.hutcheson@virgin.net]

Dalry See Balmaclellan and Kells

Dumfries: Lincluden and Holywood linked with Dumfries: Lochside
Vacant — 27 St Anne's Road, Dumfries DG2 9HZ — 01387 252912

Dumfries: Lochside See Dumfries: Lincluden and Holywood

Dumfries: Maxwelltown West (H)
Gordon M.A. Savage MA BD — 1977 1984 — Maxwelltown West Manse, 11 Laurieknowe, Dumfries DG2 7AH [E-mail: gordonsavage@uk.uumail.com] — 01387 252929

Dumfries: St George's (H)
Donald Campbell BD — 1997 — 9 Nunholm Park, Dumfries DG1 1JP [E-mail: sorges@btinternet.com] — 01387 252965

Dumfries: St Mary's-Greyfriars (H) See Caerlaverock

Dumfries: St Michael's and South
Maurice S. Bond MTh BA DipEd PhD — 1981 1999 — 39 Cardoness Street, Dumfries DG1 3AL [E-mail: maurice.bond3@tiscali.co.uk] — 01387 253849

Dumfries: Troqueer (H)
William W. Kelly BSc BD — 1994 — Troqueer Manse, Troqueer Road, Dumfries DG2 7DF [E-mail: wwkelly@dsl.pipex.com] — 01387 253043

Dunscore linked with Glencairn and Moniaive
Christine Sime (Miss) BSc BD — 1994 — Wallaceton, Auldgirth, Dumfries DG2 0TJ [E-mail: revsime@aol.com] — 01387 820245

Durisdeer See Closeburn
Gatehouse of Fleet See Borgue
Glencairn and Moniaive See Dunscore

Irongray, Lochrutton and Terregles
David J. Taylor MA BD — 1982 2002 — Shawhead Road, Dumfries DG2 9SJ [E-mail: ministerlit@aol.com] — 01387 730287

Kirkconnel (H)
David D. Melville BD — 1989 1999 — The Manse, 31 Kingsway, Kirkconnel, Sanquhar DG4 6PN [E-mail: ddm@kirkconn.freeserve.co.uk] — 01659 67241

Kirkcudbright (H)
Douglas R. Irving LLB BD WS — 1984 1998 — 6 Bourtree Avenue, Kirkcudbright DG6 4AU [E-mail: douglasirving05@tiscali.co.uk] — 01557 330489

Kirkgunzeon
Continued Vacancy

Kirkmahoe
Richard J. Hammond BA BD   1993   2005   Kirkmahoe, Dumfries DG1 1ST   01387 710572
[E-mail: libby.hammond@virgin.net]

Kirkmichael, Tinwald and Torthorwald
Louis C. Bezuidenhout MA DD   1978   2000   Manse of Tinwald, Tinwald, Dumfries DG1 3PL   01387 710246
[E-mail: macbez@btinternet.com]

Elizabeth A. Mack (Miss) DipPEd (Aux)   1994   2006   24 Roberts Crescent, Dumfries DG2 7RS   01387 264847

Lochend and New Abbey
William Holland MA   1967   1971   The Manse, 28 Main Street, New Abbey, Dumfries DG2 8BY   01387 850232
[E-mail: bilholland@aol.com]
(Charge formed by the union of Lochend and New Abbey)

Mouswald See Cummertrees

Penpont, Keir and Tynron linked with Thornhill (H)
Donald Keith MA BD   1971   2002   The Manse, Manse Park, Thornhill DG3 5ER   01848 331191
[E-mail: dnkdonald@aol.com]

Ruthwell (H) See Cummertrees

Sanquhar: St Bride's (H)
William T. Hogg MA BD   1979   2000   St Bride's Manse, Glasgow Road, Sanquhar DG6 6BZ   01659 50247
[E-mail: wthogg@yahoo.com]

Tarff and Twynholm See Balmaghie
Thornhill (H) See Penpont, Keir and Tynron
Urr See Dalbeattie

Baillie, David R.   1979 1990   (Crawford with Lowther)   4 Southwick Drive, Dalbeattie DG5 4HW   01556 610871
Bennett, David K.P. BA   1974 2000   (Kirkpatrick Irongray with Lochrutton with Terregles)   53 Anne Arundel Court, Heathhall, Dumfries DG1 3SL   01387 257755

Craig, N. Douglas MA BD   1947 1987   (Dalbeattie: Craignair with Urr)   33 Albert Road, Dumfries DG2 9DN   01387 252187
Elder, Albert B. MA   1960 1998   (Dumfries: St Michael's and South)   Charnwood Lodge, 18 Annan Road, Dumfries DG1 3AD   01387 252287
Geddes, Alexander J. MA BD   1960 1998   (Stewarton: St Columba's)   166 Georgetown Road, Dumfries DG1 4DT
[E-mail: sandy.elizabeth@virgin.net]

Gillespie, Ann M. (Miss) DCS   1956 1996   (Deaconess)   Barlochan House, Palnackie, Castle Douglas DG7 1PF   01556 600378
Greer, A. David C.
  LLB DMin DipAdultEd   (Barra)   10 Watling Street, Dumfries DG1 1HF   01387 256113
[E-mail: kandadc@greer10.fsnet.co.uk]
Hamill, Robert BA   1956 1989   (Castle Douglas: St Ringan's)   11 St Andrew Drive, Castle Douglas DG7 1EW   01556 502962
Kirk, W. Logan MA BD MTh   1988 2000   (Dalton with Hightae with St Mungo)   2 Raecroft Avenue, Collin, Dumfries DG1 4LP   01387 750489

Name	Dates	(Previous charge)	Address	Phone
Leishman, James S. LTh BD MA(Div)	1969 1999	(Kirkmichael with Tinwald with Torthorwald)	11 Hunter Avenue, Heathhall, Dumfries DG1 3UX	01387 249241
Mackay, Donald MBE FCP FSAScot	1951 1986	(Ardrossan: St John's)	8 Urquhart Crescent, Dumfries DG1 8XF	01387 259132
McKenzie, William M. DA	1958 1993	(Dumfries: Troqueer)	41 Kingholm Road, Dumfries DG1 4SR [E-mail: mckenzie.dumfries@virgin.net]	01387 253688
Miller, John G. BEd BD MTh	1983 2005	(Port Glasgow: St Martin's)	22 Lime Grove, Georgetown, Dumfries DG1 4SQ [E-mail: johnmiller22@hotmail.co.uk]	01387 272502
Miller, John R. MA BD	1958 1992	(Carsphairn with Dalry)	4 Fairgreen Court, Rhonehouse, Castle Douglas DG7 1SA	01556 680428
Morrison, James G. MBE MA	1942 1980	(Rotterdam)	1 Woodvale Lodge, Midsummer Meadows, Cambridge CB4 1HL	07812 148161
Owen, John J.C. LTh	1967 2001	(Applegarth and Sibbaldbie with Lochmaben)	5 Galla Avenue, Dalbeattie DG5 4JZ [E-mail: jj.owen@onetel.net]	01556 612125
Robertson, Ian W. MA BD	1956 1995	(Colvend, Southwick and Kirkbean)	10 Marjoriebanks, Lochmaben, Lockerbie DG11 1QH	01387 810541
Smith, Richmond OBE MA BD	1952 1983	(World Alliance of Reformed Churches)	Aignish, Merse Way, Kippford, Dalbeattie DG5 4LH	01556 620624
Strachan, Alexander E. MA BD	1974 1999	(Dumfries Health Care Chaplain)	2 Leafield Road, Dumfries DG1 2DS [E-mail: aestrachan@aol.com]	01387 279460
Vincent, C. Raymond MA FSAScot	1952 1992	(Stonehouse)	Rosebank, Newton Stewart Road, New Galloway, Castle Douglas DG7 3RT	01644 420451
Wilkie, James R. MA MTh	1957 1993	(Penpont, Keir and Tynron)	31 Morton Street, Thornhill DG3 5NF	01848 331028
Wotherspoon, Robert C. LTh	1976 1998	(Corsock and Kirkpatrick Durham with Crossmichael and Parton)	7 Hillowton Drive, Castle Douglas DG7 1LL [E-mail: robert@wotherspoon11.wanadoo.co.uk]	01556 502267
Young, John MTh DipMin	1963 1999	(Airdrie: Broomknoll)	Craigview, North Street, Moniaive, Thornhill DG3 4HR	01848 200318

DUMFRIES ADDRESSES

Lincluden	Stewartry Road
Lochside	Lochside Road
Maxwelltown West	Laurieknowe
St George's	George Street
St Mary's-Greyfriars	St Mary's Street
St Michael's and South	St Michael's Street
Troqueer	Troqueer Road

(9) WIGTOWN AND STRANRAER

Meets at Glenluce, in the church hall, on the first Tuesday of March, October and December for ordinary business; on the first Tuesday of September for formal business followed by meetings of committees; on the first Tuesday of November, February and May for worship followed by meetings of committees; and at a church designated by the Moderator on the first Tuesday of June for Holy Communion followed by ordinary business.

Clerk:	REV. DAVID W. DUTTON BA	High Kirk Manse, Leswalt High Road, Stranraer DG9 0AA [E-mail: akph79@uk.uumail.com]	01776 703268

Ervie Kirkcolm linked with Leswalt

Michael J. Sheppard BD	1997	Ervie Manse, Stranraer DG9 0QZ [E-mail: mjs@uwclub.net]	01776 854225

Glasserton and Isle of Whithorn linked with Whithorn: St Ninian's Priory
Alexander I. Currie BD CPS	1990		The Manse, Whithorn, Newton Stewart DG8 8PT	01988 500267

Inch linked with Stranraer: Town Kirk (H)
John H. Burns BSc BD | 1985 | 1988 | Bayview Road, Stranraer DG9 8BE | 01776 702383

Kirkcowan (H) linked with Wigtown (H)
Vacant | | | The Manse, Harbour Road, Wigtown, Newton Stewart DG8 9EL | 01988 402242

Kirkinner linked with Sorbie (H)
Jeffrey M. Mead BD | 1978 | 1986 | The Manse, Kirkinner, Newton Stewart DG8 9AL | 01988 840643

Kirkmabreck linked with Monigaff (H)
Peter W.I. Aiken | 1996 | 2005 | Creebridge, Newton Stewart DG8 6NR [E-mail: aikenp@btinternet.com] | 01671 403361

Kirkmaiden (H) linked with Stoneykirk
Ian McIlroy BSS BD | 1996 | | Church Street, Sandhead, Stranraer DG9 9JJ | 01776 830337

Leswalt See Ervie Kirkcolm

Mochrum (H)
Vacant | | | Manse of Mochrum, Port William, Newton Stewart DG8 9QP | 01988 700257

Monigaff (H) See Kirkmabreck

New Luce (H) linked with Old Luce (H)
Thomas M. McWhirter MA MSc BD | 1992 | 1997 | Glenluce, Newton Stewart DG8 0PU | 01581 300319

Old Luce See New Luce

Penninghame (H)
Neil G. Campbell BA BD | 1988 | 1989 | The Manse, Newton Stewart DG8 6HH [E-mail: neilcampbell@yahoo.com] | 01671 402259

Portpatrick linked with Stranraer: St Ninian's (H)
Gordon Kennedy BSc BD MTh | 1993 | 2000 | 2 Albert Terrace, London Road, Stranraer DG9 8AB [E-mail: gordon.k@tiscali.co.uk] | 01776 702443

Sorbie See Kirkinner
Stoneykirk See Kirkmaiden

Stranraer: High Kirk (H)
David W. Dutton BA | 1973 | 1986 | High Kirk Manse, Leswalt High Road, Stranraer DG9 0AA [E-mail: akph79@uk.uumail.com] | 01776 703268

Stranraer: St Ninian's See Portpatrick
Stranraer: Town Kirk See Inch
Whithorn: St Ninian's Priory See Glasserton and Isle of Whithorn
Wigtown See Kirkcowan

Name	Years	Role	Address	Phone
Cairns, Alexander B. MA	1957 1997	(Ervie Kirkcolm with Leswalt)	Beechwood, Main Street, Sandhead, Stranraer DG9 9JG [E-mail: sandy.cairns@btinternet.com]	01776 830389
Dean, Roger A.F. LTh	1983 2004	(Mochrum)	Albion Cottage, 59 Main Street, Kirkinner, Newton Stewart DG8 9AN [E-mail: roger.dean4@btopenworld.com]	01988 840621
Harkes, George	1962 1988	(Cumbernauld: Old)	11 Main Street, Sorbie, Newton Stewart DG8 8EG	01988 850255
McCreadie, David W.	1961 1995	(Kirkmabreck)	77 St John Street, Creetown, Newton Stewart DG8 7JB	01671 820390
McGill, Thomas W.	1972 1990	(Portpatrick with Stranraer: St Ninian's)	Ravenstone Moor, Dramrae, Whithorn, Newton Stewart DG8 8DS	01988 700449
Munro, Mary (Mrs) BA	1993 2004	(Auxiliary Minister)	14 Auchneel Crescent, Stranraer DG9 0JH	01776 870250
Munro, Sheila BD	1995 2003	(Chaplain: RAF)	Chaplain's Office, RAF Digby, Lincoln LN4 3LH	
Ogilvy, Oliver M.	1959 1985	(Leswalt)	8 Dale Crescent, Stranraer DG9 0HG	01776 706285

(10) AYR

Meets on the first Tuesday of every month from September to May, excluding January, and on the fourth Tuesday of June. The June meeting will be held in the Moderator's Church. One meeting will be held in a venue to be determined by the Business Committee. Other meetings will be held in Alloway Church Hall.

| Clerk: | REV. JAMES CRICHTON MA BD MTh | 30 Garden Street, Dalrymple KA6 6DG [E-mail: akph39@uk.uumail.com] | 01292 560263 |
| | Presbytery Office | [E-mail: akph40@uk.uumail.com] | 01292 560574 (Fax) / 01292 611117 (Tel/Fax) |

Alloway (H)
Neil A. McNaught BD MA | 1987 | 1999 | 1A Parkview, Alloway, Ayr KA7 4QG [E-mail: neil@mcnaught3427.freeserve.co.uk] | 01292 441252

Annbank (H) linked with Tarbolton
Alexander Shuttleworth MA BD | 2004 | 1 Kirkport, Tarbolton, Mauchline KA5 5QJ [E-mail: revshuttleworth@aol.com] | 01292 541236

Arnsheen Barrhill linked with Colmonell
John S. Lochrie BSc BD MTh PhD | 1967 | 1999 | Manse Road, Colmonell, Girvan KA26 0SA | 01465 881224

Auchinleck (H) linked with Catrine
Vacant | 28 Mauchline Road, Auchinleck KA18 2BN | 01290 421108

Ayr: Auld Kirk of Ayr (St John the Baptist) (H)
David R. Gemmell MA BD | 1991 | 1999 | 58 Monument Road, Ayr KA7 2UB [E-mail: drgemmell@aol.com] | 01292 262580 (Tel/Fax)

Ayr: Castlehill (H) Peter B. Park BD MCIBS	1997	2003	3 Old Hillfoot Road, Ayr KA7 3LF [E-mail: peterpark9@btinternet.com]	01292 267332
Ayr: Newton on Ayr (H) G. Stewart Birse CA BD BSc	1980	1989	9 Nursery Grove, Ayr KA7 3PH [E-mail: gstewart@birse21.freeserve.co.uk]	01292 264251
Ayr: St Andrew's (H) Harry B. Mealyea BArch BD	1984	2000	31 Bellevue Crescent, Ayr KA7 2DP [E-mail: mealyea@tiscali.co.uk]	01292 261126
Ayr: St Columba (H) Fraser R. Aitken MA BD	1978	1991	2 Hazelwood Road, Ayr KA7 2PY [E-mail: frasercolumba@msn.com]	01292 284177
Ayr: St James' (H) Robert McCrum BSc BD	1982	2005	1 Prestwick Road, Ayr KA8 8LD [E-mail: robert.mccrum@virgin.net]	01292 262420
Ayr: St Leonard's (H) Robert Lynn MA BD	1984	1989	7 Shawfield Avenue, Ayr KA7 4RE [E-mail: robert@shawfield200.fsnet.co.uk]	01292 442109
Ayr: St Quivox (H) David T. Ness LTh	1972	1988	11 Springfield Avenue, Prestwick KA9 2HA [E-mail: dness@fish.co.uk]	01292 478306
Ayr: Wallacetown (H) Mary C. McLauchlan (Mrs) LTh	1997	2003	87 Forehill Road, Ayr KA7 3JR [E-mail: mcmclauchlan@onetel.net]	01292 263878
Ballantrae (H) Robert P. Bell BSc	1968	1998	Ballantrae, Girvan KA26 0NH [E-mail: revbobbell@aol.com]	01465 831252 (Tel) 01465 831260 (Fax)
Barr linked with Dailly linked with Girvan South Ian K. McLachlan MA BD	1999		30 Henrietta Street, Girvan KA26 9AL [E-mail: iankmclachlan@yetiville.freeserve.co.uk]	01465 713370

Catrine See Auchinleck
Colmonell See Arnsheen Barrhill

Coylton linked with Drongan: The Schaw Kirk
Vacant — 4 Hamilton Place, Coylton, Ayr KA6 6JQ — 01292 570272

Craigie linked with Symington
Alastair M. Sanderson BA LTh — 1971 2000 — 16 Kerrix Road, Symington, Kilmarnock KA1 5QD [E-mail: revans@aol.com] — 01563 830205

Crosshill (H) linked with Dalrymple (H)
James Crichton MA BD MTh — 1969 — 30 Garden Street, Dalrymple KA6 6DG [E-mail: akph39@uk.uumail.com] — 01292 560263 (Tel) / 01292 560574 (Fax)

Dailly See Barr

Dalmellington linked with Patna: Waterside
Kenneth B. Yorke BD DipEd — 1982 1999 — 4 Carsphairn Road, Dalmellington, Ayr KA6 7RE [E-mail: kbyorke@netbreeze.co.uk] — 01292 550353
Muriel Wilson (Ms) DCS — 28 Bellevue Crescent, Ayr KA7 2DR [E-mail: murielw@fish.co.uk] — 01292 264939

Dalrymple See Crosshill
Drongan: The Schaw Kirk See Coylton

Dundonald (H)
Robert Mayes BD — 1982 1988 — 64 Main Street, Dundonald, Kilmarnock KA2 9HG [E-mail: bobmayes@fsmail.net] — 01563 850243

Fisherton (H) linked with Kirkoswald
Arrick D. Wilkinson BSc BD — 2000 2003 — The Manse, Kirkoswald, Maybole KA19 8HZ [E-mail: arrick@clergy.net] — 01655 760210

Girvan: North (Old and St Andrew's) (H)
Douglas G. McNab BA BD — 1999 — 38 The Avenue, Girvan KA26 9DS [E-mail: dougmcnab@aol.com] — 01465 713203

Girvan: South See Barr linked with Dailly

Kirkmichael linked with Straiton: St Cuthbert's
W. Gerald Jones MA BD MTh — 1984 1985 — Patna Road, Kirkmichael, Maybole KA19 7PJ [E-mail: revgerald@jonesg99.freeserve.co.uk] — 01655 750286

Kirkoswald (H) See Fisherton

Lugar linked with Old Cumnock: Old (H)
John W. Paterson BSc BD DipEd — 1994 — 33 Barrhill Road, Cumnock KA18 1PJ [E-mail: ocochurchwow@hotmail.com] — 01290 420769

Mauchline (H)
Alan B. Telfer BA BD · 1983 · 1991 · 4 Westside Gardens, Mauchline KA5 5DJ [E-mail: telferab@tiscali.co.uk] · 01290 550386

Maybole
David Whiteman BD · 1998 · 64 Culzean Road, Maybole KA19 8AH [E-mail: soohsw@aol.com] · 01655 889456
Douglas T. Moore (Aux) · 2003 · 9 Midton Avenue, Prestwick KA9 1PU [E-mail: douglastmoore@hotmail.com] · 01292 671352

Monkton and Prestwick: North (H)
Arthur A. Christie BD · 1997 · 2000 · 40 Monkton Road, Prestwick KA9 1AR [E-mail: revaac@btinternet.com] · 01292 477499

Muirkirk (H) linked with Sorn
Alex M. Welsh MA BD · 1979 · 2003 · 2 Smallburn Road, Muirkirk, Cumnock KA18 3RF · 01290 661157

New Cumnock (H)
Rona M. Young (Mrs) BD DipEd · 1991 · 2001 · 37 Castle, New Cumnock, Cumnock KA18 4AG [E-mail: revronyoung@hotmail.com] · 01290 338296

Ochiltree linked with Stair
Carolyn M. Baker (Mrs) BD · 1997 · 10 Mauchline Road, Ochiltree, Cumnock KA18 2PZ [E-mail: carolynmbaker2001@yahoo.co.uk] · 01290 700365

Old Cumnock: Old See Lugar

Old Cumnock: Trinity
Vacant · 46 Ayr Road, Cumnock KA18 1DW · 01290 422145

Patna: Waterside See Dalmellington

Prestwick: Kingcase (H) (E-mail: office@kingcase.freeserve.co.uk)
T. David Watson BSc BD · 1988 · 1997 · 15 Bellrock Avenue, Prestwick KA9 1SQ [E-mail: tdwatson@tesco.net] · 01292 479571

Prestwick: St Nicholas' (H)
George R. Fiddes BD · 1979 · 1985 · 3 Bellevue Road, Prestwick KA9 1NW [E-mail: george@gfiddes.freeserve.co.uk] · 01292 477613

Prestwick: South (H)
Kenneth C. Elliott BD BA CertMin · 1989 · 68 St Quivox Road, Prestwick KA9 1JF [E-mail: kennethc@revelliott.freeserve.co.uk] · 01292 478788

Sorn See Muirkirk
Stair See Ochiltree
Straiton: St Cuthbert's See Kirkmichael
Symington See Craigie
Tarbolton See Annbank

Troon: Old (H)

Alastair H. Symington MA BD	1972	1998	85 Bentinck Drive, Troon KA10 6HZ [E-mail: revahs@care4free.net]	01292 313644

Troon: Portland (H)

Ronald M.H. Boyd BD DipTh	1995	1999	89 South Beach, Troon KA10 6EQ [E-mail: rmhboyd@btinternet.com]	01292 313285

Troon: St Meddan's (H) (E-mail: st.meddan@virgin.net)

David L. Harper BSc BD	1972	1979	27 Bentinck Drive, Troon KA10 6HX [E-mail: d.l.harper@btinternet.com]	01292 311784

Name				Address	Phone
Andrew, R.J.M. MA	1955	1994	(Uddingston: Old)	6A Ronaldshaw Park, Ayr KA7 2TS	01292 263430
Banks, John BD	1968	2001	(Hospital Chaplain)	19 Victoria Drive, Troon KA10 6JF	01292 317758
Blyth, James G.S. BSc BD	1963	1986	(Glenmuick)	40 Robsland Avenue, Ayr KA7 2RW	01292 261276
Bogle, Thomas C. BD	1983	2003	(Fisherton with Maybole: West)	38 McEwan Crescent, Mossblown, Ayr KA6 5DR	01292 521215
Campbell, Effie C. (Mrs) BD	1981	1991	(Old Cumnock: Crichton West with St Ninian's)		
Cranston, George BD	1976	2001	(Rutherglen: Wardlawhill)	7 Lansdowne Road, Ayr KA8 8LS	01292 264282
Dickie, Michael M. BSc	1955	1994	(Ayr: Castlehill)	20 Capperview, Prestwick KA9 1BH	01292 476627
Garrity, T. Alan W. BSc BD MTh	1969	1999	Christ Church, Warwick, Bermuda	8 Noltmire Road, Ayr KA8 9ES PO Box PG88, Paget PG BX, Bermuda [E-mail: revtawg@logic.bm]	01292 618512
Glencross, William M. LTh	1968	1999	(Bellshill: Macdonald Memorial)	1 Lochay Place, Troon KA10 7HH	01292 317097
Grant, J. Gordon MA BD	1957	1997	(Edinburgh: Dean)	33 Fullarton Drive, Troon KA10 6LE	01292 311852
Guthrie, James A.	1969	2005	(Corsock and Kirkpatrick Durham with Crossmichael and Parton)	2 Barrhill Road, Pinwherry, Girvan KA26 0QE [E-mail: revjguth@fish.co.uk]	01465 841236
Hannah, William BD MCAM MIPR	1987	2001	(Muirkirk)	8 Dovecote View, Kirkintilloch, Glasgow G66 3HY	0141-776 1337
Helon, George G. BA BD	1984	2000	(Barr linked with Dailly)	9 Park Road, Maxwelltown, Dumfries DG2 7PW	01387 259255
Johnston, Kenneth L. BA LTh	1969	2001	(Annbank)	2 Rylands, Prestwick KA9 2DX [E-mail: ken@kenston.co.uk]	01292 471980
Kent, Arthur F.S.	1966	1999	(Monkton and Prestwick: North)	17 St David's Drive, Evesham, Worcs WR11 6AS	01386 421562
King, Chris (Mrs) MA BD DCS	1991	2006	Deaconess	28 Kilnford Drive, Dundonald, Kilmarnock KA2 9ET	01563 851197
Lennox, Lawrie I. MA BD DipEd	1965	1999	(Cromar)	7 Carwinshoch View, Ayr KA7 4AY	
McCrorie, William			(Free Church Chaplain: Royal Brompton Hospital)		
Macdonald, Ian U.	1960	1997	(Tarbolton)	12 Shieling Park, Ayr KA7 2UR	01292 288854
McNidder, Roderick H. BD	1987	1997	Chaplain: NHS Ayrshire and Arran Trust	18 Belmont Road, Ayr KA7 2PF	01292 283085
McPhail, Andrew M. BA	1968	2002	(Ayr: Wallacetown)	6 Hollow Park, Alloway, Ayr KA7 4SR	01292 442554
Mitchell, Sheila M. (Miss) BD MTh	1995	2002	Chaplain: NHS Ayrshire and Arran Trust	25 Maybole Road, Ayr KA7 2QA	01292 282108
Robertson, Daniel M. MA	1960	2000	(Auchinleck)	Ailsa Hospital, Ayr KA6 6BQ	01292 610556
Russell, Paul R. MA BD	1984	2006	Chaplain: NHS Ayrshire and Arran Trust	14 Corrie Place, Drongan, Ayr KA6 7DU	01292 590150
Saunders, Campbell M. MA BD	1952	1989	(Ayr: St Leonard's)	4 Hamilton Place, Coylton, Ayr KA6 6IQ	01292 570272
Stirling, Ian R. BSc BD	1990	2002	Chaplain: The Ayrshire Hospice	42 Marle Park, Ayr KA7 4RN Ayrshire Hospice, 35–37 Racecourse Road, Ayr KA7 2TG	01292 441673 01292 269200

AYR ADDRESSES

Ayr

Auld Kirk	Kirkport (116 High Street)
Castlehill	Castlehill Road x Hillfoot Road
Newton on Ayr	Main Street
St Andrew's	Park Circus
St Columba	Midton Road x Carrick Park
St James'	Prestwick Road x Falkland Park Road
St Leonard's	St Leonard's Road x Monument Road
Wallacetown	John Street x Church Street

Girvan

North	Montgomerie Street
South	Stair Park

Maybole (both buildings still in use)

Old	Centre of Cassillis Road
West	Foot of Coral Glen

Prestwick

Kingcase	Waterloo Road

Monkton and Prestwick North

St Nicholas	Monkton Road
South	Main Street
	Main Street

Troon

Old	Ayr Street
Portland	St Meddan's Street
St Meddan's	St Meddan's Street

(11) IRVINE AND KILMARNOCK

The Presbytery meets ordinarily at 6:30pm in the Hall of Howard St Andrew's Church, Kilmarnock, on the first Tuesday of each month from September to May (except January and April), and on the fourth Tuesday in June. The September meeting begins with the celebration of Holy Communion.

Clerk:	REV. COLIN G.F. BROCKIE BSc(Eng) BD		51 Portland Road, Kilmarnock KA1 2EQ [E-mail: akph57@uk.uumail.com]	01563 525311
Depute Clerk:	I. STEUART DEY LLB NP		72 Dundonald Road, Kilmarnock KA1 1RZ [E-mail: steuart.dey@btinternet.com]	01563 521686
Treasurer:	JAMES McINTOSH BA CA		15 Dundonald Road, Kilmarnock KA1 1RU	01563 523552

The Presbytery office is manned each Tuesday, Wednesday and Thursday from 9am until 12:45pm. The office telephone number is 01563 526295.

Crosshouse Vacant			27 Kilmarnock Road, Crosshouse, Kilmarnock KA2 0EZ	01563 521035
Darvel Charles M. Cameron BA BD PhD	1980	2001	46 West Main Street, Darvel KA17 0AQ	01560 322924
Dreghorn and Springside Gary E. Horsburgh BA	1976	1983	96A Townfoot, Dreghorn, Irvine KA11 4EZ	01294 217770

Dunlop
Maureen M. Duncan (Mrs) BD — 1996 — 4 Dampark, Dunlop, Kilmarnock KA3 4BZ — 01560 484083

Fenwick (H)
Geoffrey Redmayne BSc BD MPhil — 2000 — 2 Kirkton Place, Fenwick, Kilmarnock KA3 6DW
[E-mail: geoff@gredmayne.fsnet.co.uk] — 01560 600217

Galston (H)
Graeme R. Wilson MCIBS BD ThM — 2006 — 60 Brewland Street, Galston KA4 8DX
[E-mail: graeme.wilson@gmail.com] — 01563 820246
John H.B. Taylor MA BD DipEd FEIS (Assoc) — 1952 — 1990 — 62 Woodlands Grove, Kilmarnock KA3 1TZ — 01563 526698

Hurlford (H)
James D. McCulloch BD MIOP — 1996 — 12 Main Road, Crookedholm, Kilmarnock KA3 6JT — 01563 535673

Irvine: Fullarton (H)
Neil Urquhart BD DipMin — 1989 — 48 Waterside, Irvine KA12 8QJ
[E-mail: neilurquhart@beeb.net] — 01294 279909

Irvine: Girdle Toll (E) (H)
Clare B. Sutcliffe BSc BD — 2000 — 2 Littlestane Rise, Irvine KA11 2BJ
[E-mail: revclare@tesco.net] — 01294 213565

Irvine: Mure (H)
Hugh M. Adamson BD — 1976 — West Road, Irvine KA12 8RE — 01294 279916

Irvine: Old (H) (01294 273503)
Robert Travers BA BD — 1993 — 1999 — 22 Kirk Vennel, Irvine KA12 0DQ
[E-mail: robert@travers46.freeserve.co.uk] — 01294 279265

Irvine: Relief Bourtreehill (H)
Andrew R. Black BD — 1987 — 2003 — 4 Kames Court, Irvine KA11 1RT
[E-mail: andrewblack@tiscali.co.uk] — 01294 216939

Irvine: St Andrew's (H) (01294 276051)
Vacant — 206 Bank Street, Irvine KA12 0YD — 01294 211403

Kilmarnock: Grange (H) (01563 534490)
Colin G.F. Brockie BSc(Eng) BD — 1967 — 1978 — 51 Portland Road, Kilmarnock KA1 2EQ
[E-mail: revcol@revcol.demon.co.uk] — 01563 525311

Kilmarnock: Henderson (H) (01563 541302)
David W. Lacy BA BD DLitt — 1976 — 1989 — 52 London Road, Kilmarnock KA3 7AJ
[E-mail: thelacys@tinyworld.co.uk] — 01563 523113 (Tel/Fax)

Kilmarnock: Howard St Andrew's (H)
Malcolm MacLeod BA BD — 1979 — 1989 — 1 Evelyn Villas, Holehouse Road, Kilmarnock KA3 7AX
[E-mail: minister@howardstandrews.com] — 01563 522278

Kilmarnock: Laigh West High (H)
David S. Cameron BD — 2001 — 1 Holmes Farm Road, Kilmarnock KA1 1TP
[E-mail: david@cmron05.freeserve.co.uk] — 01563 525416

Kilmarnock: Old High Kirk (H)
William M. Hall BD — 1972 1979 — 107 Dundonald Road, Kilmarnock KA1 1UP
[E-mail: revwillie@tiscali.co.uk] — 01563 525608

Kilmarnock: Riccarton (H)
Vacant — 2 Jasmine Road, Kilmarnock KA1 2HD — 01563 525694

Kilmarnock: St John's Onthank (H)
Susan M. Anderson (Mrs) — 1997 — 84 Wardneuk Drive, Kilmarnock KA3 2EX
[E-mail: stjohnthank@yahoo.co.uk] — 01563 521815

Kilmarnock: St Kentigern's
S. Grant Barclay LLB BD — 1995 — 1 Thirdpart Place, Kilmarnock KA1 1UL
[E-mail: grant.barclay@bigfoot.com] — 01563 571280

Kilmarnock: St Marnock's (H) (01563 541337)
James McNaughtan BD DipMin — 1983 1989 — 35 South Gargieston Drive, Kilmarnock KA1 1TB
[E-mail: jim@mcnaughtan.demon.co.uk] — 01563 521665

Kilmarnock: St Ninian's Bellfield (01563 524705) linked with Kilmarnock: Shortlees
H. Taylor Brown BD CertMin — 1997 2002 — 14 McLelland Drive, Kilmarnock KA1 1SF
[E-mail: htaylorbrown@hotmail.com] — 01563 529920

Kilmarnock: Shortlees See Kilmarnock: St Ninian's Bellfield

Kilmaurs: St Maur's Glencairn (H)
John A. Urquhart BD — 1993 — 9 Standalane, Kilmaurs, Kilmarnock KA3 2NB — 01563 538289

Newmilns: Loudoun (H)
John Macleod MA BD — 2000 — Loudoun Manse, 116A Loudoun Road, Newmilns KA16 9HH — 01560 320174

Stewarton: John Knox
Vacant — 27 Avenue Street, Stewarton, Kilmarnock KA3 5AP — 01560 482418

Stewarton: St Columba's (H)
Vacant — 1 Kirk Glebe, Stewarton, Kilmarnock KA3 5BJ — 01560 482453

Ayrshire Mission to the Deaf

S. Grant Barclay LLB BD (Chaplain)	1991	1998	89 Mure Avenue, Kilmarnock KA3 1TT [E-mail: grant.barclay@bigfoot.com]	01563 571280

Name			Charge	Address	Phone
Campbell, George H.	1957	1992	(Stewarton: John Knox)	20 Woodlands Grove, Kilmarnock KA3 1TZ [E-mail: geen@ecampbell5.fsnet.co.uk]	01563 536365
Campbell, John A. JP FIEM	1984	1998	(Irvine: St Andrew's)	Flowerdale, Balmoral Lane, Blairgowrie PH10 7AF	01250 872795
Cant, Thomas M. MA BD	1964	2004	(Paisley: Laigh Kirk)	3 Meikle Cutstraw Farm, Stewarton, Kilmarnock KA3 5HU [E-mail: revtmcant@aol.com]	01560 480566
Christie, Robert S. MA BD ThM	1964	2001	(Kilmarnock: West High)	24 Homeroyal House, 2 Chalmers Crescent, Edinburgh EH9 1TP	01294 312515
Davidson, James BD DipAFH	1989	2002	(Wishaw: Old)	13 Redburn Place, Irvine KA12 9BQ	01560 600388
Hare, Malcolm M.W. BA BD	1956	1994	(Kilmarnock: St Kentigern's)	21 Raith Road, Fenwick, Kilmarnock KA3 6DB	01560 482799
Hay, W.J.R. MA BD	1959	1995	(Buchanan with Drymen)	18 Jamieson Place, Stewarton, Kilmarnock KA3 3AY	01563 551717
Hosain, Samuel BD MTh PhD	1979	2006	(Stewarton: John Knox)	7 Dalwhinnie Crescent, Kilmarnock KA3 1QS [E-mail: samuel.h2@ukonline.co.uk]	
Huggett, Judith A. (Miss) BA BD	1990	1998	Hospital Chaplain	4 Westmoor Crescent, Kilmarnock KA1 1TX	01563 526314
Jarvie, Thomas W. BD	1953	2005	(Kilmarnock: Riccarton)	3 Heston Place, Kilmarnock KA3 2JR	01563 573994
Kelly, Thomas A. Davidson MA BD FSAScot	1975	2002	(Glasgow: Govan Old)	2 Springhill Stables, Portland Road, Kilmarnock KA1 2EJ [E-mail: dks@springhillstables.freeserve.co.uk]	
McAlpine, Richard H.M. BA FSAScot	1968	2000	(Lochgoilhead and Kilmorich)	7 Kingsford Place, Kilmarnock KA3 6FG	01563 572075
MacDonald, James M.	1964	1987	(Kilmarnock: St John's Onthank)	29 Carmel Place, Kilmaurs, Kilmarnock KA3 2QU	01563 525254
Morrison, Alistair H. BTh DipYCS	1985	2004	(Paisley: St Mark's Oldhall)	92 St Leonard's Road, Ayr KA7 2PU [E-mail: alistairmorrison@supanet.com]	01292 266021
Roy, James BA	1967	1982	(Irvine: Girdle Toll)	23 Bowes Rigg, Stewarton, Kilmarnock KA3 5EL [E-mail: jimroy@fountainmag.fsnet.co.uk]	01560 482185
Scott, Thomas T.	1968	1989	(Kilmarnock: St Marnock's)	6 North Hamilton Place, Kilmarnock KA1 2QN [E-mail: 101725.216@compuserve.com]	01563 531415
Shaw, Catherine A.M. MA	1998	2006	(Auxiliary Minister)	40 Merrygreen Place, Stewarton, Kilmarnock KA3 5EP [E-mail: catherine.shaw@tesco.net]	01560 483352
Urquhart, Barbara (Mrs) DCS			Deaconess, Part-time Hospital Chaplain and Presbytery S.S. Adviser	9 Standalane, Kilmaurs, Kilmarnock KA3 2NB	01563 538289

IRVINE and KILMARNOCK ADDRESSES

Irvine

Dreghorn and Springside	Townfoot x Station Brae
Fullarton	Marress Road x Church Street
Girdle Toll	Bryce Knox Court
Mure	West Road
Old	Kirkgate
Relief Bourtreehill	Crofthead, Bourtreehill
St Andrew's	Caldon Road x Oaklands Ave

Kilmarnock

Ayrshire Mission to the Deaf	10 Clark Street
Grange	Woodstock Street
Henderson	London Road
Howard	5 Portland Road
Laigh	John Dickie Street
Old High Kirk	Church Street x Soulis Street
Riccarton	Old Street
St Andrew's Glencairn	St Andrew's Street
St John's Onthank	84 Wardneuk Street
St Marnock's	St Marnock's Street
St Ninian's Bellfield	Whatriggs Road
Shortlees	Central Avenue
West High	Portland Street

(12) ARDROSSAN

Meets at Saltcoats, New Trinity, on the first Tuesday of February, March, April, May, September, October, November and December, and on the second Tuesday of June.

Clerk:	REV. JOHNSTON R. McKAY MA BA	Upper Burnfoot, 27 Stanlane Place, Largs KA30 8DD [E-mail: akph38@uk.uumail.com]	01475 672960 01475 674380 (Fax) 07885 876021 (Mbl)
Depute Clerk:	MR ALAN K. SAUNDERSON	17 Union Street, Largs KA30 3DG	01475 687217

Ardrossan: Barony St John's (H) (01294 465009)
Vacant · 10 Seafield Drive, Ardrossan KA22 8NU · 01294 463868

Ardrossan: Park (01294 463711)
William R. Johnston BD 1998 · 35 Ardneil Court, Ardrossan KA22 7NQ · 01294 471808
Marion L.K. Howie (Mrs) MA ACRS (Aux) 1992 · 51 High Road, Stevenston KA20 3DY [E-mail: marion.howie@ndirect.co.uk] · 01294 466571

Beith: High (H) (01505 502686) linked with Beith: Trinity (H)
Roderick I.T. MacDonald BD CertMin 1992 2005 · 2 Glebe Court, Beith KA15 1ET · 01505 503858

Beith: Trinity (H) See Beith: High

Brodick linked with Corrie linked with Lochranza and Pirnmill linked with Shiskine (H)
Angus Adamson BD 2006 · 4 Manse Crescent, Brodick, Isle of Arran KA27 8AS · 01770 302334

Corrie See Brodick

Cumbrae
Marjory H. Mackay (Mrs) BD DipEd CCE 1998 · Marine Parade, Millport, Isle of Cumbrae KA28 0ED [E-mail: mmackay@fish.co.uk] · 01475 530416

Dalry: St Margaret's
James A.S. Boag BD 1992 2002 · Bridgend, Dalry KA24 4DA [E-mail: james@boag4458.fsnet.co.uk] · 01294 832234

Dalry: Trinity (H)
Martin Thomson BSc DipEd BD 1988 2004 · Trinity Manse, West Kilbride Road, Dalry KA24 5DX [E-mail: martin@thomsonm40.freeserve.co.uk] · 01294 832363

Fairlie (H)
James Whyte BD — 1981 — 2006 — 14 Fairlieburne Gardens, Fairlie, Largs KA29 0ER — 01475 568342

Fergushill
Vacant

Kilbirnie: Auld Kirk (H)
Ian W. Benzie BD — 1999 — 49 Holmhead, Kilbirnie KA25 6BS
[E-mail: revian@btopenworld.com] — 01505 682348

Kilbirnie: St Columba's (H) (01505 685239)
Fiona C. Ross (Miss) BD DipMin — 1996 — 2004 — Manse of St Columba's, Dipple Road, Kilbirnie KA25 7JU
[E-mail: fionaross@calvin78.freeserve.co.uk] — 01505 683342

Kilmory
Vacant

Kilwinning: Mansefield Trinity (E) (01294 550746)
Vacant — 27 Treesbank, Kilwinning KA13 6LY — 01294 558746

Kilwinning: Old
Alison Davidge MA BD — 1990 — 2006 — 54 Dalry Road, Kilwinning KA13 7HE — 01294 552606

Lamlash
Vacant

Largs: Clark Memorial (H) (01475 675186)
Stephen J. Smith BSc BD — 1993 — 1998 — 31 Douglas Street, Largs KA30 8PT
[E-mail: stephenrevsteve@aol.com] — 01475 672370

Largs: St Columba's (01475 686212)
Roderick J. Grahame BD CPS — 1991 — 2002 — 17 Beachway, Largs KA30 8QH
[E-mail: rjgrahame@supanet.com] — 01475 673107

Largs: St John's (H) (01475 674468)
Andrew F. McGurk BD — 1983 — 1993 — 1 Newhaven Grove, Largs KA30 8NS
[E-mail: afmcg.largs@talk21.com] — 01475 676123

Lochranza and Pirnmill See Brodick

Saltcoats: New Trinity (H) (01294 472001)
Elaine W. McKinnon MA BD — 1988 — 2006 — 1 Montgomerie Crescent, Saltcoats KA21 5BX — 01294 461143

Saltcoats: North (01294 464679)
Alexander B. Noble MA BD ThM — 1982 — 2003 — 25 Longfield Avenue, Saltcoats KA21 6DR — 01294 604923

Saltcoats: St Cuthbert's (H)

Brian H. Oxburgh BSc BD	1980	1988	10 Kennedy Road, Saltcoats KA21 5SF [E-mail: oxburgh9@aol.com]	01294 602674

Shiskine (H)   See Brodick

Stevenston: Ardeer linked with Stevenston: Livingstone (H)

John M.M. Lafferty BD	1999	32 High Road, Stevenston KA20 3DR	01294 464180

Stevenston: High (H) (Website: www.highkirk.com)

M. Scott Cameron MA BD	2002	Glencairn Street, Stevenston KA20 3DL [E-mail: scottie_cameron@btinternet.com]	01294 463356

Stevenston: Livingstone (H)   See Stevenston: Ardeer

West Kilbride: Overton (H)

Vacant		Goldenberry Avenue, West Kilbride KA23 9LJ	01294 823186

West Kilbride: St Andrew's (H) (01294 829902)

D. Ross Mitchell BA BD	1972	1980	7 Overton Drive, West Kilbride KA23 9LQ [E-mail: ross.mitchell@virgin.net]	01294 823142

Whiting Bay and Kildonan

Elizabeth R.L. Watson (Miss) BA BD	1981	1982	Whiting Bay, Brodick, Isle of Arran KA27 8RE [E-mail: revewatson@surefish.co.uk]	01770 700289

Name			Previous charge	Address	Phone
Bristow, Irene A. (Mrs) BD	1989	2005	(Lochgelly: Macainsh)	20 Montgomerie Road, Saltcoats KA21 5DP [E-mail: ibristow@btinternet.com]	01294 461130
Cruickshank, Norman BA BD	1983	2006	(West Kilbride: Overton)	24D Faulds Wynd, Seamill, West Kilbride KA23 9FA	01294 822239
Dailly, J.R. BD DipPS	1979	1979	Staff Chaplain: Army	DACG, HQ 42 (NW) Bde, Fulwood Barracks, Preston PR2 8AA	
Downie, Alexander S.	1975	1997	(Ardrossan: Park)	14 Korsankel Wynd, Saltcoats KA21 6HY	01294 464097
Drysdale, James H. LTh	1987	2006	(Blackbraes and Shieldhill)	10 John Clark Street, Largs KA30 9AH	01475 674870
Gordon, David C.	1953	1988	(Gigha and Cara)	Quoys of Barnhouse, Stenness, Orkney KW16 3JY	
Harbison, David J.H.	1958	1998	(Beith: High with Beith: Trinity)	42 Mill Park, Dalry KA24 5BB [E-mail: djh@harbi.fsnet.co.uk]	01294 834092
Hebenton, David J. MA BD	1958	2002	(Ayton and Burnmouth linked with Grantshouse and Houndwood and Reston)	22B Faulds Wynd, Seamill, West Kilbride KA23 9FA	01294 829228
Leask, Rebecca M. (Mrs)	1977	1985	(Callander: St Bride's)	20 Strathclyde House, 31 Shore Road, Skelmorlie PA17 5AN	01475 520765
McCallum, Alexander D. BD	1987	2005	(Saltcoats: New Trinity)	33 Greeto Falls Avenue, Largs KA30 9HJ [E-mail: sandyandjose@madasafish.com]	01475 670133
McCance, Andrew M. BSc	1986	1995	(Coatbridge: Middle)	15 The Crescent, Skelmorlie PA17 5DX	

McKay, Johnston R. MA BA	1969 1987	(Religious Broadcasting: BBC)	Upper Burnfoot, 27 Stanlane Place, Largs KA30 8DD [E-mail: johnston.mckay@btopenworld.com]	01475 672960
MacLeod, Ian LTh BA MTh PhD	1969 2006	(Brodick with Corrie)	Cromla Cottage, Corrie, Isle of Arran KA27 8JB [E-mail: revmacleod@arrannames.co.uk]	01770 810237
Paterson, John H. BD	1977 2000	(Kirkintilloch: St David's Memorial Park)	Creag Bhan, Golf Course Road, Whiting Bay, Isle of Arran KA27 8QT	01770 700569
Roy, Iain M. MA BD	1960 1997	(Stevenston: Livingstone)	2 The Fieldings, Dunlop, Kilmarnock KA3 4AU	01560 483072
Selfridge, John BTh BREd	1969 1991	(Eddrachillis)	Strathclyde House, Apt 1, Shore Road, Skelmorlie PA17 5AN	01475 529514
Taylor, Andrew S. BTh FPhS	1959 1992	(Greenock Union)	9 Raillies Avenue, Largs KA30 8QY [E-mail: andrew@taylorlargs.fsnet.co.uk]	01475 674709
Thomson, Margaret (Mrs)	1988 1993	(Saltcoats: Erskine)	72 Knockrivoch Place, Ardrossan KA22 7PZ	01294 468685
Walker, David S. MA	1939 1978	(Makerstoun with Smailholm with Stichill, Hume and Nenthorn)	The Anchorage, Baycroft, Strachur, Argyll PA27 8BY	

(13) LANARK

Meets at Lanark on the first Tuesday of February, March, April, May, September, October, November and December, and on the third Tuesday of June.

Clerk: REV. JAMES S.H. CUTLER BD CEng MIStructE   17 Mercat Loan, Biggar ML12 6DG   **01899 220625**
[E-mail: akph60@uk.uumail.com]
[E-mail: lanarkpresbytery@uk.uumail.com]

Biggar (H) (E-mail: j.francis@lanarkpresbytery.org)
James Francis BD PhD   2002 2005   61 High Street, Biggar ML12 6DA   01899 220227
[E-mail: jim.francis@btinternet.com]

Black Mount linked with Culter linked with Libberton and Quothquan (E-mail: j.cutler@lanarkpresbytery.org)
James S.H. Cutler BD CEng MIStructE   1986 2004   17 Mercat Loan, Biggar ML12 6DG   01899 220625
[E-mail: jim.cutler1@virgin.net]

Cairngryffe linked with Symington (E-mail: g.houston@lanarkpresbytery.org)
Graham R. Houston BSc BD MTh PhD   1978 2001   16 Abington Road, Symington, Biggar ML12 6JX   01899 308838
[E-mail: gandih@onetel.net]

Carluke: Kirkton (H) (01555 750778) (E-mail: i.cunningham@lanarkpresbytery.org)
Iain D. Cunningham MA BD   1979 1987   9 Station Road, Carluke ML8 5AA   01555 771262
[E-mail: iaindc@btconnect.com]

Carluke: St Andrew's (H) (E-mail: h.jamieson@lanarkpresbytery.org)
Helen E. Jamieson (Mrs) BD DipED   1989   120 Clyde Street, Carluke ML8 5BG   01555 771218
[E-mail: helen@hjamieson.wanadoo.co.uk]

Carluke: St John's (H) (Website: www.carluke-stjohns.org.uk)
Vacant   18 Old Bridgend, Carluke ML8 4HN   01555 772259

Carnwath (H) (E-mail: b.gauld@lanarkpresbytery.org)
Beverly G.D.D. Gauld MA BD   1972   1978
The Manse, Carnwath, Lanark ML11 8JY
[E-mail: bevrev.gauld@southlanarkshire.gov.uk]   01555 840259

Carstairs and Carstairs Junction, The United Church of
Iain M. Goring BSc BD   1976   2005
80 Lanark Road, Carstairs, Lanark ML11 8QH
[E-mail: imgoring@tiscali.co.uk]   01555 870250
(Charge formed by the union of Carstairs and Carstairs Junction)

Coalburn linked with Lesmahagow: Old (Church office: 01555 892425)
Aileen Robson BD   2003
9 Elm Bank, Lesmahagow, Lanark ML11 0EA
[E-mail: revamr@lopc.fsnet.co.uk]   01555 895325

Crossford linked with Kirkfieldbank (E-mail: s.reid@lanarkpresbytery.org)
Steven Reid BAcc CA BD   1989   1997
74 Lanark Road, Crossford, Carluke ML8 5RE
[E-mail: stevenreid@v21mail.co.uk]   01555 860415

Culter See Black Mount

Forth: St Paul's (H) (E-mail: s.ross@lanarkpresbytery.org)
Sarah L. Ross (Mrs) BD MTh PGDip   2004
22 Lea Rig, Forth, Lanark ML11 8EA
[E-mail: rev_sross@btinternet.com]   01555 812832

Glencaple linked with Lowther
Margaret A. Muir (Miss) MA LLB BD   1989   2001
66 Carlisle Road, Crawford, Biggar ML12 6TW   01864 502625

Kirkfieldbank See Crossford

Kirkmuirhill (H) (E-mail: i.watson@lanarkpresbytery.org)
Ian M. Watson LLB DipLP BD   1998   2003
The Manse, 2 Lanark Road, Kirkmuirhill, Lanark ML11 9RB
[E-mail: ian.watson21@btopenworld.com]   01555 892409

Lanark: Greyfriars
Vacant
2 Friarsdene, Lanark ML11 9EJ   01555 663363

Lanark: St Nicholas' (E-mail: a.meikle@lanarkpresbytery.org)
Alison A. Meikle (Mrs) BD   1999   2002
2 Kaimhill Court, Lanark ML11 9HU
[E-mail: alison@lanarkstnichs.fsnet.co.uk]   01555 662600

Law (E-mail: a.mcivor@lanarkpresbytery.org)
Anne McIvor (Miss) SRD BD   1996   2003
The Manse, 53 Lawhill Road, Law, Carluke ML8 5EZ
[E-mail: annemcivor@btinternet.com]   01698 373180

Lesmahagow: Abbeygreen (E-mail: d.carmichael@lanarkpresbytery.org)

| David S. Carmichael | 1982 | Abbeygreen Manse, Lesmahagow, Lanark ML11 0DB | 01555 893384 |

[E-mail: david@abbeygreen.freeserve.co.uk]

Lesmahagow: Old (H) See Coalburn
Libberton and Quothquan See Black Mount
Lowther See Glencaple
Symington See Cairngryffe

The Douglas Valley Church (Church office: Tel/Fax: 01555 850000) (E-mail: b.kerr@lanarkpresbytery.org; Website: www.douglasvalleychurch.org)

| Bryan Kerr BA BD | 2002 | The Manse, Douglas, Lanark ML11 0RB | 01555 851213 |

[E-mail: bryan@douglasvalleychurch.org]

Coogan, J. Melvyn LTh	1992	2004	(Carstairs with Carstairs Junction)	9E Silverdale Gardens, Largs KA30 9LT	01475 675955
Cowell, Susan G. (Miss) BA BD	1986	1998	(Budapest)	3 Gavel Lane, Regency Gardens, Lanark ML11 9FB	01555 665509
Craig, William BA LTh	1974	1997	(Cambusbarron: The Bruce Memorial)	31 Heathfield Drive, Blackwood, Lanark ML11 9SR	01555 893710
Easton, David J.C. MA BD	1965	2005	(Glasgow: Burnside-Blairbeth)	Rowanbank, Cormiston Road, Quothquan, Biggar ML12 6ND	01899 308459
				[E-mail: deaston@btinternet.com]	
Fox, George H.	1959	1977	(Coalsnaughton)	Brachead House, Crossford, Carluke ML8 5NQ	01555 860716
Jones, Philip H.	1968	1987	(Bishopbriggs: Kenmure)	39 Bankhouse, 62 Abbeygreen, Lesmahagow, Lanark ML11 0JS	
McCormick, W. Cadzow MA BD	1943	1983	(Glasgow: Maryhill Old)	82 Main Street, Symington, Biggar ML12 6LJ	01899 308221
McMahon, Robert J. BD	1959	1997	(Crossford with Kirkfieldbank)	7 Ridgepark Drive, Lanark ML11 9PG	01555 663844
Pacitti, Stephen A. MA	1963	2003	(Black Mount with Culter with Libberton and Quothquan)	157 Nithsdale Road, Glasgow G41 5RD	0141-423 5792
Seath, Thomas J.G.	1980	1992	(Motherwell: Manse Road)	Flat 11, Wallace Court, South Vennel, Lanark ML11 7LL	01555 665399
Stewart, John M. MA BD	1964	2001	(Johnstone with Kirkpatrick Juxta)	5 Rathmor Road, Biggar ML12 6QG	01899 220398
Young, David A.	1972	2003	(Kirkmuirhill)	15 Mannachie Rise, Forres IV36 2US	01309 672849
				[E-mail: youngdavid@aol.com]	

(14) GREENOCK AND PAISLEY

Meets on the second Tuesday of September, December, February and May, on the fourth Tuesday of October and March, and on the third Tuesday of June.

| Clerk: | REV. ALAN H. WARD MA BD | 72 Forsyth Street, Greenock PA16 8SX | 01475 790849 |

[E-mail: auuv93@dsl.pipex.com]

| Presbytery Office: | 'Homelea', Faith Avenue, Bridge of Weir PA11 3SX | 01505 615033 |

Barrhead: Arthurlie (H) (0141-881 8442)

| James S.A. Cowan BD DipMin | 1986 | 1998 | 10 Arthurlie Avenue, Barrhead, Glasgow G78 2BU | 0141-881 3457 |

[E-mail: jim_cowan@ntlworld.com]

Barrhead: Bourock (H) (0141-881 9813)
Maureen Leitch (Mrs) BA BD
1995
14 Maxton Avenue, Barrhead, Glasgow G78 1DY
[E-mail: maureen.leitch@ntlworld.com]
0141-881 1462

Barrhead: South and Levern (H) (0141-881 7825)
Morris M. Dutch BD BA
1998
3 Colinbar Circle, Barrhead, Glasgow G78 2BE
[E-mail: mnmdutch@yahoo.co.uk]
0141-571 4059

Bishopton (H)
Gayle J.A. Taylor (Mrs) MA BD
1999
The Manse, Newton Road, Bishopton PA7 5JP
[E-mail: gayletaylor@tiscali.co.uk]
01505 862161

Bridge of Weir: Freeland (H) (01505 612610)
Kenneth N. Gray BA BD
1988
15 Lawmarnock Crescent, Bridge of Weir PA11 3AS
[E-mail: aandkgray@btinternet.com]
01505 690918

Bridge of Weir: St Machar's Ranfurly (01505 614364)
Suzanne Dunleavy (Miss) BD DipEd
1990   1992
9 Glen Brae, Bridge of Weir PA11 3BH
[E-mail: suzanne.dunleavy@virgin.net]
01505 612975

Caldwell
John Campbell MA BA BSc
1973   2000
The Manse of Caldwell, Uplawmoor, Glasgow G78 4AL
[E-mail: campbelljohn@talktalk.net]
01505 850215

Elderslie Kirk (H) (01505 323348)
Robin N. Allison BD DipMin
1994   2005
282 Main Road, Elderslie, Johnstone PA5 9EF
[E-mail: robin@mansemob.org]
01505 321767

Erskine (0141-812 4620)
Ian W. Bell LTh
1990   1998
The Manse, 7 Leven Place, Linburn, Erskine PA8 6AS
[E-mail: rviwbepc@ntlworld.com]
0141-581 0955

Gourock: Old Gourock and Ashton (H)
Frank J. Gardner MA
1966   1979
90 Albert Road, Gourock PA19 1NN
[E-mail: frankgardner@oldgourockashton.freeserve.co.uk]
01475 631516

Gourock: St John's (H)
P. Jill Clancy (Mrs) BD
2000
6 Barrhill Road, Gourock PA19 1JX
[E-mail: jgibson@totalise.co.uk]
01475 632143

Greenock: Ardgowan
Alan H. Ward MA BD
1978   2002
72 Forsyth Street, Greenock PA16 8SX
[E-mail: alanhward@ntlworld.com]
01475 790849

Greenock: East End David J. McCarthy BSc BD	1985	2003	29 Denholm Street, Greenock PA16 8RH [E-mail: ncdgreenockeast@uk.uumail.com]	01475 722111
Eileen Manson (Mrs) DipCE (Aux)	1994	2005	1 Cambridge Avenue, Gourock PA19 1XT [E-mail jrmanson@ntlworld.com]	01475 632401
Greenock: Finnart St Paul's (H) David Mill KJSJ MA BD	1978	1979	105 Newark Street, Greenock PA16 7TW [E-mail: minister@finnart-stpauls-church.org]	01475 639602
Greenock: Mount Kirk Francis E. Murphy BEng DipDSE BD	2006		76 Finnart Street, Greenock PA16 8HJ [E-mail: francis_e_murphy@hotmail.com]	01475 722338
Greenock: Old West Kirk C. Ian W. Johnson MA BD	1997		39 Fox Street, Greenock PA16 8PD [E-mail: ian.ciw.johnson@btinternet.com]	01475 888277
Greenock: St George's North W. Douglas Hamilton BD	1975	1986	67 Forsyth Street, Greenock PA16 8SX [E-mail: revwdhamilton@lycos.co.uk]	01475 724003
Greenock: St Luke's (H) William C. Hewitt BD DipPS	1977	1994	50 Ardgowan Street, Greenock PA16 8EP [E-mail: william.hewitt@ntlworld.com]	01475 721048
Greenock: St Margaret's (01475 781953) Isobel J.M. Kelly (Miss) MA BD DipEd	1974	1998	105 Finnart Street, Greenock PA16 8HN	01475 786590
Greenock: St Ninian's Allan G. McIntyre BD	1985		5 Auchmead Road, Greenock PA16 0PY [E-mail: agmcintyre@lineone.net]	01475 631878
Greenock: Wellpark Mid Kirk Alan K. Sorensen BD MTh DipMin FSAScot	1983	2000	101 Brisbane Street, Greenock PA16 8PA [E-mail: alansorensen@beeb.net]	01475 721741
Houston and Killellan (H) Vacant			The Manse of Houston, Main Street, Houston, Johnstone PA6 7EL	01505 612569
Howwood David Stewart MA DipEd BD MTh	1977	2001	The Manse, Beith Road, Howwood, Johnstone PA9 1AS [E-mail: revdavidst@aol.com]	01505 703678
Inchinnan (H) (0141-812 1263) Marilyn MacLaine (Mrs) LTh	1995		The Manse, Inchinnan, Renfrew PA4 9PH	0141-812 1688

Charge / Name	Ord.	Ind.	Address / E-mail	Telephone
Inverkip (H) Elizabeth A. Crumlish (Mrs) BD	1995	2002	The Manse, Langhouse Road, Inverkip, Greenock PA16 0BJ [E-mail: lizcrumlish@aol.com]	01475 521207
Johnstone: High (H) (01505 336303) Ann C. McCool (Mrs) BD DSD IPA ALCM	1989	2001	76 North Road, Johnstone PA5 8NF [E-mail: ann.mccool@ntlworld.com]	01505 320006
Johnstone: St Andrew's Trinity May Bell (Mrs) LTh	1998	2002	The Manse, 7 Leven Place, Linburn, Erskine PA8 6AS [E-mail: may.bell@ntlbusiness.com]	0141-581 7352
Johnstone: St Paul's (H) (01505 321632) Alistair N. Shaw MA BD	1982	2003	9 Stanley Drive, Brookfield, Johnstone PA5 8UF [E-mail: alistairn@shaw98.freeserve.co.uk]	01505 320060
Kilbarchan: East John Owain Jones MA BD FSAScot	1981	2002	East Manse, Church Street, Kilbarchan, Johnstone PA10 2JQ [E-mail: johnowainjones@ntlworld.com]	01505 702621
Kilbarchan: West Arthur Sherratt BD	1994		West Manse, Shuttle Street, Kilbarchan, Johnstone PA10 2JR [E-mail: arthur.sherratt@ntlworld.com]	01505 342930
Kilmacolm: Old (H) (01505 873911) John C. Christie BSc BD	1990	2005	10 Cumberland Avenue, Helensburgh G84 8QG [E-mail: jcc_larchview@btinternet.com]	01436 674078 07711 336392 (Mbl)
Kilmacolm: St Columba (H) R. Douglas Cranston MA BD	1986	1992	6 Churchill Road, Kilmacolm PA13 4LH [E-mail: robert.cranston@tiscali.co.uk]	01505 873271
Langbank (T) Vacant			The Manse, Main Road, Langbank, Port Glasgow PA14 6XP	01475 540252
Linwood (H) (01505 328802) T. Edward Marshall BD	1987		49 Napier Street, Linwood, Paisley PA3 3AJ [E-mail: marshall1654@hotmail.com]	01505 325131
Lochwinnoch (T) Vacant			1 Station Rise, Lochwinnoch PA12 4NA	01505 843484

Neilston (0141-881 9445)
Vacant — The Manse, Neilston Road, Neilston, Glasgow G78 3NP — 0141-881 1958

Paisley: Abbey (H) (Tel: 0141-889 7654; Fax: 0141-887 3929)
Alan D. Birss MA BD   1979 1988 — 15 Main Road, Castlehead, Paisley PA2 6AJ [E-mail: alan.birss@paisleyabbey.com] — 0141-889 3587

Paisley: Castlehead
Esther J. Ninian (Miss) MA BD   1993 1998 — 28 Fulbar Crescent, Paisley PA2 9AS [E-mail: esther.ninian@ntlworld.com] — 01505 812304

Paisley: Glenburn (0141-884 2602)
Vacant — 10 Hawick Avenue, Paisley PA2 9LD — 0141-884 4903

Paisley: Laigh Kirk (H) (0141-889 7700)
David J. Thom BD   2000 2005 — 18 Oldhall Road, Paisley PA1 3HL [E-mail: david@thelaigh.co.uk] — 0141-882 2277

Paisley: Lylesland (H) (0141-561 7139)
Andrew W. Bradley BD   1975 1998 — 36 Potterhill Avenue, Paisley PA2 8BA — 0141-884 2882
Greta Gray (Miss) DCS — 67 Crags Avenue, Paisley PA3 6SG — 0141-884 6178

Paisley: Martyrs' (0141-889 6603)
Vacant — 12 Low Road, Paisley PA2 6AG — 0141-889 2182

Paisley: Oakshaw Trinity (H) (Tel: 0141-887 4647; Fax: 0141-848 5139)
G. Hutton B. Steel MA BD   1982 2006 — 9 Hawkhead Road, Paisley PA1 3ND [E-mail: hutton.steel@ntlworld.com] — 0141-887 0884

Paisley: St Columba Foxbar (H) (01505 812377)
Vacant — 13 Corsebar Drive, Paisley PA2 9QD — 0141-889 9988

Paisley: St James' (0141-889 2422)
Eleanor J. McMahon (Miss) BEd BD   1994 — 38 Woodland Avenue, Paisley PA2 8BH [E-mail: eleanor.mcmahon@ntlworld.com] — 0141-884 3246

Paisley: St Luke's (H)
D. Ritchie M. Gillon BD DipMin   1994 — 31 Southfield Avenue, Paisley PA2 8BX [E-mail: revgillon@hotmail.com] — 0141-884 6215

Paisley: St Mark's Oldhall (H) (0141-882 2755)
Robert G. McFarlane BD   2001 2005 — 36 Newtyle Road, Paisley PA1 3JX [E-mail: robertmcf@hotmail.com] — 0141-889 4279

Paisley: St Ninian's Ferguslie (E) (0141-887 9436) (New Charge Development)
William Wishart DCS — 10 Stanely Drive, Paisley PA2 6HE [E-mail: bill@saintninians.co.uk] — 0141-884 4177

Paisley: Sandyford (Thread Street) (0141-889 5078)
David Kay BA BD MTh — 1974 — 6 Southfield Avenue, Paisley PA2 8BY [E-mail: davidkay@ntlworld.com] — 0141-884 3600

Paisley: Sherwood Greenlaw (H) (0141-889 7060)
Alasdair F. Cameron BD CA — 1986 1993 — 5 Greenlaw Drive, Paisley PA1 3RX [E-mail: alcamron@lineone.net] — 0141-889 3057

Paisley: Wallneuk North (0141-889 9265)
Vacant — 27 Mansionhouse Road, Paisley PA1 3RG — 0141-581 1505

Port Glasgow: Hamilton Bardrainney
James A. Munro BA BD DMS — 1979 2002 — 80 Bardrainney Avenue, Port Glasgow PA14 6HD [E-mail: james@jmunro33.wanadoo.co.uk] — 01475 701213

Port Glasgow: St Andrew's (H)
Andrew T. MacLean BA BD — 1980 1993 — St Andrew's Manse, Barr's Brae, Port Glasgow PA14 5QA [E-mail: standrews.pg@mac.com] — 01475 741486

Port Glasgow: St Martin's
Archibald Speirs BD — 1995 2006 — Clunebraehead, Clune Brae, Port Glasgow PA14 5SL [E-mail: archiespeirs1@aol.com] — 01475 704115

Renfrew: North (0141-885 2154)
E. Lorna Hood (Mrs) MA BD — 1978 1979 — 1 Alexandra Drive, Renfrew PA4 8UB [E-mail: lorna.hood@ntlworld.com] — 0141-886 2074

Renfrew: Old
Alexander C. Wark MA BD STM — 1982 1998 — 31 Gibson Road, Renfrew PA4 0RH [E-mail: alecwark@yahoo.co.uk] — 0141-886 2005

Renfrew: Trinity (H) (0141-885 2129)
Stuart C. Steell BD CertMin — 1992 — 25 Paisley Road, Renfrew PA4 8JH [E-mail: ssren@tiscali.co.uk] — 0141-886 2131

Skelmorlie and Wemyss Bay
William R. Armstrong BD — 1979 — 3A Montgomerie Terrace, Skelmorlie PA17 5TD [E-mail: william@warmst.freeserve.co.uk] — 01475 520703

Name	(Charge)			Address	Tel
Abeledo, Benjamin J.A. BTh DipTh PTh	Army Chaplain	1991	2000	12 St Catherine's Close, Colchester, Essex CO2 9PP [E-mail: Babeledo@aol.com]	01206 364100
Alexander, Douglas N. MA BD	(Bishopton)	1961	1999	West Morningside, Main Road, Langbank, Port Glasgow PA4 6XP	01475 540249
Black, Janette M.K. (Mrs) BD	(Assistant: Paisley: Oakshaw Trinity)	1993	2006	5 Craigiehall Avenue, Erskine PA8 7DB	0141-812 0794
Bruce, A. William MA	(Fortingall and Glenlyon)	1942	1981	75 Union Street, Greenock PA16 8BG	01475 787534
Cameron, Margaret (Miss) DCS	(Deaconess)			2 Rowans Gate, Paisley PA2 6RD	0141-840 2479
Chestnut, Alexander MBE BA				5 Douglas Street, Largs KA30 8PS	01475 674168
Copland, Agnes M. (Mrs) MBE DCS	(Greenock: St Mark's Greenbank)	1948	1987	3 Craigmuschat Road, Gourock PA19 1SE	01475 631870
Cubie, John P. MA BD	(Deacon)	1961	1999	36 Winram Place, St Andrews KY16 8XH	01334 474708
Hetherington, Robert M. MA BD	(Caldwell)	1966	2002	31 Brodie Park Crescent, Paisley PA2 6EU [E-mail: r.hether@tiscali.co.uk]	0141-848 6560
Johnston, Mary (Miss) DCS	(Deaconess)			19 Lounsdale Drive, Paisley PA2 9ED	0141-849 1615
Lowe, Edwin MA BD	(Caldwell)	1950	1988	45 Duncarnock Crescent, Neilston, Glasgow G78 3HH [E-mail: edwin.lowe50@ntlworld.com]	0141-580 5726
McBain, Margaret (Miss) DCS				33 Quarry Road, Paisley PA2 7RD	0141-884 2920
MacColl, James C. BSc BD	(Johnstone: St Andrew's Trinity)	1966	2002	Greenways, Winton, Kirkby Stephen, Cumbria CA17 4HL	01768 372290
MacColl, John BD DipMin	Teacher: Religious Education	1989	2001	1 Birch Avenue, Johnstone PA5 0DD	01505 326506
McCully, M. Isobel (Miss) DCS	(Deacon)			10 Broadstone Avenue, Port Glasgow PA14 5BB [E-mail: mi.mccully@tesco.net]	01475 742240
Macdonald, Alexander MA BD	(Neilston)	1966	2006	35 Lochore Avenue, Paisley PA3 4BY [E-mail: alexmacdonald42@aol.com]	0141-889 0066
McDonald, Alexander BA CMIWSC DUniv	Department of Ministry	1968	1988	36 Alloway Grove, Paisley PA2 7DQ [E-mail: amcdonald1@ntlworld.com]	0141-560 1937
McLachlan, Fergus C. BD	Hospital Chaplain: Inverclyde Royal	1982	2002	46 Queen Square, Glasgow G41 2AZ [E-mail: fergus.mclachlan@rh.scot.nhs.uk]	0141-423 3830
Marshall, Fred J. BA	(Bermuda)	1946	1992	Flat 4, Varrich House, 7 Church Hill, Edinburgh EH10 4BG	0131-446 0205
Moffett, James R. BA	(Paisley: St Matthew's)	1942	1979	Arran 6, Hutton Park Care Home, 60 Greenock Road, Largs KA30 8PD	
Montgomery, Robert A. MA	(Quarrier's Village: Mount Zion)	1955	1992	11 Myreton Avenue, Kilmacolm PA13 4LJ	01505 872028
Nicol, Joyce M. (Mrs) BA DCS	(Deacon)			93 Brisbane Street, Greenock PA16 8NY [E-mail: jnicol@surefish.co.uk]	01475 723235
O'Leary, Thomas BD	(Lochwinnoch)	1983	1998	1 Carters Place, Irvine KA12 0BU	
Palmer, S.W. BD	(Kilbarchan: East)	1980	1991	4 Bream Place, Houston PA6 7ZJ	01505 615280
Prentice, George BA BTh	(Paisley: Martyrs)	1964	1997	46 Victoria Gardens, Corsebar Road, Paisley PA2 9AQ [E-mail: g.prentice04@virgin.net]	0141-842 1585
Pyper, J. Stewart BA	(Greenock: St George's North)	1951	1986	39 Brisbane Street, Greenock PA16 8NR	01475 793234
Scott, Ernest M. MA	(Port Glasgow: St Andrew's)	1957	1992	17 Brueacre Road, Wemyss Bay PA18 6ER [E-mail: ernie.scott@ernest70.fsnet.co.uk]	01475 522267
Simpson, James H. BD LLB	(Greenock: Mount Kirk)	1964	2004	82 Harbourside, Inverkip, Greenock PA16 0BF	01475 520582
Smillie, Andrew M. LTh	(Langbank)	1990	2005	7 Turnbull Avenue, West Freeland, Erskine PA8 7DL	0141-812 7030
Stone, W. Vernon MA BD	(Langbank)	1949	1985	36 Woodrow Court, Port Glasgow Road, Kilmacolm KA13 4QA [E-mail: stone@kilmacolm.fsnet.co.uk]	01505 872644
Whyte, John H. MA	(Gourock: Ashton)	1946	1986	6 Castle Levan Manor, Cloch Road, Gourock PA19 1AY	01475 636788

GREENOCK ADDRESSES

Gourock
Old Gourock and Ashton — 41 Royal Street
St John's — Bath Street x St John's Road

Greenock
Ardgowan — 31 Union Street

Finnart St Paul's — Newark Street x Bentinck Street
Mount Kirk — Dempster Street at Murdieston Park
Old West Kirk — Esplanade x Campbell Street
St George's North — George Square
St Luke's — 9 Nelson Street
St Margaret's — Finch Road x Kestrel Crescent
St Ninian's — Warwick Road, Larkfield
Wellpark Mid Kirk — Cathcart Square

Port Glasgow
Hamilton
Bardrainney — Bardrainney Avenue x Auchenbothie Road
St Andrew's — Princes Street
St Martin's — Mansion Avenue

PAISLEY ADDRESSES

Abbey — Town Centre
Castlehead — Canal Street
Glenburn — Nethercraigs Drive off Glenburn Road
Laigh Kirk — Causeyside Street

Lylesland — Rowan Street off Neilston Road
Martyrs' — Broomlands
Oakshaw Trinity — Churchill
St Columba Foxbar — Amochrie Road, Foxbar
St James' — Underwood Road
St Luke's — Neilston Road

St Mark's Oldhall — Glasgow Road, Ralston
St Ninian's Ferguslie — Blackstoun Road
Sandyford (Thread St) — Gallowhill
Sherwood Greenlaw — Glasgow Road
Wallneuk North — off Renfrew Road

(16) GLASGOW

Meets at New Govan Church, Govan Cross, Glasgow, on the second Tuesday of each month, except June when the meeting takes place on the second last Tuesday. In January, July and August there is no meeting.

Clerk: REV. DAVID W. LUNAN MA BD   260 Bath Street, Glasgow G2 4JP   0141-332 6606 (Tel/Fax)
[E-mail: akph84@uk.uumail.com]
[E-mail: cofs.glasgow.presbytery@uk.uumail.com]
[E-mail: glasgowpresbytery@yahoo.co.uk]

Hon. Treasurer: DOUGLAS BLANEY   [E-mail: glasgowpres@yahoo.co.uk]
Text Phone: 18002 0141-331 2962

1 **Banton linked with Twechar**
Alexandra Farrington LTh   2003   Manse of Banton, Kilsyth, Glasgow G65 0QL   01236 826129
[E-mail: sandra.farrington@virgin.net]

2 **Bishopbriggs: Kenmure**
Iain A. Laing MA BD   1971   1992   5 Marchfield, Bishopbriggs, Glasgow G64 3PP   0141-772 1468
[E-mail: iain@ilaing.fsnet.co.uk]

No.	Congregation / Minister	Year	Year	Address / E-mail	Telephone
3	**Bishopbriggs: Springfield** Ian Taylor BD ThM	1995	2006	64 Miller Drive, Bishopbriggs, Glasgow G64 1FB [E-mail: taylorian@btinternet.com]	0141-772 1540
4	**Broom (0141-639 3528)** Vacant Margaret McLellan (Mrs) DCS			3 Laigh Road, Newton Mearns, Glasgow G77 5EX 18 Broom Road East, Newton Mearns, Glasgow G77 5SD	0141-639 2916 (Tel) 0141-639 3528 (Fax) 0141-639 6853
5	**Burnside–Blairbeth (0141-634 4130)** Vacant Colin Ogilvie DCS			59 Blairbeth Road, Burnside, Glasgow G73 4JD 32 Upper Bourtree Court, Glasgow G73 4HT	0141-634 1233 0141-569 2750
6	**Busby (0141-644 2073)** Jeremy C. Eve BSc BD	1998		17A Carmunnock Road, Busby, Glasgow G76 8SZ [E-mail: jerry.eve@btinternet.com]	0141-644 3670
7	**Cadder (0141-772 7436)** Graham S. Finch MA BD	1977	1999	6 Balmuildy Road, Bishopbriggs, Glasgow G64 3BS [E-mail: graham@gsf57.plus.com]	0141-772 1363
8	**Cambuslang: Flemington Hallside** Neil Glover	2005		103 Overton Road, Cambuslang, Glasgow G72 7XA [E-mail: neil@naglover.plus.com]	0141-641 1049 07779 280074 (Mbl)
9	**Cambuslang: Old** Lee Messeder BD PgDipMin	2003		74 Stewarton Drive, Cambuslang, Glasgow G72 8DG [E-mail: messeder.74@tiscali.co.uk]	0141-641 3261
10	**Cambuslang: St Andrew's** Vacant James Birch PGDip FRSA FIOC (Aux)	2001		37 Brownside Road, Cambuslang, Glasgow G72 8NH 1 Kirkhill Grove, Cambuslang, Glasgow G72 8EH	0141-641 3847 0141-583 1722
11	**Cambuslang: Trinity St Paul's** Eileen M. Ross (Mrs) BD MTh	2005		4 Glasgow Road, Cambuslang, Glasgow G72 7BW [E-mail: revemr@yahoo.co.uk]	0141-641 1699
12	**Campsie (01360 310939)** David J. Torrance BD DipMin	1993		19 Redhills View, Lennoxtown, Glasgow G66 7BL [E-mail: torrance@fish.co.uk]	01360 312527
13	**Chryston (H)** Martin A.W. Allen MA BD ThM David J. McAdam BSc BD (Assoc)	1977 1990	 2000	Main Street, Chryston, Glasgow G69 9LA [E-mail: allensall@hotmail.com] 12 Dunellan Crescent, Moodiesburn, Glasgow G69 0GA [E-mail: dmca29@aol.com]	0141-779 1436 01236 870472

14	**Eaglesham (01355 302047)**			
	Lynn M. McChlery BA BD	2005	The Manse, Cheapside Street, Eaglesham, Glasgow G76 0NS [E-mail: lsmcchlery@btinternet.com]	01355 303495
15	**Fernhill and Cathkin**			
	Margaret McArthur BD DipMin	1995 2002	82 Blairbeth Road, Rutherglen, Glasgow G73 4JA	0141-634 1508
16	**Gartcosh (H) (01236 873770) linked with Glenboig (01236 875625)**			
	Alexander M. Fraser BD DipMin	1985	26 Inchknock Avenue, Gartcosh, Glasgow G69 8EA [E-mail: sandyfraser2@hotmail.com]	01236 872274
17	**Giffnock: Orchardhill (0141-638 3604)**			
	Chris Vermeulen DipLT BTh MA	1986 2005	23 Huntly Avenue, Giffnock, Glasgow G46 6LW [E-mail: chris@orchardhill.org.uk]	0141-620 3734
	Daniel Frank BA MDiv DMin (Assoc)	2003 2006	106 Ormonde Crescent, Glasgow G44 3SW	0141-586 0875
18	**Giffnock: South (0141-638 2599)**			
	Edward V. Simpson BSc BD	1972 1983	5 Langtree Avenue, Whitecraigs, Glasgow G46 7LN [E-mail: eddie.simpson3@ntlworld.com]	0141-638 8767 (Tel) 0141-620 0605 (Fax)
19	**Giffnock: The Park**			
	Calum D. Macdonald BD	1993 2001	41 Rouken Glen Road, Thornliebank, Glasgow G46 7JD [E-mail: parkhoose@msn.com]	0141-638 3023
20	**Glenboig** See Gartcosh			
21	**Greenbank (H) (0141-644 1841)**			
	Jeanne Roddick BD	2003	Greenbank Manse, 38 Eaglesham Road, Clarkston, Glasgow G76 7DJ [E-mail: jeanne.roddick@ntlworld.com]	0141-644 1395 (Tel) 0141-644 4804 (Fax)
22	**Kilsyth: Anderson**			
	Charles M. MacKinnon BD	1989 1999	Anderson Manse, Kingston Road, Kilsyth, Glasgow G65 0HR [E-mail: cm.ccmackinnon@tiscali.co.uk]	01236 822345
23	**Kilsyth: Burns and Old**			
	Robert Sloan BD	1997 2005	The Grange, Glasgow Road, Kilsyth, Glasgow G65 9AE [E-mail: robertsloan@scotnet.co.uk]	01236 823116
24	**Kirkintilloch: Hillhead**			
	Audrey Jamieson BD MTh	2004	64 Waverley Park, Kensington Gate, Kirkintilloch, Glasgow G66 2BP [E-mail: audrey.jamieson@btinternet.com]	0141-776 6270

#	Charge / Minister			Address	Telephone
25	**Kirkintilloch: St Columba's (H)** David M. White BA BD	1988	1992	14 Crossdykes, Kirkintilloch, Glasgow G66 3EU [E-mail: david.m.white@ntlworld.com]	0141-578 4357
26	**Kirkintilloch: St David's Memorial Park (H)** Bryce Calder MA BD	1995	2001	2 Roman Road, Kirkintilloch, Glasgow G66 1EA [E-mail: ministry100@aol.com]	0141-776 1434
27	**Kirkintilloch: St Mary's** Mark E. Johnstone MA BD	1993	2001	St Mary's Manse, 60 Union Street, Kirkintilloch, Glasgow G66 1DH [E-mail: mark.johnstone2@ntlworld.com]	0141-776 1252
28	**Lenzie: Old (H)** Douglas W. Clark LTh	1993	2000	41 Kirkintilloch Road, Lenzie, Glasgow G66 4LB [E-mail: douglaswclark@hotmail.com]	0141-776 2184
29	**Lenzie: Union (H)** Daniel J.M. Carmichael MA BD	1994	2003	1 Larch Avenue, Lenzie, Glasgow G66 4HX [E-mail: djm@carmichael39.fsnet.co.uk]	0141-776 3831
30	**Maxwell Mearns Castle (Tel/Fax: 0141-639 5169)** David C. Cameron BD CertMin	1993		122 Broomfield Avenue, Newton Mearns, Glasgow G77 5JR [E-mail: maxwellmearns@hotmail.com]	0141-616 0642
31	**Mearns (H) (0141-639 6555)** Joseph A. Kavanagh BD DipPTh MTh	1992	1998	Manse of Mearns, Newton Mearns, Glasgow G77 5DE [E-mail: mearnskirk@hotmail.com]	0141-616 2410 (Tel/Fax)
32	**Milton of Campsie (H)** Vacant			33 Birdston Road, Milton of Campsie, Glasgow G66 8BX	01360 310548 (Tel/Fax)
33	**Netherlee (H)** Thomas Nelson BSc BD	1992	2002	25 Ormonde Avenue, Glasgow G44 3QY [E-mail: tomnelson@ntlworld.com]	0141-585 7502 (Tel/Fax)
34	**Newton Mearns (H) (0141-639 7373)** Angus Kerr BD CertMin ThM DMin	1983	1994	28 Waterside Avenue, Newton Mearns, Glasgow G77 6TJ [E-mail: thechurch@churchatthecross.co.uk]	0141-616 2079
35	**Rutherglen: Old (H)** Alexander Thomson BSc BD MPhil PhD	1973	1985	31 Highburgh Drive, Rutherglen, Glasgow G73 3RR [E-mail: alexander.thomson6@btopenworld.com]	0141-647 6178
36	**Rutherglen: Stonelaw (0141-647 5113)** Alistair S. May LLB BD PhD	2002		80 Blairbeth Road, Rutherglen, Glasgow G73 4JA [E-mail: alistair.may@ntlworld.com]	0141-583 0157

No.	Charge / Minister			Address	Telephone
37	**Rutherglen: Wardlawhill** Ian Walker BD MEd DipMS	1973	2003	26 Parkhill Drive, Rutherglen, Glasgow G73 2PW [E-mail: walk102822@aol.com]	0141-647 1374
38	**Rutherglen: West** John W. Drummond MA BD	1971	1986	12 Albert Drive, Rutherglen, Glasgow G73 3RT	0141-569 8547
39	**Stamperland (0141-637 4999) (H)** George C. MacKay BD CertMin	1994	2004	109 Ormonde Avenue, Glasgow G44 3SN [E-mail: g.mackay3@btinternet.com]	0141-637 4976 (Tel/Fax)
40	**Stepps (H)** Neil Buchanan BD	1991	2005	2 Lenzie Road, Stepps, Glasgow G33 6DX [E-mail: neil.buchanan@talk21.com]	0141-779 5746
41	**Thornliebank (H)** Robert M. Silver BA BD	1995		19 Arthurlie Drive, Giffnock, Glasgow G46 6UR	0141-620 2133
42	**Torrance (T) (01360 620970)** Nigel L. Barge BSc BD	1991		27 Campbell Place, Meadow Rise, Torrance, Glasgow G64 4HR [E-mail: nigel@nbarge.freeserve.co.uk]	01360 622379
43	**Twechar** See Banton				
44	**Williamwood** Vacant			125 Greenwood Road, Clarkston, Glasgow G76 7LL	0141-571 7949
45	**Glasgow: Anderston Kelvingrove (0141-221 9408)** John A. Coutts BTh	1984	2004	16 Royal Terrace, Glasgow G3 7NY [E-mail: john.coutts1@btinternet.com]	0141-332 7704
46	**Glasgow: Baillieston Mure Memorial (0141-773 1216)** Allan S. Vint BSc BD	1989	1996	28 Beech Avenue, Baillieston, Glasgow G69 6LF [E-mail: allan@vint.co.uk]	0141-771 1217
47	**Glasgow: Baillieston St Andrew's (0141-771 6629)** Vacant			55 Station Park, Baillieston, Glasgow G69 7XY	0141-771 1791
48	**Glasgow: Balshagray Victoria Park** Campbell Mackinnon BSc BD	1982	2001	20 St Kilda Drive, Glasgow G14 9JN [E-mail: cmackinnon@ntlworld.com]	0141-954 9780
49	**Glasgow: Barlanark Greyfriars** David I.W. Locke MA MSc BD	2000		4 Rhindmuir Grove, Glasgow G69 6NE [E-mail: revdavidlocke@ntlworld.com]	0141-771 1240

50 Glasgow: Battlefield East (H) (0141-632 4206)
Alan C. Raeburn MA BD   1971   110 Mount Annan Drive, Glasgow G44 4RZ   0141-632 1514
                                        [E-mail: acraeburn@hotmail.com]

51 Glasgow: Blawarthill
Ian M.S. McInnes BD DipMin   1995   1997   46 Earlbank Avenue, Glasgow G14 9HL   0141-579 6521
                                                [E-mail: ian.liz1@ntlworld.com]

52 Glasgow: Bridgeton St Francis in the East (H) (L) (Church House: Tel: 0141-554 8045)
Howard R. Hudson MA BD   1982   1984   10 Albany Drive, Rutherglen, Glasgow G73 3QN   0141-587 8667
                                                [E-mail: howard.hudson@ntlworld.com]
Margaret S. Beaton (Miss) DCS   64 Gardenside Grove, Fernlee Meadows, Carmyle,   0141-646 2297
                                                Glasgow G32 8EZ

53 Glasgow: Broomhill (0141-334 2540)
William B. Ferguson BA BD   1971   1987   27 St Kilda Drive, Glasgow G14 9LN   0141-959 3204
                                                [E-mail: revferg@aol.com]

54 Glasgow: Calton Parkhead (0141-554 3866)
Vacant   98 Drumover Drive, Glasgow G31 5RP   0141-556 2520

55 Glasgow: Cardonald (0141-882 6264)
Vacant   133 Newtyle Road, Paisley PA1 3LB   0141-561 1891

56 Glasgow: Carmunnock
G. Gray Fletcher BSc BD   1989   2001   The Manse, 161 Waterside Road, Carmunnock, Glasgow G76 9AJ   0141-644 1578 (Tel/Fax)
                                                [E-mail: gray.fletcher@virgin.net]

57 Glasgow: Carmyle linked with Kenmuir Mount Vernon
Murdo Maclean BD CertMin   1997   1999   3 Meryon Road, Glasgow G32 9NW   0141-778 2625
                                                [E-mail: murdo.maclean@ntlworld.com]

58 Glasgow: Carntyne Old linked with Eastbank
Ronald A.S. Craig BAcc BD   1983   211 Sandyhills Road, Glasgow G32 9NB   0141-778 1286

59 Glasgow: Carnwadric (E)
Graeme K. Bell BA BD   1983   62 Loganswell Road, Glasgow G46 8AX   0141-638 5884
                                                [E-mail: slbellmrs@yahoo.co.uk]

60 Glasgow: Castlemilk East (H) (0141-634 2444)
John D. Miller BA BD DD   1971   15 Castlemilk Drive, Glasgow G45 9TL   0141-631 1244
                                                [E-mail: john@miller15.freeserve.co.uk]

61	**Glasgow: Castlemilk West (H) (0141-634 1480)**
	Vacant

156 Old Castle Road, Glasgow   G44 5TW

0141-637 5451

62	**Glasgow: Cathcart Old**
	Neil W. Galbraith BD CertMin	1987	1996

21 Courthill Avenue, Cathcart, Glasgow   G44 5AA
[E-mail: revneilgalbraith@hotmail.com]

0141-633 5248   (Tel/Fax)

63	**Glasgow: Cathcart Trinity (H) (0141-637 6658)**
	Ian Morrison BD	1991	2003

82 Merrylee Road, Glasgow   G43 2QZ
[E-mail: iain77@tiscali.co.uk]

0141-633 3744

Wilma Pearson (Mrs) BD (Assoc)   2004

90 Newlands Road, Glasgow   G43 2JR

0141-632 2491

64	**Glasgow: Cathedral (High or St Mungo's)**
	Vacant

65	**Glasgow: Colston Milton (0141-772 1922)**
	Vacant

118 Birsay Road, Glasgow   G22 7QP

0141-772 1958

66	**Glasgow: Colston Wellpark (H)**
	Christine M. Goldie (Miss) LLB BD MTh	1984	1999

16 Bishop's Gate Gardens, Colston, Glasgow   G21 1XS
[E-mail: christine.goldie@ntlworld.com]

0141-589 8866

67	**Glasgow: Cranhill (H) (0141-774 3344)**
	Muriel B. Pearson (Ms) MA BD		2004

31 Lethamhill Crescent, Glasgow   G33 2SH
[E-mail: muriel@pearsonL.fsnet.co.uk]

0141-770 6873
07951 888860 (Mbl)

68	**Glasgow: Croftfoot (H) (0141-637 3913)**
	John M. Lloyd BD CertMin	1984	1986

20 Victoria Road, Burnside, Rutherglen, Glasgow   G73 3QG
[E-mail: john.lloyd@croftfootparish.co.uk]

0141-647 5524

69	**Glasgow: Dennistoun Blackfriars (H) linked with Dennistoun Central (H)**
	Gordon A. McCracken BD CertMin DMin	1988	2006

45 Broompark Drive, Glasgow   G31 2JB
[E-mail: gordonangus@btinternet.com]

0141-550 2921

70	**Glasgow: Dennistoun Central (H) (0141-554 1350)** See Dennistoun Blackfriars

71	**Glasgow: Drumchapel Drumry St Mary's (0141-944 1998)**
	Brian S. Sheret MA BD DPhil	1982	2002

8 Fruin Road, Glasgow   G15 6SQ

0141-944 4493

72	**Glasgow: Drumchapel St Andrew's (0141-944 3758)**
	John S. Purves LLB BD	1983	1984

6 Firdon Crescent, Glasgow   G15 6QQ
[E-mail: john.s.purves@talk21.com]

0141-944 4566

73	**Glasgow: Drumchapel St Mark's**		146 Garscadden Road, Glasgow G15 6PR	0141-944 5440
	Vacant			
74	**Glasgow: Eastbank** See Carntyne Old			
75	**Glasgow: Easterhouse St George's and St Peter's (E) (0141-781 0800)**			
	Malcolm Cuthbertson BA BD	1984	3 Barony Gardens, Baillieston, Glasgow G69 6TS	0141-573 8200 (Tel)
			[E-mail: malcuth@aol.com]	0141-773 4878 (Fax)
76	**Glasgow: Eastwood**			
	Moyna McGlynn (Mrs) BD PhD	1999	54 Mansewood Road, Glasgow G43 1TL	0141-632 0724
			[E-mail: moyna_mcglynn@hotmail.com]	
77	**Glasgow: Gairbraid (H)**			
	Vacant			
78	**Glasgow: Gardner Street (GE)**			
	Roderick Morrison MA BD	1974	148 Beechwood Drive, Glasgow G11 7DX	0141-563 2638
79	**Glasgow: Garthamlock and Craigend East (E)**			
	Valerie J. Duff (Miss) DMin	1993	175 Tillycairn Drive, Garthamlock, Glasgow G33 5HS	0141-774 6364
			[E-mail: valduff@fish.co.uk]	
	Marion Buchanan (Mrs) MA DCS		2 Lenzie Road, Stepps, Glasgow G33 6DX	0141-779 5746
80	**Glasgow: Gorbals**			
	Ian F. Galloway BA BD	1976	44 Riverside Road, Glasgow G43 2EF	0141-649 5250
			[E-mail: ianfgalloway@msn.com]	
81	**Glasgow: Govan Old (Tel/Fax: 0141-440 2466)**			
	Norman J. Shanks MA BD DD	1983	1 Marchmont Terrace, Glasgow G12 9LT	0141-339 4421
			[E-mail: mshnks@shanks1942.freeserve.co.uk]	
82	**Glasgow: Govanhill Trinity**			
	Lily F. McKinnon MA BD	1993	12 Carleton Gate, Giffnock, Glasgow G46 6NU	0141-637 8399
83	**Glasgow: High Carntyne (0141-778 4186)**			
	Joan Ross (Miss) BSc BD PhD	1999	163 Lethamhill Road, Glasgow G33 2SQ	0141-770 9247
84	**Glasgow: Hillington Park (H)**			
	John B. MacGregor BD	1999	61 Ralston Avenue, Glasgow G52 3NB	0141-882 7000
			[E-mail: johnmacgregor494@msn.com]	
85	**Glasgow: Househillwood St Christopher's**			
	May M. Allison (Mrs) BD	1988	12 Leverndale Court, Crookston, Glasgow G53 7SJ	0141-810 5953
			[E-mail: revmayallison@hotmail.com]	

86	**Glasgow: Hyndland (H) (Website: www.hyndlandparishchurch.org)**				
	Craig Lancaster MA BD	2004		24 Hughenden Gardens, Glasgow G12 9YH [E-mail: craig@hyndlandparishchurch.org]	0141-334 1002
87	**Glasgow: Ibrox (H) (0141-427 0896)**				
	C. Blair Gillon BD	1975	1980	3 Dargarvel Avenue, Glasgow G41 5LD [E-mail: cb@gillon3.freeserve.co.uk]	0141-427 1282 (Tel/Fax) 07786 326905 (Mbl)
88	**Glasgow: John Ross Memorial Church for Deaf People**				
	(Voice Text: 0141-420 1759; Text Only: 0141-429 6682; Fax: 0141-429 6860; ISDN Video Phone: 0141-418 0579)				
	Richard C. Durno DSW CQSW (Aux)	1989	1998	31 Springfield Road, Bishopbriggs, Glasgow G64 1PJ (Voice/Text) [E-mail: richard.durno@ntlworld.com] [Website: www.deafconnections.co.uk]	0141-772 1052
89	**Glasgow: Jordanhill (Tel: 0141-959 2496)**				
	Colin C. Renwick BMus BD	1989	1996	96 Southbrae Drive, Glasgow G13 1TZ [E-mail: jordchurch@btconnect.com]	0141-959 1310
90	**Glasgow: Kelvin Stevenson Memorial (0141-339 1750)**				
	Gordon Kirkwood BSc BD	1987	2003	94 Hyndland Road, Glasgow G12 9PZ [E-mail: gordonkirkwood@tiscali.co.uk]	0141-334 5352
91	**Glasgow: Kelvinside Hillhead**				
	Jennifer Macrae (Mrs) MA BD	1998	2000	39 Athole Gardens, Glasgow G12 9BQ [E-mail: jmacrae@supanet.com]	0141-339 2865
92	**Glasgow: Kenmuir Mount Vernon** See Carmyle				
93	**Glasgow: King's Park (H) (0141-632 1131)**				
	Vacant			1101 Aikenhead Road, Glasgow G44 5SL	0141-637 2803
94	**Glasgow: Kinning Park (0141-427 3063)**				
	Margaret H. Johnston (Miss) BD	1988	2000	168 Arbroath Avenue, Cardonald, Glasgow G52 3HH	0141-810 3782
95	**Glasgow: Knightswood St Margaret's (H)**				
	Adam Dillon BD ThM	2003		26 Airthrey Avenue, Glasgow G14 9LJ [E-mail: adamdillon@ntlworld.com]	0141-959 7075
96	**Glasgow: Langside (0141-632 7520)**				
	David N. McLachlan BD	1985	2004	36 Madison Avenue, Glasgow G44 5AQ [E-mail: dmclachlan77@hotmail.com]	0141-637 0797
97	**Glasgow: Lansdowne**				
	Roy J.M. Henderson MA BD DipMin	1987	1992	18 Woodlands Drive, Glasgow G4 9EH [E-mail: roy.henderson7@ntlworld.com]	0141-339 2794

98   Glasgow: Linthouse St Kenneth's
Vacant

99   Glasgow: Lochwood (H) (0141-771 2649)
Stuart M. Duff BA   1997
42 Rhindmuir Road, Swinton, Glasgow G69 6AZ
[E-mail: stuart@duff58.freeserve.co.uk]
0141-773 2756

100   Glasgow: Martyrs', The
Ewen MacLean BA BD   1995
30 Louden Hill Road, Robroyston, Glasgow G33 1GA
[E-mail: revewenmaclean@tiscali.co.uk]
0141-558 7451

101   Glasgow: Maryhill (H) (0141-946 3512)
Anthony J.D. Craig BD   1987
111 Maxwell Avenue, Glasgow G61 1HT
[E-mail: craig.glasgow@ntlworld.com]
0141-570 0642

James Hamilton DCS
6 Beckfield Gate, Robroyston, Glasgow G33 1SW
0141-558 3195

102   Glasgow: Merrylea (0141-637 2009)
David P. Hood BD CertMin DipIOB(Scot)   1997   2001
4 Pilmuir Avenue, Glasgow G44 3HX
[E-mail: dphood3@ntlworld.com]
0141-637 6700

103   Glasgow: Mosspark (H) (0141-882 2240)
Alan H. MacKay BD   1974   2002
396 Kilmarnock Road, Glasgow G43 2DJ
[E-mail: alanhmackay@aol.com]
0141-632 1247

104   Glasgow: Mount Florida (H) (0141-561 0307)
Hugh M. Wallace MA BD   1980   1987
90 Mount Annan Drive, Glasgow G44 4RZ
[E-mail: revhugh@hotmail.com]
0141-589 5381

105   Glasgow: New Govan (H)
Vacant
19 Dumbreck Road, Glasgow G41 5LJ
0141-427 3197

106   Glasgow: Newlands South (H) (0141-632 3055)
John D. Whiteford MA BD   1989   1997
24 Monreith Road, Glasgow G43 2NY
[E-mail: jwhiteford@hotmail.com]
0141-632 2588

107   Glasgow: North Kelvinside
William G. Alston   1961   1971
41 Mitre Road, Glasgow G14 9LE
[E-mail: williamalston@hotmail.com]
0141-954 8250

108   Glasgow: Partick South (H)
Alan L. Dunnett LLB BD   1994   1997
17 Munro Road, Glasgow G13 1SQ
[E-mail: dustydunnett@prtck2.freeserve.co.uk]
0141-959 3732

109 Glasgow: Partick Trinity (H)
Stuart J. Smith BEng BD — 1994 — 99 Balshagray Avenue, Glasgow G11 7EQ [E-mail: ssmith99@ntlworld.com] — 0141-576 7149

110 Glasgow: Penilee St Andrew's (H) (0141-882 2691)
Alastair J. Cherry BA BD — 1982 2003 — 80 Tweedsmuir Road, Glasgow G52 2RX [E-mail: alastair.j.cherry@btopenworld.com] — 0141-882 2460

111 Glasgow: Pollokshaws
Margaret Whyte (Mrs) BA BD — 1988 2000 — 33 Mannering Road, Glasgow G41 3SW [E-mail: whytes@fish.co.uk] — 0141-649 0458

112 Glasgow: Pollokshields (H)
David R. Black MA BD — 1986 1997 — 36 Glencairn Drive, Glasgow G41 4PW [E-mail: davidblack@fish.co.uk] — 0141-423 4000

113 Glasgow: Possilpark
W.C. Campbell-Jack BD MTh PhD — 1979 2003 — 108 Erradale Street, Lambhill, Glasgow G22 6PT [E-mail: c.c-j@homecall.co.uk] — 0141-336 6909

114 Glasgow: Priesthill and Nitshill
Douglas M. Nicol BD CA — 1987 1996 — 36 Springkell Drive, Glasgow G41 4EZ [E-mail: dougiemnicol@aol.com] — 0141-427 7877

115 Glasgow: Queen's Park (0141-423 3654)
T. Malcolm F. Duff MA BD — 1985 2000 — 5 Alder Road, Glasgow G43 2UY [E-mail: malcolm.duff@ntlworld.com] — 0141-637 5491

116 Glasgow: Renfield St Stephen's (Tel: 0141-332 4293; Fax: 0141-332 8482)
Peter M. Gardner MA BD — 1988 2002 — 101 Hill Street, Glasgow G3 6TY [E-mail: pmg1@renfieldststephens.org] — 0141-353 0349

117 Glasgow: Robroyston (New Charge Development)
Hilary McDougall MA BD — 2004 — 86 Stewarton Drive, Cambuslang, Glasgow G72 8DJ [E-mail: ncdrobroyston@uk.uumail.com] — 0141-586 4310

118 Glasgow: Ruchazie (0141-774 2759)
William F. Hunter MA BD — 1986 1999 — 18 Borthwick Street, Glasgow G33 3UU [E-mail: billhunter@dsl.pipex.com] — 0141-774 6860

119 Glasgow: Ruchill (0141-946 0466)
John C. Matthews MA BD — 1992 — 9 Kirklee Road, Glasgow G12 0RQ [E-mail: jmatthews@kirklee9.fsnet.co.uk] — 0141-357 3249

120 Glasgow: St Andrew's East (0141-554 1485)
Janette G. Reid (Miss) BD   1991   43 Broompark Drive, Glasgow G31 2JB   0141-554 3620
[E-mail: janettegreid@aol.com]

121 Glasgow: St Columba (GE) (0141-221 3305)
Donald Michael MacInnes BD   2002   1 Reelick Avenue, Peterson Park, Glasgow G13 4NF   0141-952 0948
[E-mail: minister@highlandcathedral.org]

122 Glasgow: St David's Knightswood (0141-959 1024) (E-mail: dringlis@stdavidschurch.freeserve.co.uk)
W. Graham M. Thain LLB BD   1988   1999   60 Southbrae Drive, Glasgow G13 1QD   0141-959 2904
[E-mail: graham_thain@btopenworld.com]

123 Glasgow: St Enoch's Hogganfield (H) (Tel: 0141-770 5694; Fax: 0870 284 0084) (E-mail: church@st-enoch.org.uk) (Website: www.st-enoch.org.uk)
Vacant   43 Smithycroft Road, Glasgow G33 2RH   0141-770 7593
0870 284 0085 (Fax)

124 Glasgow: St George's Tron (0141-221 2141)
William J.U. Philip MB ChB MRCP BD   2004   12 Dargarvel Avenue, Glasgow G41 5LU   0141-427 1402
[E-mail: wp@wphilip.com]

125 Glasgow: St James' (Pollok) (0141-882 4984)
John Mann BSc MDiv DMin   2004   30 Ralston Avenue, Glasgow G52 3NA   0141-883 7405
[E-mail: drjohnmann@hotmail.com]   0141-883 2488

126 Glasgow: St John's Renfield (0141-339 7021) (Website: www.stjohns-renfield.org.uk)
Dugald J.R. Cameron BD DipMin MTh   1990   1999   26 Leicester Avenue, Glasgow G12 0LU   0141-339 4637
[E-mail: dcameron@stjohns-renfield.org.uk]

127 Glasgow: St Luke's and St Andrew's
Ian C. Fraser BA BD   1983   1995   10 Chalmers Street, Glasgow G40 2HA   0141-556 3883
[E-mail: stluke@cqm.co.uk]

128 Glasgow: St Margaret's Tollcross Park
George M. Murray LTh   1995   31 Kenmuir Avenue, Sandyhills, Glasgow G32 9LE   0141-778 5060
[E-mail: george.murray@ntlworld.com]

129 Glasgow: St Nicholas' Cardonald
Vacant   104 Lamington Road, Glasgow G52 2SE   0141-882 2065

130 Glasgow: St Paul's (0141-770 8559)
Vacant   38 Lochview Drive, Glasgow G33 1QF   0141-770 9611

131 Glasgow: St Rollox
James K. Torrens MB ChB BD   2005   42 Melville Gardens, Bishopbriggs, Glasgow G64 3DE   0141-589 8563
[E-mail: jk@torrens37.freeserve.co.uk]

No. / Church / Minister	Ordained	Inducted	Address	Phone
132 Glasgow: St Thomas' Gallowgate Peter R. Davidge BD MTh	2003		8 Helenvale Court, Glasgow G31 4LB [E-mail: rev.davidge@virgin.net]	0141-554 6816
133 Glasgow: Sandyford Henderson Memorial (H) (L) C. Peter White BVMS BD	1974	1997	66 Woodend Drive, Glasgow G13 1TG [E-mail: revcpw@ntlworld.com]	0141-954 9013
134 Glasgow: Sandyhills Graham T. Atkinson MA BD	2006		60 Wester Road, Glasgow G32 9JJ [E-mail: gtatkinson@btopenworld.com]	0141-778 2174
135 Glasgow: Scotstoun (T) Richard Cameron BD DipMin	2000		15 Northland Drive, Glasgow G14 9BE [E-mail: rev.rickycam@virgin.net]	0141-959 4637
136 Glasgow: Shawlands (0141-649 2012) Stephen A. Blakey BSc BD	1977	2005	29 St Ronan's Drive, Glasgow G41 3SQ [E-mail: shawlandskirk@aol.com]	0141-649 2034
137 Glasgow: Sherbrooke St Gilbert's (H) (0141-427 1968) Thomas L. Pollock BA BD MTh FSAScot JP	1982	2003	114 Springkell Avenue, Glasgow G41 4EW [E-mail: tompollock06@aol.com]	0141-427 2094
138 Glasgow: Shettleston Old (T) (H) (0141-778 2484) Vacant			57 Mansionhouse Road, Mount Vernon, Glasgow G32 0RP	0141-778 8904
139 Glasgow: South Carntyne (H) (0141-778 1343) Vacant			47 Broompark Drive, Glasgow G31 2JB	0141-554 3275
140 Glasgow: South Shawlands (T) (0141-649 4656) Fiona Gardner (Mrs) BD MA MLitt	1997	2000	391 Kilmarnock Road, Glasgow G43 2NU [E-mail: fionandcolin@hotmail.com]	0141-632 0013
141 Glasgow: Springburn (H) (0141-557 2345) Alan A. Ford BD AIBScot Helen Hughes (Miss) DCS	1977	2000	3 Tofthill Avenue, Bishopbriggs, Glasgow G64 3PA [E-mail: springburnchurch@dsl.pipex.com] 2/2 Burnbank Terrace, Glasgow G20 6UQ	0141-762 1844 07710 455737 (Mbl) 0141-333 9459
142 Glasgow: Temple Anniesland (0141-959 1814) John Wilson BD	1985	2000	76 Victoria Park Drive North, Glasgow G14 9PJ [E-mail: jwilson@crowroad0.freeserve.co.uk]	0141-959 5835
143 Glasgow: Toryglen (H) Sandra Black (Mrs) BSc BD	1988	2003	36 Glencairn Drive, Glasgow G41 4PW [E-mail: sblack@fish.co.uk]	0141-423 0867

144 Glasgow: Trinity Possil and Henry Drummond
Richard G. Buckley BD MTh — 1990 1995 — 50 Highfield Drive, Glasgow G12 0HL [E-mail: richardbuckley@hotmail.com] — 0141-339 2870

145 Glasgow: Tron St Mary's
William T.S. Wilson BSc BD — 1999 — 3 Hurly Hawkin', Bishopbriggs, Glasgow G64 1YL [E-mail: william.mairi@ntlworld.com] — 0141-772 8555

146 Glasgow: Victoria Tollcross
Vacant — 228 Hamilton Road, Glasgow G32 9QU — 0141-778 2413

147 Glasgow: Wallacewell
Ian C. MacKenzie MA BD — 1970 2005 — 21 Wilson Street, Motherwell ML1 1NP [E-mail: iancmackenzie@ntlworld.com] — 01698 301230

148 Glasgow: Wellington (H) (0141-339 0454)
M. Leith Fisher MA BD — 1967 1990 — 27 Kingsborough Gardens, Glasgow G12 9NH [E-mail: fleith@fish.co.uk] — 0141-339 3627

149 Glasgow: Whiteinch (New Charge Development) (Website: www.whiteinchcofs.co.uk)
Alan McWilliam BD — 1993 2000 — 65 Victoria Park Drive South, Glasgow G14 9NX [E-mail: alan@whiteinchcofs.co.uk] — 0141-576 9020

150 Glasgow: Yoker (T)
Karen E. Hendry BSc BD — 2005 — 15 Coldingham Avenue, Glasgow G14 0PX [E-mail: karen@hendry-k.fsnet.co.uk] — 0141-952 3620

Name	Years	Charge	Address	Telephone
Aitken, Andrew J. BD APhS MTh PhD	1951 1981	(Tollcross Central with Park)	18 Dorchester Avenue, Glasgow G12 0EE	0141-357 1617
Alexander, Eric J. MA BD	1958 1997	(St George's Tron)	PO Box 14725, St Andrews KY16 8WB	ex-directory
Allan, A.G.	1959 1989	(Candlish Polmadie)	30 Dalrymple Drive, East Mains, East Kilbride, Glasgow G74 4LF	01355 226190
Anderson, Colin M. BA BD STM MPhil	1968 2003	(Inverness: St Stephen's with The Old High)	83 Marlborough Avenue, Glasgow G11 7BT	0141-357 2838
Barr, Alexander C. MA BD	1950 1992	(St Nicholas' Cardonald)	25 Fisher Drive, Phoenix Park, Paisley PA1 2TP	0141-848 5941
Barr, John BSc PhD BD	1958 1979	(Kilmacolm: Old)	31 Kelvin Court, Glasgow G12 0AD	0141-357 4338
Beattie, John A.	1951 1984	(Dalmuir Overtoun)	c/o 15 Kelvindale Gardens, Glasgow G20 8DW	0141-946 5978
Bell, John L. MA BD FRSCM DUniv	1978 1988	(Iona Community)	Flat 2/1, 31 Lansdowne Crescent, Glasgow G20 6NH	0141-334 0688
Brain, Ernest J.	1955 1985	(Liverpool: St Andrew's)	14 Chesterfield Court, 1240 Great Western Road, Glasgow G12 0BJ	0141-357 2249
Brain, Isobel J. (Mrs) MA	1987 1997	(Ballantrae)	14 Chesterfield Court, 1240 Great Western Road, Glasgow G12 0BJ	0141-357 2249
Brice, Dennis G. BSc BD	1981	(Taiwan)	18 Hermitage Avenue, Benfleet, Essex SS7 1TQ	01702 555333
Brough, Robin BA	1968 2002	(Whitburn: Brucefield)	'Kildavanan', 10 Printers Lea, Lennoxtown, Glasgow G66 7GF	01360 310223
Bryden, William A. BD	1977 1984	(Yoker Old with St Matthew's)	145 Bearsden Road, Glasgow G13 1BS	0141-959 5213
Bull, Alister W. BD DipMin	1994 2001	Head of Chaplaincy Service	Chaplaincy Centre Office, First Floor, Queen Mother's Hospital, Yorkhill Division, Dalnair Street, Glasgow G3 8SJ [E-mail: alister.bull@yorkhill.scot.nhs.uk]	0141-201 0595
Campbell, A. Iain MA DipEd	1961 1997	(Busby)	430 Clarkston Road, Glasgow G44 3QF [E-mail: bellmac@sagainternet.co.uk]	0141-637 7460
Cartlidge, G.R.G. MA BD STM	1977 1993	Religious Education	5 Briar Grove, Newlands, Glasgow G43 2TG	0141-637 3228

Name	Years	Charge / Appointment	Address	Tel.
Chester, Stephen J. BA BD	1999	RE Teacher, International Christian College	42 Drumlochy Road, Ruchazie, Glasgow G33 3RE	0141-774 4666
Coley, Richard LTh	1971 2004	(Glasgow: Victoria Tollcross)	146 Hamilton Road, Glasgow G32 9QR	0141-764 1259
Collard, John K. MA BD	1986 2003	Presbytery Congregational Facilitator (Stirling: Allan Park South with the Church of the Holy Rude)	1 Nelson Terrace, East Kilbride, Glasgow G74 2EY	01355 520093
Coull, Morris C. BD	1974 2006	(Presbytery Clerk)	112 Greenock Road, Largs KA30 8PF	01475 686838
Cunningham, Alexander MA BD	1961 2002		The Glen, 103 Glenmavis Road, Airdrie ML6 0PQ	01236 763012
Cunningham, James S.A. MA BD BLitt PhD	1992 2000	(Glasgow: Barlanark Greyfriars)	'Kirkland', 5 Inveresk Place, Coatbridge ML5 2DA	01236 421541
Currie, Robert MA	1955 1990	(Community Minister)	Flat 3/2, 13 Redlands Road, Glasgow G12 0SJ	0141-334 5111
Dunnett, Linda (Mrs) DCS		Frontier Youth Trust, West of Scotland Development Officer	75B Argyle Street, Glasgow G3 8DS	0141-204 4800 (Office)
Ferguson, James B. LTh	1972 2002	(Lenzie: Union)	17 Munro Road, Glasgow G13 1SQ	0141-959 3732
Finlay, William P. MA BD	1969 2000	(Glasgow: Townhead Blochairn)	3 Bridgeway Place, Kirkintilloch, Glasgow G66 3HW	0141-588 5868
Galloway, Kathy (Mrs) BD	1977 2002	Leader: Iona Community	High Corrie, Brodick, Isle of Arran KA27 8JB	01770 810689
Gibson, H. Marshall MA BD	1957 1996	(St Thomas' Gallowgate)	20 Hamilton Park Avenue, Glasgow G12 8UU	0141-357 4079
Gibson, Michael BD STM	1974 2001	(Giffnock: The Park)	39 Burnthroom Drive, Glasgow G69 7XG	0141-771 0749
Goss, Alister BD	1975 1998	Industrial Chaplain	12 Mile End Park, Pocklington, York YO42 2TH	01475 638944
Grant, David I.M. MA BD	1969 2003	(Dalry: Trinity)	79 Weymouth Crescent, Gourock PA19 1HR	0141-770 7186
Gray, Christine (Mrs)		(Deaconess)	8 Mossbank Drive, Glasgow G33 1LS	0141-571 1008
Gregson, Elizabeth M. (Mrs) BD	1996 2001	(Drumchapel: St Andrew's)	11 Woodside Avenue, Thornliebank, Glasgow G46 7HR	0141-563 1918
Grimstone, A. Frank MA	1949 1986	(Calton Parkhead)	17 Westfields, Bishopbriggs, Glasgow G64 3PL	0141-954 1009
Haley, Derek BD DPS	1960 1999	(Chaplain: Gartnavel Royal)	144C Howth Drive, Parkview Estate, Anniesland, Glasgow G13 1RL	0141-942 9281
Harper, Anne J.M. (Miss) BD STM MTh CertSocPsych	1979 1990	Hospital Chaplain	9 Kinnaird Crescent, Bearsden, Glasgow G61 2BN	01505 862466
Harvey, W. John BA BD	1965 2002	(Edinburgh: Corstorphine Craigsbank)	122 Greenock Road, Bishopton PA7 5AS	0141-429 3774
Haughton, Frank MA BD	1942 2000	(Kirkintilloch: St Mary's)	501 Shields Road, Glasgow G41 2RF	0141-777 6802
Hope, Evelyn P. (Miss) BA BD	1990 1998	(Wishaw: Thornlie)	64 Regent Street, Kirkintilloch, Glasgow G66 1JF	0141-649 1522
Houston, Thomas C.	1975 2004	(Glasgow: Priesthill and Nitshill)	Flat 0/1, 48 Moss-side Road, Glasgow G41 3UA	0141-641 1117
Hunter, Alastair G. MSc BD	1976 1980	University of Glasgow	110 Elder Crescent, Drumsagart, Glasgow G72 7GL	0141-429 1687
Hutcheson, J. Murray MA	1943 1987	(Possilpark)	487 Shields Road, Glasgow G41 2RG	01236 631168
Hutchison, Henry MA BEd BD MLitt PhD LLCM AMusLCM	1948 1993		88 Ainslie Road, Kildrum, Cumbernauld, Glasgow G67 2ED	0141-637 2766
Irvine, Euphemia H.C. (Mrs) BD	1972 1988	(Carmunnock)	4A Briar Grove, Newlands, Glasgow G43 2TG	0141-812 2777
Johnston, Robert W.M. MA BD STM	1964 1999	(Milton of Campsie)	32 Baird Drive, Bargarran, Erskine PA8 6BB	0141-931 5862
Johnstone, H. Martin J. MA BD MTh PhD	1989 2000	(Temple Anniesland)	13 Kilmardinny Crescent, Bearsden, Glasgow G61 3NP	0141-423 3760
Keddie, David A. MA BD	1966 2005	Urban Priority Areas Adviser	3 Herries Road, Glasgow G41 4DE; 21 Ilay Road, Bearsden, Glasgow G61 1QG [E-mail: revked@hotmail.com]	0141-577 1408
Lang, I. Pat (Miss) BSc	1996 2003	(Glasgow: Linthouse St Kenneth's)	37 Crawford Drive, Glasgow G15 6TW	0141-944 2240 (Mbl) 07890 752877
Langlands, Cameron H. BD MTh ThM	1995 1999	(Dunoon: The High Kirk)	G1/28 Plantation Park Gardens, Glasgow G51 1NW	0141-334 5411
Levison, C.L. MA BD	1972 1998	Hospital Chaplain	5 Deaconsbank Avenue, Stewarton Road, Glasgow G46 7UN	0141-620 3492
Lewis, E.M.H. MA	1962 1993	Health Care Chaplaincy Training and Development Officer (Drumchapel St Andrew's)	7 Cleveden Place, Glasgow G12 0HG	0141-334 5411
Liddell, Matthew MA BD	1943 1982	(St Paul's (Outer High) and St David's (Ramshorn))	17 Traquair Drive, Glasgow G52 2TB	0141-810 3776

Name	Ord	Ind	Appointment	Address	Tel.
Lodge, Bernard P. BD	1967	2004	(Glasgow: Govanhill Trinity)	6 Darluith Park, Brookfield, Johnstone PA5 8DD	01505 320378
Lunan, David W. MA BD	1970	2002	Presbytery Clerk	142 Hill Street, Glasgow G3 6UA	0141-353 3687
Lyall, Ann (Miss) DCS	1950	2001	Chaplain: Lodging House Mission	117 Barlia Drive, Glasgow G45 0AY	0141-631 3643
McAreavey, William BA	1990	1998	(Kelvin Stevenson Memorial)	c/o Bisset, Heronbrook, Ladeside, Newmilns KA16 9BE	
Macaskill, Marjory (Mrs) LLB BD	1971	1993	Chaplain: University of Strathclyde	44 Forfar Avenue, Cardonald, Glasgow G52 3JQ	0141-883 5956
MacBain, Ian BD			(Coatbridge: Coatdyke)	24 Thornyburn Drive, Baillieston, Glasgow G69 7ER	0141-771 7030
MacDonald, Anne (Miss) BA DCS	2001	2006	Healthcare Chaplain: Levendale Hospital	510 Crookston Road, Glasgow G53 7TU	0141-211 6695
Macdonald, Kenneth MA BD			(Auxiliary Minister)	5 Henderland Road, Glasgow G61 1AH	0141-943 1103
MacFadyen, Anne M. (Mrs) BSc BD FSAScot	1995		(Auxiliary Minister)	295 Mearns Road, Glasgow G77 5LT	0141-639 3605
Macfarlane, Thomas G. BSc PhD BD	1956	1992	(South Shawlands)	Flat 0/2, 19 Corrour Road, Glasgow G43 2DY	0141-632 7966
McLachlan, Eric BD MTh	1978	2005	(Cardonald)	268 Dyke Road, Knightswood, Glasgow G13 4QX [E-mail: eric.mclachlan@ntlworld.com]	0141-954 1574
McLaren, D. Muir MA BD MTh PhD	1971	2001	(Mosspark)	House 44, 145 Shawhill Road, Glasgow G43 1SX	0141-770 9611
McLarty, R. Russell MA BD	1985	2006	Regional Interim Minister	38 Lochview Drive, Glasgow G33 1QF	0141-569 5503
McLay, Alastair D. BSc BD	1989	2004	(Glasgow: Shawlands)	183 King's Park Avenue, Glasgow G44 4HZ	
MacLeod, William J. DipTh	1963	1988	(Kirkintilloch St David's Memorial)	42 Hawthorn Drive, Banknock, Bonnybridge FK4 1LF	01324 840667
Macnaughton, J.A. MA BD	1949	1989	(Hyndland)	62 Lauderdale Gardens, Glasgow G12 9QW	0141-339 1294
MacPherson, James B. DCS			(Deacon)	0/1, 104 Cartside Street, Glasgow G42 9TQ	0141-616 6468
MacQuarrie, Stuart BD BSc JP	1984	2001	Chaplain: Glasgow University	The Chaplaincy Centre, University of Glasgow, Glasgow G12 8QQ	0141-330 5419
Martindale, John P.F. BD	1994	2005	(Glasgow: Sandyhills)	50 Springfield Park Road, Burnside, Glasgow G73 3RG	
Mitchell, David BD MSc DipPTheol	1988	1998	Chaplain: Marie Curie Hospice, Glasgow	48 Leglin Wood Drive, Wallacewell Park, Glasgow G21 3PL [E-mail: david.mitchell@mariecurie.org.uk]	0141-558 4679
Moore, William B.	1968	2002	Prison Chaplain: Low Moss	10 South Dumbreck Road, Kilsyth, Glasgow G65 9LX	
Morrice, Alastair M. MA BD	1951	2005	(Rutherglen: Stonelaw)	5 Brechin Road, Kirriemuir DD8 4BX	
Morris, William J. KCVO PhD LLD DD JP	1945	1986	(Glasgow: Cathedral)	1 Whitehill Grove, Newton Mearns, Glasgow G77 5DH	0141-639 6327
Morton, Thomas MA BD LGSM	1961	1997	(Rutherglen: Stonelaw)	54 Greystone Avenue, Burnside, Rutherglen, Glasgow G73 3SW	0141-647 2682
Muir, Fred C. MA BD ThM ARCM	1952	1978	(Stepps)	20 Alexandra Avenue, Stepps, Glasgow G33 6BP	0141-779 2504
Myers, Frank BA	1970	1986	(Springburn)	18 Birmingham Close, Grantham NG31 8SD	01476 574430
Newlands, George M. MA BD PhD	1953	1996	University of Glasgow	12 Jamaica Street North Lane, Edinburgh EH3 6HQ	(Work) 0141-339 8855
Philp, George M. MA	1937	1981	(Sandyford Henderson Memorial)	44 Beech Avenue, Bearsden, Glasgow G61 3EX	0141-942 1327
Philp, Robert A. BA BD	1953	1988	(Stepps: St Andrew's)	Bybrook Nursing Home, Middlehill, Box, Wiltshire SN13 8QP	
Porter, Richard MA	1967	1999	(Govanhill)	47 Braemar Court, Hazelden Gardens, Glasgow G44 3HF	0141-629 2887
Ramsay, W.G.			(Springburn)	53 Kelvinvale, Kirkintilloch, Glasgow G66 1RD [E-mail: billram@btopenworld.com]	0141-776 2915
Reid, Ian M.A. BD	1990	2001	Hospital Chaplain	16 Walker Court, Glasgow G11 6QP	0141-586 9925
Robertson, Archibald MA BD	1957	1999	(Eastwood)	19 Canberra Court, Braidpark Drive, Glasgow G46 6NS	0141-637 7572
Robertson, Blair MA BD ThM	1990	1998	Chaplain: Southern General Hospital	c/o Chaplain's Office, Southern General Hospital, 1345 Govan Road, Glasgow G51 4TF	0141-201 2357
Ross, Donald M. MA	1953	1994	(Industrial Mission Organiser)	14 Cartsbridge Road, Busby, Glasgow G76 8DH	0141-644 2220
Ross, James MA BD	1968	1998	(Kilsyth: Anderson)	53 Turnberry Gardens, Westerwood, Cumbernauld, Glasgow G68 0AY	01236 730501
Saunders, Keith BD	1983	1999	Hospital Chaplain	Western Infirmary, Dumbarton Road, Glasgow G11 6NT	0141-211 2000
Scrimgeour, Alice M. (Miss) DCS			(Deaconess)	265 Golfhill Drive, Glasgow G31 2PB	0141-564 9602
Shackleton, William	1960	1996	(Greenock: Wellpark West)	3 Tynwald Avenue, Burnside, Glasgow G73 4RN	0141-569 9407
Simpson, Neil A. BA BD PhD	1992	2001	(Glasgow: Yoker Old with Yoker St Matthew's)	c/o Glasgow Presbytery Office	

Name	Dates	Charge	Address	Tel
Smith, G. Stewart MA BD STM	1966 2006	(Glasgow: King's Park)	33 Brent Road, Stewartfield, East Kilbride, Glasgow G74 4RA [E-mail: stewart.smith@tinyworld.co.uk]	(Tel/Fax) 01355 226718
Smith, J. Rankine MA BD	1945 1982	(Barmulloch)	44 Middlemuir Road, Lenzie, Glasgow G66 4ND	0141-776 0870
Smith, James S.A.	1956 1991	(Drongan: The Schaw Kirk)	146 Aros Drive, Glasgow G52 1TJ	0141-883 9666
Spence, Elisabeth G.B. (Miss) BD DipEd	1995 2000	Industrial Missioner: Glasgow Area	76 Rylees Crescent, Glasgow G52 4BY [E-mail: scimglasgow@uk.uumail.com]	0141-883 8973
Spencer, John MA BD	1962 2001	(Dumfries: Lincluden with Holywood)	10 Kinkell Gardens, Kirkintilloch, Glasgow G66 2HJ	0141-777 8935
Spiers, John M. LTh MTh	1972 2004	(Giffnock: Orchardhill)	58 Woodlands Road, Thornliebank, Glasgow G46 7JQ	(Tel/Fax) 0141-638 0632
Stevenson, John LTh	1998 2006	(Cambuslang: St Andrew's)	20 Knowehead Gardens, Uddingston, Glasgow G71 7PY [E-mail: j.stevenson83@ntlworld.com]	
Stewart, Diane E. BD	1988 2006	(Milton of Campsie)	4 Miller Gardens, Bishopbriggs, Glasgow G64 1FG [E-mail: destewar@fish.co.uk]	0141-762 1358
Stewart, Norma D. (Miss) MA MEd BD	1977 2000	(Glasgow: Strathbungo Queens Park)	127 Nether Auldhouse Road, Glasgow G43 2YS	0141-637 6956
Sutherland, Denis I.	1963 1995	(Hutchesontown)	56 Lime Crescent, Cumbernauld, Glasgow G67 3PQ	01236 731723
Sutherland, Elizabeth W. (Miss) BD	1972 1996	(Balornock North with Barmulloch)	20 Kirkland Avenue, Blanefield, Glasgow G63 9BZ [E-mail: ewsutherland@aol.com]	01360 770154
Tait, Alexander	1967 1995	(St Enoch's Hogganfield)	129 Lochview Drive, Hogganfield, Glasgow G33 1LN	0141-770 6027
Turner, Angus BD	1976 1998	(Industrial Chaplain)	46 Keir Street, Pollokshields, Glasgow G41 2LA	0141-424 0493
Tuton, Robert M. MA	1957 1995	(Shettleston: Old)	6 Holmwood Gardens, Uddingston, Glasgow G71 7BH	01698 321108
Walker, A.L.	1955 1988	(Trinity Possil and Henry Drummond)	11 Dundas Avenue, Torrance, Glasgow G64 4BD	01360 622281
Walton, Ainslie MA MEd	1954 1995	(University of Aberdeen)	501 Shields Road, Glasgow G41 2RF [E-mail: revainslie@aol.com]	0141-420 3327
White, Elizabeth (Miss) DCS		(Deaconess)	Woodside House, Rodger Avenue, Rutherglen, Glasgow G73 3QZ	
Younger, Adah (Mrs) BD	1978 2004	(Glasgow: Dennistoun Central)	Flat 0/1, 101 Greenhead Street, Glasgow G40 1HR	0141-550 0878

GLASGOW ADDRESSES

Banton	Kelvinhead Road, Banton
Bishopbriggs	
Kenmure	Viewfield Road, Bishopbriggs
Springfield	Springfield Road
Broom	Mearns Road, Newton Mearns
Burnside–Blairbeth	Church Avenue, Burnside
Busby	Church Road, Busby
Cadder	Cadder Road, Glasgow
Cambuslang	
Flemington Hallside	265 Hamilton Road
Old	Cairns Road
St Andrew's	Main Street x Clydeford Road
Trinity St Paul's	Main Street
Campsie	Main Street, Lennoxtown
Chryston	Main Street, Chryston
Eaglesham	Montgomery Street, Eaglesham
Fernhill and Cathkin	Neilvaig Drive
Gartcosh	113 Lochend Road, Gartcosh
Giffnock	
South	Church Road
Orchardhill	Eastwood Toll
The Park	Ravenscliffe Drive
Glenboig	138 Main Street, Glenboig
Greenbank	Eaglesham Road, Clarkston
Kilsyth	
Anderson	Kingston Road
Burns and Old	Church Street
Kirkintilloch	
Hillhead	Newdyke Road
St Columba's	Waterside Road nr Old Aisle Road
St David's Mem Pk	Alexander Street
St Mary's	Cowgate
Lenzie	
Old	Kirkintilloch Road x Garngaber Ave
Union	Moncrieff Ave x Kirkintilloch Road
Maxwell	
Mearns Castle	Waterfoot Road
Mearns	Mearns Road, Newton Mearns
Netherlee	Ormonde Drive x Ormonde Avenue
Newton Mearns	Ayr Road, Newton Mearns
Rutherglen	
Old	Main Street at Queen Street
Stonelaw	Stonelaw Road x Dryburgh Avenue
Wardlawhill	Hamilton Road
West	Glasgow Road nr Main Street
Stamperland	Stamperland Gardens, Clarkston
Stepps	Whitehill Avenue

Thornliebank	61 Spiersbridge Road
Torrance	School Road, Torrance
Twechar	Main Street, Twechar
Williamwood	Vardar Avenue x Seres Ave, Clarkston
Glasgow	
Anderston Kelvingrove	Argyle Street x Elderslie Street
Baillieston	
Mure Memorial	Beech Avenue, Garrowhill
St Andrew's	Bredisholm Road
Balshagray Victoria Pk	Broomhill Cross
Barlanark Greyfriars	Edinburgh Road x Hallhill Road
Battlefield East	1216 Cathcart Road
Blawarthill	Millbrix Avenue
Bridgeton St Francis in the East	26 Queen Mary Street
Broomhill	Randolph Rd x Marlborough Ave
Calton Parkhead	122 Helenvale Street
Cardonald	2155 Paisley Road West
Carmunnock	Kirk Road, Carmunnock
Carmyle	South Carmyle Avenue
Carntyne Old	862 Shettleston Road
Carnwadric	556 Boydstone Road, Thornliebank
Castlemilk	
East	Barlia Terrace
West	Carmunnock Road
Cathcart	
Old	119 Carmunnock Road
Trinity	92 Clarkston Road
Cathedral	Cathedral Square
Colston Milton	Egilsay Crescent
Colston Wellpark	1378 Springburn Road
Cranhill	Bellrock Crescent x Bellrock Street
Croftfoot	Croftpark Ave x Crofthill Road
Dennistoun	
Blackfriars	Whitehill Street
Central	Armadale Street
Drumchapel	
Drumry St Mary's	Drumry Road East
St Andrew's	Garscadden Road
St Mark's	Kinfauns Drive
Eastbank	679 Old Shettleston Road
Easterhouse St George's and St Peter's	Boyndie Street
Eastwood	Mansewood Road
Gairbraid	1517 Maryhill Road
Gardner Street	Gardner Street x Muirpark Street
Garthamlock and Craigend East	Porchester Street x Balveny Street
Gorbals	Eglinton Street x Cumberland Street
Govan Old	866 Govan Road
Govanhill Trinity	Daisy Street nr Allison Street
High Carntyne	358 Carntynehall Road
Hillington Park	24 Berryknowes Road
Househillwood St Christopher's	Meikle Road
Hyndland	Hyndland Road, opp Novar Drive
Ibrox	Carillon Road x Clifford Street
John Ross Memorial	100 Norfolk Street
Jordanhill	Woodend Drive x Munro Road
Kelvin Stevenson Mem	Belmont Street at Belmont Bridge
Kelvinside Hillhead	Huntly Gardens
Kenmuir Mount Vernon	London Road, Mount Vernon
King's Park	242 Castlemilk Road
Kinning Park	Eaglesham Place
Knightswood St Margaret's	Knightswood Cross
Langside	Ledard Road x Lochleven Road
Lansdowne	Gt Western Road at Kelvin Bridge
Linthouse St Kenneth's	9 Skipness Drive
Lochwood	Liff Place
Martyrs', The	St Mungo Avenue
Maryhill	1990 Maryhill Road
Merrylea	78 Merrylee Road
Mosspark	149 Ashkirk Drive
Mount Florida	1123 Cathcart Road
New Govan	Govan Cross
Newlands South	Riverside Road x Langside Drive
North Kelvinside	153 Queen Margaret Drive
Partick	
South	Dumbarton Road
Trinity	20 Lawrence Street
Penilee St Andrew's	Bowfield Cres x Bowfield Avenue
Pollokshaws	223 Shawbridge Street
Pollokshields	Albert Drive x Shields Road
Possilpark	124 Saracen Street
Priesthill and Nitshill	Priesthill Road x Muirshiel Cresc, Dove Street
Queen's Park	170 Queen's Drive
Renfield St Stephen's	260 Bath Street
Robroyston	34 Saughs Road
Ruchazie	Elibank Street x Milncroft Road
Ruchill	Shakespeare Street nr Maryhill Rd
St Andrew's East	681 Alexandra Parade
St Columba	300 St Vincent Street
St David's Knightswood	Boreland Drive nr Lincoln Avenue
St Enoch's Hogganfield	860 Cumbernauld Road
St George's Tron	163 Buchanan Street
St James' (Pollok)	Lyoncross Road x Byrebush Road
St John's Renfield	22 Beaconsfield Road
St Luke's and St Andrew's	Bain Square at Bain Street
St Margaret's Tollcross Pk	179 Braidfauld Street
St Nicholas' Cardonald	Hartlaw Crescent nr Gladsmuir Road
St Paul's	Langdale Street x Greenrig Street
St Rollox	Fountainwell Road
St Thomas' Gallowgate	Gallowgate opp Bluevale Street
Sandyford Henderson Memorial	Kelvinhaugh Street at Argyle Street
Sandyhills	28 Baillieston Rd nr Sandyhills Rd
Scotstoun	Earlbank Avenue x Ormiston Avenue
Shawlands	Shawlands Cross
Sherbrooke St Gilbert's	Nithsdale Rd x Sherbrooke Avenue
Shettleston Old	99–111 Killin Street
South Carntyne	538 Carntyne Road
South Shawlands	Regwood Street x Deanston Drive
Springburn	Springburn Road x Atlas Street
Temple Anniesland	869 Crow Road
Toryglen	Glenmore Ave nr Prospecthill Road
Trinity Possil and Henry Drummond	Crowhill Street x Broadholm Street
Tron St Mary's	128 Red Road
Victoria Tollcross	1134 Tollcross Road
Wallacewell	57 Northgate Road, Ryehill Road x Quarrywood Rd
Wellington	University Ave x Southpark Avenue
Whiteinch	St Paul's R.C. Primary School, Primrose Street
Yoker	Dumbarton Road at Hawick Street

(17) HAMILTON

Meets at Motherwell: Dalziel St Andrew's Parish Church Halls, on the first Tuesday of February, March, May, September, October, November, December; and on the third Tuesday of June.

Presbytery Office:			18 Haddow Street, Hamilton ML3 7HX	01698 286837 (Tel/Fax)
			[E-mail: akph54@uk.uumail.com]	
Clerk:	REV. SHAW J. PATERSON BSc BD		15 Lethame Road, Strathaven ML10 6AD	01357 520019
Depute Clerk:	REV. NORMAN B. McKEE BD		1 Belmont Avenue, Uddingston, Glasgow G71 7AX	01698 814757
Acting Treasurer:	REV. JAMES G. HASTIE CA BD		Chalmers Manse, Quarry Road, Larkhall ML9 1HH	01698 882238

1 **Airdrie: Broomknoll (H)** (Tel: 01236 762101) (E-mail: airdrie-broomknoll@presbyteryofhamilton.co.uk)
linked with Calderbank (E-mail: calderbank@presbyteryofhamilton.co.uk)
Andrew Thomson BA   1976   2000   38 Commonhead Street, Airdrie ML6 6NS   01236 602538
[E-mail: andrewthomson@hotmail.com]

2 **Airdrie: Clarkston** (E-mail: airdrie-clarkston@presbyteryofhamilton.co.uk)
Lilly C. Easton (Mrs)   1999   2005   Clarkston Manse, Forrest Street, Airdrie ML6 7BE   01236 769676

3 **Airdrie: Flowerhill (H)** (E-mail: airdrie-flowerhill@presbyteryofhamilton.co.uk)
Vacant   31 Victoria Place, Airdrie ML6 9BX   01236 763025

4 **Airdrie: High** (E-mail: airdrie-high@presbyteryofhamilton.co.uk)
Vacant   17 Etive Drive, Airdrie ML6 9QL   01236 762010

5 **Airdrie: Jackson** (Tel: 01236 733508) (E-mail: airdrie-jackson@presbyteryofhamilton.co.uk)
Sharon E.F. Colvin (Mrs)   1985   1998   48 Dunrobin Road, Airdrie ML6 8LR   01236 763154
BD LRAM LTCL   [E-mail: dibley@hotmail.com]

6 **Airdrie: New Monkland (H)** (E-mail: airdrie-newmonkland@presbyteryofhamilton.co.uk)
linked with Greengairs (E-mail: greengairs@presbyteryofhamilton.co.uk)
Vacant   3 Dykehead Crescent, Airdrie ML6 6PU   01236 763554

7 **Airdrie: St Columba's** (E-mail: airdrie-stcolumbas@presbyteryofhamilton.co.uk)
Margaret F. Currie BEd BD   1980   1987   52 Kennedy Drive, Airdrie ML6 9AW   01236 763173
[E-mail: margaretfcurrie@btinternet.com]

8 **Airdrie: The New Wellwynd** (E-mail: airdrie-newwellwynd@presbyteryofhamilton.co.uk)
Robert A. Hamilton BA BD   1995   2001   20 Arthur Avenue, Airdrie ML6 9EZ   01236 763022
[E-mail: revrob13@blueyonder.co.uk]

9   Bargeddie (H) (E-mail: bargeddie@presbyteryofhamilton.co.uk)
John Fairful BD   1994   2001   The Manse, Manse Road, Bargeddie, Baillieston, Glasgow G69 6UB   0141-771 1322

10   Bellshill: Macdonald Memorial (E-mail: bellshill-macdonald@presbyteryofhamilton.co.uk) linked with Bellshill: Orbiston
Alan McKenzie BSc BD   1988   2001   32 Adamson Street, Bellshill ML4 1DT   01698 849114
[E-mail: rev.a.mckenzie@btopenworld.com]

11   Bellshill: Orbiston (E-mail: bellshill-orbiston@presbyteryofhamilton.co.uk)   See Bellshill: Macdonald Memorial

12   Bellshill: West (H) (01698 747581) (E-mail: bellshill-west@presbyteryofhamilton.co.uk)
Agnes A. Moore (Miss) BD   1987   2001   16 Croftpark Street, Bellshill ML4 1EY   01698 842877
[E-mail: revamoore@tiscali.co.uk]

13   Blantyre: Livingstone Memorial (E-mail: blantyre-livingstone@presbyteryofhamilton.co.uk)
Colin A. Sutherland LTh   1995   2003   286 Glasgow Road, Blantyre, Glasgow G72 9DB   01698 823794
[E-mail: colin.csutherland@btinternet.com]

14   Blantyre: Old (H) (E-mail: blantyre-old@presbyteryofhamilton.co.uk)
Rosemary A. Smith (Ms) BD   1997   The Manse, Craigmuir Road, High Blantyre, Glasgow G72 9UA   01698 823130
[E-mail: revrosieanne@btopenworld.com]

15   Blantyre: St Andrew's (E-mail: blantyre-standrews@presbyteryofhamilton.co.uk)
J. Peter N. Johnston BSc BD   2001   332 Glasgow Road, Blantyre, Glasgow G72 9LQ   01698 828633
[E-mail: peter.johnston@standrewsblantyre.com]

16   Bothwell (H) (E-mail: bothwell@presbyteryofhamilton.co.uk)
James M. Gibson TD LTh LRAM   1978   1989   Manse Avenue, Bothwell, Glasgow G71 8PQ   01698 853189 (Tel)
[E-mail: jamesmgibson@msn.com]   01698 854903 (Fax)

17   Calderbank   See Airdrie: Broomknoll

18   Caldercruix and Longriggend (H) (E-mail: caldercruix@presbyteryofhamilton.co.uk)
George M. Donaldson MA BD   1984   2005   Main Street, Caldercruix, Airdrie ML6 7RF   01236 842279
[E-mail: gmdonaldson@gmdonaldson.force9.co.uk]

19   Carfin (E-mail: carfin@presbyteryofhamilton.co.uk) linked with Newarthill (E-mail: newarthill@presbyteryofhamilton.co.uk)
Vacant   Church Street, Newarthill, Motherwell ML1 5HS   01698 860316

20   Chapelhall (H) (E-mail: chapelhall@presbyteryofhamilton.co.uk)
Vacant   Russell Street, Chapelhall, Airdrie ML6 8SG   01236 763439

21   Chapelton (E-mail: chapelton@presbyteryofhamilton.co.uk)
linked with Strathaven: Rankin (H) (E-mail: strathaven-rankin@presbyteryofhamilton.co.uk)
Shaw J. Paterson BSc BD   1991   15 Lethame Road, Strathaven ML10 6AD   01357 520019 (Tel)
[E-mail: shaw@patersonsj.freeserve.co.uk]   01357 529316 (Fax)

22 **Cleland (H) (E-mail: cleland@presbyteryofhamilton.co.uk)**
John A. Jackson BD   1997   The Manse, Bellside Road, Cleland, Motherwell   ML1 5NP   01698 860260
[E-mail: johnjackson@uk2.net]

23 **Coatbridge: Blairhill Dundyvan (H) (E-mail: coatbridge-blairhill@presbyteryofhamilton.co.uk)**
Patricia A. Carruth (Mrs) BD   1998   2004   18 Blairhill Street, Coatbridge   ML5 1PG   01236 432304

24 **Coatbridge: Calder (H) (E-mail: coatbridge-calder@presbyteryofhamilton.co.uk)**
Amelia Davidson (Mrs) BD   2004   26 Bute Street, Coatbridge   ML5 4HF   01236 421516
[E-mail: amelia@davidson1293.freeserve.co.uk]

25 **Coatbridge: Clifton (H) (E-mail: coatbridge-clifton@presbyteryofhamilton.co.uk)**
William G. McKaig BD   1979   2003   132 Muiryhall Street, Coatbridge   ML5 3NH   01236 421181

26 **Coatbridge: Middle (E-mail: coatbridge-middle@presbyteryofhamilton.co.uk)**
Vacant   47 Blair Road, Coatbridge   ML5 1JQ   01236 432427

27 **Coatbridge: Old Monkland (E-mail: coatbridge-oldmonkland@presbyteryofhamilton.co.uk)**
Scott Raby LTh   1991   2003   2 Brandon Way, Coatbridge   ML5 5QT   01236 423788
[E-mail: revscott@rabyfamily28.freeserve.co.uk]

28 **Coatbridge: St Andrew's (E-mail: coatbridge-standrews@presbyteryofhamilton.co.uk)**
Fiona Nicolson BA BD   1996   2005   77 Eglinton Street, Coatbridge   ML5 3JF   01236 437271

29 **Coatbridge: Townhead (H) (E-mail: coatbridge-townhead@presbyteryofhamilton.co.uk)**
Ecilo Selemani LTh MTh   1993   2004   Crinan Crescent, Coatbridge   ML5 2LH   01236 702914
[E-mail: eciloselemani@msn.com]

30 **Dalserf (E-mail: dalserf@presbyteryofhamilton.co.uk)**
D. Cameron McPherson BSc BD DMin   1982   Manse Brae, Dalserf, Larkhall   ML9 3BN   01698 882195
[E-mail: dCameronMc@aol.com]

31 **East Kilbride: Claremont (H) (Tel: 01355 238088) (E-mail: ek-claremont@presbyteryofhamilton.co.uk)**
Gordon R. Palmer MA BD STM   1986   2003   17 Deveron Road, East Kilbride, Glasgow   G74 2HR   01355 248526
[E-mail: gkrspalmer@blueyonder.co.uk]

Paul Cathcart DCS   50 Ardler Place, Greenhills, East Kilbride, Glasgow   G75 9HP   01355 521906
[E-mail: paulcathcart@msn.com]

32 **East Kilbride: Greenhills (E) (Tel: 01355 221746) (E-mail: ek-greenhills@presbyteryofhamilton.co.uk)**
John Brewster MA BD DipEd   1988   21 Turnberry Place, East Kilbride, Glasgow   G75 8TB   01355 242564
[E-mail: johnbrewster@blueyonder.co.uk]

33 **East Kilbride: Moncreiff (H) (Tel: 01355 223328) (E-mail: ek-moncreiff@presbyteryofhamilton.co.uk)**
Alastair S. Lusk BD   1974   1983   16 Almond Drive, East Kilbride, Glasgow G74 2HX
01355 238639

34 **East Kilbride: Mossneuk (E) (Tel: 01355 260954) (E-mail: ek-mossneuk@presbyteryofhamilton.co.uk)**
John L. McPake BA BD PhD   1987   2000   30 Eden Grove, Mossneuk, East Kilbride, Glasgow G75 8XU
01355 234196

35 **East Kilbride: Old (H) (E-mail: ek-old@presbyteryofhamilton.co.uk)**
Anne S. Paton BA BD   2001   40 Maxwell Drive, East Kilbride, Glasgow G74 4HJ
[E-mail: annepaton@fsmail.net]
01355 220732

36 **East Kilbride: South (H) (E-mail: ek-south@presbyteryofhamilton.co.uk)**
John C. Sharp BSc BD PhD   1980   7 Clamps Wood, East Kilbride, Glasgow G74 2HB
01355 247993

37 **East Kilbride: Stewartfield (New Charge Development)**
Douglas W. Wallace MA BD   1981   2001   8 Thistle Place, Stewartfield, East Kilbride, Glasgow G74 4RH
01355 260879

38 **East Kilbride: West (H) (E-mail: ek-west@presbyteryofhamilton.co.uk)**
Kenneth A.L. Mayne BA MSc CertEd   1976   2001   4 East Milton Grove, East Kilbride, Glasgow G75 8FN
01355 236639

39 **East Kilbride: Westwood (H) (Tel: 01355 245657) (E-mail: ek-westwood@presbyteryofhamilton.co.uk)**
Kevin Mackenzie BD DPS   1989   1996   16 Inglewood Crescent, East Kilbride, Glasgow G75 8QD
[E-mail: kevin@westwoodmanse.freeserve.co.uk]
01355 223992

40 **Glasford (E-mail: glassford@presbyteryofhamilton.co.uk) linked with Strathaven: East (E-mail: strathaven-east@presbyteryofhamilton.co.uk)**
William T. Stewart   1980   68 Townhead Street, Strathaven ML10 6DJ
01357 521138

41 **Greengairs** See Airdrie: New Monkland

42 **Hamilton: Burnbank (E-mail: hamilton-burnbank@presbyteryofhamilton.co.uk)**
linked with Hamilton: North (H) (E-mail: hamilton-north@presbyteryofhamilton.co.uk)
Raymond D. McKenzie BD   1978   1987   9 South Park Road, Hamilton ML3 6PJ
01698 424609

43 **Hamilton: Cadzow (H) (Tel: 01698 428695) (E-mail: hamilton-cadzow@presbyteryofhamilton.co.uk)**
Arthur P. Barrie LTh   1973   1979   3 Carlisle Road, Hamilton ML3 7BZ
[E-mail: elizabeth@elsiebarrie.wanadoo.co.uk]
01698 421664 (Tel)
01698 891126 (Fax)

44 **Hamilton: Gilmour and Whitehill (H) (E-mail: hamilton-gilmourwhitehill@presbyteryofhamilton.co.uk)**
Ronald J. Maxwell Stitt   1977   2000   86 Burnbank Centre, Burnbank, Hamilton ML3 0NA
LTh BA ThM BREd DMin FSAScot
01698 284201

45 **Hamilton: Hillhouse (E-mail: hamilton-hillhouse@presbyteryofhamilton.co.uk)**
David W.G. Burt BD DipMin   1989   1998   66 Wellhall Road, Hamilton ML3 9BY
[E-mail: dwgburt@blueyonder.co.uk]
01698 422300

46   **Hamilton: North** See Hamilton: Burnbank

47   **Hamilton: Old (H) (Tel: 01698 281905) (E-mail: hamilton-old@presbyteryofhamilton.co.uk)**
John M.A. Thomson TD JP BD ThM   1978   2001   1 Chateau Grove, Hamilton ML3 7DS
[E-mail: jt@john1949.plus.com]
01698 422511

48   **Hamilton: St Andrew's (T) (E-mail: hamilton-standrews@presbyteryofhamilton.co.uk)**
Norman MacLeod BTh   1999   2005   15 Bent Road, Hamilton ML3 6QB
[E-mail: normanmacleod@btopenworld.com]
01698 283264

49   **Hamilton: St John's (H) (Tel: 01698 283492) (E-mail: hamilton-stjohns@presbyteryofhamilton.co.uk)**
Robert M. Kent MA BD   1973   1981   12 Castlehill Crescent, Hamilton ML3 7DG
[E-mail: robertmkent@btinternet.com]
01698 425002

50   **Hamilton: South (H) (Tel: 01698 281014) (E-mail: hamilton-south@presbyteryofhamilton.co.uk)**
linked with Quarter (E-mail: quarter@presbyteryofhamilton.co.uk)
George MacDonald BTh   2004   The Manse, Limekilnburn Road, Quarter, Hamilton ML3 7XA
[E-mail: george.macdonald1@btinternet.com]
01698 424511

51   **Hamilton: Trinity (Tel: 01698 284254) (E-mail: hamilton-trinity@presbyteryofhamilton.co.uk)**
Karen E. Harbison (Mrs) MA BD   1991   69 Buchan Street, Hamilton ML3 8JY
01698 425326

52   **Hamilton: West (H) (Tel: 01698 284670) (E-mail: hamilton-west@presbyteryofhamilton.co.uk)**
Elizabeth A. Waddell (Mrs) BD   1999   2005   43 Bothwell Road, Hamilton ML3 0BB
01698 458770

53   **Holytown (E-mail: holytown@presbyteryofhamilton.co.uk)**
Vacant   Holytown, Motherwell ML1 5RU
01698 832622

54   **Kirk o' Shotts (H) (E-mail: kirk-o-shotts@presbyteryofhamilton.co.uk)**
Sheila M. Spence (Mrs) MA BD   1979   The Manse, Kirk o' Shotts, Salsburgh, Shotts ML7 4NS
[E-mail: sm_spence@hotmail.com]
01698 870208

55   **Larkhall: Chalmers (H) (E-mail: larkhall-chalmers@presbyteryofhamilton.co.uk)**
James S.G. Hastie CA BD   1990   Quarry Road, Larkhall ML9 1HH
[E-mail: jHastie@chalmers0.demon.co.uk]
01698 882238
08700 562133 (Fax)

56   **Larkhall: St Machan's (H) (E-mail: larkhall-stmachans@presbyteryofhamilton.co.uk)**
Alastair McKillop BD DipMin   1995   2004   2 Orchard Gate, Larkhall ML9 1HG
01698 321976

57   **Larkhall: Trinity (E-mail: larkhall-trinity@presbyteryofhamilton.co.uk)**
Lindsay Schluter (Miss) ThE CertMin   1995   13 Machan Avenue, Larkhall ML9 2HE
01698 881401

58 Motherwell: Crosshill (H) (E-mail: mwell-crosshill@presbyteryofhamilton.co.uk)
Vacant   15 Orchard Street, Motherwell ML1 3JE   01698 263410

59 Motherwell: Dalziel St Andrew's (H) (Tel: 01698 264097) (E-mail: mwell-dalzielstandrews@presbyteryofhamilton.co.uk)
Derek W. Hughes BSc BD DipEd   1990   1996   4 Pollock Street, Motherwell ML1 1LP   01698 263414
                                                          [E-mail: derekthecleric@btinternet.com]

60 Motherwell: Manse Road (E-mail: mwell-manseroad@presbyteryofhamilton.co.uk)
Vacant   10 Hamilton Drive, Motherwell ML1 2QA   01698 267345

61 Motherwell: North (E-mail: mwell-north@presbyteryofhamilton.co.uk)
Derek H.N. Pope BD   1987   1995   35 Birrens Road, Motherwell ML1 3NS   01698 266716
                                                          [E-mail: derekpopemotherwell@hotmail.com]

62 Motherwell: St Margaret's (E-mail: mwell-stmargarets@presbyteryofhamilton.co.uk)
Andrew M. Campbell BD   1984   70 Baron's Road, Motherwell ML1 2NB   01698 263803
                                                          [E-mail: drewdorca@hotmail.com]

63 Motherwell: St Mary's (H) (E-mail: mwell-stmarys@presbyteryofhamilton.co.uk)
David W. Doyle MA BD   1977   1987   19 Orchard Street, Motherwell ML1 3JE   01698 263472

64 Motherwell: South Dalziel (H) (E-mail: mwell-southdalziel@presbyteryofhamilton.co.uk)
Phyllis M. Wilson (Mrs) DipCom DipRE   1985   1994   62 Manse Road, Motherwell ML1 2PT   01698 263054
                                                          [E-mail: thomas.wilson38@btinternet.com]

65 Newarthill See Carfin

66 Newmains: Bonkle (H) (E-mail: bonkle@presbyteryofhamilton.co.uk)
linked with Newmains: Coltness Memorial (H) (E-mail: coltness@presbyteryofhamilton.co.uk)
Graham Raeburn MTh   2004   5 Kirkgate, Newmains, Wishaw ML2 9BT   01698 383858
                                                          [E-mail: grahamraeburn@tiscali.co.uk]

67 Newmains: Coltness Memorial See Newmains: Bonkle

68 New Stevenston: Wrangholm Kirk (E-mail: wrangholm@presbyteryofhamilton.co.uk)
Vacant   222 Clydesdale Street, New Stevenston, Motherwell ML1 4JQ   01698 832533

69 Overtown (E-mail: overtown@presbyteryofhamilton.co.uk)
Nan Low (Mrs) BD   2002   The Manse, Main Street, Overtown, Wishaw ML2 0QP   01698 372330
                                                          [E-mail: nanlow@supanet.com]

70 Quarter See Hamilton: South

71 Shotts: Calderhead Erskine (E-mail: calderhead-erskine@presbyteryofhamilton.co.uk)
Ian G. Thom BSc PhD BD   1990   2000   The Manse, 9 Kirk Road, Shotts ML7 5ET   01501 820042
                                                          [E-mail: the.thoms@btinternet.com]

72 **Stonehouse: St Ninian's (H) (E-mail: stonehouse@presbyteryofhamilton.co.uk)**
Paul G.R. Grant BD MTh   2003   4 Hamilton Way, Stonehouse, Larkhall ML9 3PU   01698 792947
[E-mail: agrg@surefish.co.uk]

73 **Strathaven: Avendale Old and Drumclog (H) (Tel: 01357 529748) (E-mail: strathaven-avendaleold@presbyteryofhamilton.co.uk and**
E-mail: drumclog@presbyteryofhamilton.co.uk)
Alan W. Gibson BA BD   2001   Kirk Street, Strathaven ML10 6BA   01357 520077
[E-mail: awgibson82@hotmail.com]

74 **Strathaven: East** See Glasford
75 **Strathaven: Rankin** See Chapelton

76 **Strathaven: West (E-mail: strathaven-west@presbyteryofhamilton.co.uk)**
Una B. Stewart (Ms) BD DipEd   1995   2002   6 Avenel Crescent, Strathaven ML10 6JF   01357 529086
[E-mail: rev.ubs@virgin.net]

77 **Uddingston: Burnhead (H) (E-mail: uddingston-burnhead@presbyteryofhamilton.co.uk)**
Sandi McGill (Ms) BD   2002   90 Laburnum Road, Uddingston, Glasgow G71 5DB   01698 813716
[E-mail: smcgillbox-mail@yahoo.co.uk]

78 **Uddingston: Old (H) (Tel: 01698 814015) (E-mail: uddingston-old@presbyteryofhamilton.co.uk)**
Norman B. McKee BD   1987   1994   1 Belmont Avenue, Uddingston, Glasgow G71 7AX   01698 814757
[E-mail: n.mckee1@btinternet.com]

79 **Uddingston: Park (T) (H) (E-mail: uddingston-park@presbyteryofhamilton.co.uk)**
W. Bruce McDowall BA BD   1989   1999   25 Douglas Gardens, Uddingston, Glasgow G71 7HB   01698 817256

80 **Uddingston: Viewpark (H) (E-mail: uddingston-viewpark@presbyteryofhamilton.co.uk)**
Michael G. Lyall BD   1993   2001   14 Holmbrae Road, Uddingston, Glasgow G71 6AP   01698 813113
[E-mail: michaellyall@blueyonder.co.uk]

81 **Wishaw: Cambusnethan North (H) (E-mail: wishaw-cambusnethannorth@presbyteryofhamilton.co.uk)**
Mhorag Macdonald (Ms) MA BD   1989   350 Kirk Road, Wishaw ML2 8LH   01698 381305
[E-mail: mhorag@mhorag.force9.co.uk]

82 **Wishaw: Cambusnethan Old (E-mail: wishaw-cambusnethanold@presbyteryofhamilton.co.uk)**
and Morningside (E-mail: wishaw-morningside@presbyteryofhamilton.co.uk)
Iain C. Murdoch MA LLB DipEd BD   1995   22 Coronation Street, Wishaw ML2 8LF   01698 384235
[E-mail: iaincmurdoch@btopenworld.com]

83 Wishaw: Craigneuk and Belhaven (H) (E-mail: wishaw-craigneukbelhaven@presbyteryofhamilton.co.uk) linked with Wishaw: Old

Vacant 100 Glen Road, Wishaw ML2 7NP 01698 372495

84 Wishaw: Old (H) (Tel: 01698 376080) (E-mail: wishaw-old@presbyteryofhamilton.co.uk) See Wishaw: Craigneuk and Belhaven

85 Wishaw: St Mark's (E-mail: wishaw-stmarks@presbyteryofhamilton.co.uk)

Vacant Coltness Road, Wishaw ML2 7EX 01698 384596

86 Wishaw: South Wishaw (H)

Klaus O.F. Buwert LLB BD 1984 1999 Wishaw South Manse, West Thornlie Street, Wishaw ML2 7AR 01698 372356
[E-mail: k.buwert@btinternet.com]

Name			Charge	Address	Tel
Anderson, Catherine B. (Mrs) DCS	1951	1986	(Deaconess)	13 Mosshill Road, Bellshill ML4 1NQ	01698 745907
Beattie, William G. BD BSc	1963	2002	(Hamilton: St Andrew's)	33 Dungavel Gardens, Hamilton ML3 7PE	01698 423804
Black, John M. MA BD	1995	2003	(Coatbridge: Blairhill Dundyvan)	3 Grantown Avenue, Airdrie ML6 8HH	01236 750638
Brown, Allan B. BD MTh			Chaplain: Shotts Prison	HMP Shotts, Scott Drive, Shotts ML7 4LE [E-mail: alan.brown3@sps.gov.uk]	01501 824071
Cook, J. Stanley BD Dip PSS	1974	2001	(Hamilton: West)	Mansend, 137A Old Manse Road, Netherton, Wishaw ML2 0EW [E-mail: stancook@blueyonder.co.uk]	01698 299600
Cullen, William T. BA LTh	1984	1996	(Kilmarnock: St John's Onthank)	6 Laurel Wynd, Cambuslang, Glasgow G72 7BA	0141-641 4337
Currie, David E.P. BSc BD	1983	2000	Congregational Development Consultant	21 Rosa Burn Avenue, Lindsayfield, East Kilbride, Glasgow G75 9DE	01355 248510
Currie, R. David BSc BD	1984	2004	(Cambuslang: Flemington Hallside)	69 Kethers Street, Motherwell ML1 3HN	01698 323424
Dunn, W. Stuart LTh	1970	2006	(Motherwell: Crosshill)	10 Macrostie Gardens, Crieff PH7 4LP	01764 655178
Fraser, James P.	1951	1988	(Strathaven: Avendale Old and Drumclog)	26 Hamilton Road, Strathaven ML10 6JA	01357 522758
Gilchrist, Kay (Miss) BD	1996	1999	Part-time Chaplain: Polmont Young Offenders Institution	45 Hawthorn Drive, Craigneuk, Airdrie ML6 8AP	01698 742545
Grier, James BD	1991	2005	(Coatbridge: Middle)	14 Love Drive, Bellshill ML4 1BY	01698 262733
Handley, John	1954	1993	(Motherwell: Clason Memorial)	12 Airbles Crescent, Motherwell ML1 3AR	01698 826177
Hunter, James E. LTh	1974	1997	(Blantyre: Livingstone Memorial)	57 Dalwhinnie Avenue, Blantyre, Glasgow G72 9NQ	
King, Crawford S. MA	1958	1984	(Glenboig)	Rawyards House, Motherwell Street, Airdrie ML6 7HP	
McAlpine, John BSc	1998	2004	(Auxiliary Minister)	201 Bonkle Road, Newmains, Wishaw ML2 9AA	01698 384610
McCabe, George	1963	1996	(Airdrie: High)	Flat 8, Park Court, 2 Craighouse Park, Edinburgh EH10 5LD	0131-447 9522
McDonald, John A. MA BD	1978	1997	(Cumbernauld: Condorrat)	17 Thomson Drive, Bellshill ML4 3ND	
Martin, James MA BD DD	1946	1987	(Glasgow: High Carntyne)	9 Magnolia Street, Wishaw ML2 7EQ	01698 385825
Melrose, J.H. Loudon MA BD MEd	1955	1996	(Gourock: Old Gourock and Ashton [Assoc])	1 Laverock Avenue, Hamilton ML3 7DD	01698 427958
Munton, James G. BA	1969	2002	(Coatbridge: Old Monkland)	2 Moorcroft Drive, Airdrie ML6 8ES [E-mail: jacjim@supanet.com]	01236 754848
Price, Peter O. CBE QHC BA FPhS	1960	1996	(Blantyre: Old)	22 Old Bothwell Road, Bothwell, Glasgow G71 8AW [E-mail: peteroprice@aol.com]	01698 854032
Rogerson, Stuart D. BSc BD	1980	2001	(Strathaven: West)	17 Westfield Park, Strathaven ML10 6XH [E-mail: srogerson@cnetwork.co.uk]	01357 523321
Salmond, James S. BA BD MTh ThD	1979	2003	(Holytown)	165 Torbothie Road, Shotts ML7 5NE	01501 826852

Thorne, Leslie W. BA LTh	1987 2001	(Coatbridge: Clifton)	'Hatherleigh', 9 Chatton Walk, Coatbridge ML5 4FH [E-mail: lesthorne@tiscali.co.uk]	01236 432241 (Mbl) 07963 199921
Wilson, James H. LTh	1970 1996	(Cleland)	21 Austine Drive, Hamilton ML3 7YE [E-mail: wilsonjh@blueyonder.co.uk]	01698 457042
Wyllie, Hugh R. MA DD FCIBS	1962 2000	(Hamilton: Old)	18 Chantinghall Road, Hamilton ML3 8NP	01698 420002
Zambonini, James LIADip	1997	Auxiliary Minister	100 Old Manse Road, Wishaw ML2 0EP	01698 350887

HAMILTON ADDRESSES

Airdrie

Broomknoll	Broomknoll Street
Clarkston	Forrest Street
Flowerhill	89 Graham Street
High	North Bridge Street
Jackson	Glen Road
New Monkland	Glenmavis
St Columba's	Thrashbush Road
The New Wellwynd	Wellwynd

Coatbridge

Blairhill Dundyvan	Blairhill Street
Calder	Calder Street
Clifton	Muiryhall Street x Jackson Street
Middle	Bank Street
Old Monkland	Woodside Street
St Andrew's	Church Street
Townhead	Crinan Crescent

East Kilbride

Claremont	High Common Road, St Leonard's
Greenhills	Greenhills Centre

Moncreiff	Calderwood Road
Mossneuk	Eden Drive
Old	Montgomery Street
South	Baird Hill, Murray
West	Kittoch Street
Westwood	Belmont Drive, Westwood

Hamilton

Burnbank	High Blantyre Road
Cadzow	Woodside Walk
Gilmour and Whitehill	Glasgow Road, Burnbank Abbotsford Road, Whitehill
Hillhouse	Clerkwell Road
North	Windmill Road
Old	Leechlee Road
St Andrew's	Avon Street
St John's	Duke Street
South	Strathaven Road
Trinity	Neilsland Square off North Road
West	Burnbank Road

Motherwell

Crosshill	Windmillhill Street x Airbles Street
Dalziel St Andrew's	Merry Street and Muir Street

Manse Road	
North	St Margaret's
St Mary's	
South Dalziel	

Uddingston

Burnhead	
Old	Park
Viewpark	

Wishaw

Cambusnethan North	
Old	
Chalmers	
Craigneuk and Belhaven	
Old	
St Mark's	
Thornlie	

Gavin Street	
Chesters Crescent	
Shields Road	
Avon Street	
504 Windmillhill Street	
Laburnum Road	
Old Glasgow Road.	
Main Street	
Old Edinburgh Road	
Kirk Road	
Kirk Road	
East Academy Street	
Craigneuk Street	
Main Street	
Coltness Road	
West Thornlie Street	

(18) DUMBARTON

Meets at Dumbarton, in Riverside Church Halls, on the first Tuesday of February, March, April, May, October, November and December; on the second Tuesday of June and September (and April when the first Tuesday falls in Holy Week), and at the incoming Moderator's church on the first Tuesday of June for the installation of the Moderator.

Clerk:	REV. J. COLIN CASKIE BA BD	11 Ardenconnel Way, Rhu, Helensburgh G84 8LX [E-mail: akph43@uk.uumail.com] [E-mail: pres.dumbarton@uk.uumail.com]	01436 820213

Alexandria
Elizabeth W. Houston (Miss) MA BD DipEd | 1985 | 1995 | 32 Ledrish Avenue, Balloch, Alexandria G83 8JB | 01389 751933

Arrochar linked with Luss
H. Dane Sherrard BD DMin | 1971 | 1998 | The Manse, Luss, Alexandria G83 8NZ [E-mail: dane@cadder.demon.co.uk] | 01436 860240 / 07801 939138 (Mbl)

Baldernock (H)
Andrew P. Lees BD | 1984 | 2002 | The Manse, Bardowie, Milngavie, Glasgow G62 6ES [E-mail: thereverend@alees.fsnet.co.uk] | 01360 620471

Bearsden: Killermont (H)
Alan J. Hamilton LLB BD | 2003 | | 8 Clathic Avenue, Bearsden, Glasgow G61 2HF [E-mail: alanj@hamilton63.freeserve.co.uk] | 0141-942 0021

Bearsden: New Kilpatrick (H) (0141-942 8827) (E-mail: mail@nkchurch.org.uk)
David D. Scott BSc BD | 1981 | 1999 | 51 Manse Road, Bearsden, Glasgow G61 3PN [E-mail: nkbearsden@btopenworld.com] | 0141-942 0035

Bearsden: North (H) (0141-942 2818)
Keith T. Blackwood BD Dip Min | 1997 | | 5 Fintry Gardens, Bearsden, Glasgow G61 4RJ [E-mail: k2blackwood@btinternet.com] | 0141-942 0366 / 07903 319943 (Mbl)

Bearsden: South (H)
John W.F. Harris MA | 1967 | 1987 | 61 Drymen Road, Bearsden, Glasgow G61 2SU [E-mail: jwfh@bearsdensouth.org] | 0141-942 0507 / 07711 573877 (Mbl)

Bearsden: Westerton Fairlie Memorial (H) (0141-942 6960)
Eric V. Hudson LTh | 1971 | 1990 | 3 Canniesburn Road, Bearsden, Glasgow G61 1PW [E-mail: evhudson@canniesburn.fsnet.co.uk] | 0141-942 2672

Bonhill (H) (01389 756516)
Ian H. Miller BA BD | 1975 | | 1 Glebe Gardens, Bonhill, Alexandria G83 9NZ [E-mail: ianmiller@bonhillchurch.freeserve.co.uk] | 01389 753039

Cardross (H) (01389 841322)
Andrew J. Scobie MA BD | 1963 | 1965 | The Manse, Main Road, Cardross, Dumbarton G82 5LB [E-mail: ascobie55@cardross.dunbartonshire.co.uk] | 01389 841289 / 07889 670252 (Mbl)

Clydebank: Abbotsford (E-mail: abbotsford@lineone.net) (Website: www.abbotsford.org.uk)
Roderick G. Hamilton MA BD | 1992 | 1996 | 35 Montrose Street, Clydebank G81 2PA [E-mail: rghamilton@ntlworld.com] | 0141-952 5151

Clydebank: Faifley
Gregor McIntyre BSc BD — 1991
Kirklea, Cochno Road, Hardgate, Clydebank G81 6PT
[E-mail: mail@gregormcintyre.com]
01389 876836

Clydebank: Kilbowie St Andrew's
Peggy Roberts (Mrs) BA BD — 2003
5 Melfort Avenue, Clydebank G81 2HX
[E-mail: peggy.r@ntlworld.com]
0141-951 2455

Clydebank: Radnor Park (H)
Margaret J.B. Yule (Mrs) BD — 1992
Church Manse, Spencer Street, Clydebank G81 3AS
[E-mail: mjbyule@yahoo.co.uk]
0141-951 1007

Clydebank: St Cuthbert's (T) linked with Duntocher (H)
David Donaldson MA BD DMin — 1969 2002
The Manse, Roman Road, Duntocher, Clydebank G81 6BT
[E-mail: david.donaldson3@btopenworld.com]
01389 873471

Craigrownie linked with Rosneath: St Modan's (H)
William M. Murdoch BSc PhD BD STM — 1980 2004
Edenkiln, Argyll Road, Kilcreggan, Helensburgh G84 0JW
[E-mail: wmccmurdoch@aol.com]
01436 842274
07818 051243 (Mbl)

Dalmuir: Barclay (0141-941 3988)
Fiona E. Maxwell BA BD — 2004
16 Parkhall Road, Dalmuir, Clydebank G81 3RJ
[E-mail: fionamaxi@btinternet.com]
0141-941 3317

Dumbarton: Riverside (H) (01389 742551)
Robert J. Watt BD — 1994 2002
5 Kirkton Road, Dumbarton G82 4AS
[E-mail: robertjwatt@blueyonder.co.uk]
01389 762512

Dumbarton: St Andrew's (H)
Vacant
17 Mansewood Drive, Dumbarton G82 3EU
01389 604259

Dumbarton: West Kirk (H)
Christine Liddell (Miss) BD — 1999
3 Havoc Road, Dumbarton G82 4JW
[E-mail: christineliddell@blueyonder.co.uk]
01389 604840

Duntocher (H) See Clydebank: St Cuthbert's

Garelochhead (01436 810589)
Alastair S. Duncan MA BD — 1989
Old School Road, Garelochhead, Helensburgh G84 0AT
[E-mail: gpc@churchuk.fsnet.co.uk]
01436 810022

Helensburgh: Park (H) (01436 674825)
Vacant
35 East Argyle Street, Helensburgh G84 7EL
01436 672209

Helensburgh: St Columba (H)
Vacant   46 Suffolk Street, Helensburgh G84 9QZ   01436 672054

Helensburgh: The West Kirk (H) (01436 676880)
David W. Clark MA BD   1975   37 Campbell Street, Helensburgh G84 9NH   01436 674063
                                                                           [E-mail: clarkdw@lineone.net]

Jamestown (H)
Norma Moore (Ms) MA BD   1995   1986   26 Kessog's Gardens, Balloch, Alexandria G83 8QJ   01389 756447
                                                                           [E-mail: norma.moore5@btinternet.com]

Kilmaronock Gartocharn
Janet P.H. MacMahon (Mrs) MSc BD   1992   2004   Kilmaronock Manse, Alexandria G83 8SB   01360 660295
                                                                           [E-mail: janetmacmahon@yahoo.co.uk]

Luss See Arrochar

Milngavie: Cairns (H) (0141-956 4868)
Andrew Frater BA BD   1987   2006   4 Cairns Drive, Milngavie, Glasgow G62 8AJ   0141-956 1717
                                                                           [E-mail: office@cairnschurch.org.uk]

Milngavie: St Luke's (0141-956 4226)
Ramsay B. Shields BA BD   1990   1994   70 Hunter Road, Milngavie, Glasgow G62 7BY   0141-577 9171 (Tel)
                                                                           [E-mail: rbs@minister.com]   0141-577 9181 (Fax)

Milngavie: St Paul's (H) (0141-956 4405)
Fergus C. Buchanan MA BD MTh   1982   1997   8 Buchanan Street, Milngavie, Glasgow G62 8DD   0141-956 1043
                                                                           [E-mail: f.c.buchanan@ntlworld.com]

Old Kilpatrick Bowling
Jeanette Whitecross (Mrs) BD   2002   1988   The Manse, 175 Dumbarton Road, Old Kilpatrick,   01389 873130
                                                                           Glasgow G60 5JQ
                                                                           [E-mail: jeanettewx@yahoo.com]

Renton: Trinity (H)
Ian Wilkie BD PGCE   2001   2002   38 Main Street, Renton, Dumbarton G82 4PU   01389 752017
                                                                           [E-mail: rtpccofs@aol.com]   07751 155552 (Mbl)

Rhu and Shandon (H)
J. Colin Caskie BA BD   1977   2001   11 Ardenconnel Way, Rhu, Helensburgh G84 8LX   01436 820213
                                                                           [E-mail: colin@jcaskie.freeserve.co.uk]

Rosneath: St Modan's See Craigrownie

Name			Position / Parish	Address	Tel
Booth, Frederick M. LTh	1970	2005	(Helensburgh: St Columba)	Achnashie Coach House, Clynder, Helensburgh G84 0QD	01436 831522
Crombie, W.M.D. MA BD	1947	1987	(Calton New with St Andrew's)	32 Westbourne Drive, Bearsden, Glasgow G61 4BH	0141-943 0235
Davidson, Professor Robert MA BD DD FRSE	1956	1991	(University of Glasgow)	30 Dumgoyne Drive, Bearsden, Glasgow G61 3AP	0141-942 1810
Donaghy, Leslie G. BD DipMin PGCE FSAScot	1990	2004	(Dumbarton: St Andrew's)	130 Dumbuck Road, Dumbarton G82 3LZ	01389 604251
Easton, I.A.G. MA FIPM	1945	1988	Lecturer	6 Edgehill Road, Bearsden, Glasgow G61 3AD	0141-942 4214
Ferguson, Archibald M. MSc PhD CEng FRINA	1989	2004	Auxiliary Minister with Clerk	The Whins, Barrowfield, Cardross, Dumbarton G82 5NL [E-mail: archieferguson@supanet.com]	01389 841517
Houston, Peter M. FPhS	1952	1997	(Renfrew: Old)	25 Honeysuckle Lane, Jamestown, Alexandria G83 8PL	01389 721165 (Mbl) 07770 390936
Jack, Robert MA BD	1950	1996	(Bearsden: Killermont)	142 Turnhill Drive, Erskine PA8 7AH	0141-812 8370
Kemp, Tina MA		2005	Auxiliary Minister	12 Oaktree Gardens, Dumbarton G82 1EU	01389 730477
Lawson, Alexander H. ThM ThD FPhS	1950	1988	(Clydebank: Kilbowie)	1 Glebe Park, Mansewood, Dumbarton G82 3HE	01389 742030
McIntyre, J. Ainslie MA BD	1963	1984	(University of Glasgow)	60 Bonnaughton Road, Bearsden, Glasgow G61 4DB [E-mail: jamcintyre@hotmail.com]	0141-942 5143 (Mbl) 07050 295103
Mackenzie, Ian M. MA	1967	1989	(BBC)	1 Glenman Gardens, Helensburgh G84 8XT	01436 673429
Munro, David P. MA BD STM	1953	1996	(Bearsden: North)	14 Birch Road, Killearn, Glasgow G63 9SQ	01360 550098
Paul, Alison (Miss) MA BD Dip Theol	1986	2001	(Rhu and Shandon)	30 Perrays Drive, Lennox Gardens, Dumbarton G82 5HT	01389 733698
Ramage, Alistair E. BA ADB CertEd	1996	2004	Auxiliary Minister with Clerk	6 Claremont Gardens, Milngavie, Glasgow G62 6PG [E-mail: ara3@waitrose.com]	0141-956 2897
Shackleton, Scott J.S. BA BD PhD	1993	1993	Chaplain: Royal Navy	HMS Neptune, HMNB Clyde, Faslane, Helensburgh G84 8HL	
Spence, C.K.O. MC TD MA BD	1949	1983	(Craigrownie)	8B Cairndhu Gardens, Helensburgh G84 8PG	01436 678838
Steven, Harold A.M. LTh FSA Scot	1970	2001	(Baldernock)	9 Cairnhill Road, Bearsden, Glasgow G61 1AT	0141-942 1598
Wright, Malcolm LTh	1970	2003	(Craigrownie with Rosneath: St Modan's)	30 Clairinsh, Drumkinnon Gate, Balloch, Alexandria G83 8SE	01389 720338

DUMBARTON ADDRESSES

Clydebank
Abbotsford	Town Centre
Faifley	Faifley Road
Kilbowie St Andrew's	Kilbowie Road
Radnor Park	Radnor Street
St Cuthbert's	Linnvale

Dumbarton
Riverside	High Street
St Andrew's	Aitkenbar Circle
West Kirk	West Bridgend

Helensburgh
Park	Charlotte Street
St Columba	Sinclair Street
The West Kirk	Colquhoun Square

(19) ARGYLL

Meets at various locations in Argyll on the first Tuesday or Wednesday of March, June, September and December. For details, contact the Presbytery Clerk.

Clerk:	MR IAN MACLAGAN LLB FSAScot	Carmonadh, Eastlands Road, Rothesay, Isle of Bute PA20 9JZ [E-mail: argyll.pres@uk.uumail.com]	01700 503015
Depute Clerk:	REV. GEORGE G. CRINGLES BD	St Oran's Manse, Connel, Oban PA37 1PJ [E-mail: george.cringles@btinternet.com]	01631 710242
Treasurer:	MRS PAMELA A. GIBSON	Allt Ban, Portsonachan, Dalmally PA33 1BJ [E-mail: macgills1234@aol.com]	01866 833344

Appin linked with Lismore
John A.H. Murdoch BA BD DPSS 1979 2001 The Manse, Appin PA38 4DD   01631 730206
[E-mail: jmurdoch@toucansurf.com]

Ardchattan (H)
Jeffrey A. McCormick BD 1984 Ardchattan Manse, North Connel, Oban PA37 1RG   01631 710364
[E-mail: jeff.mcc@virgin.net]

Ardrishaig (H) linked with South Knapdale
David Carruthers BD 1998 The Manse, Park Road, Ardrishaig, Lochgilphead PA30 8HE   01546 603269

Campbeltown: Highland (H)
Michael J. Lind LLB BD 1984 1997 Highland Church Manse, Kirk Street, Campbeltown PA28 6BN   01586 551146
[E-mail: myknan@tiscali.co.uk]

Campbeltown: Lorne and Lowland (H)
Philip D. Burroughs BSc BTh DTS 1998 2004 Lorne and Lowland Manse, Castlehill, Campbeltown PA28 6AN   01586 552468

Coll linked with Connel
George G. Cringles BD 1981 2002 St Oran's Manse, Connel, Oban PA37 1PJ   01631 710242
[E-mail: george.cringles@btinternet.com]

Colonsay and Oronsay linked with Kilbrandon and Kilchattan (Website: www.islandchurches.org.uk)
Vacant   The Manse, Winterton Road, Balvicar, Oban PA34 4TF

Connel See Coll

Craignish linked with Kilninver and Kilmelford
T. Alastair McLachlan BSc 1972 2004 The Manse, Kilmelford, Oban PA34 4XA   01852 200565
[E-mail: talastair@tesco.net]

01852 300240

Cumlodden, Lochfyneside and Lochgair
Roderick MacLeod
MA BD PhD(Edin) PhD(Open)   1966   1985   Cumlodden Manse, Furnace, Inveraray PA32 8XU   01499 500288
[E-mail: revroddy@yahoo.co.uk]

Dunoon: St John's linked with Sandbank (H)
Joseph Stewart LTh   1979   1989   23 Bullwood Road, Dunoon PA23 7QJ   01369 702128

Dunoon: The High Kirk (H) linked with Innellan linked with Toward
David P. Anderson BSc BD   2002   7A Matheson Lane, Innellan, Dunoon PA23 7SH   01369 830276
[E-mail: davidshar.anderson@ntlworld.com]
Ruth I. Griffiths (Mrs) (Aux)   2004   Kirkwood, Matheson Lane, Innellan, Dunoon PA23 7TA   01369 830145
[E-mail: ruth.griffiths@surefish.co.uk]

Gigha and Cara (H) (GD)
Rosemary Legge (Mrs) BSc BD MTh   1992   2002   The Manse, Isle of Gigha PA41 7AA   01583 505245
[E-mail: Leggesongigha@aol.com]

Glassary, Kilmartin and Ford linked with North Knapdale
Richard B. West   1994   2005   The Manse, Kilmichael Glassary, Lochgilphead PA31 8QA   01546 606926
[E-mail: rickangelawest@hotmail.com]

Glenaray and Inveraray
W. Brian Wilkinson MA BD   1968   1993   The Manse, Inveraray PA32 8XT   01499 302060
[E-mail: brianwilkinson@f2s.com]

Glenorchy and Innishael linked with Strathfillan
Vacant   The Manse, Dalmally PA33 1AA   01838 200386

Innellan (H) See Dunoon: The High Kirk

Iona linked with Kilfinichen and Kilvickeon and the Ross of Mull
Sydney S. Graham BD DipYL MPhil   1987   2004   The Manse, Bunessan, Isle of Mull PA67 6DW   01681 700227
[E-mail: syd@sydgraham.force9.co.uk]

Jura (GD)
Vacant   Church of Scotland Manse, Craighouse, Isle of Jura PA60 7XG   01496 820384

Kilarrow (H) linked with Kilmeny
Vacant   The Manse, Bowmore, Isle of Islay PA43 7LH   01496 810271

Kilberry linked with Tarbert (H)
Vacant — Glenakil Cottage, Tarbert, Argyll PA29 6XX — 01880 820156

Kilbrandon and Kilchattan See Colonsay and Oronsay

Kilcalmonell
Vacant — The Manse, Whitehouse, Tarbert, Argyll PA29 6XS — 01880 730224

Kilchoman (GD) linked with Portnahaven (GD)
Stephen Fulcher BA MA   1993   2003 — The Manse, Port Charlotte, Isle of Islay PA48 7TW [E-mail: scr@fish.co.uk] — 01496 850241

Kilchrenan and Dalavich linked with Muckairn
Margaret R.M. Millar (Miss) BTh   1977   1996 — Muckairn Manse, Taynuilt PA35 1HW [E-mail: macoje@aol.com] — 01866 822204

Kildalton and Oa (GD) (H)
Vacant — The Manse, Port Ellen, Isle of Islay PA42 7DB — 01496 302447

Kilfinan linked with Kilmodan and Colintraive linked with Kyles (H)
Vacant — West Cowal Manse, Tighnabruaich PA21 2AD

Kilfinichen and Kilvickeon and the Ross of Mull See Iona

Killean and Kilchenzie (H)
John H. Paton JP BSc BD   1983   1984 — The Manse, Muasdale, Tarbert, Argyll PA29 6XD [E-mail: jonymar@globalnet.co.uk] — 01583 421249

Kilmeny See Kilarrow
Kilmodan and Colintraive See Kilfinan

Kilmore (GD) and Oban (E-mail: obancofs@btinternet.com)
Vacant
Elizabeth Gibson (Mrs) MA MLitt BD (Assoc) 2003 — Kilmore and Oban Manse, Ganavan Road, Oban PA34 5TU Rudha-na-Cloiche, Esplanade, Oban PA34 5AQ [E-mail: lizgibson@phonecoop.coop] — 01631 562322 / 01631 562759

Kilmun (St Munn's) (H) linked with Strone (H) and Ardentinny
Franklin G. Wyatt MA MDiv DMin   1974   2004 — The Manse, Blairmore, Dunoon PA23 8TE [E-mail: shorechurches@tesco.net] — 01369 840313

Kilninver and Kilmelford See Craignish

Kirn (H)
Grahame M. Henderson BD — 1974 — 2004 — Kirn Manse, 13 Dhailling Park, Hunter Street, Kirn, Dunoon PA23 8FK [E-mail: ghende5884@aol.com] — 01369 702256

Kyles See Kilfinan
Lismore See Appin

Lochgilphead
Hilda C. Smith (Miss) MA BD MSc — 1992 — 2005 — Parish Church Manse, Manse Brae, Lochgilphead PA31 8QZ [E-mail: hilda.smith2@btinternet.com] — 01546 602238

Lochgoilhead (H) and Kilmorich
James Macfarlane PhD — 1991 — 2000 — The Manse, Lochgoilhead, Cairndow PA24 8AA [E-mail: macfarlane-cofs@beeb.net] — 01301 703059

Muckairn See Kilchrenan

Mull, Isle of, Kilninian and Kilmore linked with Salen (H) and Ulva linked with Tobermory (GD) (H) linked with Torosay (H) and Kinlochspelvie
Vacant
Robert C. Nelson BA BD (Assoc) — 1980 — 2003 — Trewince, Western Road, Strongarbh, Tobermory, Isle of Mull PA75 6RA [E-mail: robertnelson@onetel.com] — 01688 302356

North Knapdale See Glassary, Kilmartin and Ford
Portnahaven See Kilchoman

Rothesay: Trinity (H)
Samuel McC. Harris BA BD — 1974 — 2004 — 12 Crichton Road, Rothesay, Isle of Bute PA20 9JR — 01700 503010

Saddell and Carradale (H) linked with Skipness
Vacant — The Manse, Carradale, Campbeltown PA28 6QN — 01583 431253

Salen and Ulva See Mull
Sandbank See Dunoon: St John's
Skipness See Saddell and Carradale
South Knapdale See Ardrishaig

Southend (H)
Martin R. Forrest BA MA BD — 1988 — 2001 — St Blaans Manse, Southend, Campbeltown PA28 6RQ [E-mail: jmr.forrest@btopenworld.com] — 01586 830274

Strachur and Strathlachlan
Robert K. Mackenzie MA BD PhD   1976   1998   The Manse, Strachur, Cairndow PA27 8DG   01369 860246
[E-mail: rkmackenzie@strachurmanse.fsnet.co.uk]

Strathfillan See Glenorchy
Strone (H) and Ardentinny See Kilmun
Tarbert See Kilberry

The United Church of Bute
Ian S. Currie MBE BD   1975   2005   10 Bishop Terrace, Rothesay, Isle of Bute PA20 9HF   01700 504502
[E-mail: iancurrie@ntlworld.com]

Tiree (GD)
Irene C. Gillespie (Mrs) BD   1991   2005   The Manse, Scarinish, Isle of Tiree PA77 6TN   01879 220377
[E-mail: revicg@btinternet.com]

Tobermory See Mull
Torosay and Kinlochspelvie See Mull
Toward (H) See Dunoon: The High Kirk

Name			Charge	Address	Phone
Bell, Douglas W. MA LLB BD	1975	1993	(Alexandria: North)	3 Cairnbaan Lea, Cairnbaan, Lochgilphead PA31 8BA	01546 606815
Bristow, W.H.G. BEd HDipRE DipSpecEd	1951	2002	Part-time Hospital Chaplain: Campbeltown	Laith Cottage, Southend, Campbeltown PA28 6RU	01586 830667
Dunlop, Alistair J. MA FSAScot	1965	2004	(Saddell and Carradale)	8 Pipers Road, Cairnbaan, Lochgilphead PA31 8UF [E-mail: dunrevn@btinternet.com]	01546 600316
Erskine, Austin U.	1986	2001	(Anwoth and Girthon with Borgue)	'Anwoth', 8 Dunloskin View, Kirn, Dunoon PA23 8HW	01369 701295
Fenemore, John H.C.	1980	1993	(Edinburgh: Colinton Mains)	Seaford Cottage, 74E Shore Road, Innellan, Dunoon PA23 7TR	01369 830678
Forrest, Alan B. MA	1956	1993	(Uphall: South)	126 Shore Road, Innellan, Dunoon PA23 7SX	01369 830424
Forrest, Janice (Mrs) DCS			Part-time Hospital Chaplain: Campbeltown	St Blaans Manse, Southend, Campbeltown PA28 6RQ	01586 830274
Gibson, Frank S. BL BD STM DSWA DD	1963	1995	(Kilarrow with Kilmeny)	163 Gilbertstoun, Edinburgh EH15 2RG	0131-657 5208
Grainger, Ian G.	1985	1991	(Maxton with Newtown)	Seaview, Ardtun, Bunessan, Isle of Mull PA67 6DH	01681 700457
Gray, William LTh	1971	2006	(Kilberry with Tarbert)	Lochnagar, Longsdale Road, Oban PA34 5DZ [E-mail: gray98@hotmail.com]	01631 567471
Henderson, Charles M.	1952	1989	(Campbeltown: Highland)	Springbank House, Askomill Walk, Campbeltown PA28 6EP	01586 552759
Hood, H. Stanley C. MA BD	1966	2000	(London: Crown Court)	10 Dalriada Place, Kilmichael Glassary, Lochgilphead PA31 8QA	01546 606168
Inglis, David B.C. MA MEd BD	1975	2000	(Turriff: St Andrew's)	'Lindores', 11 Bullwood Road, Dunoon PA23 7QJ	01369 701334
Lamont, Archibald	1952	1994	(Kilcalmonell with Skipness)	8 Achlonan, Taynuilt PA35 1JJ	01866 822385
MacKechnie, J.M. MBE MA	1938	1978	(Kilchrenan and Dalavich)	c/o Montgomery, 185 Mill Road, Hamilton ML3 8PE	
Mackenzie, Iain MA BD	1967	2000	(Tarbat)	3 Southern Beeches, Sandbank, Dunoon PA23 8PD [E-mail: iain84mackenzie@btinternet.com]	01369 703507
Marshall, Freda (Mrs) BD FCII	1993	2005	(Colonsay and Oronsay with Kilbrandon and Kilchattan)	All Mhaluidh, Glenview, Dalmally PA33 1BE [E-mail: mail@freda.org.uk]	01838 200693

Miller, Harry Galbraith MA BD	1941 1985	(Iona and Ross of Mull)	16 Lobnitz Avenue, Renfrew PA4 0TG	0141-886 2147
Montgomery, David	1961 1996	(North Knapdale)	185 Mill Road, Hamilton ML3 8PE	
Morrison, Angus W. MA BD	1959 1999	(Kildalton and Oa)	1 Livingstone Way, Port Ellen, Isle of Islay PA42 7EP	01496 300043
Pollock, William MA BD PhD	1987 2002	(Isle of Mull Parishes)	Correay, Salen, Aros, Isle of Mull PA72 6JF	01680 300507
Ritchie, Malcolm A.	1955 1990	(Kilbrandon and Kilchattan)	Roadside Cottage, Tayvallich, Lochgilphead PA31 8PN	01546 870616
Ritchie, Walter M.	1973 1999	(Uphall: South)	Hazel Cottage, Barr Mor View, Kilmartin, Lochgilphead PA31 8UN	01546 510343
Stewart, Jean E. (Mrs)	1983 1989	(Kildalton and Oa)	Tigh-na-Truain, Port Ellen, Isle of Islay PA42 7AH	01496 302068
Taylor, Alan T. BD	1980 2005	(Isle of Mull Parishes)	Erray Road, Tobermory, Isle of Mull PA75 6PS	01688 302496
Troup, Harold J.G. MA	1951 1980	(Garelochhead)	Tighshee, Isle of Iona PA76 6SP	01681 700309
Watson, James LTh	1968 1994	(Bowden with Lilliesleaf)	7 Lochan Avenue, Kirn, Dunoon PA23 8HT	01369 702851

Communion Sundays

Ardrishaig	4th Apr, 1st Nov
Campbeltown	
Highland	1st May, Nov
Lorne and Lowland	1st May, Nov
Craignish	1st Jun, Nov
Cumlodden, Lochfyneside	
and Lochgair	1st May, 3rd Nov
Dunoon	
St John's	1st Mar, Jun, Nov
The High Kirk	1st Feb, Jun, Oct
Gigha and Cara	1st May, Nov
Glassary, Kilmartin and Ford	1st Apr, Sep
Glenaray and Inveraray	1st Apr, Jul, Oct, Dec
Innellan	1st Mar, Jun, Sep, Dec
Inverlussa and Bellanoch	2nd May, Nov
Jura	Passion Sun., 2nd Jul, 3rd Nov
Kilarrow	1st Mar, Jun, Sep, Dec
Kilberry with Tarbert	1st May, Oct
Kilcalmonell	1st Jul, 3rd Nov
Kilchoman	1st Jul, 2nd Dec, Easter
Kildalton	Last Jan, Jun, Oct, Easter
Kilfinan	Last Apr, Oct
Killean and Kilchenzie	1st Mar, Jul, Oct
Kilmeny	2nd May, 3rd Nov
Kilmodan and	
Colintraive	1st Apr, Sep
Kilmun	Last Jan, Nov
Kilninver and Kilmelford	Last Feb, Jun, Oct
Kirn	2nd Jun, Oct
Kyles	1st May, Nov
Lochgair	Last Apr, Oct
Lochgilphead	2nd Oct (Gaelic)
	1st Apr, Nov
Lochgoilhead and	
Kilmorich	2nd Mar, Jun, Sep, Nov
North Knapdale	1st Aug, Easter
Portnahaven	3rd Oct, 2nd May
Rothesay Trinity	3rd Jul
Saddell and Carradale	1st Feb, May, Nov
Sandbank	2nd May, 1st Nov
Skipness	1st Jan, May, Nov
Southend	2nd May, Nov
South Knapdale	1st Jun, Dec
Strachur and Strathlachlan	4th Apr, 1st Nov
Strone and Ardentinny	1st Mar, Jun, Nov
Tayvallich	Last Feb, Jun, Oct
The United Church of Bute	2nd May, Nov
Toward	1st Feb, May, Nov
	Last Feb, May, Aug, Nov

(22) FALKIRK

Meets at St Andrew's West, Falkirk, on the first Tuesday of September, October, November, December and March, on the fourth Tuesday of January and on the third Tuesday of June; and in Kildrum Church, Cumbernauld on the first Tuesday in May.

Clerk:	REV. IAN W. BLACK MA BD	Zetland Manse, Ronaldshay Crescent, Grangemouth FK3 9JH [E-mail: akph51@uk.uumail.com]	01324 472868 / 01324 471656 (Presby)
Associate Clerk:	REV. JEROME O'BRIEN BA LLB BTh	3 Orchard Grove, Polmont, Falkirk FK2 0XE	01324 718677
Treasurer:	MR. I. MACDONALD	1 Jones Avenue, Larbert FK5 3ER	01324 553603

Airth (H)
Vacant — The Manse, Airth, Falkirk FK2 8LS — 01324 831474

Blackbraes and Shieldhill
Vacant — Shieldhill, Falkirk FK1 2EG — 01324 621938

Bo'ness: Old (H)
David S. Randall BA BD 2003 — 10 Dundas Street, Bo'ness EH51 0DG — 01506 822206

Bo'ness: St Andrew's (Website: www.standonline.org.uk)
Albert O. Bogle BD MTh 1981 — St Andrew's Manse, 11 Erngath Road, Bo'ness EH51 9DP [E-mail: a.bogle@blueyonder.co.uk] — 01506 822195

Bonnybridge: St Helen's (H) (01324 815756)
Alisdair T. MacLeod-Mair MEd DipTheol 2001 — 133 Falkirk Road, Bonnybridge FK4 1BA — 01324 812621 (Tel/Fax)

Bothkennar and Carronshore
Vacant — 11 Hunter Place, Greenmount Park, Carronshore, Falkirk FK2 8QS — 01324 570525

Brightons (H)
Vacant — The Manse, Maddiston Road, Brightons, Falkirk FK2 0JP — 01324 712062

Carriden (H)
R. Gordon Reid BSc BD MIEE 1993 — The Spires, Foredale Terrace, Carriden, Bo'ness EH51 9LW — 01506 822141

Cumbernauld: Abronhill (H)
Joyce A. Keyes (Mrs) BD 1996 2003 — 26 Ash Road, Cumbernauld, Glasgow G67 3ED — 01236 723833
Linda Black (Miss) BSc DCS — 148 Rowan Road, Cumbernauld, Glasgow G67 3DA — 01236 786265

Cumbernauld: Condorrat (H)

Name	Ord.	Ind.	Address	Phone
William Jackson BD CertMin	1994	2004	11 Rosehill Drive, Cumbernauld, Glasgow G67 4EQ [E-mail: wiljcksn4@aol.com]	01236 721464
Janette McNaughton (Miss) DCS			4 Dunellan Avenue, Moodiesburn, Glasgow G69 0GB	01236 870180

Cumbernauld: Kildrum (H)

Name	Ord.	Ind.	Address	Phone
Elinor J. Gordon (Miss) BD	1988	2004	64 Southfield Road, Balloch, Cumbernauld, Glasgow G68 9DZ [E-mail: elinorgordon@aol.com]	01236 723204
David Nicholson DCS			2D Doon Side, Kildrum, Cumbernauld, Glasgow G67 2HX [E-mail: deacdave@btopenworld.com]	01236 732260

Cumbernauld: Old (H)

Name	Ord.	Ind.	Address	Phone
Catriona Ogilvie (Mrs) MA BD	1999		The Manse, 23 Baronhill, Cumbernauld, Glasgow G67 2SD	01236 721912
Valerie Cuthbertson (Miss) DCS			105 Bellshill Road, Motherwell ML1 3SJ	01698 259001

Cumbernauld: St Mungo's

Name	Ord.	Ind.	Address	Phone
Neil MacKinnon BD	1990	1999	18 Fergusson Road, Cumbernauld, Glasgow G67 1LS [E-mail: neil.mackinnon@homecall.co.uk]	01236 721513
Ronald M. Mackinnon DCS			71 Cromary Road, Cairnhill, Airdrie ML6 9RL	01236 762024

Denny: Dunipace (H)

Name	Ord.	Ind.	Address	Phone
Jean W. Gallacher (Miss) BD CMin CTheol DMin	1989		Dunipace Manse, Denny FK6 6QJ	01324 824540

Denny: Old

Name	Ord.	Ind.	Address	Phone
John Murning BD	1988	2002	31 Duke Street, Denny FK6 6NR [E-mail: bridgebuilder@supanet.com]	01324 824508

Denny: Westpark (H) (Website: www.westparkchurch.org.uk)

Name	Ord.	Ind.	Address	Phone
Andrew Barrie BSc BD	1984	2000	13 Baxter Crescent, Denny FK6 5EZ [E-mail: andrew.barrie@blueyonder.co.uk]	01324 876224
David Wandrum (Aux)	1993	2005	5 Cawder View, Carrickstone Meadows, Cumbernauld, Glasgow G68 0BN	01236 723288

Falkirk: Bainsford

Name	Ord.	Ind.	Address	Phone
Michael R. Philip BD	1978	2001	1 Valleyview Place, Newcarron Village, Falkirk FK2 7JB [E-mail: mrphilip@btinternet.com]	01324 621087

Falkirk: Camelon

Name	Ord.	Ind.	Address	Phone
Stuart Sharp MTheol DipPA	2001		30 Cotland Drive, Falkirk FK2 7GE	01324 623631
Margaret Corrie (Miss) DCS			44 Sunnyside Street, Falkirk FK1 4BH	01324 670656

Falkirk: Erskine (H)

Name	Ord.	Ind.	Address	Phone
Glen D. Macaulay BD	1999		Burnbrae Road, Falkirk FK1 5SD	01324 623701

Falkirk: Grahamston United (H) Vacant			30 Russel Street, Falkirk FK2 7HS	01324 624461
Falkirk: Laurieston linked with Redding and Westquarter Geoffrey H. Smart LTh	1994	2002	11 Polmont Road, Laurieston, Falkirk FK2 9QQ	01324 621196
Falkirk: Old and St Modan's (H) Robert S.T. Allan LLB DipLP BD	1991	2003	9 Major's Loan, Falkirk FK1 5QF	01324 625124
Falkirk: St Andrew's West (H) Alastair M. Horne BSc BD	1989	1997	1 Maggiewood's Loan, Falkirk FK1 5SJ	01324 623308
Falkirk: St James' Vacant			13 Wallace Place, Falkirk FK2 7EN	01324 622757
Grangemouth: Abbotsgrange Vacant			8 Naismith Court, Grangemouth FK3 9BQ	01324 482109
(Charge formed by the union of Grangemouth: Dundas and Grangemouth: Kerse)				
Grangemouth: Kirk of the Holy Rood David J. Smith BD DipMin	1992	2003	The Manse, Bowhouse Road, Grangemouth FK3 0EX	01324 471595
Grangemouth: Zetland (H) Ian W. Black MA BD	1976	1991	Ronaldshay Crescent, Grangemouth FK3 9JH	01324 472868
Haggs (H) Helen F. Christie (Mrs) BD	1998		5 Watson Place, Dennyloanhead, Bonnybridge FK4 2BG	01324 813786
Larbert: East Melville D. Crosthwaite BD DipEd DipMin Lorna A. MacDougall (Miss) MA (Aux)	1984 2003	1995	1 Cortachy Avenue, Carron, Falkirk FK2 8DH 34 Millar Place, Carron, Falkirk FK2 8QB	01324 562402 01324 552739
Larbert: Old (H) Clifford A.J. Rennie MA BD	1973	1985	The Manse, 38 South Broomage Avenue, Larbert FK5 3ED	01324 562868
Larbert: West (H) Gavin Boswell BTheol	1993	1999	11 Carronvale Road, Larbert FK5 3LZ	01324 562878
Muiravonside Vacant			The Manse, South Brae, Main Road, Maddiston, Falkirk FK2 0LX	01324 712876
Polmont: Old Jerome O'Brien BA LLB BTh	2001	2005	3 Orchard Grove, Polmont, Falkirk FK2 0XE	01324 718677

Redding and Westquarter See Falkirk: Laurieston

Slamannan

Name	Year	Address	Tel
Raymond Thomson BD DipMin	1992	Slamannan, Falkirk FK1 3EN	01324 851307

Stenhouse and Carron (H)

Name	Address	Tel
Vacant	Stenhouse Church Manse, Church Street, Stenhousemuir, Larbert FK5 4BU	01324 562393

Name			Charge / Position	Address	Tel
Barclay, Neil W. BSc BEd BD	1986	2006	(Falkirk: Grahamston United)	4 Gibsongray Street, Falkirk FK2 7LN	01324 874681
Blair, Douglas B. LTh	1969	2004	(Grangemouth: Dundas)	Flat 6, Hanover Grange, Forth Street, Grangemouth FK3 8LF	01324 484414
Brown, James BA BD DipHSW DipPsychol	1973	2001	(Abercorn with Dalmeny)	Fern Cottage, 3 Philpingstone Lane, Bo'ness EH51 9JP	01506 822454
Chalmers, George A. MA BD MLitt	1962	2002	(Catrine with Sorn)	3 Cricket Place, Brightons, Falkirk FK2 0HZ	01324 712030
Goodman, Richard A.	1976	1986	(Isle of Mull Associate)	13/2 Glenbrae Court, Falkirk FK1 1YT	01324 621315
Hardie, Robert K. MA BD	1968	2005	(Stenhouse and Carron)	33 Palace Street, Berwick-upon-Tweed TD15 1HN	01324 711352
Heriot, Charles R. JP BA	1962	1996	(Brightons)	20 Eastcroft Drive, Polmont, Falkirk FK2 0SU	01324 634483
Hill, Stanley LTh	1967	1998	(Muiravonside)	28 Creteil Court, Falkirk FK1 1UL	01324 880109
Holland, John C.	1976	1985	(Strone and Ardentinny)	7 Polmont Park, Polmont, Falkirk FK2 0XT	
Jenkinson, John J. JP LTCL ALCM DipEd DipSen	1991	2006	(Auxiliary Minister)	8 Rosehall Terrace, Falkirk FK1 1PY	01324 625498
Kellock, Chris N. MA BD		1998	Chaplain: RAF Sqn Leader	The Chaplaincy Centre, RAF Akrotiri, BFPO 57	00 357 2567 6220
Kesting, Sheilagh M. (Miss) BA BD	1980	1993	Ecumenical Relations	12 Glenview Drive, Falkirk FK1 5JU	01324 671489
Kirkland, Scott R.McL. BD MAR	1996	2005	Lucaya Presbyterian Kirk, Bahamas	PO Box F-40777, Freeport	001 242 373 2568 / 001 242 373 4961 (Fax)
McCallum, John	1962	1998	(Falkirk: Irving Camelon)	11 Burnbrae Gardens, Falkirk FK1 5SB	01324 619766
McDonald, William G. MA BD	1959	1975	(Falkirk: Grahamston United)	38 St Mary Street, St Andrews KY16 8AZ	01334 470481
McDowall, Ronald J. BD	1980	2001	(Falkirk: Laurieston with Redding and Westquarter)		
McMullin, J. Andrew MA	1960	1996	(Blackbraes and Shieldhill)	'Kailas', Windsor Road, Falkirk FK1 5EJ	01324 871947
Martin, Neil DCS			(Deacon)	33 Eastcroft Drive, Polmont, Falkirk FK2 0SU	01324 624938
Mathers, Daniel L. BD	1982	2001	(Grangemouth: Charing Cross and West)	3 Strathmiglo Place, Stenhousemuir, Larbert FK5 4UQ	01324 551362
Maxton, Ronald M. MA	1955	1995	(Dollar: Associate)	10 Ercall Road, Brightons, Falkirk FK2 0RS	01324 872253
Miller, Elsie M. (Miss) DCS			(Deaconess)	5 Rulley View, Denny FK6 6QQ	01324 825441
Munro, Henry BA LTh LTI	1971	1988	(Denny: Dunipace North with Old)	30 Swinton Avenue, Rowansbank, Baillieston, Glasgow G69 6JR	0141-771 0857
Paul, Iain BSc PhD BD PhD	1976	1991	(Wishaw: Craigneuk and Belhaven)	Viewforth, High Road, Maddiston, Falkirk FK2 0BL	01324 712446
Ross, Evan J. LTh	1986	1998	(Cowdenbeath: West with Mossgreen and Crossgates)	116 Tryst Road, Larbert FK5 4QJ	01324 562641
Scott, Donald H. BA BD	1987	2002	Prison Chaplain	5 Arneil Place, Brightons, Falkirk FK2 0NJ / Polmont Young Offenders' Institution, Newlands Road, Brightons, Falkirk FK2 0DE	01324 719936 / 01324 711558
Smith, Richard BD	1976	2002	(Denny: Old)	Easter Wayside, 46 Kennedy Way, Airth, Falkirk FK2 8GB [E-mail: richards@uklinux.net]	01324 831386
Talman, Hugh MA	1943	1987	(Polmont: Old)	Niagara, 70 Lawers Crescent, Polmont, Falkirk FK2 0QU	01324 711240
Whiteford, Robert S. MA	1945	1986	(Shapinsay)	3 Wellside Court, Wellside Place, Falkirk FK1 5RG	01324 610562

FALKIRK ADDRESSES

Falkirk		Main Falkirk Road	**Grangemouth**	
Bainsford	Hendry Street, Bainsford		Abbotsgrange	Abbot's Road
Camelon	Dorrator Road	Kirk Wynd	Kirk of the Holy Rood	Bowhouse Road
Erskine	Cockburn Street x Hodge Street	Newmarket Street	Zetland	Ronaldshay Crescent
Grahamston	Bute Street	Thornhill Road x Firs Street		
	Laurieston			
	Old and St Modan's			
	St Andrew's West			
	St James'			

(23) STIRLING

Meets at the Moderator's Church on the second Thursday of September; and at Stirling Management Centre, Stirling University on the second Thursday of every other month except January, July and August when there is no meeting.

Clerk: MOIRA G. MacCORMICK BA LTh — Presbytery Office, St Columba's Church, Park Terrace, Stirling FK8 2NA
[E-mail: akph75@uk.uumail.com]
[E-mail: stirling-presbytery@uk.uumail.com]
01786 449522 (Tel)
01786 473930 (Fax)
(Mon–Fri: 9:30am–12 noon)

Treasurer: MR GILMOUR CUTHBERTSON — 'Denovan', 1 Doune Road, Dunblane FK15 9AR
01786 823487

Aberfoyle (H) linked with Port of Menteith (H)
James Daniel Gibb BA LTh | 1994 | 2000 | The Manse, Loch Ard Road, Aberfoyle, Stirling FK8 3SZ | 01877 382391
[E-mail: dannygibb@hotmail.co.uk]

Alloa: North (H)
Elizabeth Clelland (Mrs) BD | 2002 | 30 Claremont, Alloa FK10 2DF | 01259 210403

Alloa: St Mungo's (H)
Alan F.M. Downie MA BD | 1977 | 1996 | 37a Claremont, Alloa FK10 2DG | 01259 213872
[E-mail: alan@stmungos.freeserve.co.uk]

Alloa: West
Vacant | 29 Claremont, Alloa FK10 2DF | 01259 214204

Alva
James N.R. McNeil BSc BD | 1990 | 1997 | The Manse, 34 Ochil Road, Alva FK12 5JT | 01259 760262

Balfron linked with Fintry (H)
John Turnbull LTh | 1994 | 7 Station Road, Balfron, Glasgow G63 0SX | 01360 440285

Balquhidder linked with Killin and Ardeonaig (H)

John Lincoln MPhil BD	1986 1997	The Manse, Killin FK21 8TN [E-mail: gm0jol@zetnet.co.uk]	01567 820247

Bannockburn: Allan (H) (Website: www.allanchurch.org.uk)

Jim Landels BD CertMin	1990	The Manse, Bogend Road, Bannockburn, Stirling FK7 8NP [E-mail: revjimlandels@btinternet.com]	01786 814692

Bannockburn: Ladywell (H)

Elizabeth M.D. Robertson (Miss) BD CertMin	1997	57 The Firs, Bannockburn FK7 0EG [E-mail: lizr@tinyonline.uk]	01786 812467

Bridge of Allan (H) (01786 834155)

Gillian Weighton (Mrs) BD STM	1992 2004	19 Keir Street, Bridge of Allan, Stirling FK9 4QJ [E-mail: gillweighton@aol.com]	01786 832753

Buchanan linked with Drymen

Alexander J. MacPherson BD	1986 1997	Buchanan Manse, Drymen, Glasgow G63 0AQ	01360 870212

Buchlyvie (H) linked with Gartmore (H)

Elaine H. MacRae (Mrs) BD	1985 2004	The Manse, Kippen, Stirling FK8 3DN	01786 871170

Callander (H) (Tel/Fax: 01877 331409)

Stanley A. Brook BD MTh	1977 2004	3 Aveland Park Road, Callander FK17 8FD [E-mail: stan_brook@hotmail.com]	01877 330097
June Cloggie (Mrs) (Aux)	1997 1998	11A Tulipan Crescent, Callander FK17 8AR	01877 331021

Cambusbarron: The Bruce Memorial (H)

Brian G. Webster BSc BD	1998	14 Woodside Court, Cambusbarron, Stirling FK7 9PH [E-mail: revwebby@aol.com]	01786 450579

Clackmannan (H)

J. Gordon Mathew MA BD	1973 1999	The Manse, Port Street, Clackmannan FK10 4JH [E-mail: jgmathew@lineone.net]	01259 211255

Cowie (H) and Plean linked with Fallin

Vacant		The Manse, Plean, Stirling FK7 8BX	01786 813287

Dollar (H) linked with Glendevon linked with Muckhart (Website: www.dollarparishchurch.org.uk)

Suzanne G. Fletcher (Mrs) BA MDiv MA	2001 2004	2 Manse Road, Dollar FK14 7AJ [E-mail: revfletcher@btinternet.com]	01259 743432
J. Mary Henderson (Miss) MA BD DipEd PhD (Assoc)	1990 2005	58 The Ness, Dollar FK14 7EB	01259 743503

Drymen See Buchanan

Dunblane: Cathedral (H)
Colin G. McIntosh BSc BD — 1976 1988 — Cathedral Manse, The Cross, Dunblane FK15 0AQ — 01786 822205

Dunblane: St Blane's (H)
Alexander B. Mitchell — 1981 2003 — 49 Roman Way, Dunblane FK15 9DJ [E-mail: alex.mitchell6@btopenworld.com] — 01786 822268

Fallin See Cowie and Plean

Fintry See Balfron

Gargunnock linked with Kilmadock linked with Kincardine-in-Menteith
Richard S. Campbell LTh — 1993 2001 — The Manse, Gargunnock, Stirling FK8 3BQ — 01786 860678

Gartmore See Buchlyvie

Glendevon See Dollar

Killearn (H)
Philip R.M. Malloch LLB BD — 1970 1993 — 2 The Oaks, Killearn, Glasgow G63 9SF [E-mail: minister@killearnkirk.org.uk] — 01360 550045

Killin and Ardeonaig (H) See Balquhidder

Kilmadock See Gargunnock

Kincardine-in-Menteith See Gargunnock

Kippen (H) linked with Norrieston
Gordon MacRae BA BD — 1985 1998 — The Manse, Kippen, Stirling FK8 3DN — 01786 870229

Lecropt (H)
William M. Gilmour MA BD — 1969 1983 — 5 Henderson Street, Bridge of Allan, Stirling FK9 4NA — 01786 832382

Logie (H)
Vacant — 21 Craiglea, Causewayhead, Stirling FK9 5EE — 01786 463060

Menstrie (H)
Mairi F. Lovett BSc BA DipPS MTh — 2005 — The Manse, 7 Long Row, Menstrie FK11 7BA [E-mail: mairi.lovett@kanyo.co.uk] — 01259 761461

Muckhart See Dollar

Norrieston See Kippen

Port of Menteith See Aberfoyle

Sauchie and Coalsnaughton Alan T. McKean BD	1982	2003	19 Graygoran, Sauchie, Alloa FK10 3ET [E-mail: almack@freeuk.com]	01259 212037
Stirling: Allan Park South (H) linked with Church of the Holy Rude (H) Vacant			22 Laurelhill Place, Stirling FK8 2JH	01786 473999
Stirling: Church of the Holy Rude (H) See Stirling: Allan Park South				
Stirling: North (H) (01786 463376) (Website: www.northparishchurch.com) Calum Jack BSc BD	2004		18 Shirra's Brae Road, Stirling FK7 0BA [E-mail: info@northparishchurch.com]	01786 475378
Stirling: St Columba's (H) (01786 449516) Kenneth G. Russell BD CCE	1986	2001	5 Clifford Road, Stirling FK8 2AQ [E-mail: kenrussell1000@hotmail.com]	01786 475802
Stirling: St Mark's Vacant			176 Drip Road, Stirling FK8 1RR	01786 473716
Stirling: St Ninian's Old (H) Gary J. McIntyre BD DipMin	1993	1998	7 Randolph Road, Stirling FK8 2AJ	01786 474421
Stirling: Viewfield (T) (H) Vacant			7 Windsor Place, Stirling FK8 2HY	01786 474534
Strathblane (H) Alex H. Green MA BD	1986	1995	The Manse, Strathblane, Glasgow G63 9AB	01360 770226
Tillicoultry (H) James Cochrane LTh	1994	2000	The Manse, Dollar Road, Tillicoultry FK13 6PD [E-mail: jc@cochranemail.co.uk]	01259 750340 01259 752951 (Fax)
Tullibody: St Serf's (H) John Brown MA BD	1995	2000	16 Menstrie Road, Tullibody, Alloa FK10 2RG [E-mail: john@browntj.fsnet.co.uk]	01259 213236

Aitken, E. Douglas MA	1961 1998	(Clackmannan)	1 Dolan Grove, Saline, Dunfermline KY12 9UP	01383 852730
Benson, James W. BA BD DipEd	1975 1996	(Balquhidder)	1 Sunnyside, Dunblane FK15 9HA	01786 822624
Blackley, Jean R.M. (Mrs) BD	1989 2001	(Banton with Twechar)	8 Rodders Grove, Alva FK12 5RR	01259 760198
Brown, James H. BD	1977 2005	(Helensburgh: Park)	14 Gullipen View, Callander FK17 8HN	01877 339425

Name	Dates	Role	Address	Tel
Craig, Maxwell D. BD ThM	1966 2000	(Jerusalem: St Andrew's: Locum)	3 Queen's Road, Stirling FK8 2QY	01786 472319
Cruickshank, Alistair A.B. MA	1991 2004	(Auxiliary Minister)	2A Chapel Place, Dollar FK14 7DW	01259 742549
Doherty, Arthur James DipTh	1957 1993	(Fintry)	1 Murdiston Avenue, Callander FK17 8AY	
Fleming, Alexander F. MA BD	1966 1995	(Strathblane)	4 Horsburgh Avenue, Kilsyth, Glasgow G65 9BZ	01236 821461
Izett, William A.F.	1968 2000	(Law)	1 Duke Street, Clackmannan FK10 4EF	01259 724203
Jamieson, G.T. BA	1936 1969	(Stirling: Viewfield)	10 Grendon Court, Snowdon Place, Stirling FK8 2JX	01786 461646
MacCormick, Moira G. BA LTh	1986 2003	(Buchlyvie with Gartmore)	12 Rankine Wynd, Tullibody, Alloa FK10 2UW	01259 724619
McIntosh, Hamish N.M. MA	1949 1987	(Fintry)	1 Forth Crescent, Stirling FK8 1LE	01786 470453
Murray, Douglas R. MA BD	1994 2004	(Lausanne)	32 Forth Park, Bridge of Allan, Stirling FK9 5NT	01786 831081
Nicol, John C. MA BD	1965 2002	(Bridge of Allan: Holy Trinity)	37 King O'Muirs Drive, Tullibody, Alloa FK10 3AY	01259 212305
Ovens, Samuel B. BD	1982 1993	(Slamannan)	21 Bevan Drive, Alva FK12 5PD	01259 222723
Paterson, John L. MA BD STM	1964 2003	(Linlithgow: St Michael's)	'Kirkmichael', 22 Waterfront Way, Stirling FK9 5GH [E-mail: lormandian.paterson@virgin.net]	01786 447165
Pryce, Stuart F.A.	1963 1997	(Dumfries: St George's)	36 Forth Park, Bridge of Allan, Stirling FK9 5NT	01786 831026
Rennie, James B. MA	1959 1992	(Leochel Cushnie and Lynturk with Tough)	17 Oliphant Court, Riverside, Stirling FK8 1US	
Robertson, Alex	1974 1993	(Baldernock)	4 Moray Park, Moray Street, Doune FK16 6DJ	01786 841894
Sangster, Ernest G. BD ThM	1958 1997	(Alva)	6 Law Hill Road, Dollar FK14 7BG	
Scott, James F.	1957 1997	(Dyce)	5 Gullipen View, Callander FK17 8HN	01877 330565
Scoular, J. Marshall	1954 1996	(Kippen)	2H Buccleuch Court, Dunblane FK15 0AH	01786 825976
Sherry, George T. LTh	1977 2004	(Menstrie)	37 Moubray Gardens, Silver Meadows, Cambus, Alloa FK10 2NQ	01259 220665
Silcox, John R. BD DipPhilEd CPP CF TD	1976 1984	School Chaplain	Queen Victoria School, Dunblane FK15 0JY	01786 824944
Sinclair, James H. MA BD	1966 2004	(Auchencairn and Rerrick with Buittle and Kelton)	25 The Shielings, Cambus, Alloa FK10 2NN	01259 729001
Stewart, Angus T. MA BD PhD	1962 1999	(Glasgow: Greenbank)	Mansefield, Station Road, Buchlyvie, Stirling FK8 3NE	01360 850117
Todd, A. Stewart MA BD DD	1952 1993	(Aberdeen: St Machar's Cathedral)	Ferntoun House, 11 Bedford Place, Alloa FK10 1LJ	01259 212737
Watson, Jean S. (Miss) MA	1993 2004	(Auxiliary Minister)	29 Strachan Crescent, Dollar FK14 7HL	01259 742872
Watt, Robert MA BD	1943 1982	(Aberdeen: Woodside South)	1 Coldstream Avenue, Dunblane FK15 9JN	01786 823632
Wright, John P. BD	1977 2000	(Glasgow: New Govan)	Plane Castle, Airth, Falkirk FK2 8SF	01786 480840

STIRLING ADDRESSES

Allan Park South	Dumbarton Road	
Holy Rude	St John Street	
North	Springfield Road	
St Columba's	Park Terrace	
St Mark's	Drip Road	
St Ninian's Old	Kirk Wynd, St Ninians	
Viewfield	Barnton Street	

(24) DUNFERMLINE

Meets at Dunfermline in the Abbey Church Hall, Abbey Park Place, on the first Thursday of each month, except January, July and August when there is no meeting, and June when it meets on the last Thursday.

Clerk: REV. ELIZABETH S.S. KENNY BD RGN SCM   The Manse, Carnock, Dunfermline KY12 9JG   01383 850327
[E-mail: akph46@uk.uumail.com]

Aberdour: St Fillan's (H) (Website: www.stfillans.presbytery.org)
Peter S. Gerbrandy-Baird   2004   St Fillan's Manse, 36 Bellhouse Road, Aberdour, Fife KY3 0TL   01383 861522
MA BD MSc FRSA FRGS

Beath and Cowdenbeath: North (H)
David W. Redmayne BSc BD   2001   10 Stuart Place, Cowdenbeath KY4 9BN   01383 511033
[E-mail: david@redmayne.freeserve.co.uk]

Cairneyhill (H) (01383 882352) linked with Limekilns (H) (01383 873337)
Norman M. Grant BD   1990   The Manse, 10 Church Street, Limekilns, Dunfermline KY11 3HT   01383 872341
[E-mail: norman.grant@which.net]

Carnock and Oakley (H)
Elizabeth S.S. Kenny BD RGN SCM   1989   The Manse, Carnock, Dunfermline KY12 9JG   01383 850327
[E-mail: esskenny@ecosse.net]

Cowdenbeath: Trinity (H)
David G. Adams BD   1991   1999   66 Barclay Street, Cowdenbeath KY4 9LD   01383 515089
[E-mail: trinity@fsmail.net]

Culross and Torryburn (H)
Thomas Moffat BSc BD   1976   2000   Culross, Dunfermline KY12 8JD   01383 880231
[E-mail: ctm@fish.co.uk]

Dalgety (H) (01383 824092) (E-mail: office@dalgety-church.co.uk) (Website: www.dalgety-church.co.uk)
Donald G.B. McCorkindale BD DipMin   1992   2000   9 St Colme Drive, Dalgety Bay, Dunfermline KY11 9LQ   01383 822316 (Tel/Fax)
[E-mail: donald@dalgety-church.co.uk]

Dunfermline: Abbey (H) (Website: www.dunfabbey.freeserve.co.uk)
Alistair L. Jessamine MA BD   1979   1991   12 Garvock Hill, Dunfermline KY12 7UU   01383 721022
[E-mail: alistairjessamine@dunfermlineabbey.wanadoo.co.uk]

Dunfermline: Gillespie Memorial (H) (01383 621253) (E-mail: gillespie.church@btopenworld.com)
A. Gordon Reid BSc BD   1982   1988   4 Killin Court, Dunfermline KY12 7XF   01383 723329
[E-mail: reid501@fsmail.net]

Dunfermline: North
Vacant
Andrew E. Paterson (Aux)   13 Barbour Grove, Dunfermline KY12 9YB   01383 851078
                                             6 The Willows, Kelty KY4 0FQ   01383 830998

Dunfermline: St Andrew's Erskine (01383 841660)
Ann Allison BSc PhD BD   2000   71A Townhill Road, Dunfermline KY12 0BN   01383 734657
[E-mail: ann.allison@homecall.co.uk]

Dunfermline: St Leonard's (01383 620106) (E-mail: stleonards_dunf@lineone.net) (Website: www.stleonardsparishchurch.org.uk)
Andrew J. Philip BSc BD   1996   2004   12 Torvean Place, Dunfermline KY11 4YY   01383 721054 (Tel)
[E-mail: andrewphilip@minister.com]   0871 242 5222 (Fax)

Dunfermline: St Margaret's
Vacant   38 Garvock Hill, Dunfermline KY12 7UU   01383 723955

Dunfermline: St Ninian's
Elizabeth A. Fisk (Mrs) BD   1996   51 St John's Drive, Dunfermline KY12 7TL   01383 722256
Jacqueline Thomson (Mrs) DCS   2004   1 Barron Terrace, Leven KY8 4DL   01333 301115

Dunfermline: St Paul's East (New Charge Development)
Alan Childs BA BD MBA   2000   2003   9 Dover Drive, Dunfermline KY11 8HQ   01383 620704
[E-mail: alan@kingdomkirk.org.uk]

Dunfermline: Townhill and Kingseat (H)
William E. Farquhar BA BD   1987   161 Main Street, Townhill, Dunfermline KY12 0EZ   01383 723835
[E-mail: akph46@uk.uumail.com]

Inverkeithing: St John's linked with North Queensferry (T)
Christopher D. Park BSc BD   1977   2005   1 Dover Way, Dunfermline KY11 8HR

Inverkeithing: St Peter's (01383 412626)
George G. Nicol BD DPhil   1982   1988   20 Struan Drive, Inverkeithing KY11 1AR   01383 410032
[E-mail: ggnicol@totalise.co.uk]

Kelty (Website: www.keltykirk.org.uk)
Scott Burton BD DipMin   1999   15 Arlick Road, Kelty KY4 0BH   01383 830291
[E-mail: minister@keltykirk.org.uk]

Limekilns See Cairneyhill

Lochgelly and Benarty: St Serf's

Elisabeth M. Stenhouse (Ms) BD — 2006 — 82 Main Street, Lochgelly KY5 9AA [E-mail: lissten@tiscali.co.uk] — 01592 780435

North Queensferry   See Inverkeithing: St John's

Rosyth

Violet C.C. McKay (Mrs) BD — 1988 2002 — 42 Woodside Avenue, Rosyth KY11 2LA [E-mail: v.mckay@btinternet.com] — 01383 412776

Morag Crawford (Miss) MSc DCS — 118 Wester Drylaw Place, Edinburgh EH4 2TG [E-mail: morag.crawford@virgin.net] — 0131-332 2253

Saline and Blairingone

Robert P. Boyle LTh — 1990 2003 — 8 The Glebe, Saline, Dunfermline KY12 9UT [E-mail: boab.boyle@btinternet.com] — 01383 853062

Tulliallan and Kincardine

Jock Stein MA BD — 1973 2002 — 62 Toll Road, Kincardine, Alloa FK10 4QZ [E-mail: handsel@dial.pipex.com] — 01259 730538

Margaret E. Stein (Mrs) DA BD DipRE — 1984 2002 — 62 Toll Road, Kincardine, Alloa FK10 4QZ [E-mail: handsel@dial.pipex.com] — 01259 730538

Brown, Peter MA BD FRAScot	1953 1987	(Holm)	24 Inchmickery Avenue, Dalgety Bay, Dunfermline KY11 5NF	01383 822456
Campbell, John MA	1943 1978	(Urquhart)	40A Couston Street, Dunfermline KY12 7QW	01383 738055
Findlay, Henry J.W. MA BD	1965 2005	(Wishaw: St Mark's)	94 Dewar Street, Dunfermline KY12 8AA	01383 724345
Jenkins, Gordon F.C. MA BD PhD	1968 2006	(Dunfermline: North)	59 Porterfield, Comrie, Dunfermline KY12 9XQ	01383 851078
Macpherson, Stewart M. MA	1953 1990	(Dunfermline: Abbey)	176 Halbeath Road, Dunfermline KY11 4LB	01383 722851
Orr, J. McMichael MA BD PhD	1949 1986	(Aberfoyle with Port of Menteith)	9 Overhaven, Limekilns, Dunfermline KY11 3JH	01383 872245
Pogue, Victor C. BA BD	1945 1980	(Baird Research Fellow)	5/2 Plewlands Court, Edinburgh EH10 5JY	0131-445 1628
Reid, David MSc LTh FSAScot	1961 1992	(St Monans with Largoward)	North Lethans, Saline, Dunfermline KY12 9TE	01383 733144
Scott, John LTh	1969 1996	(Aberdour: St Fillan's)	32 White's Quay, St David's Harbour, Dalgety Bay, Dunfermline	01383 82089
Shewan, Frederick D.F. MA BD	1970 2005	(Edinburgh: Muirhouse St Andrew's)	38 Tremayne Place, Dunfermline KY12 9YH	01383 734354
Stuart, Anne (Miss) DCS		(Deaconess)	19 St Colme Crescent, Aberdour, Burntisland KY3 0ST	01383 860049
Whyte, Isabel H. (Mrs) BD	1993	(Chaplain: Queen Margaret Hospital, Dunfermline)	14 Carlingnose Point, North Queensferry, Inverkeithing KY11 1ER [E-mail: iainisabel@whytes28.fsnet.co.uk]	01383 410732

(25) KIRKCALDY

Meets at Kirkcaldy, in St Brycedale Hall, on the first Tuesday of February, March, April, May, November and December, on the second Tuesday of September, and on the fourth Tuesday of June.

Clerk:	MR ANDREW F. MOORE BL	Annandale, Linksfield Street, Leven KY8 4HX [E-mail: akph59@uk.uumail.com]	01333 422644
Depute Clerk:	MR DOUGLAS G. HAMILL BEM	41 Abbots Mill, Kirkcaldy KY2 5PE [E-mail: hamilldg@tiscali.co.uk]	01592 267500

Auchterderran: St Fothad's linked with Kinglassie
Vacant — 7 Woodend Road, Cardenden, Lochgelly KY5 0NE — 01592 720213

Auchtertool linked with Kirkcaldy: Linktown (H) (01592 641080)
Catriona M. Morrison (Mrs) MA BD — 1995 2000 — 16 Raith Crescent, Kirkcaldy KY2 5NN — 01592 265536

Buckhaven (01592 715577)
Wilma Cairns (Miss) BD — 1999 2004 — 181 Wellesley Road, Buckhaven, Leven KY8 1JA — 01592 712870

Burntisland (H)
Alan Sharp BSc BD — 1980 2001 — 21 Ramsay Crescent, Burntisland KY3 9JL
[E-mail: alansharp03@aol.com] — 01592 874303

Denbeath linked with Methilhill
Elisabeth F. Cranfield (Miss) MA BD — 1988 — 9 Chemiss Road, Methilhill, Leven KY8 2BS
[E-mail: ecranfield@btinternet.com] — 01592 713142

Dysart (H)
Tilly Wilson (Miss) MTh — 1990 1998 — 1 School Brae, Dysart, Kirkcaldy KY1 2XB — 01592 655887

Glenrothes: Christ's Kirk (H)
Peter A.D. Berrill MA BD — 1983 2005 — 12 The Limekilns, Glenrothes KY6 3QJ
[E-mail: peterberrill@hotmail.com] — 01592 620536

Glenrothes: St Columba's (01592 752539)
Diane L. Hobson (Mrs) BA BD — 2002 2005 — 40 Liberton Drive, Glenrothes KY6 3PB
[E-mail: diane.hobson@btclick.com] — 01592 741215
Sarah McDowall (Mrs) DCS — 116 Scot Road, Glenrothes KY6 1AE — 01592 562386

Glenrothes: St Margaret's (H) (01592 610310)
John P. McLean BSc BPhil BD — 1994 — 8 Alburne Park, Glenrothes KY7 5RB
[E-mail: john@stmargaretschurch.org.uk] — 01592 752241

Glenrothes: St Ninian's (H) (01592 610560) (E-mail: st-ninians@tiscali.co.uk)
Vacant — 1 Cawdor Drive, Glenrothes KY6 2HN — 01592 611963

Innerleven: East (H)
James L. Templeton BSc BD — 1975 — 77 McDonald Street, Methil, Leven KY8 3AJ — 01333 426310

Kennoway, Windygates and Balgonie: St Kenneth's (01333 351372) (E-mail: administration@st-kenneths.freeserve.co.uk)
Richard Baxter MA BD — 1997 — 2 Fernhill Gardens, Windygates, Leven KY8 5DZ — 01333 352329
[E-mail: richard-baxter@msn.com]

Maureen Paterson (Mrs) BSc (Aux) — 1992 1994 — 91 Dalmahoy Crescent, Kirkcaldy KY2 6TA — 01592 262300

Kinghorn
James Reid BD — 1985 1997 — 17 Myre Crescent, Kinghorn, Burntisland KY3 9UB — 01592 890269
[E-mail: jim17reid@aol.com]

Kinglassie See Auchterderran: St Fothad's

Kirkcaldy: Abbotshall (H)
Rosemary Frew (Mrs) MA BD — 1988 2005 — 83 Milton Road, Kirkcaldy KY1 1TP — 01592 260315
[E-mail: rosiefrew@blueyonder.co.uk]

Kirkcaldy: Linktown (01592 641080) See Auchtertool

Kirkcaldy: Pathhead (H) (Tel/Fax: 01592 204635) (E-mail: pathhead@btinternet.com) (Website: www.pathheadparishchurch.co.uk)
Andrew C. Donald BD DPS — 1992 2005 — 73 Loughborough Road, Kirkcaldy KY1 3DD — 01592 652215
[E-mail: andrewdonald@blueyonder.co.uk]

Kirkcaldy: St Andrew's (H)
Donald M. Thomson BD — 1975 — 15 Harcourt Road, Kirkcaldy KY2 5HQ — 01592 260816
[E-mail: dmaclthomson@aol.com]

Kirkcaldy: St Bryce Kirk (H) (01592 640016) (E-mail: office@stbee.freeserve.co.uk)
Ken Froude MA BD — 1979 — 6 East Fergus Place, Kirkcaldy KY1 1XT — 01592 264480
[E-mail: kenfroude@blueyonder.co.uk]

Kirkcaldy: St John's
Nicola Frail BLE MBA MDiv — 2000 2004 — 25 Bennochy Avenue, Kirkcaldy KY2 5QE — 01592 263821

Kirkcaldy: Templehall (H)
Anthony J.R. Fowler BSc BD — 1982 2004 — 35 Appin Crescent, Kirkcaldy KY2 6EJ — 01592 260156

Kirkcaldy: Torbain
Ian Elston BD MTh — 1999 — 91 Sauchenbush Road, Kirkcaldy KY2 5RN — 01592 263015

Name	Year	Year	Position / Charge	Address	Phone
Kirkcaldy: Viewforth (H) linked with Thornton Anne J. Job	2000			66 Viewforth Street, Kirkcaldy KY1 3DJ	01592 652502
Leslie: Trinity Melvyn J. Griffiths BTh DipTheol	1978	2006		4 Valley Drive, Leslie, Glenrothes KY6 3BQ [E-mail: mel@thehavyn.wanadoo.co.uk]	01592 741008
Leven Vacant				5 Forman Road, Leven KY8 4HH	01333 303339
Markinch Alexander R. Forsyth TD BA MTh	1973	2002		7 Guthrie Crescent, Markinch, Glenrothes KY7 6AY	01592 758264
Methil (H) Vacant				Alma House, 2 School Brae, Methilhill, Leven KY8 2BT	01592 713708
Methilhill See Denbeath					
Thornton See Kirkcaldy: Viewforth					
Wemyss Kenneth W. Donald BA BD	1982	1999		33 Main Road, East Wemyss, Kirkcaldy KY1 4RE [E-mail: kenneth@kdonald.freeserve.co.uk]	01592 713260
Campbell, J. Ewen R. MA BD	1967	2005	(Auchterderran: St Fothad's with Kinglassie)	93 The Moorings, Dalgety Bay, Dunfermline KY11 9GP	01383 820765
Collins, Mitchell BD CPS	1996	2005	(Creich, Flisk and Kilmany with Monimail)	6 Netherby Park, Glenrothes KY6 3PL	
Connolly, Daniel BD DipTheol DipMin	1983		Army Chaplain	2 CS Reg, RLC, BFPO 47	
Cooper, M.W. MA	1944	1979	(Kirkcaldy: Abbotshall)	Applegarth, Sunny Park, Kinross KY13 7BX	01577 263204
Dick, James S. MA BTh	1988	1997	(Glasgow: Ruchazie)	1 Hawkmuir, Kirkcaldy KY1 2AN	01592 260289
Duncan, John C. BD MPhil	1987	2001	Army Chaplain	British Forces Episkopi Support Unit, BFPO 53	
Elston, Peter K.	1963	2000	(Dalgety)	6 Cairngorm Crescent, Kirkcaldy KY2 5RF	01592 205622
Ferguson, David J.	1966	2001	(Bellie with Speymouth)	4 Russell Gardens, Ladybank, Cupar KY15 7LI	01337 831406
Forrester, Ian L. MA	1964	1996	(Friockheim, Kinnell with Inverkeilor and Lunan)		
Gatt, David W.	1981	1995	(Thornton)	8 Bennochy Avenue, Kirkcaldy KY2 5QE	01592 260251
Gibson, Ivor MA	1957	1993	(Abercorn with Dalmeny)	15 Beech Avenue, Thornton, Kirkcaldy KY1 4AT	01592 774328
Gordon, Ian D. LTh	1972	2001	(Markinch)	15 McInnes Road, Glenrothes KY7 6BA	01592 759982
				2 Somerville Way, Glenrothes KY7 5GE	01592 742487
Howden, Margaret (Miss) DCS			(Deaconess)	38 Munro Street, Kirkcaldy KY1 1PY	01592 205913
McAlpine, Robin J. BDS BD	1988	1997	Adviser in Mission and Evangelism	10 Seton Place, Kirkcaldy KY2 6UX [E-mail: robin.mcalpine@virgin.net]	01592 643518
McDonald, Ian J.M. MA BD	1984	1996	Chaplain, Kirkcaldy Acute Hospitals	11 James Grove, Kirkcaldy KY1 1TN	01592 203775
McKenzie, Donald M. TD MA	1947	1986	(Auchtertool with Burntisland)	76 Forth Park Gardens, Kirkcaldy KY2 5TD	01592 263012
McLeod, Alistair G.	1988	2005	(Glenrothes: St Columba's)	13 Greenmantle Way, Glenrothes KY6 3QG [E-mail: alistair@mcleod3246.freeserve.co.uk]	01592 744558
MacLeod, Norman	1960	1988	(Orwell with Portmoak)	324 Muirfield Drive, Glenrothes KY6 2PZ	01592 610281

McNaught, Samuel M. MA BD MTh	1968	2002	(Kirkcaldy: St John's)	6 Munro Court, Glenrothes KY7 5GD	01592 742352
Munro, Andrew MA BD PhD	1972	2000	(Glencaple with Lowther)	7 Dunvegan Avenue, Kirkcaldy KY2 5SG	01592 566129
Reid, Martin R.B.C. BD	1960	1990	(Falkirk: West)	13 Rothes Park, Leslie, Glenrothes KY6 3LL	01592 620053
Simpson, Gordon M. MA BD	1959	1996	(Leslie: Trinity)	37 Spottiswoode Gardens, St Andrews KY16 8SA	01334 473406
Sutherland, William	1964	1993	(Bo'ness Old)	88 Dunrobin Road, Kirkcaldy KY2 5YT	01592 205510
Thomson, Gilbert L. BA	1965	1996	(Glenrothes: Christ's Kirk)	3 Fortharfield, Freuchie, Cupar KY15 7JJ	01337 857431
Thomson, John D. BD	1985	2005	(Kirkcaldy: Pathhead)	3 Tottenham Court, Hill Street, Dysart, Kirkcaldy KY1 2XY	01592 655313
Tomlinson, Bryan L. TD	1969	2003	(Kirkcaldy: Abbotshall)	2 Duddingston Drive, Kirkcaldy KY2 6JP	01592 564843
				[E-mail: abbkirk@blueyonder.co.uk]	
Webster, Elspeth H. (Miss) DCS			(Deaconess)	82 Broomhill Avenue, Burntisland KY3 0BP	01592 873616

KIRKCALDY ADDRESSES

Abbotshall	Abbotshall Road	Pathhead	Harriet Street x Church Street
Linktown	Nicol Street x High Street	St Andrew's	Victoria Road x Victoria Gdns
		St Bryce Kirk	St Brycedale Avenue x Kirk Wynd
		St John's	Elgin Street
Templehall	Beauly Place		
Torbain	Lindores Drive		
Viewforth	Viewforth Street x Viewforth Terrace		

(26) ST ANDREWS

Meets at Cupar, in St John's Church Hall, on the second Wednesday of February, March, April, May, September, October, November and December, and on the last Wednesday of June.

Clerk:	**DR RAYMOND K. MACKIE**	c/o The Scottish Churches Parliamentary Office, The Scottish	**0131-652 3270**
Depute Clerk:	**REV. DAVID I. SINCLAIR BSc BD PhD DipSW**	Storytelling Centre, 43–45 High Street, Edinburgh EH1 1SR	
		[E-mail: akph74@uk.uumail.com]	

Abdie and Dunbog (H) linked with Newburgh (H)

Lynn Brady (Miss) BD DipMin	1996	2002	2 Guthrie Court, Cupar Road, Newburgh, Cupar KY14 6HA	01337 842228
			[E-mail: lynn@revbrady.freeserve.co.uk]	

Anstruther

Ian A. Cathcart BSc BD	1994	The James Melville Manse, Anstruther KY10 3EX	01333 311808

Auchtermuchty (H)

Ann G. Fraser (Mrs) BD CertMin	1990	2 Burnside, Auchtermuchty, Cupar KY14 7AJ	01337 828519
		[E-mail: anngilfraser@bushinternet.com]	

Balmerino (H) linked with Wormit (H)

James Connolly DipTh CertMin	1982	2004	5 Westwater Place, Newport-on-Tay DD6 8NS	01382 542626
		[E-mail: jim@connollyuk.wanadoo.co.uk]	

Boarhills and Dunino linked with St Andrews: Martyrs'
Vacant
49 Irvine Crescent, St Andrews KY16 8LG
01334 472948

Cameron linked with St Andrews: St Leonard's (01334 478702)
Alan D. McDonald LLB BD MTh   1979   1998
1 Cairnhill Gardens, St Andrews KY16 8QY
[E-mail: alan.d.mcdonald@talk21.com]
01334 472793

Carnbee linked with Pittenweem
Vacant
29 Milton Road, Pittenweem, Anstruther KY10 2LN
01333 312838

Cellardyke (H) linked with Kilrenny
David J.H. Laing BD DPS   1976   1999
Toll Road, Cellardyke, Anstruther KY10 3BH
[E-mail: davith@v21mail.co.uk]
01333 310810

Ceres, Kemback and Springfield
Eric G. McKimmon BA BD MTh   1983   2005
The Manse, St Andrews Road, Ceres, Cupar KY15 5NQ
[E-mail: McKimmonCeres@aol.com]
01334 829466

Crail linked with Kingsbarns (H)
Michael J. Erskine MA BD   1985   2002
Church Manse, St Andrews Road, Crail, Anstruther KY10 3UH
01333 450358

Creich, Flisk and Kilmany linked with Monimail
Vacant
Creich Manse, Brunton, Cupar KY15 4PA
01337 870332

Cupar: Old (H) and St Michael of Tarvit
Kenneth S. Jeffrey BA BD PhD   2002
76 Hogarth Drive, Cupar KY15 5YH
[E-mail: ksjeffrey@btopenworld.com]
01334 653196

Cupar: St John's linked with Dairsie
A. Sheila Blount (Mrs) BD BA   1978   2002
23 Hogarth Drive, Cupar KY15 5YH
[E-mail: asblount@fish.co.uk]
01334 656408

Dairsie See Cupar: St John's

Edenshead and Strathmiglo
James G. Redpath BD DipPTh   1988   2006
The Manse, Kirk Wynd, Strathmiglo, Cupar KY14 7QS
[E-mail: james.redpath1@btinternet.com]
01337 860256

Elie (H) linked with Kilconquhar and Colinsburgh (H)
Vacant
30 Bank Street, Elie, Leven KY9 1BW
01333 330685

Falkland (01337 858442) linked with Freuchie (H)
Vacant
1 Newton Road, Falkland, Cupar KY15 7AQ
01337 857696

Freuchie (H) See Falkland

Howe of Fife
Marion J. Paton (Miss) BMus BD   1991   1994   83 Church Street, Ladybank, Cupar KY15 7ND   01337 830513
[E-mail: marion@marionpaton.f9.co.uk]

Cameron Harrison (Aux)   2006   Woodfield House, Prior Muir, St Andrews KY16 8LP   01334 478067

Kilconquhar and Colinsburgh See Elie
Kilrenny See Cellardyke
Kingsbarns See Crail

Largo and Newburn (H) linked with Largo: St David's
Vacant   The Manse, Church Place, Upper Largo, Leven KY8 6EH   01333 360286

Largo: St David's See Largo and Newburn

Largoward (H) linked with St Monans (H)
Donald G. MacEwan MA BD PhD   2001   The Manse, St Monans, Anstruther KY10 2DD   01333 730258
[E-mail: maiadona@fish.co.uk]

Leuchars: St Athernase
Caroline Taylor (Mrs) MA BD   1995   2003   7 David Wilson Park, Balmullo, St Andrews KY16 0NP   01334 870038
[E-mail: enilorac@fish.co.uk]

Monimail See Creich, Flisk and Kilmany
Newburgh See Abdie and Dunbog

Newport-on-Tay (H)
W. Kenneth Pryde DA BD   1994   57 Cupar Road, Newport-on-Tay DD6 8DF   01382 543165 (Tel/Fax)
[E-mail: wkpryde@hotmail.com]

Pittenweem See Carnbee

St Andrews: Holy Trinity
Rory MacLeod BA MBA BD   1994   2004   19 Priory Gardens, St Andrews KY16 8XX   01334 461098
[E-mail: annicerory@hotmail.com]

St Andrews: Hope Park (H) linked with Strathkinness
A. David K. Arnott MA BD   1971   1996   20 Priory Gardens, St Andrews KY16 8XX   01334 472912 (Tel/Fax)
[E-mail: adka@st-andrews.ac.uk]

St Andrews: Martyrs' (H) See Boarhills and Dunino
St Andrews: St Leonard's (H) See Cameron
St Monans See Largoward
Strathkinness See St Andrews: Hope Park

Tayport
Colin J. Dempster BD CertMin   1990   27 Bell Street, Tayport DD6 9AP   01382 552861
[E-mail: demps@tayportc.fsnet.co.uk]

Wormit See Balmerino

Name			Charge	Address	Tel
Alexander, James S. MA BD BA PhD	1966	1973	University of St Andrews	5 Strathkinness High Road, St Andrews KY16 9RP	01334 472680
Bennett, G. Alestair A. TD MA	1938	1976	(Strathkinness)	7 Bonfield Park, Strathkinness, St Andrews KY16 9SY	01334 850249
Bews, James MA	1942	1981	(Dundee: Craigiebank)	21 Balrymonth Court, St Andrews KY16 8XT	01334 476087
Blount, Graham K. LLB BD PhD	1976	1998	Parliamentary Officer	23 Hogarth Drive, Cupar KY15 5YH	01334 656408
Bradley, Ian MA BD DPhil	1990	1990	University of St Andrews	4 Donaldson Gardens, St Andrews KY16 9DN	01334 475389
Brown, Lawson R. MA	1960	1997	(Cameron with St Andrew's: St Leonard's)	10 Park Street, St Andrews KY16 8AQ	01334 473413
Buchan, Alexander MA BD	1975	1992	(North Ronaldsay with Sanday)	6 Allan Robertson Drive, St Andrews KY16 8EY	01334 473875 / 07709 024018 (Mbl)
				[E-mail: revabuchan@bluebucket.org]	
Cameron, James K. MA BD PhD FRHistS	1953	1989	(University of St Andrews)	Priorscroft, 71 Hepburn Gardens, St Andrews KY16 9LS	01334 473996
Casebow, Brian C. MA BD	1959	1993	(Edinburgh: Salisbury)	'The Rowans', 67 St Michael's Drive, Cupar KY15 5BP	01334 656385
Craig, Gordon W. MBE MA BD	1972	2006	(Carnbee with Pittenweem)	1 Beley Bridge, Dunino, St Andrews KY16 8LT	01334 880285
Douglas, Peter C. JP	1966	1993	(Boarhills linked with Dunino)	The Old Schoolhouse, Flisk, Newburgh, Cupar KY14 6HN	01337 870218
Earnshaw, Philip BA BSc BD	1986	1996	(Glasgow: Pollokshields)	22 Castle Street, St Monans, Anstruther KY10 2AP	01333 730640
Edington, George L.	1952	1989	(Tayport)	64B Burghmuir Road, Perth PH1 1LH	
Fairlie, George BD BVMS MRCVS	1971	2002	(Crail with Kingsbarns)	41 Warrack Street, St Andrews KY16 8DR	01334 475868
Galloway, Robert W.C. LTh	1970	1998	(Cromarty)	22 Haughgate, Leven KY8 4SG	01333 426223
Gibson, Henry M. MA BD PhD	1960	1999	(Dundee: The High Kirk)	4 Comerton Place, Drumoig, Leuchars, St Andrews KY16 0NQ	01382 542199
Gordon, Peter M. MA BD	1958	1995	(Airdrie: West)	3 Cupar Road, Cuparmuir, Cupar KY15 5RH	01334 652341
Hegarty, John D. LTh ABSC	1988	2004	(Buckie: South and West with Enzie)	26 Montgomery Way, Kinross KY13 8FD	01577 863829
				[E-mail: john.hegarty@tesco.net]	
Henney, William MA DD	1957	1996	(St Andrews: Hope Park)	30 Doocot Road, St Andrews KY16 9LP	01334 472560
Hill, Roy MA	1962	1997	(Lisbon)	Forgan Cottage, Kinnessburn Road, St Andrews KY16 8AD	01334 472121
Jarvie, John W. BD CertMin MTh	1990	2005	(Falkland with Freuchie)	62 Glebe Park, Kirkcaldy KY1 1BL	07740 256120 (Mbl)
				[E-mail: john@jarvie.info]	
Learmonth, Walter LTh	1968	1997	(Ceres with Springfield)	14 Marionfield Place, Cupar KY15 5JN	01334 656290
Lithgow, Thomas MA	1945	1982	(Banchory Devenick with Maryculter)	c/o Milne, Bairds (Lawyers), 7 St Catherine Street, Cupar KY15 4LS	
McCartney, Alexander C. BTh	1973	1995	(Caputh and Clunie with Kinclaven)	10 The Glebe, Crail, Anstruther KY10 3UT	01333 451194
McGregor, Duncan J. MIFM	1982	1996	(Channelkirk with Lauder: Old)	14 Mount Melville, St Andrews KY16 8NG	01334 478314
Macintyre, William J. MA BD DD	1951	1989	(Crail with Kingsbarns)	Tigh a' Ghobhainn, Lochton, Crail, Anstruther KY10 3XE	01333 450327
Mackenzie, A. Cameron MA	1955	1995	(Biggar)	Hedgerow, 5 Shiels Avenue, Freuchie, Cupar KY15 7JD	01337 857763
MacNab, Hamish S.D. MA	1948	1987	(Kilrenny)	Fairhill, Northmuir, Kirriemuir DD8 4PF	01575 572564
McPhail, Peter MA BD	1940	1982	(Creich, Flisk and Kilmany)	12 Deeside Terrace, Aberdeen AB15 7PZ	
Meager, Peter MA BD CertMgmt(Open)	1971	1998	(Elie with Kilconquhar and Colinsburgh)	7 Lorraine Drive, Cupar KY15 5DY	01334 656991
Ord, J.K.	1963	1968	(Falkirk: Condorrat)	24 Forth Street, St Monance, Anstruther KY10 2AX	01333 730461
Paton, Iain F. BD FCIS	1980	2006	(Elie with Kilconquhar and Colinsburgh)	Lindisfarne, 19 Links Road, Lundin Links, Leven KY8 6AS	01333 320765

Name			Charge	Address	Telephone
Patterson, John W. BA BD	1948	1989	(St Andrews: Martyrs)	34 Claybraes, St Andrews KY16 8RS	01334 473606
Portchmouth, Roland John NDD ATD	1980	1989	(Bendochy)	1 West Braes, Pittenweem, Anstruther KY10 2PS	01333 311448
Porteous, James K. DD	1944	1997	(Cupar: St John's)	16 Market Street, St Andrews KY16 9NS	
Reid, Alan A.S. MA BD STM	1962	1995	(Bridge of Allan: Chalmers)	Wayside Cottage, Bridgend, Ceres, Cupar KY15 5LS	01334 828509
Robb, Nigel J. FCP MA BD ThM MTh	1981	1998	Associate Secretary: Worship and Doctrine: Mission and Discipleship Council	c/o 121 George Street, Edinburgh EH2 4YN [E-mail: nrobb@cofscotland.org.uk]	0131-225 5722
Robertson, Norma P. (Miss) BD DMin	1993	2002	(Kincardine O'Neil with Lumphanan)	82 Hogarth Drive, Cupar KY15 5YU [E-mail: normapr@fish.co.uk]	01334 650595
Roy, Alan J. BSc BD	1960	1999	(Aberuthven with Dunning)	14 Comerton Place, Drumoig; Leuchars, St Andrews KY16 0NQ [E-mail: roma.roy@btopenworld.com]	01382 542225
Salters, Robert B. MA BD PhD	1966	1971	(University of St Andrews)	Vine Cottage, 119 South Street, St Andrews KY16 9UH	01334 473198
Scott, J. Miller MA BD FSAScot DD	1949	1988	(Jerusalem)	St Martins, 6 Trinity Place, St Andrews KY16 8SG	01334 479518
Sinclair, David I. BSc BD PhD DipSW	1990	1998	Secretary: Church and Society Council	42 South Road, Cupar KY15 5JF	01334 656957
Stevenson, A.L. LLB MLitt DPA FPEA	1984	1993	(Balmerino linked with Wormit)	41 Main Street, Dairsie, Cupar KY15 4SR	01334 870582
Stoddart, David L.	1961	1987	(Laggan with Newtonmore)	3 Castle Street, Anstruther KY10 3DD	01333 310668
Strickland, Alexander JP LTh	1971	2005	(Dairsie with Kemback with Strathkinness)	12 Ballumbie Braes, Dundee DD4 0UN	01382 505551
Strong, Clifford LTh	1983	1995	(Creich, Flisk and Kilmany with Monimail)		
Taylor, Ian BSc MA LTh DipEd	1983	1997	(Abdie and Dunbog with Newburgh)	60 Maryknowe, Gauldry, Newport-on-Tay DD6 8SL	01382 330445
Thomson, P.G. MA BD MTh ThD	1947	1989	(Irvine: Fullarton)	Lundie Cottage, Arncroach, Anstruther KY10 2RN	01333 720222
Thrower, Charles G. BSc	1965	2002	(Carnbee with Pittenweem)	Fullarton, 2 Beech Walk, Crail, Anstruther KY10 3UN	01333 450423
				Grange House, Wester Grangemuir, Pittenweem, Anstruther KY10 2RB [E-mail: c-thrower@pittenweem2.freeserve.co.uk]	01333 312631
Torrance, Alan J. MA BD DrTheol	1984	1999	University of St Andrews	Kincaple House, Kincaple, St Andrews KY16 9SH	01334 850755 (Home) / 01334 462843 (Office)
Turnbull, James J. MA	1940	1981	(Arbirlot with Colliston)	Woodlands, Beech Avenue, Ladybank, Cupar KY15 7NG	01337 830279
Walker, James B. MA BD DPhil	1975	1993	Chaplain: University of St Andrews	1 Gillespie Terrace, The Scores, St Andrews KY16 9AT [E-mail: james.walker@st-andrews.ac.uk]	01334 462866 (Tel) / 01334 462868 (Fax)
Watson, Valerie G.C. MA BD STM	1987	2006	Locum: Cameron with St Andrews: St Leonard's	11 Carron Place, St Andrews KY16 8QU [E-mail: valerie@watson30.wanadoo.co.uk]	01334 479117
Wilson, Robert McL. MA BD PhD DD FBA	1946	1983	(University of St Andrews)	10 Murrayfield Road, St Andrews KY16 9NB	01334 474331
Wotherspoon, Ian G. BA LTh	1967	2004	(Coatbridge: St Andrew's)	10 South Union Street, Cupar KY15 5BB [E-mail: wotherspoonrig@aol.com]	01334 654245
Wright, Lynda (Miss) BEd DCS			Deacon: Retreat Leader, Key House (Kilmun (St Munn's) with Strone and Ardentinny)	6 Key Cottage, High Street, Falkland, Cupar KY15 7BD	01337 857705
Young, Evelyn M. (Mrs) BSc BD	1984	2003		2 Priestden Place, St Andrews KY16 8DP	01334 479662

(27) DUNKELD AND MEIGLE

Meets at Pitlochry on the first Tuesday of September and December, on the third Tuesday of February, April and October, and at the Moderator's church on the third Tuesday of June.

Clerk:	REV. JOHN RUSSELL MA	Kilblaan, Gladstone Terrace, Birnam, Dunkeld PH8 0DP [E-mail: akph47@uk.uumail.com]	01350 728896

Aberfeldy (H) linked with Amulree and Strathbraan linked with Dull and Weem
Vacant (from 1 November 2006) — Taybridge Terrace, Aberfeldy PH15 2BS — 01887 820656

Alyth (H)
Vacant *Sheila Kirk* — Cambridge Street, Alyth, Blairgowrie PH11 8AW — 01828 632104

Amulree and Strathbraan See Aberfeldy

Ardler, Kettins and Meigle
Linda Stewart (Mrs) BD — 2001 — The Manse, Dundee Road, Meigle, Blairgowrie PH12 8SB — 01828 640278

Bendochy linked with Coupar Angus: Abbey
Bruce Dempsey BD — 1997 — Caddam Road, Coupar Angus, Blairgowrie PH13 9EF — 01828 627331
[E-mail: revbruce.dempsey@btopenworld.com]

Blair Atholl and Struan linked with Tenandry
Brian Ian Murray BD — 2002 — Blair Atholl, Pitlochry PH18 5SX — 01796 481213
[E-mail: athollkirks@yahoo.co.uk]

Blairgowrie
Donald Macleod BD LRAM DRSAM — 1987 — 2002 — The Manse, Upper David Street, Blairgowrie PH10 6HB — 01250 872146
[E-mail: donmac@fish.co.uk]

Braes of Rannoch linked with Foss and Rannoch (H)
Christine A.Y. Ritchie (Mrs) BD DipMin — 2002 — 2005 — The Manse, Kinloch Rannoch, Pitlochry PH16 5QA — 01882 632381
[E-mail: critchie@fish.co.uk]

Caputh and Clunie (H) linked with Kinclaven (H) (T)
William Ewart BSc BD — 1972 — 2004 — Caputh Manse, Caputh, Perth PH1 4JH — 01738 710520
[E-mail: ewe@surefish.co.uk]

Coupar Angus: Abbey See Bendochy
Dull and Weem See Aberfeldy

Dunkeld (H)
R. Fraser Penny BA BD — 1984 — 2001 — Cathedral Manse, Dunkeld PH8 0AW — 01350 727249
[E-mail: fraserpenn@aol.com] — 01350 727102 (Fax)

Fortingall and Glenlyon linked with Kenmore and Lawers
Anne J. Brennan BSc BD MTh   1999   The Manse, Balnaskeag, Kenmore, Aberfeldy PH15 2HB   01887 830218
[E-mail: annebrennan@yahoo.co.uk]

Foss and Rannoch See Braes of Rannoch

Grantully, Logierait and Strathtay
Vacant *Rosemary Legge*   The Manse, Strathtay, Pitlochry PH9 0PG   01887 840251

Kenmore and Lawers (H) See Fortingall and Glenlyon
Kinclaven See Caputh and Clunie

Kirkmichael, Straloch and Glenshee linked with Rattray (H)
Malcolm H. MacRae MA PhD   1971   2005   The Manse, Alyth Road, Rattray, Blairgowrie PH10 7HF   01250 872462
[E-mail: malcolm.macrae1@btopenworld.com]

Pitlochry (H) (01796 472160)
Malcolm Ramsay BA LLB DipMin   1986   1998   Manse Road, Moulin, Pitlochry PH16 5EP   01796 472774
[E-mail: amramsay@aol.com]

Rattray See Kirkmichael, Straloch and Glenshee
Tenandry See Blair Atholl and Struan

Barbour, Robin A.S. KCVO MC BD STM DD		(University of Aberdeen)	Old Fincastle, Pitlochry PH16 5RJ	01796 473209
Cassells, Alexander K. MA BD	1954	1982 (Leuchars: St Athernase and Guardbridge)	Balloch Cottage, Keltneyburn, Aberfeldy PH15 2LS	01887 830758
Creegan, Christine M. (Mrs) MTh	1961	1997 (Grantully, Logierait and Strathtay)	Lonaig, 28 Lettoch Terrace, Pitlochry PH16 5BA	01796 472422
	1993	2005	[E-mail: christine@creegans.co.uk]	
Dick, Tom MA	1951	1990 (Dunkeld)	Mo Dhachaidh, Callybrae, Dunkeld PH8 0EP	01350 727338
Duncan, James BTh FSAScot	1980	1995 (Blair Atholl and Struan)	25 Knockard Avenue, Pitlochry PH16 5JE	01796 474096
Forsyth, David Stuart MA	1948	1992 (Belhelvie)	Birchlea, 38 Fonab Crescent, Pitlochry PH16 5SR	01796 473708
Fulton, Frederick H. MA	1942	1983 (Clunie, Lethendy and Kinloch)	Grampian Cottage, Chapel Brae, Braemar, Ballater AB35 5YT	01339 741277
Gisbey, John E. MA BD MSc DipEd	1964	2002 (Thornhill)	Cherry House, Perth Road, Rosemount, Blairgowrie PH10 6QB	01250 872573
Gunn, Alexander M. MA BD	1967	2006 (Aberfeldy with Amulree and Strathbraan with Dull and Weem)	12 Cornhill Road, Perth PH1 1LR	07703 469020
			[E-mail: sandygunn@btinternet.com]	
Hamilton, David G. MA BD	1971	2004 (Braes of Rannoch with Foss and Rannoch)	79 Finlay Rise, Milngavie, Glasgow G62 6QL	(Mbl) 0141-956 4202
			[E-mail: davidhamilton@onetel.com]	
Henderson, John D. MA BD	1953	1992 (Cluny with Monymusk)	Aldersyde, George Street, Blairgowrie PH10 6HP	01250 875181
Knox, John W. MTheol	1992	1997 (Lochgelly: Macainsh)	Heatherlea, Main Street, Ardler, Blairgowrie PH12 8SR	01828 640731
McAlister, D.J.B. MA BD PhD	1951	1989 (North Berwick: Blackadder)	2 Duff Avenue, Moulin, Pitlochry PH16 5EN	01796 473591
MacVicar, Kenneth MBE DFC TD MA	1950	1990 (Kenmore with Lawers with Fortingall and Glenlyon)	Illeray, Kenmore, Aberfeldy PH15 2HE	01887 830514
Ormiston, Hugh C. BSc BD MPhil PhD	1969	2004 (Kirkmichael, Straloch and Glenshee with Rattray)	Cedar Lea, Main Road, Woodside, Blairgowrie PH13 9NP	01828 670539

Robertson, Iain M. MA	1967	1992	(Carriden)	St Colme's, Perth Road, Birnam, Dunkeld PH8 0BH	01350 727455
Robertson, Matthew LTh	1968	2002	(Cawdor with Croy and Dalcross)	Inver, Strathtay, Pitlochry PH9 0PG	01887 840780
Russell, John MA	1959	2000	(Tillicoultry)	Kilblaan, Gladstone Terrace, Birnam, Dunkeld PH8 0DP	01350 728896
Shannon, W.G. MA BD	1955	1998	(Pitlochry)	19 Knockard Road, Pitlochry PH16 5HJ	01796 473533
Stewart, Walter T.A.	1964	1999	(Barry)	7A Tummel Crescent, Pitlochry PH16 5DF	01796 473422
Tait, Thomas W. BD	1972	1997	(Rattray)	20 Cedar Avenue, Blairgowrie PH10 6TT	01250 874833
White, Brock A. LTh	1971	2001	(Kirkcaldy: Templehall)	1 Littlewood Gardens, Blairgowrie PH10 6XZ	01250 870399
Whyte, William B. BD	1973	2003	(Nairn: St Ninian's)	The Old Inn, Park Hill Road, Rattray, Blairgowrie PH10 7DS	01250 874401
Wilson, John M. MA BD	1965	2004	(Altnaharra and Farr)	Berbice, The Terrace, Blair Atholl, Pitlochry PH18 5SZ	01796 481619
Wilson, Mary D. (Mrs) RGN SCM DTM	1990	2004	(Auxiliary Minister)	Berbice, The Terrace, Blair Atholl, Pitlochry PH18 5SZ	01796 481619
Young, G. Stuart	1961	1996	(Blairgowrie: St Andrew's)	7 James Place, Stanley, Perth PH1 4PD	01738 828473

(28) PERTH

Meets at Scone: Old, at 7:00pm, in the Elizabeth Ashton Hall, on the second Tuesday of February, March, June, September, November and December in each year.

Clerk:	**REV. DOUGLAS M. MAIN BD**			
Presbytery Office:			**209 High Street, Perth PH1 5PB**	**01738 451177** (Tel)
			[E-mail: akph70@uk.uumail.com]	**01738 638226** (Fax)

Abernethy and Dron linked with Arngask
Vacant — 3 Manse Road, Abernethy, Perth PH2 9JP — 01738 850607

Almondbank Tibbermore
Donald Campbell BD — 1998 — The Manse, Pitcairngreen, Perth PH1 3EA — 01738 583217
[E-mail: revdonald@almondbankchurch.co.uk]

Ardoch (H) linked with Blackford (H)
Stuart D.B. Picken MA BD PhD — 1966 2005 — 3 Millhill Crescent, Greenloaning, Dunblane FK15 0LH — 01786 880217
[E-mail: picken@eikoku.demon.co.uk]

Arngask See Abernethy and Dron

Auchterarder (H)
Michael R.R. Shewan MA BD CPS — 1985 1998 — 24 High Street, Auchterarder, Perth PH3 1DF — 01764 662210
[E-mail: michael.shewan@lineone.net]

Auchtergaven and Moneydie
Iain McFadzean MA BD — 1989 2005 — Bankfoot, Perth PH1 4BS — 01738 787235
[E-mail: iainmcfadzean@hotmail.com]

Blackford See Ardoch

Cargill Burrelton linked with Collace
Jose R. Carvalho BD — 2002 — Manse Road, Woodside, Blairgowrie PH13 9NQ [E-mail: joecarvalho@btinternet.com] — 01828 670352

Cleish (H) linked with Fossoway: St Serf's and Devonside
Joanne G. Finlay (Mrs) DipTMus BD AdvDipCouns — 1996 2005 — The Manse, Cleish, Kinross KY13 7LR [E-mail: joanne.finlay196@btinternet.com] — 01577 850231

Collace See Cargill and Burrelton

Comrie (H) linked with Dundurn (H)
Graham McWilliams BSc BD — 2005 — The Manse, Strowan Road, Comrie, Crieff PH6 2ES [E-mail: Themansefamily@aol.com] — 01764 671045 (Tel/Fax)

Crieff (H)
James W. MacDonald BD — 1976 2002 — 8 Strathearn Terrace, Crieff PH7 3AQ [E-mail: revup@tesco.net] — 01764 653907

Dunbarney (H) and Forgandenny
Vacant — Dunbarney Manse, Bridge of Earn, Perth PH2 9DY — 01738 812463
(Charge formed by the union of Dunbarney and Forgandenny)

Dundurn See Comrie

Errol (H) linked with Kilspindie and Rait
Douglas M. Main BD — 1986 2005 — South Bank, Errol, Perth PH2 7PZ [E-mail: revdmain@aol.com] — 01821 642279

Fossoway: St Serf's and Devonside See Cleish

Fowlis Wester linked with Madderty linked with Monzie
Alexander F. Bonar LTh LRIC — 1988 1996 — Beechview, Abercairney, Crieff PH7 3NF [E-mail: sandy.bonar@btinternet.com] — 01764 652116

Gask (H) linked with Methven and Logiealmond (H)
Brian Bain LTh — 1980 1986 — Sauchob Road, Methven, Perth PH1 3QD [E-mail: brian.bain4@btinternet.com] — 01738 840274 (Tel/Fax)

Kilspindie and Rait See Errol

Kinross (H)
John P.L. Munro MA BD PhD — 1977 1998 — 15 Station Road, Kinross KY13 8TG [E-mail: john@lochleven.freeserve.co.uk] — 01577 862952

Madderty See Fowlis Wester
Methven and Logiealmond See Gask
Monzie See Fowlis Wester

Muthill (H) linked with Trinity Gask and Kinkell
John Oswald BSc PhD BD   1997   2002   Muthill, Crieff PH5 2AR
[E-mail: revdocoz@bigfoot.com]   01764 681205

Orwell (H) and Portmoak (H)
Robert G.D.W. Pickles BD MPhil   2003   3 Perth Road, Milnathort, Kinross KY13 9XU
[E-mail: robert.pickles1@btopenworld.com]   01577 863461
(Charge formed by the union of Orwell and Portmoak)

Perth: Craigie (H)
William Thomson BD   2001   46 Abbot Street, Perth PH2 0EE   01738 623748
[handwritten: Vacant Jan 07. → Stephanus Fakooh Thredasjun]
[handwritten: IH Bruce Thomson]

Perth: Kinnoull (H)
David I. Souter BD   1996   2001   1 Mount Tabor Avenue, Perth PH2 7BT
[E-mail: d.souter@virgin.net]   01738 626046

Perth: Letham St Mark's (H)
James C. Stewart BD DipMin   1997   1997   35 Rose Crescent, Perth PH1 1NT
[E-mail: jimstewartrev@lineone.net]   01738 624167
Kenneth McKay DCS   11F Balgowan Road, Perth PH1 2JG
[E-mail: kennydandcs@hotmail.com]   01738 621169

Perth: Moncreiffe (T)
Isobel Birrell (Mrs) BD   1994   1999   2 Rhynd Lane, Perth PH2 8QT
[E-mail: isobel.birrell@tiscali.co.uk]   01738 625694

Perth: North (01738 622298)
David W. Denniston BD DipMin   1981   1996   127 Glasgow Road, Perth PH2 0LU
[E-mail: david.denniston@blueyonder.co.uk]   01738 625728

Perth: Riverside (New Charge Development)
Vacant
Christine Palmer (Miss) DCS   2003   2005   44 Hay Street, Perth PH1 5HS   01738 621305
                                        39 Fortingall Place, Perth PH1 2NF   01738 587488
[E-mail: chrispalmer@blueyonder.co.uk]

Perth: St John the Baptist's (H) (01738 626159)
David D. Ogston MA BD   1970   1980   15 Comely Bank, Perth PH2 7HU
[E-mail: ogston@cwcom.net]   01738 621755
Elizabeth Brown (Mrs)   1996   25 Highfield Road, Scone, Perth PH2 6RN
[E-mail: liz.brown@blueyonder.co.uk]   01738 552391 (Tel/Fax)

Perth: St Leonard's-in-the-Fields and Trinity (H) (01738 632238)
Gilbert C. Nisbet CA BD 1993 2000 5 Stratheam Terrace, Perth PH2 0LS 01738 621709
[E-mail: gcnisbet@stleonardsmanse.fsnet.co.uk]

Perth: St Matthew's (Office: 01738 6367757; Vestry: 01738 630725)
Vacant 23 Kincarrathie Crescent, Perth PH2 7HH 01738 626828

Redgorton and Stanley
Derek G. Lawson LLB BD 1998 22 King Street, Stanley, Perth PH1 4ND 01738 828247
[E-mail: lawson@stanley9835.freeserve.co.uk]
(Charge formed by the union of Redgorton and Stanley)

St Madoes and Kinfauns
Marc F. Bircham BD MTh 2000 Glencarse, Perth PH2 7NF 01738 860837
[E-mail: mark.bircham@btinternet.com]

St Martin's linked with Scone: New (H) (01738 553900)
Vacant 24 Victoria Road, Scone, Perth PH2 6JW 01738 551467

Scone: New See St Martin's

Scone: Old (H)
J. Bruce Thomson JP MA BD 1972 1983 Burnside, Scone, Perth PH2 6LP 01738 552030
[E-mail: jock.tamson@talk21.com]

The Stewartry of Strathearn (H) (01738 621674) (E-mail: office@stewartryofstrathearn.org.uk)
Colin R. Williamson LLB BD 1972 2000 Manse of Aberdalgie, Aberdalgie, Perth PH2 0QD 01738 625854
[E-mail: stewartry@beeb.net]

Trinity Gask and Kinkell See Muthill

Barr, George K. ARIBA BD PhD 1967 1993 (Uddingston: Viewpark) 7 Tay Avenue, Comrie, Crieff PH6 2PE 01764 670454
[E-mail: gbarr2@compuserve.com]

Barr, T. Leslie LTh 1969 1997 (Kinross) 8 Fairfield Road, Kelty KY4 0BY 01383 839330
Bartholomew, Julia (Mrs) BSc BD 2002 Auchterarder: Associate Kippenhill, Dunning, Perth PH2 0RA 01764 684929
Bertram, Thomas A. 1972 1995 (Patna: Waterside) 3 Scrimgeours Corner, 29 West High Street, Crieff PH7 4AP 01764 652066
Birrell, John M. MA LLB BD 1974 1996 Hospital Chaplain: Perth Royal Infirmary 2 Rhynd Lane, Perth PH2 8QT 01738 625694
[E-mail: john.birrell@tuht.scot.nhs.uk]

Buchan, William DipTheol BD 1987 2001 (Kilwinning: Abbey) 34 Bridgewater Avenue, Auchterarder PH3 1DQ 01764 660306
[E-mail: wbuchan3@aol.com]

Cairns, Evelyn BD 2004 Chaplain: Rachel House 15 Tala Park, Kinross KY13 8AB 01577 863990
[E-mail: revelyn@chas.org.uk]

Campbell, Andrew B. BD DPS MTh 1979 2006 Mission and Discipleship Council The Haven, 21 Skye Crescent, Crieff PH7 3FB 01764 654226
[E-mail: acampbell@cofscotland.org.uk]

Name			Charge	Address	Tel
Carr, W. Stanley MA	1951	1991	(Largs: St Columba's)	16 Gannochy Walk, Perth PH2 7LW	01738 627422
Coleman, Sidney H. BA BD MTh	1961	2001	(Glasgow: Merrylea)	'Blaven', 11 Clyde Place, Perth PH2 0EZ [E-mail: sidney.coleman@blueyonder.co.uk]	01738 565072
Craig, Joan H. (Miss) MTheol	1986	2005	(Orkney: East Mainland)	7 Jedburgh Place, Perth PH1 1SJ [E-mail: joanhcraig@bigfoot.com]	01738 580180
Denniston, Jane MA BD	2002		Ministries Council	127 Glasgow Road, Perth PH2 0LU [E-mail: jdenniston@cofscotland.org.uk]	01738 565379
Donaldson, Robert B. BSocSc	1953	1997	(Kilchoman with Portnahaven)	11 Strathearn Court, Crieff PH7 3DS	01764 654976
Drummond, Alfred G. BD DMin	1991	2006	Scottish General Secretary: Evangelical Alliance		
Fleming, Hamish K. MA	1966	2001	(Banchory Ternan: East)	10 Errochty Court, Perth PH1 2SU	01764 679178
Galbraith, W. James L. BSc BD MICE	1973	1996	(Kilchrenan and Dalavich with Muckairn)	36 Earnmuir Road, Comrie, Crieff PH6 2EY	01577 863887
Gaston, A. Ray C. MA BD	1969	2002	(Leuchars: St Athernase)	19 Mayfield Gardens, Kinross KY13 9GD	01259 743202
Gregory, J.C. LTh	1968	1992	(Blantyre: St Andrew's)	'Hamewith', 13 Manse Road, Dollar FK14 7AL	01764 664594
Grimson, John A. MA	1950	1986	(Glasgow: Wellington: Associate)	2 Southlands Road, Auchterarder PH3 1BA	01764 653063
Halliday, Archibald R. BD MTh	1964	1999	(Duffus, Spynie and Hopeman)	29 Highland Road, Turret Park, Crieff PH7 4LE	01764 656464
Henry, Malcolm N. MA BD	1951	1987	(Perth: Craigie)	2 Pittenzie Place, Crieff PH7 3JL	01556 504144
Houston, Alexander McR	1939	1977	(Tibbermore)	Kelton, Castle Douglas DG7 1RU	01738 628056
Hughes, Clifford E. MA BD	1993	2001	(Haddington: St Mary's)	120 Glasgow Road, Perth PH2 0LU	01577 840506
Kelly, T. Clifford	1973	1995	(Ferintosh)	Pavilion Cottage, Bnglands, Rumbling Bridge, Kinross KY13 0PS	01592 840387
Lacey, Eric R. BD	1971	1992	(Creich with Rosehall)	7 Bankfoot Park, Scotlandwell, Kinross KY13 7JP	01764 684041
				The Bungalow, Forteviot, Perth PH2 9BT [E-mail: revela.cey@homecall.co.uk]	
Lawson, James B. MA BD	1961	2002	(South Uist)	4 Cowden Way, Comrie, Crieff PH6 2NW	01764 679180
Lawson, Ronald G. MA BD	1964	1999	(Greenock: Wellpark Mid Kirk)	6 East Brougham Street, Stanley, Perth PH1 4NJ	01738 828871
Low, J.E. Stewart MA	1957	1997	(Tarbat)	15 Stormont Place, Scone, Perth PH2 6SR	01738 552023
McCormick, Alastair F.	1962	1998	(Creich with Rosehall)	54 Balmanno Park, Bridge of Earn, Perth PH2 9RJ	01738 813588
McGregor, William LTh	1987	2003	(Auchtergaven and Moneydie)	Ard Choille, 7 Taypark Road, Luncarty, Perth PH1 3FE [E-mail: bill.mcgregor@ukonline.co.uk]	01738 827866
MacKenzie, Donald W. MA	1941	1983	(Auchterarder: The Barony)	81 Kingswell Terrace, Perth PH1 2DA	01738 633716
MacLean, Nigel R. MA BD	1940	1986	(Perth: St Paul's)	9 Hay Street, Perth PH1 5HS	01738 626728
MacMillan, Riada M. (Mrs) BD	1991	1998	(Perth: Craigend Moncreiffe with Rhynd)	73 Muirend Gardens, Perth PH1 1JR	01738 628867
McNaughton, David J.H. BA CA	1976	1995	(Killin and Ardeonaig)	30 Hollybush Road, Crieff PH7 3HB	01764 653028
MacPhee, Duncan P.	1951	1980	(Braemar with Crathie: Associate)	Braemar Cottage, Ben Alder Place, Kirkcaldy KY2 5RH	01592 201984
McQuilken, John E. MA BD	1969	1992	(Glenaray and Inveraray)	18 Clark Terrace, Crieff PH7 3QE	01764 655764
Millar, Alexander M. MA BD MBA	1980	2001	Associate Secretary: Mission and Discipleship Council	c/o 121 George Street, Edinburgh EH2 4YN [E-mail: amillar@cofscotland.org.uk]	0131-225 5722
Millar, Archibald E. DipTh	1965	1991	(Perth: St Stephen's)	7 Maple Place, Perth PH1 1RT	01738 621813
Millar, Jennifer M. (Mrs) BD DipMin	1986	1995	Teacher: Religious and Moral Education	17 Mapledene Road, Scone, Perth PH2 6NX	01738 550270
Munro, Gillian (Miss) BSc BD	1989	2003	Head of Department of Spiritual Care, NHS Tayside		
Pattison, Kenneth J. MA BD STM	1967	2004	(Kilmuir and Logie Easter)	Royal Dundee Liff Hospital, Liff, Dundee DD2 5ND	01382 423116
				2 Castle Way, St Madoes, Glencarse, Perth PH2 7NY [E-mail: ken@thepattisons.fsnet.co.uk]	01738 860340
Reid, David T. BA BD	1954	1993	(Cleish with Fossoway: St Serf's and Devonside)	Benarty, Wester Balgedie, Kinross KY13 9HE	01592 840214
Robertson, Thomas G.M. LTh	1971	2004	(Edenshead and Strathmiglo)	23 Muirend Avenue, Perth PH1 1JL	01738 624432
Shirra, James MA	1945	1987	(St Martin's with Scone: New)	17 Dunbarney Avenue, Bridge of Earn, Perth PH2 9BP	01738 812610
Simpson, James A. BSc BD STM DD	1960	2000	(Dornoch Cathedral)	'Dornoch', Perth Road, Bankfoot, Perth PH1 4ED	01738 787710

Stenhouse, W. Duncan MA BD	1989 2006	(Dunbarney and Forgandenny)	32 Sandport Gait, Kinross KY13 8FB [E-mail: d.stenhouse@tiscali.co.uk]	01577 866992
Stewart, Gordon G. MA	1961 2000	(Perth: St Leonard's-in-the-Fields and Trinity)	'Balnoe', South Street, Rattray, Blairgowrie PH10 7BZ	01250 870626
Stewart, Robin J. MA BD STM	1959 1995	(Orwell with Portmoak)	Oakbrae, Perth Road, Murthly, Perth PH1 4HF	01738 710220
Tait, Henry A.G. MA BD	1966 1997	(Crieff: South and Monzievaird)	14 Shieling Hill Place, Crieff PH7 4ER	01764 652325
Taylor, A.H.S. MA BA BD	1957 1992	(Brydekirk with Hoddam)	41 Anderson Drive, Perth PH1 1LF	01738 626579
Thomson, Peter D. MA BD	1968 2004	(Comrie with Dundurn)	34 Queen Street, Perth PH2 0EJ [E-mail: revpdt@the-manse.freeserve.co.uk]	01738 622418

PERTH ADDRESSES

Craigie	Abbot Street
Kinnoull	Dundee Rd near Queen's Bridge
Letham St Mark's	Rannoch Road
Moncreiffe	Glenbruar Crescent
North	Mill Street near Kinnoull Street
Riverside	Bute Drive
St John's	St John's Street
St Leonard's-in-the-Fields and Trinity	Marshall Place
St Matthew's	Tay Street

(29) DUNDEE

Meets at Dundee, Meadowside St Paul's Church Halls, Nethergate, on the second Wednesday of February, March, May, September, October, November and December, and on the fourth Wednesday of June.

Clerk:	REV. JAMES L. WILSON BD CPS		[E-mail: akph45@uk.uumail.com]	01382 459249 (Home) 07885 618659 (Mobile)
Presbytery Office:			Whitfield Parish Church, Haddington Crescent, Dundee DD4 0NA	01382 503012

Abernyte linked with Inchture and Kinnaird linked with Longforgan (H)

Vacant				
Elizabeth Kay (Miss) DipYCS (Aux)	1993 1999		[E-mail: r3vjw@aol.com] The Manse, Longforgan, Dundee DD2 5EU	01382 360238
			1 Kintail Walk, Inchture, Perth PH14 9RY [E-mail: lizkay@clara.co.uk]	01828 686029

Auchterhouse (H) linked with Murroes and Tealing (T)

David A. Collins BSc BD	1993 2006		New Kirk Manse, 25 Ballinard Gardens, Broughty Ferry, Dundee DD5 1BZ	01382 778874

Dundee: Balgay (H)

George K. Robson LTh DPS BA	1983 1987		150 City Road, Dundee DD2 2PW [E-mail: gkrobson@tiscali.co.uk]	01382 668806

Dundee: Barnhill St Margaret's (H)

Fraser M.C. Stewart BSc BD	1980 2000		The Manse, Invermark Terrace, Broughty Ferry, Dundee DD5 2QU	01382 779278

Dundee: Broughty Ferry New Kirk (H)
Catherine E.E. Collins (Mrs) MA BD 1993 2006 New Kirk Manse, 25 Ballinard Gardens, Broughty Ferry, Dundee DD5 1BZ 01382 778874
[E-mail: catherine.collins@dundeepresbytery.org.uk]

Dundee: Broughty Ferry St James' (H)
Alberto A. de Paula BD MTh 1991 2005 2 Ferry Road, Monifieth, Dundee DD5 4NT 01382 534468
[E-mail: albertodepaula@aol.com]

Dundee: Broughty Ferry St Luke's and Queen Street
C. Graham Taylor BSc BD FIAB 2001 22 Albert Road, Broughty Ferry, Dundee DD5 1AZ 01382 779212
[E-mail: cgdtaylor@surefish.co.uk]

Dundee: Broughty Ferry St Stephen's and West (H)
John U. Cameron BA BSc PhD BD ThD 1974 33 Camperdown Street, Broughty Ferry, Dundee DD5 3AA 01382 477403

Dundee: Camperdown (H) (01382 623958)
Vacant Camperdown Manse, Myrekirk Road, Dundee DD2 4SF 01382 621383

Dundee: Chalmers Ardler (H)
Kenneth D. Stott MA BD 1989 1997 The Manse, Turnberry Avenue, Dundee DD2 3TP 01382 827439
[E-mail: arkstotts@aol.com]
Jane Martin (Miss) DCS 12A Carnoustie Court, Ardler, Dundee DD2 3RB 01382 813786

Dundee: Clepington and Fairmuir
Vacant 9 Abercorn Street, Dundee DD4 7HY 01382 458314

Dundee: Craigiebank (H) (01382 457951) linked with Dundee: Douglas and Mid Craigie
Michael V.A. Mair MA BD 1967 1998 244 Arbroath Road, Dundee DD4 7SB 01382 452337
Edith F. McMillan (Mrs) MA BD (Assoc) 1981 1999 19 Americanmuir Road, Dundee DD3 9AA 01382 812423
Jean Allan (Mrs) DCS 2005 12C Hindmarsh Avenue, Dundee DD3 7LW 01382 827299

Dundee: Douglas and Mid Craigie See Dundee: Craigiebank
(New charge formed by the union of Dundee: Douglas and Angus with Dundee: Mid Craigie)

Dundee: Downfield South (H) (01382 810624)
Lezley J. Kennedy BD ThM MTh 2000 15 Elgin Street, Dundee DD3 8NL 01382 889498
[E-mail: lezleykennedy@btinternet.com]

Dundee: Dundee (St Mary's) (H) (01382 226271)
Keith F. Hall MA BD 1980 1994 33 Strathern Road, West Ferry, Dundee DD5 1PP 01382 778808

Dundee: Lochee Old and St Luke's (T)
Hazel Wilson (Ms) MA BD DipEd DMS 1991 2004 32 Clayhills Drive, Dundee DD2 1SX 01382 561989
[E-mail: hazel@feddal.freeserve.co.uk]

Dundee: Lochee West (H) James A. Roy MA BD	1965	1973	Beechwood, 7 Northwood Terrace, Wormit, Newport-on-Tay DD6 8PP [E-mail: j.roy@btinternet.com]	01382 543578
Dundee: Logie and St John's Cross (H) David S. Scott MA BD	1987	1999	7 Hyndford Street, Dundee DD2 1HQ	01382 641572
Dundee: Mains (H) (01382 812166) John M. Pickering BSc BD DipEd	1997	2004	9 Elgin Street, Dundee DD3 8NL	01382 827207
Dundee: Mains of Fintry (01382 508191) Colin M. Brough BSc BD	1998	2002	4 Clive Street, Dundee DD4 7AW [E-mail: colin.brough@btinternet.com]	01382 458629
Dundee: Meadowside St Paul's (H) (01382 225420) Maudeen I. MacDougall (Miss) BA BD	1978	1984	36 Blackness Avenue, Dundee DD2 1HH	01382 668828
Dundee: Menzieshill Harry J. Brown LTh	1991	1996	The Manse, Charleston Drive, Dundee DD2 4ED [E-mail: harrybrown@aol.com]	01382 667446
David Sutherland (Aux)			6 Cromarty Drive, Dundee DD2 2UQ [E-mail: dave.sutherland@tesco.net]	01382 621473
Dundee: St Andrew's (H) (01382 224860) Ian D. Petrie MA BD	1970	1986	77 Blackness Avenue, Dundee DD2 1JN	01382 641695
Dundee: St David's High Kirk (H) Vacant			6 Adelaide Place, Dundee DD3 6LF	01382 322955
Dundee: Steeple (H) (01382 223880) David M. Clark MA BD	1989	2000	128 Arbroath Road, Dundee DD4 7HR	01382 455411
Dundee: Stobswell (H) Vacant			23 Shamrock Street, Dundee DD4 7AH	01382 459119
Dundee: Strathmartine (H) (01382 825817) Stewart McMillan BD	1983	1990	19 Americanmuir Road, Dundee DD3 9AA	01382 812423
Dundee: Trinity (H) (01382 459997) Vacant			5 Castlewood Avenue, Emmock Woods, The Barns of Claverhouse, Dundee DD4 9FP	01382 501334

Dundee: West

Andrew T. Greaves BD	1985	2000	22 Hyndford Street, Dundee DD2 1HX [E-mail: andrew@greaves49.fsnet.co.uk]	01382 646586

Dundee: Whitfield (E) (H) (01382 503012) (New Charge Development)

James L. Wilson BD CPS	1986	2001	53 Old Craigie Road, Dundee DD4 7JD [E-mail: r3vjw@aol.com]	01382 459249

Fowlis and Liff linked with Lundie and Muirhead of Liff (H) (01382 580550)

Donna M. Hays (Mrs) MTheol DipEd DipTMHA	2004	149 Coupar Angus Road, Muirhead of Liff, Dundee DD2 5QN [E-mail: dmhays32@aol.com]	01382 580210

Inchture and Kinnaird See Abernyte

Invergowrie (H)

Robert J. Ramsay LLB NP BD	1986	1997	2 Boniface Place, Invergowrie, Dundee DD2 5DW [E-mail: robert@r-j-ramsay.fsnet.co.uk]	01382 561118

Longforgan See Abernyte
Lundie and Muirhead of Liff See Fowlis and Liff

Monifieth: Panmure (H)

David B. Jamieson MA BD STM	1974	8A Albert Street, Monifieth, Dundee DD5 4JS	01382 532772

Monifieth: St Rule's (H)

Robert W. Massie LTh	1989	1999	Church Street, Monifieth, Dundee DD5 4JP [E-mail: revrwm@lineone.net]	01382 532607

Monifieth: South

Donald W. Fraser MA	1958	1959	Queen Street, Monifieth, Dundee DD5 4HG	01382 532646

Monikie and Newbigging

Vacant	59B Broomwell Gardens, Monikie, Dundee DD5 3QP	01382 370200

Murroes and Tealing See Auchterhouse

Barrett, Leslie M. BD FRICS	1991	2001	Chaplain: University of Abertay, Dundee	Dunelm Cottage, Logie, Cupar KY15 4SJ [E-mail: l.barrett@abertay.ac.uk]	01334 870396
Campbell, Gordon MA CDipAF DipHSM MCMI MIHM MRIN ARSGS FRGS FSAScot			Auxiliary Minister: Chaplain: University of Dundee	2 Falkland Place, Kingoodie, Invergowrie, Dundee DD2 5DY [E-mail: gordon.campbell@dundeepresbytery.org.uk]	01382 561383
Clarkson, Robert G.	1950	1989	(Dundee: Strathmartine)	320 Strathmartine Road, Dundee DD3 8QG [E-mail: rob.gov@virgin.net]	01382 825380

Name			Charge / Role	Address	Tel
Craig, Iain R. MA	1948	1988	(Invergowrie)	Hope View, Burton Row, Brent Knoll, Highbridge, Somerset TA9 4BX	01278 760719
Craik, Sheila (Mrs) BD	1989	2001	(Dundee: Camperdown)	35 Haldane Terrace, Dundee DD3 0HT	01382 802078
Cramb, Erik M. LTh	1973	1989	(Industrial Mission Organiser)	Flat 35, Brachead, Methven Walk, Dundee DD2 3FJ [E-mail: erikcramb@aol.com]	01382 526196
Donald, Robert M. LTh BA	1969	2005	(Kilmodan and Colintraive)	2 Blacklaw Drive, Birkhill, Dundee DD2 5RJ [E-mail: robandmoiradonald@yahoo.com]	01382 581337
Douglas, Fiona C. (Miss) MA BD PhD	1989	1997	Chaplain: University of Dundee	10 Springfield, Dundee DD1 4JE	01382 344157
Ferguson, John F. MA BD	1987	2001	(Perth: Kinnoull)	10 Glamis Crescent, Inchture, Perth PH14 9QU	01828 687881
Gammack, George BD	1985	1999	(Dundee: Whitfield)	13A Hill Street, Broughty Ferry, Dundee DD5 2JP	01382 778636
Hawdon, John E. BA MTh AICS	1961	1995	(Dundee: Clepington)	53 Hillside Road, Dundee DD2 1QT [E-mail: jandjhawdon@btopenworld.com]	01382 646212
Hudson, J. Harrison DipTh MA BD	1961	1999	(Dundee: St Peter's McCheyne)	22 Hamilton Avenue, Tayport DD6 9BW	01382 552052
Ingram, J.R.	1954	1978	(Chaplain: RAF)	48 Marlee Road, Broughty Ferry, Dundee DD5 3EX	01382 736400
Laidlaw, John J. MA	1964	1973	(Adviser in Religious Education)	14 Dalhousie Road, Barnhill, Dundee DD5 2SQ	01382 477458
McLeod, David C. BSc MEng BD	1969	2001	(Dundee: Fairmuir)	6 Carseview Gardens, Dundee DD2 1NE [E-mail: david@mcleod6098.freeserve.co.uk]	01382 641371
McMillan, Charles D. LTh	1979	2004	(Elgin: High)	11 Troon Terrace, The Orchard, Ardler, Dundee DD2 3FX	01382 831358
Malvenan, Dorothy DCS	1964	1990	The Deaf Association, Dundee	Flat 19, 6 Craigie Street, Dundee DD4 6PF	01382 462495
Miller, Charles W. MA	1953	1994	(Fowlis and Liff)	'Palm Springs', Parkside, Auchterhouse, Dundee DD3 0RF	01382 320407
Milroy, Tom	1960	1992	(Monifieth: St Rule's)	9 Long Row, Westhaven, Carnoustie DD7 6BE	01241 856654
Mitchell, Jack MA BD CTh	1987	1996	(Dundee: Menzieshill)	10 Invergowrie Drive, Dundee DD2 1RF	01382 642301
Mowat, Gilbert M. MA	1948	1986	(Dundee: Albany-Butterburn)	7 Dunmore Gardens, Dundee DD2 1PP	01382 566013
Powrie, James E. LTh	1969	1995	(Dundee: Chalmers Ardler)	3 Kirktonhill Road, Kirriemuir DD8 4HU	01575 572503
Rae, Robert LTh	1968	1983	Chaplain: Dundee Acute Hospitals	14 Neddertoun View, Liff, Dundee DD3 5RU	01382 581790
Robertson, Thomas P.	1963	2001	(Dundee: Broughty Ferry St James')	20 Kilnburn, Newport-on-Tay DD6 8DE [E-mail: tp.robertson@ukonline.co.uk]	01382 542422
Rogers, James M. BA DB DCult	1955	1996	(Gibraltar)	24 Mansion Drive, Dalclaverhouse, Dundee DD4 9DD	01382 506162
Scroggie, John C.	1951	1985	(Mains)	23 Cliffburn Gardens, Broughty Ferry, Dundee DD5 3NB	01382 739354
Scoular, Stanley	1963	2000	(Rosyth)	31 Duns Crescent, Dundee DD4 0RY	01382 501653
Simpson, James H. BSc	1996	2005	(Auxiliary Minister)	11 Claypotts Place, Broughty Ferry, Dundee DD5 1LG	01382 776520
Smith, Lilian MA DCS			(Deaconess)	6 Fintry Mains, Dundee DD4 9HF	01382 500052

DUNDEE ADDRESSES

Balgay	200 Lochee Road
Barnhill St Margaret's	10 Invermark Terrace
Broughty Ferry	
New Kirk	5 Fort Street
St James'	5 West Queen Street
St Luke's and Queen Street	96 Dundee Road
St Stephen's and West	22 Brownhill Road
Camperdown	Turnberry Avenue
Chalmers Ardler	Isla Street x Main Street
Clepington	
Craigiebank	Craigie Avenue at Greendyke Road
Douglas and Angus	Balbeggie Place
Downfield South	Haldane Street off Strathmartine Road
Dundee (St Mary's)	Nethergate
Fairmuir	329 Clepington Road
Lochee	
Old and St Luke's	Bright Street, Lochee
West	191 High Street, Lochee
Logie and	
St John's (Cross)	Shaftesbury Rd x Blackness Ave
Mains	Foot of Old Glamis Road
Mains of Fintry	Fintry Road x Fintry Drive
Meadowside St Paul's	114 Nethergate
Menzieshill	Charleston Drive, Lochee
Mid Craigie	Longtown Terrace
St Andrew's	2 King Street
St David's High Kirk	119A Kinghorne Road and 273 Strathmore Avenue
Steeple	Nethergate
Stobswell	Top of Albert Street
Strathmartine	513 Strathmartine Road
Trinity	73 Crescent Street
West	130 Perth Road
Whitfield	Haddington Crescent

(30) ANGUS

Meets at Forfar in St Margaret's Church Hall, on the first Tuesday of each month, except June when it meets on the last Tuesday, and January, July and August when there is no meeting.

Clerk:	REV. MATTHEW S. BICKET BD		
Depute Clerk:	MRS HELEN McLEOD MA		
Presbytery Office:		St Margaret's Church, West High Street, Forfar DD8 1BJ [E-mail: akph36@uk.uumail.com]	01307 464224

Aberlemno (H) linked with Guthrie and Rescobie
Brian Ramsay BD DPS MLitt	1980	1984	The Manse, Guthrie, Forfar DD8 2TP	01241 828243

Arbirlot linked with Carmyllie
Ian O. Coltart CA BD	1988	2004	The Manse, Arbirlot, Arbroath DD11 2NX	01241 434479

Arbroath: Knox's (H) linked with Arbroath: St Vigeans (H)
Ian G. Gough MA BD MTh DMin	1974	1990	The Manse, St Vigeans, Arbroath DD11 4RD [E-mail: ianggough@btinternet.com]	01241 873206

Arbroath: Old and Abbey (H) (Church office: 01241 877068)
Valerie L. Allen (Ms) BMus MDiv	1990	1996	51 Cliffburn Road, Arbroath DD11 5BA [E-mail: VL2allen@aol.com]	01241 872196 (Tel/Fax)

Arbroath: St Andrew's (H) (E-mail: st_andrews_arbroath@lineone.net)
W. Martin Fair BA BD DMin	1992		92 Grampian Gardens, Arbroath DD11 4AQ [E-mail: martinfair@aol.com]	01241 873238 (Tel/Fax)

Arbroath: St Vigeans See Arbroath: Knox's

Arbroath: West Kirk (H)
Alasdair G. Graham BD DipMin	1981	1986	1 Charles Avenue, Arbroath DD11 2EY [E-mail: alasdair.graham@lineone.net]	01241 872244

Barry linked with Carnoustie
Michael S. Goss BD DPS	1991	2003	44 Terrace Road, Carnoustie DD7 7AR [E-mail: michaelgoss@blueyonder.co.uk]	01241 410194 (Tel/Fax) 07787 141567 (Mbl)

Brechin: Cathedral (H)
Scott Rennie MA BD STM — 1999 — Chanonry Wynd, Brechin DD9 6JS [E-mail: scott.rennie@onetel.com] — 01356 622783

Brechin: Gardner Memorial (H)
Moira Herkes (Mrs) BD — 1985 1999 — 15 Caldhame Gardens, Brechin DD9 1JJ [E-mail: mossherkes@aol.com] — 01356 622789

Carmyllie See Arbirlot
Carnoustie See Barry

Carnoustie: Panbride (H)
Matthew S. Bicket BD — 1989 — 8 Arbroath Road, Carnoustie DD7 6BL [E-mail: matthew@bicket.freeserve.co.uk] — 01241 854478 (Tel) / 01241 855088 (Fax)

Colliston linked with Friockheim Kinnell linked with Inverkeilor and Lunan (H)
Peter A. Phillips BA — 1995 2004 — 18 Middlegate, Friockheim, Arbroath DD11 4TS [E-mail: peter-rona@revphillips.freeserve.co.uk] — 01241 828781

Dun and Hillside
Linda J. Broadley (Mrs) LTh DipEd — 1996 2004 — 4 Manse Road, Hillside, Montrose DD10 9FB [E-mail: linda.broadley@tesco.net] — 01674 830288

Dunnichen, Letham and Kirkden
Allan F. Webster MA BD — 1978 1990 — 7 Braehead Road, Letham, Forfar DD8 2PG [E-mail: allanfwebster@aol.com] — 01307 818916
Shirley Thomas (Mrs) (Aux) — 2000 2002 — 14 Kirkgait, Letham, Forfar DD8 2XQ [E-mail: martyn-shirley@thomas447.fsnet.co.uk] — 01307 818084

Eassie and Nevay linked with Newtyle
Carleen Robertson (Miss) BD — 1992 — 2 Kirkton Road, Newtyle, Blairgowrie PH12 8TS [E-mail: carleen.robertson@tesco.net] — 01828 650461

Edzell Lethnot (H) linked with Fern, Careston and Menmuir linked with Glenesk
Alan G.N. Watt MTh DipCommEd CQSW — 1996 2003 — Glenesk Cottage, Dunlappie Road, Edzell, Brechin DD9 7UB [E-mail: alangnwatt@aol.com] — 01356 648455

Farnell
Vacant — 01674 672060

Fern, Careston and Menmuir See Edzell Lethnot

Forfar: East and Old (H)
Graham Norrie MA BD — 1967 1978 — The Manse, Lour Road, Forfar DD8 2BB — 01307 464303

Forfar: Lowson Memorial (H)
Vacant
1 Jamieson Street, Forfar DD8 2HY
01307 462248

Forfar: St Margaret's (H) (Church office: 01307 464224)
Vacant
15 Potters Park Crescent, Forfar DD8 1HH
01307 466390

Friockheim Kinnell See Colliston

Glamis (H), Inverarity and Kinnettles
John F. Davidson BSc DipEdTech   1970   2005
12 Turfbeg Road, Forfar DD8 3LT
[E-mail: jfraserdavid@tiscali.co.uk]
01307 466038

Glenesk See Edzell Lethnot
Guthrie and Rescobie See Aberlemno

Inchbrayock linked with Montrose: Melville South
David S. Dixon MA BD   1976   1994
The Manse, Ferryden, Montrose DD10 9SD
[E-mail: david@inchbrayock.wanadoo.co.uk]
01674 672108

Inverkeilor and Lunan See Colliston

Kirriemuir: St Andrew's (H) linked with Oathlaw Tannadice
David J. Taverner MCIBS ACIS BD   1996   2002
26 Quarry Park, Kirriemuir DD8 4DR
[E-mail: rahereuk@hotmail.com]
01575 575561

Montrose: Melville South See Inchbrayock

Montrose: Old and St Andrew's
Laurence A.B. Whitley MA BD PhD   1975   1985
2 Rosehill Road, Montrose DD10 8ST
[E-mail: labwhitley@btinternet.com]
01674 672447
07870 733721 (Mbl)

Newtyle See Eassie and Nevay
Oathlaw Tannadice See Kirriemuir: St Andrew's

The Glens and Kirriemuir: Old (H) (Church office: 01575 572819) (Website: www.gkopc.co.uk)
Malcolm I.G. Rooney DPE BEd BD   1993   1999
20 Strathmore Avenue, Kirriemuir DD8 4DJ
[E-mail: malcolm@gkopc.co.uk]
01575 573724
07909 993233 (Mbl)

Linda Stevens (Mrs) BSc BD (Team Minister) 2006
17 North Latch Road, Brechin DD9 6LE
[E-mail: Linda@gkopc.co.uk]
01356 623415
07801 192730 (Mbl)

The Isla Parishes
Ben Pieterse BA BTh LTh   2001
Balduff House, Kilry, Blairgowrie PH11 8HS
[E-mail: benhp@angus.seriouslyinternet.com]
01575 560260
(Charge formed by the union of Airlie Ruthven Kingoldrum and Glenisla Kilry Lintrathen)

Anderson, James W. BSc MTh	1986	1997	(Kincardine O'Neil with Lumphanan)	47 Glebe Road, Arbroath DD11 4HJ	01241 873298
Anderson, Kenneth G. MA BD	1967	2006	(Abernethy and Dron with Arngask)	26 Andrew Welsh Way, Arbroath DD11 1LS	01241 411078
Brodie, James BEM MA BD STM	1955	1974	(Hurlford)	25A Keptie Road, Arbroath DD11 3ED	01241 828030
Bruce, William C. MA BD	1961	1995	(Motherwell: Dalziel)	31 Kirkton Terrace, Carnoustie DD7 7BZ	01241 828717
Butters, David	1964	1998	(Turriff: St Ninian's and Forglen)	68A Millgate, Friockheim, Arbroath DD11 4TN	01356 625201
Douglas, Iain M. MA BD MPhil DipEd	1960	2002	(Farnell with Montrose: St Andrew's)	Old School House, Kinnell, Friockheim, Arbroath DD11 4UL	01575 573973
Drysdale James P.R.	1967	1999	(Brechin: Gardner Memorial)	51 Airlie Street, Brechin DD9 6JX	
Duncan, Robert F. MTheol	1986	2001	(Lochgelly: St Andrew's)	25 Rowan Avenue, Kirriemuir DD8 4TB	01307 461944
Finlay, Quintin BA BD	1975	1996	(North Bute)	Ivy Cottage, Greenlees Farm, Kelso TD5 8BT	01307 463193
Hodge, William N.T.	1966	1995	(Longside)	'Tullochgorum', 61 South Street, Forfar DD8 2BS	01241 854928
Jones, William	1952	1987	(Kirriemuir: St Andrew's)	14 Muir Street, Forfar DD8 3JY	01307 818741
Milton, Eric G. RD	1963	1994	(Blairdaff)	16 Bruce Court, Links Parade, Carnoustie DD7 7JE	01307 818416
Perry, Joseph B.	1955	1989	(Farnell)	19 Guthrie Street, Letham, Forfar DD8 2PS	01356 647322
Reid, Albert B. BD BSc	1996	2001	(Ardler, Kettins and Meigle)	1 Dundee Street, Letham, Forfar DD8 2PQ	
Robertson, George R. LTh	1985	2004	(Udny and Pitmedden)	3 Slateford Gardens, Edzell, Brechin DD9 7SX [E-mail: george.robertson@tesco.net]	
Searle, David C. MA DipTh	1965	2003	(Warden: Rutherford House)	12 Cairnie Road, Arbroath DD11 3DY	01241 872794
Smith, Hamish G.	1965	1993	(Auchterless with Rothienorman)	11A Guthrie Street, Letham, Forfar DD8 2PS	01307 818973
Thomas, Martyn R.H. CEng MIStructE	1987	2002	(Fowlis and Liff with Lundie and Muirhead of Liff)	14 Kirkgait, Letham, Forfar DD8 2XQ	01307 818084
Tyre, Robert	1960	1998	(Aberdeen: St Ninian's with Stockethill)	8 Borrowfield Crescent, Montrose DD10 9BR	01674 676961
Warnock, Denis MA	1952	1990	(Kirkcaldy: Torbain)	19 Keptie Road, Arbroath DD11 3ED	01241 872740
Youngson, Peter	1961	1996	(Kirriemuir: St Andrew's)	Coreen, Woodside, Northmuir, Kirriemuir DD8 4PG	01575 572832

ANGUS ADDRESSES

Arbroath
Knox's — Howard Street
Old and Abbey — West Abbey Street
St Andrew's — Hamilton Green
West Kirk — Keptie Street

Brechin
Cathedral — Bishops Close
Gardner Memorial — South Esk Street

Carnoustie — Dundee Street
Panbride — Arbroath Road

Forfar
East and Old — East High Street
Lowson Memorial — Jamieson Street
St Margaret's — West High Street

Kirriemuir
Old — High Street
St Andrew's — Glamis Road

Montrose
Melville South — Castle Street
Old and St Andrew's — High Street

(31) ABERDEEN

Meets at Queen's Cross Church, Albyn Place, Aberdeen AB10 1UN, on the first Tuesday of February, March, April, May, September, October, November and December, and on the fourth Tuesday of June.

Clerk:	REV. IAN A. McLEAN BSc BD DMin		
Presbytery Office:		Mastrick Church, Greenfern Road, Aberdeen AB16 6TR [E-mail: akph34@uk.uumail.com] [E-mail: aberdeen.presbytery@uk.uumail.com]	01224 690494
Hon. Treasurer:	MR A. SHARP	27 Hutchison Terrace, Aberdeen AB10 7NN	01224 315702

Aberdeen: Bridge of Don Oldmachar (01224 709299) (Website: www.oldmacharchurch.org) (New Charge Development)
Jim Ritchie BD MTh	2000	2004	60 Newburgh Circle, Aberdeen AB22 8QZ [E-mail: jim.ritchie@btopenworld.com]	01224 708137

Aberdeen: Cove (E)
David Swan BVMS BD	2005		4 Charleston Way, Cove, Aberdeen AB12 3FA [E-mail: ncdcove@uk.uumail.com]	01224 899933
Mark Johnston BSc BD DipMin (Assoc)	1998	2003	5 Bruce Walk, Redmoss, Aberdeen AB12 3LX [E-mail: ncdcove2@uk.uumail.com]	01224 874269

Aberdeen: Craigiebuckler (H) (01224 315649)
Kenneth L. Petrie MA BD	1984	1999	185 Springfield Road, Aberdeen AB15 8AA [E-mail: patandkenneth@aol.com]	01224 315125

Aberdeen: Ferryhill (H) (01224 213093)
John H.A. Dick MA MSc BD	1982		54 Polmuir Road, Aberdeen AB11 7RT [E-mail: jhadick@fish.co.uk]	01224 586933

Aberdeen: Garthdee (H)
Vacant			27 Ramsay Gardens, Aberdeen AB10 7AE	01224 317452

Aberdeen: Gilcomston South (H) (01224 647144)
D. Dominic Smart BSc BD MTh	1988		37 Richmondhill Road, Aberdeen AB15 5EQ [E-mail: smartdd@btconnect.com]	01224 314326

Aberdeen: High Hilton (H) (01224 494717)
A. Peter Dickson BSc BD	1996		24 Rosehill Drive, Aberdeen AB24 4JJ [E-mail: peter@highhilton.com]	01224 484155

Aberdeen: Holburn West (H) (01224 571120)
Duncan C. Eddie MA BD   1992   1999   31 Cranford Road, Aberdeen AB10 7NJ   01224 325873
[E-mail: nacnud@ceddie.freeserve.co.uk]

Aberdeen: Mannofield (H) (01224 310087) (E-mail: mannofieldchurch@xalt.co.uk)
John F. Anderson MA BD FSAScot   1966   1975   21 Forest Avenue, Aberdeen AB15 4TU   01224 315748
[E-mail: jfa941@aol.com]

Aberdeen: Mastrick (H) (01224 694121)
Lesley P. Risby (Mrs) BD   1994   2005   8 Corse Wynd, Kingswells, Aberdeen AB15 8TP   01224 749346
[E-mail: mrsrisby@hotmail.com]

Aberdeen: Middlefield (H)
Vacant
Michael Phillippo   73 Manor Avenue, Aberdeen AB16 7UT   01224 685214
MTh BSc BVetMed MRCVS (Aux)   25 Deeside Crescent, Aberdeen AB15 7PT   01224 318317

Aberdeen: Midstocket
Marian Cowie MA BD MTh   1990   2006   54 Woodstock Road, Aberdeen AB15 5JF
[E-mail: mcowieou@aol.com]
(Charge formed by the union of Aberdeen: Beechgrove and Aberdeen: St Ninian's)

Aberdeen: New Stockethill (New Charge Development)
Ian M. Aitken MA BD   1999   52 Ashgrove Road West, Aberdeen AB16 5EE   01224 686929
[E-mail: ncdstockethill@uk.uumail.com]

Aberdeen: Northfield
Scott C. Guy BD   1989   1999   28 Byron Crescent, Aberdeen AB16 7EX   01224 692332
[E-mail: scguy@fish.co.uk]

Aberdeen: Queen Street
Vacant   51 Osborne Place, Aberdeen AB25 2BX   01224 646429

Aberdeen: Queen's Cross (H) (01224 644742)
Robert F. Brown MA BD ThM   1971   1984   1 St Swithin Street, Aberdeen AB10 6XH   01224 322549
[E-mail: minister@queenscrosschurch.org.uk]

Aberdeen: Rubislaw (H) (01224 645477)
Andrew G.N. Wilson MA BD DMin   1977   1987   45 Rubislaw Den South, Aberdeen AB15 4BD   01224 314878
[E-mail: agn.wilson@virgin.net]

Aberdeen: Ruthrieston West (H)
Sean Swindells BD DipMin   1996   451 Great Western Road, Aberdeen AB10 6NL   01224 313075
[E-mail: seanswinl@aol.com]

Aberdeen: St Columba's Bridge of Don (H) (01224 825653)
Louis Kinsey BD DipMin — 1991
151 Jesmond Avenue, Aberdeen AB22 8UG — 01224 705337
[E-mail: revkinsey@aol.com]

Aberdeen: St George's Tillydrone (H) (01224 482204)
James Weir BD — 1991 — 2003
127 Clifton Road, Aberdeen AB24 4RH — 01224 483976
[E-mail: rjweir@tiscali.co.uk]

Ann V. Lundie (Miss) DCS
20 Langdykes Drive, Cove, Aberdeen AB12 3HW — 01224 898416

Aberdeen: St John's Church for Deaf People (H) (01224 494566)
John R. Osbeck BD — 1979 — 1991
15 Deeside Crescent, Aberdeen AB15 7PT — (Voice/Text) 01224 315595
[E-mail: info@aneds.org.uk]

Aberdeen: St Machar's Cathedral (H) (01224 485988)
Alan D. Falconer MA BD DLitt
18 The Chanonry, Old Aberdeen AB24 1RQ — 01224 483688
[E-mail: minister@stmachar.com]

Aberdeen: St Mark's (H) (01224 640672)
John M. Watson LTh — 1989
65 Mile-end Avenue, Aberdeen AB15 5PU — 01224 622470
[E-mail: drjohn@johnmutchwatson.wanadoo.co.uk]

Aberdeen: St Mary's (H) (01224 487227)
Elsie J. Fortune (Mrs) BSc BD — 2003
456 King Street, Aberdeen AB24 3DE — 01224 633778

Aberdeen: St Nicholas Kincorth, South of
Edward C. McKenna BD DPS — 1989 — 2002
The Manse, Kincorth Circle, Aberdeen AB12 5NX — 01224 872820

Aberdeen: St Nicholas Uniting, Kirk of (H) (01224 643494)
B. Stephen C. Taylor BA BBS MA MDiv — 1984 — 2005
12 Louisville Avenue, Aberdeen AB15 4TX — 01224 314318
[E-mail: minister@kirk-of-st-nicholas.org.uk] — 01224 649242 (Fax)

Aberdeen: St Stephen's (H) (01224 624443)
James M. Davies BSc BD — 1982 — 1989
6 Belvidere Street, Aberdeen AB25 2QS — 01224 635694
[E-mail: daviesjim@btinternet.com]

Aberdeen: South Holburn (H) (01224 211730)
George S. Cowie BSc BD — 1991 — 2006
54 Woodstock Road, Aberdeen AB15 5JF
[E-mail: gscowie@aol.com]
(Charge formed by the union of Aberdeen: Holburn Central and Aberdeen: Ruthrieston South)

Aberdeen: Summerhill (H)
Ian A. McLean BSc BD DMin — 1981
36 Stronsay Drive, Aberdeen AB15 6JL — 01224 324669
[E-mail: iamclean@lineone.net]

Aberdeen: Torry St Fittick's (H) (01224 899183)
Iain C. Barclay 1976 1999 11 Devanha Gardens East, Aberdeen AB11 7UH 01224 588245
MBE TD MA BD MTh MPhil PhD [E-mail: i.c.barclay@virgin.net] 07968 131930 (Mbl)
  07625 383830 (Pager)

Aberdeen: Woodside (H) (01224 277249)
Markus Auffermann DipTheol 1999 2006 322 Clifton Road, Aberdeen AB24 4HQ 01224 484562
Ann V. Lundie DCS 20 Langdykes Drive, Cove, Aberdeen AB12 3HW 01224 898416

Bucksburn Stoneywood (H) (01224 712411)
Nigel Parker BD MTh DMin 1994 25 Gilbert Road, Bucksburn, Aberdeen AB21 9AN 01224 712635
  [E-mail: nigel@revparker.fsnet.co.uk]

Cults (H)
Ewen J. Gilchrist BD DipMin DipComm 1982 2005 1 Cairnlee Terrace, Bieldside, Aberdeen AB15 9AE 01224 861692
  [E-mail: ewengilchrist@btconnect.com]

Dyce (H) (01224 771295)
Russel Moffat BD MTh PhD 1986 1998 144 Victoria Street, Dyce, Aberdeen AB21 7BE 01224 722380

Kingswells
Dolly Purnell BD 2003 2004 Kingswells Manse, Lang Stracht, Aberdeen AB15 8PL 01224 740229
  [E-mail: neilanddolly.purnell@btinternet.com]

Newhills (H) (Tel/Fax: 01224 716161)
Norman Maciver MA BD DMin 1976 Newhills Manse, Bucksburn, Aberdeen AB21 9SS 01224 712655
  [E-mail: newhillsnm@aol.com]

Peterculter (H) (01224 735845)
John A. Ferguson BD DipMin DMin 1988 1999 7 Howie Lane, Peterculter AB14 0LJ 01224 735041
  [E-mail: jc.ferguson@virgin.net]

Aitchison, James W. BD	1993	Chaplain: Army	2 Bn Prince of Wales Royal Regiment, Clive Barracks, Tern Hill, Shropshire TF9 3QE
Alexander, William M. BD	1971 1998	(Berriedale and Dunbeath with Latheron)	110 Fairview Circle, Danestone, Aberdeen AB22 8YR 01224 703752
Beattie, Walter G. MA BD	1956 1995	(Arbroath: Old and Abbey)	126 Seafield Road, Aberdeen AB15 7YQ 01224 329259
Black, W. Graham MA BD	1983 1999	Urban Prayer Ministry	72 Linksview, Linksfield Road, Aberdeen AB24 5RG 01224 492491
Bryden, Agnes Y. (Mrs) DCS		(Deaconess)	Angusfield House, 226 Queen's Road, Aberdeen AB15 8DN 07761 235815
Campbell, W.M.M. BD CPS	1970 2003	(Hospital Chaplain)	43 Murray Terrace, Aberdeen AB11 7SA 01224 583805
Coutts, Fred MA BD	1973 1989	Hospital Chaplain	9A Millburn Street, Aberdeen AB11 6SS 01224 208341
Crawford, Michael S.M. LTh	1966 2002	(Aberdeen: St Mary's)	9 Craigton Avenue, Aberdeen AB15 7RP 01330 826236
Dickson, John C. MA	1950 1987	(Aberdeen: St Fittick's)	36 Queen Victoria Park, Inchmarlo, Banchory AB31 4AL

Name	Position			Address	Tel
Douglas, Andrew M. MA	(High Hilton)	1957	1995	219 Countesswells Road, Aberdeen AB15 7RD	01224 311932
Falconer, James B. BD	Hospital Chaplain	1982	1991	3 Brimmond Walk, Westhill AB32 6XH	01224 744621
Finlayson, Ena (Miss) DCS	(Deaconess)			16E Denwood, Aberdeen AB15 6JF	01224 321147
Goldie, George D. ALCM	(Greyfriars)	1953	1995	27 Broomhill Avenue, Aberdeen AB10 6JL	01224 322503
Gordon, Laurie Y.	(John Knox)	1960	1995	1 Alder Drive, Portlethen, Aberdeen AB12 4WA	01224 782703
Graham, A. David M. BA BD	(Aberdeen: Rosemount)	1971	2005	Elmhill House, 27 Shaw Crescent, Aberdeen AB25 3BT	01224 648041
Grainger, Harvey L. LTh	(Kingswells)	1975	2004	13 St Ronan's Crescent, Peterculter, Aberdeen AB14 0RL	01224 739824
				[E-mail: harveygrainger@tiscali.co.uk]	07768 333216 (Mbl)
Haddow, Angus BSc	(Methlick)	1963	1999	25 Lerwick Road, Aberdeen AB16 6RF	01224 696362
Hamilton, Helen (Miss) BD	(Glasgow: St James' Pollok)	1991	2003	The Cottage, West Tilbouries, Maryculter, Aberdeen AB12 5GD	01224 739632
Hutchison, A. Scott MA BD DD	(Hospital Chaplain)	1957	1991	Ashfield, Drumoak, Banchory AB31 5AG	01330 811309
Hutchison, Alison M. (Mrs) BD DipMin	Hospital Chaplain	1988	1988	Ashfield, Drumoak, Banchory AB31 5AG	01330 811309
				[E-mail: amhutch62@aol.com]	
Hutchison, David S. BSc BD ThM	(Aberdeen: Torry St Fittick's)	1991	1999	51 Don Street, Aberdeen AB24 1UH	01224 276122
Jack, David LTh	(West Mearns)	1984	1999	7 Cromwell Road, Aberdeen AB15 4UH	01224 325355
				[E-mail: david@cromwell7.fsnet.co.uk]	
Johnstone, William MA BD	(University of Aberdeen)	1963	2001	9/5 Mount Alvernia, Edinburgh EH16 6AW	0131-664 3140
Jolly, Andrew J. BD CertMin	Chaplain to the Oil Industry	1983	2006	Chaplain's Office, Total E and P (UK) PLC, Crawpeel Road, Altens, Aberdeen AB12 3FG	01224 297532/3
Kerr, Hugh F. MA BD	(Aberdeen: Ruthrieston South)	1968	2006	134C Great Western Road, Aberdeen AB10 6QE	01224 580091
McCallum, Moyra (Miss) MA BD DCS	(Deaconess)			176 Hilton Drive, Aberdeen AB24 4LT	01224 486240
				[E-mail: moymac@aol.com]	
Main, Alan TD MA BD STM PhD	(University of Aberdeen)	1963	2001	Kirkfield, Barthol Chapel, Inverurie AB51 8TD	01651 806773
				[E-mail: amain@fish.co.uk]	
Mirrilees, J.B. MA BD	(High Hilton)	1937	1977	22 King's Gate, Aberdeen AB15 4EJ	01224 638351
Montgomerie, Jean B. (Miss) MA BD	(Forfar: St Margaret's)	1973	2005	12 St Ronan's Place, Peterculter, Aberdeen AB14 0QX	01224 732350
				[E-mail: revjeanb@tiscali.co.uk]	
Patterson, James BSc BD	(Aberdeen: Denburn)	2003	2006	122 Desswood Place, Aberdeen AB15 4DQ	01224 641033
Richardson, Thomas C. LTh ThB	(Cults: West)	1971	2004	19 Kinkell Road, Aberdeen AB15 8HR	01224 315328
				[E-mail: thomas.richardson7@btinternet.com]	
Rodgers, D. Mark BA BD MTh	Hospital Chaplain	1987	2003	152D Gray Street, Aberdeen AB10 6JW	01224 210810
Sefton, Henry R. MA BD STM PhD	(University of Aberdeen)	1957	1992	25 Albury Place, Aberdeen AB11 6TQ	01224 572305
Skakle, George S. MA	(Aberdeen: Powis)	1945	1987	30 Whitehall Terrace, Aberdeen AB25 2RY	01224 646478
Smith, Angus MA LTh	(Industrial Chaplain)	1965	2006	3/7 West Powburn, West Savile Gait, Edinburgh EH9 3EW	0131-667 1761
Stewart, James C. MA BD STM	(Aberdeen: Kirk of St Nicholas)	1960	2000	54 Murray Terrace, Aberdeen AB11 7SB	01224 587071
Strachan, Ian M. MA BD	(Ashkirk with Selkirk)	1959	1994	'Cardenwell', Glen Drive, Dyce, Aberdeen AB21 7EN	01224 772028
Swindells, Alison J. (Mrs) LLB BD	(Aberdeen: St Ninian's)	1998	2005	451 Great Western Road, Aberdeen AB10 6NL	01224 313075
				[E-mail: alisonswindells@aol.com]	
Swinton, John BD PhD	University of Aberdeen	1999		51 Newburgh Circle, Bridge of Don, Aberdeen AB22 8XA	01224 825637
				[E-mail: j.swinton@abdn.ac.uk]	
Torrance, Iain R. TD MA BD DPhil DD	President: Princeton Theological Seminary	1982	2005	64 Mercer Street, PO Box 552, Princeton, NJ 08542-0803, USA	001 609 497 7800
Watt, William G.	(Aberdeen: South of St Nicholas Kincorth)	1970	1977	50 Rosewell Gardens, Aberdeen AB15 6HZ	01224 321915
Wilkie, William E. LTh	(Aberdeen: St Nicholas Kincorth, South of)	1978	2001	32 Broomfield Park, Portlethen, Aberdeen AB12 4XT	01224 782052
Wilson, Thomas F. BD	Education	1984	1996	55 Allison Close, Cove, Aberdeen AB12 3WG	01224 873501
Wood, James L.K.	(Ruthrieston West)	1967	1995	1 Glen Drive, Dyce, Aberdeen AB21 7EN	01224 722543

ABERDEEN ADDRESSES

Bridge of Don
   Oldmachar — Ashwood Park
Cove — Loirston Primary School, Loirston Avenue
Craigiebuckler — Springfield Road
Cults — Quarry Road, Cults
Dyce — Victoria Street, Dyce
Ferryhill — Fonthill Road x Polmuir Road
Garthdee — Ramsay Gardens
Gilcomston South — Union Street x Summer Street
High Hilton — Hilton Drive
Holburn West — Great Western Road

Kingswells — Old Skene Road, Kingswells
Mannofield — Great Western Road x Craigton Road
Mastrick — Greenfern Road
Middlefield — Manor Avenue
Midstocket — Mid Stocket Road
New Stockethill
Northfield — Byron Crescent
Peterculter — Craigton Crescent
Queen Street — Queen Street
Queen's Cross — Albyn Place
Rubislaw — Queen's Gardens
Ruthrieston West — Broomhill Road
St Columba's — Brachead Way, Bridge of Don
St George's — Hayton Road, Tillydrone
St John's for the Deaf — Smithfield Road

St Machar's — The Chanonry
St Mark's — Rosemount Viaduct
St Mary's — King Street
St Nicholas Kincorth, South of — Kincorth Circle
St Nicholas Uniting, Kirk of — Union Street
St Ninian's — Mid Stocket Road
St Stephen's — Powis Place
South Holburn — Holburn Street
Summerhill — Stronsay Drive
Torry St Fittick's — Walker Road
Woodside — Church Street, Woodside

(32) KINCARDINE AND DEESIDE

Meets in Birse and Feughside Church, Finzean, Banchory on the first Tuesday of September, October, December, March and May and on the last Tuesday of June at 7pm.

Clerk: **REV. JACK HOLT BSc BD**   The Manse, Finzean, Banchory AB31 6PB   01330 850339
[E-mail: akph58@uk.uumail.com]
[E-mail: kincardinedeeside.presbytery@uk.uumail.com]

Aberluthnott linked with Laurencekirk (H)
Ronald Gall BSc BD   1985   2001   Aberdeen Road, Laurencekirk AB30 1AJ   01561 378838
[E-mail: ronniegall@aol.com]

Aboyne – Dinnet (H) (01339 886989) linked with Cromar (E-mail: aboynedinnet.cos@virgin.net)
Douglas I. Campbell BD DPS   2004   49 Charlton Crescent, Aboyne AB34 5GN   01339 886447
[E-mail: douglas.campbell@btinternet.com]

Arbuthnott and Bervie
Georgina M. Baxendale (Mrs) BD   1981   2006   10 Kirkburn, Inverbervie, Montrose DD10 0RT   01561 362633

Banchory-Devenick and Maryculter/Cookney

Bruce K. Gardner MA BD PhD	1988	2002	The Manse, Kirkton of Maryculter, Aberdeen AB12 5FS [E-mail: ministerofbdmc@aol.com]	01224 735776

Banchory-Ternan: East (H) (Tel: 01330 820380) (E-mail: eastchurch@banchory.fsbusiness.co.uk)

Mary M. Haddow (Mrs) BD	2001		East Manse, Station Road, Banchory AB31 5YP [E-mail: mary_haddow@ntlworld.com]	01330 822481
Anthony Stephen MA BD (Assistant Minister and Youth Leader)	2001		72 Grant Road, Banchory AB31 5UU	01330 825038

Banchory-Ternan: West (H)

Donald K. Walker BD	1979	1995	2 Wilson Road, Banchory AB31 5UY [E-mail: btw@uk2.net]	01330 822811
Anthony Stephen MA BD (Assistant Minister and Youth Leader)	2001		72 Grant Road, Banchory AB31 5UU	01330 825038

Birse and Feughside

Jack Holt BSc BD	1985	1994	The Manse, Finzean, Banchory AB31 6PB [E-mail: jholt@finzeanmanse.wanadoo.co.uk]	01330 850237

Braemar and Crathie

Kenneth I. Mackenzie BD CPS	1990	2005	Manse, Crathie, Ballater AB35 5UL	01339 742208

Cromar See Aboyne – Dinnet

Drumoak (H) and Durris (H)

James Scott MA BD	1973	1992	Manse, Durris, Banchory AB31 6BU [E-mail: jimscott@durrismanse.freeserve.co.uk]	01330 844557

Glenmuick (Ballater) (H)

Anthony Watts BD DipTechEd JP	1999		The Manse, Craigendarroch Walk, Ballater AB35 5ZB	01339 754014

Kinneff linked with Stonehaven: South (H)

David J. Stewart BD MTh DipMin	2000		South Church Manse, Cameron Street, Stonehaven AB39 2HE [E-mail: brigodon@clara.co.uk]	01569 762576

Laurencekirk See Aberluthnott

Mearns Coastal

George I. Hastie MA BD	1971	1998	The Manse, Kirkton, St Cyrus, Montrose DD10 0BW	01674 850880 (Tel/Fax)

Mid Deeside
Norman Nicoll BD — 2003 — The Manse, Torphins, Banchory AB31 4GQ — 01339 882276

Newtonhill
Hugh Conkey BSc BD — 1987 2001 — 39 St Ternans Road, Newtonhill, Stonehaven AB39 3PF [E-mail: hugh@conkey.plus.com] — 01569 730143

Portlethen (H) (01224 782883)
Flora J. Munro (Mrs) BD — 1993 2004 — 18 Rowanbank Road, Portlethen, Aberdeen AB12 4QY [E-mail: flora.munro@surefish.co.uk] — 01224 780211

Stonehaven: Dunnottar (H)
Gordon Farquharson MA BD DipEd — 1998 — Dunnottar Manse, Stonehaven AB39 3XL [E-mail: gfarqu@lineone.net] — 01569 762874

Stonehaven: Fetteresso (H) (Tel: 01569 767689) (E-mail: office@fetteressokirk.org.uk)
John R. Notman BSc BD — 1990 2001 — 11 South Lodge Drive, Stonehaven AB39 2PN [E-mail: notman@clara.co.uk] — 01569 762876

Stonehaven: South See Kinneff

West Mearns
Catherine A. Hepburn (Miss) BA BD — 1982 2000 — West Mearns Parish Church Manse, Fettercairn, Laurencekirk AB30 1UE [E-mail: chepburn@fish.co.uk] — 01561 340203

Name	Dates	Charge	Address	Tel
Brown, J.W.S. BTh	1960 1995	(Cronar)	10 Forestside Road, Banchory AB31 5ZH	01330 824353
Christie, Andrew C. LTh	1975 2000	(Banchory-Devenick and Maryculter/Cookney)	17 Broadstraik Close, Elrick, Aberdeen AB32 6JP	01224 746888
Forbes, John W.A. BD	1973 1999	(Edzell Lethnot with Fern, Careston and Menmuir with Glenesk)	Mid Clune, Finzean, Banchory AB31 6PL	01330 850283
Gray, Robert MA BD	1942 1982	(Stonehaven: Fetteresso)	4 Park Drive, Stonehaven AB39 2NW	01569 767027
Kinniburgh, Elizabeth B.F. (Miss) MA BD	1970 1986	(Birse with Finzean with Strachan)	7 Huntly Cottages, Aboyne AB31 5HD	01339 886757
Lamb, A. Douglas MA	1964 2002	(Dalry: St Margaret's)	130 Denstrath Road, Edzell Woods, Brechin DD9 7XF [E-mail: lamb.edzell@talk21.com]	01356 648139
Nicholson, William	1949 1986	(Banchory-Ternan: East with Durris)	10 Pantoch Gardens, Banchory AB31 5ZD	01330 823875
Rennie, Donald B. MA	1956 1996	(Industrial Chaplain)	Mernis Howe, Inverurie Street, Auchenblae, Laurencekirk AB30 1XS	01561 320622
Smith, Albert E. BD	1983 2006	(Methlick)	42 Haulkerton Crescent, Laurencekirk AB30 1FB [E-mail: aesmethlick@aol.com]	01561 376111
Taylor, Peter R. JP BD	1977 2001	(Torphins)	42 Beltie Road, Torphins, Banchory AB31 4JT	01339 882780

Name		Charge / note	Address	Telephone
Tierney, John P. MA	1945 1985	(Peterhead West Associate)	3 Queenshill Drive, Aboyne AB34 5DG	01339 886741
Watt, William D. LTh	1978 1996	(Aboyne – Dinnet)	2 West Toll Crescent, Aboyne AB34 5GB	01339 886943

(33) GORDON

Meets at various locations on the first Tuesday of February, March, April, May, September, October, November and December, and on the fourth Tuesday of June.

Clerk: **REV. G. EUAN D. GLEN BSc BD**   **The Manse, 26 St Ninian's, Monymusk, Inverurie AB51 7HF   01467 651941**
[E-mail: akph52@uk.uumail.com]

Barthol Chapel linked with Tarves
Vacant   8 Murray Avenue, Tarves, Ellon AB41 7LZ   01651 851250

Belhelvie (H)
Paul McKeown BSc PhD BD   2000 2005   Belhelvie Manse, Balmedie, Aberdeen AB23 8YR   01358 742227
[E-mail: prmckeown@tiscali.co.uk]

Blairdaff linked with Chapel of Garioch
Kim Cran (Mrs) MDiv BA   1993 2000   The Manse, Chapel of Garioch, Inverurie AB51 5HE   01467 681619
[E-mail: blairdaff.chapelofgariochparish@btinternet.com]

John C. Mack JP (Aux)   1985 2004   The Willows, Auchleven, Insch AB52 6QB   01464 820387

Chapel of Garioch See Blairdaff

Cluny (H) linked with Monymusk (H)
G. Euan D. Glen BSc BD   1992   The Manse, 26 St Ninian's, Monymusk, Inverurie AB51 7HF   01467 651470
[E-mail: euanglen@aol.com]

Culsalmond and Rayne linked with Daviot (H)
Mary M. Cranfield (Miss) MA BD DMin   1989   The Manse, Daviot, Inverurie AB51 0HY   01467 671241
[E-mail: marymc@ukgateway.net]

Cushnie and Tough (T) (H)
Margaret J. Garden (Miss) BD   1993 2000   The Manse, Muir of Fowlis, Alford AB33 8JU   01975 581239
[E-mail: m.garden@virgin.net]

Daviot See Culsalmond and Rayne

Drumblade linked with Huntly Strathbogie
Neil I.M. MacGregor BD   1995   Deveron Road, Huntly AB54 8DU   01466 792702

Echt linked with Midmar (T) Alan Murray BSc BD PhD	2003	The Manse, Echt, Westhill AB32 7AB [E-mail: ladecottage@btinternet.com]	01330 860004
Ellon Eleanor E. Macalister (Mrs) BD	1994 1999	The Manse, Union Street, Ellon AB41 9BA [E-mail: maca11ster@aol.com]	01358 720476
Sheila Craggs (Mrs) (Aux)	2001	7 Morar Court, Ellon AB41 9GG	01358 723055
Fintray Kinellar Keithhall Vacant		20 Kinmhor Rise, Blackburn, Aberdeen AB21 0LJ (The name for the united charge of Fintray and Kinellar and Keithhall)	01224 790701
Foveran Neil Gow BSc MEd BD	1996 2001	The Manse, Foveran, Ellon AB41 6AP [E-mail: ngow@beeb.net]	01358 789288
Howe Trinity John A. Cook MA BD	1986 2000	The Manse, 110 Main Street, Alford AB33 8AD [E-mail: j-a-cook@howe-trinity.freeserve.co.uk]	01975 562282
Huntly Cairnie Glass Thomas R. Calder LLB BD WS	1994	The Manse, Queen Street, Huntly AB54 8EB	01466 792630
Huntly Strathbogie See Drumblade			
Insch-Leslie-Premnay-Oyne (H) Jane C. Taylor (Miss) BD DipMin	1990 2001	22 Western Road, Insch AB52 6JR	01464 820914
Inverurie: St Andrew's T. Graeme Longmuir KGSJ MA BEd	1976 2001	St Andrew's Manse, 1 Ury Dale, Inverurie AB51 3XW [E-mail: standrew@ukonline.co.uk]	01467 620468
Inverurie: West Ian B. Groves BD CPS	1989	West Manse, 1 Westburn Place, Inverurie AB51 5QS [E-mail: i.groves@inveruriewestchurch.org]	01467 620285
Kennay John P. Renton BA LTh	1976 1990	Kennay, Inverurie AB51 9ND [E-mail: johnrenton@btinternet.com]	01467 642219 (Tel/Fax)

Kintore (H)

Alan Greig BSc BD	1977	1992	6 Forest Road, Kintore, Inverurie AB51 0XG [E-mail: greig@kincarr.free-online.co.uk]	01467 632219 (Tel/Fax)

Meldrum and Bourtie

Hugh O'Brien CSS MTheol	2001		The Manse, Urquhart Road, Oldmeldrum, Inverurie AB51 0EX [E-mail: minister@meldrum-bourtiechurch.org]	01651 872250

Methlick

Vacant			Methlick, Ellon AB41 0DS	01651 806215

Midmar See Echt
Monymusk See Cluny

New Machar

Manson C. Merchant BD CPS	1992	2001	The Manse, Disblair Road, Newmachar, Aberdeen AB21 0RD [E-mail: mcmerchant@btopenworld.com]	01651 862278

Noth

John McCallum BD DipPTh	1989		Manse of Noth, Kennethmont, Huntly AB54 4NP [E-mail: rev.john@btopenworld.com]	01464 831244

Skene (H)

Iain U. Thomson MA BD	1970	1972	The Manse, Kirkton of Skene, Skene AB32 6LX	01224 743277
Marion G. Stewart (Miss) DCS			Kirk Cottage, Kirkton of Skene, Skene AB32 6XE	01224 743407

Tarves See Barthol Chapel

Udny and Pitmedden

Regine U. Cheyne (Mrs) MA BSc BD	1988	2005	Manse Road, Udny Green, Udny, Ellon AB41 0RS	01651 842052

Upper Donside (H)

Brian Dingwall BTh CQSW	1999	2006	The Manse, Lumsden, Huntly AB54 4GQ	01464 861757

Andrew, John MA BD DipRE DipEd	1961	1995	(Teacher: Religious Education)	Cartar's Croft, Midmar, Inverurie AB51 7NJ	01330 833208
Bowie, Alfred LTh	1974	1998	(Alford with Keig with Tullynessle Forbes)	17 Stewart Road, Alford AB33 8UA	01975 563824
Collie, Joyce P. (Miss) MA PhD	1966	1994	(Corgarff Strathdon and Glenbuchat Towie)	35 Foudland Court, Insch AB52 6LG	01464 820945
Dryden, Ian MA DipEd	1988	2001	(New Machar)	16 Glenhome Gardens, Dyce, Aberdeen AB21 7FG	01224 722820
Hawthorn, Daniel MA BD DMin	1965	2004	(Belhelvie)	7 Crimond Drive, Ellon AB41 8BT [E-mail: donhawthorn@compuserve.com]	01358 723981
Jones, Robert A. LTh CA	1966	1997	(Marnoch)	13 Gordon Terrace, Inverurie AB51 4GT	01467 622691
Lister, Douglas	1945	1986	(Largo and Newburn)	Gowanbank, Port Elphinstone, Inverurie AB51 3UN [E-mail: pastillister@surf.scotland.uk]	01467 621262
Macallan, Gerald B.	1954	1992	(Kintore)	38 Thorngrove House, 500 Great Western Road, Aberdeen AB10 6PF	01224 316125

McLean, John MA BD	1967	2003	(Bathgate: Boghall)	16 Eastside Drive, Westhill AB32 6QN	01224 747701
McLeish, Robert S.	1970	2000	(Insch-Leslie-Premnay-Oyne)	19 Western Road, Insch AB52 6JR	01464 820749
Mellis, Robert J. BTh CA	1982	1998	(Shapinsay)	81 Western Avenue, Ellon AB41 9EX	01358 721929
Rodger, Matthew A. BD	1978	1999	(Ellon)	57 Eilean Rise, Ellon AB41 9NF	01358 724556
Scott, Allan D. BD	1977	1989	(Culsalmond with Daviot with Rayne)	20 Barclay Road, Inverurie AB51 3QP	01467 625161
Stewart, George C. MA	1952	1995	(Drumblade with Huntly Strathbogie)	104 Scott Drive, Huntly AB54 8PF	01466 792503
Stoddart, A. Grainger	1975	2001	(Meldrum and Bourtie)	6 Mayfield Gardens, Insch AB52 6XL	01464 821124
Wallace, R.J. Stuart MA	1947	1986	(Foveran)	Manse View, Manse Road, Methlick, Ellon AB41 7DW	01651 806843

(34) BUCHAN

Meets at St Kane's Centre, New Deer, Turriff on the first Tuesday of each month with the exception of January, July and August.

| Clerk: | MR GEORGE W. BERSTAN | | Faithlie, Victoria Terrace, Turriff AB53 4EE | **01888 562392** |
| | | | [E-mail: akph41@uk.uumail.com] | |

Aberdour linked with Pitsligo linked with Sandhaven
Vacant — The Manse, 49 Pitsligo Street, Rosehearty, Fraserburgh AB43 7JL — 01346 571237

Auchaber United linked with Auchterless
Alison Jaffrey (Mrs) MA BD — 1990 1999 — The Manse, Auchterless, Turriff AB53 8BA — 01888 511217
[E-mail: alison.jaffrey@bigfoot.com]

Auchterless See Auchaber United

Banff linked with King Edward
Alan Macgregor BA BD — 1992 1998 — 7 Colleonard Road, Banff AB45 1DZ — 01261 812107
[E-mail: banffkirk@btinternet.com]

Crimond linked with Lonmay linked with St Fergus
Vacant — The Manse, Crimond, Fraserburgh AB43 8QJ — 01346 532431

Cruden
Rodger Neilson JP BSc BD — 1972 1974 — Hatton, Peterhead AB42 0QQ — 01779 841229
[E-mail: rodger.neilson@virgin.net]

Deer (H)
James Wishart JP BD — 1986 — The Manse, Old Deer, Peterhead AB42 5JB — 01771 623582
[E-mail: jameswishart@freeola.com]

Fordyce
Iain A. Sutherland BSc BD   1996   2000   Seafield Terrace, Portsoy, Banff AB45 2QB   01261 842272
[E-mail: revsuthy@aol.com]

Fraserburgh: Old
Vacant   The Old Parish Church Manse, 4 Robbies Road, Fraserburgh   01346 518536
AB43 7AF

Fraserburgh: South (H) linked with Inverallochy and Rathen: East
Ronald F. Yule   1982   15 Victoria Street, Fraserburgh AB43 9PJ   01346 518244 (Tel)
0870 055 4665 (Fax)

Fraserburgh: West (H) linked with Rathen: West
B. Andrew Lyon LTh   1971   1978   23 Strichen Road, Fraserburgh AB43 9SA   01346 513303 (Tel)
[E-mail: rathen@tiscali.co.uk]   01346 512398 (Fax)

Fyvie linked with Rothienorman
Robert J. Thorburn BD   1978   2004   The Manse, Fyvie, Turriff AB53 8RD   01651 891230
[E-mail: rjthorburn@aol.com]

Gardenstown
Donald N. Martin BD   1996   The Manse, Fernie Brae, Gardenstown, Banff AB45 3YL   01261 851256
[E-mail: dnm@gamrie.plus.com]

Inverallochy and Rathen: East See Fraserburgh: South
King Edward See Banff

Longside
Vacant   9 Anderson Drive, Longside, Peterhead AB42 4XG   01779 821224

Lonmay See Crimond

Macduff
David J. Randall MA BD ThM   1971   The Manse, Macduff AB45 3QL   01261 832316
[E-mail: djrandall@macduff.force9.co.uk]

Marnoch
Vacant   Marnoch Manse, Aberchirder, Huntly AB54 7TS   01466 780276

Maud and Savoch linked with New Deer: St Kane's
Alistair P. Donald MA PhD BD   1999   The Manse, New Deer, Turriff AB53 6TD   01771 644216
[E-mail: alistair.donald@v21.me.uk]

Monquhitter and New Byth linked with Turriff: St Andrew's
James Cook MA MDiv   1999 2002   Balmellie Road, Turriff AB53 4SP   01888 560304
                                                                     [E-mail: jmscook9@aol.com]

New Deer: St Kane's See Maud and Savoch

New Pitsligo linked with Strichen and Tyrie
Iain Macnee LTh BD MA PhD   1975   Kingsville, Strichen, Fraserburgh AB43 6SQ   01771 637365
                                                                     [E-mail: strchtyr@fish.co.uk]

Ordiquhill and Cornhill (H) linked with Whitehills
Brian Hendrie BD   1992 2005   6 Craigneen Place, Whitehills, Banff AB45 2NE   01261 861671
                                                                     [E-mail: brianandyvonne@98duncansby.freeserve.co.uk]

Peterhead: Old
Vacant   1 Hawthorn Road, Peterhead AB42 2DW

Peterhead: St Andrew's (H)
David G. Pitkeathly LLB BD   1996   1 Landale Road, Peterhead AB42 1QN   01779 472141
                                                                     [E-mail: david-gp@fish.co.uk]

Peterhead: Trinity
L. Paul McClenaghan BA   1973   18 Landale Road, Peterhead AB42 1QP   01779 472405
                                                                     [E-mail: paul.mcclenaghan@gmail.com]

Pitsligo See Aberdour
Rathen: West See Fraserburgh: West
Rothienorman See Fyvie
St Fergus See Crimond
Sandhaven See Aberdour
Strichen and Tyrie See New Pitsligo
Turriff: St Andrew's See Monquhitter and New Byth

Turriff: St Ninian's and Forglen
Murdo C. MacDonald MA BD   2002   4 Deveronside Drive, Turriff AB53 4SP   01888 563850

Whitehills See Ordiquhill and Cornhill

Birnie, Charles J. MA   1969 1995   (Aberdour and Tyrie)   'The Dookit', 23 Water Street, Strichen, Fraserburgh AB43 6ST   01771 637775
Blaikie, James BD   1972 1997   (Berwick-on-Tweed: St Andrew's   57 Glenugie View, Peterhead AB42 2BW   01779 490625
                                                          Wallace Green and Lowick)

Douglas, Ian P. LTh	1974 1998	(Aberdeen: Craigiebuckler)	'Stonecroft', 1 Tortorston Drive, Tortorston, Blackhills, Peterhead AB42 3LY	01779 474728
Dunlop, M. William B. LLB BD	1981 1995	(Peterhead: St Andrew's)	18 Iona Avenue, Peterhead AB42 1NZ	01779 479189
Fawkes, G.M. Allan BA BSc JP	1979 2000	(Lonmay with Rathen: West)	3 Northfield Gardens, Hatton, Peterhead AB42 0SW	01779 841814
McKay, Margaret (Mrs) MA BD MTh	1991 2003	(Auchaber United with Auchterless)	The Smithy, Knowes of Elrick, Aberchirder, Huntly AB54 7PP [E-mail: mgt_mckay@yahoo.com.uk]	01466 780208 (Tel) 01466 780015 (Fax)
Mackenzie, Seoras L. BD	1996 1998	Chaplain: Army	1 RHF, BFPO 38	
McMillan, William J. CA LTh BD	1969 2004	(Sandsting and Aithsting with Walls and Sandness)	7 Ardinn Drive, Turriff AB53 4PR [E-mail: revbillymcmillan@aol.com]	01888 560727
Noble, George S. DipTh	1972 2000	(Carfin with Newarthill)	Craigowan, 3 Main Street, Inverallochy, Fraserburgh AB43 8XX	01346 582749
Ross, David S. MSc PhD BD	1978 2003	Prison Chaplain Service	3–5 Abbey Street, Old Deer, Peterhead AB42 5LN [E-mail: padsross@btinternet.com]	01771 623994
Taylor, William MA MEd	1984 1996	(Buckie: North)	23 York Street, Peterhead AB42 6SN	01779 481798

(35) MORAY

Meets at St Andrew's-Lhanbryd and Urquhart on the first Tuesday of February, March, April, May, September, October, November and December; and at the Moderator's church on the fourth Tuesday of June.

| Clerk: | REV. HUGH M.C. SMITH LTh | Mortlach Manse, Dufftown, Keith AB55 4AR [E-mail: akph67@uk.uumail.com] [E-mail: clerk@moraypresbytery.plus.com] | 01340 820538 |
| Depute Clerk: | REV. GRAHAM W. CRAWFORD BSc BD STM | The Manse, Prospect Terrace, Lossiemouth IV31 6JS | 01343 810676 |

Aberlour (H)

| Elizabeth M. Curran (Miss) BD | 1995 | 1998 | Mary Avenue, Aberlour AB38 9QN [E-mail: ecurran8@aol.com] | 01340 871027 |

Alves and Burghead linked with Kinloss and Findhorn

| Duncan Shaw LTh CPS | 1984 | 2006 | The Manse, 4 Manse Road, Kinloss, Forres IV36 3GH | 01309 690931 |

Bellie linked with Speymouth

| Alison C. Mehigan BD DPS | 2003 | 11 The Square, Fochabers IV32 7DG [E-mail: alisonc@mehigan-ug.fsnet.co.uk] | 01343 820256 |

Birnie and Pluscarden linked with Elgin High

| Julie M. Woods (Mrs) BTh | 2005 | Daisy Bank, 5 Forteath Avenue, Elgin IV30 1TQ [E-mail: missjulie@btinternet.com] | 01343 542449 |

Buckie: North (H)

| Vacant | 14 St Peter's Road, Buckie AB56 1DL | 01542 831328 |

Buckie: South and West (H) linked with Enzie
Vacant
41 East Church Street, Buckie AB56 1ES
01542 832103

Cullen and Deskford
Wilma A. Johnston MTheol MTh   2006
3 Seafield Place, Cullen, Buckie AB56 4UU
[E-mail: revwilmaj@btinternet.com]
01542 841851

Dallas linked with Forres: St Leonard's (H) linked with Rafford
Paul Amed LTh DPS   1992   2000
St Leonard's Manse, Nelson Road, Forres IV36 1DR
[E-mail: paulamed@stleonardsmanse.freeserve.co.uk]
01309 672380

Duffus, Spynie and Hopeman (H)
Bruce B. Lawrie BD   1974   2001
The Manse, Duffus, Elgin IV30 5QP
[E-mail: blawrie@zetnet.co.uk]
01343 830276

Dyke linked with Edinkillie
Gordon R. Mackenzie BScAgr BD   1977   2003
Manse of Dyke, Brodie, Forres IV36 2TD
[E-mail: rev.g.mackenzie@btopenworld.com]
01309 641239

Edinkillie See Dyke
Elgin: High See Birnie and Pluscarden

Elgin: St Giles' (H) and St Columba's South (01343 551501)
George B. Rollo BD   1974   1986
(Office and Church Halls: Greyfriars Street, Elgin IV30 1LF)
18 Reidhaven Street, Elgin IV30 1QH
[E-mail: gbrstgiles@hotmail.com]
01343 547208

Enzie See Buckie South and West

Findochty linked with Portknockie linked with Rathven
Graham Austin BD   1997
20 Netherton Terrace, Findochty, Buckie AB56 4QD
[E-mail: grahamaustin1@btopenworld.com]
01542 833484

Forres: St Laurence (H)
Barry J. Boyd LTh DPS   1993
12 Mackenzie Drive, Forres IV36 2JP
[E-mail: barryj.boydstlaurence@btinternet.com]
01309 672260
07778 731018 (Mbl)

Forres: St Leonard's See Dallas

Keith: North, Newmill, Boharm and Rothiemay (H) (01542 886390)
T. Douglas McRoberts BD CPS FRSA   1975   2002
North Manse, Church Road, Keith AB55 5BR
[E-mail: doug.mcroberts@btinternet.com]
01542 882559

Ian Cunningham DCS
The Manse, Rothiemay, Huntly AB54 7NE
[E-mail: icunninghamdcs@btinternet.com]
01466 711334

Keith: St Rufus, Botriphnie and Grange (H)
Ranald S.R. Gauld MA LLB BD   1991   1995   Church Road, Keith AB55 5BR   01542 882799
Kay Gauld (Mrs) BD STM PhD (Assoc)   1999   Church Road, Keith AB55 5BR   01542 882799
[E-mail: kay_gauld@strufus.fsnet.co.uk]

Kinloss and Findhorn   See Alves and Burghead

Knockando, Elchies and Archiestown (H) linked with Rothes
Robert J.M. Anderson BD   1993   2000   Manse Brae, Rothes, Aberlour AB38 7AF   01340 831381 (Tel/Fax)
[E-mail: robert@carmanse.freeserve.co.uk]

Lossiemouth: St Gerardine's High (H)
Thomas M. Bryson BD   1997   2002   The Manse, St Gerardine's Road, Lossiemouth IV31 6RA   01343 813146
[E-mail: thomas@bryson547.fsworld.co.uk]

Lossiemouth: St James'
Graham W. Crawford BSc BD STM   1991   2003   The Manse, Prospect Terrace, Lossiemouth IV31 6JS   01343 810676
[E-mail: pictishreiver@aol.com]

Mortlach and Cabrach (H)
Hugh M.C. Smith LTh   1973   1982   Mortlach Manse, Dufftown, Keith AB55 4AR   01340 820380
[E-mail: clerk@moraypresbytery.plus.com]

Pluscarden   See Birnie
Portknockie   See Findochty
Rafford   See Dallas
Rathven   See Findochty
Rothes   See Knockando, Elchies and Archiestown

St Andrew's-Lhanbryd (H) and Urquhart
Rolf H. Billes BD   1996   2001   39 St Andrews Road, Lhanbryde, Elgin IV30 8PU   01343 843995
[E-mail: rolf.billes@lineone.net]

Speymouth   See Bellie

Davidson, A.A.B. MA BD   1960   1997   (Grange with Rothiemay)   11 Sutors Rise, Nairn IV12 5BU
Douglas, Christina A. (Mrs)   1987   1993   (Inveraven and Glenlivet)   White Cottage, St Fillans, Crieff PH6 2ND
Evans, John W. MA BD   1945   1984   (Elgin High)   15 Weaver Place, Elgin IV30 1HB   01343 543607
Henig, Gordon BSc BD   1997   2003   (Bellie with Speymouth)   59 Woodside Drive, Forres IV36 2UF   01309 672558
King, Margaret R. (Miss) MA DCS   2002   56 Murrayfield, Fochabers IV32 7EZ   01343 820937
[E-mail: margaretrking@aol.com]
Macaulay, Alick Hugh MA   1943   1981   (Bellie with Speymouth)   5 Duke Street, Fochabers IV32 7DN   01343 820726

Miller, William B.	1950	1987	(Cawdor with Croy and Dalcross)	10 Kirkhill Drive, Lhanbryde, Elgin IV30 8QA	01343 842368
Morton, Alasdair J. MA BD DipEd FEIS	1960	2000	(Bowden with Newtown)	16 St Leonard's Road, Forres IV36 1DW	01309 671719
				[E-mail: alasgilmor@compuserve.com]	
Morton, Gillian M. (Mrs) MA BD PGCE	1983	1996	(Hospital Chaplain)	16 St Leonard's Road, Forres IV36 1DW	01309 671719
				[E-mail: alasgilmor@compuserve.com]	
Poole, Ann McColl (Mrs) DipEd ACE LTh	1983	2003	(Dyke with Edinkillie)	Kirkside Cottage, Dyke, Forres IV36 2TF	01309 641046
Scotland, Ronald J. BD	1993	2003	(Birnie with Pluscarden)	7A Rose Avenue, Elgin IV30 1NX	01343 543086
Spence, Alexander	1944	1989	(Elgin: St Giles': Associate)	16 Inglis Court, Edzell, Brechin DD9 7SR	01356 648502
Wright, David L. MA BD	1957	1998	(Stornoway: St Columba)	84 Wyvis Drive, Nairn IV12 4TP	01667 451613
Thomson, James M. BA	1952	2000	(Elgin: St Giles' and St Columba's South: Associate)	48 Mayne Road, Elgin IV30 1PD	01343 547664

(36) ABERNETHY

Meets at Boat of Garten on the first Tuesday of February, March, April, June, September, October, November and December.

Clerk: REV. JAMES A.I. MACEWAN MA BD   The Manse, Nethy Bridge PH25 3DG   **01479 821280**
[E-mail: akph35@uk.uumail.com]

Abernethy (H) linked with Cromdale (H) and Advie
James A.I. MacEwan MA BD   1973   1980   The Manse, Nethy Bridge PH25 3DG   01479 821280
[E-mail: manse@nethybridge.freeserve.co.uk]

Alvie and Insh (T) (H)
Vacant   Kincraig, Kingussie PH21 1NA

Boat of Garten (H) and Kincardine linked with Duthil (H)
David W. Whyte LTh   1993   1999   Deshar Road, Boat of Garten PH24 3BN   01479 831252
[E-mail: djwhyte@fish.co.uk]

Cromdale and Advie See Abernethy

Dulnain Bridge (H) linked with Grantown-on-Spey (H)
Morris Smith BD   1988   The Manse, Golf Course Road, Grantown-on-Spey   PH26 3HY   01479 872084
[E-mail: mosmith.themanse@virgin.net]

Duthil See Boat of Garten and Kincardine

Grantown-on-Spey See Dulnain Bridge

Kingussie (H)
Helen Cook (Mrs) BD — 1974 2003 — The Manse, 18 Hillside Avenue, Kingussie PH21 1PA [E-mail: bhja@cookville.fsnet.co.uk] — 01540 661311

Laggan linked with Newtonmore (H)
Douglas F. Stevenson BD DipMin — 1991 2001 — The Manse, Fort William Road, Newtonmore PH20 1DG [E-mail: dfstevenson@aol.com] — 01540 673238

Newtonmore See Laggan

Rothiemurchus and Aviemore (H)
Ron C. Whyte BD CPS — 1990 — The Manse, 8 Dalfaber Park, Aviemore PH22 1QF [E-mail: ron4xst@aol.com] — 01479 810280

Tomintoul (H), Glenlivet and Inveraven
Sven S. Bjarnason CandTheol — 1975 1992 — The Manse, Tomintoul, Ballindalloch AB37 9HA [E-mail: sven@bjarnason.org.uk] — 01807 580254

(37) INVERNESS

Meets at Inverness, in the Dr Black Memorial Hall, on the first Tuesday of February, March, April, May, September, October, November and December, and at the Moderator's church on the fourth Tuesday of June.

Clerk: REV. ALASTAIR S. YOUNGER BScEcon ASCC — 3 Elm Park, Inverness IV2 4WN [E-mail: akph55@uk.uumail.com] [E-mail: inverness.presbytery@uk.uumail.com] — 01463 232462 (Tel/Fax)

Ardersier (H) linked with Petty
Alexander Whiteford LTh — 1996 — Ardersier, Inverness IV2 7SX [E-mail: a.whiteford@ukonline.co.uk] — 01667 462224

Auldearn and Dalmore linked with Nairn: St Ninian's
Richard Reid BSc BD MTh — 1991 2005 — The Manse, Auldearn, Nairn IV12 5SX — 01667 451675

Cawdor (H) linked with Croy and Dalcross (H)
Janet S. Mathieson MA BD — 2003 — The Manse, Croy, Inverness IV2 5PH [E-mail: jan@mathieson99.fsnet.co.uk] — 01667 493217

Croy and Dalcross See Cawdor

Culloden: The Barn (H) James H. Robertson BSc BD	1975	1994	45 Oakdene Court, Culloden IV2 7XL [E-mail: revjimrobertson@netscape.net]	01463 790504
Daviot and Dunlichity linked with Moy, Dalarossie and Tomatin Reginald F. Campbell BD DipChEd	1979	2003	The Manse, Daviot, Inverness IV2 5XL	01463 772242
Dores and Boleskine Vacant			The Manse, Foyers, Inverness IV2 6XU	01456 486206
Inverness: Crown (H) (01463 238929) Peter H. Donald MA PhD BD	1991	1998	39 Southside Road, Inverness IV2 4XA [E-mail: pdonald7@aol.com]	01463 230537
Inverness: Dalneigh and Bona (GD) (H) Fergus A. Robertson MA BD	1971	1999	9 St Mungo Road, Inverness IV3 5AS	01463 232339
Inverness: East (H) Aonghas I. MacDonald MA BD	1967	1981	2 Victoria Drive, Inverness IV2 3QD [E-mail: aonghas@ukonline.co.uk]	01463 231269
Inverness: Hilton Duncan MacPherson LLB BD	1994		66 Culduthel Mains Crescent, Inverness IV2 6RG [E-mail: duncan@hiltonchurch.freeserve.uk]	01463 231417
Inverness: Inshes (H) Alistair Malcolm BD DPS	1976	1992	48 Redwood Crescent, Milton of Leys, Inverness IV2 6HB [E-mail: alimalcolm@7inverness.freeserve.co.uk]	01463 772402
Inverness: Kinmylies (E) (H) Peter M. Humphris BSc BD	1976	2001	2 Balnafettack Place, Inverness IV3 8TQ [E-mail: peter@humphris.co.uk]	01463 709893
Inverness: Ness Bank (T) (H) S. John Chambers OBE BSc	1972	1998	15 Ballifeary Road, Inverness IV3 5PJ [E-mail: chambers@ballifeary.freeserve.co.uk]	01463 234653
Inverness: Old High St Stephen's Peter W. Nimmo BD ThM	1996	2004	24 Damfield Road, Inverness IV2 3HU [E-mail: peternimmo@minister.com]	01463 250802

Inverness: St Columba High (H)
Alastair S. Younger BScEcon ASCC — 1969 1976 — 3 Elm Park, Inverness IV2 4WN [E-mail: asyounger@aol.com] — 01463 232462 (Tel/Fax)

Inverness: Trinity (H)
Alistair Murray BD — 1984 2004 — 60 Kenneth Street, Inverness IV3 5PZ [E-mail: ally.murray@btopenworld.com] — 01463 234756

Kilmorack and Erchless
Vacant — 'Roselynn', Croyard Road, Beauly IV4 7DJ — 01463 782260

Kiltarlity linked with Kirkhill
Fraser K. Turner LTh — 1994 2002 — Wardlaw Manse, Wardlaw Road, Kirkhill, Inverness IV5 7NZ [E-mail: fraseratq@yahoo.co.uk] — 01463 831662

Kirkhill See Kiltarlity
Moy, Dalarossie and Tomatin See Daviot and Dunlichity

Nairn: Old (H)
Ian W.F. Hamilton BD LTh ALCM AVCM — 1978 1986 — 3 Manse Road, Nairn IV12 4RN [E-mail: reviwfh@btinternet.com] — 01667 452203

Nairn: St Ninian's (H) See Auldearn and Dalmore
Petty See Ardersier

Urquhart and Glenmoriston (H)
Hugh F. Watt BD DPS — 1986 1996 — Blairbeg, Drumnadrochit, Inverness IV3 6UG [E-mail: hw@tinyworld.co.uk] — 01456 450231

Name			Charge	Address	Tel
Black, Archibald T. BSc	1964	1997	(Inverness: Ness Bank)	16 Elm Park, Inverness IV2 4WN	01463 230588
Brown, Derek G. BD DipMin DMin	1989	1994	Chaplain: NHS Highland	Cathedral Manse, Cnoc-an-Lobht, Dornoch IV25 3HN [E-mail: revsbrown@aol.com]	01862 810296
Buell, F. Bart BA MDiv	1980	1995	(Urquhart and Glenmoriston)	6 Towerhill Place, Cradlehall, Inverness IV2 5FN [E-mail: bart@tower22.freeserve.co.uk]	01463 794634
Charlton, George W.	1952	1992	(Fort Augustus with Glengarry)	61 Drumfield Road, Inverness IV12 4XL	01463 242802
Chisholm, Archibald F. MA	1957	1997	(Braes of Rannoch with Foss and Rannoch)	32 Seabank Road, Nairn IV12 4EU	01667 452001
Christie, James LTh	1993	2003	(Dores and Boleskine)	20 Wester Inshes Crescent, Inverness IV2 5HL	01463 710534
Clyne, Douglas R. BD	1973	2004	(Fraserburgh: Old)	27 River Park, Nairn IV12 5SP [E-mail: manse1@supanet.com]	01667 456372
Donaldson, Moses	1972	2000	(Fort Augustus with Glengarry)	'Tabgha', 10 Garden Place, Beauly IV4 7AW	(Tel/Fax) 01463 783701
Donn, Thomas M. MA	1932	1969	(Duthil)	Clachnaharry Residential Home, Inverness	
Frizzell, R. Stewart BD	1961	2000	(Wick: Old)	98 Boswell Road, Inverness IV2 3EW	01463 231907
Gibbons, Richard BD	1997		Adviser in Mission and Evangelism	3 Holm Burn Place, Inverness IV2 6WT [E-mail: nmadvisernorth@uk.uumail.com]	01463 226889

Name	Dates	Charge	Address	Tel
Jeffrey, Stewart D. BSc BD	1962 1997	(Banff with King Edward)	10 Grigor Drive, Inverness IV2 4LP	
Livesley, Anthony LTh	1979 1997	(Kiltearn)	87 Beech Avenue, Nairn IV12 5SX [E-mail: a.livesley@tesco.net]	01667 455126
Logan, Robert J.V. MA BD	1962 2001	(Abdie and Dunbog with Newburgh)	Lindores, 1 Murray Place, Smithton, Inverness IV2 7PX [E-mail: rjvlogan@aol.com]	01463 790226
Macritchie, Iain A.M. BSc BD STM PhD	1987 1998	Chaplain: Inverness Hospitals	7 Merlin Crescent, Inverness IV2 3TE	01463 235204
Morrison, Hector BSc BD MTh	1981 1994	Lecturer: Highland Theological College	24 Oak Avenue, Inverness IV2 4NX	01463 238561
Rettie, James A. BTh	1981 1999	(Melness and Eriboll with Tongue)	2 Trantham Drive, Westhill, Inverness IV2 5QT	01463 798896
Robb, Rodney P.T.	1995 2004	(Stirling: St Mark's)	2A Mayfield Road, Inverness IV2 4AE	
Stirling, G. Alan S. MA	1960 1999	(Leochel Cushnie and Lynturk linked with Tough)	97 Lochlann Road, Culloden, Inverness IV2 7HJ	01463 798313
Waugh, John L. LTh	1973 2002		58 Wyvis Drive, Nairn IV12 4TP [E-mail: jswaugh@care4free.net]	(Tel/Fax) 01667 456397
Wilson, Ian M.	1988 1993	(Cawdor with Croy and Dalcross)	17 Spires Crescent, Nairn IV12 5PZ	01667 452977

INVERNESS ADDRESSES

Inverness

Crown	Kingsmills Road x Midmills Road	
Dalneigh and Bona	St Mary's Avenue	
East	Academy Street x Margaret Street	
Hilton	Druid Road x Tomatin Road	
Inshes	Inshes Retail Park	
Kinmylies	Kinmylies Way	
Ness Bank	Ness Bank x Castle Road	
St Columba High	Bank Street x Fraser Street	
St Stephen's	Old Edinburgh Road x Southside Road	
	The Old High	Church Street x Church Lane
	Trinity	Huntly Place x Upper Kessock Street

Nairn

Old	Academy Street x Seabank Road
St Ninian's	High Street x Queen Street

(38) LOCHABER

Meets at Caol, Fort William, in Kilmallie Church Hall at 7pm, on the first Tuesday of September, December and February, the last Tuesday in October and the fourth Tuesday in March. The June meeting is held on the first Tuesday in the church of the incoming Moderator.

Clerk: REV. DAVID M. ANDERSON MSc FCOptom   'Mirlos', 1 Dumfries Place, Fort William PH33 6UQ [E-mail: akph62@uk.uumail.com]   01397 703203

Acharacle (H) linked with Ardnamurchan
Vacant   The Manse, Acharacle, Argyll PH36 4JU   01967 431561

Ardgour linked with Strontian
Vacant   The Manse, Ardgour, Fort William PH33 7AH   01855 841230

Ardnamurchan See Acharacle

Arisaig and the Small Isles linked with Mallaig: St Columba and Knoydart
Vacant
Janet Anderson (Miss) DCS   4 Clanranald Place, Arisaig PH39 4NN

Duror (H) linked with Glencoe: St Munda's (H) (T)
                                    1991   2002
Alison H. Burnside (Mrs) MA BD   The Manse, Ballachulish PH49 4JG   01855 811998
                                             [E-mail: alisonskyona@aol.com]

Fort Augustus linked with Glengarry
Adrian P.J. Varwell BA BD PhD   1983   2001   The Manse, Fort Augustus PH32 4BH   01320 366210
                                             [E-mail: a-varwell@ecosse.net]

Fort William: Duncansburgh (H) linked with Kilmonivaig
                                    1979   1990
Donald A. MacQuarrie BSc BD   The Manse of Duncansburgh, The Parade, Fort William   01397 702297
                                             PH33 6BA
                                             [E-mail: pdmacq@ukgateway.net]

Fort William: MacIntosh Memorial (H)
Alan Ramsay MA   1967   The Manse, 26 Riverside Park, Lochyside, Fort William PH33 7RB   01397 702054
                                             [E-mail: limandalan@btopenworld.com]
Ruth E. Lawson BA BSc PhD (Aux)   2004   4 Torlundy Courtyard, Torlundy, Fort William PH33 6SW   01397 700833
                                             [E-mail: correspondence@ruthlawson.sol.co.uk]

Glencoe: St Munda's See Duror
Glengarry See Fort Augustus

Kilmallie
Richard T. Corbett BSc MSc PhD BD   1992   2005   Kilmallie Manse, Corpach, Fort William PH33 7JS   01397 772736
                                             [E-mail: revcorbett@pgen.net]

Kilmonivaig See Fort William: Duncansburgh

Kinlochleven (H) linked with Nether Lochaber (H)
Vacant   Lochaber Road, Kinlochleven, Argyll PA40 4QW   01855 831227

Mallaig: St Columba and Knoydart See Arisaig and the Small Isles

Morvern
Vacant   The Manse, Lochaline, Morvern, Oban PA34 5UU   01967 421267

Nether Lochaber See Kinlochleven
Strontian See Ardgour

Anderson, David M. MSc FCOptom	1984	Auxiliary Minister: Presbytery Clerk	'Mirlos', 1 Dumfries Place, Fort William PH33 6UQ [E-mail: akph62@uk.uumail.com]	01397 703203
Beaton, Jamesina (Miss) DCS		(Deaconess)	Farhills, Fort Augustus PH32 4DS	01320 366252
Burnside, William A.M. MA BD PGCE	1990	Teacher: Religious Education	The Manse, Ballachulish PH49 4JG	01855 811998
Carmichael, James A. LTh	1976 2006	(Ardgour with Strontian)	Limhe View, 5 Clovulin, Ardgour, Fort William PH33 7AB	01855 841351
Lamb, Alan H.W. BA MTh	1959 2005	(Associate Minister)	The Manse, 5 Mid Road, Arisaig PH39 4NJ	01687 450227
Millar, John L. MA BD	1981 1990	(Fort William: Duncansburgh with Kilmonivaig)	17 Whittinghame Court, 1350 Great Western Road, Glasgow G12 0BH	0141-339 4098
Olsen, Heather C. (Miss) BD	1978 2003	(Creich with Rosehall)	4 Riverside Park, Lochyside, Coull, Fort William PH33 7RA	01397 700023
Rae, Peter C. BSc BD	1968 2000	(Beath and Cowdenbeath North)	Rodane, Badabrie, Banavie, Fort William PH33 7LX	01397 772603
Winning, A. Ann MA DipEd BD	1984 2006	(Morvern)	'Westering', 13C Carnoch, Glencoe, Ballachulish PH49 4HQ [E-mail: annw@morvern13.fslife.co.uk]	01855 811929

LOCHABER Communion Sundays

Acharacle	1st Mar, Jun, Sep, Dec	Kilmonivaig	1st May, Nov
Ardgour	1st Jun, Sep, Dec, Easter	Kinlochleven	1st Feb, Apr, Jun, Oct, Dec
Ardnamurchan	1st Apr, Aug, Dec	Mallaig	4th May, 3rd Nov
Arisaig and Moidart	1st May, Nov	Morvern	Easter, 1st Jul, 4th Sep, 1st Dec
Duror	2nd Jun, 3rd Nov	Nether Lochaber	1st Apr, Oct
Fort Augustus	1st Jan, Apr, Jul, Oct	Strontian	1st Jun, Sep, Dec
Fort William			
Duncansburgh	1st Apr, Jun, Oct		
MacIntosh Memorial	1st Mar, Jun, Sep, Dec		
Glencoe	1st Apr, Oct		
Glengarry	1st Jan, Apr, Jul, Oct		
Kilmallie	3rd Mar, May, Sep, 1st Dec		

(39) ROSS

Meets in Dingwall on the first Tuesday of each month, except January, May, July and August.

Clerk:	REV. THOMAS M. McWILLIAM MA BD	Guidhadden, 7 Woodholme Crescent, Culbokie, Dingwall IV7 8JH [E-mail: akph71@uk.uumail.com]	01349 877014

Alness

Ronald Morrison BD	1996	27 Darroch Brae, Alness IV17 0SD	01349 882238

Avoch linked with Fortrose and Rosemarkie

Alison J. Grainger BD	1995 2006	5 Nessway, Fortrose IV10 8SS	01381 620068

Contin

Gordon McLean LTh	1972 2005	The Manse, Contin, Strathpeffer IV14 9ES	01997 421380

Cromarty

John Tallach MA MLitt	1970 1999	Denny Road, Cromarty IV11 8YT [E-mail: john.t@ecosse.net]	01381 600802

Dingwall: Castle Street (H) Bruce Ritchie BSc BD	1977	2006	16 Achany Road, Dingwall IV15 9JB	01349 863167
Dingwall: St Clement's (H) Russel Smith BD	1994		8 Castlehill Road, Dingwall IV15 9PB	01349 861011
Fearn Abbey and Nigg linked with Tarbat Vacant			The Manse, Fearn, Tain IV20 1TN	01862 832626
Ferintosh Andrew F. Graham BTh DPS	2001	2006	Ferintosh Manse, Leanaig Road, Conon Bridge, Dingwall IV7 8BE [E-mail: andy@afg1.fsnet.co.uk]	01349 861275
Fodderty and Strathpeffer Ivan C. Warwick MA BD TD	1980	1999	The Manse, Strathpeffer IV14 9DL [E-mail: L70rev@btinternet.com]	01997 421398 07775 530709 (Mbl)
Fortrose and Rosemarkie See Avoch				
Invergordon Kenneth Donald Macleod BD CPS	1989	2000	The Manse, Cromlet Drive, Invergordon IV18 0BA	01349 852273
Killearnan linked with Knockbain Iain Ramsden BTh	1999		The Church of Scotland Manse, Coldwell Road, Artafallie, North Kessock, Inverness IV1 3ZE [E-mail: s4rev@cqm.co.uk]	01463 731333
Kilmuir and Logie Easter Thomas J.R. Mackinnon LTh DipMin	1996	2005	Delny, Invergordon IV18 0NW [E-mail: tmackinnon@aol.com]	01862 842280
Kiltearn (H) Donald A. MacSween BD	1991	1998	The Manse, Swordale Road, Evanton, Dingwall IV16 9UZ	01349 830472
Knockbain See Killearnan				
Lochbroom and Ullapool (GD) James Gemmell BD MTh	1999		The Manse, Garve Road, Ullapool IV26 2SX [E-mail: jasgemmell@aol.com]	01854 612050
Resolis and Urquhart (T) C.J. Grant Bell	1983	2002	The Manse, Culbokie, Dingwall IV7 8JN	01349 877452
Rosskeen Robert Jones BSc BD	1990		Rosskeen Manse, Perrins Road, Alness IV17 0SX [E-mail: rob-jones@freeuk.com]	01349 882265

Tain

Douglas A. Horne BD — 1977 — 14 Kingsway Avenue, Tain IV19 1NJ [E-mail: douglas.horne@virgin.net] — 01862 894140

Tarbat (T) See Fearn Abbey and Nigg

Urray and Kilchrist

J. Alastair Gordon BSc BD — 2000 — The Manse, Corrie Road, Muir of Ord IV6 7TL — 01463 870259

Buchan, John BD MTh — 1968 1993 — (Fodderty and Strathpeffer) — 'Faithlie', 45 Swanston Avenue, Inverness IV3 6QW — 01463 713114

Dupar, Kenneth W. BA BD PhD — 1965 1993 — (Christ's College, Aberdeen) — The Old Manse, The Causeway, Cromarty IV11 8XJ — 01381 600428

Forsyth, James LTh — 1970 2000 — (Fearn Abbey with Nigg Chapelhill) — Rhives Lodge, Golspie, Sutherland KW10 6DD

Glass, Alexander OBE MA — 1998 — Auxiliary Minister: Attached to Presbytery Clerk — Craigton, Tulloch Avenue, Dingwall IV15 9TU — 01349 863258

Harries, David A. — 1950 1990 — (British Sailors Society) — Odessey, 5 Farm Lane, Englands Road, Acle, Norfolk

Holroyd, Gordon BTh FPhS FSAScot — 1959 1993 — (Dingwall: St Clement's) — 22 Stuarthill Drive, Maryburgh, Dingwall IV15 9HU — 01349 863379

Liddell, Margaret (Miss) BD DipTh — 1987 1997 — (Contin) — 20 Wyvis Crescent, Conon Bridge, Dingwall IV7 8BZ [E-mail: margaretliddell@ecosse.net] — 01349 865997

McGowan, Prof. Andrew T.B. BD STM PhD — 1979 1994 — Highland Theological College — 4 Kintail Place, Dingwall IV15 9RL [E-mail: andrew.mcgowan@htc.uhi.ac.uk] — (Home) 01349 867639 (Work) 01349 780208 (Fax) 01349 780001

Macgregor, John BD — 2001 2006 — Chaplain: Army — 5 Oackway, Milton Bridge, Penicuik EH26 0EN — 01349 866293

Mackinnon, R.M. LTh — 1968 1995 — (Kilmuir and Logie Easter) — 27 Riverford Crescent, Conon Bridge, Dingwall IV7 8HL — 01463 870704

MacLennan, Alasdair J. BD DCE — 1978 2001 — (Resolis and Urquhart) — Airdale, Seaforth Road, Muir of Ord IV6 7TA — 01463 871286

Macleod, John MA — 1959 1993 — (Resolis and Urquhart) — 'Benview', 19 Balvaird, Muir of Ord IV6 7RG — 01463 877014

McWilliam, Thomas M. MA BD — 1964 2003 — (Contin) — Guidhadden, 7 Woodholme Crescent, Culbokie, Dingwall IV7 8JH

Niven, William W. BTh — 1982 1995 — (Alness) — 4 Obsdale Park, Alness IV17 0TP — 01349 882427

Rutherford, Ellen B. (Miss) MBE DCS — — (Deaconess) — 41 Duncanston, Conon Bridge, Dingwall IV7 8JB — 01349 877439

---

(40) SUTHERLAND

Meets at Lairg on the first Tuesday of March, May, September, November and December; and on the first Tuesday of June at the Moderator's church.

Clerk: REV. J.L. GOSKIRK LTh — The Manse, Lairg, Sutherland IV27 4EH [E-mail: akph76@uk.uumail.com] — 01549 402373

Altnaharra and Farr

Vacant — The Manse, Bettyhill, Thurso KW14 7SZ — 01641 521208

Assynt and Stoer
Vacant
Canisp Road, Lochinver, Lairg IV27 4LH — 01571 844342

Clyne (H)
Ian W. McCree BD — 1971 — Golf Road, Brora KW9 6QS
[E-mail: ian@mccree.f9.co.uk] — 01408 621239

Creich linked with Rosehall
Robert R. Te Whaiti BTh — 1986 — 2005 — Church of Scotland Manse, Dornoch Road, Bonar Bridge, Ardgay IV24 3EB
[E-mail: robert.tewhaiti@tesco.net] — 01863 766256

Dornoch Cathedral (H)
Susan M. Brown (Mrs) BD DipMin — 1985 — 1998 — Cnoc-an-Lobht, Dornoch IV25 3HN
[E-mail: revsbrown@aol.com] — 01862 810296

Durness and Kinlochbervie
John T. Mann BSc BD — 1990 — 1998 — Manse Road, Kinlochbervie, Lairg IV27 4RG
[E-mail: jtmklb@aol.com] — 01971 521287

Eddrachillis
John MacPherson BSc BD — 1993 — Church of Scotland Manse, Scourie, Lairg IV27 4TQ — 01971 502431

Golspie
Vacant
The Manse, Fountain Road, Golspie KW10 6TH — 01408 633295

Kildonan and Loth Helmsdale (H)
Vacant

Kincardine Croick and Edderton
Graeme W.M. Muckart MTh MSc FSAScot — 1983 — 2004 — The Manse, Ardgay IV24 3BG
[E-mail: gw2m@clara.net] — 01863 766285

Lairg (H) linked with Rogart (H)
J.L. Goskirk LTh — 1968 — The Manse, Lairg IV27 4EH — 01549 402373

Melness and Tongue (H)
John F. Mackie BD — 1979 — 2000 — New Manse, Glebelands, Tongue, Lairg IV27 4XL
[E-mail: john.mackie1@virgin.net] — 01847 611230

Rogart See Lairg
Rosehall See Creich

(41) CAITHNESS

Meets alternately at Wick and Thurso on the first Tuesday of February, March, May, September, November and December, and the third Tuesday of June.

Clerk: MR JAMES R.H. HOUSTON MBA MA Lyndene House, Weydale, Thurso KW14 8YN [E-mail: akph42@uk.uumail.com] 01847 893955

Bower linked with Watten
Alastair H. Gray MA BD 1978 2005 Station Road, Watten, Wick KW1 5YN [E-mail: alastairgray@hotmail.co.uk] 01955 621220

Canisbay linked with Keiss
Vacant The Manse, Canisbay, Wick KW1 4YH 01955 611309

Dunnet linked with Olrig
James F. Todd BD CPS 1984 1999 Olrig, Castletown, Thurso KW14 8TP 01847 821221

Halkirk and Westerdale
Kenneth Warner BD DA DipTD 1981 Abbey Manse, Halkirk KW12 6UU [E-mail: wrnrkenn@aol.com] 01847 831227

Keiss See Canisbay
Olrig See Dunnet

The North Coast Parish
Paul R. Read BSc MA 2000 2006 Church of Scotland Manse, Reay, Thurso KW14 7RE [E-mail: PRead747@aol.com]
(The name now given to the charge formed by the union of Reay with Strathy and Halladale)

The Parish of Latheron
Vacant Central Manse, Lybster KW3 6BN 01593 721231
(Charge formed by the union of Berriedale and Dunbeath with Latheron and with Lybster and Bruan)

Thurso: St Peter's and St Andrew's (H)
Vacant 46 Rose Street, Thurso KW14 7HN 01847 895186

Thurso: West (H)
Ronald Johnstone BD   1977 1984   Thorkel Road, Thurso KW14 7LW   01847 892663
[E-mail: ronaldjohnstone@tiscali.co.uk]

Watten See Bower

Wick: Bridge Street
A.A. Roy MA BD   1955   Mansfield, Miller Avenue, Wick KW1 4DF   01955 602822

Wick: Old (H) (L)
Vacant   The Old Manse, Miller Avenue, Wick KW1 4DF   01955 604252

Wick: Pulteneytown (H) and Thrumster
William F. Wallace BDS BD   1968 1974   The Manse, Coronation Street, Wick KW1 5LS   01955 603166
[E-mail: williamwallace39@btopenworld.com]

Craw, John DCS   (Bower with Watten)
Mappin, Michael G. BA   1961 1998   'Craiglockhart', Latheronwheel, Latheron KW5 6DW   01593 741779
Mundays, Banks Road, Watten, Wick KW1 5YL   01955 621720

CAITHNESS Communion Sundays

Bower	North Coast	1st Jul, Dec		
Canisbay	Olrig	1st Jun, Nov	Watten	Mar, Easter, Jun, Sep, Dec	1st Jul, Dec
Dunnet	Thurso	last May, Nov	Wick	last May, Nov	
Halkirk and Westerdale	St Peter's and	Apr, Jul, Oct	Bridge Street		1st Apr, Oct
	St Andrew's	1st May, 3rd Nov	Old		4th Apr, Sep
Keiss	West	Apr, Jul, Sep, Nov	Pulteneytown and	Mar, Jun, Sep, Dec	1st Mar, Jun, Sep, Dec
Latheron			Thrumster	4th Mar, Jun, Nov	

(42) LOCHCARRON – SKYE

Meets in Kyle on the first Tuesday of each month, except January, May, July and August.

Clerk: REV. ALLAN J. MACARTHUR BD   High Barn, Croft Road, Lochcarron, Strathcarron IV54 8YA   01520 722278 (Tel)
[E-mail: akph63@uk.uumail.com]   01520 722674 (Fax)
[E-mail: a.macarthur@btinternet.com]

Applecross, Lochcarron and Torridon (GD)
Vacant
David V. Scott BTh (Assoc) — 1994 — The Manse, Lochcarron, Strathcarron IV54 8YD / Camusterrach, Applecross, Strathcarron IV54 8LU — 01520 722829 / 01520 744263 (Tel/Fax)

Bracadale and Duirinish (GD)
Gary Wilson BD — 1996 — 2000 — Kinloch Manse, Dunvegan, Isle of Skye IV55 8WQ [E-mail: rev.gary@onetel.com] — 01470 521457

Gairloch and Dundonnell
Derek Morrison — 1995 — 2000 — Church of Scotland Manse, The Glebe, Gairloch IV21 2BT [E-mail: derek@morrison92.wanadoo.co.uk] — 01445 712053 (Tel/Fax)

Glenelg and Kintail
Roderick N. MacRae BTh — 2001 — 2004 — Church of Scotland Manse, Inverinate, Kyle IV40 8HE [E-mail: barvalous@msn.com] — 01599 511245

Kilmuir and Stenscholl (GD)
Ivor MacDonald BSc MSc BD — 1993 — 2000 — Staffin, Portree, Isle of Skye IV51 9JX [E-mail: ivormacdonald@btinternet.com] — 01470 562759 (Tel/Fax)

Lochalsh
John M. Macdonald — 2002 — The Church of Scotland Manse, Main Street, Kyle IV40 8DA [E-mail: john.macdonald53@btinternet.com] — 01599 534294

Portree (GD)
Vacant — Viewfield Road, Portree, Isle of Skye IV51 9ES — 01478 611868

Snizort (H) (GD)
Iain M. Greenshields BD DipRS ACMA MSc MTh — 1985 — 2002 — The Manse, Kensaleyre, Snizort, Portree, Isle of Skye IV51 9XE [E-mail: rev_imaclg@hotmail.com] — 01470 532260

Strath and Sleat (GD)
Ben Johnstone MA BD DMin — 1973 — 2003 — The Manse, 6 Upper Breakish, Isle of Skye IV42 8PY [E-mail: benonskye@onetel.com] — 01471 820063
John D. Urquhart BA BD — 1998 — 2003 — The Manse, The Glebe, Kilmore, Teangue, Isle of Skye IV44 8RG [E-mail: ministear@hotmail.co.uk] — 01471 844469

Beaton, Donald MA BD MTh — 1961 2002 — (Glenelg and Kintail) — Kilmaluag Croft, North Duntulm, Isle of Skye IV51 9UF — 01470 552296
Ferguson, John LTh BD DD — 1973 2002 — (Portree) — 9 Braeview Park, Beauly, Inverness IV4 7ED — 01463 783900
Kellas, David J. MA BD — 1966 2004 — (Kilfinan with Kyles) — Babhann, Glenelg, Kyle IV40 8LA [E-mail: davidkellas@britishlibrary.net] — 01599 522257

Macarthur, Allan J. BD — 1973 1998 — (Applecross, Lochcarron and Torridon) — High Barn, Croft Road, Lochcarron, Strathcarron IV54 8YA — (Tel) 01520 722278 / (Fax) 01520 722674

McCulloch, Alen J.R. MA BD	1990 1995	Chaplain: Royal Navy	6 The Terrace, Morice Yard, HMNB Devonport, Plymouth PL1 4SB	01752 605424
MacDonald, Kenneth	1965 1992	(Associate: Applecross l/w Lochcarron)	Tigharry, Main Street, Lochcarron, Strathcarron IV54 8YB	01520 722433
Macleod, Donald LTh	1988 2000	(Snizort)	20 Caulfield Avenue, Cradlehall, Inverness IV1 2GA	01463 798093
Martin, George M. MA BD	1987 2005	(Applecross, Lochcarron and Torridon)	8(1) Buckingham Terrace, Edinburgh EH4 3AA	0131-343 3937
Matheson, James G. MA BD DD	1936 1979	(Portree)	The Elms, 148 Whitehouse Loan, Edinburgh EH9 2EZ	0131-446 6211
Murray, John W.	2003	Auxiliary Minister	Totescore, Kilmuir, Portree, Isle of Skye IV51 9YN	01470 542297
Nicolson, John M. BD DipMin	1997 2006	(Portree)	3 Marybank, Stornoway, Isle of Lewis HS2 0DF	01851 704205
			[E-mail: johnjehunicolson@aol.com]	
Williamson, Tom MA BD	1941 1982	(Dyke with Edinkillie)	16 Cove, Inverasdale, Poolewe, Achnasheen IV22 2LT	01445 781423

LOCHCARRON – SKYE Communion Sundays

Applecross	4th Jun	Kilmuir	1st Mar, Sep	Portree	Easter, Pentecost, Christmas, 2nd Mar, Aug, 1st Nov
Arnisort	1st Sep	Kintail	3rd Apr, Jul	Sleat	2nd Jun, Dec
Bracadale	3rd Mar, Sep	Kyleakin	Easter, 1st Nov	Snizort	1st Jan, 4th Mar
Duirinish	3rd Jan, Easter, 2nd Jun, 3rd Sep	Lochalsh and Stromeferry		Stenscholl	1st Jun, Dec
Dundonnell	4th Jun		4th Jan, Jun, Sep, Christmas, Easter	Strath	2nd Mar, Sep
Gairloch	3rd Jun, Nov	Lochcarron and Shieldaig	Easter, 3rd Jun, 1st Oct	Torridon and Kinlochewe	2nd May
Glenelg	2nd Jun, Nov	Plockton and Kyle	2nd May, 1st Oct		
Glenshiel	1st Jul				

(43) UIST

Meets on the fourth Wednesday of January, March, September and November in Berneray, and the fourth Wednesday of June in Leverburgh.

Clerk:	**REV. MURDO SMITH MA BD**	Scarista, Isle of Harris HS3 3HX	**01859 550200**
		[E-mail: akph77@uk.uumail.com]	

Barra (GD)

Eleanor D. Muir (Miss) MTheol DipPTheol	1986	2005	Cuithir, Castlebay, Isle of Barra HS9 5XD	01871 810230

Benbecula (GD) (H)

Andrew A. Downie BD BSc DipEd DipMin ThB	1994	2006	Church of Scotland Manse, Griminish, Isle of Benbecula HS7 5QA	01870 602180
			[E-mail: andownie@yahoo.co.uk]	

Berneray and Lochmaddy (GD) (H)

Donald Campbell MA BD DipTh	1997	2004	Church of Scotland Manse, Lochmaddy, Isle of North Uist HS6 5AA	01876 500414
			[E-mail: donald13712@aol.com]	

Carinish (GD) (H)

Vacant	Church of Scotland Manse, Clachan, Locheport, Lochmaddy, Isle of North Uist HS6 5HD	01876 580219

Kilmuir and Paible (GE)
Iain M. Campbell BD — 2004 — Paible, Isle of North Uist HS6 5ED [E-mail: ianmstudy@aol.com] — 01876 510310

Manish-Scarista (GD) (H)
Murdo Smith MA BD — 1988 — Scarista, Isle of Harris HS3 3HX [E-mail: akph77@uk.uumail.com] — 01859 550200

South Uist (GD)
Jackie G. Petrie — 1989 2004 — Daliburgh, Isle of South Uist HS8 5SS [E-mail: jackiegpetrie@yahoo.com] — 01878 700265

Tarbert (GE) (H)
Norman MacIver BD — 1976 1988 — The Manse, Manse Road, Tarbert, Isle of Harris HS3 3DF [E-mail: norman@n-cmaciver.freeserve.co.uk] — 01859 502231

Name	Years	Charge	Address	Telephone
MacDonald, Angus J. BSc BD	1995 2001	(Lochmaddy and Trumisgarry)	7 Memorial Avenue, Stornoway, Isle of Lewis HS1 2QR	01851 706634
MacInnes, David MA BD	1966 1999	(Kilmuir and Paible)	9 Golf View Road, Kinmylies, Inverness IV3 8SZ	01463 717377
Macpherson, Kenneth J. BD	1988 2002	(Benbecula)	70 Baile na Cille, Balivanich, Isle of Benbecula HS7 5ND	01870 602751
Morrison, Donald John	2001	Auxiliary Minister	Lagnam, Brisgean 22, Kyles, Isle of Harris HS3 3BS	01859 502341
Muir, Alexander MA BD	1982 1996	(Carinish)	14 West Mackenzie Park, Inverness IV2 3ST	01463 712096
Smith, John M.	1956 1992	(Lochmaddy)	Hamersay, Clachan, Isle of North Uist HS6 5HD	01876 580332

UIST Communion Sundays

Barra	2nd Mar, June, Sep, Easter, Advent	Carinish	4th Mar, Aug
Benbecula	2nd Mar, Sep	Kilmuir and Paible	1st Jun, 3rd Nov
Berneray and Lochmaddy	4th Jun, last Oct	Manish-Scarista	3rd Apr, 1st Oct
		South Uist – Iochdar	1st Mar
		Howmore	1st Jun
		Daliburgh	1st Sep
		Tarbert	2nd Mar, 3rd Sep

(44) LEWIS

Meets at Stornoway, in St Columba's Church Hall, on the first Tuesday of February, March, June, September and November. It also meets if required in April and December on dates to be decided.

Clerk: REV. THOMAS S. SINCLAIR MA LTh BD — An Caladh, East Tarbert, Tarbert, Isle of Harris HS3 3DB [E-mail: akph61@uk.uumail.com] [E-mail: thomas@sinclair0438.freeserve.co.uk] — 01859 502849 / 07766 700110 (Mbl)

Congregation / Minister	Year(s)	Address	Telephone
Barvas (GD) (H) Vacant		Barvas, Isle of Lewis HS2 0QY	01851 840218
Carloway (GD) (H) Murdo M. Campbell BD DipMin	1997	Knock, Carloway, Isle of Lewis HS2 9AU [E-mail: murdocampbell@hotmail.com]	01851 643255
Cross Ness (GE) (H) Ian Murdo M. Macdonald DPA BD	2001	Cross Manse, Swainbost, Ness, Isle of Lewis HS2 0TB [E-mail: ianmurdo@crosschurch.fsnet.co.uk]	01851 810375
Kinloch (GE) (H) Vacant		Laxay, Lochs, Isle of Lewis HS2 9LA	01851 830218
Knock (GE) (H) Fergus J. MacBain BD DipMin	1999 2002	Knock Manse, Garrabost, Point, Isle of Lewis HS2 0PW [E-mail: fergusjohn@macbain.freeserve.co.uk]	01851 870362
Lochs-Crossbost (GD) (H) Andrew W.F. Coghill BD DPS	1993	Leurbost, Lochs, Isle of Lewis HS2 9NS [E-mail: andcoghill@aol.com]	01851 860243 (Tel/Fax) 07776 480748 (Mbl)
Lochs-in-Bernera (GD) (H) Vacant		Great Bernera, Isle of Lewis HS2 9LU	
Stornoway: High (GD) (H) William B. Black MA BD	1972 1998	1 Goathill Road, Stornoway, Isle of Lewis HS1 2NJ [E-mail: willieblack@lineone.net]	01851 703106
Stornoway: Martin's Memorial (H) Thomas MacNeil MA BD	2002 2006	Matheson Road, Stornoway, Isle of Lewis HS1 2LR [E-mail: tommymacneil@hotmail.com]	01851 704238
Stornoway: St Columba (GD) (H) (Church office: 01851 701546) Angus Morrison MA BD PhD	1979 2000	Lewis Street, Stornoway, Isle of Lewis HS1 2JF [E-mail: morrisonangus@btconnect.com]	01851 703350
Uig (GE) (H) Vacant		Miavaig, Uig, Isle of Lewis HS2 9HW	01851 672216
Macdonald, Alexander	1957 1991	(Cross Ness)	5 Urquhart Gardens, Stornoway, Isle of Lewis HS1 2TX — 01851 702825
Macdonald, James LTh CPS	1984 2001	(Knock)	Elim, 8A Lower Bayble, Point, Isle of Lewis HS2 0QA — 01851 870173
Maclean, Donald A. DCS		(Deacon)	8 Upper Barvas, Isle of Lewis HS2 0QX — 01851 840454

MacLennan, Donald Angus   1975 2006   (Kinloch)   4 Kestrel Place, Inverness IV2 3YH   01463 243750
 [E-mail: maclennankinloch@btinternet.com]   (Mbl) 07799 668270
Macleod, William   1957 2006   (Uig)   54 Lower Barvas, Isle of Lewis HS2 0QY   01851 840217
MacSween, Norman   1952 1986   (Kinloch)   7 Balmerino Drive, Stornoway, Isle of Lewis HS1 2TD   01851 703369
Sinclair, Thomas Suter MA LTh BD   1966 2004   (Stornoway: Martin's Memorial)   An Caladh, East Tarbert, Tarbert, Isle of Harris HS3 3DB   01859 502849
 [E-mail: akph61@uk.uumail.com]   (Mbl) 07766 700110
 [E-mail: thomas@sinclair0438.freeserve.co.uk]

LEWIS Communion Sundays

Barvas	3rd Mar, Sep	Lochs-Crossbost	4th Mar, Sep
Carloway	1st Mar, last Sep	Lochs-in-Bernera	1st Apr, 2nd Sep
Cross Ness	2nd Mar, Oct	Stornoway	
Kinloch	3rd Mar, 2nd Jun, 2nd Sep	High	3rd Feb, last Aug
Knock	1st Apr, Nov	Martin's Memorial	3rd Feb, last Aug, 1st Dec, Easter
Stornoway			
St Columba	3rd Feb, last Aug		
Uig	3rd Jun, 1st Sep		

(45) ORKNEY

Normally meets at Kirkwall, in the East Church King Street Halls, on the second Tuesday of September, February and May, and on the last Tuesday of November.

Clerk: REV. TREVOR G. HUNT BA BD   The Manse, Finstown, Orkney KW17 2EG   01856 761328 (Tel/Fax)
 [E-mail: akph68@uk.uumail.com]   07753 423333 (Mbl)
 [E-mail (personal): trevorghunt@yahoo.co.uk]

Birsay, Harray and Sandwick
Andrea E. Price (Mrs)   1997   2001   The Manse, North Biggings Road, Dounby, Orkney KW17 2HZ   01856 771803
 [E-mail: andrea@andreaneil.plus.com]

East Mainland
Vacant   West Manse, Holm, Orkney KW17 2SB   01856 781422 (Tel/Fax)

Eday linked with Stronsay: Moncur Memorial (H)
Jennifer D. George (Ms) BA MDiv PhD   2000   2005   Manse, Stronsay, Orkney KW17 2AF   01857 616311
 [E-mail: jennifergeorge@btinternet.com]

Evie linked with Firth (H) linked with Rendall
Trevor G. Hunt BA BD   1986   Manse, Finstown, Orkney KW17 2EG   01856 761328 (Tel/Fax)
 [E-mail: trevorghunt@yahoo.co.uk]   07753 423333 (Mbl)

Firth (H) (01856 761117) See Evie

Flotta linked with Hoy and Walls
Vacant
South Isles Manse, Longhope, Stromness, Orkney KW16 3PG
01856 701325

Hoy and Walls See Flotta

Kirkwall: East (H)
Allan McCafferty BSc BD   1993
East Church Manse, Thoms Street, Kirkwall, Orkney KW15 1PF
[E-mail: amccafferty@beeb.net]
01856 875469

Kirkwall: St Magnus Cathedral (H)
G. Fraser H. Macnaughton MA BD   1982   2002
Berstane Road, Kirkwall, Orkney KW15 1NA
[E-mail: fmacnaug@fish.co.uk]
01856 873312

North Ronaldsay linked with Sanday (H)
John L. McNab MA BD   1997   2002
The Manse, Sanday, Orkney KW17 2BW
01857 600429

Orphir (H) linked with Stenness (H)
Thomas L. Clark BD   1985
Stenness Manse, Stenness, Stromness, Orkney KW16 3HH
[E-mail: toml.clark@btopenworld.com]
01856 761331

Papa Westray linked with Westray
Iain D. MacDonald BD   1993
The Manse, Hilldavale, Westray, Orkney KW17 2DW
[E-mail: macdonald@rapnessmanse.freeserve.co.uk]
01857 677357 (Tel/Fax)
07710 443780 (Mbl)

Rendall See Evie

Rousay
Continuing Vacancy

Sanday See North Ronaldsay

Shapinsay (50 per cent part-time)
Vacant

South Ronaldsay and Burray
Graham D.S. Deans MA BD MTh DMin   1978   2002
St Margaret's Manse, Church Road, St Margaret's Hope,
Orkney KW17 2SR
[E-mail: graham.deans@btopenworld.com]
01856 831288

Stenness See Orphir

Stromness (H)
Fiona L. Lillie (Mrs) BA BD MLitt   1995   1999   5 Manse Lane, Stromness, Orkney KW16 3AP   01856 850203
                                                                  [E-mail: fiona@lilliput23.freeserve.co.uk]

Stronsay: Moncur Memorial See Eday
Westray See Papa Westray

Brown, R. Graeme BA BD   1961 1998   (Birsay with Rousay)   Bring Deeps, Orphir, Orkney KW17 2LX   (Tel/Fax) 01856 811707
                                                                                   [E-mail: grasibrown@bringdeeps.fsnet.co.uk]
Cant, H.W.M. MA BD STM   1951 1990   (Kirkwall: St Magnus Cathedral)   Quoylobs, Holm, Orkney KW17 2RY   01856 781300

(46) SHETLAND

Meets at Lerwick on the first Tuesday of March, April, June, September, October, November and December.

Clerk: REV. CHARLES H.M. GREIG MA BD   The Manse, Sandwick, Shetland ZE2 9HW   **01950 431244**
                                                       [E-mail: akph72@uk.uumail.com]

Burra Isle linked with Tingwall
Edgar J. Ogston BSc BD   1976   2001   Park Neuk, Meadowfield Place, Scalloway, Shetland ZE1 0UE   01595 880865
                                                                  [E-mail: edgar.ogston@macfish.com]

Delting linked with Northmavine
Winnie Munson (Ms) BD   1996   2001   The Manse, Grindwell, Brae, Shetland ZE2 9QJ   01806 522219
                                                                  [E-mail: shetlandsafety@aol.com]
Robert M. MacGregor (Aux)   2004   Olna Cottage, Brae, Shetland ZE2 9QS   01806 522773
   MIOSH DipOSH RSP

Dunrossness and St Ninian's inc. Fair Isle linked with Sandwick, Cunningsburgh and Quarff
Charles H.M. Greig MA BD   1976   1997   The Manse, Sandwick, Shetland ZE2 9HW   01950 431244
                                                                  [E-mail: chm.greig@btopenworld.com]

Fetlar linked with Unst linked with Yell
Vacant

Lerwick and Bressay
Gordon Oliver BD   1979   2002   The Manse, 82 St Olaf Street, Lerwick, Shetland ZE1 0ES   01595 692125
                                                                  [E-mail: stolaf@tiscali.co.uk]

Nesting and Lunnasting linked with Whalsay and Skerries

Irene A. Charlton (Mrs) BTh   1994 1997   The Manse, Marrister, Symbister, Whalsay, Shetland ZE2 9AE   01806 566767
[E-mail: irene.charlton@virgin.net]

Richard M. Charlton (Aux)   2001   The Manse, Marrister, Symbister, Whalsay, Shetland ZE2 9AE   01806 566767
[E-mail: richardm.charlton@virgin.net]

Northmavine See Delting

Sandsting and Aithsting linked with Walls and Sandness

Thomas Macintyre MA BD   1972 2006   The Rock, Whiteness, Shetland ZE2 9LJ   01595 810386
[E-mail: the2macs.macintyre@btinternet.com]

Sandwick, Cunningsburgh and Quarff See Dunrossness and St Ninian's
Tingwall See Burra Isle
Unst See Fetlar
Walls and Sandness See Sandsting and Aithsting
Whalsay and Skerries See Nesting and Lunnasting
Yell See Fetlar

Name				Address	Phone
Blair, James N.	1962	1986	(Sandsting and Aithsting with Walls)	2 Swinister, Sandwick, Shetland ZE2 9HH	01950 431472
Douglas, Marilyn (Miss) DCS	1988	2004	Presbytery Assistant	Heimdal, Quarff, Shetland ZE2 9EZ	01950 477584
Kirkpatrick, Alice H. (Miss) MA BD FSAScot	1987	2000	(Northmavine)	3 Stendaal, South Nesting, Shetland ZE2 9XA	
Knox, R. Alan MA LTh AInstAM	1965	2005	(Fetlar with Unst with Yell)	27 Killyvalley Road, Garvagh, Co. Londonderry, Northern Ireland BT51 5LX	
Smith, Catherine (Mrs) DCS	1964	2003	(Presbytery Assistant)	21 Lingaro, Bixter, Shetland ZE2 9NN	01595 810207
Williamson, Magnus J.C.	1982	1999	(Fetlar with Yell)	Creekhaven, Houll Road, Scalloway, Shetland ZE1 0XA	01595 880023
Wilson, W. Stewart DA	1980	1997	(Kirkcudbright)	Aesterhoull, Fair Isle, Shetland ZE2 9JU	01595 760273

(47) ENGLAND

Meets at London, in Crown Court Church, on the second Tuesday of March and December, and at St Columba's, Pont Street, on the second Tuesday of June and October.

Clerk: REV. SCOTT J. BROWN BD RN   35 Stag Way, Funtley, Fareham, Hants PO15 6TW   01329 236895 (Home)
[E-mail: akph14@uk.uumail.com]   02392 625553 (Work)
[E-mail: clerk@presbyteryofengland.org.uk]   07867 584820 (Mbl)

Corby: St Andrew's (H)

W. Alexander Cairns BD   1978 2001   6 Honiton Gardens, Corby, Northants NN18 8BW   01536 203175
[E-mail: sandy.cairns@btinternet.com]

Marjory Burns (Mrs) DCS   2003 1998   25 Barnsley Square, Corby, Northants NN18 0PQ   01536 264819
[E-mail: mburns8069@aol.com]

Corby: St Ninian's (H) (01536 265245)
Vacant
Marjory Burns (Mrs) DCS   2003 1998   46 Glyndebourne Gardens, Corby, Northants NN18 0PZ   01536 747378
25 Barnsley Square, Corby, Northants NN18 0PQ   01536 264819
[E-mail: mburns8069@aol.com]

Guernsey: St Andrew's in the Grange (H)
Graeme W. Beebee BD   1993 2003   The Manse, Le Villocq, Castel, Guernsey GY5 7SB   01481 257345
[E-mail: beehive@cwgsy.net]

Jersey: St Columba's (H)
Randolph Scott MA BD   1991 2006   18 Claremont Avenue, St Saviour, Jersey JE2 7SF   01534 730659
[E-mail: rev.rs@tinyworld.co.uk]

Liverpool: St Andrew's
Continued Vacancy
Session Clerk: Mr Robert Cottle   0151-524 1915

London: Crown Court (H) (020 7836 5643)
Sigrid Marten   1997 2001   53 Sidmouth Street, London WC1H 8JX   020 7278 5022
[E-mail: minister@crowncourtchurch.org.uk]
Timothy Fletcher BA FCMA (Aux)   1998   37 Harestone Valley Road, Caterham, Surrey CR3 6HN   01883 340826

London: St Columba's (H) (020 7584 2321) linked with Newcastle: St Andrew's (H)
Barry W. Dunsmore MA BD   1982 2000   29 Hollywood Road, Chelsea, London SW10 9HT   020 7376 5230
[E-mail: office@stcolumbas.org.uk]
Dorothy Lunn (Aux)   2001 2002   14 Bellerby Drive, Ouston, Co. Durham DH2 1TW   0191-492 0647
[E-mail: dorothy.lunn2@btopenworld.com]
Patricia Munro (Miss) BSc DCS   2002   11 Hurlingham Square, Peterborough Road, London SW6 3DZ   020 7610 6994
[E-mail: patmunro@tiscali.co.uk]

Newcastle: St Andrews   See London: St Columba's

Bowie, A. Glen CBE BA BSc   1954 1984   (Principal Chaplain: RAF)   16 Weir Road, Hemingford Grey, Huntingdon PE18 9EH   01480 381425
MA BD   1987 1992
Britchfield, Alison E.P. (Mrs)   Chaplain: RN   Director RN, Armed Forces Chaplaincy Centre, Amport House, Amport, Andover, Hants
Brown, Scott J. BD RN   1993   Chaplain: RN   Staff Chaplain to the Chaplain of the Fleet, Second Sea Lord and   02392 625553
Commander in Chief Naval Home Command, MP 1.2,
Leach Building, Whale Island, Portsmouth PO2 8BY
[E-mail: clerk@presbyteryofengland.org.uk]
Cameron, R. Neil   1975 1981   Chaplain: Community   The Church Centre, Rhine Area Support Unit, BFPO 40   0049 2161 472770
1989 1994
Coulter, David G.   Chaplain: Army   8 Ashdown Terrace, Tidworth, Wilts SP9 7SQ   01980 842175
BA BD MDA PhD CF   [E-mail: padredgoulter@aol.com]
Craig, Gordon T. BD   1988 1988   Chaplain: RAF   40 Aiden Road, Quarrington, Sleaford, Lincs NG34 8UU   01529 300264
Dalton, Mark BD DipMin   2002 2002   Chaplain: RN   Fleet Pool Chaplain, Room 112, Defiance Building, HMNB Devonport,   01752 555921
Plymouth, Devon PL2 2BG
[E-mail: mark.dalton242@mod.uk]

Name			Position	Address	Telephone
Devenney, David J. BD	1997	2003	Chaplain: RN	8 Hunton Close, Lympstone, Exmouth, Devon EX8 5JG [E-mail: davidjdevenney@freeuk.com]	01395 266570
Dowswell, James A.M.	1991	2001	(Lerwick and Bressay)	Mill House, High Street, Staplehurst, Tonbridge, Kent TN12 0AV	01580 891271
Drummond, J.S. MA	1949	1978	(Corby: St Ninian's)	77 Low Road, Hellesdon, Norwich NR6 5AG	01603 417736
Duncan, Denis M. BD PhD	1944	1986	(Editor: *The British Weekly*)	80A Woodland Rise, London N10 3UJ	020 8883 1831 / 020 8374 4708 (Tel) / 020 8201 1397 (Fax)
Fields, James MA BD STM	1988	1997	School Chaplain	The Bungalow, The Ridgeway, Mill Hill, London NW7 1QX	
Hood, Adam J.J. MA BD DPhil	1989		Lecturer	67A Farquhar Road, Edgbaston, Birmingham B15 2QP [E-mail: adamhood1@hotmail.com]	0121-452 2606
Hughes, O. Tudor MBE BA	1934	1976	(Guernsey: St Andrew's in the Grange)	4 Belcher Court, Dorchester on Thames, Oxon	01865 340779 (Work)
Kingston, David V.F. BD DipPTH	1993	1993	Chaplain: Army	101 Logistic Brigade Headquarters, Bullen Barracks, Aldershot GU11 2BX	01252 347062 (Home) / 01252 331123 (Tel/Fax)
Lugton, George L. MA BD	1955	1997	(Guernsey: St Andrew's in the Grange)	6 Clos de Beauvoir, Rue Cohu, Guernsey GY5 7TE	01481 254285
McEnhill, Peter BD PhD	1992	1996	Lecturer	Westminster College, Madingley Road, Cambridge CB3 0AA	01223 353997
Macfarlane, Peter T. BA LTh	1970	1994	(Chaplain: Army)	4 rue de Rives, 37160 Abilly, France	
McIndoe, John H. MA BD STM DD	1966	2000	(London: St Columba's with Newcastle: St Andrew's	5 Dunlin, Westerlands Park, Glasgow G12 0FE	0141-579 1366
Mackenzie, James G. BA BD	1980	2005	(Jersey: St Columba's)	10 Sandpiper Crescent, Carnbroe, Coatbridge ML5 4UW	
MacLaughlan, Grant BA BD	1998	2006	Director of the Market Place Partnership, St Nicholas' Church, Durham	23 Staindrop Road, Newton Hall, Durham DH1 5XS	0191-370 9725
MacLeod, C. Angus BD	1996		Chaplain: Army	1 Mechanised Brigade, Delhi Barracks, Tidworth, Wilts SP9 7DX [E-mail: padreangusmac@hotmail.com]	01980 602326 (Work) / 01980 842380 (Home)
MacLeod, R.N. MA BD	1986	1992	Chaplain: Army	25 Redford Gardens, Edinburgh EH13 0AP	0131-441 6522
Majcher, Philip L. BD	1982	1987	Chaplain: Army	Assistant Chaplain General, HQ 4th Division, Steeles Road, Aldershot GU11 2DP	01252 347058 (Work) / 01256 398868 (Home)
Martin, Anthony M. BA BD	1989	1989	Chaplain: Army	Army Technical Foundation College, Rowcroft Barracks, Arborfield, Reading, Berks RG2 9NJ [E-mail: am_km_martin@hotmail.com]	01189 763409
Milloy, A. Miller DPE LTh DipTrMan	1979	1998	General Secretary: United Bible Societies	3 Lea Wood Road, Fleet, Hants GU51 5AL	01252 628455
Mills, Peter W. BD CPS	1984		Chaplain-in-Chief, Royal Air Force	Ripon College, Cuddesdon, Oxford OX4 9HP	01865 877408
Milton, A. Leslie MA BD PhD	1996	2001	Lecturer	6 Kempton Close, Thundersley, Benfleet, Essex SS7 3SG	01268 747219
Norwood, David W. BA	1948	1980	(Lisbon)	Seme Bordon, Hampshire GU35 0JE	
Prentice, Donald K. BSc BD	1989	1992	Army Chaplain		
Rae, Scott M. MBE BD CPS	1976	2002	Principal Chaplain: Royal Navy	Principal Church of Scotland and Free Churches Chaplain (Naval) and Director Royal Naval Chaplaincy Service (Pastoral Provision and Operations), Second Sea Lord and Commander in Chief Naval Home Command, MP 1.2, Leach Building, Whale Island, Portsmouth PO2 8BY [E-mail: scott.rae420@mod.uk]	02392 625552
Rennie, Alistair M. MA BD	1939	1986	(Kincardine Croick and Edderton)	Noble's Yard, St Mary's Gate, Wirksworth, Derbyshire DE4 4DQ [E-mail: alistairrennie@lineone.net]	01629 820289
Stewart, Charles E. BSc BD PhD	1976	2000	School Chaplain	The Royal Hospital School, Holbrook, Ipswich IP9 2RX	01473 326200
Thomson, Steven	2001	2004	Chaplain: Royal Navy	Fleet Pool Chaplain, Lancelot Building, HMNB Portsmouth, Hants PO1 3LS	
Trevorrow, James A. LTh	1971	2003	(Glasgow: Cranhill)	12 Test Green, Corby, Northants NN17 2HA [E-mail: jimtrevorrow@compuserve.com]	01536 264018
Walker, R. Forbes BSc BD ThM	1987	2000	School Chaplain	2 Holmleigh, Priory Road, Ascot, Berks SL5 8EA	01344 883272
Wallace, Donald S.	1950	1980	(Chaplain: RAF)	7 Delfield Close, Watford, Herts WD1 3BL	01923 223289
Ward, Michael J. BSc BD PhD MA	1983	2004	Chaplain: College	19 Devonshire Avenue, Grimsby, Lincs DN32 0BW [E-mail: revmw@btopenworld.com]	01472 877079
Whitton, John P.	1977	1999	Deputy Chaplain General	Trenchard Lines, Upavon, Wilts SN9 6BE	01980 615802

ENGLAND – Church Addresses

Corby		
St Andrew's	Occupation Road	
St Ninian's	Beanfield Avenue	
Liverpool	The Western Rooms, Anglican Cathedral	
London	Crown Court	Crown Court WC2
	St Columba's	Pont Street SW1
Newcastle		Sandyford Road

(48) EUROPE

Clerk: REV. JOHN A. COWIE BSc BD   Jan Willem Brouwersstraat 9, NL-1071 LH Amsterdam   **Tel: 0031 20 672 2288**
[E-mail: j.cowie@chello.nl]   **Fax: 0031 842 221513**

Amsterdam
John A. Cowie BSc BD   1983   1989   Jan Willem Brouwersstraat 9, NL-1071 LH Amsterdam, The Netherlands   0031 20 672 2288
[E-mail: j.cowie@chello.nl]   Fax: 0031 842 221513

Brussels (E-mail: secretary@churchofscotland.be)
Andrew Gardner BSc BD PhD   1997   2004   23 Square des Nations, B-1000 Brussels, Belgium   0032 2 672 40 56
[E-mail: minister@churchofscotland.be]

Budapest
Vacant   St Columba's Scottish Mission,   0036 1 343 8479
Vorosmarty utca 51, H-1064 Budapest, Hungary   0036 1 246 2258
Oltvany Arok 25, H-1112 Budapest, Hungary (Manse)

Costa del Sol
John Shedden CBE BD DipPSS   1971   2005   La Loma de Los Pacos, Portal 6 4B, Malaga District, Spain   0034 654 328016
[E-mail: scotskirk@terra.es]

Geneva
Ian A. Manson BA BD   1989   2001   20 Ancienne Route, 1218 Grand Saconnex, Geneva, Switzerland   0041 22 798 29 09
[E-mail: cofsg@pingnet.ch]   (Office)   0041 22 788 08 31

Gibraltar
Stewart J. Lamont BSc BD   1972   2003   St Andrew's Manse, 29 Scud Hill, Gibraltar   00350 77040
[E-mail: lamont@gibraltar.gi]

Lausanne

G. Melvyn Wood MA BD	1982	2004	26 Avenue de Rumine, CH-1005 Lausanne, Switzerland [E-mail: scotskirklausanne@bluewin.ch]	(Tel/Fax)	0041 21 323 98 28

Lisbon

William B. Ross LTh CPS	1988	2006	R. do Viveiro 537, Edificio Costa do Sol, 7c, 2765–295 Monte Estoril, Portugal [E-mail: cofscotlx@netcabo.pt]		00351 21468 0853

Malta

David Morris	2002		La Romagnola, 13 Triq is-Seiqja, Mosra Kola, Attard BZN 05, Malta [E-mail: djlmorris@onvol.net] Church address: 210 Old Baker Street, Valletta, Malta	(Tel/Fax)	00356 214 15465

Paris

Alan Miller BA MA BD	2000	2006	10 Rue Thimmonier, F-75009 Paris, France		0033 1 48 78 47 94

Regensburg (University)

Rhona Dunphy (Mrs)	2005		Hirtensteig 1, 93155 Hemau-Laufenthal, Germany [E-mail: rhona@dunphy.de]		0049 (949) 1903666

Rome: St Andrew's

William B. McCulloch BD	1997	2002	Via XX Settembre 7, 00187 Rome, Italy [E-mail: revwbmcculloch@hotmail.com]	(Tel) (Fax)	0039 06 482 7627 0039 06 487 4370

Rotterdam

Robert A. Calvert BSc BD DMin	1983	1995	Gelebrem 59, NL-3068 TJ Rotterdam, The Netherlands [E-mail: scotsintchurch@cs.com]		0031 10 220 4199
Joanne Evans-Boiten BD (Community Minister)	2004		Oude Veerdam 2, NL-3212 MA Simonshaven, The Netherlands		0031 181 454229

Turin

Vacant			Via Sant Anselmo 6, 10125 Turin, Italy		0039 011 650 9467

Conference of European Churches

Matthew Z. Ross LLB BD MTh FSAScot	1998	2003	Church and Society Commission, Ecumenical Centre, Rue Joseph II 174, B-1000 Brussels, Belgium [E-mail: mzr@cec-kek.be]	(Tel) (Fax) (Mbl)	0032 2 230 1732 0032 2 231 1413 0044 7711 706950

CORRESPONDING MEMBERS

James M. Brown MA BD	1982		Neustrasse 15, D-4630 Bochum, Germany [E-mail: j.brown@web.de]		0049 234 133 65
R. Graeme Dunphy	1988	1993	Institut für Anglistik, Universitätsstrasse 31, D-93053 Regensburg, Germany		

Professor A.I.C. Heron BD DTheol	1975	1987	University of Erlangen, Kochstrasse 6, D-91054 Erlangen, Germany [E-mail: arheron@theologie.uni-erlangen.de]	0049 9131 852202
Jane M. Howitt (Miss) MA BD	1996		21 Rodger Drive, Rutherglen, Glasgow G73 3QY [E-mail: jane_m_howitt@yahoo.co.uk]	0141-647 5228
Bertalan Tamas			St Columba's Scottish Mission, Vorosmarty utca 51, H-1064 Budapest, Hungary [E-mail: rch@mail.elender.hu]	0036 1 343 8479
Derek Yarwood			Chaplain's Department, Garrison HQ, Princess Royal Barracks, BFPO 47, Germany	0044 5241 77924
(Rome) David F. Huie MA BD	1962	(2001)	15 Rosebank Gardens, Largs KA30 8TD [E-mail: david.huie@btopenworld.com]	01475 670733
(Brussels) Charles C. McNeill OBE BD	1962	(1991)	17 All Saints Way, Beachamwell, Swaffham, Norfolk PE37 8BU	
(Gibraltar) John R. Page BD DipMin	1988	2003	Flat 01 'Toward', The Lighthouses, Greenock Road, Wemyss Bay PA18 6DT	01475 520281
(Gibraltar) D. Stuart Philip MA	1952	(1990)	6 St Bernard's Crescent, Edinburgh EH4 1NP	0131-332 7499
(Brussels) Thomas C. Pitkeathly MA CA BD	1984	2004	1 Lammermuir Court, Gullane EH31 2HU	01620 843373
(Rotterdam) Joost Pot BSc (Aux)	1992	2004	[E-mail: j.pot@wanadoo.nl]	

(49) JERUSALEM

Jerusalem: St Andrew's

Jane L. Barron (Mrs) BA DipEd BD	1999	2006	PO Box 8619, Jerusalem 91086, Israel [E-mail: stachjer@netvision.net.il]	(Tel) 00972 2 673 2401 (Fax) 00972 2 673 1711

Tiberias: St Andrew's

Jennifer C. Zielinski (Mrs) (Reader)			PO Box 104, Tiberias 14100, Israel [E-mail: scottie2@netvision.net.il]	(Tel) 00972 4 671 0710 (Fax) 00972 4 671 0711

SECTION 6

Additional Lists
of Personnel

LIST A – AUXILIARY MINISTERS

NAME	ORD	ADDRESS	TEL	PR
Anderson, David M. MSc FCOptom	1984	1 Dumfries Place, Fort William PH33 6UQ	01397 703203	38
Birch, Jim PGDip FRSA FIOC	2001	1 Kirkhill Grove, Cambuslang, Glasgow G72 8EH	0141-583 1722	16
Brown, Elizabeth (Mrs) JP RGN	1996	25 Highfield Road, Scone, Perth PH2 6RN	01738 552391	28
Cameron, Ann	2005	30 Wilson Road, Banchory AB31 5UY	01330 825953	32
Campbell, Gordon MA CDipAF DipHSM MCMI MIHM MRIN ARSGS FRGS FSAScot	2001	2 Falkland Place, Kingoodie, Invergowrie, Dundee DD2 5DY	01382 561383	29
Charlton, Richard	2001	The Manse, Symbister, Whalsay, Shetland ZE2 9AE	01806 566767	46
Cloggie, June (Mrs)	1997	11A Tulipan Crescent, Callander FK17 8AR	01877 331021	23
Craggs, Sheila (Mrs)	2001	7 Morar Court, Ellon AB41 9GG	01358 723055	33
Cruikshank, Alistair A.B. MA (Retired)	1991	Thistle Cottage, 2A Chapel Place, Dollar FK14 7DW	01259 742549	23
Durno, Richard C. DSW CQSW (Community Minister)	1989	Durnada House, 31 Springfield Road, Bishopbriggs, Glasgow G64 1PJ	0141-772 1052	16
Ferguson, Archibald M. MSc PhD CEng FRINA	1989	The Whins, 2 Barrowfield, Station Road, Cardross, Dumbarton G82 5NL	01389 841517	18
Fletcher, Timothy E.G. BA FCMA	1998	37 Hareston Valley Road, Caterham, Surrey CR3 6HN	01883 340826	47
Glass, Alexander OBE MA	1998	Craigton, Tulloch Avenue, Dingwall IV15 9TU	01349 863258	39
Griffiths, Ruth (Mrs)	2004	Kirkwood, Mathieson Lane, Innellan, Dunoon PA23 7TA	01369 830145	19
Harrison, Cameron	2006	Woodfield House, Priormuir, St Andrews KY16 8LP	01334 478067	26
Howie, Marion L.K. (Mrs) MA ARCS	1992	51 High Road, Stevenston KA20 3DY	01294 466571	12
Jenkinson, John J. JP LTCL ALCM DipEd DipSen (Retired)	1991	8 Rosehall Terrace, Falkirk FK1 1PY	01324 625498	22
Kay, Elizabeth (Miss) Dip YCS	1993	1 Kintail Walk, Inchture, Perth PH14 9RY	01828 686029	29
Kemp, Tina MA	2005	12 Oaktree Gardens, Dumbarton G82 1EV	01389 730477	18
Landale, William	2005	Green Hope Guest House, Green Hope, Duns TD11 3SG	01361 890242	5
Lawson, Ruth E. BA BSc PhD	2004	4 Torlundy Courtyard, Torlundy, Fort William PH33 6SW	01397 700833	38
Lunn, Dorothy	2002	14 Bellerby Drive, Ouston, Co. Durham DH2 1TN	0191-492 0647	47
McAlpine, John BSc (Retired)	1988	Braeside, 201 Bonkle Road, Newmains, Wishaw ML2 9AA	01698 384610	17
McCann, George McD. BSc ATI (Retired)	1994	Rosbeg, Parsonage Road, Galashiels TD1 3HS	01896 752055	4
MacDonald, Kenneth MA BA (Retired)	2001	5 Henderland Road, Bearsden, Glasgow G61 1AH	0141-943 1103	16
Macdonald, Michael	2004	73 Firhill, Alness IV17 0RT	01349 884268	40
MacDougall, Lorna A. MA	2003	34 Miller Place, Greenmount Park, Falkirk FK2 9QB	01324 552739	22
MacGregor, Robert M. MIOSH DipOSH RSP	2004	Olna Cottage, Brae, Shetland ZE2 9QS	01806 522604	46
Mack, Elizabeth (Miss) Dip PEd	1994	24 Roberts Crescent, Dumfries DG2 7RS	01387 264847	8
Mack, John C. JP	1985	The Willows, Auchleven, Insch AB52 6QD	01464 820387	33
Mailer, Colin (Retired)	2000	Innis Chonain, Back Row, Polmont, Falkirk FK2 0RD	01324 712401	22
Manson, Eileen (Mrs) DCE	1994	1 Cambridge Avenue, Gourock PA19 1XT	01475 632401	14
Mills, Iain	2006	4 Farden Place, Prestwick KA9 2HS	01292 475212	10
Moore, Douglas T.	2003	9 Midton Avenue, Prestwick KA9 1PU	01292 671352	10
Morrison, Donald John	2001	22 Kyles, Tarbert, Isle of Harris HS3 3BS	01859 502341	43

Name	Address	Phone	Page
Munro, Mary (Mrs) BA (Retired)	14 Auchneel Crescent, Stranraer DG9 0JH	01776 870250	9
Murray, John W.	1 Totescore, Kilmuir, Portree, Isle of Skye IV51 9YN	01470 542297	42
Paterson, Andrew E. JP	6 The Willows, Kelty KY4 0FQ	01383 830998	24
Paterson, Maureen (Mrs) BSc	91 Dalmahoy Crescent, Kirkcaldy KY2 6TA	01592 262300	25
Phillippo, Michael MTh BSc BVetMed MRCVS	25 Deeside Crescent, Aberdeen AB15 7PT		31
Pot, Joost BSc (Retired)	Rijksstraatweg 12, NL-2988 BJ Ridderkerk, The Netherlands	0031 18 042 0894	48
Ramage, Alistair E. MA BA ADB CertEd	16 Claremont Gardens, Milngavie, Glasgow G62 6PG	0141-956 2897	18
Riddell, Thomas S. BSc CEng FIChemE	4 The Maltings, Linlithgow EH49 6DS	01506 843251	2
Robson, Brenda (Dr)	Old School House, 2 Baird Road, Ratho, Newbridge EH28 8RA	0131-333 2746	1
Sharp, James	102 Rue des Eaux-Vivres, CH-1207 Geneva, Switzerland		48
Shaw, Catherine A.M. MA (Retired)	40 Merrygreen Place, Stewarton, Kilmarnock KA3 5EP	01560 483352	11
Simpson, James H. BSc (Retired)	11 Claypotts Place, Broughty Ferry, Dundee DD5 1LG	01382 776520	29
Sutherland, David	6 Cromarty Drive, Dundee DD2 2UQ	01382 621473	29
Thomas, Shirley A. (Mrs) DipSocSci AMIA	14 Kirkgait, Letham, Forfar DD8 2XQ	01307 818084	30
Vivers, Katherine (Mrs)	Blacket House, Eaglesfield, Lockerbie DG11 3AA	01461 500412	7
Wandrum, David	5 Cawder View, Carrickstone Meadows, Cumbernauld, Glasgow G68 0BN	01236 723288	22
Watson, Jean S. (Miss) MA (Retired)	29 Strachan Crescent, Dollar FK14 9HL	01259 742872	23
Wilson, Mary D. (Mrs) RGN SCM DTM	'Berbice', The Terrace, Bridge of Tilt, Blair Atholl, Pitlochry PH18 5SZ	01796 481619	27
Zambonini, James LIADip	100 Old Manse Road, Netherton, Wishaw ML2 0EP	01698 350889	17

LIST B – CHAPLAINS TO HM FORCES

NAME	ORD	COM	BCH	ADDRESS
Abeledo, Benjamin J.A. BTh DipTh PTh	1991	1999	A	3 Bn The Parachute Regiment, Hyderabad Barracks, Mersea Road, Colchester CO2 7TB
Aitchison, James W. BD	1993	1993	A	2 Bn The Parachute Regiment, Clive Barracks, Tern Hill, Shropshire TF9 3QE
Britchfield, Alison E.P. (Mrs) MA BD	1987	1992	RN	Director Royal Navy, Armed Forces Chaplaincy Centre, Amport House, Amport, Andover SP11 8BG
Brown, Scott J. BD	1993	1993	RN	Staff Chaplain to the Chaplain of the Fleet, Directorate Royal Naval Chaplaincy Service, MP 1.2, Leach Building, Whale Island, Portsmouth, Hants PO2 8BY
Connolly, Daniel BD DipTheol DipMin	1983	1994	A	1 Bn Infantry Training Centre, Vimy Barracks, Catterick Garrison, North Yorks DL9 3PS
Coulter, David G. BA BD PhD	1989	1994	A	Headquarters 3 (UK) Division, Bulford Camp, Salisbury SP4 9NY
Craig, Gordon T. BD DipMin	1988	1988	RAF	Deputy Director Chaplaincy Operations and Training, HQ Strike Command, RAF High Wycombe, Bucks HP14 4UE
Dailly, J.R. BD DipPS	1979	1979	A	Warminster Training Centre, Warminster, Wiltshire BA12 0DJ
Dalton, Mark BD DipMin	2002	2002	RN	c/o The Chaplaincy, Fleet Pool, Devonport, Water Front Office, Room 132 Defence Building, HMNB Devonport, Plymouth PL2 2BG
Devenney, David BD	1997	2002	RN	The Chaplaincy Centre, Command Training Centre, Royal Marines, Lympstone, Exmouth, Devon EX8 5AR

Duncan, John C. BD MPhil	1987	2001	A	2 Royal Tank Regiment, BFPO 38
Kellock, Chris N. MA BD	1998		RAF	Chaplaincy Centre, Building 150, Jacaramda Drive, RAF Akrotiri, BFPO 57
Kennon, Stan MA BD	1992	2000	RN	c/o The Chaplaincy, Fleet Pool, Devonport, Water Front Office, Room 132 Defence Building, HMNB Devonport, Plymouth PL2 2BG
Kingston, David V.F. BD DipPTH	1993		A	Senior Chaplain, 101 Brigade, Buller Barracks, Aldershot, Hants GU11 2BX
McCulloch, Alen J.R. MA BD	1990	1995	RN	c/o The Chaplaincy, Fleet Pool, Devonport, Water Front Office, Room 132 Defence Building, HMNB Devonport, Plymouth PL2 2BG
Macgregor, John BD	2001		A	Royal Highland Fusiliers, Glencorse Barracks, Penicuik EH26
Mackenzie, Seoras L. BD	1996		A	Royal Armoured Corps Training Centre, Bovington, Wareham, Dorset BH20 6JA
MacLeod, C. Angus MA BD	1996		A	1 Argyll and Southern Highlanders, Howe Barracks, Canterbury CT16 1JU
MacLeod, Rory N. MA BD	1986		A	2 Bn The Light Infantry, Redford Barracks, Edinburgh EH13 0PP
MacPherson Duncan J. BSc BD	1993		A	1 Bn The Royal Highland Fusiliers, BFPO 38
Majcher, Philip L. BD	1982	1987	A	Assistant Chaplain General, HQ 4 Division, Alison House, Steele's Road, Aldershot GU11 2DP
Mills, Peter W. BD CPS	1984	1984	RAF	Chaplain-in-Chief and Principal Chaplain (Church of Scotland and Free Churches), HQ Strike Command, RAF High Wycombe, Bucks HP14 4UE
Munro, Sheila BD	1995		RAF	Chaplaincy Centre, RAF Digby, Lincoln LN4 3LH
Prentice, Donald K. BSc BD	1987		A	Senior Chaplain, Serne Bordon, Hampshire GU35 0JE
Rae, Scott M. MBE BD CPS	1976		RN	Director Naval Chaplaincy Service (Pastoral Provision and Operations) and Principal Chaplain (Church of Scotland and Free Churches), MP 1.2 Leach Building, Whale Island, Portsmouth, Hants PO2 8BY
Shackleton, Scott J.S. BA BD	1993		RN	The Chaplaincy Centre, HMS Neptune, HM Naval Base Clyde, Faslane, Helensburgh G84 8HL
Thomson, Steven BSc BD	2001		RN	Fleetpool Portsmouth, The Water Front Chaplaincy, Lancelot Building, HMNB Portsmouth PO1 3NT
Whitton, John P. MA BD	1977		A	Deputy Chaplain General, MOD Chaplains (Army), Trenchard Lines, Upavon, Pewsey, Wilts SN9 6BE

CHAPLAINS TO HM FORCES (Territorial Army)
CHAPLAINS TO HM FORCES (Army Cadet Force)
CHAPLAINS TO HM FORCES (Royal Naval Reserve)

In recent years, the *Year Book* has included details of those serving as Chaplains with the Territorial Army and with the Army Cadet Force. These lists have not always been as complete as those concerned with full-time Chaplains to the Forces. Fresh consideration is being given to the preparation and updating of these lists so that they can be included in future editions of the *Year Book* in accurate and appropriate forms. It is also intended that these lists will include the new category of Chaplains to the Royal Naval Reserve. The Rev. Marjory A. MacLean LLB BD PhD has completed her training in this regard and has been commissioned as Chaplain Royal Naval Reserve at HMS *Scotia*. It is anticipated that some further appointment(s) may be made in the foreseeable future.

LIST C – HOSPITAL CHAPLAINS ('Full-time' Chaplains are listed first in each area)

LOTHIAN

EDINBURGH – LOTHIAN UNIVERSITY HOSPITALS
ROYAL INFIRMARY
Rev. Alexander Young — 32 Alnwickhill Park, Edinburgh EH16 6UH — 0131-242 1991
Anne Mulligan — 27A Craigour Avenue, Edinburgh EH17 7NH — 0131-242 1996
WESTERN GENERAL HOSPITAL [0131-537 1000]
Rev. Alistair K. Ridland — 13 Stewart Place, Kirkliston EH29 2BQ — 0131-537 1400
LOTHIAN PRIMARY CARE
ROYAL EDINBURGH HOSPITAL [0131-537 6734]
Rev. Lynne MacMurchie
Rev. Patricia Allen
ROYAL HOSPITAL FOR SICK CHILDREN [0131-536 0000]
Rev. Caroline Upton — 1 Westgate, Dunbar EH42 1JL — 0131-536 0144
EDINBURGH COMMUNITY MENTAL HEALTH
Rev. Lynne MacMurchie — 10 (3FL) Montagu Terrace, Edinburgh EH3 5QX
LIVINGSTON – ST JOHN'S HOSPITAL [01506 419666]
Rev. John McMahon — 41 George IV Bridge, Edinburgh EH1 1EL — 0131-220 5150
Rev. Dr Georgina Nelson — Chaplain's Office, St John's Hospital, Livingston
6 Pentland Park, Craigshill, Livingston EH54 5NR

HOSPICES

MARIE CURIE CENTRE — Rev. Tom Gordon — Frogston Road West, Edinburgh EH10 7DR — (Tel) 0131-445 2141 / (Fax) 0131-445 5845
ST COLUMBA'S HOSPICE — Rev. Ewan Kelly — 15 Boswall Road, Edinburgh EH5 3RW — 0131-551 1381

HOSPITALS

CORSTORPHINE — Rev. J. William Hill — 33/9 Murrayfield Road, Edinburgh EH12 6EP — 0131-554 1842
EASTERN GENERAL — Rev. John Tait — 52 Pilrig Street, Edinburgh EH6 5AS — 01506 419666
LINLITHGOW ST MICHAEL'S — Rev. John McMahon — Chaplain's Office, St John's Hospital, Livingston — 01368 863098
BELHAVEN — Rev. Laurence H. Twaddle — The Manse, Belhaven Road, Dunbar EH42 1NH — 01875 614442
EDENHALL — Rev. Anne M. Jones — 7 North Elphinstone Farm, Tranent EH33 2ND — 01875 614442
HERDMANFLAT — Rev. Anne M. Jones — 7 North Elphinstone Farm, Tranent EH33 2ND — 0131-667 2995
LOANHEAD — Mrs Susan Duncan — 35 Kilmaurs Road, Edinburgh EH16 5DB — 01620 880378
ROODLANDS — Rev. Kenneth D.F. Walker — The Manse, Athelstaneford, North Berwick EH39 5BE

Location	Chaplain	Address	Tel
ROSSLYNLEE	Rev. John W. Fraser	North Manse, Penicuik EH26 8AG	01968 672213
	Mrs Diane Kettles	10 Millway, Pencaitland, Tranent EH34 5HQ	07812 032226

BORDERS

Location	Chaplain	Address	Tel
MELROSE – BORDERS GENERAL HOSPITAL [01896 754333]	Rev. J. Ronald Dick	Chaplaincy Centre, Borders General Hospital, Melrose TD6 9BS	
DINGLETON	Rev. John Riddell	42 High Street, Jedburgh TD8 6NQ	01835 863223
HAY LODGE, PEEBLES	Rev. James H. Wallace	Innerleithen Road, Peebles EH45 8BD	01721 721749
KNOLL	Rev. Andrew Morrice	The Manse, Castle Street, Duns TD11 3DG	01361 883755
INCH	Rev. Robin McHaffie	Kirk Yetholm, Kelso TD5 8RD	01573 420308

DUMFRIES AND GALLOWAY

Location	Chaplain	Address	Tel
DUMFRIES HOSPITALS [01387 246246]	Rev. Alexander E. Strachan	2 Leafield Road, Dumfries DG1 2DS	01387 279460
THOMAS HOPE, LANGHOLM	Rev. Robert B. Milne	The Manse, Langholm DG13 0BL	01896 668577
LOCHMABEN	Rev. Alexander C. Stoddart	The Manse, Hightae, Lockerbie DG11 1JL	01387 811499
MOFFAT	Rev. David M. McKay	The Manse, Moffat DG10 9LR	01683 220128
NEW ANNAN	Rev. Mairi C. Byers	Meadowbank, Plumdon Road, Annan DG12 6SJ	01461 206512
CASTLE DOUGLAS	Rev. Robert Malloch	1 Castle View, Castle Douglas DG7 1BG	01556 502171
DUMFRIES AND GALLOWAY ROYAL INFIRMARY			
KIRKCUDBRIGHT	Rev. Douglas R. Irving	6 Bourtree Avenue, Kirkcudbright DG6 4AU	01557 330489
THORNHILL	Rev. Donald Keith	The Manse, Mansepark, Thornhill D63 5ER	01848 331191
DALRYMPLE	Rev. Ian McIlroy	The Manse, Church Street, Sandhead, Stranraer DG9 9JJ	01776 830337
GARRICK	Rev. Ian McIlroy	The Manse, Church Street, Sandhead, Stranraer DG9 9JJ	01776 830337
NEWTON STEWART	Rev. Neil Campbell	The Manse, Newton Stewart DG8 6HH	01671 402259

AYRSHIRE AND ARRAN

Location	Chaplain	Address	Tel
AYRSHIRE AND ARRAN PRIMARY CARE [01292 513023] AILSA HOSPITAL, AYR	Rev. Sheila Mitchell	Chaplaincy Centre, Dalmellington Road, Ayr KA6 6AB	
	Mrs Norma Livingstone	31 Victoria Drive, Troon KA10 6JF	
	Rev. Andrew Graham	33 Morton Avenue, Ayr KA7 2NJ	

AYRSHIRE AND ARRAN ACUTE HOSPITALS [01563 521133]

Hospital	Chaplain	Address	Tel
CROSSHOUSE HOSPITAL KILMARNOCK	Rev. Paul Russell	4 Westmoor Crescent, Kilmarnock KA1 1TX	
	Rev. Judith Huggett	6 Hollow Park, Alloway, Ayr KA7 4SR	01292 442554

AYR/BIGGART HOSPITALS [01292 610555]

Hospital	Chaplain	Address	Tel
AILSA	Rev. Roderick H. McNidder	31 Victoria Drive, Troon KA10 6JF	01292 478788
AYR	Mrs Norma Livingstone	68 St Quivox Road, Prestwick KA9 1JF	01292 441252
	Rev. Kenneth Elliott	1A Parkview, Alloway, Ayr KA7 4QG	
BIGGART	Rev. Neil A. McNaught	33 Barrhill Road, Cumnock KA18 1PJ	01290 420769
EAST AYRSHIRE COMMUNITY	Rev. John Paterson		
WAR MEMORIAL, ARRAN	Rev. Elizabeth Watson	The Manse, Whiting Bay, Isle of Arran KA27 8RE	01770 700289
LADY MARGARET, MILLPORT	Rev. Marjory H. Mackay	The Manse, Millport, Isle of Cumbrae KA28 0ED	01475 530416

LANARKSHIRE

Hospital	Chaplain	Address	Tel
LOCKHART	Rev. Alison Meikle	2 Kaimhill Court, Lanark ML11 9HU	01555 662600
CLELAND	Rev. John Jackson	The Manse, Bellside Road, Cleland, Motherwell ML1 5NP	01698 860260
KELLO	Rev. James Francis	61 High Street, Biggar ML12 6DA	01899 220227
LADY HOME	Rev. Bryan Kerr	The Manse, Douglas, Lanark ML11 0RB	01555 851213
ROADMEETINGS	Rev. Geoff McKee	Kirkstyle Manse, Church Street, Carluke ML8 4BA	
WISHAW GENERAL	Rev. James S.G. Hastie	Chalmers Manse, Quarry Road, Larkhall ML9 1HH	01698 882238
	Rev. J. Allardyce	6 Kelso Crescent, Wishaw ML2 7HD	01698 372657
	Rev. Sharon Colvin	48 Dunrobin Road, Airdrie ML6 8LR	01236 763154
	Rev. Mhorag MacDonald	350 Kirk Road, Wishaw ML2 8LH	01698 381305
STRATHCLYDE	Rev. David W. Doyle	19 Orchard Street, Motherwell ML1 3JE	01698 263472
HAIRMYRES	Rev. John Brewster	21 Turnberry Place, East Kilbride, Glasgow G75 8TB	01355 242564
	Rev. Dr John McPake	30 Eden Grove, East Kilbride, Glasgow G75 8XY	01355 234196
KIRKLANDS	Rev. Marjorie Taylor	1 Kirkhill Road, Strathaven ML10 6HN	01357 520643
STONEHOUSE	Rev. James S.G. Hastie	Chalmers Manse, Quarry Road, Larkhall ML9 1HH	01698 882238
UDSTON	Rev. Rosemary Smith	Blantyre Old Manse, High Blantyre, Glasgow G72 9UA	01698 823130
COATHILL	Rev. James P. Fraser	26 Hamilton Road, Strathaven ML10 6JA	01357 522758
	Rev. J. Stanley Cook	137A Old Manse Road, Netherton, Wishaw ML2 0EW	01698 299600
	Rev. William Beattie	33 Dungavel Gardens, Hamilton ML3 7PE	01698 423804
MONKLANDS GENERAL	Rev. James Munton	2 Moorcroft Drive, Airdrie ML6 8ES	01236 754848
	Rev. Andrew Thomson	38 Commonhead Street, Airdrie ML6 6NS	01236 602538
	Rev. James Grier	47 Blair Road, Coatbridge ML5 1JQ	01236 432427
WESTER MOFFAT	Rev. James Munton	2 Moorcroft Drive, Airdrie ML6 8ES	01236 754848
HARTWOODHILL	Rev. Derek Pope	35 Birrens Road, Motherwell ML1 3NS	01698 266716
HATTONLEA	Rev. Colin Cuthbert	Yieldshields Farm, Carluke ML8 4QB	01555 771157
MOTHERWELL PSYCHIATRIC	Rev. Agnes Moore	16 Croftpark Street, Bellshill ML4 1EY	01698 842877
	Rev. John Handley	12 Airbles Crescent, Motherwell ML1 3AR	01698 262733
COMMUNITY MENTAL HEALTH CARE	Rev. J. Stanley Cook	137A Old Manse Road, Netherton, Wishaw ML2 0EW	01698 299600
	Rev. Sharon Colvin	48 Dunrobin Road, Airdrie ML6 8LR	01236 763154
	Rev. Rosemary Smith	Blantyre Old Manse, High Blantyre, Glasgow G72 9UA	01698 823130

GREATER GLASGOW

NORTH GLASGOW UNIVERSITY HOSPITALS			
GLASGOW ROYAL INFIRMARY [0141-211 4000/4661]	Rev. Patricia McDonald	4 Whithope Terrace, Glasgow G53 7LT	
	Rev. Anne J.M. Harper	122 Greenock Road, Bishopton PA7 5AS	
WESTERN INFIRMARY [0141-211 2000]	Rev. Keith Saunders	1 Beckfield Drive, Robroyston, Glasgow G33 1SR	0141-211 2000/2812
GARTNAVEL GENERAL [0141-211 3000]	Rev. Keith Saunders	1 Beckfield Drive, Robroyston, Glasgow G33 1SR	0141-211 3000/3026
GLASGOW HOMEOPATHIC [0141-211 1600]	Rev. Keith Saunders	1 Beckfield Drive, Robroyston, Glasgow G33 1SR	0141-211 1600
GREATER GLASGOW PRIMARY CARE	Rev. Cameron H. Langlands: Co-ordinator		
GARTNAVEL ROYAL HOSPITAL [0141-211 3686]	Rev. Gordon B. Armstrong: North/East Sector	Chaplain's Office, Old College of Nursing, Stobhill Hospital, 133 Balornock Road, Glasgow G21 3UW	0141-232 0609
	Ms Anne MacDonald: South Sector	Chaplain's Office, Leverndale Hospital, 510 Crookston Road, Glasgow G53 7TU	0141-211 6695
SOUTH GLASGOW UNIVERSITY HOSPITALS			
SOUTHERN GENERAL HOSPITAL [0141-201 2156]	Rev. Ann Purdie		
	Rev. Blair Robertson: Co-ordinator		
VICTORIA INFIRMARY	Rev. Iain Reid	Chaplain's Office, Langside Road, Glasgow G42 9TT	0141-201 5164
YORKHILL NHS TRUST [0141-201 0595]	Rev. Alistair Bull	Royal Hospital for Sick Children, Glasgow G3 8SG	01360 312527
GREATER GLASGOW PRIMARY CARE	Rev. David Torrance	19 Redhills View, Lennoxtown, Glasgow G65 7BL	
	Rev. Alastair MacDonald	42 Roman Way, Dunblane FK15 9DJ	
ROYAL INFIRMARY	Mrs Sandra Bell	62 Loganswell Road, Thornliebank, Glasgow G46 8AX	
	Rev. Norma Stewart	127 Nether Auldhouse Road, Glasgow G43 2YS	0141-637 6956
STOBHILL	Rev. Elizabeth W. Sutherland	54 Etive Crescent, Bishopbriggs, Glasgow G54 1ES	0141-772 1453
	Rev. John Beaton	33 North Birbiston Road, Lennoxtown, Glasgow G65 7LZ	
	Rev. Kenneth Coulter	8 Abbotsford Avenue, Rutherglen, Glasgow G73 3NX	0141-647 6250
	Miss Anne MacDonald	62 Berwick Drive, Glasgow G52 3JA	0141-883 5618
LEVERNDALE			
DARNLEY COURT			
VICTORIA INFIRMARY/MEARNSKIRK	Rev. Alan Raeburn	110 Mount Annan Drive, Glasgow G44 4RZ	0141-632 1514
GARTNAVEL GENERAL	Rev. Annette Morrison	1055 Great Western Road, Glasgow G12 0XH	0141-211 3026
WESTERN INFIRMARY	Rev. David Vogan	Dumbarton Road, Glasgow G11 6NT	0141-211 2812
	Miss Helen Bunce	Dumbarton Road, Glasgow G11 6NT	0141-211 2812
BLAWARTHILL	Rev. Annette Morrison	Knightswood, Glasgow G13 3TG	0141-959 1864
KNIGHTSWOOD/DRUMCHAPEL	Rev. Andrew McMillan	1 Swallow Gardens, Glasgow G13 4QD	0141-959 7158
RUTHERGLEN TAKARE	Rev. J.W. Drummond	12 Albert Drive, Rutherglen, Glasgow G73 3RT	0141-569 8547
	Rev. Alexander Thomson	31 Highburgh Drive, Rutherglen, Glasgow G73 3RR	0141-647 6178
PRINCE AND PRINCESS OF WALES HOSPICE	Rev. Alan Donald	71 Carlton Place, Glasgow G5 9TD	0141-429 5599
FOURHILLS NURSING HOME	Rev. W.G. Ramsay	3 Tofthill Avenue, Bishopbriggs, Glasgow G64 3PN	0141-762 1844

HUNTERS HILL MARIE CURIE CENTRE	Miss Dawn Allan	1 Belmont Road, Glasgow G21 3AY	0141-531 1346
NATIONAL SERVICES SCOTLAND	Rev. Thomas Pollock	114 Springkell Avenue, Glasgow G41 4EW	0141-427 2094
INVERCLYDE ROYAL HOSPITAL (Whole-time) GREENOCK [01475 633777]	Rev. Janet McMahon	156 Old Castle Road, Glasgow G44 5TW	0141-637 5451
	Rev. Fergus McLachlan	Chaplain's Office, Inverclyde Royal Hospital, Larkfield Road, Greenock PA16 0XN	
(Part-time)	Mrs Joyce Nicol	93 Brisbane Street, Greenock PA16 8NY	01475 723235
DYKEBAR	Rev. Alistair Morrison	92 St Leonard's Road, Ayr KA7 2PU	01292 266121
	Rev. Alexander MacDonald	The Manse, Neilston, Glasgow G78 3NP	0141-881 1958
	Rev. George Mackay	109 Ormonde Avenue, Glasgow G44 3SN	0141-637 4976
MERCHISTON HOUSE	Miss Margaret McBain	33 Quarry Road, Paisley PA2 7RD	0141-884 2920
JOHNSTONE	Rev. Thomas Cant	18 Oldhall Road, Paisley PA1 3HL	0141-882 2277
ROYAL ALEXANDRA	Rev. Thomas Cant	18 Oldhall Road, Paisley PA1 3HL	0141-882 2277
	Rev. Arthur Sherratt	West Manse, Kilbarchan, Johnstone PA10 2JR	01805 702669
	Rev. Douglas Ralph	24 Kinpurnie Road, Paisley PA1 3HH	0141-883 3505
	Rev. Esther J. Ninian	28 Fulbar Crescent, Paisley PA2 9AS	01505 812304
	Rev. Ritchie Gillon	31 Southfield Avenue, Paisley PA2 8BX	0141-884 6215
	Rev. David Kay	6 Southfield Avenue, Paisley PA2 8BY	0141-884 3600
	Rev. E. Lorna Hood (Mrs)	North Manse, 1 Alexandra Drive, Renfrew PA4 8UB	0141-886 2074
RAVENSCRAIG	Rev. Owain Jones	East Manse, Kilbarchan PA10 2JQ	01505 702621
	Rev. David Mill	105 Newark Street, Greenock PA16 7TW	01475 639602
	Rev. Douglas Cranston	6 Churchill Road, Kilmacolm PA13 4LH	01505 873271
DUMBARTON JOINT	Rev. Christine Liddell	3 Havoc Road, Dumbarton G82 4JW	01389 604840
VALE OF LEVEN GENERAL	Rev. Ian Miller	1 Glebe Gardens, Bonhill, Alexandria G83 9HB	01389 753039
VALE OF LEVEN GERIATRIC	Rev. Ian Wilkie	38 Main Street, Renton, Dumbarton G82 4PU	01389 752017

FORTH VALLEY

BELLSDYKE	Rev. Ann Smith	16 Mannerston Holdings, Linlithgow EH49 7ND	01506 834350
	Rev. Henry Munroe	Viewforth, High Road, Maddiston, Falkirk FK2 0BL	01324 712446
	Rev. Robert MacLeod	13 Cannons Way, Falkirk FK2 7QG	01324 631008
BO'NESS	Rev. Stuart Webster	36 Blair Avenue, Bo'ness EH51 0QT	01506 204485
BONNYBRIDGE	Rev. Alisdair MacLeod-Mair	133 Falkirk Road, Bonnybridge FK4 1BA	01324 812621
FALKIRK ROYAL INFIRMARY	Rev. Helen Christie	5 Watson Place, Dennyloanhead, Bonnybridge FK4 2BG	01324 813786
RSNH LARBERT	Rev. Margery Collin	2 Saughtonhall Crescent, Edinburgh EH12 5RF	0131-337 7153
	Rev. Robert Philip	35 Belmont Avenue, Shieldhill, Falkirk FK1 2BS	01324 716231
BANNOCKBURN	Rev. James Landels	Allan Manse, Bogend Road, Bannockburn, Stirling FK7 8NP	01786 814692
CLACKMANNAN COUNTY	Rev. Eleanor Forgan	18 Alexandra Drive, Alloa FK10 2DQ	01259 212836
KILDEAN	Rev. George T. Sherry	37 Moubray Gardens, Silver Meadows, Cambus, Alloa FK10 2NQ	01259 220665
SAUCHIE	Rev. George T. Sherry	37 Moubray Gardens, Silver Meadows, Cambus, Alloa FK10 2NQ	01259 220665
STIRLING ROYAL INFIRMARY	Rev. Gary McIntyre	7 Randolph Road, Stirling FK8 2AJ	01786 474421
	Rev. Kenneth Russell	5 Clifford Road, Stirling FK8 2QU	01786 475802

FIFE

QUEEN MARGARET HOSPITAL, DUNFERMLINE [01383 674136]

	Mr Mark Evans DCS	Queen Margaret Hospital, Whitefield Road, Dunfermline KY12 0SU	

VICTORIA HOSPITAL, KIRKCALDY [01592 643355]

Institution	Chaplain	Address	Telephone
	Rev. Ian J.M. McDonald	11 James Grove, Kirkcaldy KY1 1TN	01592 203775
LYNEBANK	Rev. Elizabeth Fisk	51 St John's Drive, Dunfermline KY12 7TL	01383 720256
CAMERON	Rev. James L. Templeton	Innerleven Manse, McDonald Street, Methil, Leven KY8 3AJ	01333 426310
	Rev. Kenneth Donald	33 Main Road, East Wemyss, Kirkcaldy KY1 4RE	01592 713260
GLENROTHES	Rev. Ian D. Gordon	7 Guthrie Crescent, Markinch, Glenrothes KY7 6AY	01592 758264
RANDOLPH WEMYSS	Rev. Elizabeth Cranfield	9 Chemiss Road, Methilhill, Leven KY8 2BS	01592 713142
ADAMSON, CUPAR	Rev. Lynn Brady	2 Guthrie Court, Cupar Road, Newburgh, Cupar KY14 6HA	01337 842228
NETHERLEA, NEWPORT	Rev. Colin Dempster	27 Bell Street, Tayport DD6 9AP	01382 552861
STRATHEDEN, CUPAR	Mr Allan Grant	6 Normandy Place, Rosyth, Dunfermline KY11 2HJ	01383 428760
ST ANDREWS MEMORIAL	Rev. David Arnott	20 Priory Gardens, St Andrews KY16 8XX	01334 472912

TAYSIDE

Head of Spiritual Care

	Rev. Gillian Munro	Royal Dundee Liff Hospital, Dundee DD2 5NF	01382 423116

DUNDEE NINEWELLS HOSPITAL [01382 660111]

	Chaplain	Address	Telephone
	Rev. David J. Gordon		

PERTH ROYAL INFIRMARY [01738 473896]

	Rev. John M. Birrell	2 Rhynd Lane, Perth PH2 8TP	01738 625694
ABERFELDY	Rev. Ian Knox	Heatherlea, Main Street, Ardler, Blairgowrie PH12 8SR	01828 640731
BLAIRGOWRIE RATTRAY	Rev. Ian Murray	The Manse, Blair Atholl, Pitlochry PH18 5SX	01796 481213
IRVINE MEMORIAL	Rev. James W. MacDonald	8 Strathearn Terrace, Crieff PH7 3AQ	01764 653907
CRIEFF COTTAGE	Rev. John M. Birrell	2 Rhynd Lane, Perth PH2 8TP	01738 625694
MACMILLAN HOSPICE	Rev. Peter Meager	7 Lorraine Drive, Cupar KY15 5DY	01334 656991
MURRAY ROYAL	Rev. Randal MacAlister	St Kessog's Rectory, High Street, Auchterarder PH3 1AD	01764 662525
ST MARGARET'S COTTAGE	Rev. Roy Massie	St Rule's Manse, 8 Church Street, Monifieth DD5 4JP	01382 532607
ASHLUDIE	Rev. David Jamieson	Panmure Manse, 8A Albert Street, Monifieth DD5 4JS	01382 532772
DUNDEE, ROYAL LIFF	Rev. Janet Foggie	39 Tullidelph Road, Dundee DD2 2JD	01382 660152
ROYAL VICTORIA	Rev. Janet Foggie	39 Tullidelph Road, Dundee DD2 2JD	01382 660152
NINEWELLS			
STRATHMARTINE	Rev. Janet Foggie	39 Tullidelph Road, Dundee DD2 2JD	01382 660152
ARBROATH INFIRMARY	Rev. Alasdair G. Graham	1 Charles Avenue, Arbroath DD11 2EZ	01241 872244
BRECHIN INFIRMARY	Mr Gordon Anderson	33 Grampian View, Montrose DD10 9SU	01674 674915
FORFAR INFIRMARY	Rev. Graham Norrie	East Manse, Lour Road, Forfar DD8 2BB	01307 464303
LITTLE CAIRNIE	Rev. Ian G. Gough	St Vigeans Manse, Arbroath DD11 4RD	01241 873206

MONTROSE ROYAL	Rev. Iain Coltart	The Manse, Arbirlot, Arbroath DD11 2NX	01241 434479
STRACATHRO	Mr Gordon Anderson	33 Grampian View, Montrose DD10 9SU	01674 674915
SUNNYSIDE ROYAL	Mr Gordon Anderson	33 Grampian View, Montrose DD10 9SU	01674 674915

GRAMPIAN

Head of Spiritual Care:
Rev. Fred Coutts, Chaplains' Office, Aberdeen Royal Infirmary, Foresterhill, Aberdeen AB25 2ZN   01224 553166

1. ACUTE SECTOR
ABERDEEN ROYAL INFIRMARY, ABERDEEN MATERNITY HOSPITAL
Chaplains' Office, Aberdeen Royal Infirmary, Foresterhill, Aberdeen AB25 2ZN   01224 553316
Rev. Fred Coutts
Mrs Trudy Noble (Chaplain's Assistant)
Rev. Sylvia Spencer (Chaplain's Assistant)
Ms Monica Stewart (Chaplain's Assistant)

ROYAL ABERDEEN CHILDREN'S HOSPITAL
Chaplain's Office, Royal Aberdeen Children's Hospital, Westburn Drive, Aberdeen AB25 2ZG   01224 554905
Rev. James Falconer

ROXBURGHE HOUSE
Chaplain's Office, Roxburghe House, Ashgrove Road, Aberdeen AB25 2ZH   01224 557077
Rev. Alison Hutchison
Ms Monica Stewart

WOODEND HOSPITAL
Chaplain's Office, Woodend Hospital, Eday Road, Aberdeen AB15 6XS   01224 556788
Rev. Mark Rodgers

DR GRAY'S HOSPITAL, ELGIN
Rev. George Rollo, 18 Reidhaven Street, Elgin IV30 1QH   01343 547208
Rev. Andrew Willis, Deanshaugh Croft, Mulben, Keith AB55 6YJ   01542 860240

THE OAKS, ELGIN
Rev. Stuart Macdonald, 55 Forsyth Street, Hopeman, Elgin IV30 2SY   01343 831175

2. MENTAL HEALTH
ROYAL CORNHILL HOSPITAL, WOODLANDS
Chaplain's Office, Royal Cornhill Hospital, Cornhill Road, Aberdeen AB25 2ZH.   01224 557293
Rev. Muriel Knox
Miss Pamela Adam (Chaplain's Assistant)
Mr Donald Meston (Chaplain's Assistant)

3. COMMUNITY HOSPITALS

Hospital	Chaplain	Address	Tel.
ABOYNE	Rev. Douglas Campbell	49 Charlton Crescent, Aboyne AB24 5GN	01339 886447
GLEN O'DEE, BANCHORY	Rev. Donald Walker	2 Wilson Road, Banchory AB31 3UY	01330 822811
CAMPBELL, PORTSOY	Rev. Iain Sutherland	The Manse, Portsoy, Banff AB45 2QB	01261 842272
CHALMERS, BANFF	Rev. Alan Macgregor	7 Colleonard Road, Banff AB45 1DZ	01261 812107
FLEMING, ABERLOUR	Rev. Andrew Willis	Deanshaugh Croft, Mulben, Keith AB55 6YJ	01542 860240
FRASERBURGH	Rev. Andrew Lyon	23 Strichen Road, Fraserburgh AB43 9SA	01346 513303
INVERURIE	Rev. Ian B. Groves	1 Westburn Place, Inverurie AB51 5QS	01467 620285
INSCH	Rev. Jane Taylor	22 Western Road, Insch AB52 6JR	01464 820914
JUBILEE, HUNTLY	Rev. Thomas Calder	The Manse, Queen Street, Huntly AB54 5EB	01466 792630
KINCARDINE COMMUNITY,	Rev. Gordon Farquharson	Dunnottar Manse, Stonehaven AB39 3XL	01569 762874
STONEHAVEN	Rev. David Stewart	South Manse, Cameron Street, Stonehaven AB39 2HE	01569 762576
LEANCHOIL, FORRES	Rev. David Young	15 Mannachie Rise, Forres IV36 2US	01309 672284
LINKS UNIT, ABERDEEN	Rev. Marian Cowie	Chaplain's Office, Woodend Hospital, Aberdeen	01224 556788
MAUD	Rev. Alastair Donald	New Deer Manse, Turriff AB53 6TG	01771 644216
PETERHEAD COMMUNITY	Rev. David S. Ross	3–5 Abbey Street, Deer, Peterhead AB42 5LN	01771 623994
SEAFIELD, BUCKIE	Rev. Andrew Willis	Deanshaugh Croft, Mulben, Keith AB55 6YJ	01542 860240
STEPHEN, DUFFTOWN	Rev. Hugh M.C. Smith	The Manse, Church Street, Dufftown, Keith AB55 4AR	01340 820380
TURNER, KEITH	Rev. Kay Gauld	The Manse, Church Road, Keith AB55 5BR	01542 882799
TURRIFF	Rev. Sylvia Dyer	The Shieling, Westfield Road, Turriff AB53 4AF	01888 562530
UGIE, PETERHEAD	Mrs Sena Allen	Berea Cottage, Kirk Street, Peterhead AB42 1RY	01779 477327

HIGHLAND

Hospital	Chaplain	Address	Tel.
THE RAIGMORE HOSPITAL [01463 704000]	Rev. Iain MacRitchie	7 Merlin Crescent, Inverness IV2 3TE	
	Rev. Derek Brown	Cathedral Manse, Dornoch IV25 3HV	
IAN CHARLES	Rev. Morris Smith	Golf Course Road, Grantown-on-Spey PH26 3HY	01479 872084
ST VINCENT	Rev. Helen Cook	The Manse, West Terrace, Kingussie PH21 1HA	01340 661311
NEW CRAIGS	Rev. Michael Hickford	Chaplain's Office, New Craigs Hospital, Leachkin Road, Inverness IV3 8NP	01463 704000
NAIRN TOWN AND COUNTY	Rev. Ian Hamilton	3 Manse Road, Nairn IV12 4RN	01667 452203
BELFORD AND BELHAVEN	Rev. Donald A. MacQuarrie	Manse of Duncansburgh, Fort William PH33 6BA	01397 702297
GLENCOE	Rev. Alison Burnside	The Manse, Ballachulish PH49 4JG	01855 811998
ROSS MEMORIAL, DINGWALL	Rev. Russel Smith	8 Castlehill Road, Dingwall IV15 9PB	01349 861011
	Rev. Grahame M. Henderson	16 Achany Road, Dingwall IV15 9JB	01349 863167
INVERGORDON COUNTY	Rev. Kenneth D. Macleod	The Manse, Cromlet Drive, Invergordon IV18 0BA	01349 852273
LAWSON MEMORIAL	Rev. Eric Paterson	Free Church Manse, Golspie KW10 6TT	01408 633529
MIGDALE	Rev. Kenneth Hunter	Free Church Manse, Gower Street, Brora KW9 6PU	01408 621271
CAITHNESS GENERAL	Rev. William F. Wallace	The Manse, Coronation Street, Wick KW1 5LS	01955 603166
	Mr John Craw	'Craiglockhart', Latheronwheel, Latheron KW5 6DW	01593 741779
	Mr Howard Espie	The Cottage, Achorn Road, Dunbeath KW6 6ET	

DUNBAR	Rev. Ronald Johnstone	West Church Manse, Thorkel Road, Thurso KW14 7LW	01847 892663
BROADFORD MACKINNON MEMORIAL	Rev. Dr Ben Johnstone	The Shiants, 5 Upper Breakish, Breakish, Isle of Skye IV42 8PY	01471 822538
PORTREE	Rev. Iain Greenshields	The Manse, Kensaleyre, Snizort, Portree, Isle of Skye IV51 9XE	01470 532260
CAMPBELTOWN	Mrs Janice Forrest	The Manse, Southend, Campbeltown PA28 6RQ	01586 830274
LOCHGILPHEAD	Mrs Margaret Sinclair	2 Quarry Park, Furnace, Inveraray PA32 8XW	01499 500633
ISLAY	Rev. Stephen Fulcher	The Manse, Main Street, Port Charlotte, Isle of Islay PA48 7TW	01496 850241
DUNOON	Rev. Austin Erskine	99 Sandhaven, Sandbank, Dunoon PA23 8QW	01369 701295
DUNOON ARGYLL UNIT	Rev. Austin Erskine	99 Sandhaven, Sandbank, Dunoon PA23 8QW	01369 701295
ROTHESAY	Mr Raymond Deans	60 Ardmory Road, Rothesay PA20 0PG	01700 504893
LORN AND THE ISLANDS DISTRICT GENERAL	Rev. Elizabeth Gibson	Rudha-na-Cloiche, The Esplanade, Oban PA34 5AQ	01631 562759

WESTERN ISLES HEALTH BOARD

UIST AND BARRA HOSPITAL WESTERN ISLES, STORNOWAY	Rev. James MacDonald	8A Lower Bayble, Point, Lewis HS2 0QA	01851 870173

ORKNEY HEALTH BOARD

BALFOUR AND EASTBANK	Mrs Marion Dicken	6 Claymore Brae, Kirkwall KW15 1UQ	01856 879509

LIST D – FULL-TIME INDUSTRIAL CHAPLAINS

EDINBURGH (Edinburgh City Mission Appointment)	Mr John Hopper	26 Mulberry Drive, Dunfermline KY11 5BZ	01383 737189
EDINBURGH (Methodist Appointment)	Rev. Linda Bandelier	5 Dudley Terrace, Edinburgh EH6 4QQ	0131-554 1636
EDINBURGH (part-time)	Mrs Dorothy Robertson	45 Kirklands Park Crescent, Kirkliston EH29 9EP	0131-333 5414
GLASGOW	Rev. Elisabeth Spence	45 Selvieland Road, Glasgow G52 4ES	0141-883 8973 (Office) 0141-332 4458
WEST OF SCOTLAND	Rev. Alister Goss	79 Weymouth Crescent, Gourock PA19 1HR	01475 638944
OFFSHORE OIL INDUSTRY	Rev. Andrew Jolly	Total E and P UK PLC, Crawpeel Road, Aberdeen AB12 3FG	(Office) 01224 297532

	Mrs Cate Adams	15 Rousay Place, Aberdeen AB15 6HG	01224 643494/647470
ABERDEEN CITY CENTRE (part-time)			
NORTH OF SCOTLAND and NATIONAL CO-ORDINATOR	Mr Lewis Rose DCS	16 Gean Drive, Blackburn, Aberdeen AB21 0YN	01224 790145
TAYSIDE	Rev. Gareth T. Jones	65 Clepington Road, Dundee DD4 7BQ	01382 458764

LIST E – PRISON CHAPLAINS

CO-ORDINATOR (NATIONAL)	Rev. William Taylor	HM Prison, Edinburgh EH11 3LN	0131-444 3082
ABERDEEN CRAIGINCHES	Rev. Dr David Ross	HM Prison, Aberdeen AB1 2NE	01224 238300
	Rev. Louis Kinsey	HM Prison, Aberdeen AB1 2NE	01224 238300
CASTLE HUNTLY			
CORNTON VALE	Rev. Kay Gilchrist	HM Prison, Cornton Vale, Stirling FK9 5NU	01786 832591
DUMFRIES	Rev. Mark Rimmer	HM Prison, Dumfries DG2 9AX	01387 261218
	Rev. Neil Campbell	The Manse, Newton Stewart DG8 6HH	01671 402259
EDINBURGH: SAUGHTON	Rev. Colin Reed	Chaplaincy Centre, HMP Edinburgh EH11 3LN	0131-444 3115
	Rev. William Taylor	HM Prison, Edinburgh EH11 3LN	0131-444 3082
	Rev. Robert Akroyd	HM Prison, Edinburgh EH11 3LN	0131-444 3115
GLASGOW: BARLINNIE	Rev. Edward V. Simpson	5 Langtree Avenue, Glasgow G46 7LN	0141-638 8767
	Rev. Ian McInnes	46 Earlbank Avenue, Glasgow G14 9HL	0141-954 0328
	Rev. Douglas Clark	41 Kirkintilloch Road, Lenzie, Glasgow G66 4LB	0141-770 2184
	Rev. Alexander Wilson	HM Prison, Barlinnie, Glasgow G33 2QX	0141-770 2059
LOW MOSS	Rev. Dr William D. Moore	Chaplaincy Centre, HMP Low Moss, Glasgow G64 2QB	0141-762 4848
GLENOCHIL	Rev. Alan F.M. Downie	37A Claremont, Alloa FK10 2DG	01259 213872
GREENOCK	Rev. James Munro	80 Bardrainney Avenue, Port Glasgow PA14 6UD	01475 701213
INVERNESS	Rev. James Robertson	45 Oakdene Court, Culloden, Inverness IV2 7XZ	01463 790504
	Rev. Alexander Shaw	HM Prison, Inverness IV2 3HN	01463 229000
	Rev. Christopher Smart	HM Prison, Inverness IV2 3HN	01463 229000
KILMARNOCK	Rev. Andrew Black	HMP Bowhouse, Mauchline Road, Kilmarnock KA1 5AA	01563 548928
	Rev. Morag Dawson	206 Bank Street, Irvine KA12 0YB	01294 211403

NORANSIDE			
PERTH INCLUDING FRIARTON	Rev. Graham Matthews Mrs Deirdre Yellowlees	Chaplaincy Centre, HMP Perth PH2 8AT Ringmill House, Gannochy Farm, Perth PH2 7JH	01738 622293 01738 633773
PETERHEAD	Rev. Dr David Ross	HM Prison, Peterhead AB42 6YY	01779 479101
POLMONT	Rev. Donald H. Scott Rev. Daniel L. Mathers	Chaplaincy Centre, HMYOI Polmont, Falkirk FK2 0AB 10 Ercall Road, Brightons, Falkirk FK2 0RS	01324 711558 01324 872253
SHOTTS	Rev. Allan Brown	Chaplaincy Centre, HMP Shotts ML7 4LE	01501 824071

LIST F – UNIVERSITY CHAPLAINS

ABERDEEN	Easter Smart MDiv	01224 484271
ABERTAY, DUNDEE	Leslie M. Barrett BD FRICS	01382 308447
CALEDONIAN	Ewen MacLean BA BD (Honorary)	0141-558 7451
CAMBRIDGE	Keith Riglin (U.R.C. and C. of S.)	01223 503726
DUNDEE	Fiona C. Douglas BD PhD	01382 34157
EDINBURGH	Diane Williams	0131-650 2595
GLASGOW	Stuart D. MacQuarrie JP BD BSc	0141-330 5419
HERIOT-WATT	Howard G. Taylor BSc BD	0131-449 5111 (ext 4508)
NAPIER	Marion Chatterley	0131-455 4694
OXFORD	Susan Durber (U.R.C. and C. of S.)	01865 554358
PAISLEY	Morris M. Dutch BD BA	0141-571 4059
ROBERT GORDON	George Cowie BSc BD (Honorary)	01224 262000 (ext 3506)
ST ANDREWS	James B. Walker MA BD DPhil	01334 462866
STIRLING	Gillian Weighton BD STM (Honorary)	01786 832753
STRATHCLYDE	Marjory Macaskill LLB BD	0141-553 4144

LIST G – THE DIACONATE

NAME	COM	APP	ADDRESS	TEL	PRES
Allan, Jean (Mrs) DCS	1989	1988	12C Hindmarsh Avenue, Dundee DD3 7LW	01382 827299	29
Anderson, Janet (Miss) DCS	1979	1982	4 Clanranald Place, Arisaig PH39 4NN		38
Beaton, Margaret (Miss) DCS	1989	1988	64 Gardenside Grove, Carmyle, Glasgow G32 8EZ	0141-646 2297	16

Name	Year	Address / E-mail	Telephone	No.
Bell, Sandra (Mrs)	2001	62 Loganswell Road, Thornliebank, Glasgow G46 8AX	0141-638 5884	16
Black, Linda (Miss) BSc DCS	1993	148 Rowan Road, Abronhill, Cumbernauld, Glasgow G67 3DA [E-mail: lnan@blueyonder.co.uk]	01236 786265	22
Buchanan, John (Mr) DCS	1988	19 Gillespie Crescent, Edinburgh EH10 4HJ	0131-229 0794	3
Buchanan, Marion (Mrs) MA DCS	1983	2 Lenzie Road, Stepps, Glasgow G33 6DX	0141-779 5746	16
Burns, Marjorie (Mrs) DCS	1997	25 Barnsley Square, Corby, Northants NN18 0PQ [E-mail: mburns8069@aol.com]	01536 264819 / 07989 148464 (Mbl)	47
Cathcart, John Paul (Mr) DCS	1998	50 Alder Place, Greenhills, East Kilbride, Glasgow G75 9HP [E-mail: paulcathcart@msn.com]	01355 521906	17
Clark, Jean (Ms) DCS	2006	Flat 1/1, 15 Colston Grove, Bishopbriggs, Glasgow G64 1BF	07729 316321 (Mbl)	16
Corrie, Margaret (Miss) DCS	1989	44 Sunnyside Street, Camelon, Falkirk FK1 4BH	01324 670656	22
Craw, John (Mr) DCS	1998	'Craiglockhart', Latheronwheel, Latheron KW5 6DW	01593 741779	41
Crawford, Morag (Miss) MSc DCS	1977	118 Wester Drylaw Place, Edinburgh EH4 2TG [E-mail: morag.crawford@virgin.net]	0131-332 2253 (Tel/Fax) / 07970 982563 (Mbl)	24
Crocker, Elizabeth (Mrs) DCS DipComEd	1985	77C Craigcrook Road, Edinburgh EH4 3PH [E-mail: crock@crook77c.freeserve.co.uk]	0131-332 0227	1
Cunningham, Ian (Mr) DCS	1994	The Manse, Rothiemay, Huntly AB54 7NE	01466 711334	35
Cuthbertson, Valerie DipTMus DCS	2003	105 Bellshill Road, Motherwell ML1 3SJ [E-mail: vcuthbertson@tiscali.co.uk]	01698 259001	22
Deans, Raymond (Mr) DCS	1998	60 Ardmory Road, Rothesay, Isle of Bute PA20 0PG [E-mail: deans@fish.co.uk]	01700 504893	19
Douglas, Marilyn (Miss) DCS	1988	Heimdal, Quarff, Shetland ZE2 9JA	01950 447584	46
Dunnett, Linda (Mrs)	1976	17 Munro Road, Glasgow G13 1SQ	0141-959 3732	[16]
Evans, Mark (Mr) RGN DCS	1988	13 Easter Drylaw Drive, Edinburgh EH4 2QA [E-mail: mevansdcs@aol.com]	0141-552 4040 / 0131-343 3089 (Office)	1
Gargrave, Mary (Mrs) DCS	1989	229/2 Calder Road, Edinburgh EH11 4RG	0131-476 3493 / 0131-443 9452 (Office)	1
Gordon, Margaret (Mrs) DCS	1998	92 Lanark Road West, Currie EH14 5LA	0131-449 2554	1
Gray, Greta (Miss) DCS	1992	67 Crags Avenue, Paisley PA2 6SG	0141-884 6178	14
Hamilton, James (Mr) DCS	1997	6 Beckfield Gate, Glasgow G33 1SW [E-mail: j.hamilton111@btinternet.com]	0141-558 3195	16
Hamilton, Karen (Mrs) DCS	1995	6 Beckfield Gate, Glasgow G33 1SW [E-mail: k.hamilton6@btinternet.com]	0141-558 3195	16
Hughes, Helen (Miss) DCS	1977	2/2, 43 Burnbank Terrace, Glasgow G20 6UQ [E-mail: helenhughes@fish.co.uk]	0141-333 9459	16
King, Chris (Mrs) DCS	2002	28 Kinford, Dundonald, Kilmarnock KA2 9ET [E-mail: chrisking99@tiscali.co.uk]	01563 851197	10
King, Margaret (Miss) DCS	2002	56 Murrayfield, Fochabers IV32 7EZ	01343 820937	35
Lundie, Ann V. (Miss) DCS	1972	20 Langdykes Drive, Cove, Aberdeen AB12 3HW	01224 898416	31
Lyall, Ann (Miss) DCS	1980	117 Barria Drive, Glasgow G45 0AY [E-mail: annlyall@btinternet.com]	0141-631 3643	16
MacDonald, Anne (Miss) BA	1980	21 Campsie Road, East Kilbride, Glasgow G75 9GE	07976 786174 (Mbl)	16
McDowall, Sarah (Mrs) DCS	1991	116 Scott Road, Glenrothes KY6 1AE	01592 562386	25

Name			Address	Tel	No.
McKay, Kenneth (Mr) DCS	1996	1995	11F Balgowan Road, Letham, Perth PH1 2JG [E-mail: kennydandcs@hotmail.com]	01738 621169 (Mbl) 07952 076331	28
MacKinnon, Ronald (Mr) DCS	1996	1995	71 Cromarty Road, Cairnhill, Airdrie ML6 9RL	01236 762024	22
McLellan, Margaret (Mrs)	1986	1997	18 Broom Road East, Newton Mearns, Glasgow G77 5SD	0141-639 6853	16
McNaughton, Janette (Miss) DCS	1982	1997	4 Dunellan Avenue, Moodiesburn, Glasgow G69 0GB	01236 870180	22
McPheat, Elspeth (Miss)	1985	1997	11/5 New Orchardfield, Edinburgh EH6 5ET	0131-554 4143	1
Martin, Jane (Miss) DCS	1979	1979	16 Wentworth Road, Dundee DD2 3SD [E-mail: janimar@aol.com]	01382 813786	29
Mitchell, Joyce (Mrs) DCS	1994	1993	16/4 Murrayburn Place, Edinburgh EH14 2RR [E-mail: joyce@mitchell71.freeserve.co.uk]	0131-453 6548	1
Mulligan, Anne MA DCS	1974	1986	27A Craigour Avenue, Edinburgh EH17 7NH [E-mail: mulliganne@aol.com]	0131-664 3426 0131-242 1996	1
Munro, Patricia (Miss) BSc DCS	1986	2002	11 Hurlingham Square, Peterborough Road, London SW6 3DZ [E-mail: patmunro@tiscali.co.uk]	(Office) 020 7610 6994	47
Nicholson, David (Mr) DCS	1994	1993	2D Doonside, Kildrum, Cumbernauld, Glasgow G67 2HX	01236 732260 (Mbl) 07703 332270	22
Nicol, Joyce (Mrs) BA DCS	1974	1998	93 Brisbane Street, Greenock PA16 8NY	01475 723235 (Mbl) 07957 642709	14
Ogilvie, Colin (Mr) DCS	1998	1998	32 Upper Bairtree Court, Glasgow G67 2HX	0141-569 2750	16
Palmer, Christine (Ms) DCS	2003	2005	39 Fortingall Place, Perth PH1 2NF [E-mail: chrispalmer@blueyonder.co.uk]	01738 587488	28
Rennie, Agnes M. (Miss) DCS	1974	1979	3/1 Craigmillar Court, Edinburgh EH16 4AD	0131-661 8475	1
Rose, Lewis (Mr) DCS	1993	1998	16 Gean Drive, Blackburn, Aberdeen AB21 0YN [E-mail: scinmorth@uk.uumail.com]	01224 790145 (Mbl) 07899 790466	31
Ross, Duncan (Mr) DCS	1996	2006	4 Glasgow Road, Cambuslang, Glasgow G72 7BW [E-mail: ssornacnud@hotmail.com]	0141-641 1699	16
Rycroft-Sadi, Pauline (Mrs) DCS	2003		6 Ashville Terrace, Edinburgh EH6 8DD	0131-554 6564 (Mbl) 07759 436303	1
Steele, Marilynn J. (Mrs) BD DCS			2 Northfield Gardens, Prestonpans EH32 9LQ	01875 811497	1
Steven, Gordon BD DCS	1997		51 Nantwich Drive, Edinburgh EH7 6RB	0131-669 2054 (Mbl) 07904 385256	3
Stewart, Marion (Miss) DCS	1991	1994	Kirk Cottage, Kirkton of Skene, Westhill, Skene AB32 6XE	01224 743407	33
Thomson, Jacqueline (Mrs) MTh DCS			1 Barron Terrace, Leven KY8 4DL [E-mail: jacquelinethomson@blueyonder.co.uk]	01333 301115	24
Thomson, Phyllis (Miss) DCS	2003		63 Caroline Park, Mid Calder, Livingston EH53 0SJ	01506 883207	2
Urquhart, Barbara (Mrs) DCS	1986	1994	9 Standalane, Kilmaurs, Kilmarnock KA3 2NB	01563 538289	11
Wilson, Glenda (Mrs) DCS	1990	2006	Charity Cottage, Blairmore, Dunoon PA23 8TP	01369 810397	19
Wilson, Muriel (Miss) MA BD DCS	1997	2001	28 Bellevue Crescent, Ayr KA7 2DR	01292 264939	10
Wishart, William (Mr) DCS	1994	1993	10 Stanley Drive, Paisley PA2 6HE	0141-884 4177 (Mbl) 07971 422201	14
Wright, Lynda (Miss) BEd DCS	1979	1992	Key Cottage, High Street, Falkland, Cupar KY15 7BU	01337 857705	26

THE DIACONATE (Retired List)

NAME	COM	ADDRESS	TEL	PRES
Anderson, Catherine B. (Mrs) DCS	1975	13 Mosshill Road, Bellshill, Motherwell ML4 1NQ	01698 745907	17
Anderson, Mary (Miss) DCS	1955	33 Ryehill Terrace, Edinburgh EH6 8EN	0131-553 2818	1
Bayes, Muriel C. (Mrs) DCS	1963	Flat 6, Carleton Court, 10 Fenwick Road, Glasgow G46 4AN	0141-633 0865	16
Beaton, Jamesina (Miss) DCS	1953	Fairhills, Fort Augustus PH32 4DS	01320 366252	38
Bryden, Agnes Y. (Mrs) DCS	1963	Angusfield House, 226 Queen's Road, Aberdeen AB15 8DN		31
Cameron, Margaret (Miss) DCS	1961	2 Rowans Gate, Paisley PA2 6RD	0141-840 2479	14
Copland, Agnes M. (Mrs) MBE DCS	1950	3 Craigmuschat Road, Gourock PA19 1SE	01475 631870	14
Cunningham, Alison W. (Miss) DCS	1961	23 Strathblane Road, Milngavie, Glasgow G62 8DL	0141-563 9232	18
Drummond, Rhoda (Miss) DCS	1960	23 Grange Loan, Edinburgh EH9 2ER	0131-668 3631	1
Erskine, Morag (Miss) DCS	1979	111 Mains Drive, Park Mains, Erskine PA8 7JJ	0141-812 6096	14
Finlayson, Ellena B. (Miss) DCS	1963	16E Denwood, Summerhill, Aberdeen AB15 6JF	01224 321147	31
Flockhart, Andrew (Mr) DCS	1988	Flat 0/1, 8 Hardie Avenue, Rutherglen, Glasgow G73 3AS		16
Gillespie, Ann M. (Miss) DCS	1969	Barlochan House, Palnackie, Castle Douglas DG7 1PF	01556 600378	8
Gillon, Phyllis (Miss) DCS	1957	The Hermitage Home, 15 Hermitage Drive, Edinburgh EH10 6BX	0131-447 0664	1
Gordon, Fiona S. (Mrs) MA DCS	1958	Machrie, 3 Cupar Road, Cuparmuir, Cupar KY15 5RH [E-mail: machrie@madasafish.com]	01334 652341	26
Gray, Catherine (Miss) DCS	1969	10C Eastern View, Gourock PA19 1RJ	01475 637479	14
Gray, Christine (Mrs) DCS	1969	11 Woodside Avenue, Thornliebank, Glasgow G46 7HR	0141-571 1008	16
Howden, Margaret (Miss) DCS	1954	38 Munro Street, Kirkcaldy KY1 1PY	01592 205913	25
Hutchison, Alan E.W. (Mr) DCS	1988	132 Lochbridge Road, North Berwick EH39 4DR	01620 894077	3
Hutchison, Maureen (Mrs) DCS	1961	23 Drylaw Crescent, Edinburgh EH4 2AU	0131-332 8020	1
Johnston, Mary (Miss) DCS	1987	19 Lounsdale Drive, Paisley PA2 9ED	0141-849 1615	14
McBain, Margaret (Miss) DCS	1974	33 Quarry Road, Paisley PA2 7RD	0141-884 2920	14
McCallum, Moyra (Miss) MA BD DCS	1965	176 Hilton Drive, Aberdeen AB24 4LT [E-mail: moymac@aol.com]	01224 486240	31
McCully, M. Isobel (Miss) DCS	1974	10 Broadstone Avenue, Port Glasgow PA14 5BB	01475 742240	14
MacLean, Donald A. (Mr) DCS	1988	8 Upper Barvas, Isle of Lewis HS2 0QX	01851 840454	44
MacPherson, James B. (Mr) DCS	1988	104 Cartside Street, Glasgow G42 9TQ	0141-616 6468	16
MacQuien, Duncan (Mr) DCS	1988	35 Criffel Road, Mount Vernon, Glasgow G32 9JE	0141-575 1137	14
Malvenan, Dorothy (Miss) DCS	1937	Flat 19, 6 Craigie Street, Dundee DD4 6PF	01382 462495	29
Martin, Neil (Mr) DCS	1988	3 Strathmiglo Place, Stenhousemuir, Larbert FK5 4UQ	01324 551362	22
Merrilees, Ann (Miss) DCS	1994	0/1, 15 Crookston Grove, Glasgow G52 3PN [E-mail: ann@merrilees.freeserve.co.uk]	0141-883 2488	16
Miller, Elsie M. (Miss) DCS	1974	30 Swinton Avenue, Rowanbank, Baillieston, Glasgow G69 6JR	0141-771 0857	22

Name		Year	Address	Phone	No.
Morrison, Jean (Dr) DCS		1964	45 Corslet Road, Currie EH14 5LZ [E-mail: jean.morrison@blueyonder.co.uk]	0131-449 6859	1
Mortimer, Aileen (Miss) BSc DCS		1976	38 Sinclair Way, Knightsridge, Livingston EH54 8HW	01506 430504	2
Moyes, Sheila (Miss) DCS		1957	158 Pilton Avenue, Edinburgh EH5 2JZ	0131-551 1731	1
Nicol, Senga (Miss) DCS		1993	Forthbank Nursing Home, Drip Road, Raploch, Stirling FK8 1RR		16
Potts, Jean M. (Miss) DCS		1973	28B East Claremont Street, Edinburgh EH7 4JP	0131-557 2144	1
Ramsay, Katherine (Miss) MA DCS		1958	25 Homeroyal House, 2 Chalmers Crescent, Edinburgh EH9 1TP	0131-667 4791	1
Ronald, Norma A. (Miss) MBE DCS		1961	2B Saughton Road North, Edinburgh EH12 7HG	0131-334 8736	1
Rutherford, Ellen B. (Miss) MBE DCS		1962	41 Duncanston, Conon Bridge, Dingwall IV7 8JB	01349 877439	39
Scrimgeour, Alice M. (Miss) DCS		1950	265 Golfhill Drive, Glasgow G31 2PB	0141-564 9602	16
Smith, Catherine (Mrs) DCS		1964	21 Lingaro, Bixter, Shetland ZE2 9NN	01595 810207	46
Smith, Lillian (Miss) MA DCS		1977	6 Fintry Mains, Dundee DD4 9HF	01382 500052	29
Stuart, Anne (Miss) DCS		1966	19 St Colme Crescent, Aberdour, Burntisland KY3 0ST	01383 860049	24
Tait, Agnes (Mrs) DCS		1995	(Currently in Malawi)		
Teague, Yvonne (Mrs) DCS		1965	46 Craigcrook Avenue, Edinburgh EH4 3PX	0131-336 3113	1
Thom, Helen (Miss) BA DipEd MA DCS		1959	84 Great King Street, Edinburgh EH3 6QU	0131-556 5687	1
Trimble, Robert DCS		1988	5 Templar Rise, Livingston EH54 6PJ	01506 412504	2
Webster, Elspeth H. (Miss) DCS		1950	82 Broomhill Avenue, Burntisland KY3 0BP	01592 873616	25
Weir, Minnie Mullo (Miss) MA DCS		1934	37 Strathearn Court, Strathearn Terrace, Crieff PH7 3DS	01764 654189	
White, Elizabeth (Miss) DCS		1950	Rodger Park Nursing Home, Rutherglen, Glasgow G73 3QZ		16

THE DIACONATE (Supplementary List)

Name	Year	Address	Phone
Carson, Christine (Miss) MA DCS	1992	The Manse, Southend, Campbeltown PA28 6RQ	01586 830274
Forrest, Janice (Mrs)	1990	5 Bluebell Drive, Cheverel Court, Bedward CV12 0GE	02476 366031
Gilroy, Lorraine (Mrs)	1988	14 Eskview Terrace, Ferryden, Montrose DD10 9RD	01674 660345
Guthrie, Jennifer M. (Miss) DCS	1993	243 Western Avenue, Sandfields, Port Talbot, West Glamorgan SA12 7NF	01639 884855
Harris, Judith (Mrs)	1988	67C Farquhar Road, Edgbaston, Birmingham B18 2QP	
Hood, Katrina (Mrs)	1982	10 Albany Drive, Rutherglen, Glasgow G73 3QN	
Hudson, Sandra (Mrs)	1990	4 Jacklin Green, Livingston EH54 8PZ	01506 495472
McIntosh, Kay (Mrs) DCS	1969	77 Arthur Street, Dunfermline KY12 0JJ	
Muir, Alison M. (Mrs)	1978	2 Wykeham Close, Bassett, Southampton SO16 7LZ	
Ramsden, Christine (Miss)	1970	24 Brodie's Yard, Queen Street, Coupar Angus PH13 9RA	01828 628251
Walker, Wikje (Mrs)		4 Thornwood Court, Setauket, NY 11733, USA	
Wallace, Catherine (Mrs)			

LIST H – MINISTERS HAVING RESIGNED MEMBERSHIP OF PRESBYTERY

(in Terms of Act III 1992)

(Resignation of Presbytery membership does not imply the lack of a practising certificate.)

NAME	ORD	ADDRESS	TEL	PRES
Bailey, W. Grahame MA BD	1939	148 Craiglea Drive, Edinburgh EH10 5PU	0131-447 1663	1
Beck, John C. BD	1975	43A Balvenie Street, Dufftown, Keith AB55 4AS		35
Brown, Alastair BD	1986	52 Henderson Drive, Kintore, Inverurie AB51 0FB	01467 632787	32
Caie, Albert LTh	1983	34 Ringwell Gardens, Stonehouse, Larkhall ML9 3QW	01698 792187	32
Cooper, George MA BD	1943	8 Leighton Square, Alyth, Blairgowrie PH11 8AQ	01828 633746	27
Craig, Eric MA BD BA	1959	5 West Relugas Road, Edinburgh EH9 2PW	0131-667 8210	1
Craig, John W. MA BD	1951	83 Milton Road East, Edinburgh EH15 2NL	0131-657 2309	1
Crawford, Victor	1980	Crofton, 65 Main Road, East Wemyss, Kirkcaldy KY1 4RL	01592 712325	25
Cumming, David P.L. MA	1957	Shillong, Tarbat Ness Road, Portmahomack, Tain IV20 1YA	01862 871794	19
Drummond, R. Hugh	1953	19 Winton Park, Edinburgh EH10 7EX [E-mail: hughdrummond1@activemail.co.uk]	0131-445 3634	1
Ferguson, Ronald MA BD ThM	1972	Vinbreck, Orphir, Orkney KW17 2RE [E-mail: ronbluebrazil@aol.com]	01856 811378	45
Finlayson, Duncan MA	1943	Flat 3, Nicholson Court, Kinnettas Road, Strathpeffer IV14 9BG	01997 420014	39
Gordon, Alasdair B. BD LLB EdD	1970	31 Binghill Park, Milltimber, Aberdeen AB13 0EE [E-mail: alasdairbgordon@hotmail.com]	01224 732464	31
Greig, James C.G. MA BD STM	1955	Block 2, Flat 2, Station Lofts, Strathblane, Glasgow G63 9BD [E-mail: jgreig@netcomuk.co.uk]	01360 771915	16
Grubb, George D.W. BA BD BPhil DMin	1962	10 Wellhead Close, South Queensferry EH30 9WA	0131-331 2072	1
Hamilton, David S.M. MA BD STM	1958	2 Roselea Drive, Milngavie, Glasgow G62 8HQ	0141-956 1839	18
Hosie, James MA BD MTh	1959	Hilbre, Baycrofts, Strachur, Cairndow, Argyll PA27 8BY	01369 860634	19
Howie, William MA BD STM	1964	26 Morgan Road, Aberdeen AB16 5JY	01224 483669	31
Hurst, Frederick R. MA	1965	Apartment 10, 20 Abbey Drive, Glasgow G14 9JX	0141-959 2604	40
Lambie, Andrew BD	1957	1 Mercat Loan, Biggar ML12 6DG	01899 221352	13
Levison, Mary I. (Mrs) BA BD DD	1978	2 Gillsland Road, Edinburgh EH10 5BW	0131-228 3118	1
Lindsay, W. Douglas BD CPS	1978	3 Drummond Place, Calderwood, East Kilbride, Glasgow G74 3AD	01355 234169	16
Lynn, Joyce (Mrs) MIPM BD	1995	Calle San Jose No. 7, 04858 Codbar, Almería, Spain		29
McCaskill, George I.L. MA BD	1953	19 Tyler's Acre Road, Edinburgh EH12 7HY	0131-334 7451	1
Macfarlane, Alwyn J.C. MA	1957	Flat 12, Homeburn House, 177 Fenwick Road, Giffnock, Glasgow G46 6JD	0141-620 3235	1
Macfarlane, Donald MA	1940	8 Muirfield Gardens, Inverness IV2 4HF	01463 231977	37
Macfarlane, Kenneth	1963	9 Bonnington Road, Peebles EH45 9HF	01721 723609	4
Mackenzie, J.A.R. MA	1947	West Lodge, Inverness Road, Nairn IV12 4SD	01667 452827	26
McKenzie, Mary O. (Miss)	1976	4 Dunellan Avenue, Moodiesburn, Glasgow G69 0GB	01236 870180	16

Mackie, Steven G. MA BD	1956	38 Grange Loan, Edinburgh EH9 2NR	0131-667 9532	1
MacLeod, Ian I.S. MA BD	1954	St Margaret's, St Margaret's Crescent, Polmont, Falkirk FK2 0UP		22
Mair, John BSc	1965	21 Kenilworth Avenue, Helensburgh G84 7JR	01436 671744	18
Marshall, James S. MA PhD	1939	25 St Mary's Street, St Andrews KY16 8AZ	01334 476136	26
Miller, Irene B. (Mrs) MA BD	1984	5 Braeside Park, Aberfeldy PH15 2DT	01887 829396	27
Monro, George D. TD MA	1935			1
Morton, Andrew Q. MA BSc BD FRSE	1949	Sunnyside, 4A Manse Street, Aberdour, Burntisland KY3 0TY	0131-440 3321	18
Nelson, John MA BD	1941	7 Manse Road, Roslin EH25 9LF		3
Paterson, Ian M. MA	1947	45/15 Maidencraig Crescent, Edinburgh EH4 2UU	0131-332 9735	1
Reid, William M. MA BD	1966	10 Rue Rossini, F-75009 Paris, France		48
Shaw of Chapelverna, Duncan Bundesverdienstkreuz PhD ThDr Drhc JP				
Shaw, D.W.D. BA BD LLB WS DD	1951	4 Sydney Terrace, Edinburgh EH7 6SL	0131-669 1089	19
Skinner, Silvester MA	1960	4/13 Succoth Court, Edinburgh EH12 6BZ	0131-337 2130	26
Smith, J.A. Wemyss MA	1941	29 Silverbank Gardens, Banchory AB31 5YZ	0131 823032	32
Smith, Ralph C.P. MA STM	1947	Rapplaroan, 42 Beltie Road, Torphins, Banchory AB31 4JT	01339 882780	32
	1960	2A Waverley Road, Eskbank, Dalkeith EH22 3DJ [E-mail: rcpsmith@waitrose.com]	0131-663 1234	3
Speed, David K. LTh	1969	153 West Princes Street, Helensburgh G84 8EZ	01436 674493	16
Spowart, Mary G. (Mrs) BD	1978	Aldersyde, St Abbs Road, Coldingham, Eyemouth TD14 5NR	01890 771697	26
Swan, Andrew MA	1941	11 The Terrace, Ardbeg, Rothesay, Isle of Bute PA20 0NP	01700 502138	14
Taylor, Alexander T.H. MA BD	1938	4 The Pleasance, Strathkinness, St Andrews KY16 9SD	01334 850585	26
Urie, D.M.L. MA BD PhD	1940	7 Glebe Park, Kincardine O'Neil, Aboyne AB34 5ED	01339 884204	32
Weatherhead, James L. CBE MA LLB DD	1960	59 Brechin Road, Kirriemuir DD8 4DE	01575 572237	30
Webster, John BSc	1964	Plane Tree, King's Cross, Brodick, Isle of Arran KA27 8RG	01770 700747	16
Westmarland, Colin A.	1971	PO Box 5, Cospicua, CSPOI, Malta	00356 216 923552	48
Wilkie, George D. OBE BL	1948	2/37 Barnton Avenue West, Edinburgh EH4 6EB	0131-339 3973	1
Wylie, W. Andrew	1953	Well Rose Cottage, Peat Inn, Cupar KY15 5LH	01334 840600	26

LIST I – MINISTERS HOLDING PRACTISING CERTIFICATES (under Act II, as amended by Act VIII 2000)

NAME	ORD	ADDRESS	TEL	PRES
Aitken, Ewan R. BA BD	1992	159 Restalrig Avenue, Edinburgh EH7 6PJ	0131-447 4519	1
Alexander, Ian W. BA BD STM	1990	5 Comiston Gardens, Edinburgh EH10 5QH		1
Anderson, David MA BD	1975	Rowan Cottage, Aberlour Gardens, Aberlour AB38 9LD	01340 871906	35
Arbuthnott, Joan (Mrs) MA BD	1993	139/1 New Street, Musselburgh EH21 6DH	0131-665 6736	3

Name	Year	Address	Telephone	No.
Archer, Nicholas D.C. BA BD	1971	Hillview, Edderton, Tain IV19 4AJ	01862 821494	47
Bardgett, Frank D. MA BD PhD	1987	Tigh an Iasgair, Street of Kincardine, Boat of Garten PH24 3BY [E-mail: frank@bardgett.plus.com]	01479 831751	36
Beattie, Warren BSc BD	1991	33A Chancery Lane, Singapore 908554	0065 256 3208	1
Black, James S. BD DPS	1976	7 Breck Terrace, Penicuik EH26 0RJ [E-mail: jsb.black@btopenworld.com]	01968 677559	3
Blane, Quintin A. BSc BD MSc	1979	18D Kirkhill Road, Penicuik EH26 8HZ [E-mail: quintin@qab.org.uk]	01968 670017	3
Bowman, Norman M. MA BD	1940	18 Eglinton Court, Saltcoats KA21 5DN	01294 463453	12
Boyd, Ian R. MA BD PhD	1989	33 Castleton Drive, Newton Mearns, Glasgow G77 3LE		16
Boyd, Kenneth M. MA BD PhD	1970	1 Doune Terrace, Edinburgh EH3 6DY	0131-225 6485	1
Buchan, Isabel C. (Mrs) BSc BD RE(PgCE)	1975	26 Allan Robertson Drive, St Andrews KY16 8EY [E-mail: revicbuchan@bluebucket.org]	01334 473875	26
Caie, Albert LTh	1983	34 Ringwell Gardens, Stonehouse, Larkhall ML9 3QW	01698 792187	32
Campbell, Thomas R. MA BD	1986	Craigleith, Bowfield Road, Howwood, Johnstone PA9 1BS	01505 702461	14
Cobain, Alan R. BD	2000	39F Spa Street, Aberdeen AB25 1PT	01224 637133	31
Currie, Gordon C.M. MA BD	1975	43 Deanburn Park, Linlithgow EH49 6HA	01506 842759	2
Davies, Gareth W. BA BD	1979	Pitadro House, Fordell Gardens, Dunfermline KY11 7EY	01383 417634	24
Dickson, Graham T. MA BD	1985	19/4 Stead's Place, Edinburgh EH6 5DY [E-mail: gtd22@blueyonder.co.uk]	0131-476 0187	1
Drummond, Norman W. MA BD	1976	c/o Columba 1400 Ltd, Staffin, Isle of Skye IV51 9JY	01478 611400	42
Ellis, David W. GIMechE GIProdE	1962	4 Wester Tarsappie, Rhynd Road, Perth PH2 8PT	01738 449618	16
Ferguson, Sinclair B. MA BD PhD	1971	Westminster Seminary, 3878 Oak Lawn Avenue, Dallas, TX 75219, USA		16
Fleming, Thomas G.	1961			22
Flockhart, D. Ross OBE BA BD DUniv	1955	Longwood, Humbie EH36 5PN [E-mail: rossflock@ednet.co.uk]	01875 833208	3
Fowler, Richard C.A. BSc MSc BD	1978	4 Gardentown, Whalsay, Shetland ZE2 9AB	01806 566538	46
Fraser, Ian M. MA BD PhD	1946	Ferndale, Gargunnock, Stirling FK8 3BW	01786 860612	23
Frew, John M. MA BD	1946	17 The Furrows, Walton-on-Thames KT12 3JQ		16
Fyall, Robert S. MA BD PhD	1986	Rutherford House, 17 Claremont Park, Edinburgh EH6 7PJ	0131-554 1206	1
Gillies, Jan E. (Mrs) BD	1998	18 McInyre Lane, Macmerry, Tranent EH33 1QL [E-mail: jgillies@fish.co.uk]		3
Gilmour, Robert M. MA BD	1942	'Bellevue', Station Road, Watten, Wick KW1 5YN	01955 621317	37
Grubb, George D.W. BA BD BPhil DMin	1962	10 Wellhead Close, South Queensferry EH30 9WA	0131-331 2072	1
Gunn, F Derek BD	1986	6 Yardley Place, Falkirk FK2 7FH	01324 624938	22
Hamilton David S.M. MA BD STM	1958	2 Roselea Drive, Milngavie, Glasgow G62 8HQ	0141-956 1839	18
Hendrie, Yvonne (Mrs)	1995	6 Craigneen Place, Whitehills, Banff AB45 2NE	01261 861671	34
Hibbert, Frederick W. BD	1986	4 Cemydd Terrace, Senghemydd, Caerphilly, Mid Glamorgan CF83 4HL	02920 831653	1
Higgins, G.K.	1957	150 Broughty Ferry Road, Dundee DD4 6JJ	01382 461288	29
Howitt, Jane M. (Miss) MA BD	1996	PO Box 476, LV-1050 Riga 50, Latvia		16
Ireland, Andrew BA BTh DipRD	1963	48 Jubilee Court, St Margaret's Street, Dunfermline KY12 7PE	01383 732223	24
Jack, Alison M. MA BD PhD	1998	Glenallan, Doune Road, Dunblane FK15 9AT	01786 823241	23

Name	Year	Address	Phone	No.
Jamieson, Esther M.M. (Mrs) BD	1984	1 Redburn, Bayview, Stornoway HS1 2UV [E-mail: ejamieson@freeuk.com]	01851 704789	44
Johnstone, Donald B.	1969	22 Glenhove Road, Cumbernauld, Glasgow G67 2JZ	01236 612479	22
Johnstone, Robert MTheol	1973	59 Cliffburn Road, Arbroath DD11 5BA	01241 439292	32
Lawrie, Robert M. BD MSc DipMin LLCM(TD)	1994	West Benview, Main Road, Langbank, Port Glasgow PA14 6XP	01475 540240	14
Liddiard, F.G.B. MA	1957	34 Trinity Fields Crescent, Brechin DD9 6YF	01356 622966	30
Logan, Thomas M. LTh	1971	3 Duncan Court, Kilmarnock KA3 7TF	01563 524398	11
Macaskill, Donald MA BD PhD	1994	44 Forfar Avenue, Glasgow G52 3JQ	0141-883 5956	16
McCaskill, George I.L. MA BD	1953	19 Tyler's Acre Road, Edinburgh EH12 7HY	0131-334 7451	1
McDonald, Ross J. BA BD ThM	1998			
Macfarlane, Kenneth	1963	9 Bonnington Road, Peebles EH45 9HF	01721 723609	4
McKean, Martin J. BD DipMin	1984	56 Kingsknowe Drive, Edinburgh EH14 2JX	0131-466 1157	1
Mackie, Steven G. MA BD	1956	38 Grange Loan, Edinburgh EH9 2NR	0131-667 9532	1
McLean-Foreman, Anthony R.C.	1995			
McLellan, Andrew MA BD STM DD	1970	4 Liggars Place, Dunfermline KY12 7XZ	01383 725959	1
MacPherson, Gordon C.	1963	203 Capelrig Road, Patterton, Newton Mearns, Glasgow G77 6ND	0141-616 2107	16
McPherson, William BD DipEd	1993	83 Laburnum Avenue, Port Seton, Prestonpans EH32 0UD	01875 812252	22
Mailer, Colin (Aux)	1996	Innis Chonain, Back Row, Polmont, Falkirk FK2 0RD	01324 712401	
Main, Arthur W.A. BD	1954	13/3 Eildon Terrace, Edinburgh EH3 5NL	0131-556 1344	16
Manners, Stephen MA BD	1989	124 Fernieside Crescent, Edinburgh EH17 7DH	0131-620 0589	1
Marr, Ian MA BD	1984	116 Jeanfield Road, Perth PH1 1LP	01738 632530	28
Masson, John D. MA BD PhD BSc	1984	2 Beechgrove, Craw Hall, Brampton CA8 1TS	ex-directory	7
Matheson, Iain G. BD BMus	1985	16 New Street, Musselburgh EH21 6JP [E-mail: igmatheson@tiscali.co.uk]	0131-665 2128	3
Millar, Peter W. MA BD PhD	1971	35/6 Mid Steil, Edinburgh EH10 5XB [E-mail: ionacottage@hotmail.com]	0131-447 6186	1
Miller, Irene B. (Mrs) MA BD	1984	5 Braeside Park, Aberfeldy PH15 2DT	01887 829396	27
Mills, Archibald MA PhD	1953	32 High Street, South Queensferry EH30 9PP	0131-331 3906	1
Moodie, Alastair R. MA BD	1978	5 Buckingham Terrace, Glasgow G12 8EB		16
Morton, Andrew Q. MA BSc BD FRSE	1949	Sunnyside, 4A Manse Street, Aberdour, Burntisland KY3 0TY	01575 574937	18
Mowbray, Harry (Aux)	2003	Viewlands, Beechwood Place, Kirriemuir DD8 5DZ	01704 543044	30
Munro, Alexander W. MA BD	1978	Columba House, 12 Alexandra Road, Southport PR9 0NB	0131-556 3505	47
Newell, Alison M. (Mrs) BD	1986	1A Inverleith Terrace, Edinburgh EH3 5NS [E-mail: alinewell@aol.com]		1
Newell, J. Philip	1982	1A Inverleith Terrace, Edinburgh EH3 5NS	0131-556 3505	1
Ostler, John H. MA LTh	1975	52E Middleshot Square, Prestonpans EH32 9RJ	01875 814358	3
Owen, Catherine W. MTh	1984	10 Waverley Park, Kirkintilloch, Glasgow G66 2BP	0141-776 0407	16
Provan, Iain W. MA BA PhD	1991	Regent College, 5800 University Boulevard, Vancouver BC V6T 2E4, Canada	001 604 224 3245	1
Quigley, Barbara D. (Mrs) MTheol ThM DPS	1979			
Reamonn, Paraic BA BD	1982	7 Albany Terrace, Dundee DD3 6HQ	01382 223059	29
Rodwell, Anna J. (Mrs) BD DipMin	1998	Stewards House, Whitton, Morebattle, Kelso TD5 8QX	01573 440761	6

Name	Year	Address	Phone	
Sawers, Hugh BA	1968	2 Rosemount Meadows, Castlepark, Bothwell, Glasgow G71 8EL	01698 853960	17
Scouller, Hugh BSc BD	1985	The Mercat Hotel, High Street, Haddington EH41 3EP [E-mail: hughscouller@hotmail.com]		3
Shaw, D.W.D. BA BD LLB WS DD	1960	4/13 Succoth Court, Edinburgh EH12 6BZ	0131-337 2130	26
Squires, J. Finlay R. MA BD	1964	16 Bath Street, Stonehaven AB39 2DH	01569 762458	32
Steenbergen, Pauline (Ms) MA BD		1 Landale Road, Peterhead AB42 1QN	01779 472141	34
Stewart, Anne S. (Mrs) BD	1998	35 Rose Crescent, Perth PH1 1NT	01738 624167	28
Stewart, Margaret L. (Mrs) BSc MB ChB BD	1985	28 Inch Crescent, Bathgate EH48 1EU	01506 653428	2
Storrar, William F. MA BD PhD	1984	Director, Centre of Theological Enquiry, 50 Stockton Street, Princeton, NJ 08540, USA		1
Strachan, David G. BD DPS	1978	1 Deeside Park, Aberdeen AB15 7PQ	01224 324101	31
Strachan, Gordon MA BD PhD	1963	59 Merchiston Crescent, Edinburgh EH10 5AH	0131-229 3654	1
Tollick, Frank BSc DipEd	1958	3 Bellhouse Road, Aberdour, Burntisland KY3 0TL	01383 860559	24
Turnbull, Julian S. BSc BD MSc CEng MBCS	1980	25 Hamilton Road, Gullane EH31 2HP [E-mail: jules-turnbull@zetnet.co.uk]	01620 842958	3
Weatherhead, James L. CBE MA LLB DD	1960	59 Brechin Road, Kirriemuir DD8 4DE	01575 572237	30
Weir, Mary K. (Mrs) BD PhD	1968	1249 Millar Road RR1, SITEH-46, BC V0N 1G0, Canada	001 604 947 0636	1
Williams, Linda J. (Mrs) BD	1993	The Manse, Kirtlebridge, Lockerbie DG11 3LY [E-mail: ljpwilliams@btopenworld.com]	01461 500378	7
Winn, Fiona M.M. MA BD RGN	1994	35 Ashwood Avenue, Melbourne 3190, Australia	0061 3 9555 2038	1
Wood, Peter J. MA BD	1993	97 Broad Street, Cambourne, Cambridgeshire CB3 6DH	01954 205216	47

LIST J – PRESBYTERY ADVISERS AND FACILITATOR

ANGUS PRESBYTERY CONGREGATIONAL DEVELOPMENT ADVISER	Mr Gordon Anderson	33 Grampian View, Ferryden, Montrose DD10 9SU	01674 674915
GLASGOW PRESBYTERY CONGREGATIONAL FACILITATOR	Rev. John K. Collard MA BD	1 Nelson Terrace, East Kilbride, Glasgow G74 2EY	01355 520093
HAMILTON PRESBYTERY CONGREGATIONAL DEVELOPMENT OFFICER	Mr David Geddes	108 Maxwelton Avenue, East Kilbride, Glasgow G74 3DU	01355 235998

LIST K – OVERSEAS LOCATIONS

EUROPE

AMSTERDAM
Rev. John A. Cowie (1990) and Mrs Gillian Cowie
Jan Willem Brouwersstraat 9, NL-1071 LH Amsterdam, The Netherlands
[E-mail: j.cowie2@chello.nl; Website: www.ercadam.nl]
The English Reformed Church, The Begijnhof (off the Spui). Service each Sunday at 10:30am.
(Tel) 0031 20 672 2288
(Fax) 0031 20 676 4895

BRUSSELS
Rev. Dr Andrew Gardner (2004) and Mrs Julie Gardner
23 Square des Nations, B-1000 Brussels, Belgium
[E-mail: andrewgar@pro.tiscali.be; Website: www.welcome.to/st-andrews]
St Andrew's Church, Chaussée de Vleurgat 181 (off Ave. Louise). Service each Sunday at 11:00am.
[E-mail: st-andrews@welcome.to]
(Tel/Fax) 0032 2 672 40 56

BUDAPEST
St Columba's Scottish Mission, Vorosmarty utca 51, H-1064 Budapest, Hungary
Service in English and Sunday School each Sunday at 11:00am.
The General Synod of the Reformed Church in Hungary, 1440 Budapest, PF5, Hungary
[E-mail: zsinat.kulugy@zsinatiroda.hu]
(Church Tel) 0036 1 343 8479

(Tel/Fax) 0036 1 460 0708

COSTA DEL SOL
Rev. John Shedden and Mrs Jeannie Shedden (2005)
Services at Lux Mundi Ecumenical Centre, Calle Nueva 7, Fuengirola. Service each Sunday at 10:30am.

GENEVA
Rev. Ian A. Manson (2001) and Mrs Roberta Manson
[E-mail: cofsg@pingnet.ch; Website: www.churchofscotlandgeneva.com]
20 Ancienne Route, CH-1218 Grand Saconnex, Geneva, Switzerland
The Calvin Auditoire, Place de la Taconnerie (beside Cathedral of St Pierre). Service each Sunday at 11:00am.
(Tel/Fax) 0041 22 798 29 09

GIBRALTAR
Rev. Stewart J. Lamont (2003) and Mrs Lara Lamont
St Andrew's Manse, 29 Scud Hill, Gibraltar
St Andrew's Church, Governor's Parade. Service each Sunday at 10:30am.
[E-mail: lamont@gibraltar.gi]
(Tel) 00350 77040
(Fax) 00350 40852

LAUSANNE
Rev. Melvyn Wood (2004) and Mrs Doreen Wood
26 Avenue de Rumine, CH-1005 Lausanne, Switzerland
[E-mail: scotskirklausanne@bluewin.ch]
Service each Sunday at 10:30am.
(Tel/Fax) 0041 21 323 98 28

LISBON
Rev. William B. Ross and Mrs Maureen Ross (2006)
St Andrew's Church, Rua da Arriaga 13–15, Lisbon. Service each Sunday at 11:00am.

MALTA

Rev. David Morris (2003) and Mrs Jacky Morris (not Church of Scotland)
[E-mail: djlmorris@onvol.net]
La Romagnola, 13 Triq is-Sieqjamisrah Eola, Attard BZN 05
St Andrew's Church, 210 Old Bakery Street, Valletta. Service each Sunday at 10:30am.
(Tel/Fax) 00356 222 643

PARIS

Vacant
10 Rue Thimonnier, F-75009 Paris, France
[E-mail: scotskirk@wanadoo.fr; Website: www.scotskirkparis.com]
The Scots Kirk, 17 Rue Bayard, F-75008 Paris (Metro: Roosevelt)
Service each Sunday at 10:30am.
(Tel/Fax) 0033 1 48 78 47 94

ROME

Rev. William B. McCulloch (2001) and Mrs Jean McCulloch
[E-mail: revwbmcculloch@hotmail.com]
Via XX Settembre 7, 00187 Rome, Italy. Service each Sunday at 11:00am.
(Tel) 0039 06 482 7627
(Fax) 0039 06 487 4370

ROTTERDAM

Rev. Robert A. Calvert (1995) and Mrs Lesley-Ann Calvert
Gelebrem 59, NL-3068 TJ Rotterdam, The Netherlands
[E-mail: scotsintchurch@cs.com; Website: www.scotsintchurch.com]
The Scots Kirk, Schiedamsevest 121, Rotterdam. Service each Sunday at 10:30am.
Informal service at 9:15am.
(Tel/Fax) 0031 10 220 4199
(Tel) 0031 10 412 4779

AFRICA

KENYA

Presbyterian Church of East Africa
Dr Alison Wilkinson (1992)
PCEA Chogoria Hospital, PO Box 35, Chogoria, Kenya   (Fax) 00254 166 22122
[E-mail: alisonjwilkinson@swiftkenya.com]

MALAWI

Church of Central Africa Presbyterian
Synod of Blantyre

Synod of Livingstonia
Dr Andrew and Mrs Felicity Gaston (1997)
Miss Helen Scott (2000, held previous appointment)
LISAP, PO Box 279, Ekwendeni, Malawi
CCAP Girls' Secondary School, PO Box 2, Ekwendeni, Malawi

SOUTH AFRICA

Rev. Graham Duncan (1998, held previous appointment)
and Mrs Sandra Duncan (1998)
56 Daphne Road, Maroelana 00081, Pretoria, South Africa

ZAMBIA

United Church of Zambia
Rev. Colin D. Johnston (1994) (Ecum)
PO Box 21225, Kitwe, Zambia
[E-mail: revcdj@zamnet.zm]
Mr Brian Payne (2002) and Mrs Georgina Payne (2002) (Ecum)
United Church of Zambia Synod Office, Lusaka, Zambia
[E-mail: uczsynod@zamnet.zm]
(Tel) 00260 1 250 641
(Fax) 00260 1 252 198

THE CARIBBEAN, CENTRAL AND SOUTH AMERICA

BAHAMAS

Rev. Terry Purvis-Smith (2006) — St Andrew's Manse, PO Box N1099, Nassau
(Tel) 001 242 322 5475
(Fax) 001 242 323 1960

Rev. Scott R.McL. Kirkland (2006) — Lucaya Presbyterian Kirk, PO Box F-40777, Freeport
(Tel) 001 242 373 2568
(Fax) 001 242 373 4961

BERMUDA

Rev. T. Alan W. Garrity (1999) and Mrs Elizabeth Garrity — The Manse, PO Box PG88, Paget PGBX, Bermuda [E-mail: revtawg@logic.bm *and* christchurch@logic.bml] and [Church website: www.christchurch.bm]
(Tel) 001 441 236 0400
(Tel) 001 441 236 1882
(Fax) 001 441 232 0552

JAMAICA

United Church of Jamaica and Grand Cayman

Rev. Margaret Fowler (1988) — PO Box 3097, Negril, Westmoreland, Jamaica [E-mail: revm@cwjamaica.com]
(Tel) 001 876 640 0846

TRINIDAD

Rev. Garwell Bacchas — Church of Scotland Greyfriars St Ann's, 50 Frederick Street, Port of Spain, Trinidad [E-mail: greyfriars@tstt.net.tt]
(Tel) 001 868 623 6634

ASIA

BANGLADESH

Church of Bangladesh

Mr James Pender (2004) (Ecum) — c/o St Thomas' Church, 54 Johnston Road, Dhaka 1100, Bangladesh [E-mail: ohenepender@yahoo.co.uk]

Mr David Hall and Mrs Sarah Hall (2005) (Ecum) — c/o St Thomas' Church, 54 Johnston Road, Dhaka 1100, Bangladesh

Dr Helen Brannam (2006) (Ecum) — c/o St Thomas' Church, 54 Johnston Road, Dhaka 1100, Bangladesh

Ecumenical Appointments

CHINA

Together with Scottish Churches China Group

Mr Ian Groves (1996)

Mr Mick and Mrs Anne Kavanagh (1997) — Amity Foundation, Overseas Office, 4 Jordan Road, Kowloon, Hong Kong Nanping Teachers' College, 16 Wuyi Dadao, Wuyi Shan, Fusdan Province 354800, PR of China

Kate Keir (2004) — Dingxi Teachers' College, Dingxi, Gansu Province 743000, PR of China

Margaret Scarlett (2005) — Yousiang Teachers' College for Nationalists, Baise City, Guangxi Zhuang Minority Autonomous Region, Guangxi Province 533000, PR of China

Michelle Adams (2005) — Wuwei Occupational College, 21 Xian Jian Road, Xi Guan Street, Wuwei, Gansu Province 733000, PR of China

Andrew MacLeod (2005) — Hexi College, 87 Bei Huan Road, Zhangye, Gansu Province 734000, PR of China

Placements for Kate Jarman, Christine Green, Angela Evans and David Clements are not yet known.

NEPAL

United Mission to Nepal

Mrs Marianne Karsgaard (2001) — PO Box 126, Kathmandu, Nepal [E-mail: marianne@wlink.com.np]
(Fax) 00977 1 225 559

SRI LANKA	**Presbytery of Lanka**	
	Rev. John P.S. Purves BSc BD (2003)	St Andrew's Scots Kirk, Colombo
		St Andrew's Church Manse, 73 Galle Road, Colombo 3, (Tel) 0094 1386 774
		Sri Lanka
		[E-mail: reverend@sltnet.lk]

MIDDLE EAST AND NORTH AFRICA

ISRAEL	[NOTE: Church Services are held in St Andrew's Scots Memorial Church, Jerusalem, each Sunday at 10am, and at St Andrew's, Galilee (contact minister for worship time)]
	Jerusalem
	Rev. Clarence W. Musgrave (2000) St Andrew's, Jerusalem, PO Box 8619, Jerusalem 91086, Israel
	and Mrs Joan Musgrave (Tel: 00972 2 6732401; Fax: 00972 2 673 1711)
	[E-mail: standjer@netvision.net.il; Private E-mail: stachjer@netvision.net.il;
	Website: www.scothotels.co.il]
	Tiberias
	Vacant St Andrew's, Galilee, PO Box 104, Tiberias, Israel
	[E-mail: scottie@netvision.net.il] (Tel: 00972 6 6721165; Fax: 00972 6 6790145)
	[Website: www.scothotels.co.il]
	Jaffa
	Ms Malti Joshi (2005) Tabeetha School, PO Box 8170, 21 Yefet Street, Jaffa, Israel
	(Tel: 00972 3 6821581; Fax: 00972 3 6819357)
	[E-mail: costab@zahav.net.il;
	Website: www.tabeetha.htmlplant.com]
	Tabeetha School
	Mrs Karen Anderson (1992) Tabeetha School

LIST L – OVERSEAS RESIGNED AND RETIRED MISSION PARTNERS (ten or more years' service)

NAME	APP	RET	AREA	ADDRESS
Aitken, Faith (Mrs)	1957	1968	Nigeria	High West, Urlar Road, Aberfeldy PH15 2ET
	1987	1990	Zambia	
Anderson, Kathleen (Mrs)	1955	1968	Pakistan	1A Elms Avenue, Great Shelford, Cambridge CB2 5LN
Archibald, Mary L. (Miss)	1964	1982	Nigeria/Ghana	490 Low Main Street, Wishaw ML2 7PL
Barbour, Edith R. (Miss)	1952	1983	North India	13/11 Pratik Nagar, Yerwada, Pune 411006, Maharashtra, India

Name	Year	Country	Address
Baxter, Rev. Richard and Mrs Ray	1954	Malawi	138 Braid Road, Edinburgh EH10 6JB
Berkeley, Dr John and Dr Muriel	1967	Bhutan	Drumbeg, Coylumbridge, Aviemore PH22 1QU
Boyle, Lexa (Miss)	1995	Yemen	7 Maxwell Grove, Glasgow G41 5JP
Bone, Mr David and Mrs Isobel	1959, 1977	Aden/Yemen/Sudan; Malawi	315 Blackness Road, Dundee DD2 1SH
Bone, Elizabeth (Mrs)	1950, 1980	Malawi; Malawi	2A Elm Street, Dundee DD2 2AY
Brodie, Rev. Jim	1955, 1996	North India; Nepal	25A Keptie Road, Arbroath DD11 3ED
Brown, Janet H. (Miss)	1967	Pakistan	6 Baxter Park Terrace, Dundee DD4 6NL
Burnett, Dr Fiona	1988	Zambia	The Glenholm Centre, Broughton, Biggar ML12 6JF
Burnett, Dr Robin and Mrs Storm	1964, 1968	Nigeria; South Africa	79 Bank Street, Irvine KA12 0LL
Burt, M.R.C. (Miss)	1940	Kenya	22 The Loaning, Chirnside, Duns TD11 3YE
Byers, Rev. Alan and Rev. Mairi	1960, 1957	Ghana; Livingstonia	Meadowbank, Plumdon Road, Annan DG12 6SJ
Campbell, George H.	1967	North India	20 Woodlands Grove, Kilmarnock KA3 1TZ
Coltart, Rev. Ian O.	1963	India	The Manse, Arbirlot, Arbroath DD11 2NX
Conacher, Marion (Miss)	1966	Kenya	41 Magdalene Drive, Edinburgh EH15 3BG
Cooper, Rev. George	1969	North India	69 Montpelier Park, Edinburgh EH10 4WD
Cowan, Dr Betty	1955	Nigeria	2 Sunningdale Square, Kilwinning KA13 6PH
Crosbie, Ann R. (Miss)	1976	Malawi	21 Fieldhead Square, Glasgow G43 IHL
Dawson, Miss Anne	1954	North India	5 Cattle Market, Clackmannan FK10 4EH
Dick, Dr James and Mrs Anne	1957	Nepal	1 Tummel Place, Comrie, Crieff PH6 2PG
Dodman, Rev. Roy and Mrs Jane	1983	Jamaica	PO Box 64, Stony Hill, Kingston 9, Jamaica
Dougall, Ian C.	1960	Kenya	60B Craigmillar Park, Edinburgh EH16 5PU
Drever, Dr Bryan	1962	Aden/Yemen/Pakistan	188 Addison Road, King's Head, Birmingham
Duncan, Mr David and Mrs Allison	1952	Nigeria	7 Newhailes Avenue, Musselburgh EH21 6DW
Dunlop, Mr Walter T. and Mrs Jennifer	1979	Malawi/Israel	50 Oxgangs Road, Edinburgh EH13 9DR
Fauchelle, Rev. Don and Mrs Margaret	1971, 1991	Zambia, Malawi, Zimbabwe	Flat 3, 22 North Avenue, Devonport, Auckland 1309, New Zealand
Ferguson, Mr John K.P.	1977	Pakistan	15 Ashgrove, Craigshill, Livingston EH54 5JQ
Finlay, Carol (Ms)	1990	Malawi	96 Broomfield Crescent, Edinburgh EH12 7LX
Fischbacher, Dr Colin M. and Mrs Sally	1986, 1968	Malawi; Kenya	11 Barclay Square, Gosforth, Newcastle-upon-Tyne NE3 2JB
Foster, Joyce (Miss) BSc	1972	Malawi	99 Sixth Street, Newtongrange EH22 4LA

Name			Country	Address
Fucella, Rev. Mike and Mrs Jane	1990	2006	Thailand	95/5 Sathorn SOI 9, Pikul, Sathorn Road, Yannawa, Sathorn, Bangkok 10120, Thailand
Gall, E.G. (Miss)	1940	1962	Blantyre	151 Raeburn Heights, Glenrothes KY16 1BW
Hutchison, C.M. (Mr)	1951	1972	Calabar	75 Grampian Road, Torry, Aberdeen AB11 8ED
Irvine, Mr Clive and Mrs Su	1984	1999	Nepal	McGregor Flat, 92 Blackford Avenue, Edinburgh EH9 3ES
Irvine, Elsabe (Mrs)	1951	1987	Malawi	60 Thirlestane Road, Edinburgh EH9 1AR
Irvine, Dr Geoffrey C. and Mrs Dorothy	1952	1989	Kenya	Lakeside, PO Box 1356 Naivasha, Kenya
Karam, Ishbel (Mrs)	1968	1985	Pakistan	Hillsgarth, Baltasound, Unst, Shetland ZE2 9DY
King, Dr Alistair and Mrs Betty	1955	1971	North India	23 Main Street, Newstead, Melrose TD6 9DX
Knowles, Dr John K. and Mrs Heather	1976	1992	Malawi	Trollopes Hill, Monton Combe, Bath BA2 7HX
Laidlay, Dr Rorie and Mrs Una	1961	1968	Yemen	Isles View, 5 Bell's Road, Lerwick, Shetland ZE1 0QB
	1968	1971	Pakistan	
	1971	1978	Yemen	
Liddell, Margaret (Miss)	1964	1980	Zambia	20 Wyvis Crescent, Conon Bridge, Dingwall IV7 8BZ
Logie, Robina (Mrs)	1950	1960	North India	23 Stonefield Drive, Inverurie AB5 9DZ
Lyon, Rev. D.H.S.	1952	1972	Nagpur	30 Mansfield Road, Balerno EH14 7JZ
McArthur, G. (Mr)	1956	1972	South Africa	3 Craigcrook Road, Edinburgh EH4 3NQ
McCulloch, Lesley (Mrs)	1982	1992	Malawi/Pakistan	316 North Jones Street, Port Angeles, WA 98362-4218, USA
McCutcheon, Agnes W.F. (Miss)	1957	1989	India	10A Hugh Murray Grove, Cambuslang, Glasgow G72 7NG
MacDonald, Dr Alistair and Mrs Freda	1949	1962	Nigeria	10 Millside, Morpeth, Northumberland NE61 1PN
McDougall, Rev. John N.	1935	1960	West Pakistan	Everill Orr Home, Allendale Road, Mount Albert, Auckland 3, New Zealand
McGoff, A.W. (Miss)	1954	1974	Kolhapur	6 Mossvale Walk, Craigend, Glasgow G33 5PF
MacGregor, Rev. Margaret	1959	1994	India	Gordon Flat, 16 Learmonth Court, Edinburgh EH4 1PB
McKenzie, Rev. Robert P.	1936	1951	India	23 Foulis Crescent, Edinburgh EH14 5BN
McKenzie, Rev. W.M.	1958	1974	Zambia	Troqueer Road, Dumfries DG2 7DF
MacKinnon, E.L. (Miss)	1952	1972	Nigeria	
McMahon, Rev. Robert and Mrs Jessie	1959	1976	North India	7 Ridgepark Drive, Lanark ML11 7PG
McMillan, Helen (Miss)	1981	2003	Pakistan	17/1 New Orchardfield, Edinburgh EH6 5ET
Macrae, Rev. Norman	1943	1960	Nigeria	49 Lixmount Avenue, Edinburgh EH5 3EW
Malley, Beryl Stevenson (Miss)	1982	1992	Malawi	272/2 Craigcrook Road, Edinburgh EH4 7TF
Marshall, Rev. Fred J.	1946	1992	Bermuda	Flat 3, 31 Oswald Road, Edinburgh EH9 2HT
Millar, Rev. Margaret R.M.	1967	1996	Malawi/Zambia	
Millar, Rev. Peter	1976	1989	South India	The Manse, Taynuilt, Argyll PA35 1HW
Moir, Rev. Ian and Mrs Elsie	1962	1973	South Africa	28/6 Comely Bank Avenue, Edinburgh EH4 1EL

Moore, Rev. J. Wilfred and Mrs Lillian	1943	1957	Ghana	31 Lennox Gardens, Linlithgow EH49 7PZ
Morrice, Rev. Dr Charles and Mrs Margaret	1971	1998	Buenos Aires/Kenya	104 Baron's Hill Avenue, Linlithgow EH49 7JG
Morton, Rev. Alasdair J.	1960	1973	Zambia	St Leonard's, 16 St Leonard's Road, Forres IV36 1DW
Morton, Rev. Colin	1988	1998	Israel	313 Lanark Road West, Currie EH14 5RS
Munro, Harriet (Miss)	1959	1969	Malawi	26 The Forge, Braidpark Drive, Glasgow G46 6LB
Murison, Rev. W.G.	1951	1971	Santalia	21 Hailes Gardens, Edinburgh EH13 0JL
Murray, Rev. Douglas and Mrs Sheila	1994	2004	Switzerland	Flat 9, 4 Bonnington Gait, Edinburgh EH6 5NZ
Murray, Mr Ian and Mrs Isabel	1962	2000	Pakistan	17 Piershill Terrace, Edinburgh EH8 7EY
Musk, Mrs Lily	1959	1959	Malawi	1 Tulloch Place, St Andrews KY16 8XJ
	1959	1974	Zambia	
Nelson, Rev. John and Mrs Anne	1947	1952	Pakistan	7 Manse Road, Roslin EH25 9LF
	1952	1959	North India	
	1970	1973	North India	
Nicholson, Rev. Thomas S.	1981	1995	Taiwan	Todholes, Greenlaw, Duns TD10 6XD
Nicol, Catherine (Miss)	1960	2000	Pakistan	St Columba Christian Girls' RTC, Barah Patthar, Sialkot 2, Pakistan
Nutter, Margaret (Miss)	1966	1979	Pakistan	Kilmorich, 14 Balloch Road, Balloch, Alexandria G83 8SR
Pacitti, Rev. Stephen A.	1977	1996	Taiwan	157 Nithsdale Road, Pollokshields, Glasgow G41 5RD
Pattison, Rev. Kenneth and Mrs Susan	1966	1977	Malawi	2 Castle Way, St Madoes, Glencarse, Perth PH2 7NY
Philip, Rev. David Stuart	1978	1991	Gibraltar	6 St Bernard's Crescent, Edinburgh EH4 1NP
Philip, Mrs Margaret	1951	1968	Nigeria	Penlan, Holm Farm Road, Catrine, Mauchline KA5 6TA
Philp, Rev. Robert	1937	1961	Kenya	Bybrook Nursing Home, Middlehill, Box, Wilts SN13 8QP
Philpot, Rev. David	1981	1995	WCC Geneva	2/27 Pentland Drive, Edinburgh EH10 6PX
Rae, Rev. David	1953	1989	India	29 Falcon Avenue, Edinburgh EH10 4AL
Reid, Dr Ann	1988	1996	Ghana	19 Cloughwood Crescent, Shevington, Lancs WN6 8EP
Reid, Margaret I. (Miss)	1964	1982	Malawi	26A Angle Park Terrace, Edinburgh EH11 2JT
Rennie, Rev. Alistair M.	1939	1976	Malawi	Noble's Yard, St Mary's Gate, Wirksworth, Derbyshire DE4 4DQ
Ritchie, Ishbel M. (Miss)	1955	1996	Eastern Himalaya	8 Ross Street, Dunfermline KY12 0AN
Ritchie, Rev. J.M.	1974	1977	Yemen	46 St James' Gardens, Penicuik EH26 9DU
Ritchie, Margaret (Miss)	1968	1978	Zambia	1 Afton Bridgend, New Cumnock KA18 4AX
Ritchie, Mary Scott (Miss)	1968	1991	Malawi/Zambia/Israel	Afton Villa, 1 Afton Bridgend, New Cumnock KA18 4AX
Ross, Rev. Prof. Kenneth and Mrs Hester	1988	1998	Malawi	35 Madeira Street, Edinburgh EH6 4AJ
Rough, Mary E. (Miss)	1966	1987	Blantyre	6 Glebe Street, Dumfries DG1 2LF
Roy, Rev. Alan J.	1960	1972	Zambia	14 Comerton Place, Drumoig, St Andrews KY16 0NQ
Russell, M.M. (Miss)	1946	1969	Nigeria	14 Hozier Street, Carluke ML8 5DW
Samuel, Lynda (Mrs)	1974	1990	Madras	28 Braehead, Methven Walk, Dundee DD2 3FJ [E-mail: rasam42@onetel.com]
Shepherd, Dr Clyne	1956	1968	Nigeria	10 Kingsknowe Road South, Edinburgh EH14 2JE

Smith, Mr Harry and Mrs Margaret	1959	1967	Nigeria	31 Woodville Crescent, Sunderland SR4 8RE
Smith, M.L. (Miss)	1968	1970	Malawi	6 Fintry Mains, Dundee DD4 9HF
Smith, Rev. W. Ewing	1956	1973	Madras	8 Hardy Gardens, Bathgate EH48 1NH
Sneddon, Mr Sandy and Mrs Marie	1962	1978	Delhi	84 Greenend Gardens, Edinburgh EH17 7QH
Steedman, Martha (Mrs) (née Hamilton)	1986	2003	Pakistan	
Stewart, Marion G. (Miss)	1955	1966	North India	Muir of Blebo, Blebo Craigs, Cupar KY15 5TZ
Stiven, Rev. Iain	1976	1989	Malawi/Israel	Kirk Cottage, Kirkton of Skene, Westhill, Skene AB32 6XX
Stone, W. Vernon MA BD	1959	1969	Pakistan	7 Gloucester Place, Edinburgh EH3 6EE
Taylor, Rev. A.T.H.	1949	1966	Zambia	36 Woodrow Court, Port Glasgow Road, Kilmacolm PA13 4QA
Tennant, Frances (Miss)	1938	1972	Nigeria/Jamaica	4 The Pleasance, Strathkinness, St Andrews KY16 9SD
Wallace, A. Dorothy (Miss)	1965	1977	Pakistan	101 St John's Road, Edinburgh EH12 6NN
Walker, Rev. Donald and Mrs Judith	1953	1991	North India	7 Bynack Place, Nethy Bridge PH25 3DU
Westmarland, Rev. Colin	1981	1994	Zambia	2 Wilson Road, Banchory AB31 3UY
Wilkie, Rev. James L.	1975	2001	Malta	PO Box 5, Cospicua, CSPO1, Malta
Wilkinson, Rev. John	1959	1976	Zambia	7 Comely Bank Avenue, Edinburgh EH4 1EW
Wilson, Irene (Ms)	1946	1975	Kenya	70 Craigleith Hill Gardens, Edinburgh EH4 2JH
Wilson, M.H. (Miss)	1993	2004	Israel	7 Lady's Well, Moat Road, Annan DG12 5AD
Wilson, Rev. Mark	1946	1977	Nasik	37 Kings Avenue, Longniddry EH32 0QN
	1953	1978	Nagpur	

LIST M – PARISH ASSISTANTS AND PROJECT WORKERS

NAME	APP	ADDRESS	APPOINTMENT	TEL	PRES
Adam, Dougie	2001	175 Fairview Drive, Danestone, Aberdeen AB22 8ZZ	Aberdeen: Bridge of Don	07729 781634	31
Bauer, Alex (Mrs)	2001	26 Netherhouse Avenue, Lenzie, Glasgow G66 5NG	Linwood	07900 531196	14
Black, Colm	2001	2B Mason Road, Inverness IV2 3SZ	Inverness: Hilton	01463 717208	37
Brown, Sarah (Miss)	2003	2/1, 3 Bathgate Street, Glasgow G31 1DZ	Govan Old, Linthouse St Kenneth's and New Govan	0141-556 2959	16
Campbell, Alasdair	2000	3 Gellatly Road, Dunfermline KY11 4BH	Dunfermline: Dalgety	01383 726238	24
Close, David	2001	5 Shortroods Road, Paisley PA3 2NT	The Star Project: Paisley North	0141-889 5850	14

Name	Year	Address	Charge	Telephone	
Conlin, Melodie	2000	Bridgeton Business Centre, Suite 313, 285 Abercromby Street, Glasgow G40 2DD	Glasgow East End	0141-554 0997	16
Cowie, Marjorie	2002	35 Balbirnie Avenue, Markinch, Glenrothes KY7 6BS	Glenrothes: St Margaret's	01592 758402	25
Douglas, Jessie (Mrs)	1999	24 Niddrie Marischal Crescent, Edinburgh EH16 4LA	Edinburgh: Richmond Craigmillar	0131-669 6848	1
Falconer, Alexander J.	1996	59 Waldegrave Road, Carlisle CA2 6EW	The Border Kirk	01228 544757	7
Finch, John	2002	71 Maxwell Avenue, Glasgow G61 8NZ	Glasgow: St Francis in the East	0141-587 7390	16
Haringman, Paul	2003	81/5 Kirk Brae, Edinburgh EH16 6JJ	Newbattle	0131-620 3586	3
Hutchison, John BA	2001	30/4 West Pilton Gardens, Edinburgh EH4 4EA	Edinburgh: The Old Kirk	0131-538 1622	1
Johnston, Mark (Rev.)	2003	5 Bruce Walk, Redmoss, Nigg, Aberdeen AB12 3LX	Cove New Charge Development	01224 874269	31
MacLauchlan, Dorothy Jean (Mrs)	2001	114 Brownside Road, Glasgow G72 8AF	Glasgow: Cranhill	0141-641 3171	16
Philip, Elizabeth MA BA	2001	12 Torvean Place, Dunfermline KY11 4YY [E-mail: elizabethphilip@cheerful.com]		01383 721054	16
Reford, Susan	2001	32 Jedburgh Street, Blantyre, Glasgow G72 0SU	East Kilbride: Moncreiff	01698 820122	17
Smith, David	2003	66 Hendry Road, Kirkcaldy KY2 5DB	Benarty and Lochgelly	07748 808488	24
Young, Neil James	2001	1/2, 33 Alexandra Park Street, Glasgow G31 2UB	Glasgow: St Paul's		16

LIST N – READERS

1. EDINBURGH

Beasley, Ronald E.	37 Warrender Park Terrace, Edinburgh EH9 1EB	0131-229 8383
Davies, Ruth (Mrs) (attached to Liberton)	4 Hawkhead Grove, Edinburgh EH16 6LS	0131-664 3608
Farrant, Yvonne (Mrs)	Flat 7, 14 Duddingston Mills, Edinburgh EH8 7NF [E-mail: yfarrant@charis.org.uk]	0131-661 0672
Farrell, William J.	50 Ulster Crescent, Edinburgh EH8 7JS [E-mail: will.farrell@free.uk.com]	0131-661 1026
Farrow, Edmund	14 Brunswick Terrace, Edinburgh EH7 5PG [E-mail: efsc18422@blueyonder.co.uk]	0131-558 8210
Kerrigan, Herbert A. MA LLB QC	Airdene, 20 Edinburgh Road, Dalkeith EH22 1JY [E-mail: kerriganqc@btconnect.com]	0131-660 3007
Kinnear, Dr Malcolm	25 Thorburn Road, Edinburgh EH13 0BH [E-mail: andrewk@kinnear25.fsnet.co.uk]	0131-441 3150
McPherson, Alistair	77 Bonaly Wester, Edinburgh EH13 0RQ [E-mail: amjhmcpherson@blueyonder.co.uk]	0131-478 5384
Morrison, Peter K.	14 Eildon Terrace, Edinburgh EH3 5LU [E-mail: pmorriso@fish.co.uk]	0131-556 1962

Pearce, Martin — 4 Corbiehill Avenue, Edinburgh EH4 5DR [E-mail: martin.j.pearce@blueyonder.co.uk] — 0131-336 4864

Wyllie, Anne (Miss) — 46 Jordan Lane, Edinburgh EH10 4QX — 0131-447 9035

2. WEST LOTHIAN

Blackwood, Michael — Inshaig Cottage, Hatton, Kirknewton EH27 8DZ — 0131-333 1448

Coyle, Charlotte (Mrs) — 28 The Avenue, Whitburn EH47 0DA — 01501 740687

Elliott, Sarah (Miss) — 105 Seafield, Bathgate EH47 7AW — 01506 654950

Notman, Jean G.S. (Miss) — 31 South Loch Park, Bathgate EH48 2QZ — 01506 633820

Rankin, Stuart A.D. — 7 Watson Green, Deer Park, Livingston EH54 8RP [E-mail: stuart@sadrankin.com] — 01506 439911

Scoular, Iain W. — 'The Wee Hoose', Ecclesmachan Road, Uphall, Broxburn EH52 6JP [E-mail: iain@iwsconsultants.com] — 01506 855794

Wilkie, David — 53 Goschen Place, Broxburn EH52 5JH — 01506 854777

3. LOTHIAN

Booth, Sidney J. IEng CCME — 6 Winton Court, Cockenzie, Prestonpans EH32 0JW [E-mail: sidjbooth@aol.com] — 01875 813978

Cannon, S. Christopher MA — Briarwood, Winterfield Place, Belhaven, Dunbar EH42 1QQ — 01368 864991

Evans, W. John IEng MIIE(Elec) — Edenwood, 29 Smileyknowes Court, North Berwick EH39 4RG [E-mail: jevans7is@hotmail.com] — 01620 894309

Gibson, C.B. Stewart — 27 King's Avenue, Longniddry EH32 0QN [E-mail: stewartgibson27@tiscali.co.uk] — 01875 853464

Hogg, David MA — 82 Eskhill, Penicuik EH26 8DQ — 01968 676350

Lyall, George JP — Mossgiel, 13 Park Road, Bonnyrigg EH19 2AW [E-mail: george.lyall@bigfoot.com] — 0131-663 9343

Millan, Mary (Mrs) — 33 Polton Vale, Loanhead EH20 9DF — 0131-440 1624

Trevor, A. Hugh MA MTh — 29A Fidra Road, North Berwick EH39 4NE [E-mail: htrevor@onetel.com] — 01620 894924

Yeoman, Edward T.N. FSAScot — 75 Newhailes Crescent, Musselburgh EH21 6EF — 0131-653 2291

4. MELROSE AND PEEBLES

Butcher, John W. — 'Sandal', 13 Ormiston Grove, Melrose TD6 9SR — 01896 822339

Cashman, Margaret D. (Mrs) — 38 Abbotsford Road, Galashiels TD1 3HR — 01896 752711

Selkirk, Frances (Mrs) — 2 The Glebe, Ashkirk, Selkirk TD7 4PJ — 01750 32204

5. DUNS

Bennett, Michael A. — 1 South Moor Farm Cottages, Ancroft, Berwick-upon-Tweed TD15 — 01289 387405

Deans, M. (Mrs) BA — The Lodge, Edrington House, Mordington, Berwick-on-Tweed TD15 1UF — 01289 386222

Elphinston, Enid (Mrs) — Edrington House, Berwick-on-Tweed TD15 1UF — 01289 386359

6. JEDBURGH

Findlay, Elizabeth (Mrs) — 10 Inch Park, Kelso TD5 7EQ [E-mail: elizabeth@findlay8124.fsworld.co.uk] — 01573 226641

Knox, Dagmar (Mrs) — 3 Stichill Road, Ednam, Kelso TD5 7QQ [E-mail: dagmar@knox-riding.wanadoo.co.uk] — 01573 224883

Thomson, Robert R. — 34/36 Fisher Avenue, Hawick TD9 9NB — 01450 373851

7. ANNANDALE AND ESKDALE

Boncey, David — Redbrae, Beattock, Moffat DG10 9RF [E-mail: bonceyofredbrae@yahoo.co.uk] — 01683 300613

Brown, Martin J. — Lochhouse Farm, Beattock, Moffat DG10 9SG [E-mail: martin@lochhousefarm.com] — 01683 300451

Brown, S. Jeffrey BA — Skara Brae, 8 Ballplay Road, Moffat DG10 9AR — 01683 220475

Chisholm, Dennis A.G. MA BSc — Moss-side, Hightae, Lockerbie DG11 1JR — 01387 811803

Dodds, Alan — Trinco, Battlehill, Annan DG12 6SN [E-mail: alan-dodds@supanet.com] — 01461 201235

Jackson, Susan (Mrs) — 48 Springbells Road, Annan DG12 6LQ [E-mail: shjackson@supanet.com] — 01461 204159

Morton, Andrew A. BSc — 19 Sherwood Park, Lockerbie DG11 2DX [E-mail: andrew_a_morton@btinternet.com] — 01576 203164

8. DUMFRIES AND KIRKCUDBRIGHT

Carroll, J. Scott — 17 Downs Place, Heathhall, Dumfries DG1 3RF — 01387 265350

Greer, Kathleen (Mrs) MEd — 10 Watling Street, Dumfries DG1 1HF — 01387 256113

Harvey, Joyce (Mrs) — Lochside Cottage, Balmaclellan, Castle Douglas DG7 3QA — 01644 420763

Ogilvie, D.W. MA FSAScot — Lingerwood, 2 Nelson Street, Dumfries DG2 9AY — 01387 264267

Paterson, Ronald M. (Dr) — Mirkwood, Ringford, Castle Douglas DG7 2AL — 01557 820202

Piggins, Janette (Mrs) — Clengh Wood, Dalbeattie DG5 4PF — 01387 780655

Wallace, Mhairi (Mrs) — The Manse, Twynholm, Kirkcudbright DG6 4NY — 01557 860381

9. WIGTOWN AND STRANRAER

Clough, Alan — Dowiesbank, Whauphill, Newton Stewart DG8 9PN — 01988 700824

Connery, Graham — Skellies Knowe, West Ervie, Stranraer DG9 — 01776 854277

McQuistan, Robert — Old School House, Carsluith, Newton Stewart DG8 7DT — 01671 820327

Williams, Roy — 120 Belmont Road, Stranraer DG9 7BG

10. AYR

Anderson, James (Dr) BVMS PhD DVM FRCPath FIBiol MRCVS — 67 Henrietta Street, Girvan KA26 9AN — 01465 710059

Jamieson, I. — 2 Whinfield Avenue, Prestwick KA9 2BH — 01242 476898

Morrison, James — 27 Monkton Road, Prestwick KA9 1AP — 01292 479313

Murphy, I. — 56 Lamont Crescent, Cumnock KA18 3DU — 01290 423675

Riome, Elizabeth (Mrs) — Monkwood Mains, Minishant, Maybole KA19 8EY — 01292 443440

11. IRVINE AND KILMARNOCK

Bircham, James	8 Holmlea Place, Kilmarnock KA1 1UU	01563 532287
Cuthbert, Helen (Miss) MA MSc	63 Haining Avenue, Kilmarnock KA1 3QN	01563 550403
Crosbie, Shona (Mrs)	4 Campbell Street, Darvel KA17 0PA	01560 322229
Findlay, Elizabeth (Mrs)	19 Keith Place, Kilmarnock KA3 7NS	01563 528084
Hamilton, Margaret A. (Mrs)	59 South Hamilton Street, Kilmarnock KA1 2DT	01563 534431
Jamieson, John BSc(Hons) DEP AFBPSS	22 Moorfield Avenue, Kilmarnock KA1 1TS	01563 534065
Lightbody, Hunter B.	36 Rannoch Place, Irvine KA12 9NQ	01294 273955
McAllister, Anne C. (Mrs)	39 Bowes Rigg, Stewarton KA3 5EN	01560 483191
McLean, Donald	1 Four Acres Drive, Kilmaurs, Kilmarnock KA3 2ND	01563 381475
MacTaggart, Elspeth (Miss)	21 Scargie Road, Kilmarnock KA3 1QR	01563 527713
Mills, Catherine (Mrs)	59 Crossdene Road, Crosshouse, Kilmarnock KA2 0JU	01563 535305
Raleigh, Gavin	21 Landsborough Drive, Kilmarnock KA3 1RY	01563 520836
Scott, William BA DipEd	6 Elgin Avenue, Stewarton, Kilmarnock KA3 3HJ	01560 484273
Storm, Iain	17 Kilwinning Road, Irvine KA12 8RR	01294 277647
Wilson, Robert L.S. MA BD	57 West Woodstock Street, Kilmarnock KA1 2JH	01563 526658

12. ARDROSSAN

Barclay, Elizabeth (Mrs)	2 Jacks Road, Saltcoats KA21 5NT	01294 471855
Currie, Archie	55 Central Avenue, Kilbirnie KA25 6JP	01505 681474
Hunter, Jean C.Q. (Mrs) BD	The Manse, Lamlash, Brodick, Isle of Arran KA27 8LE	01770 860380
McCool, Robert	17 McGregor Avenue, Stevenston KA20 4BA	01294 466548
Mackay, Brenda H. (Mrs)	19 Eglinton Square, Ardrossan KA22 8LN	01294 464491
Ross, Magnus	13 Northfield Park, Largs KA30 8NZ	01475 689572
Smith, N. (Mrs)	5 Kames Street, Millport, Isle of Cumbrae KA28 0BN	01475 530747

13. LANARK

Allan, Robert	59 Jennie Lee Drive, Overtown, Wishaw ML2 0EE	01698 376738
Grant, Alan	25 Moss-side Avenue, Carluke ML8 5UG	01555 771419
Kerr, Sheilah I. (Mrs)	Dunvegan, 29 Wilsontown Road, Forth, Lanark ML11 8ER	01555 812214

14. GREENOCK AND PAISLEY

Banks, Russell	18 Aboyne Drive, Paisley PA2 7SJ [E-mail: cbanks25@aol.com]	0141-884 6925
Campbell, Tom BA DipCPC	100 Craigielea Road, Renfrew PA4 8NJ [E-mail: thomas.campbell1180@ntlworld.co.uk]	0141-886 2503
Davey, Charles L.	16 Divert Road, Gourock PA19 1DT [E-mail: charles@davey2.freeserve.co.uk]	01475 631544
Glenny, John C.	49 Cloch Road, Gourock PA19 1AT [E-mail: jacklizg@aol.com]	01475 636415
Hood, Eleanor (Mrs)	12 Clochoderick Avenue, Kilbarchan, Johnstone PA10 2ES [E-mail: eleanor.hood.kilbarchan@ntlworld.com]	01505 704208
Jamieson, J.A.	148 Finnart Street, Greenock PA16 8HY	01475 729531

McFarlan, Elizabeth (Miss) — 20 Fauldswood Crescent, Paisley PA2 9PA [E-mail: elizabeth.mcfarlan@ntlworld.com] — 01505 358411

McHugh, Jack — 'Earlshaugh', Earl Place, Bridge of Weir PA11 3HA [E-mail: jrmchugh@btinternet.com] — 01505 612789

Marshall, Leon M. — Glenisla, Gryffe Road, Kilmacolm PA13 4BA [E-mail: lm@stevenson-kyles.co.uk] — 01505 872247

Maxwell, Margaret (Mrs) BD — 2 Grants Avenue, Paisley PA2 6AZ [E-mail: sandra1.maxwell@virgin.net] — 0141-884 3710

Orry, Geoff — 'Rhu Ellan', 4 Seaforth Crescent, Barrhead, Glasgow G78 1PL — 0141-881 9748

Robertson, William — 69 Colinbar Circle, Barrhead, Glasgow G78 2BG — 0141-571 4338

Shaw, Ian — The Grove, 8 Commercial Road, Barrhead, Glasgow G78 1AJ — 0141-881 2038

16. GLASGOW

Birchall, Edwin R. — 11 Sunnybank Grove, Clarkston, Glasgow G76 7SU — 0141-638 4332

Callander, Thomas M.S. — 31 Dalkeith Avenue, Bishopbriggs, Glasgow G64 2HQ — 0141-563 6955

Campbell, Jack T. BD BEd — 40 Kenmure Avenue, Bishopbriggs, Glasgow G64 2DE — 0141-563 5837

Dickson, Hector — 'Gwito', 61 Whitton Drive, Giffnock, Glasgow G46 6EF — 0141-637 0080

Galbraith, Iain B. — Beechwood, Overton Road, Alexandria G83 0LJ — 01389 753563

Gibson, James N. — 153 Peveril Avenue, Glasgow G41 3SF — 0141-632 4162

Hunt, Roland BSc PhD CertEd — 4 Flora Gardens, Bishopbriggs, Glasgow G64 1DS — 0141-548 3658 (Daytime – Mon-Fri) / 0141-563 3257 (Evenings and weekends)

McFarlane, Robert — 25 Avenel Road, Glasgow G13 2PB — 0141-954 5540

McLaughlin, Cathy (Mrs) — 8 Lamlash Place, Glasgow G33 3XH — 0141-774 2483

MacLeod, John — 2 Shuna Place, Newton Mearns, Glasgow G77 6TN — 0141-639 6862

Phillips, John B. — 2/3, 30 Handel Place, Glasgow G5 0TP [E-mail: johnphillips@fish.co.uk] — 0141-429 7716

Robertson, Adam — 423 Amulree Street, Glasgow G32 7SS — 0141-573 6662

Stuart, Alex — 107 Baldorran Crescent, Cumbernauld, Glasgow G68 9EX — 01236 727710

Tindall, Margaret (Mrs) — 23 Ashcroft Avenue, Lennoxtown, Glasgow G65 7EN [E-mail: margarettindall@aol.com] — 01360 310911

Wilson, George A. — 46 Maxwell Drive, Garrowhill, Baillieston, Glasgow G69 6LS — 0141-771 3862

17. HAMILTON

Anderson, Malcolm — 5 Anford Place, Blantyre, Glasgow G72 0NR [E-mail: andersoncalvin1@aol.com] — 01698 820510

Beattie, Richard — 4 Bent Road, Hamilton ML3 6QB — 01698 420806

Bell, Sheena — 2 Langdale, East Kilbride, Glasgow G74 4RP — 01355 248217

Clemenson, Anne — 25 Dempsey Road, Lochview, Bellshill ML4 2UF [E-mail: aclemenson@msn.com] — 01698 291019

Cruickshanks, William — 63 Progress Drive, Caldercruix, Airdrie ML6 7PU — 01236 843352

Haggarty, Frank — 46 Glen Road, Caldercruix, Airdrie ML6 7PZ — 01236 842182

Hawthorne, William G. MBE — 172 Main Street, Plains, Airdrie ML6 7JH — 01236 842230

Hewitt, Samuel — 3 Corrie Court, Earnock, Hamilton ML3 9XE — 01698 457403

Hislop, Eric — 1 Castlegait, Strathaven ML10 6FF — 01357 520003

Name	Address	Telephone
Keir, Dickson	46 Brackenhill Drive, Hamilton ML3 8AY	01698 457351
Leckie, Elizabeth	41 Church Street, Larkhall ML9 1EZ	01698 308933
McCleary, Isaac	719 Coatbridge Road, Bargeddie, Glasgow G69 7PH	0141-236 0158
MacMillan, Georgina	1 Darngaber Gardens, Quarter, Hamilton ML3 7XX	01698 424040
McRae, James	36 Crosshill Road, Strathaven ML10 6DS	01357 520053
Queen, Leslie	60 Loch Assynt, East Kilbride, Glasgow G74 2DW	01355 233932
Robertson, Rowan	68 Townhead Road, Coatbridge ML5 2HU	01236 425703
Smith, Alexander	6 Coronation Street, Wishaw ML2 8LF	01698 385797
Stevenson, Thomas	34 Castle Wynd, Quarter, Hamilton ML3 7XD	01698 282263
White, Ian	21 Muirhead, Stonehouse, Larkhall ML9 3HG	01698 792772
Wilson, William	115 Chatelherault Crescent, Low Waters Estate, Hamilton ML3 9PL	01698 421856

18. DUMBARTON

Name	Address	Telephone
Foster, Peter	The Forge, Colgrain Steading, Colgrain, Cardross, Dumbarton G82 5JL	01389 849200
Giles, Donald (Dr)	Levern House, Stuckenduff, Shandon, Helensburgh G84 8NW	01436 820565
Harold, Sandy	The Laurels, Risk Street, Clydebank G81 3LW	0141-952 3673
Hart, R.J.M. BSc	7 Kidston Drive, Helensburgh G84 8QA	01436 672039
Nutter, Margaret (Miss)	14 Balloch Road, Balloch, Alexandria G83 8SR	01436 754505
Rettie, Sara (Mrs)	86 Denniston Crescent, Helensburgh G84 7JF	01436 677984
Robertson, Ishbell (Miss)	81 Bonhill Road, Dumbarton G82 2DU	01389 763436

19. ARGYLL

Binner, Aileen (Mrs)	'Ailand', Connel, Oban PA37 1QX	01631 710264
Challis, John O.	Bay Villa, Strachur, Cairndow PA27 8DE	01369 860436
Elwis, Michael	Erray Farm, Tobermory, Mull PA75 6PS	01688 302331
Goodison, Michael	Dalriada Cottage, Bridge of Awe, Taynuilt PA35 1HT [E-mail: dalriada@btinternet.com]	01866 822479
Holden, Robert	Orsay, West Bank Road, Ardrishaig, Lochgilphead PA30 8HG	01546 603211
Logue, David	3 Braeface, Tayvallich, Lochgilphead PA31 8PN	01546 870647
McLellan, James A.	West Drimvore, Lochgilphead PA31 8SU [E-mail: james.mclellan@argyll-bute.gov.uk]	01546 606403
Mitchell, James S.	4 Main Street, Port Charlotte, Isle of Islay PA48 7TX	01496 850650
Morrison, John L.	Tigh na Barnashaig, Tayvallich, Lochgilphead PA31 8PN	01546 870637
Ramsay, Matthew M.	Portnastorm, Carradale, Campbeltown PA28 6SB [E-mail: portnastorm@tiscali.co.uk]	01583 431381
Roberts, John V.	20 Toberonochy, Isle of Luing, Oban PA34 4UE	01852 314301 (Prefix 18001 Text, prefix 18002 Voice)
Sinclair, Margaret (Mrs)	2 Quarry Place, Furnace, Inveraray PA32 8XW [E-mail: margaret_sinclair@btinternet.com]	01499 500633
Stather, Angela (Mrs)	9 Gartness Cottages, Ballygrant, Isle of Islay PA45 7QN	01496 840527
Stewart, Agnes (Mrs)	Creagdhu Mansions, New Quay Street, Campbeltown PA28 6BB	01586 552805

22. FALKIRK

Duncan, Lorna (Mrs) BA	Richmond, 28 Solway Drive, Head of Muir, Denny FK5 5NS	01324 813020
Mathers, S. (Mrs)	10 Ercall Road, Brightons, Falkirk FK2 0RS	01324 872253
O'Rourke, Edith (Mrs)	16 Achray Road, Cumbernauld, Glasgow G67 4JH	01236 732813
Sarle, Andrew BSc BD	114 High Station Road, Falkirk FK1 5LN	01324 621648
Stewart, Arthur MA	51 Bonnymuir Crescent, Bonnybridge FK4 1GD	01324 812667
Struthers, I.	7 McVean Place, Bonnybridge FK4 1QZ	01324 841145
	[E-mail: ivar.struthers@btinternet.com]	

23. STIRLING

Brown, Kathryn (Mrs)	The Manse, Tullibody, Alloa FK10 2RG	01259 213236
Durie, Alastair	25 Forth Place, Stirling FK8 1UD	01786 451029
Grier, Hunter	17 Station Road, Bannockburn, Stirling FK7 8LG	01786 815192
Kimmitt, Alan	111 Glasgow Road, Stirling FK7 0PF	01786 817014
Lamont, John BD	62 Parkdyke, Stirling FK7 9LS	01786 474515
Mack, Lynne (Mrs)	36 Middleton, Menstrie FK11 7HD	01259 761465
Ross, Alastair	7 Elm Court, Doune FK16 6JG	01786 841648
Tilly, Patricia	4 Innerdownie Place, Dollar FK14 7BY	01259 742094
Weir, Andrew (Dr)	16 The Oaks, Killearn, Glasgow G63 9SF	01360 550779

24. DUNFERMLINE

Adams, William	24 Foulford Street, Cowdenbeath KY4 0EQ	01383 822293
Arnott, Robert G.K.	25 Sealstrand, Dalgety Bay, Dunfermline KY11 5GH	01383 830442
Conway, Bernard	4 Centre Street, Kelty KY4 0DU	
Grant, Allan	6 Normandy Place, Rosyth KY11 2HJ	ex-directory
McCaffery, Joyce (Mrs)	53 Foulford Street, Cowdenbeath KY4 9ND	01383 880231
McDonald, Elizabeth (Mrs)	Parleyhill, Culross, Dunfermline KY12 8JD	01383 731550
Meiklejohn, Barry	40 Lilac Grove, Dunfermline KY11 8AP	01383 416240
Mitchell, Ian G. QC	17 Carlingnose Point, North Queensferry, Inverkeithing KY11 1ER	

25. KIRKCALDY

Biernat, Ian	2 Formonthills Road, Glenrothes KY6 3EF	01592 741487
Weatherston, Catriona M.A. (Miss) BSc	'Cruachan', Church Road, Leven KY8 4JB	01333 424636

26. ST ANDREWS

Allan, Angus J.	Craigmore, The Barony, Cupar KY15 5ER	01334 653369
Elder, Morag (Mrs)	5 Provost Road, Tayport DD6 9JE	01382 552218
King, C.M. (Mrs)	8 Bankwell Road, Anstruther KY10 3DA	01333 310017
Kinnis, W.K.B. (Dr)	4 Dempster Court, St Andrews KY16 9EU	01334 476959
Sherriffs, Irene (Mrs)	Cragganmhor, 79 Tay Street, Newport-on-Tay DD1 8AQ	01382 542193
Smith, Elspeth (Mrs)	Whinstead, Dalgairn, Cupar KY15 4PH	01334 653269

27. DUNKELD AND MEIGLE

Carr, Graham	St Helens, Meigle Road, Alyth PH11 8EU	01828 632474
Howat, David	Lilybank Cottage, Newton Street, Blairgowrie PH10 6MZ	01250 874715

Macmartin, Duncan M.	Teallach, Old Crieff Road, Aberfeldy PH15 2DG	01887 820693
Peacock, Graham	7 Glenisla View, Alyth, Blairgowrie PH11 8LW	01828 633341
Saunders, Grace (Ms)	40 Perth Street, Blairgowrie PH10 6DQ	01250 873981
Templeton, Elizabeth (Mrs)	Milton of Pitgur Farmhouse, Dalcapon, Pitlochry PH9 0ND	01796 482232
28. PERTH		
Begg, James	Benholm, 12 Commissioner Street, Crieff PH7 3AY	01764 655907
	[E-mail: beggjlcrieff@tinyworld.co.uk]	
Brown, Stanley	14 Buchan Drive, Perth PH1 1NQ	01738 628818
Chappell, E. (Mrs)	Fiscal's House, Flat B, 1 South Street, Perth PH2 8NJ	01738 587808
	[E-mail: chappell@fish.co.uk]	
Coulter, Hamish	95 Cedar Drive, Perth PH1 1RW	01738 636761
	[E-mail: hamish@coulter9530.freeserve.co.uk]	
Hastings, W.P.	5 Craigroyston Road, Scone, Perth PH2 6NB	01738 560498
Johnstone, David	92 Duncansby Way, Perth PH1 5XF	01738 442051
	[E-mail: dcmj@fish.co.uk]	
Laing, John	10 Graybank Road, Perth PH2 0GZ	01738 623888
	[E-mail: laing_middlechurch@hotmail.com]	
Livingstone, Alan	Strathmore House, 6 Lauder Crescent, Perth PH1 1SU	
Michie, Margaret (Mrs)	3 Loch Leven Court, Wester Balgedie, Kinross KY13 9NE	01592 840602
	[E-mail: margaretmichie@balgedie.freeserve.co.uk]	
Ogilvie, Brian	67 Whitecraigs, Kinnesswood, Kinross KY13 9JN	01592 840823
	[E-mail: brianj.ogilvie1@btopenworld.com]	
Packer, Joan (Miss)	11 Moredun Terrace, Perth PH2 0DA	01738 623873
Thorburn, Susan (Mrs) MTh	3 Daleally Cottages, St Madoes Road, Errol, Perth PH2 7TJ	
	[E-mail: s_thor2@yahoo.com]	
Wilkie, Robert	24 Huntingtower Road, Perth PH1 2JS	01738 628301
Yellowlees, Deirdre (Mrs)	Ringmill House, Gannochy Farm, Perth PH2 7JH	01738 633773
	[E-mail: d.yellowlees@btinternet.com]	
29. DUNDEE		
Baxter, John T.G.	2 Garten Street, Broughty Ferry, Dundee DD5 3HH	01382 739997
Bell, Stephen (Dr)	10 Victoria Street, Newport-on-Tay DD6 8DJ	01382 542315
	[E-mail: stephen.bell@dundeepresbytery.org.uk]	
Brown, Isobel (Mrs)	10 School Wynd, Muirhead, Dundee DD2 5LW	01382 580545
Brown, Janet (Miss)	G2, 6 Baxter Park Terrace, Dundee DD4 6NL	01382 453066
Doig, Andrew	6 Lyndhurst Terrace, Dundee DD2 3HP	01382 610596
Owler, Harry G. (Emeritus)	43 Brownhill Road, Dundee DD2 4LH	01382 622902
Rodgers, Mary (Mrs)	12 Balmerino Road, Dundee DD4 8RN	01382 500291
Shepherd, E.	34 Dalmahoy Drive, Dundee DD2 3UT	01382 815825
Simpson, Webster	51 Wemyss Crescent, Monifieth, Dundee DD5 4RA	01382 535218
Webster, Charles A.	16 Bath Street, Broughty Ferry, Dundee DD5 2BY	01382 739520
	[E-mail: charles.webster@dundeepresbytery.org.uk]	

Woodley, Alan G. (Dr) — 67 Marlee Road, Broughty Ferry, Dundee DD5 3EU [E-mail: alan.woodley@dundeepresbytery.org.uk] — 01382 739820

30. ANGUS

Anderson, Gordon — 33 Grampian View, Ferryden, Montrose DD10 9SU — 01674 674915
Beedie, A. W. — 62 Newton Crescent, Arbroath DD11 3JZ — 01241 875001
Davidson, P.I. — 95 Bridge Street, Montrose DD10 8AF — 01674 674098
Edwards, Dougal — 25 Mackenzie Street, Carnoustie DD7 6HD — 01241 852666
Gray, Ian — 'The Mallards', 15 Rossie Island Road, Montrose DD10 9NH — 01674 677126
Gray, Linda (Mrs) — 8 Inchgarth Street, Forfar DD8 3LY — 01307 464039
Ironside, Colin (Emeritus) — 21 Tailyour Crescent, Montrose DD10 9BL — 01674 673959
Leslie Melville, Ruth (Hon. Mrs) — Little Deuchar, Fern, Forfar DD8 3RA — 01356 650279
Nicol, Douglas C. — Edenbank, 16 New Road, Forfar DD8 2AE — 01307 463264
Stevens, Peter J. BSc BA — 7 Union Street, Montrose DD10 8PZ — 01674 673710
Thompson, Anne — 22 Braehead Drive, Carnoustie DD7 7SX — 01241 852084
Wheat, M. — 16A South Esk Street, Montrose DD10 8BJ — 01674 676083

31. ABERDEEN

Anderson, William — 1 Farepark Circle, Westhill, Skene AB32 6WJ — 01224 740017
Gray, Peter PhD — 165 Countesswells Road, Aberdeen AB15 7RA — 01224 318172
Morgan, Richard — 73A Bon-Accord Street, Aberdeen AB11 6ED — 01224 210270
Sinton, George P. (Emeritus) FIMLS — 12 North Donside Road, Bridge of Don, Aberdeen AB23 8PA — 01224 702273

32. KINCARDINE AND DEESIDE

Atkins, Sally (Mrs) — 9 Feugh View, Strachan, Banchory AB31 6NF — 01330 850434
Broere, Teresa (Mrs) — 3 Balnastraid Cottages, Dinnet, Aboyne AB34 5NE — 01339 880058
Coles, Stephen — 43 Mearns Walk, Laurencekirk AB30 1FA — 01561 378400
Harris, Michael — The Gables, Netherley Park, Netherley, Stonehaven AB39 3QM — 01569 731091
McCafferty, W. John — Lynwood, Cammachmore, Stonehaven AB39 3NR [E-mail: john.mccafferty@opuscompany.com] — 01569 730281
McLuckie, John — 7 Monaltrie Close, Ballater AB35 5PT [E-mail: j-r-mcluckie@supanet.com] — 01339 755489
Middleton, Robbie (Capt.) — 7 St Ternan's Road, Newtonhill, Stonehaven AB39 2PF — 01569 730852
Platt, David — 2 St Michael's Road, Newtonhill, Stonehaven AB39 3RW — 01569 730465
Simpson, Elizabeth (Mrs) — 33 Golf Road, Ballater AB35 5QX [E-mail: connemara33@yahoo.com] — 01339 755597

33. GORDON

Doak, Alan B. — 17 Chievres Place, Ellon AB41 9WH — 01358 721819
Findlay, Patricia (Mrs) — Douglas View, Tullynessle, Alford AB33 8QR — 01975 562379
Hart, Elsie (Mrs) — The Knoll, Craigearn, Kemnay AB51 9LN — 01467 642105
Mitchell, Jean (Mrs) — 6 Cowgate, Oldmeldrum, Inverurie AB51 0EN — 01651 872745
Rennie, Lyall — Dunisla, Oyne, Insch AB52 6QU — 01464 851587
Robb, Margaret (Mrs) — Chrislouan, Keithhall, Inverurie AB51 0LN — 01651 882310

Robertson, James Y.   1 Nicol Road, Kintore, Inverurie AB51 0QA   01467 633001
Sutherland, Susan (Mrs)   53 Westhill Grange, Westhill, Skene AB32 6QJ   01224 741889

34. BUCHAN
Brown, Lillian (Mrs)   Bank House, 45 Main Street, Aberchirder, Huntly AB54 7ST   01466 780330
Davidson, James   19 Great Stuart Street, Peterhead AB42 1JX   01779 470242
Forsyth, Alisia (Mrs)   Rothie Inn Farm, Rothienorman, Inverurie AB51 8YH   01651 821359
Lumsden, Vera (Mrs)   8 Queen's Crescent, Portsoy, Banff AB45 2PX   01261 842712
    [E-mail: ivsd@lumsden77.freeserve.co.uk]
McColl, John   East Cairnchina, Lonmay, Fraserburgh AB43 8RH   01346 532558
Macnee, Anthea (Mrs)   Kingsville, Strichen, Fraserburgh AB43 6SQ   01771 637941
Mair, Dorothy (Miss)   53 Dennyduff Road, Fraserburgh AB43 9LY   01346 513879
Michie, William   34 Seafield Street, Whitehills, Banff AB45 2NR   01261 861439
Noble, John   44 Henderson Park, Peterhead AB42 2WR   01779 472522
    [E-mail: john.noble@onetel.net]
Ogston, Norman   Rowandale, 6 Rectory Road, Turriff AB53 4SU   01888 560342
    [E-mail: norman.ogston@virgin.net]
Simpson, Andrew C.   10 Wood Street, Banff AB45 1JX   01261 812538
Smith, Ian M.G. MA   Chomriach, 2 Hill Street, Cruden Bay, Peterhead AB42 0HF   01779 812698
Smith, Jenny (Mrs)   5 Seatown Place, Cairnbulg, Fraserburgh AB43 8YN   01346 582980
Sneddon, Richard   8 School Road, Peterhead AB42 2BE   01779 480803
    [E-mail: carichcarich@aol.com]
Yule, Joseph   5 Staffa Street, Peterhead AB42 1NF   01779 476400

35. MORAY
Benson, F. Stewart   8 Springfield Court, Forres IV36 3WY   01309 671525
Carson, John   2 Woodside Drive, Forres IV36 2UF   01309 674541
Forbes, Jean (Mrs)   Greenmoss, Drybridge, Buckie AB56 5JB   01542 831646
MacKenzie, Stuart G. MA   Woodend Cottage, Blackburn, Fochabers IV32 7LN   01343 843248
Middleton, Alex   Coral Cottage, Pilmuir Road West, Forres IV36 2HL   01309 676912

36. ABERNETHY
Bardgett, Alison (Mrs)   Tigh an Iasgair, Street of Kincardine, Boat of Garten PH24 3BY   01479 831751
    [E-mail: alison@bardgett.plus.com]
Berkeley, John S. (Dr)   Drumbeg, Coylumbridge, Aviemore PH22 1QU   01479 811055
    [E-mail: john@berkeleyj.freeserve.co.uk]
Duncanson, Mary (Mrs)   Falas-an-Duin, Catlodge, Laggan, Newtonmore PH20 1BS   01528 544399
    [E-mail: maryb@mduncanson.freeserve.co.uk]

37. INVERNESS
Barry, Dennis   50 Holm Park, Inverness IV2 4XU   01463 225883
Cazaly, Leonard   9 Moray Park, Culloden, Inverness IV2 4SX   01463 794469
Cook, Arnett D.   128 Laurel Avenue, Inverness IV3 5RS   01463 242586

Name	Address	Telephone
Davidson, Margaret (Mrs)	11 Souters Rise, Nairn IV12 5BU	01667 859838
Robertson, Hendry	'Park House', 51 Glenurquhart Road, Inverness IV3 5PB	01463 231858
Robertson, Stewart J.H.	27 Towerhill Drive, Inverness IV2 5FD	01463 793144
Roden, Vivien	15 Oldmill Road, Tomatin, Inverness IV13 7YW	01808 511355

38. LOCHABER

Chalkley, Andrew BSc	2 Telford Place, Claggan, Fort William PH33 6QG [E-mail: andrew.chalkley@btinternet.com]	01397 700271
Dick, Robert MA	8 Lanark Place, Fort William PH33 6UD	01397 704833
Fraser, John A. BA	26 Clunes Avenue, Caol, Fort William PH33 7BJ [E-mail: john.afraser@btopenworld.com]	01397 703467
Maitland, John	St Monance, Ardgour, Fort William PH33 7AA	01855 841267
Thomas, Geoff	Drumcannach, Station Road, Arisaig PH39 4NJ [E-mail: geoffthomas@tiscali.co.uk]	01687 450230

39. ROSS

Finlayson, Michael R.	Amberlea, Evanton, Dingwall IV16 9UY	01349 830598
Gilbertson, Ian	Firth View, Craigrory, North Kessock, Inverness IV1 1XH	01463 731538
McCreadie, Frederick	Highfield, Highfield Park, Conon Bridge, Dingwall IV7 8AP	01349 862171
Riddell, Keith	2 Station Cottages, Fearn, Tain IV20 1RR	01862 832867
Woodham, Maisey F. (Mrs)	Scardroy, Greenhill, Dingwall IV15 9JQ	01349 862116

40. SUTHERLAND

Stobo, Mary (Mrs)	Druim-an-Sgairnich, Lower Gledfield, Ardgay IV24 3BG	01863 766868
Weidner, Karl	St Vincent Road, Tain IV19 1JR	01862 894202

41. CAITHNESS

Name	Address	Telephone
Duncan, Esme (Miss)	Avalon, Upper Warse, Canisbay, Wick KW1 4YD	01955 611455

42. LOCHCARRON – SKYE

Name	Address	Telephone
Mackenzie, Hector	53 Strath, Gairloch IV21 2DB	01445 712433
Macrae, D.E.	Nethania, 52 Strath, Gairloch IV21 2DB	01445 712235
Ross, R. Ian	St Conal's, Inverinate, Kyle IV40 8HB	01599 511371

43. UIST

Name	Address	Telephone
Browning, Margaret	1 Middlequarter, Sollar, Lochmaddy, Isle of North Uist HS6	01876 560392
Lines, Charles	Flat 1/02, 8 Queen Margaret Road, Glasgow G20 6DP	0141-946 2142
MacAulay, John	Flodabay, Isle of Harris HS3 3HA	01859 530340
MacNab, Ann (Mrs)	Druim Skilivat, Scolpaig, Lochmaddy, Isle of North Uist HS6 5DH	01876 510701
MacSween, John	5 Scott Road, Tarbert, Isle of Harris HS3 3DL	01859 502338
Taylor, Hamish	Tigh na Tobair, Flodabay, Isle of Harris HS3 3HA	01859 530310

44. LEWIS

Name	Address	Telephone
Forsyth, William	1 Berisay Place, Stornoway, Isle of Lewis HS1 2TF	01851 702332
McAlpin, Robert J.G. MA FEIS	42A Upper Coll, Back, Isle of Lewis HS2 0LS	01851 820288

Murray, Angus — 4 Ceann Chilleagraidh, Stornoway, Isle of Lewis HS1 2UJ — 01851 703550

45. ORKNEY
Robertson, Johan (Mrs) — Old Manse, Eday, Orkney KW17 2AA — 01857 622251
Steer, John — Beckington, Hillside Road, Stromness, Orkney KW16 3AH — 01856 850815

46. SHETLAND
Christie, William C. — 11 Fullaburn, Bressay, Shetland ZE2 9ET — 01595 820244
Greig, Diane (Mrs) MA — The Manse, Sandwick, Shetland ZE2 9HW — 01950 431244
Harrison, Christine (Mrs) BA — Gerdavatn, Baltasound, Unst, Shetland ZE2 9DY — 01957 711578
Jamieson, Ian MA — Linksview, Ringesta, Quendale, Shetland ZE2 9JD — 01950 460477
Laidlay, Una (Mrs) — 5 Bells Road, Lerwick, Shetland ZE1 0QB — 01595 695147
Ogston, Jean (Mrs) DRSAM — Park Neuk, Meadowfield Place, Scalloway, Shetland ZE1 0UE — 01595 880865
Smith, M. Beryl (Mrs) DCE MSc — Vakterlee, Cumliewick, Sandwick, Shetland ZE2 9HH — 01950 431280

47. ENGLAND
Dick, R.G. — Duneagle, Church Road, Sparkford, Somerset — 01963 40475
Green, Peter (Dr) — Samburu Cottage, Russells Green Road, Ninfield, East Sussex — 01424 892033
Mackay, Donald (Reader Emeritus) — 90 Hallgarth Street, Elvet, Durham DH1 3AS — 0191-383 2110
Menzies, Rena (Mrs) — 49 Elizabeth Avenue, St Brelade's, Jersey JE3 8GR — 01534 741095

48. EUROPE
Ross, David — URB EL Campanario, EDF Granada, Esc 14, Baja B, Ctra Cadiz N-340, Km 168, 29680 Estepona, Malaga, Spain [E-mail: rosselcampanario@yahoo.co.uk] — (Tel/Fax) 0034 952 88 26 34
Sharp, James — 102 Rue des Eaux-Vives, CH-1207 Geneva, Switzerland [E-mail: jsharp@world.scout.org] — 0041 22 786 48 47

49. JERUSALEM
Zielinski, Jennifer C. (Mrs) — PO Box 104, Tiberias 14100, Israel [E-mail: scottie2@netvision.net.il] — (Tel) 00972 4 671 0710 / (Fax) 00972 4 671 0711

LIST O – REPRESENTATIVES ON COUNCIL EDUCATION COMMITTEES

COUNCIL	NAME	ADDRESS
ABERDEEN CITY	Mr Ronald Riddell	66 Hammersmith Road, Aberdeen AB10 6ND
ABERDEENSHIRE	Mr Alexander Corner	4 Bain Road, Mintlaw, Peterhead AB42 5EW

ANGUS	Rev. Allan Webster	7 Brachead Road, Letham, Forfar DD8 2PG
ARGYLL and BUTE	Miss Fiona Fisher	2 Nursery Cottages, Kilmun, Dunoon PA23 8SE
BORDERS	Professor George O.B. Thomson	Rathmore, Springhill Road, Peebles EH45 9ER
CLACKMANNAN	Rev. T. John Brown	The Manse, 16 Menstrie Road, Tullibody, Alloa FK10 2RG
DUMFRIES and GALLOWAY	Mr Robert McQuistan	Kirkdale Schoolhouse, Carsluith, Newton Stewart DG8 7DT
DUNDEE	Rev. James L. Wilson	53 Old Craigie Road, Dundee DD4 7JD
EAST AYRSHIRE	Mr William McGregor	25 Blackburn Drive, Ayr KA7 2XW
EAST DUNBARTONSHIRE	Mrs Barbara Jarvie	18 Cannerton Crescent, Milton of Campsie, Glasgow G66 8DR
EAST LOTHIAN	Mrs Marjorie K. Goldsmith	20 St Lawrence, Haddington EH41 3RL
EAST RENFREWSHIRE	Rev. Maureen Leitch	14 Maxton Avenue, Barrhead, Glasgow G78 1DY
EDINBURGH CITY	Mr A. Craig Duncan	2 East Barnton Gardens, Edinburgh EH4 6AR
EDINBURGH SCRUTINY PANEL	Dr J. Mitchell Manson	17 Huntingdon Place, Edinburgh EH7 4AX
FALKIRK	Mrs Margaret Coutts	34 Pirleyhill Gardens, Falkirk FK1 5NB
FIFE	Rev. Alistair McLeod	13 Greenmantle Way, Glenrothes KY6 2QG
GLASGOW CITY	Rev. Graham Cartlidge	5 Briar Grove, Newlands, Glasgow G43 2TD
HIGHLAND	Rev. Alexander Glass	Craigton, Tulloch Avenue, Dingwall IV15 9LH
INVERCLYDE	Rev. William Armstrong	3A Montgomerie Terrace, Skelmorlie PA17 5TD
MIDLOTHIAN	Mr Paul Hayes	Kingsway Management Services Ltd, 127 Deanburn, Penicuik EH26 0JA
MORAY	Mrs Mary Nelson	Skeoberry, Mosstowie, Elgin IV30 8TX
NORTH AYRSHIRE	Mr John S. Scott	2 West Lynn, Dalry KA24 4LJ
NORTH LANARKSHIRE	Mr Alistair MacLeod	21 Cairnhill Avenue, Airdrie ML6 9HQ
ORKNEY	Mrs Carole Macnaughton	The Cathedral Manse, Berstane Road, Kirkwall, Orkney KW15 1NA
PERTH and KINROSS	Mr Alex Dunlop	3 Auchmore Drive, Rosemount, Blairgowrie PH10 6LZ
RENFREWSHIRE	Mr George Hamilton	33 St Ninian's Road, Paisley PA2 6TP
SHETLAND	Rev. Winnie Munson	The Manse, Grindwell, Brae, Shetland ZE2 9QJ
SOUTH AYRSHIRE	Rev. Dr John Lochrie	Manse Road, Colmonell, Girvan KA26 0SA
SOUTH LANARKSHIRE	Mrs Marion Dickie	2 Murchison Drive, East Kilbride, Glasgow G75 8HF
STIRLING	Mr George Bennie	3 Baron Court, Buchlyvie, Stirling FK8 3NJ
WEST DUNBARTONSHIRE	Miss Sheila Rennie	128 Dumbuie Avenue, Dumbarton G82 2JW
WEST LOTHIAN	Rev. Dr Robert A. Anderson	The Manse, 5 MacDonald Gardens, Blackburn, Bathgate EH47 7RE
WESTERN ISLES	Rev. Andrew W.F. Coghill	Leurbost, Lochs, Isle of Lewis HS2 9NS

LIST P – RETIRED LAY AGENTS

Forrester, Arthur A.   158 Lee Crescent North, Bridge of Don, Aberdeen AB22 8FR
Scott, John W.   15 Manor Court, Forfar DD8 1BR
Shepherd, Dennis   Mission House, Norby, Sandness, Shetland ZE2 9PL

LIST Q – MINISTERS ORDAINED FOR SIXTY YEARS AND UPWARDS

Until 1992, the *Year Book* contained each year a list of those ministers who had been ordained 'for fifty years and upwards'. For a number of reasons, that list was thereafter discontinued. The current Editor was encouraged to reinstate such a list, and the edition for 2002 included the names of those ordained for sixty years and upwards. With ministers, no less than the rest of society, living longer, it was felt reasonable to proceed on that basis. Correspondence made it clear that this list was welcomed, and it has been included in an appropriately revised form each year since then. Again this year, an updated version is offered following the best enquiries that could be made. The date of ordination is given in full where it is known.

1932	14 August	Thomas Mackenzie Donn (Duthil)
1933	20 October	The Very Rev. William Roy Sanderson (Stenton with Whittingehame)
1934	3 November	Owain Tudor Hughes (Guernsey: St Andrew's in the Grange)
1935	10 April	George Douglas Monro (Yester)
1936	5 April	George Thomas Jamieson (Stirling: Viewfield)
	September	The Very Rev. James Gunn Matheson (Portree)
1937	31 March	James Brown Mirrilees (Aberdeen: High Hilton)
	15 October	Robert Anderson Philp (Stepps: St Andrew's)
1938	26 February	John Macgregor MacKechnie (Kilchrenan and Dalavich)
	29 June	George Alestair Alison Bennett (Strathkinness)
	1 July	Alexander Thomas Hain Taylor (Dunoon: Old and St Cuthbert's)
	13 October	Robert Hamilton (Kelso: Old)
1939	2 June	David Noel Fisher (Glasgow: Sherbrooke St Gilbert's)
	27 October	James Scott Marshall (Associate Minister: Leith South)
	12 November	Alexander McRae Houston (Tibbermore)
	18 November	David Sloan Walker (Makerstoun with Smailholm with Stichill, Hume and Nethorn)
	10 December	Wellesley Grahame Bailey (Ladykirk with Whitsome)
	22 December	Alastair McRae Rennie (Kincardine Croick and Edderton)
1940	24 February	James Johnstone Turnbull (Arbirlot with Colliston)
	20 March	The Very Rev. Thomas Forsyth Torrance (Professor of Christian Dogmatics: Edinburgh University)
	22 March	Donald MacKellar Leitch Urie (Kincardine O'Neil)
	29 May	Norman McGathan Bowman (Edinburgh: St Mary's)
	14 July	Nigel Ross MacLean (Perth: St Paul's)
	21 August	Donald MacFarlane (Inverness: East)

	3 September	Arthur Thomas Hill (Ormiston with Prestonpans: Grange)
	6 September	Peter McPhail (Creich, Flisk and Kilmany)
1941	29 May	Harry Galbraith Miller (Iona and Ross of Mull)
	1 June	Robert Bernard William Walker (Lesmahagow: Abbeygreen)
	6 June	Thomas Williamson (Dyke with Edinkillie)
	3 July	Donald William MacKenzie (Auchterarder: The Barony)
	21 September	Silvester Skinner (Lumphanan)
	21 September	Andrew Swan (Greenock: St Margaret's)
	9 December	John Nelson (Crawford and Elvanfoot with Leadhills and Wanlockhead)
1942	2 January	James Gilbert Morrison (Rotterdam)
	4 February	Robert Macbean Gilmour (Kiltarlity)
	15 April	Frank Haughton (Kirkintilloch: St Mary's)
	5 July	Norman Christopher Macrae (Loanhead)
	26 August	Arthur William Bruce (Fortingall and Glenlyon)
	3 September	James Robert Moffett (Paisley: St Matthew's)
	22 November	Robert Gray (Stonehaven: Fetteresso)
	23 November	Frederick Haslehurst Fulton (Clunie, Lethendy and Kinloch)
	24 December	James Bews (Dundee: Craigiebank)
1943	4 March	Matthew Liddell (Glasgow: St Paul's (Outer High) and St David's (Ramshorn))
	11 May	Leon David Levison (Ormiston with Pencaitland)
	2 June	Duncan Finlayson (Morvern)
	22 June	William Cadzow McCormick (Glasgow: Maryhill Old)
	24 June	James Murray Hutcheson (Glasgow: Possilpark)
	3 September	George Cooper (Delting with Nesting and Lunnasting)
	21 September	John Campbell (Urquhart)
	1 October	Alick Hugh McAulay (Bellie with Speymouth)
	7 October	Hugh Talman (Polmont: Old)
	28 November	David Hutchison Whiteford (Gullane)
1944	3 January	Magnus William Cooper (Kirkcaldy: Abbotshall)
	21 June	Denis Macdonald Duncan (Editor: The British Weekly)
	12 July	James Kirk Porteous (Cupar: St John's)
	10 November	Alexander Spence (Elgin: St Giles': Associate)
1945	4 January	Victor Charles Pogue (Baird Research Fellow)
	24 January	Thomas Morton (Rutherglen: Stonelaw)
	4 February	James Shirra (St Martin's with Scone New)
	1 March	John Rankine Smith (Glasgow: Barmulloch)

20 April	Thomas Lithgow (Banchory-Devenick with Maryculter)
5 May	Robert Stockbridge Whiteford (Shapinsay)
27 June	Ian Arthur Girdwood Easton (University of Strathclyde)
4 July	Douglas Lister (Largo and Newburn)
1 August	John Walter Evans (Elgin: High)
5 August	Richard Anderson Baigrie (Kirkurd with Newlands)
4 September	John Paul Tierney (Peterhead West: Associate)
5 September	Allan MacInnes Macleod (Gordon: St Michael's with Legerwood with Westruther)
7 October	George Scott Skakle (Aberdeen: Powis)
1946	
11 April	James Martin (Glasgow: High Carntyne)
19 May	John McClymont Frew (Glasgow: Dennistoun)
3 June	John Geddes Sim (Kirkcaldy: Old)
6 June	Robert McLachlan Wilson (University of St Andrews)
23 June	Ian Masson Fraser (Selly Oak Colleges)
18 September	John Wilkinson (Kikuyu)
25 September	Frederick John Marshall (Bermuda)
3 October	John Henry Whyte (Gourock: Ashton)
13 November	Ian Bruce Doyle (Department of National Mission)
18 December	Ronald Neil Grant Murray (Pardovan and Kingscavil with Winchburgh)

LIST R – DECEASED MINISTERS

The Editor has been made aware of the following ministers who have died since the publication of the previous volume of the *Year Book*.

Baird, George Wilson	(Crimond with St Fergus)
Balfour, Thomas	(Department of Ministry and Mission)
Ballantyne, Samuel	(Aberdeen: Rutherford)
Birnie, Norman	(Monquhitter)
Blair, Thomas James Loudon	(Galston)
Bogie, Albert Penman	(Forgan)
Burnett, John Bain	(Associate: Dollar)
Campbell, Colin	(Glasgow: Williamwood)
Campbell, James Alexander	(Stoneykirk)
Carmichael, Robert Craig Miller	(Craignish with Kilninver and Kilmelford)
Cheyne, Alexander Campbell	(University of Edinburgh)
Cowie, Gordon Strachan	(Birnie with Pluscarden)

Duthie, George (Kilmorack and Erchless)
Elders, Iain Alasdair (Edinburgh: Broughton St Mary's)
Ewing, James (Ardrossan: Barony)
Fisher, Kenneth Harold (Stronsay with Eday)
Gallan, Alexander (Wishaw: Cambusnethan North)
Galloway, Allan Douglas (University of Glasgow)
Grubb, Anthony James (Deer)
Hamilton, Patrick John Rogers (East Kilbride: South)
Hood, Ebenezer Craigie Purvis (Methlick)
Hutchison, Mrs Fiona Esther Taylor (Associate: Edinburgh: St Cuthbert's)
Jolly, John (Glasgow: Old Partick)
Jones, Edward Gwynfai (Glasgow: St Rollox)
Knight, Barry (Lamlash with Lochranza and Pirnmill with Shiskine)
Lamont, Allan Donald (Nakuru)
Macaskill, Duncan (Lochs-in-Bernera)
Macaulay, Donald (Park)
McDonald, George Ferguson (Methil)
McIntyre, John (University of Edinburgh)
Mackenzie, Robert Paterson (Dunfermline: St Leonard's)
Maclagan, David Willox (Largs: St John's)
Macleod, Alexander John (Brussels)
MacRitchie, Murdanie (Acharacle)
Maule-Brown, Robert (Strathy and Halladale)
Morris, Gordon Cumming (Buenos Aires)
Orrock, Archibald Alexander (Teacher: Religious Instruction)
Petty, Philip Wilfred Powell (Prestwick: North)
Richmond, James (University of Lancaster)
Robertson, John Thomas (Keith: North, Newmill and Boharm)
Robertson, Thomas Roberts (Broughton, Glenholm and Kilbucho with Skirling)
Ross, John Hugh Gunn (Dundurn)
Rule, James Aitken (Renfrew: Moorpark)
Russell, Andrew Montgomery (Aberdeen: Woodside North)
Sawers, Edward Anthony Howarth (Cranstoun, Crichton and Ford with Fala and Soutra)
Smith, Andrew McLaren (Cumbrae)
Stobie, Charles Ian Graham (Fyvie)
Symington, Robert Cambridge (Community Minister: Lorn and Mull)
Walker, Colin Douglas (Auchindoir and Kildrummy)
Wallace, Ronald Stewart (Edinburgh: Lothian Road)
White, Earlsley Mabin (Uddingston: Park)
Young, William Finlayson (Kinglassie)

IS YOUR CHURCH SHOWING ITS AGE?

Clock face showing a few tell-tale wrinkles?
Weather vane a little unsteady on its feet?
Roof going bald?
Stonework requiring a little plastic surgery?
Steeple suffering from lightning headaches?

If you can say yes to any of these questions, then
why not give your church a facelift or maybe just a little
check-up. Contact us today to take advantage of our
inspection service, including a thorough examination of
the spire by our experts and photographs of any defects.

24 HOUR EMERGENCY SERVICE

Balmore Specialist Contracts Limited.
107 Dalsetter Avenue, Glasgow, G15 8TE, G15 8TE
Tel: 0141 944 6100, Fax: 0141 944 7100
Mobile: 07710 417067
email: sales@balmore-ltd.co.uk   www.balmore-ltd.co.uk

SECTION 7

Congregational Statistics
2005

CHURCH OF SCOTLAND STATISTICS
FOR 2005

Congregations 1,523
Communicants 520,940
Elders 41,218

NOTES ON CONGREGATIONAL STATISTICS

Com   Number of communicants at 31 December 2005.

Eld   Number of elders at 31 December 2005.

G   Membership of the Guild including Young Woman's Group. The letter 'j' beside a figure indicates that the figure is a joint figure for all the congregations making up the charge.

In 05   Ordinary General Income for 2005. Ordinary General Income consists of members' offerings, contributions from congregational organisations, regular fund-raising events, income from investments, deposits and so on. This figure does not include extraordinary or special income, or income from special collections and fund-raising for other charities.

Ass   Amount allocated to congregations for the Mission and Renewal Fund in 2005.

Gvn   Amount contributed by congregations to the Mission and Renewal Fund in 2005. The amount shown includes contributions to allocation and voluntary extra contributions. The figures do not take into account late payments made in 2006 for 2005 but may contain late payments made in 2005 for 2004 and prior years.

–18   This figure shows 'the number of children and young people aged 17 years and under who are involved in the life of the congregation'.

(NB Figures may not be available for new charges created or for congregations which have entered into readjustment late in 2005 or during 2006.)

Congregation	Com	Eld	G	In 05	Ass	Gvn	–18
1. Edinburgh							
Albany Deaf Church of Edinburgh	127	13	–	–	–	–	–
Balerno	817	62	50	112,082	14,700	16,157	60
Barclay	293	33	–	113,355	19,960	20,435	46
Blackhall St Columba	1,086	87	46	162,631	39,787	39,787	87
Bristo Memorial Craigmillar	127	7	22	–	110	4,110	48
Broughton St Mary's	278	29	30	52,367	7,341	7,341	87
Canongate	406	52	–	68,823	10,927	12,238	20
Carrick Knowe	509	52	85	60,331	10,044	11,240	186
Colinton	1,030	79	–	196,245	46,550	51,887	261
Colinton Mains	211	15	–	47,753	3,309	3,709	45
Corstorphine Craigsbank	644	34	–	104,309	18,750	18,750	98
Corstorphine Old	564	54	59	73,658	15,988	15,988	26
Corstorphine St Anne's	473	50	58	75,182	15,705	15,705	51
Corstorphine St Ninian's	1,000	77	61	142,980	38,514	38,514	70
Craigentinny St Christopher's	153	12	–	27,821	550	550	14
Craiglockhart	543	61	39	143,528	27,700	27,700	390
Craigmillar Park	293	24	30	85,837	15,637	15,637	27
Cramond	1,305	102	26	201,136	53,470	53,470	56
Currie	757	69	83	147,778	33,322	34,072	104
Dalmeny	122	9	–	11,409	180	180	–
Davidson's Mains	822	70	54	194,666	39,846	39,846	200
Dean	233	26	–	57,235	10,282	10,581	22
Drylaw	207	15	–	20,887	110	111	1
Duddingston	875	64	42	96,455	15,344	13,810	180
Fairmilehead	851	60	34	94,169	23,896	24,321	95
Gilmerton	–	–	–	–	29	128	–
Gorgie	315	33	–	74,987	14,048	14,048	125
Granton	339	32	–	–	1,280	1,280	45
Greenbank	946	89	77	235,155	53,014	53,014	92
Greenside	221	32	–	–	7,055	7,055	30
Greyfriars Tolbooth and Highland	394	53	19	102,326	22,297	22,297	14
High (St Giles')	587	39	–	250,591	43,418	43,418	8
Holyrood Abbey	264	34	16	139,141	39,690	39,690	75
Holy Trinity	184	24	–	76,233	7,186	7,959	55
Inverleith	354	44	–	91,343	16,548	16,548	14
Juniper Green	420	32	–	85,045	15,165	15,165	50
Kaimes Lockhart Memorial	89	7	12	14,594	110	110	–
Kirkliston	343	36	51	75,336	6,543	6,543	50
Kirk o' Field	207	28	–	33,320	6,406	6,406	3
Leith North	456	42	–	65,447	14,343	14,343	170
Leith St Andrew's	291	31	–	52,684	6,911	6,911	182
Leith St Serf's	307	28	23	52,804	7,322	7,322	130
Leith St Thomas' Junction Road	271	26	–	49,796	4,400	4,400	8
Leith South	575	79	–	103,342	12,540	12,540	126
Leith Wardie	570	73	35	113,702	24,484	25,787	138
Liberton	865	85	63	138,009	28,445	28,445	108

Congregation	Com	Eld	G	In 05	Ass	Gvn	–18
Liberton Northfield.	303	8	30	63,402	2,230	2,230	–
London Road	372	30	40	53,096	6,245	6,245	57
Marchmont St Giles'	290	40	28	60,444	16,509	18,010	45
Mayfield Salisbury	737	71	27	228,755	50,526	52,045	48
Morningside	762	105	29	165,418	31,305	31,305	26
Morningside United	232	30	–	83,501	5,793	9,443	46
Muirhouse St Andrew's	119	7	–	15,742	29	55	74
Murrayfield.	562	98	–	124,744	20,850	20,850	53
Newhaven	249	17	47	63,403	11,000	11,000	55
New Restalrig	270	16	24	108,290	19,742	19,758	63
Old Kirk	137	15	–	21,894	110	286	9
Palmerston Place	479	63	–	146,607	43,288	43,288	126
Pilrig St Paul's	317	29	–	45,199	1,639	1,639	62
Polwarth	332	22	18	71,605	14,255	14,255	20
Portobello Old	388	40	39	64,963	9,035	9,035	12
Portobello St James'.	390	35	–	55,892	6,408	6,408	94
Portobello St Philip's Joppa	658	67	81	123,662	30,481	30,481	135
Priestfield	233	20	23	59,875	7,797	7,156	–
Queensferry	789	53	72	90,380	5,910	5,910	140
Ratho	232	23	21	38,693	1,650	1,650	45
Reid Memorial	427	26	–	104,674	18,179	18,605	25
Richmond Craigmillar	115	10	–	14,527	110	110	11
St Andrew's and St George's	357	42	16	148,311	36,330	39,343	14
St Andrew's Clermiston	328	22	–	40,280	2,767	2,767	15
St Catherine's Argyle	296	29	20	126,345	32,126	32,126	152
St Colm's	153	18	26	29,959	2,700	2,700	15
St Cuthbert's.	493	59	–	165,217	44,267	44,267	25
St David's Broomhouse	189	15	–	39,397	5,174	5,307	–
St George's West	178	40	–	78,945	18,382	18,753	10
St John's Oxgangs	298	25	37	29,002	401	401	18
St Margaret's	433	44	22	50,758	7,792	7,792	77
St Martin's	117	15	–	17,562	109	109	90
St Michael's	485	29	–	54,953	9,688	12,613	23
St Nicholas' Sighthill	510	31	22	52,048	6,415	6,477	30
St Stephen's Comely Bank.	426	26	40	106,628	20,079	20,079	100
Slateford Longstone	313	25	51	–	6,310	9,517	–
Stenhouse St Aidan's	216	16	–	29,561	110	110	30
Stockbridge.	353	34	34	46,774	8,367	8,367	14
Tron Moredun.	146	12	–	–	109	109	23
Viewforth	225	28	–	56,993	8,910	8,910	20
2. West Lothian							
Abercorn.	95	9	9	12,088	1,000	1,600	–
Pardovan, Kingscavil and Winchburgh	303	30	16	48,413	2,750	2,750	48
Armadale	637	31	31	63,166	8,170	8,170	192
Avonbridge	94	10	10	14,848	250	250	11
Torphichen	276	19	–	–	2,753	3,059	35
Bathgate: Boghall.	288	36	22	61,789	6,400	12,400	80

Congregation	Com	Eld	G	In 05	Ass	Gvn	–18
Bathgate: High	567	42	35	76,306	12,000	12,000	120
Bathgate: St David's	284	13	15	48,943	5,500	10,910	6
Bathgate: St John's	377	25	35	55,792	6,358	6,358	120
Blackburn and Seafield	544	41	–	46,168	5,052	5,052	80
Blackridge	109	7	–	18,315	2,119	2,119	–
Harthill: St Andrew's	247	19	40	50,823	7,231	7,231	98
Breich Valley	221	10	–	23,677	250	250	–
Broxburn	511	31	45	51,531	6,340	6,340	145
Fauldhouse: St Andrew's	267	14	18	48,123	2,550	2,550	8
Kirknewton and East Calder	535	41	27	92,791	12,649	12,649	86
Kirk of Calder	647	43	23	72,845	8,150	8,150	80
Linlithgow: St Michael's	1,506	103	65	256,193	56,875	60,738	353
Linlithgow: St Ninian's Craigmailen	531	49	69	67,506	7,763	7,763	117
Livingston Ecumenical	810	48	–	–	272	272	350
Livingston: Old	456	32	26	63,466	10,100	9,258	59
Polbeth Harwood	235	31	–	29,477	600	600	6
West Kirk of Calder	339	28	51	41,486	6,000	6,600	24
Strathbrock	368	44	24	96,849	16,706	16,706	65
Uphall South	216	22	–	–	700	700	77
Whitburn: Brucefield	471	27	20	90,978	6,940	6,940	25
Whitburn: South	423	35	38	70,111	8,570	8,570	117

3. Lothian

Aberlady	304	30	–	34,758	6,991	6,991	–
Gullane	465	38	50	55,937	9,937	9,937	39
Athelstaneford	217	18	–	19,412	2,573	5,057	10
Whitekirk and Tyninghame	160	16	–	–	4,585	4,585	16
Belhaven	761	41	67	67,407	9,277	9,377	120
Spott	104	7	–	10,685	1,333	1,333	10
Bilston	108	5	20	9,992	984	984	–
Glencorse	354	11	–	24,259	2,965	2,965	14
Roslin	288	9	–	24,820	2,720	2,720	–
Bolton and Saltoun	163	16	18	23,610	4,030	4,030	12
Humbie	87	9	12	12,450	2,943	2,943	15
Yester	213	21	19	27,661	3,200	3,200	19
Bonnyrigg	859	72	54	92,780	16,385	16,385	50
Borthwick	80	8	–	23,403	175	1,000	15
Cranstoun, Crichton and Ford	267	20	–	40,771	4,784	4,784	12
Fala and Soutra	72	6	14	8,298	1,683	1,683	3
Cockenzie and Port Seton Chalmers: M'r'l	282	33	45	60,200	7,954	7,954	55
Cockenzie and Port Seton: Old	443	14	28	40,207	217	217	30
Cockpen and Carrington	342	24	46	23,472	2,923	5,630	32
Lasswade	336	24	–	25,228	4,122	4,122	12
Rosewell	138	9	–	12,100	1,704	1,704	–
Dalkeith: St John's and King's Park	571	46	26	80,580	10,076	10,076	45
Dalkeith: St Nicholas Buccleuch	507	29	–	45,477	7,051	7,051	15
Dirleton	265	18	15	21,201	6,116	6,116	13

Congregation	Com	Eld	G	In 05	Ass	Gvn	–18
North Berwick: Abbey	335	30	47	63,968	14,471	14,471	57
Dunbar	822	23	52	83,081	11,087	11,087	37
Dunglass	353	14	19	32,461	325	325	3
Garvald and Morham	53	9	–	–	2,055	2,055	32
Haddington: West	514	39	41	70,180	10,257	10,257	54
Gladsmuir	219	11	–	20,977	3,038	3,038	–
Longniddry	435	35	38	73,678	13,851	14,652	36
Gorebridge	475	18	40	72,704	4,794	4,794	30
Haddington: St Mary's	674	61	–	85,265	24,687	26,557	60
Howgate	39	5	7	15,096	2,404	2,404	2
Penicuik: South	227	14	–	84,271	21,888	21,999	40
Loanhead	398	28	41	49,711	3,850	4,735	45
Musselburgh: Northesk	427	35	40	66,771	8,545	8,545	108
Musselburgh: St Andrew's High	392	34	25	55,675	4,630	4,630	17
Musselburgh: St Clement's and St Ninian's	383	27	12	32,884	284	284	29
Musselburgh: St Michael's Inveresk	524	36	27	–	7,776	7,776	25
Newbattle	661	49	–	65,360	1,100	1,100	177
Newton	176	6	15	16,280	174	174	–
North Berwick: St Andrew Blackadder	714	50	33	90,745	18,449	18,449	160
Ormiston	179	8	27	34,716	4,278	4,278	–
Pencaitland	267	12	12	–	9,303	5,943	65
Penicuik: North	638	40	–	90,556	12,770	13,125	75
Penicuik: St Mungo's	485	22	30	61,967	8,290	8,290	8
Prestonpans: Prestongrange	379	48	28	41,049	4,204	4,204	24
Tranent	324	15	26	45,445	4,657	4,657	20
Traprain	524	36	–	52,142	9,088	9,088	8

4. Melrose and Peebles

Ashkirk	68	6	12	7,400	1,696	2,196	4
Selkirk	602	25	33	56,768	10,803	11,103	14
Bowden	96	14	–	20,848	2,641	2,641	–
Newtown	193	12	–	13,480	2,311	2,311	–
Broughton, Glenholm and Kilbucho	175	14	28	15,739	1,046	1,046	8
Skirling	91	8	–	9,021	713	713	12
Stobo and Drumelzier	103	8	–	13,718	1,090	1,090	4
Tweedsmuir	44	6	–	7,344	692	692	12
Caddonfoot	227	16	–	18,153	1,070	1,070	17
Galashiels: St Aidan's and St Ninian's	979	66	–	84,823	5,644	2,129	16
Carlops	69	11	–	12,702	1,499	1,499	12
Kirkurd and Newlands	110	8	10	17,154	2,218	2,218	–
West Linton: St Andrew's	248	17	–	31,451	4,470	4,520	–
Channelkirk and Lauder	418	26	–	42,368	1,051	1,051	28
Earlston	516	15	13	41,636	3,279	3,279	20
Eddleston	121	7	11	11,120	787	787	13
Peebles: Old	663	48	–	85,650	14,288	14,288	107
Ettrick and Yarrow	220	23	–	32,377	547	547	16
Galashiels: Old and St Paul's	351	25	33	60,749	8,831	8,831	45

Congregation	Com	Eld	G	In 05	Ass	Gvn	–18
Galashiels: St John's	262	16	–	36,886	656	656	84
Innerleithen, Traquair and Walkerburn	480	36	–	60,470	9,198	9,198	97
Lyne and Manor	104	11	–	25,780	219	219	28
Maxton and Mertoun	156	11	12	16,993	2,959	2,959	6
St Boswells	332	24	25	34,032	4,375	4,375	15
Melrose	896	48	53	104,030	18,350	19,629	45
Peebles: St Andrew's Leckie	701	40	–	87,869	12,483	12,483	50
Stow: St Mary of Wedale and Heriot	196	14	–	31,009	459	459	37

5. Duns

Ayton and Burnmouth	200	9	–	16,442	592	592	14
Grantshouse and Houndwood and Reston	122	8	–	10,145	528	528	–
Berwick-upon-Tweed: St Andrew's Wallace Green and Lowick	491	34	50	53,096	3,506	3,709	–
Bonkyl and Preston	87	7	–	8,223	614	614	–
Chirnside	332	21	–	32,369	1,407	2,007	15
Edrom: Allanton	83	10	–	7,066	586	586	–
Coldingham and St Abb's	111	9	–	24,334	1,834	1,834	16
Eyemouth	281	23	49	35,647	4,791	4,921	36
Coldstream	408	23	23	39,173	2,923	2,923	–
Eccles	102	10	16	7,788	895	895	5
Duns	556	25	46	46,435	3,010	3,010	50
Fogo and Swinton	136	7	–	10,755	437	437	–
Ladykirk	38	6	11	9,321	414	414	–
Leitholm	92	9	–	–	370	370	–
Whitsome	51	5	11	4,727	210	210	–
Foulden and Mordington	93	10	10	5,406	123	123	6
Hutton and Fishwick and Paxton	95	8	12	12,935	113	113	6
Gordon: St Michael's	72	7	–	9,792	831	831	6
Greenlaw	154	10	22	17,540	2,020	2,020	12
Legerwood	66	7	–	6,765	645	645	4
Westruther	45	6	12	6,691	781	781	9
Kirk of Lammermuir	83	10	–	15,842	902	902	12
Langton and Polwarth	107	7	27	21,255	808	808	1

6. Jedburgh

Ale and Teviot United	490	36	–	37,079	4,490	4,690	25
Cavers and Kirkton	151	8	–	7,100	2,117	2,117	–
Hawick: Trinity	863	33	50	48,894	7,023	7,023	80
Hawick: Burnfoot	200	14	12	22,922	218	218	82
Hawick: St Mary's and Old	611	26	48	33,375	7,160	7,160	110
Hawick: Teviot and Roberton	368	12	9	49,431	5,107	5,107	29
Hawick: Wilton	427	28	40	40,639	1,993	1,993	22
Teviothead	76	6	7	5,745	1,075	1,075	–
Hobkirk and Southdean	182	15	14	11,154	779	779	12
Ruberslaw	323	25	–	30,292	1,246	1,246	22
Jedburgh: Old and Edgerston	718	22	21	41,386	3,590	3,590	–

Congregation	Com	Eld	G	In 05	Ass	Gvn	–18
Jedburgh: Trinity	247	12	29	38,157	2,778	2,778	2
Kelso: North and Ednam	1,467	73	71	106,941	20,596	20,596	30
Kelso: Old and Sprouston	637	45	–	50,579	5,327	5,420	8
Linton, Morebattle, Hownam and Yetholm	475	31	–	58,126	4,340	4,340	23
Makerstoun, Smailholm, Roxburgh and Stichill, Hume and Nenthorn	228	17	–	27,439	985	985	–
Oxnam	107	8	–	6,623	404	404	2
7. Annandale and Eskdale							
Annan: Old	432	37	51	61,815	7,580	7,580	60
Annan: St Andrew's	788	41	97	62,414	8,300	8,901	120
Brydekirk	58	5	–	7,742	1,086	–	–
Applegarth, Sibbaldbie and Johnstone	198	12	–	10,217	1,713	1,713	3
Lochmaben	555	24	42	52,544	3,768	4,968	18
Canonbie United	142	13	–	22,602	219	219	180
Liddesdale	158	9	–	38,707	437	749	36
Dalton	121	8	5	16,402	980	980	12
Hightae	91	8	15	13,018	826	826	28
St Mungo	141	10	16	12,923	930	725	6
Dornock	154	13	–	–	100	100	40
Eskdalemuir	32	–	–	4,998	62	62	–
Hutton and Corrie	79	6	–	7,424	198	–	–
Tundergarth	76	8	11	7,967	79	79	–
Gretna: Old, Gretna: St Andrew's and Half Morton and Kirkpatrick Fleming	410	29	22	–	710	829	80
Hoddam	153	9	–	10,641	884	1,207	–
Kirtle-Eaglesfield	93	10	18	14,626	1,081	840	–
Middlebie	102	9	14	5,400	693	–	3
Waterbeck	70	5	–	5,854	291	197	–
Kirkpatrick Juxta	156	9	–	12,647	383	549	6
Moffat: St Andrew's	524	47	43	80,056	10,207	10,207	35
Wamphray	61	6	–	6,490	1,125	1,125	–
Langholm, Ewes and Westerkirk	532	30	61	37,804	3,700	3,824	31
Lockerbie: Dryfesdale	852	45	42	49,929	3,680	3,680	29
The Border Kirk	390	52	–	63,554	3,260	3,260	25
8. Dumfries and Kirkcudbright							
Auchencairn and Rerrick	117	11	–	8,249	998	998	2
Buittle and Kelton	217	20	15	20,589	1,609	1,609	12
Balmaclellan and Kells	140	11	15	14,517	305	305	9
Carsphairn	108	8	–	7,896	147	147	6
Dalry	194	15	25	12,310	179	179	15
Balmaghie	132	7	17	15,621	650	1,233	5
Tarff and Twynholm	198	19	26	24,224	2,951	2,951	6
Borgue	59	7	13	5,381	245	245	5
Gatehouse of Fleet	330	24	33	44,391	7,347	7,493	10
Caerlaverock	164	10	–	8,342	1,554	1,554	18

Congregation	Com	Eld	G	In 05	Ass	Gvn	–18
Dumfries: St Mary's-Greyfriars	862	64	–	64,952	10,126	10,126	16
Castle Douglas	558	36	54	54,676	4,121	4,121	28
Closeburn	256	13	–	19,388	1,842	1,842	6
Durisdeer	173	6	22	17,903	1,538	1,538	20
Colvend, Southwick and Kirkbean	367	25	48	52,876	8,777	8,777	12
Corsock and Kirkpatrick Durham	139	16	23	17,740	1,837	1,837	30
Crossmichael and Parton	183	12	20	20,566	2,244	2,244	20
Cummertrees	50	4	–	5,605	223	203	–
Mouswald	84	7	16	6,909	404	404	–
Ruthwell	101	8	19	11,389	854	854	12
Dalbeattie	651	37	64	45,963	7,112	7,112	60
Urr	219	12	–	15,836	1,990	1,990	18
Dumfries: Lincluden and Holywood	292	18	–	23,754	1,438	1,438	32
Dumfries: Lochside	389	18	30	21,380	110	110	60
Dumfries: Maxwelltown West	681	52	51	71,165	7,317	7,317	140
Dumfries: St George's	566	49	37	73,526	8,925	8,925	109
Dumfries: St Michael's and South	932	52	34	74,451	8,158	8,158	35
Dumfries: Troqueer	426	29	22	84,006	10,608	10,608	48
Dunscore	249	17	11	27,197	2,989	2,989	34
Glencairn and Moniaive	216	12	–	25,245	2,591	2,591	18
Irongray, Lochrutton and Terregles	515	33	–	30,322	2,308	2,308	16
Kirkconnel	364	11	15	45,382	3,991	3,991	8
Kirkcudbright	715	35	–	64,292	11,453	11,453	70
Kirkgunzeon	55	9	–	6,709	100	100	–
Kirkmahoe	380	18	37	22,329	350	350	12
Kirkmichael, Tinwald and Torthorwald	574	44	–	45,498	7,638	7,638	45
Lochend	49	4	8	2,897	32	32	–
New Abbey	234	16	13	20,393	110	110	12
Penpont Keir and Tynron	190	12	–	17,579	268	268	15
Thornhill	277	12	18	22,911	1,065	1,065	–
Sanquhar: St Bride's	518	27	24	40,604	3,743	4,548	47

9. Wigtown and Stranraer

Congregation	Com	Eld	G	In 05	Ass	Gvn	–18
Ervie Kirkcolm	251	17	–	19,185	1,513	1,513	17
Leswalt	306	14	19	26,135	1,892	1,892	15
Glasserton and Isle of Whithorn	111	7	–	14,875	1,122	1,122	–
Whithorn: St Ninian's Priory	324	15	33	24,762	1,738	1,993	12
Inch	267	18	14	15,991	3,915	7,253	22
Stranraer: Town Kirk	725	46	–	67,370	17,402	17,402	96
Kirkcowan	151	10	–	24,126	1,415	1,557	11
Wigtown	238	12	16	30,648	2,407	2,407	36
Kirkinner	173	6	14	12,370	273	273	–
Sorbie	163	11	9	15,120	317	–	20
Kirkmabreck	183	13	27	19,076	2,468	2,468	16
Monigaff	450	27	–	25,042	4,885	4,885	25
Kirkmaiden	241	22	16	21,474	3,528	3,831	21
Stoneykirk	381	27	18	30,984	3,845	3,845	34
Mochrum	285	22	40	26,623	177	177	30

Congregation	Com	Eld	G	In 05	Ass	Gvn	−18
New Luce	109	10	–	8,522	1,357	1,357	14
Old Luce	178	24	35	36,165	3,565	3,946	36
Penninghame	591	44	–	54,124	12,068	17,381	25
Portpatrick	256	10	27	19,268	2,512	2,512	18
Stranraer: St Ninian's	451	25	23	41,167	5,922	6,022	24
Stranraer: High Kirk	632	38	30	67,941	5,241	5,241	85

10. Ayr

Congregation	Com	Eld	G	In 05	Ass	Gvn	−18
Alloway	1,276	96	37	187,157	51,011	63,011	170
Annbank	305	21	23	28,073	3,518	3,518	22
Tarbolton	544	33	28	44,520	7,013	7,013	16
Arnsheen Barrhill	75	5	–	–	109	208	–
Colmonell	212	14	–	18,550	168	168	–
Auchinleck	383	22	34	–	5,513	5,513	24
Catrine	117	17	28	22,106	2,966	2,966	–
Ayr: Auld Kirk of Ayr	658	83	39	84,478	19,922	19,922	–
Ayr: Castlehill	731	43	66	85,400	15,270	15,270	30
Ayr: Newton on Ayr	432	41	44	105,140	11,320	11,570	371
Ayr: St Andrew's	541	–	16	77,847	12,935	14,085	89
Ayr: St Columba	1,464	138	52	185,923	40,580	40,580	160
Ayr: St James'	534	28	54	57,843	7,443	7,443	109
Ayr: St Leonard's	649	52	38	76,400	12,143	13,018	46
Ayr: St Quivox	388	37	22	49,356	4,799	4,799	17
Ayr: Wallacetown	381	26	31	42,574	6,340	6,520	5
Ballantrae	286	24	43	36,376	2,150	2,150	15
Barr	73	5	11	5,085	263	263	–
Dailly	184	13	19	13,332	277	277	20
Girvan: South	333	23	37	34,147	1,877	1,877	36
Coylton	349	17	–	25,394	1,619	1,619	130
Drongan: The Schaw Kirk	285	–	20	22,023	1,349	1,349	–
Craigie	124	8	–	12,912	1,825	1,825	14
Symington	398	18	30	55,319	9,714	9,714	24
Crosshill	197	11	26	15,554	895	895	12
Dalrymple	265	15	–	25,086	2,356	2,356	–
Dalmellington	321	26	76	46,730	3,319	3,319	–
Patna Waterside	161	15	–	24,843	160	160	40
Dundonald	549	49	66	–	10,036	10,036	116
Fisherton	147	9	11	10,710	129	129	–
Kirkoswald	267	18	16	30,180	1,780	1,780	6
Girvan: North (Old and St Andrew's)	1,004	67	–	65,496	11,791	13,791	155
Kirkmichael	231	20	22	–	837	837	11
Straiton: St Cuthbert's	169	14	14	13,367	612	612	18
Lugar	173	10	20	20,763	2,415	2,465	5
Old Cumnock: Old	424	20	46	72,101	3,023	3,027	62
Mauchline	596	24	67	69,330	9,139	9,139	78
Maybole	613	29	–	61,654	150	150	15
Monkton and Prestwick: North	522	40	41	103,485	12,816	12,816	90
Muirkirk	241	16	25	33,849	1,960	2,109	8

Congregation	Com	Eld	G	In 05	Ass	Gvn	–18
Sorn	173	14	25	21,431	2,679	2,679	11
New Cumnock	605	43	53	58,794	4,593	4,593	75
Ochiltree	283	21	20	20,589	3,474	3,474	41
Stair	223	14	12	24,216	3,844	3,994	49
Old Cumnock: Trinity	419	27	–	49,248	3,715	3,022	43
Prestwick: Kingcase	1,006	94	63	117,882	18,207	18,207	270
Prestwick: St Nicholas'	788	75	78	96,585	17,363	17,363	85
Prestwick: South	374	35	49	79,133	11,819	11,819	100
Troon: Old	1,211	77	–	140,219	29,487	29,487	118
Troon: Portland	703	49	42	99,340	20,792	20,792	48
Troon: St Meddan's	1,098	132	70	160,966	35,697	35,697	85

11. Irvine and Kilmarnock

Congregation	Com	Eld	G	In 05	Ass	Gvn	–18
Crosshouse	347	28	24	39,134	970	873	25
Darvel	603	37	55	41,765	2,920	2,920	16
Dreghorn and Springside	624	69	43	66,506	10,960	10,960	21
Dunlop	425	38	45	54,572	5,860	6,160	45
Fenwick	398	25	27	55,834	6,230	6,230	33
Galston	804	67	80	109,077	18,794	18,794	125
Hurlford	581	26	36	59,251	4,566	4,566	31
Irvine: Fullarton	498	35	55	102,397	16,500	16,780	145
Irvine: Girdle Toll	212	18	25	39,499	619	619	125
Irvine: Mure	447	29	32	67,669	12,410	14,773	24
Irvine: Old	531	31	29	85,139	17,330	17,330	102
Irvine: Relief Bourtreehill	385	32	30	43,926	2,440	2,440	12
Irvine: St Andrew's	343	21	40	38,315	4,450	4,452	20
Kilmarnock: Grange	429	37	55	61,888	8,650	8,650	30
Kilmarnock: Henderson	624	85	66	112,799	22,161	22,161	35
Kilmarnock: Howard St Andrew's	420	40	36	68,103	13,400	13,400	25
Kilmarnock: Laigh West High	921	72	–	132,272	38,115	38,115	205
Kilmarnock: Old High Kirk	284	18	20	–	2,120	4,240	24
Kilmarnock: Riccarton	361	33	32	65,546	7,927	7,927	134
Kilmarnock: St John's Onthank	309	28	24	55,560	2,040	2,040	76
Kilmarnock: St Kentigern's	298	29	–	49,510	3,870	3,877	140
Kilmarnock: St Marnock's	753	80	–	117,910	17,752	17,752	342
Kilmarnock: St Ninian's Bellfield	233	19	26	29,450	1,745	7,325	35
Kilmarnock: Shortlees	120	13	20	29,883	2,367	2,367	2
Kilmaurs: St Maur's Glencairn	349	23	24	51,249	4,710	4,710	25
Newmilns: Loudoun	373	11	–	87,769	10,270	10,270	25
Stewarton: John Knox	276	36	21	72,641	8,890	8,890	100
Stewarton: St Columba's	500	44	54	64,882	11,560	11,560	48

12. Ardrossan

Congregation	Com	Eld	G	In 05	Ass	Gvn	–18
Ardrossan: Barony St John's	348	20	43	44,416	3,955	3,955	20
Ardrossan: Park	471	37	41	57,674	6,522	6,552	132
Beith: High	866	78	29	54,889	9,936	10,356	65
Beith: Trinity	248	25	34	40,627	7,269	7,269	35
Brodick	208	24	–	37,558	2,330	2,330	13

Congregation	Com	Eld	G	In 05	Ass	Gvn	–18
Corrie	74	8	–	15,379	882	1,114	–
Cumbrae	303	26	62	47,896	2,945	3,345	35
Dalry: St Margaret's	1,028	56	39	91,903	18,664	18,664	135
Dalry: Trinity	263	23	37	72,413	11,652	11,933	58
Fairlie	276	28	54	56,821	5,427	5,427	24
Fergushill	50	5	–	4,930	169	405	9
Kilbirnie: Auld Kirk	524	30	20	52,222	3,183	3,183	43
Kilbirnie: St Columba's	622	35	36	54,883	5,090	5,090	117
Kilmory	46	8	–	9,278	100	100	7
Kilwinning: Mansefield Trinity	243	13	43	39,464	1,181	1,181	10
Kilwinning: Old	766	54	–	78,943	4,267	4,267	82
Lamlash	150	13	28	29,921	3,520	3,520	15
Lochranza and Pirnmill	62	7	22	12,690	1,976	1,976	–
Shiskine	63	6	15	15,352	2,527	2,527	12
Largs: Clark Memorial	986	91	55	108,342	20,073	20,073	60
Largs: St Columba's	552	55	60	86,531	14,190	14,190	55
Largs: St John's	935	52	85	135,041	28,079	28,079	125
Saltcoats: New Trinity	367	47	30	56,378	7,671	7,671	23
Saltcoats: North	362	24	31	51,271	3,933	4,248	98
Saltcoats: St Cuthbert's	516	50	61	86,156	17,076	17,076	85
Stevenston: Ardeer	335	29	30	37,926	3,748	3,748	96
Stevenston: Livingstone	372	42	39	47,194	4,689	4,689	17
Stevenston: High	278	26	53	72,898	8,364	8,364	36
West Kilbride: Overton	353	30	26	51,006	4,726	4,726	150
West Kilbride: St Andrew's	706	60	30	–	10,426	10,426	170
Whiting Bay and Kildonan	121	15	–	36,465	1,003	1,003	15

13. Lanark

Biggar	684	39	65	76,503	11,904	11,904	30
Black Mount	108	7	15	11,093	1,137	1,166	–
Culter	91	11	–	10,449	855	855	3
Libberton and Quothquan	88	8	–	11,087	546	546	12
Cairngryffe	256	17	22	24,805	3,374	3,374	12
Symington	245	20	27	32,215	3,356	3,356	29
Carluke: Kirkton	845	50	25	94,614	15,484	15,692	355
Carluke: St Andrew's	377	19	17	47,051	3,362	4,608	31
Carluke: St John's	821	61	51	80,058	12,398	12,398	52
Carnwath	339	16	25	39,126	1,400	1,400	35
Carstairs	230	17	23	23,605	842	842	26
Carstairs Junction	93	6	17	18,030	987	2,382	3
Coalburn	167	8	20	15,013	442	567	5
Lesmahagow: Old	687	36	30	40,412	8,329	8,329	75
Crossford	199	9	–	26,615	2,230	2,230	32
Kirkfieldbank	128	8	14	18,748	175	175	–
Forth: St Paul's	415	32	54	46,031	2,421	2,421	35
Glencaple	256	17	18	23,204	778	778	21
Lowther	40	5	–	8,236	269	269	4
Kirkmuirhill	315	17	66	106,479	17,298	17,298	76

Congregation	Com	Eld	G	In 05	Ass	Gvn	–18
Lanark: Greyfriars	866	50	48	90,529	10,851	10,851	103
Lanark: St Nicholas'	664	54	35	82,688	11,815	13,115	98
Law	174	20	37	–	412	412	140
Lesmahagow: Abbeygreen	233	18	4	76,582	10,157	10,157	32
The Douglas Valley Church	428	38	–	48,110	1,178	1,178	20

14. Greenock and Paisley

Congregation	Com	Eld	G	In 05	Ass	Gvn	–18
Barrhead: Arthurlie	350	26	30	90,471	11,092	11,092	75
Barrhead: Bourock	535	51	57	76,088	12,669	12,669	308
Barrhead: South and Levern	457	33	27	67,827	13,290	13,840	28
Bishopton	826	61	–	88,685	14,161	14,161	127
Bridge of Weir: Freeland	428	56	–	108,195	21,845	21,845	105
Bridge of Weir: St Machar's Ranfurly	497	42	38	83,277	13,030	20,993	43
Caldwell	269	16	–	59,948	5,252	5,252	65
Elderslie Kirk	599	62	59	87,356	22,654	22,654	211
Erskine	412	34	55	104,767	17,139	17,139	254
Gourock: Old Gourock and Ashton	1,025	70	64	115,412	30,713	30,713	270
Gourock: St John's	717	73	33	97,608	17,225	17,547	340
Greenock: Ardgowan	476	46	32	79,268	11,664	11,740	25
Greenock: East End	–	–	–	–	148	–	–
Greenock: Finnart St Paul's	377	32	–	74,145	12,321	12,321	25
Greenock: Mount Kirk	354	45	18	54,340	10,948	10,948	170
Greenock: Old West Kirk	334	26	40	74,027	15,665	15,665	23
Greenock: St George's North	342	36	–	–	8,753	9,871	68
Greenock: St Luke's	727	88	54	117,646	29,579	29,698	219
Greenock: St Margaret's	198	19	26	31,293	441	441	93
Greenock: St Ninian's	258	20	–	28,319	213	263	103
Greenock: Wellpark Mid Kirk	642	47	28	79,157	12,705	12,705	124
Houston and Killellan	758	60	55	130,670	25,457	25,457	375
Howwood	225	15	23	50,160	3,414	3,414	25
Inchinnan	418	40	20	62,763	6,799	7,417	189
Inverkip	439	31	36	52,867	4,111	4,111	90
Johnstone: High	339	40	37	84,400	11,304	11,304	42
Johnstone: St Andrew's Trinity	262	32	43	48,038	2,398	2,398	137
Johnstone: St Paul's	611	68	25	75,978	10,962	10,962	38
Kilbarchan: East	403	44	25	70,544	7,671	7,671	30
Kilbarchan: West	482	50	30	95,454	22,149	24,149	61
Kilmacolm: Old	824	66	–	122,540	29,617	30,523	50
Kilmacolm: St Columba	582	35	23	100,232	18,145	18,145	–
Langbank	147	12	–	32,006	1,154	1,154	10
Linwood	489	45	36	65,193	7,681	7,681	65
Lochwinnoch	160	14	–	–	1,147	1,147	174
Neilston	684	43	30	94,597	13,484	17,019	–
Paisley: Abbey	790	57	–	143,303	22,855	22,855	135
Paisley: Castlehead	283	36	20	53,371	6,538	6,538	26
Paisley: Glenburn	296	22	–	43,426	1,186	1,186	42
Paisley: Laigh Kirk	512	85	65	61,782	12,835	11,552	58
Paisley: Lylesland	465	66	48	82,423	13,103	13,103	53

Congregation	Com	Eld	G	In 05	Ass	Gvn	–18
Paisley: Martyrs'	493	57	–	70,030	14,330	14,330	113
Paisley: Oakshaw Trinity	683	110	56	115,228	18,420	18,420	127
Paisley: St Columba Foxbar	237	29	28	37,488	1,186	1,186	28
Paisley: St James'	373	32	–	53,368	6,583	7,128	30
Paisley: St Luke's	293	33	–	59,493	4,718	4,718	13
Paisley: St Mark's Oldhall	615	62	104	99,041	22,612	22,612	215
Paisley: St Ninian's Ferguslie	40	–	–	9,532	85	77	–
Paisley: Sandyford (Thread Street)	302	16	20	45,282	5,252	1,252	139
Paisley: Sherwood Greenlaw	773	88	52	119,234	23,364	23,364	57
Paisley: Wallneuk North	493	55	–	77,233	11,240	12,490	55
Port Glasgow: Hamilton Bardrainney	369	17	21	42,057	2,272	2,272	76
Port Glasgow: St Andrew's	678	59	51	81,805	14,190	14,190	272
Port Glasgow: St Martin's	168	16	–	20,633	171	171	18
Renfrew: North	681	66	43	106,686	17,670	17,670	150
Renfrew: Old	629	46	60	66,050	13,188	14,520	–
Renfrew: Trinity	399	36	69	70,758	11,378	11,378	70
Skelmorlie and Wemyss Bay	416	31	–	69,376	9,020	9,090	–

16. Glasgow

Congregation	Com	Eld	G	In 05	Ass	Gvn	–18
Banton	86	12	–	–	108	108	17
Twechar	76	–	–	14,473	90	90	–
Bishopbriggs: Kenmure	343	30	47	76,275	12,090	12,642	140
Bishopbriggs: Springfield	938	52	82	94,125	19,132	19,132	198
Broom	888	63	46	147,546	28,080	28,080	75
Burnside–Blairbeth	719	54	–	218,217	52,383	52,383	265
Busby	377	44	40	61,513	8,280	8,280	24
Cadder	917	89	64	141,503	38,403	38,653	240
Cambuslang: Flemington Hallside	204	15	21	29,034	616	616	125
Cambuslang: Old	406	53	38	71,493	14,748	14,748	26
Cambuslang: St Andrew's	425	40	–	63,860	13,222	8,000	39
Cambuslang: Trinity St Paul's	313	22	–	63,045	9,810	9,810	65
Campsie	214	20	20	–	3,938	3,938	90
Chryston	697	43	25	162,373	28,851	28,851	99
Eaglesham	680	56	72	114,957	21,775	21,775	55
Fernhill and Cathkin	322	23	40	43,135	2,000	2,000	58
Gartcosh	148	8	10	17,809	669	669	60
Glenboig	143	8	14	–	461	461	11
Giffnock: Orchardhill	530	55	27	162,050	47,090	47,090	362
Giffnock: South	975	97	60	147,693	53,364	56,467	127
Giffnock: The Park	315	27	–	54,698	3,800	3,800	98
Greenbank	1,094	77	49	203,711	62,496	62,996	300
Kilsyth: Anderson	421	20	60	81,107	12,089	13,089	132
Kilsyth: Burns and Old	490	38	45	68,798	7,813	7,813	117
Kirkintilloch: Hillhead	153	8	15	–	160	160	6
Kirkintilloch: St Columba's	572	51	45	83,745	16,410	16,410	100
Kirkintilloch: St David's Memorial Park	732	62	37	113,492	26,956	26,956	141
Kirkintilloch: St Mary's	798	66	77	131,239	24,155	24,155	300

Congregation	Com	Eld	G	In 05	Ass	Gvn	–18
Lenzie: Old	497	47	–	106,055	12,589	14,189	44
Lenzie: Union	829	76	85	152,644	40,690	41,320	330
Maxwell Mearns Castle	344	32	–	155,005	30,296	30,296	196
Mearns	879	45	–	155,256	37,111	37,111	90
Milton of Campsie	366	41	38	49,053	3,938	3,938	118
Netherlee	844	72	60	183,949	54,255	55,802	430
Newton Mearns	725	55	31	114,982	25,419	25,419	155
Rutherglen: Old	395	32	–	58,406	4,620	4,620	80
Rutherglen: Stonelaw	464	–	55	122,919	24,425	24,425	–
Rutherglen: Wardlawhill	378	43	45	51,312	3,430	3,430	50
Rutherglen: West	506	32	32	71,381	6,880	6,880	27
Stamperland	443	32	30	76,487	14,923	14,923	250
Stepps	391	27	18	56,045	4,310	4,310	150
Thornliebank	243	18	50	53,197	3,910	3,910	72
Torrance	306	16	–	64,610	3,289	4,462	150
Williamwood	553	74	48	126,536	28,831	28,831	233
Glasgow: Anderston Kelvingrove	69	19	10	17,642	240	–	20
Glasgow: Baillieston Mure Memorial	538	32	104	84,927	14,801	14,801	330
Glasgow: Baillieston St Andrew's	386	28	51	57,939	8,190	8,190	128
Glasgow: Balshagray Victoria Park	291	240	34	73,018	14,109	14,109	–
Glasgow: Barlanark Greyfriars	158	20	22	36,701	540	540	160
Glasgow: Battlefield East	164	13	36	43,546	2,050	2,050	5
Glasgow: Blawarthill	199	27	48	–	242	116	97
Glasgow: Bridgeton St Francis in the East	109	17	8	30,564	410	410	88
Glasgow: Broomhill	629	65	60	137,181	34,195	34,195	140
Glasgow: Calton Parkhead	120	13	10	20,890	230	234	5
Glasgow: Cardonald	498	49	107	125,719	30,887	34,193	189
Glasgow: Carmunnock	361	28	32	53,022	7,490	7,490	50
Glasgow: Carmyle	127	6	25	–	2,035	2,035	42
Glasgow: Kenmuir Mount Vernon	179	10	40	51,244	4,956	4,956	95
Glasgow: Carntyne Old	154	22	14	39,276	6,717	6,717	98
Glasgow: Eastbank	161	17	25	35,377	5,330	5,330	45
Glasgow: Carnwadric	155	19	24	30,654	220	220	50
Glasgow: Castlemilk East	166	12	16	29,182	396	396	40
Glasgow: Castlemilk West	138	21	16	22,234	–	200	–
Glasgow: Cathcart Old	326	53	47	66,002	13,039	13,039	375
Glasgow: Cathcart Trinity	605	68	–	149,558	36,925	37,525	157
Glasgow: Cathedral (High or St Mungo's)	417	57	–	98,567	17,849	17,850	14
Glasgow: Colston Milton	122	19	–	27,801	220	220	80
Glasgow: Colston Wellpark	187	16	–	33,809	616	616	56
Glasgow: Cranhill	41	7	–	10,921	99	199	31
Glasgow: Croftfoot	339	46	44	71,078	12,640	12,773	63
Glasgow: Dennistoun Blackfriars	147	20	22	42,597	3,300	3,300	8
Glasgow: Dennistoun Central	266	24	23	40,420	4,180	4,180	150
Glasgow: Drumchapel Drumry St Mary's	116	10	–	8,563	99	99	12
Glasgow: Drumchapel St Andrew's	440	47	–	49,238	5,410	11,480	30

Congregation	Com	Eld	G	In 05	Ass	Gvn	–18
Glasgow: Drumchapel St Mark's	77	10	–	16,296	100	100	9
Glasgow: Easterhouse St George's and St Peter's	53	8	–	–	1	–	3
Glasgow: Eastwood	369	48	45	77,726	15,897	15,897	93
Glasgow: Gairbraid	235	22	22	37,680	1,700	1,700	24
Glasgow: Gardner Street	40	8	–	40,167	4,150	2,251	7
Glasgow: Garthamlock and Craigend East	86	10	–	–	99	198	48
Glasgow: Gorbals	101	11	–	25,703	240	240	9
Glasgow: Govan Old	161	32	23	49,275	2,310	2,310	45
Glasgow: Govanhill Trinity	130	17	30	26,085	1,080	1,080	5
Glasgow: High Carntyne	429	33	77	76,102	13,620	13,620	126
Glasgow: Hillington Park	409	26	50	66,180	9,850	9,980	130
Glasgow: Househillwood St Christopher's	128	–	28	–	180	165	–
Glasgow: Hyndland	276	40	40	91,356	16,789	16,789	35
Glasgow: Ibrox	226	18	32	49,031	4,460	5,260	94
Glasgow: John Ross Memorial (for the Deaf)	70	8	–	–	–	–	–
Glasgow: Jordanhill	661	79	35	163,169	40,955	41,967	239
Glasgow: Kelvin Stevenson Memorial	171	30	20	40,194	2,580	2,580	100
Glasgow: Kelvinside Hillhead	184	27	–	63,985	8,450	8,450	82
Glasgow: King's Park	826	80	59	145,539	38,690	38,690	326
Glasgow: Kinning Park	169	17	20	33,056	1,310	1,310	15
Glasgow: Knightswood St Margaret's	659	31	43	55,905	5,020	5,330	94
Glasgow: Langside	251	44	30	71,342	3,278	3,278	120
Glasgow: Lansdowne	107	12	–	7,481	140	–	5
Glasgow: Linthouse St Kenneth's	105	18	15	23,220	230	230	53
Glasgow: Lochwood	77	5	12	–	–	60	80
Glasgow: Martyrs', The	126	5	–	–	230	140	4
Glasgow: Maryhill	207	15	–	37,470	1,920	1,920	90
Glasgow: Merrylea	465	73	40	89,924	15,986	15,986	152
Glasgow: Mosspark	201	37	50	61,308	7,970	7,970	68
Glasgow: Mount Florida	286	34	54	99,597	15,190	21,700	163
Glasgow: New Govan	110	16	25	50,362	1,401	1,401	52
Glasgow: Newlands South	628	69	33	173,995	44,891	44,891	50
Glasgow: North Kelvinside	68	4	25	38,077	700	700	20
Glasgow: Partick South	195	36	32	59,297	4,917	4,917	135
Glasgow: Partick Trinity	196	25	–	60,455	1,716	1,716	60
Glasgow: Penilee St Andrew's	160	25	–	42,445	1,350	1,350	36
Glasgow: Pollokshaws	172	24	38	41,824	1,771	1,771	83
Glasgow: Pollokshields	312	37	60	110,819	23,130	23,130	47
Glasgow: Possilpark	182	21	19	30,905	980	980	52
Glasgow: Priesthill and Nitshill	132	19	19	34,559	540	565	17
Glasgow: Queen's Park	256	30	–	74,960	11,569	11,569	27
Glasgow: Renfield St Stephen's	181	27	41	72,473	11,420	12,340	24
Glasgow: Robroyston	58	–	–	6,444	1	1	–
Glasgow: Ruchazie	72	10	–	14,743	120	80	39

Congregation	Com	Eld	G	In 05	Ass	Gvn	–18
Glasgow: Ruchill	94	21	–	41,696	2,959	2,959	20
Glasgow: St Andrew's East	124	22	28	37,757	660	660	76
Glasgow: St Columba	141	12	18	–	550	487	38
Glasgow: St David's Knightswood	483	30	51	90,155	15,430	15,730	65
Glasgow: St Enoch's Hogganfield	206	–	35	40,707	3,230	4,230	–
Glasgow: St George's Tron	419	31	–	231,209	55,733	55,733	50
Glasgow: St James' (Pollok)	177	28	24	53,531	901	901	60
Glasgow: St John's Renfield	439	47	–	151,178	31,627	31,627	140
Glasgow: St Luke's and St Andrew's	81	9	12	18,106	190	84	–
Glasgow: St Margaret's Tollcross Park	156	5	–	28,284	700	630	40
Glasgow: St Nicholas' Cardonald	352	35	10	55,729	7,120	7,420	292
Glasgow: St Paul's	69	7	–	–	99	99	12
Glasgow: St Rollox	123	13	–	23,536	230	230	35
Glasgow: St Thomas' Gallowgate	29	–	–	5,507	–	100	–
Glasgow: Sandyford Henderson Memorial	195	25	18	132,979	21,228	21,228	40
Glasgow: Sandyhills	344	31	56	71,228	12,133	12,133	75
Glasgow: Scotstoun	269	15	–	68,676	9,400	9,400	60
Glasgow: Shawlands	452	30	–	93,484	23,560	5,000	33
Glasgow: Sherbrooke St Gilbert's	401	49	35	129,313	24,528	24,528	82
Glasgow: Shettleston Old	230	23	26	33,911	4,210	4,210	75
Glasgow: South Carntyne	84	10	–	24,434	220	220	50
Glasgow: South Shawlands	210	26	–	64,415	4,480	4,480	121
Glasgow: Springburn	320	41	27	63,104	11,240	11,240	134
Glasgow: Temple Anniesland	437	34	56	78,607	13,596	13,596	81
Glasgow: Toryglen	125	12	23	21,506	190	190	15
Glasgow: Trinity Possil and Henry Drummond	130	6	–	47,272	2,112	2,112	15
Glasgow: Tron St Mary's	149	21	–	40,509	–	833	120
Glasgow: Victoria Tollcross	147	9	22	22,343	–	–	39
Glasgow: Wallacewell	142	14	–	29,535	920	920	29
Glasgow: Wellington	279	33	–	79,144	16,579	16,579	20
Glasgow: Whiteinch	34	–	–	49,206	200	200	150
Glasgow: Yoker	112	10	–	26,586	230	230	3
17. Hamilton							
Airdrie: Broomknoll	366	41	36	58,258	9,846	9,846	136
Calderbank	134	10	19	21,626	1,857	1,857	28
Airdrie: Clarkston	442	39	36	54,048	10,596	11,619	130
Airdrie: Flowerhill	739	68	23	100,546	16,506	17,946	194
Airdrie: High	409	29	–	47,912	5,010	5,010	77
Airdrie: Jackson	334	47	21	59,257	6,020	6,020	94
Airdrie: New Monkland	374	27	23	43,331	4,708	4,708	120
Greengairs	150	7	–	22,668	2,032	2,032	–
Airdrie: St Columba's	242	13	9	21,439	230	230	60
Airdrie: The New Wellwynd	732	87	32	100,536	16,454	16,454	250
Bargeddie	147	11	–	63,603	3,770	3,770	9
Bellshill: Macdonald Memorial	296	22	24	41,011	4,941	4,941	18

Congregation	Com	Eld	G	In 05	Ass	Gvn	–18
Bellshill: Orbiston	248	22	16	18,584	2,089	2,089	10
Bellshill: West	794	66	44	66,565	7,680	7,680	75
Blantyre: Livingstone Memorial	282	23	31	57,023	870	870	144
Blantyre: Old	363	21	22	–	7,786	7,786	52
Blantyre: St Andrew's	284	25	26	67,970	6,720	6,720	110
Bothwell	545	53	47	106,705	23,590	25,557	72
Caldercruix and Longriggend	226	10	22	49,144	4,520	4,520	2
Carfin	61	7	–	6,366	1,177	1,177	–
Newarthill	459	32	20	47,001	6,423	6,423	127
Chapelhall	293	25	38	38,827	2,780	2,780	90
Chapelton	204	15	27	24,298	4,216	4,216	47
Strathaven: Rankin	591	59	36	77,960	16,465	16,465	184
Cleland	229	18	13	27,865	230	230	24
Coatbridge: Blairhill Dundyvan	399	29	26	60,431	6,220	6,220	–
Coatbridge: Calder	461	31	43	59,681	4,100	4,100	109
Coatbridge: Clifton	250	27	21	44,652	3,150	3,150	40
Coatbridge: Middle	395	35	50	47,835	3,420	3,420	157
Coatbridge: Old Monkland	332	22	30	42,716	1,750	1,750	73
Coatbridge: St Andrew's	688	65	42	80,846	16,353	16,353	240
Coatbridge: Townhead	355	26	32	55,382	2,960	2,466	111
Dalserf	256	20	25	56,450	10,063	10,063	74
East Kilbride: Claremont	760	85	44	109,703	14,569	15,897	168
East Kilbride: Greenhills	173	16	35	32,600	210	210	10
East Kilbride: Moncrieff	897	74	48	106,770	18,426	18,426	300
East Kilbride: Mossneuk	268	22	–	34,249	1,055	1,055	265
East Kilbride: Old	696	65	87	86,794	14,570	14,570	140
East Kilbride: South	393	49	46	79,464	17,015	17,015	30
East Kilbride: Stewartfield	–	–	–	9,518	–	–	–
East Kilbride: West	653	35	80	61,796	9,136	9,305	195
East Kilbride: Westwood	734	49	132	75,362	13,985	13,985	30
Glasford	188	10	23	18,726	2,602	2,602	6
Strathaven: East	299	32	30	44,241	5,718	5,718	46
Hamilton: Burnbank	136	13	–	25,106	3,185	4,144	9
Hamilton: North	162	31	29	35,426	4,675	4,675	21
Hamilton: Cadzow	764	68	70	100,638	20,740	20,740	139
Hamilton: Gilmour and Whitehill	187	24	–	31,629	1,500	1,548	73
Hamilton: Hillhouse	446	50	32	81,253	14,165	11,344	219
Hamilton: Old	629	77	40	115,481	30,405	30,405	120
Hamilton: St Andrew's	353	35	36	51,099	7,250	7,450	137
Hamilton: St John's	589	59	66	114,278	24,304	24,304	260
Hamilton: South	310	31	30	51,884	6,692	6,692	39
Quarter	97	12	15	20,854	2,232	2,232	16
Hamilton: Trinity	322	30	–	41,058	1,510	1,510	116
Hamilton: West	384	32	–	64,321	9,427	9,427	33
Holytown	326	25	30	42,296	3,650	3,650	95
Kirk o' Shotts	203	11	14	25,306	300	300	20
Larkhall: Chalmers	158	16	32	32,213	1,170	2,824	50
Larkhall: St Machan's	590	54	52	89,723	14,987	15,237	75

Congregation	Com	Eld	G	In 05	Ass	Gvn	–18
Larkhall: Trinity	325	21	38	49,792	3,690	3,690	134
Motherwell: Crosshill	505	59	59	72,729	11,912	11,912	120
Motherwell: Dalziel St Andrew's	589	78	60	99,322	22,513	30,006	210
Motherwell: Manse Road	239	33	25	40,898	2,390	2,390	130
Motherwell: North	212	31	40	44,137	2,340	2,340	250
Motherwell: St Margaret's	385	18	24	–	1,180	1,180	151
Motherwell: St Mary's	954	110	101	113,911	23,472	23,472	270
Motherwell: South Dalziel	396	60	68	83,715	15,466	16,549	90
Newmains: Bonkle	179	20	–	28,401	4,971	5,041	24
Newmains: Coltness Memorial	240	28	23	43,981	6,629	6,629	70
New Stevenston: Wrangholm Kirk	186	9	29	36,703	820	820	38
Overtown	299	29	46	45,094	2,170	2,420	192
Shotts: Calderhead Erskine	603	35	40	–	9,035	9,035	160
Stonehouse: St Ninian's	451	47	45	73,158	10,387	10,387	29
Strathaven: Avendale Old and Drumclog	781	64	44	–	30,085	30,085	198
Strathaven: West	241	20	38	43,567	2,320	2,320	50
Uddingston: Burnhead	283	25	14	38,719	1,310	1,310	100
Uddingston: Old	697	65	78	103,203	20,343	23,343	140
Uddingston: Park	208	15	30	69,667	7,180	7,385	46
Uddingston: Viewpark	474	35	37	72,762	9,884	10,487	300
Wishaw: Cambusnethan North	541	44	–	73,801	13,534	13,798	150
Wishaw: Cambusnethan Old & Morningside	546	70	19	68,096	14,162	14,660	165
Wishaw: Craigneuk and Belhaven	226	26	28	48,660	11,145	11,145	24
Wishaw: Old	367	36	–	39,586	10,167	10,277	85
Wishaw: St Mark's	475	41	47	72,210	10,163	10,163	193
Wishaw: South Wishaw	621	42	–	90,592	19,827	20,002	38

18. Dumbarton

Alexandria	447	35	27	60,199	8,778	8,778	52
Arrochar	56	8	14	15,648	591	591	52
Luss	85	9	16	31,980	610	610	30
Baldernock	228	20	–	42,205	3,006	3,112	20
Bearsden: Killermont	726	62	69	138,186	29,930	29,930	112
Bearsden: New Kilpatrick	1,705	131	111	291,435	84,411	84,411	170
Bearsden: North	653	71	69	102,429	22,150	22,450	60
Bearsden: South	952	90	42	165,262	40,550	40,550	93
Bearsden: Westerton Fairlie Memorial	483	51	48	78,806	14,680	14,680	45
Bonhill	916	61	–	64,832	13,470	13,470	120
Cardross	453	36	34	94,778	17,995	17,995	60
Clydebank: Abbotsford	341	26	33	50,811	6,244	6,244	28
Clydebank: Faifley	236	24	45	34,444	730	952	19
Clydebank: Kilbowie St Andrew's	315	25	38	44,843	4,836	4,836	149
Clydebank: Radnor Park	242	32	36	43,349	4,650	4,650	–
Clydebank: St Cuthbert's	139	17	23	–	1,600	1,600	6
Duntocher	323	30	28	59,852	2,853	2,853	–
Craigrownie	231	23	20	34,767	5,765	5,765	23
Rosneath: St Modan's	179	11	28	23,474	3,012	3,012	6

Congregation	Com	Eld	G	In 05	Ass	Gvn	–18
Dalmuir: Barclay	312	18	34	37,873	4,851	4,850	18
Dumbarton: Riverside	719	83	84	110,875	20,430	20,430	340
Dumbarton: St Andrew's	135	27	16	30,209	510	510	12
Dumbarton: West Kirk	338	45	38	–	6,391	6,894	50
Garelochhead	180	17	–	51,933	5,480	5,480	119
Helensburgh: Park	490	45	35	78,512	15,215	15,459	27
Helensburgh: St Columba	549	50	38	92,256	17,637	17,637	99
Helensburgh: The West Kirk	623	56	50	111,575	30,860	30,860	50
Jamestown	402	23	28	50,386	6,953	7,726	14
Kilmaronock Gartocharn	274	10	–	25,279	540	540	16
Milngavie: Cairns	697	45	–	110,398	21,580	21,580	68
Milngavie: St Luke's	413	39	27	64,846	10,456	14,244	–
Milngavie: St Paul's	1,136	98	98	214,318	46,390	46,390	175
Old Kilpatrick Bowling	318	30	39	50,517	721	721	146
Renton: Trinity	293	24	–	32,063	1,150	1,150	8
Rhu and Shandon	312	36	50	78,248	11,600	11,600	17
19. Argyll							
Appin	88	11	21	18,832	165	165	30
Lismore	54	8	15	12,962	92	92	12
Ardchattan	146	12	10	17,360	206	206	15
Ardrishaig	181	26	39	35,395	3,349	3,349	43
South Knapdale	37	6	–	6,651	613	613	8
Campbeltown: Highland	496	38	30	54,296	4,498	4,498	15
Campbeltown: Lorne and Lowland	929	65	60	70,752	12,258	12,258	76
Coll	17	3	–	3,670	94	94	–
Connel	149	19	24	42,955	1,141	1,141	21
Colonsay and Oronsay	15	–	–	3,232	198	198	–
Kilbrandon and Kilchattan	90	14	–	25,531	561	561	30
Craignish	41	–	–	–	105	105	–
Kilninver and Kilmelford	59	6	–	10,053	112	112	4
Cumlodden, Lochfyneside and Lochgair	103	13	14	18,844	184	184	18
Dunoon: St John's	244	30	40	38,134	5,415	5,415	24
Sandbank	151	–	–	18,146	2,429	2,429	4
Dunoon: The High Kirk	430	38	36	–	5,859	5,859	16
Innellan	149	12	–	25,846	2,288	2,288	7
Toward	113	14	–	17,911	1,729	1,729	20
Gigha and Cara	44	7	–	10,226	99	99	14
Glassary, Kilmartin and Ford	121	11	10	21,248	2,606	725	10
North Knapdale	71	10	–	27,392	3,207	3,207	–
Glenaray and Inveraray	125	16	11	21,383	219	219	7
Glenorchy and Innishael	82	7	–	11,354	109	109	26
Strathfillan	48	5	–	11,723	77	77	–
Iona	23	6	–	5,029	65	265	6
Kilfinichen and Kilvickeon and the Ross of Mull	33	–	–	12,954	103	253	–
Jura	40	6	–	12,756	99	99	18
Kilarrow	108	17	17	27,895	1,191	1,191	12

Congregation	Com	Eld	G	In 05	Ass	Gvn	–18
Kilmeny	43	6	–	10,048	577	577	21
Kilberry	12	3	–	1,018	21	21	2
Tarbert	171	19	30	30,852	274	274	15
Kilcalmonell	56	7	10	8,425	78	78	8
Kilchoman	89	8	–	16,355	554	554	26
Portnahaven	19	4	16	6,329	316	316	3
Kilchrenan and Dalavich	34	4	7	8,565	395	395	–
Muckairn	133	15	13	23,131	516	516	25
Kildalton and Oa	125	15	16	36,321	434	434	28
Kilfinan	28	–	9	5,083	173	173	–
Kyles	185	17	26	25,419	876	876	14
Killean and Kilchenzie	183	13	16	29,771	492	581	38
Kilmodan and Colintraive	138	13	–	17,225	230	230	25
Kilmore and Oban	679	–	44	88,781	12,495	12,495	–
Kilmun (St Munn's)	118	11	30	14,915	371	371	9
Strone and Ardentinny	131	10	12	21,730	396	399	8
Kirn	363	24	28	80,020	9,224	9,224	15
Lochgilphead	217	18	17	28,086	420	420	18
Lochgoilhead and Kilmorich	116	12	19	26,856	339	439	7
Mull, Isle of, Kilninian and Kilmore	40	2	–	10,222	1,227	1,227	–
Salen and Ulva	31	8	–	11,282	1,170	1,170	6
Tobermory	85	14	–	23,284	662	662	16
Torosay and Kinlochspelvie	25	4	–	5,789	646	646	5
Rothesay: Trinity	467	45	48	58,060	6,765	6,765	92
Saddell and Carradale	228	15	27	29,976	459	859	2
Skipness	32	2	–	7,392	65	65	6
Southend	250	14	22	–	262	412	25
Strachur and Strachlachlan	140	18	20	25,939	862	862	12
The United Church of Bute	674	41	–	72,385	13,478	13,478	16
Tiree	106	9	22	19,879	217	366	18

22. Falkirk

Congregation	Com	Eld	G	In 05	Ass	Gvn	–18
Airth	157	8	16	–	2,388	2,388	35
Blackbraes and Shieldhill	190	16	18	21,036	100	209	20
Bo'ness: Old	524	37	33	60,964	7,610	7,610	87
Bo'ness: St Andrew's	572	32	–	63,703	9,662	9,662	125
Bonnybridge: St Helen's	359	19	31	43,753	4,423	4,423	149
Bothkennar and Carronshore	278	31	–	30,719	2,449	2,449	5
Brightons	752	42	73	127,531	16,062	17,228	233
Carriden	534	50	22	42,870	5,937	5,937	30
Cumbernauld: Abronhill	301	34	35	57,219	2,145	2,416	315
Cumbernauld: Condorrat	471	39	32	61,877	7,177	7,178	139
Cumbernauld: Kildrum	427	43	–	44,068	3,608	3,674	227
Cumbernauld: Old	488	39	–	62,268	7,583	7,583	101
Cumbernauld: St Mungo's	336	32	–	49,446	3,736	3,736	99
Denny: Dunipace	403	32	24	57,935	4,965	4,965	100
Denny: Old	475	50	30	62,094	9,552	9,552	100
Denny: Westpark	698	61	40	77,087	13,454	11,780	100

Congregation	Com	Eld	G	In 05	Ass	Gvn	–18
Falkirk: Bainsford.	320	13	–	38,717	3,434	3,434	76
Falkirk: Camelon	418	27	–	71,695	11,990	11,990	42
Falkirk: Erskine	535	42	41	75,021	12,134	12,609	–
Falkirk: Grahamston United.	470	53	41	71,515	12,288	12,288	98
Falkirk: Laurieston	257	19	32	37,250	4,358	4,358	20
Redding and Westquarter	183	13	40	23,933	2,560	2,560	24
Falkirk: Old and St Modan's	998	73	26	101,084	18,656	18,656	110
Falkirk: St Andrew's West	586	41	23	–	23,308	23,308	54
Falkirk: St James'.	272	25	16	34,176	3,580	3,580	67
Grangemouth: Dundas	210	21	–	36,167	2,114	2,114	13
Grangemouth: Kerse.	588	48	34	50,906	5,283	5,283	169
Grangemouth: Kirk of the Holy Rood	674	49	–	–	7,598	7,598	86
Grangemouth: Zetland	893	81	76	97,006	20,929	20,929	142
Haggs	307	30	17	38,575	3,507	3,507	78
Larbert: East	639	41	38	85,692	12,652	12,652	221
Larbert: Old	664	38	21	89,627	16,609	16,609	206
Larbert: West	541	44	39	68,288	9,801	9,801	225
Muiravonside	235	18	12	29,929	1,037	1,037	8
Polmont: Old	433	28	64	71,101	11,325	11,325	20
Slamannan	258	8	–	–	635	635	24
Stenhouse and Carron	512	47	23	82,532	9,940	10,152	21

23. Stirling

Aberfoyle	134	11	20	20,938	729	729	17
Port of Menteith	69	7	7	13,457	427	1,000	13
Alloa: North	282	19	25	52,552	4,579	4,579	23
Alloa: St Mungo's	654	49	50	62,970	10,790	10,788	18
Alloa: West	225	14	32	45,493	2,683	2,662	8
Alva	605	56	32	63,840	8,946	8,946	163
Balfron	178	18	22	60,806	10,359	10,359	15
Fintry	156	10	17	12,752	3,001	3,001	10
Balquhidder	99	5	–	18,077	1,747	1,747	6
Killin and Ardeonaig	160	10	15	24,235	1,752	1,752	9
Bannockburn: Allan	513	39	21	48,517	5,984	5,984	75
Bannockburn: Ladywell	497	34	21	–	1,000	1,000	17
Bridge of Allan	813	55	–	107,777	25,212	25,507	67
Buchanan	107	8	–	22,764	2,740	2,740	17
Drymen.	313	20	29	55,778	7,146	7,146	25
Buchlyvie	241	13	19	21,739	2,316	2,316	21
Gartmore.	79	10	–	16,443	1,868	1,868	11
Callander	693	47	49	114,323	23,011	23,011	120
Cambusbarron: The Bruce Memorial.	422	30	–	42,326	2,263	2,404	18
Clackmannan	503	38	40	67,078	12,362	12,562	50
Cowie	110	12	9	12,681	349	522	–
Plean.	219	6	–	21,680	437	437	–
Dollar	661	45	54	115,345	17,068	17,068	75
Glendevon.	52	10	–	–	542	542	–
Muckhart	141	10	–	–	3,428	–	14

Congregation	Com	Eld	G	In 05	Ass	Gvn	-18
Dunblane: Cathedral	1,042	89	89	224,044	46,220	46,220	285
Dunblane: St Blane's	413	43	35	88,076	15,818	15,818	30
Fallin	266	7	–	40,188	854	854	164
Gargunnock	196	14	–	17,167	2,622	2,622	22
Kilmadock	203	10	–	8,246	300	330	6
Kincardine-in-Menteith	112	8	–	11,823	600	600	15
Killearn	567	40	49	74,719	10,500	10,528	70
Kippen	300	22	25	30,714	4,236	4,236	7
Norrieston	145	13	16	17,482	1,565	1,565	10
Lecropt	263	16	26	43,877	3,658	3,658	20
Logie	577	54	52	88,651	16,189	19,189	61
Menstrie	403	29	25	56,994	7,972	7,972	23
Sauchie and Coalsnaughton	834	37	36	61,091	8,711	8,813	24
Stirling: Allan Park South	254	44	33	48,470	7,291	7,291	24
Stirling: Church of the Holy Rude	267	34	–	44,893	5,060	5,060	21
Stirling: North	537	41	24	56,661	8,294	8,294	155
Stirling: St Columba's	561	58	–	91,114	14,595	15,060	85
Stirling: St Mark's	283	10	–	31,124	300	300	–
Stirling: St Ninian's Old	818	60	–	78,531	14,031	14,031	41
Stirling: Viewfield	441	30	35	67,398	10,258	10,488	28
Strathblane	205	27	41	59,020	8,196	8,196	49
Tillicoultry	857	63	49	82,636	16,246	16,623	118
Tullibody: St Serf's	530	22	30	62,976	7,777	7,777	124

24. Dunfermline

Aberdour: St Fillan's	394	30	–	59,487	9,100	9,100	40
Beath and Cowdenbeath: North	210	17	–	44,246	320	320	54
Cairneyhill	195	21	–	22,009	4,100	4,100	40
Limekilns	329	49	–	62,120	13,200	13,200	30
Carnock and Oakley	220	22	16	50,883	3,900	3,900	26
Cowdenbeath: Trinity	425	25	–	50,978	2,000	2,000	61
Culross and Torryburn	317	21	–	39,738	2,569	6,054	14
Dalgety	645	46	41	110,137	16,200	16,200	69
Dunfermline: Abbey	781	71	–	125,855	24,000	24,000	200
Dunfermline: Gillespie Memorial	384	68	23	111,736	19,000	19,000	85
Dunfermline: North	217	19	–	34,870	330	330	17
Dunfermline: St Andrew's Erskine	248	23	14	38,197	1,350	1,350	170
Dunfermline: St Leonard's	511	40	36	66,374	8,379	8,379	92
Dunfermline: St Margaret's	405	49	29	51,273	6,300	6,300	33
Dunfermline: St Ninian's	340	31	50	38,343	1,200	2,867	63
Dunfermline: St Paul's East	–	–	–	–	–	–	–
Dunfermline: Townhill and Kingseat	432	32	37	66,159	6,500	6,621	30
Inverkeithing: St John's	186	19	19	30,562	3,000	4,130	82
North Queensferry	90	7	–	16,871	1,500	1,956	25
Inverkeithing: St Peter's	310	7	–	22,251	500	500	20
Kelty	368	30	55	61,823	5,100	5,100	90
Lochgelly and Benarty: St Serf's	600	69	–	62,082	4,808	4,808	34
Rosyth	313	24	–	34,788	800	800	35

Congregation	Com	Eld	G	In 05	Ass	Gvn	–18
Saline and Blairingone	219	14	20	41,851	5,100	5,300	30
Tulliallan and Kincardine	571	49	60	58,445	4,900	4,900	29
25. Kirkcaldy							
Auchterderran: St Fothad's	419	25	–	36,809	5,781	5,781	17
Kinglassie	196	12	–	–	2,840	2,840	4
Auchtertool	83	6	–	8,249	1,405	1,405	8
Kirkcaldy: Linktown	416	42	35	52,607	7,245	7,605	20
Buckhaven	246	24	–	39,419	640	640	15
Burntisland	598	42	54	41,446	9,049	9,049	57
Denbeath	81	4	24	7,091	87	–	10
Methilhill	165	16	36	21,125	173	200	17
Dysart	387	39	20	49,687	5,427	5,427	9
Glenrothes: Christ's Kirk	358	24	50	–	600	600	20
Glenrothes: St Columba's	622	35	25	56,006	7,131	7,131	47
Glenrothes: St Margaret's	407	37	35	54,619	6,152	6,152	74
Glenrothes: St Ninian's	309	45	17	59,887	6,883	6,883	28
Innerleven: East	177	8	25	27,239	186	186	45
Kennoway, Windygates and Balgonie: St Kenneth's	740	49	78	80,068	7,760	7,760	65
Kinghorn	449	29	–	77,831	8,564	7,708	33
Kirkcaldy: Abbotshall	686	60	–	72,031	13,323	13,323	89
Kirkcaldy: Pathhead	574	44	69	74,207	13,887	14,087	176
Kirkcaldy: St Andrew's	288	26	33	44,878	3,676	3,676	15
Kirkcaldy: St Bryce Kirk	810	50	–	81,066	18,220	19,207	48
Kirkcaldy: St John's	406	50	57	72,166	8,331	8,542	14
Kirkcaldy: Templehall	359	21	22	42,618	1,323	1,323	12
Kirkcaldy: Torbain	267	30	21	37,020	768	888	30
Kirkcaldy: Viewforth	348	14	–	33,351	3,848	3,848	65
Thornton	228	10	–	19,388	2,319	2,419	40
Leslie: Trinity	297	23	32	27,382	163	163	5
Leven	749	45	–	89,186	12,041	12,226	111
Markinch	625	40	41	72,730	7,314	7,314	28
Methil	380	21	29	32,910	1,100	1,100	6
Wemyss	161	10	28	26,496	582	582	7
26. St Andrews							
Abdie and Dunbog	176	18	–	16,363	1,076	1,076	–
Newburgh	275	16	–	22,740	880	–	22
Anstruther	364	21	–	44,142	2,830	2,830	28
Auchtermuchty	311	24	19	31,702	740	604	25
Balmerino	159	18	14	26,207	3,438	3,438	10
Wormit	295	23	41	30,302	4,400	4,400	41
Boarhills and Dunino	166	8	–	14,862	2,962	2,962	1
St Andrews: Martyrs'	335	30	31	36,549	7,307	7,307	4
Cameron	96	11	14	16,414	2,863	2,863	20
St Andrews: St Leonard's	637	52	31	101,561	23,515	23,515	40
Carnbee	114	16	22	15,285	1,361	1,361	8

Congregation	Com	Eld	G	In 05	Ass	Gvn	–18
Pittenweem	307	18	36	30,558	3,349	3,349	30
Cellardyke	304	23	48	36,384	3,979	3,979	12
Kilrenny	115	11	20	22,229	2,981	2,981	30
Ceres, Kemback and Springfield	473	35	–	50,730	12,447	12,447	36
Crail	433	31	47	44,193	7,270	7,270	10
Kingsbarns	101	9	–	–	2,305	2,305	–
Creich, Flisk and Kilmany	122	9	19	18,377	2,258	2,258	8
Monimail	120	16	–	21,622	2,650	2,650	28
Cupar: Old and St Michael of Tarvit	644	42	20	102,088	17,940	17,940	85
Cupar: St John's	828	44	64	69,911	9,608	9,608	54
Dairsie	138	10	18	19,038	1,855	1,855	6
Edenshead and Strathmiglo	234	13	19	24,088	333	333	8
Elie	405	34	73	58,104	15,555	15,555	15
Kilconquhar and Colinsburgh	222	20	–	34,159	5,156	5,156	23
Falkland	322	23	–	28,741	4,940	8,744	16
Freuchie	244	16	22	25,549	4,132	4,132	–
Howe of Fife	792	36	–	54,833	7,898	7,898	27
Largo and Newburn	270	15	–	34,549	5,962	5,962	10
Largo: St David's	188	17	47	28,889	4,353	8,972	4
Largoward	89	6	–	12,241	625	625	18
St Monans	312	15	45	54,237	5,562	5,562	75
Leuchars: St Athernase	503	17	36	53,260	5,323	5,323	14
Newport-on-Tay	404	44	–	65,820	10,516	10,716	73
St Andrews: Holy Trinity	638	31	54	58,547	8,932	8,932	30
St Andrews: Hope Park	753	75	56	119,646	29,600	29,600	45
Strathkinness	146	12	12	20,672	2,956	2,956	3
Tayport	472	188	27	40,691	3,285	3,285	25

27. Dunkeld and Meigle

Congregation	Com	Eld	G	In 05	Ass	Gvn	–18
Aberfeldy	260	17	19	43,529	2,865	3,015	122
Amulree and Strathbraan	17	3	–	–	574	574	1
Dull and Weem	95	10	20	14,336	1,515	1,515	15
Alyth	831	40	40	73,018	8,779	8,829	55
Ardler Kettins and Meigle	473	26	43	41,899	5,216	5,216	28
Bendochy	82	11	–	16,205	1,500	1,500	4
Coupar Angus: Abbey	383	32	17	45,238	3,360	3,360	80
Blair Atholl and Struan	149	20	22	20,078	158	158	10
Tenandry	73	9	8	21,329	219	219	9
Blairgowrie	980	57	–	96,237	13,490	13,490	27
Braes of Rannoch	34	9	–	14,698	219	1,019	–
Foss and Rannoch	126	17	23	22,744	494	494	14
Caputh and Clunie	201	25	13	21,481	2,314	2,314	22
Kinclaven	154	14	12	18,352	1,810	2,341	–
Dunkeld	443	31	20	86,435	16,597	16,597	50
Fortingall and Glenlyon	51	9	–	15,471	981	981	30
Kenmore and Lawers	95	8	21	–	1,085	3,726	–
Grantully, Logierait and Strathtay	164	16	12	37,664	950	950	23
Kirkmichael, Straloch and Glenshee	144	15	11	15,653	982	1,265	11

Congregation	Com	Eld	G	In 05	Ass	Gvn	–18
Rattray	497	20	32	42,124	4,212	4,212	21
Pitlochry	502	42	30	83,025	12,303	12,520	48

28. Perth

Congregation	Com	Eld	G	In 05	Ass	Gvn	–18
Abernethy and Dron	251	18	17	21,833	1,980	1,980	12
Arngask	149	13	26	16,364	1,976	1,976	35
Almondbank Tibbermore	332	25	42	32,845	837	837	70
Ardoch	172	10	34	28,319	2,859	2,859	20
Blackford	87	12	–	19,140	1,514	1,514	12
Auchterarder	711	34	58	82,209	13,972	14,283	35
Auchtergaven and Moneydie	526	23	34	40,666	3,442	3,442	–
Cargill Burrelton	351	18	38	42,682	3,605	3,605	20
Collace	133	9	21	17,384	3,086	3,086	12
Cleish	262	17	20	58,918	9,612	10,165	15
Fossoway: St Serf's and Devonside	231	16	–	36,847	7,036	7,036	37
Comrie	496	29	34	60,636	9,290	9,528	–
Dundurn	65	7	–	16,271	1,850	1,850	–
Crieff	975	54	48	98,807	12,555	12,555	73
Dunbarney	557	30	50	–	9,670	9,670	35
Forgandenny	91	9	9	12,951	1,966	1,966	8
Errol	300	13	18	43,765	4,228	4,228	14
Kilspindie and Rait	73	8	–	10,241	1,103	1,103	8
Fowlis Wester	123	12	–	16,942	994	994	10
Madderty	106	14	13	17,380	1,041	2,041	17
Monzie	103	9	–	14,207	1,082	1,082	–
Gask	126	12	13	10,650	2,919	2,919	–
Methven and Logiealmond	360	25	18	26,423	3,522	3,522	–
Kinross	666	32	36	69,745	12,130	12,130	80
Muthill	302	22	13	–	2,209	2,454	69
Trinity Gask and Kinkell	63	5	–	10,229	583	583	–
Orwell	380	27	28	39,783	4,842	4,952	40
Portmoak	151	16	–	21,831	4,139	4,238	1
Perth: Craigie	693	32	42	56,259	8,643	8,643	25
Perth: Kinnoull	462	34	30	58,987	9,137	9,137	52
Perth: Letham St Mark's	615	8	32	71,524	4,478	4,478	60
Perth: Moncrieffe	256	14	–	9,342	109	109	412
Perth: North	1,330	104	29	180,178	44,955	44,955	59
Perth: Riverside	62	–	–	–	143	–	–
Perth: St John the Baptist's	760	44	–	91,828	15,611	15,611	–
Perth: St Leonard's-in-the-Fields and Trinity	612	74	34	101,615	18,585	18,585	25
Perth: St Matthew's	965	61	42	102,503	17,555	17,555	46
Redgorton	156	14	48	18,526	1,353	1,353	20
Stanley	272	21	–	28,135	4,147	4,147	12
St Madoes and Kinfauns	345	24	28	37,469	525	525	65
St Martin's	193	6	14	10,364	1,632	2,003	10
Scone: New	568	41	65	61,165	9,542	9,542	52

Congregation	Com	Eld	G	In 05	Ass	Gvn	–18
Scone: Old	689	44	34	58,306	7,849	7,849	47
The Stewartry of Strathearn	512	40	–	54,783	3,004	4,404	30

29. Dundee

Congregation	Com	Eld	G	In 05	Ass	Gvn	–18
Abernyte	92	10	–	11,851	1,715	1,715	25
Inchture and Kinnaird	247	28	–	27,875	3,667	–	40
Longforgan	219	21	17	33,960	5,581	5,581	10
Auchterhouse	157	13	22	20,395	3,216	3,216	18
Murroes and Tealing	307	18	19	27,936	2,608	2,608	7
Dundee: Balgay	524	44	35	74,483	9,534	9,534	72
Dundee: Barnhill St Margaret's	834	67	54	111,723	26,812	26,812	33
Dundee: Broughty Ferry New Kirk	1,139	94	–	134,783	18,159	18,159	48
Dundee: Broughty Ferry St James'	233	11	37	42,430	5,467	5,467	39
Dundee: Broughty Ferry St Luke's and Queen Street	514	47	47	78,351	14,006	14,006	–
Dundee: Broughty Ferry St Stephen's and West	359	23	–	39,474	3,742	3,742	–
Dundee: Camperdown	192	20	18	29,036	262	262	10
Dundee: Chalmers Ardler	244	20	25	68,405	7,386	7,386	155
Dundee: Clepington and Fairmuir	487	36	–	54,701	3,514	3,514	50
Dundee: Craigiebank	303	12	20	45,749	7,573	–	162
Dundee: Douglas and Angus	189	22	25	29,804	3,754	3,754	64
Dundee: Downfield South	369	32	36	69,313	8,599	8,599	176
Dundee: Dundee (St Mary's)	674	63	37	85,110	20,891	20,891	20
Dundee: Lochee Old and St Luke's	250	22	21	37,184	2,180	2,180	6
Dundee: Lochee West	524	38	14	37,394	3,412	3,412	62
Dundee: Logie and St John's Cross	368	18	30	108,270	16,501	16,501	50
Dundee: Mains	222	11	–	17,930	228	–	12
Dundee: Mains of Fintry	144	6	–	45,703	5,111	10,927	23
Dundee: Meadowside St Paul's	538	44	30	69,063	11,348	11,908	86
Dundee: Menzieshill	419	26	–	41,150	2,745	3,645	140
Dundee: Mid Craigie	22	3	–	5,271	99	599	3
Dundee: St Andrew's	749	75	35	–	14,984	15,084	37
Dundee: St David's High Kirk	409	52	–	53,276	7,469	7,469	98
Dundee: Steeple	354	42	–	115,913	16,749	16,749	34
Dundee: Stobswell	590	–	–	72,249	10,246	10,246	–
Dundee: Strathmartine	493	37	38	52,856	7,347	7,344	12
Dundee: Trinity	698	55	35	53,025	4,479	4,479	96
Dundee: West	450	30	–	69,203	12,367	12,367	20
Dundee: Whitfield	–	–	–	12,752	99	99	–
Fowlis and Liff	157	16	13	19,948	2,457	2,457	16
Lundie and Muirhead of Liff	355	25	–	38,293	5,779	5,779	38
Invergowrie	474	46	63	58,758	5,789	5,939	115
Monifieth: Panmure	435	39	26	42,716	5,346	5,346	19
Monifieth: St Rule's	729	30	42	53,109	6,799	6,799	20
Monifieth: South	419	20	42	49,677	3,448	4,118	151
Monikie and Newbigging	256	19	–	–	250	250	–

Congregation	Com	Eld	G	In 05	Ass	Gvn	–18
30. Angus							
Aberlemno	200	11	–	18,902	1,336	1,336	11
Guthrie and Rescobie	226	9	18	22,165	1,401	1,401	16
Arbirlot	214	13	–	17,438	3,394	3,394	3
Carmyllie	134	8	10	19,246	2,823	2,823	9
Arbroath: Knox's	405	27	36	–	6,568	6,643	15
Arbroath: St Vigeans	649	46	–	60,166	11,510	11,738	21
Arbroath: Old and Abbey	688	43	45	83,963	11,568	11,568	86
Arbroath: St Andrew's	771	48	43	90,684	16,330	16,330	150
Arbroath: West Kirk	1,043	90	46	89,598	16,627	16,627	80
Barry	292	16	16	26,004	1,892	1,892	12
Carnoustie	540	43	32	65,300	12,588	12,588	12
Brechin: Cathedral	1,010	44	17	116,386	7,762	7,762	20
Brechin: Gardner Memorial	563	36	11	44,595	6,569	7,569	8
Carnoustie: Panbride	757	39	–	58,417	8,043	8,043	49
Colliston	205	11	11	16,166	3,050	3,050	20
Friockheim Kinnell	233	17	22	17,478	1,475	1,475	10
Inverkeilor and Lunan	211	10	19	–	2,574	2,574	–
Dun and Hillside	473	41	8	48,028	4,626	5,258	35
Dunnichen, Letham and Kirkden	371	19	32	44,963	994	1,652	26
Eassie and Nevay	63	9	–	5,963	491	937	3
Newtyle	304	15	57	26,567	2,317	4,891	15
Edzell Lethnot	417	24	47	44,148	6,998	6,998	22
Fern, Careston and Menmuir	132	9	–	12,806	2,278	2,278	4
Glenesk	60	2	–	4,617	1,196	–	–
Farnell	111	8	–	4,552	1,001	1,001	–
Forfar: East and Old	1,396	52	43	90,157	15,893	15,893	93
Forfar: Lowson Memorial	1,036	41	27	69,320	9,507	9,507	118
Forfar: St Margaret's	977	43	27	75,113	13,519	13,694	54
Glamis, Inverarity and Kinettles	423	31	–	45,050	3,783	3,783	27
Inchbrayock	220	11	–	36,520	5,354	5,979	–
Montrose: Melville South	347	19	–	33,755	6,026	6,026	–
Kirriemuir: St Andrew's	386	27	49	64,734	5,607	5,607	17
Oathlaw Tannadice	174	8	–	14,114	1,409	1,409	22
Montrose: Old and St Andrew's	1,016	55	–	105,937	15,286	16,112	141
The Glens and Kirriemuir: Old	1,182	96	–	158,013	29,204	29,204	60
The Isla Parishes	315	29	12	35,044	853	853	20
31. Aberdeen							
Aberdeen: Bridge of Don Oldmachar	279	5	–	121,898	2,465	2,465	300
Aberdeen: Cove	78	–	–	14,721	89	188	43
Aberdeen: Craigiebuckler	846	69	54	102,672	18,313	18,313	191
Aberdeen: Denburn	364	37	20	39,721	1,010	1,010	9
Aberdeen: Ferryhill	500	66	30	66,473	9,148	9,148	25
Aberdeen: Garthdee	283	17	26	31,393	380	380	14
Aberdeen: Gilcomston South	287	29	–	130,247	25,678	25,678	54
Aberdeen: High Hilton	579	53	47	–	18,316	18,316	55
Aberdeen: Holburn Central	443	45	20	57,373	7,375	7,375	8

Congregation	Com	Eld	G	In 05	Ass	Gvn	−18
Aberdeen: Holburn West	543	47	31	94,422	23,701	23,701	31
Aberdeen: Mannofield	1,689	129	67	180,646	51,325	51,325	193
Aberdeen: Mastrick	436	26	18	45,928	2,570	3,632	170
Aberdeen: Middlefield	179	11	–	–	88	88	2
Aberdeen: Midstocket	856	82	–	125,368	–	–	186
Aberdeen: New Stockethill	86	–	–	22,233	64	64	18
Aberdeen: Northfield	315	14	20	30,235	1,600	1,600	80
Aberdeen: Queen Street	955	81	–	–	19,100	19,640	33
Aberdeen: Queen's Cross	657	53	39	138,070	39,052	42,052	55
Aberdeen: Rosemount	129	21	–	20,208	267	267	1
Aberdeen: Rubislaw	657	89	53	134,083	33,741	33,741	50
Aberdeen: Ruthrieston South	644	45	56	–	8,124	9,124	97
Aberdeen: Ruthrieston West	417	37	24	58,973	5,952	5,952	16
Aberdeen: St Columba's Bridge of Don	382	24	–	78,416	15,160	15,160	46
Aberdeen: St George's Tillydrone	161	10	20	19,771	110	110	19
Aberdeen: St John's Church for the Deaf	108	4	–	–	–	–	–
Aberdeen: St Machar's Cathedral	635	43	–	102,556	24,222	24,222	25
Aberdeen: St Mark's	530	49	28	80,412	12,924	11,847	67
Aberdeen: St Mary's	513	45	21	48,538	105	105	–
Aberdeen: St Nicholas Kincorth, South of	477	33	35	51,706	5,268	5,268	45
Aberdeen: St Nicholas Uniting, Kirk of	525	61	22	75,841	7,268	7,268	6
Aberdeen: St Stephen's	268	29	22	53,605	3,935	4,243	50
Aberdeen: Summerhill	205	19	–	25,827	250	229	45
Aberdeen: Torry St Fittick's	557	31	28	50,223	80	80	3
Aberdeen: Woodside	359	33	26	44,360	500	670	67
Bucksburn Stoneywood	573	22	20	44,452	4,408	4,408	30
Cults	871	65	–	129,785	19,771	20,100	45
Dyce	1,326	75	43	–	14,681	14,681	283
Kingswells	441	32	29	47,687	2,997	2,997	42
Newhills	947	44	70	93,541	17,636	17,636	227
Peterculter	723	53	–	76,820	12,835	12,835	210

32. Kincardine and Deeside

Congregation	Com	Eld	G	In 05	Ass	Gvn	−18
Aberluthnott	231	9	19	17,285	2,000	2,000	10
Laurencekirk	516	13	50	29,538	3,265	3,264	16
Aboyne – Dinnet	480	13	32	–	6,286	6,286	20
Arbuthnott and Bervie	588	36	–	50,114	2,854	2,854	71
Banchory-Devenick and Maryculter/Cookney	385	17	–	39,115	1,849	1,849	27
Banchory-Ternan: East	1,096	53	45	89,927	11,118	11,118	115
Banchory-Ternan: West	678	43	42	99,028	12,444	13,087	60
Birse and Feughside	285	31	20	35,058	3,991	4,392	12
Braemar and Crathie	288	25	–	68,774	7,797	7,797	–
Cromar	262	12	–	–	219	176	20
Drumoak and Durris	462	25	–	58,863	1,320	1,320	73
Glenmuick (Ballater)	360	25	31	45,069	3,235	3,235	6

Congregation . . . . Com	Eld	G	In 05	Ass	Gvn	–18
Kinneff 164	5	6	9,082	571	421	–
Stonehaven: South 301	24	12	43,702	3,401	3,401	15
Mearns Coastal. 347	16	–	30,830	1,539	1,539	3
Mid Deeside 847	53	32	49,908	7,178	7,178	30
Newtonhill 400	18	20	34,297	1,390	1,390	139
Portlethen 512	21	–	51,919	8,089	8,089	205
Stonehaven: Dunnottar. 882	35	23	63,361	10,411	10,411	20
Stonehaven: Fetteresso. 936	54	40	127,931	18,349	18,349	194
West Mearns. 562	28	54	41,224	5,191	5,191	27
33. Gordon						
Barthol Chapel 101	7	10	5,735	918	1,058	25
Tarves 501	–	34	38,117	4,139	4,139	–
Belhelvie. 393	35	17	64,016	4,177	4,177	61
Blairdaff 103	11	–	9,423	1,037	1,037	7
Chapel of Garioch 321	30	18	31,561	2,396	2,396	40
Cluny 205	12	9	21,725	1,720	1,720	9
Monymusk 125	4	7	16,597	1,013	1,013	22
Culsalmond and Rayne 236	7	–	9,813	220	290	15
Daviot. 158	9	–	15,530	1,409	1,445	10
Cushnie and Tough. 293	–	–	30,924	656	3,656	15
Drumblade 130	9	13	7,180	2,004	2,004	10
Huntly Strathbogie 803	43	23	65,784	8,706	8,706	85
Echt. 291	15	14	28,883	1,675	1,675	15
Midmar. 166	7	–	14,769	1,519	1,519	8
Ellon 1,761	101	–	128,158	21,256	21,256	23
Fintray and Kinellar 173	12	14	17,755	956	869	15
Keithhall. 66	–	–	6,110	709	1,497	–
Foveran. 370	17	–	31,544	1,528	1,524	40
Howe Trinity. 696	32	44	46,025	5,781	6,016	35
Huntly Cairnie Glass 813	24	38	40,747	4,009	4,009	9
Insch-Leslie-Premnay-Oyne. 569	43	38	–	5,541	6,738	31
Inverurie: St Andrew's. 1,301	41	45	100,392	14,709	14,709	11
Inverurie: West 787	62	38	77,759	9,312	9,312	82
Kemnay. 639	36	–	41,122	6,106	8,050	105
Kintore 881	47	32	84,951	14,629	15,629	50
Meldrum and Bourtie 545	34	45	60,423	5,003	5,003	42
Methlick 367	23	30	41,317	3,386	3,386	15
New Machar. 516	27	25	41,536	4,173	4,173	85
Noth 364	13	–	–	110	100	14
Skene 1,565	99	66	126,242	18,325	21,579	209
Udny and Pitmedden 488	31	15	51,200	5,447	5,447	65
Upper Donside 457	19	–	37,742	1,041	1,000	20
34. Buchan						
Aberdour. 148	10	13	9,914	695	695	27
Pitsligo 139	12	–	–	1,285	–	45
Sandhaven. 84	7	–	8,571	626	626	28

Congregation	Com	Eld	G	In 05	Ass	Gvn	–18
Auchaber United	170	13	16	13,739	974	885	9
Auchterless	209	19	16	25,768	1,657	1,717	11
Banff	837	36	33	72,149	16,865	17,049	185
King Edward	167	18	10	18,122	4,133	4,133	12
Crimond	270	12	15	18,595	219	219	21
Lonmay	174	14	11	10,252	982	982	–
St Fergus	213	11	16	10,035	219	219	–
Cruden	492	33	24	51,658	4,601	4,601	45
Deer	885	32	23	47,521	4,414	4,414	24
Fordyce	528	30	27	51,906	6,423	6,503	40
Fraserburgh: Old	840	62	82	115,829	31,560	31,560	258
Fraserburgh: South	337	27	–	38,033	4,242	4,242	43
Inverallochy and Rathen: East	92	12	–	16,923	2,592	2,592	12
Fraserburgh: West	672	40	–	48,646	7,047	7,047	40
Rathen: West	113	8	–	7,314	862	862	10
Fyvie	402	26	44	39,502	5,420	5,420	20
Rothienorman	181	10	18	11,095	1,033	1,033	4
Gardenstown	70	10	30	45,312	2,831	2,831	63
Longside	552	27	–	45,187	4,981	4,981	160
Macduff	881	44	67	83,965	13,381	15,921	80
Marnoch	393	18	12	29,142	2,178	2,302	6
Maud and Savoch	255	16	24	23,659	842	842	12
New Deer: St Kane's	472	21	21	39,458	5,729	5,729	100
Monquhitter and New Byth	393	22	14	21,115	2,731	2,731	18
Turriff: St Andrew's	569	28	17	42,410	4,820	4,820	49
New Pitsligo	359	10	–	21,377	1,224	1,224	19
Strichen and Tyrie	643	22	–	42,961	3,777	3,777	23
Ordiquhill and Cornhill	158	10	10	11,228	356	573	20
Whitehills	309	16	39	28,294	2,666	3,257	24
Peterhead: Old	492	36	36	54,374	6,124	6,124	25
Peterhead: St Andrew's	587	37	31	50,087	6,172	6,170	59
Peterhead: Trinity	378	27	27	86,909	16,920	16,920	22
Turriff: St Ninian's and Forglen	987	43	57	71,953	9,725	9,932	104

35. Moray

Aberlour	355	28	26	38,255	3,241	3,241	28
Alves and Burghead	165	18	46	20,709	1,734	1,734	10
Kinloss and Findhorn	92	16	10	12,203	1,429	1,479	7
Bellie	317	17	42	42,576	7,642	7,642	36
Speymouth	236	11	25	17,876	2,404	2,404	10
Birnie and Pluscarden	306	28	–	32,903	6,253	6,253	14
Elgin: High	728	50	39	72,069	13,755	13,755	61
Buckie: North	517	45	58	54,733	6,229	6,479	42
Buckie: South and West	326	30	33	36,153	4,743	4,743	218
Enzie	101	7	13	9,728	750	750	10
Cullen and Deskford	395	33	44	50,169	4,781	4,781	12
Dallas	59	7	14	9,203	1,916	1,916	16
Forres: St Leonard's	294	18	45	66,432	9,100	9,100	18

Congregation	Com	Eld	G	In 05	Ass	Gvn	–18
Rafford	77	5	–	9,896	1,829	1,829	8
Duffus, Spynie and Hopeman	373	41	29	45,678	4,886	4,886	21
Dyke	161	13	18	19,358	2,579	2,579	25
Edinkillie	90	13	–	16,083	1,951	1,951	8
Elgin: St Giles' and St Columba's South	1,425	102	–	124,580	23,916	23,916	168
Findochty	54	10	12	23,344	560	560	44
Portknockie	95	8	34	23,628	763	763	70
Rathven	115	14	27	18,632	1,090	1,090	9
Forres: St Laurence	616	41	53	67,768	10,153	10,153	15
Keith: North, Newmill, Boharm and Rothiemay	682	54	–	84,238	12,715	13,015	132
Keith: St Rufus, Botriphnie and Grange	1,072	61	–	65,464	6,489	6,489	122
Knockando, Elchies and Archiestown	277	16	12	19,674	1,174	1,500	–
Rothes	330	20	24	27,356	3,519	3,519	41
Lossiemouth: St Gerardine's High	391	21	39	53,384	6,666	6,666	25
Lossiemouth: St James'	344	20	42	47,804	3,943	3,943	22
Mortlach and Cabrach	410	22	33	–	750	895	7
St Andrew's-Lhanbryd and Urquhart	506	28	27	54,240	7,352	7,352	30

36. Abernethy

Abernethy	160	19	–	36,997	2,943	2,943	65
Cromdale and Advie	97	3	–	13,276	526	1,035	5
Alvie and Insh	75	8	–	22,952	2,035	2,035	11
Boat of Garten and Kincardine	94	10	20	22,724	409	409	12
Duthil	72	10	17	9,784	169	169	15
Dulnain Bridge	38	6	–	9,951	907	907	4
Grantown-on-Spey	271	21	27	39,352	3,976	3,976	8
Kingussie	131	15	–	21,616	216	216	22
Laggan	35	5	–	11,990	333	333	17
Newtonmore	87	14	–	24,169	540	540	11
Rothiemurchus and Aviemore	93	4	–	20,090	179	179	9
Tomintoul, Glenlivet and Inveraven	174	14	–	–	216	425	20

37. Inverness

Ardersier	67	14	12	15,474	646	646	12
Petty	73	12	9	18,260	741	741	21
Auldearn and Dalmore	81	7	17	11,817	105	105	6
Cawdor	185	18	–	26,349	1,920	1,920	19
Croy and Dalcross	58	9	13	10,346	752	752	8
Culloden: The Barn	351	25	26	61,937	8,700	8,700	170
Daviot and Dunlichity	63	9	–	15,935	489	489	17
Moy, Dalarossie and Tomatin	34	5	10	11,629	434	434	31
Dores and Boleskine	100	7	–	16,527	206	545	5
Inverness: Crown	809	89	81	121,635	23,231	23,231	207
Inverness: Dalneigh and Bona	285	19	27	82,799	12,530	12,530	72
Inverness: East	327	40	–	129,866	26,906	26,906	151

Congregation	Com	Eld	G	In 05	Ass	Gvn	–18
Inverness: Hilton	271	10	28	80,542	2,754	–	114
Inverness: Inshes	181	16	–	99,690	13,202	13,202	31
Inverness: Kinmylies	154	12	–	45,458	426	526	15
Inverness: Ness Bank	619	68	35	104,884	16,171	16,171	119
Inverness: Old High St Stephen's	550	64	–	96,328	21,060	21,060	61
Inverness: St Columba High	232	26	19	44,201	8,270	8,420	–
Inverness: Trinity	367	36	30	60,579	11,350	11,350	90
Kilmorack and Erchless	133	16	25	45,640	1,716	1,716	52
Kiltarlity	46	7	8	12,812	525	525	–
Kirkhill	74	5	13	13,890	361	361	–
Nairn: Old	893	62	35	105,132	18,611	18,611	70
Nairn: St Ninian's	263	17	32	34,727	2,085	2,085	30
Urquhart and Glenmoriston	133	7	14	50,604	4,431	4,431	32

38. Lochaber

Congregation	Com	Eld	G	In 05	Ass	Gvn	–18
Acharacle	39	2	–	20,110	111	111	7
Ardnamurchan	20	4	–	6,428	75	75	12
Ardgour	53	7	11	15,524	125	125	14
Strontian	27	4	10	8,925	72	72	19
Arisaig and the Small Isles	65	8	17	13,992	99	282	15
Mallaig: St Columba and Knoydart	57	4	–	26,637	250	250	48
Duror	45	7	14	11,798	238	238	20
Glencoe: St Munda's	68	8	27	14,785	261	261	8
Fort Augustus	73	7	15	19,714	279	387	–
Glengarry	37	7	12	13,002	179	179	12
Fort William: Duncansburgh	293	26	28	59,187	8,177	9,445	79
Kilmonivaig	82	5	11	17,378	5,331	5,331	10
Fort William: MacIntosh Memorial	205	27	24	45,838	3,531	3,531	15
Kilmallie	173	19	34	–	3,613	3,613	42
Kinlochleven	69	12	18	21,299	586	586	13
Nether Lochaber	52	10	–	–	504	604	17
Morvern	48	6	10	11,539	152	152	10

39. Ross

Congregation	Com	Eld	G	In 05	Ass	Gvn	–18
Alness	94	14	–	25,910	830	830	19
Avoch	35	5	15	16,567	1,833	1,833	14
Fortrose and Rosemarkie	123	17	–	30,658	4,287	4,287	4
Contin	64	10	–	19,734	200	990	–
Cromarty	72	7	14	19,507	180	180	50
Dingwall: Castle Street	126	16	22	37,174	3,457	3,457	2
Dingwall: St Clement's	254	28	24	56,171	5,053	5,053	45
Fearn Abbey and Nigg	117	16	–	23,106	240	240	7
Tarbat	69	10	–	14,017	240	240	–
Ferintosh	197	23	37	46,688	2,757	2,957	25
Fodderty and Strathpeffer	143	16	23	31,783	330	619	16
Invergordon	172	13	–	49,130	4,589	4,589	30
Killearnan	139	20	–	34,459	1,562	1,562	19
Knockbain	70	11	–	16,155	781	840	–

Congregation . . . . Com	Eld	G	In 05	Ass	Gvn	–18
Kilmuir and Logie Easter. 75	10	19	–	404	787	12
Kiltearn. 89	7	–	28,787	300	300	47
Lochbroom and Ullapool 58	5	12	34,765	490	490	25
Resolis and Urquhart 92	8	–	22,256	370	370	24
Rosskeen. 138	11	20	43,428	2,110	2,310	50
Tain. 167	12	21	77,317	5,237	5,237	25
Urray and Kilchrist. 117	15	19	38,725	1,201	1,201	36

40. Sutherland

Altnaharra and Farr 34	–	–	13,266	99	99	8
Assynt and Stoer 28	2	–	–	119	119	18
Clyne 75	10	–	18,800	87	87	17
Kildonan and Loth Helmsdale 31	4	16	17,263	174	174	–
Creich 38	6	–	9,681	102	102	14
Rosehall 26	4	–	5,509	82	82	6
Dornoch Cathedral 393	38	68	107,647	13,961	13,961	75
Durness and Kinlochbervie 37	3	13	–	206	206	15
Eddrachillis. 18	2	–	17,063	108	108	3
Golspie 91	22	18	30,948	336	336	20
Kincardine Croick and Edderton 76	11	16	23,550	411	411	17
Lairg 50	6	22	25,340	165	391	19
Rogart. 25	4	9	11,889	132	132	4
Melness and Tongue. 51	6	–	14,652	99	99	8

41. Caithness

Bower 39	6	12	12,337	101	495	14
Watten. 46	4	–	13,934	116	410	25
Canisbay. 46	3	21	12,656	145	285	19
Keiss 27	2	9	10,789	81	101	5
Dunnet 18	3	7	–	61	61	–
Olrig 56	4	10	9,081	75	75	16
Halkirk and Westerdale 80	6	18	18,990	75	75	20
Reay 25	8	13	8,532	104	104	5
Strathy and Halladale. 23	6	17	8,746	111	111	5
The Parish of Latheron. 78	11	–	18,990	–	–	20
Thurso: St Peter's and St Andrew's 233	16	44	65,636	6,791	6,791	25
Thurso: West. 289	26	37	49,417	4,395	4,392	26
Wick: Bridge Street 168	9	–	37,271	2,515	2,515	–
Wick: Old 230	40	37	–	6,083	6,178	24
Wick: Pulteneytown and Thrumster. 238	14	25	–	6,379	–	268

42. Lochcarron – Skye

Applecross, Lochcarron and Torridon 84	6	–	36,221	835	1,523	27
Bracadale and Duirinish. 82	6	–	31,293	500	500	80
Gairloch and Dundonnell 98	5	–	63,895	5,672	5,672	30
Glenelg and Kintail 56	11	–	26,040	393	847	29
Kilmuir and Stenscholl. 73	9	–	37,310	950	948	45
Lochalsh 86	10	28	41,408	1,169	1,536	54

Congregation . . . . Com	Eld	G	In 05	Ass	Gvn	–18
Portree 132	8	–	48,091	3,917	3,917	30
Snizort 70	8	–	47,298	2,439	3,439	37
Strath and Sleat 195	11	33	83,061	8,727	8,741	73

43. Uist

Barra. 38	2	–	13,653	99	99	19
Benbecula. 72	11	15	30,508	286	286	30
Berneray and Lochmaddy 59	5	–	32,491	206	206	7
Carinish 80	10	20	39,734	2,032	2,032	35
Kilmuir and Paible 31	4	–	38,318	383	383	33
Manish-Scarista 43	3	–	29,532	601	601	14
South Uist. 60	10	10	20,118	228	228	17
Tarbert. 148	14	–	79,957	11,145	11,145	63

44. Lewis

Barvas. 93	10	–	60,806	3,629	3,629	40
Carloway. 40	1	–	29,106	219	919	21
Cross Ness 56	8	–	55,421	1,777	1,777	25
Kinloch. 46	9	–	28,474	249	249	22
Knock 58	2	–	45,740	1,595	1,595	25
Lochs-Crossbost. 26	4	–	23,272	184	184	18
Lochs-in-Bernera 32	3	–	20,031	100	100	12
Stornoway: High. 256	17	–	121,405	22,411	22,411	80
Stornoway: Martin's Memorial 125	8	17	54,021	4,981	4,981	72
Stornoway: St Columba 140	16	55	72,780	8,878	8,878	130
Uig 38	6	–	23,791	228	228	–

45. Orkney

Birsay, Harray and Sandwick. 383	31	–	35,192	2,096	2,096	35
East Mainland. 291	25	–	25,935	704	704	10
Eday 6	1	–	2,525	29	29	–
Stronsay: Moncur Memorial 72	9	18	11,106	98	98	17
Evie. 41	3	–	6,243	692	692	–
Firth 120	8	19	25,341	2,389	2,389	40
Rendall 55	3	15	8,211	503	804	12
Flotta. 27	4	–	2,822	44	44	–
Hoy and Walls 65	11	13	–	64	64	6
Kirkwall: East. 476	47	39	55,410	7,610	7,610	51
Kirkwall: St Magnus Cathedral 793	67	34	69,090	12,093	12,093	–
North Ronaldsay. 16	1	–	1,848	23	12	–
Sanday 83	10	13	8,674	107	–	10
Orphir. 131	12	16	18,746	556	1,134	12
Stenness 89	9	–	14,941	474	607	3
Papa Westray 11	3	–	5,894	44	44	7
Westray. 72	16	24	20,103	194	194	25
Rousay 28	4	8	1,404	99	99	–
Shapinsay 63	8	–	4,255	99	99	–
South Ronaldsay and Burray 177	12	14	17,609	174	174	12

Congregation .... Com	Eld	G	In 05	Ass	Gvn	–18
Stromness 388	27	26	38,827	5,767	5,543	20
46. Shetland						
Burra Isle 43	6	25	8,486	296	271	17
Tingwall 166	19	11	31,272	1,673	1,673	36
Delting 94	8	–	19,608	9	9	19
Northmavine 84	10	–	11,062	88	88	11
Dunrossness and St Ninian's						
inc. Fair Isle 69	18	–	17,208	779	779	28
Sandwick, Cunningsburgh and Quarff 138	11	30	23,676	1,304	1,304	53
Fetlar 20	5	–	1,330	53	–	–
Unst 132	10	25	17,860	32	32	–
Yell 122	10	14	11,297	194	194	–
Lerwick and Bressay 520	–	9	69,985	8,076	8,076	90
Nesting and Lunnasting 40	5	18	6,898	265	265	–
Whalsay and Skerries 239	18	20	23,501	741	741	15
Sandsting and Aithsting 48	8	–	6,285	6	50	28
Walls and Sandness 42	9	5	5,941	80	80	10
47. England						
Corby: St Andrew's 309	23	33	53,682	1,850	1,850	15
Corby: St Ninian's 299	20	12	37,565	3,210	3,951	12
Guernsey: St Andrew's in the Grange 242	20	–	48,129	4,376	4,376	20
Jersey: St Columba's 125	18	–	55,224	4,937	4,937	23
Liverpool: St Andrew's 38	5	7	18,201	1,601	1,600	8
London: Crown Court 246	41	8	78,616	16,189	16,189	30
London: St Columba's 1,115	49	–	224,498	59,363	61,363	102
Newcastle: St Andrew's 111	21	–	–	1,035	1,035	12

INDEX OF MINISTERS

NOTE: Ministers who are members of a Presbytery are designated 'A' if holding a parochial appointment in that Presbytery, or 'B' if otherwise qualifying for membership.

'A-1, A-2' etc. indicate the numerical order of congregations in the Presbyteries of Edinburgh, Glasgow and Hamilton.

Also included are:

(1) Ministers who have resigned their seat in Presbytery (List 6-H)
(2) Ministers who hold a Practising Certificate (List 6-I)
(3) Ministers serving overseas (List 6-K)
(4) Auxiliary Ministers (List 6-A)
(5) Ministers ordained for sixty years and upwards (List 6-Q)
(6) Ministers who have died since the publication of the last *Year Book* (List 6-R)

NB *For a list of the Diaconate, see List 6-G.*

Abeledo, B.J.	Greenock/Paisley 14B	Andrews, J.E.	Lothian 3B
Acklam, C.R.	West Lothian 2A	Annand, J.M.	Annandale/Eskdale 7B
Adams, D.G.	Dunfermline 24A	Arbuthnott, Mrs J.	List 6-I
Adamson, A.	Ardrossan 12A	Archer, N.D.C.	List 6-I
Adamson, H.	Irvine/Kilmarnock 11A	Armitage, W.L.	Edinburgh 1B
Aiken, P.W.I.	Wigtown/Stranraer 9A	Armstrong, W.R.	G'ock/Paisley 14A
Aitchison, J.W.	Aberdeen 31B	Arnott, A.D.K.	St Andrews 26A
Aitken, A.J.	Glasgow 16B	Atkins, Mrs Y.E.S.	Lothian 3A
Aitken, A.R.	Edinburgh 1B	Atkinson, G.T.	Glasgow 16A-134
Aitken, E.D.	Stirling 23B	Auffermann, M.	Aberdeen 31A
Aitken, E.R.	List 6-I	Auld, A.G.	Edinburgh 1B
Aitken, F.R.	Ayr 10A	Austin, G.	Moray 35A
Aitken, I.M.	Aberdeen 31A		
Aitken, J.D.	Edinburgh 1A-79	Baigrie, R.A.	Edinburgh 1B
Albon, D.W.	West Lothian 2A	Bailey, W.G.	List 6-H
Alexander, D.N.	G'ock/Paisley 14B	Baillie, D.	Dum'/Kirkcudbright 8B
Alexander, E.J.	Glasgow 16B	Bain, B.	Perth 28A
Alexander, I.W.	List 6-I	Baird, G.W.	List 6-R
Alexander, J.S.	St Andrews 26B	Baird, K.S.	Edinburgh 1A-40
Alexander, W.M.	Aberdeen 31B	Baker, Mrs C.	Ayr 10A
Allan, A.G.	Glasgow 16B	Balfour, T.	List 6-R
Allan, R.T.	Falkirk 22A	Ballantyne, S.	List 6-R
Allen, M.A.W.	Glasgow 16A-13	Ballentine, Miss A.M.	W' Lothian 2A
Allen, Ms V.L.	Angus 30A	Banks, J.	Ayr 10B
Allison, A.	Dunfermline 24A	Barber, P.I.	Edinburgh 1A-27
Allison, Ms M.M.	Glasgow 16A-85	Barbour, R.A.	Dunkeld/Meigle 27B
Allison, R.N.	G'ock/Paisley 14A	Barclay, I.C.	Aberdeen 31A
Almond, D.	Annandale/Eskdale 7A	Barclay, N.W.	Falkirk 22B
Alston, W.G.	Glasgow 16A-107	Barclay, S.G.	Irvine/Kilmarnock 11A
Amed, P.	Moray 35A	Bardgett, F.D.	List 6-I
Anderson, A.F.	Edinburgh 1A-30	Barge, N.L.	Glasgow 16A-42
Anderson, C.M.	Glasgow 16B	Barr, A.C.	Glasgow 16B
Anderson, D.	List 6-I	Barr, G.K.	Perth 28B
Anderson, D.M.	Lochaber 38B	Barr, G.R.	Edinburgh 1A-18
Anderson, D.P.	Argyll 19A	Barr, J.	Glasgow 16B
Anderson, D.U.	Edinburgh 1A-69	Barr, T.L.	Perth 28B
Anderson, J.F.	Aberdeen 31A	Barrett, L.	Dundee 29B
Anderson, J.W.	Angus 30B	Barrie, A.	Falkirk 22A
Anderson, K.G.	Angus 30B	Barrie, A.P.	Hamilton 17A-43
Anderson, R.A.	West Lothian 2A	Barrington, C.W.H.	Edinburgh 1A-2
Anderson, R.J.M.	Moray 35A	Barron, Mrs J.L.	Jerusalem 49A
Anderson, R.S.	Edinburgh 1B	Bartholomew, D.S.	Dum'/K'cud' 8A
Anderson, Mrs S.M.	Irv'/K'nock 11A	Baxendale, Mrs G.M.	Kincardine/Deeside 32A
Andrew, J.	Gordon 33B	Baxter, R.	Kirkcaldy 25A
Andrew, R.J.M.	Ayr 10B		
Baxter, R.F.	Edinburgh 1B		
Bayne, A.L.	Lothian 3B		
Beaton, D.	Lochcarron/Skye 42B		
Beattie, J.A.	Glasgow 16B		
Beattie, W.	List 6-I		
Beattie, W.G.	Hamilton 17B		
Beattie, W.G.	Aberdeen 31B		
Beautyman, P.H.	Edinburgh 1A-26		
Beck, J.C.	List 6-H		
Beckett, D.M.	Edinburgh 1B		
Beebee, G.W.	England 47A		
Bell, C.J.G.	Ross 39A		
Bell, D.W.	Argyll 19B		
Bell, G.K.	Glasgow 16A-59		
Bell, I.W.	Greenock/Paisley 14A		
Bell, J.L.	Glasgow 16B		
Bell, Mrs M.	Greenock/Paisley 14A		
Bell, R.P.	Ayr 10A		
Bennett, A.	St Andrews 26B		
Bennett, A.G.	Melrose/Peebles 4A		
Bennett, D.K.P.	Dum'/K'cudbright 8B		
Benson, J.W.	Stirling 23B		
Benzie, I.W.	Ardrossan 12A		
Berrill, P.A.D.	Kirkcaldy 25A		
Bertram, T.A.	Perth 28B		
Beveridge, S.E.P.	Annan'/Eskdale 7B		
Bews, J.	St Andrews 26B		
Bezuidenhout, L.C.	Dum'/K'cudbright 8A		
Bicket, M.S.	Angus 30A		
Billes, R.H.	Moray 35A		
Birch, J.	Glasgow 16A-11		
Bircham, M.F.	Perth 28A		
Birnie, C.J.	Buchan 34B		
Birnie, N.	List 6-R		
Birrell, Mrs I.	Perth 28A		
Birrell, J.M.	Perth 28B		
Birse, G.S.	Ayr 10A		
Birss, A.D.	Greenock/Paisley 14A		
Bjarnason, S.	Abernethy 36A		
Black, A.G.	Lothian 3B		
Black, A.R.	Irv'/Kilmarnock 11A		
Black, A.T.	Inverness 37B		
Black, D.R.	Glasgow 16A-112		
Black, D.W.	West Lothian 2A		

Duncan, R.F.	Angus 30B	Ferguson, S.B.	List 6-I	Frizzell, R.S.	Inverness 37B
Dundas, T.B.S.	West Lothian 2B	Ferguson, W.B.	Glasgow 16A-53	Froude, K.	Kirkcaldy 25A
Dunleavy, Miss S.	G'ock/Paisley 14A	Fergusson, D.A.S.	Edinburgh 1B	Fulcher, S	Argyll 19A
Dunlop, A.J.	Argyll 19B	Fiddes, G.R.	Ayr 10A	Fulton, F.H.	Dunkeld/Meigle 27B
Dunlop, M.W.B.	Buchan 34B	Fields, J.T.	England 47B	Fyall, R.S.	List 6-I
Dunn, W.I.C.	Edinburgh 1B	Finch, G.S.	Glasgow 16A-7		
Dunn, W.S.	Hamilton 17B	Findlay, H.J.W.	Dunfermline 24B	Gaddes, D.R.	Duns 5B
Dunnett, A.L.	Glasgow 16A-108	Finlay, Mrs J.G.	Perth 28A	Galbraith, D.	Edinburgh 1B
Dunphy, Mrs R.	Europe 48A	Finlay, Q.	Angus 30B	Galbraith, N.W.	Glasgow 16A-62
(Dunphy, R.G.	Europe 48)	Finlay, W.P.	Glasgow 16B	Galbraith, W.J.L.	Perth 28B
Dunsmore, B.W.	England 47A	Finlayson, D.	List 6-H	Gale, R.A.A.	Duns 5B
Dupar, K.W.	Ross 39B	Finnie, C.J.	Jedburgh 6A	Gall, R.	Kincardine/Deeside 32A
Durno, R.C.	Glasgow 16A-88	Fisher, D.N.	Annandale/Eskdale 7B	Gallacher, Miss J.W.	Falkirk 22A
Dutch, M.M.	Greenock/Paisley 14A	Fisher, K.H.	List 6-R	Gallan, A.	List 6-R
Duthie, G.	List 6-R	Fisher, M.L.	Glasgow 16A-148	Galloway, A.D.	List 6-R
Dutton, D.W.	Wigtown/Stranraer 9A	Fisk, Mrs E.A.	Dunfermline 24A	Galloway, I.F.	Glasgow 16A-80
		Fleming, A.F.	Stirling 23B	Galloway, Mrs K.	Glasgow 16B
Earnshaw, P.	St Andrews 26B	Fleming, H.K.	Perth 28B	Galloway, R.W.C.	St Andrews 26B
Easton, D.J.C.	Lanark 13B	Fleming, T.G.	List 6-I	Gammack, G.	Dundee 29B
Easton, I.A.G.	Dumbarton 18B	Fletcher, G.G.	Glasgow 16A-56	Garden, Miss M.J.	Gordon 33A
Easton, Mrs L.C.	Hamilton 17A-2	Fletcher, Mrs S.G.	Stirling 23A	Gardner, A.	Europe 48A
Eddie, D.C.	Aberdeen 31A	Fletcher, T.	England 47A	Gardner, B.K.	Kin'/Deeside 32A
Edington, G.L.	St Andrews 26B	Flockhart, D.R.	List 6-I	Gardner, Mrs F.	Glasgow 16A-140
Elder, A.B.	Dum'/K'cudbright 8B	Foggitt, E.W.	Lothian 3A	Gardner, F.J.	Greenock/Paisley 14A
Elders, I.A.	List 6-R	Forbes, I.M.	Lothian 3B	Gardner, J.V.	Edinburgh 1B
Elliott, G.J.	Edinburgh 1B	Forbes, J.W.A.	Kincard'/Deeside 32B	Gardner, N.N.	Edinburgh 1A-7
Elliott, K.C.	Ayr 10A	Ford, A.A.	Glasgow 16A-141	Gardner, P.M.	Glasgow 16A-116
Ellis, D.W.	List 6-I	Ford, C.H.M.	Edinburgh 1A-77	Garrity, T.A.W.	Ayr 10B and List 6-K
Elston, I.	Kirkcaldy 25A	Forrest, A.B.	Argyll 19B	Gaston, A.R.C.	Perth 28B
Elston, P.K.	Kirkcaldy 25B	Forrest, M.R.	Argyll 19A	Gatherer, J.F.	Dum'/K'cudbright 8A
Embleton, B.M.	Edinburgh 1A-67	Forrester, D.B.	Edinburgh 1B	Gatt, D.W.	Kirkcaldy 25B
Embleton, Mrs S.R.	Edinburgh 1A-42	Forrester, I.L.	Kirkcaldy 25B	Gauld, B.G.D.D.	Lanark 13A
Erskine, A.U.	Argyll 19B	Forrester, Mrs M.R.	Edinburgh 1B	Gauld, Mrs K.	Moray 35A
Erskine, M.J.	St Andrews 26A	Forsyth, A.R.	Kirkcaldy 25A	Gauld, R.S.R.	Moray 35A
Evans, J.W.	Moray 35B	Forsyth, D.S.	Dunkeld/Meigle 27B	Geddes, A.J.	Dum'/K'cudbright 8A
Evans-Boiten, J.	Europe 48A	Forsyth, J.	Ross 39B	Gehrke, R.	West Lothian 2A
Eve, J.C.	Glasgow 16A-6	Fortune, Mrs E.J.	Aberdeen 31A	Gemmell, D.R.	Ayr 10A
Ewart, W.	Dunkeld/Meigle 27A	Foster, M.	Edinburgh 1A-22	Gemmell, J.	Ross 39A
Ewing, J.	List 6-R	Fowler, A.J.R.	Kirkcaldy 25A	George, Ms J.D.	Orkney 45A
		Fowler, R.C.A.	List 6-I	Gerbrandy-Baird, P.S.	Dunfermline 24A
Fair, W.M.	Angus 30A	Fox, G.D.A.	Jedburgh 6A	Gibb, J.D.	Stirling 23A
Fairful, J.	Hamilton 17A-9	Fox, G.H.	Lanark 13B	Gibbons, R.	Inverness 37B
Fairlie, G.	St Andrews 26B	Frail, N.	Kirkcaldy 25A	Gibson, A.W.	Hamilton 17A-73
Falconer, A.D.	Aberdeen 31A	Francis, J.	Lanark 13A	Gibson, E.	Argyll 19A
Falconer, J.B.	Aberdeen 31B	Frank, D.	Glasgow 16A-17	Gibson, F.S.	Argyll 19B
Faris, Mrs J.M.	Melrose/Peebles 4A	Fraser, Mrs A.G.	St Andrews 26A	Gibson, H.M.	Glasgow 16B
Farquhar, W.E.	Dunfermline 24A	Fraser, A.M.	Glasgow 16A-16	Gibson, H.M.	St Andrews 26B
Farquharson, G.	Kin'/Deeside 32A	Fraser, D.W.	Dundee 29A	Gibson, I.	Kirkcaldy 25B
Farrington, A.	Glasgow 16A-1	Fraser, I.C.	Glasgow 16A-127	Gibson, J.C.L.	Edinburgh 1B
Faulds, N.L.	Edinburgh 1B	Fraser, I.M.	List 6-I	Gibson, J.M.	Hamilton 17A-16
Fawkes, G.M.A.	Buchan 34B	Fraser, J.P.	Hamilton 17B	Gibson, M.	Glasgow 16B
Fenemore, J.C.	Argyll 19B	Fraser, J.W.	Lothian 3A	Gilchrist, E.J.	Aberdeen 31A
Ferguson, A.M.	Dumbarton 18B	Fraser, J.W.	Lothian 3B	Gilchrist, Miss K.	Hamilton 17B
Ferguson, D.J.	Kirkcaldy 25B	Fraser, Miss S.A.	Edinburgh 1B	Gilfillan, J.	Lothian 3B
Ferguson, J.	Lochcarron/Skye 42B	Frater, A.	Dumbarton 18A	Gillan, D.S.	West Lothian 2A
Ferguson, J.A.	Aberdeen 31A	Frazer, R.E.	Edinburgh 1A-31	Gillespie, Mrs I.C.	Argyll 19A
Ferguson, J.B.	Glasgow 16B	Frew, J.M.	List 6-I	Gillies, Mrs J.E.	List 6-I
Ferguson, J.F.	Dundee 29B	Frew, M.W.	Edinburgh 1A-82	Gillon, C.B.	Glasgow 16A-87
Ferguson, R.	List 6-H	Frew, Mrs R.	Kirkcaldy 25A	Gillon, D.R.M.	G'ock/Paisley 14A

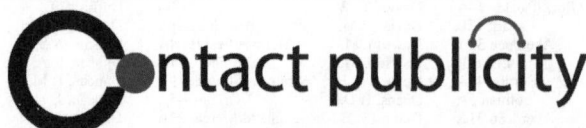

Sinclair, T.S.	Lewis 44B	Stewart, A.T.	Stirling 23B	Taylor, C.G.	Dundee 29A
Siroky, S.	Melrose/Peebles 4A	Stewart, C.E.	England 47B	Taylor, D.J.	Dum'/Kirkcudbright 8A
Skakle, G.S.	Aberdeen 31B	Stewart, D.	G'ock/Paisley 14A	Taylor, G.J.A.	G'ock/Paisley 14A
Skinner, D.M.	Edinburgh 1B	Stewart, Ms D.E.	Glasgow 16B	Taylor, H.G.	Edinburgh 1B
Skinner, S.	List 6-I	Stewart, D.J.	Kin'/Deeside 32A	Taylor, I.	Glasgow 16A-3
Sloan, R.	Glasgow 16A-23	Stewart, F.M.C.	Dundee 29A	Taylor, I.	St Andrews 26B
Sloan, R.P.	West Lothian 2A	Stewart, G.C.	Gordon 33B	Taylor, Miss J.C.	Gordon 33A
Slorach, A.	Edinburgh 1B	Stewart, G.G.	Perth 28B	Taylor, J.H.B.	Irv'/Kilmarnock 11A
Smart, D.D.	Aberdeen 31A	Stewart, J.	Argyll 19A	Taylor, P.R.	Kincardine/Deeside 32B
Smart, G.H.	Falkirk 22A	Stewart, J.C.	Perth 28A	Taylor, T.	West Lothian 2A
Smillie, A.M.	Greenock/Paisley 14B	Stewart, J.C.	Aberdeen 31B	Taylor, W.	Buchan 34B
Smith, A.	Aberdeen 31B	Stewart, Mrs J.E.	Argyll 19B	Taylor, W.R.	Edinburgh 1B
Smith, A.E.	Kincard'/Deeside 32B	Stewart, J.M.	Lanark 13B	Te Whaiti, R.R.	Sutherland 40A
Smith, A.McL.	List 6-R	Stewart, L.	Dunkeld/Meigle 27A	Telfer, A.B.	Ayr 10A
Smith, D.J.	Falkirk 22A	Stewart, Mrs M.L.	List 6-I	Telfer, I.J.M.	Edinburgh 1B
Smith, Mrs E.	West Lothian 2A	Stewart, Ms N.D.	Glasgow 16B	Templeton, J.L.	Kirkcaldy 25A
Smith, G.S.	Glasgow 16B	Stewart, R.J.	Perth 28B	Thain, W.G.M.	Glasgow 16A-122
Smith, G.W.	West Lothian 2A	Stewart, Miss U.B.	Hamilton 17A-76	Thom, D.J.	Greenock/Paisley 14A
Smith, Miss H.C.	Argyll 19A	Stewart, W.T.	Hamilton 17A-40	Thom, I.G.	Hamilton 17A-71
Smith, H.G.	Angus 30B	Stewart, W.T.A.	Dunkeld/Meigle 27B	Thomas, M.R.H.	Angus 30B
Smith, H.M.C.	Moray 35A	Stirling, A.D.	Edinburgh 1B	Thomas, Mrs S.	Angus 30A
Smith, Miss H.W.	Edinburgh 1A-32	Stirling, G.A.S.	Inverness 37B	Thompson, W.M.D.	Jedburgh 6B
Smith, J.A.W.	List 6-H	Stirling, I.R.	Ayr 10B	Thomson, A.	Glasgow 16A-35
Smith, J.M.	Uist 43B	Stitt, R.J.M.	Hamilton 17A-44	Thomson, A.	Hamilton 17A-1
(Smith, J.R.	Edinburgh 1A-52)	Stiven, I.K.	Edinburgh 1B	Thomson, D.M.	Kirkcaldy 25A
Smith, J.R.	Glasgow 16B	Stobie, C.I.G.	List 6-R	Thomson, E.P.L.	Jedburgh 6A
Smith, J.S.A.	Glasgow 16B	Stoddart, A.C.	Annandale/Eskdale 7A	Thomson, G.F.M.	Melrose/Peebles 4B
Smith, M.	Abernethy 36A	Stoddart, A.G.	Gordon 33B	Thomson, G.L.	Kirkcaldy 25B
Smith, M.	Uist 43A	Stoddart, D.L.	St Andrews 26B	Thomson, I.U.	Gordon 33A
Smith, N.A.	Edinburgh 1A-28	Stone, W.V.	Greenock/Paisley 14B	Thomson, J.B.	Perth 28A
Smith, R.	Dum'/Kirkcudbright 8B	Storrar, W.F.	List 6-I	Thomson, J.D.	Kirkcaldy 25B
Smith, R.	Lothian 3A	Stott, K.D.	Dundee 29A	Thomson, J.M.	Moray 35B
Smith, R.	Ross 39A	Strachan, A.E.	Dum'/K'cudbright 8B	Thomson, J.M.A.	Hamilton 17A-47
Smith, Ms R.A.	Hamilton 17A-14	Strachan, D.G.	List 6-I	Thomson, M.	Ardrossan 12A
Smith, R.C.P.	List 6-H	Strachan, G.	List 6-I	Thomson, Mrs M.	Ardrossan 12B
Smith, R.W.	Falkirk 22A	Strachan, I.M.	Aberdeen 31B	Thomson, P.D.	Perth 28B
Smith, S.J.	Glasgow 16A-109	Strickland, A.	St Andrews 26B	Thomson, P.G.	St Andrews 26B
Smith, S.J.	Ardrossan 12A	Strong, C.	St Andrews 26B	Thomson, R.	Falkirk 22A
Smith, W.E.	West Lothian 2B	Strong, C.A.	Edinburgh 1A-83	Thomson, S.	England 47B
Sorensen, A.K.	G'ock/Paisley 14A	Sutcliffe, Miss C.B.	Irv'/K'nock 11A	Thomson, W.	Perth 28A
Souter, D.I.	Perth 28A	Sutherland, C.A.	Hamilton 17A-13	Thomson, W.H.	Lothian 3B
Speed, D.K.	List 6-H	Sutherland, D.	Dundee 29A	Thorburn, R.J.	Buchan 34A
Speirs, A.	Greenock/Paisley 14A	Sutherland, D.I.	Glasgow 16B	Thorne, L.W.	Hamilton 17B
Spence, A.	Moray 35B	Sutherland, Miss E.W.	Glasgow 16B	Thornthwaite, A.P.	Edinburgh 1A-86
Spence, C.K.O.	Dumbarton 18B	Sutherland, I.A.	Buchan 34A	Thrower, C.G.	St Andrews 26B
Spence, Miss E.G.B.	Glasgow 16B	Sutherland, W.	Kirkcaldy 25B	Tierney, J.P.	Kincardine/Deeside 32B
Spence, Mrs S.M.	Hamilton 17A-54	Swan, A.	List 6-H	Todd, A.S.	Stirling 23B
Spencer, J.	Glasgow 16B	Swan, A.F.	Lothian 3B	Todd, J.F.	Caithness 41A
Spiers, J.M.	Glasgow 16B	Swan, D.	Aberdeen 31A	Tollick, F.	List 6-I
Spowart, Mrs M.G.	List 6-H	Swinburne, N.	Annan'/Eskdale 7B	Tomlinson, B.L.	Kirkcaldy 25B
Squires, J.F.R.	List 6-I	Swindells, Mrs A.J.	Aberdeen 31B	Torrance, A.	St Andrews 26B
Steel, G.H.B.	Greenock/Paisley 14A	Swindells, S.	Aberdeen 31A	Torrance, D.J.	Glasgow 16A-12
Steele, H.D.	Annan'/Eskdale 7A	Swinton, J.	Aberdeen 31B	Torrance, D.W.	Lothian 3B
Steele, L.M.	Melrose/Peebles 4A	Symington, A.H.	Ayr 10A	Torrance, I.R.	Aberdeen 31B
Steele, Miss M.	West Lothian 2A	Symington, R.C.	List 6-R	Torrance, T.F.	Edinburgh 1B
Steell, S.C.	G'ock/Paisley 14A			Torrens, J.K.	Glasgow 16A-131
Steenbergen, Ms P.	List 6-I	Tait, A.	Glasgow 16B	Torrens, S.A.R.	Edinburgh 1A-3
Stein, J.	Dunfermline 24A	Tait, H.A.G.	Perth 28B	Travers, R.	Irvine/Kilmarnock 11A
Stein, Mrs M.E.	Dunfermline 24A	Tait, J.M.	Edinburgh 1A-59	Trevorrow, J.A.	England 47B
Stenhouse, Ms E.M.	Dunfermline 24A	Tait, T.W.	Dunkeld/Meigle 27B	Troup, H.J.G.	Argyll 19B
Stenhouse, W.D.	Perth 28B	Tallach, J.	Ross 39A	Turnbull, J.	Stirling 23A
Stephen, A.	Kin'/Deeside 32A	Talman, H.	Falkirk 22B	Turnbull, J.J.	St Andrews 26B
Stephen, D.M.	Edinburgh 1B	(Tamas, B.	Europe 48A)	Turnbull, J.S.	List 6-I
Steven, H.A.M.	Dumbarton 18B	Taverner, D.J.	Angus 30A	Turner, A.	Glasgow 16B
Stevens, L.	Angus 30A	Taverner, G.R.	Melrose/Peebles 4B	Turner, F.K.	Inverness 37A
Stevenson, A.L.	St Andrews 26B	Taylor, A.H.S.	Perth 28B	Tuton, R.M.	Glasgow 16B
Stevenson, D.F.	Abernethy 36A	Taylor, A.S.	Ardrossan 12B	Twaddle, L.H.	Lothian 3A
Stevenson, J.	Edinburgh 1B	Taylor, A.T.	Argyll 19B	Tyre, R.	Angus 30B
Stevenson, J.	Glasgow 16B	Taylor, A.T.H.	List 6-H		
Stewart, Mrs A.	List 6-I	Taylor, B.S.C.	Aberdeen 31A	Underwood, Mrs F.A.	Lothian 3B
Stewart, A.T.	Edinburgh 1A-14	Taylor, Mrs C.	St Andrews 26A	Underwood, G.H.	Lothian 3B

INDEX OF PARISHES AND PLACES

NOTE: Numbers on the right of the column refer to the Presbytery in which the district lies. Names in brackets are given for ease of identification. They may refer to the name of the Parish, which may be different from that of the district, or they distinguish places with the same name, or they indicate the first named charge in a union.

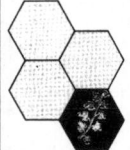

INDEX OF FORMER PARISHES AND CONGREGATIONS

The following index updates and corrects the 'Index of Former Parishes and Congregations' printed in the previous edition of the *Year Book*. As before, it contains the names of parishes of the Church of Scotland and of congregations of the Free Church, the United Free Church and the United Presbyterian Church (and its constituent denominations) which no longer have a separate existence, largely as a consequence of union.

It should be stressed that this index is not intended to be a comprehensive guide to readjustment in the Church of Scotland and does not therefore include the names of *all* parishes and congregations which no longer exist as independent entities. Its purpose is rather to assist those who are trying to identify the present successor of some former parish or congregation whose name may no longer be recognisable. Where a connection between the former name and the present name may easily be established, the former name has not been included, as the following examples will illustrate.

- Where all the former congregations in a town have been united into one, as in the case of Melrose or Selkirk, the names of these former congregations have not been included; but in the case of towns with more than one congregation, such as Galashiels or Hawick, the names of the various constituent congregations are listed.
- Where a prefix such as North, Old, Little, Mid or the like has been lost but the substantive part of the name has been retained, the former name has not been included: it is assumed that someone searching for Little Dalton or Mid Yell will have no difficulty in connecting these with Dalton or Yell.
- Where the present name of a united congregation includes the names of some or all of its constituent parts, these former names do not appear in the index: thus, neither Glasgow: Anderston nor Glasgow: Kelvingrove appears, since both names are easily traceable to Glasgow: Anderston Kelvingrove.
- Some parishes and congregations have disappeared, and their names have been lost, as a consequence of suppression, dissolution or secession. The names of rural parishes in this category have been included, together with the names of their Presbyteries to assist with identification, but those in towns and cities have not been included, as there will clearly be no difficulty in establishing the general location of the parish or congregation in question.

Since 1929, a small number of rural parishes have adopted a new name (for example Whitehills, formerly Boyndie). The former names of these parishes have been included, but it would have been too unwieldy to include either the vast numbers of such changes of name in towns and cities, especially those which occurred at the time of the 1900 and 1929 unions, or the very many older names of pre-Reformation parishes which were abandoned in earlier centuries (however fascinating a list of such long-vanished names as Fothmuref, Kinbathock and Toskertoun might have been).

In this index, the following abbreviations have been used:

C of S	Church of Scotland
FC	Free Church
R	Relief Church
RP	Reformed Presbyterian Church
UF	United Free Church
UP	United Presbyterian Church
US	United Secession Church

Name no longer used	Present name of parish
Abbey St Bathan's	Kirk of Lammermuir
Abbotrule	charge suppressed: Presbytery of Jedburgh
Aberargie	charge dissolved: Presbytery of Perth
Aberchirder	Marnoch
Aberdalgie	The Stewartry of Strathearn
Aberdeen: Beechgrove	Aberdeen: Midstocket
Aberdeen: Belmont Street	Aberdeen: St Mark's
Aberdeen: Carden Place	Aberdeen: Queen's Cross
Aberdeen: Causewayend	Aberdeen: St Stephen's
Aberdeen: East	Aberdeen: St Mark's
Aberdeen: Gallowgate	Aberdeen: St Mary's
Aberdeen: Greyfriars	Aberdeen: Queen Street
Aberdeen: Hilton	Aberdeen: Woodside
Aberdeen: John Knox Gerrard Street	Aberdeen: Queen Street
Aberdeen: John Knox's (Mounthooly)	Aberdeen: Queen Street
Aberdeen: King Street	Aberdeen: Queen Street
Aberdeen: Melville	Aberdeen: Queen's Cross
Aberdeen: Nelson Street	Aberdeen: Queen Street
Aberdeen: North	Aberdeen: Queen Street
Aberdeen: North of St Andrew	Aberdeen: Queen Street
Aberdeen: Pittodrie	Aberdeen: St Mary's
Aberdeen: Powis	Aberdeen: St Stephen's
Aberdeen: South (C of S)	Aberdeen: South of St Nicholas, Kincorth
Aberdeen: South (FC)	Aberdeen: St Mark's
Aberdeen: St Andrew's	Aberdeen: Queen Street
Aberdeen: St Columba's	Aberdeen: High Hilton
Aberdeen: St Mary's	Aberdeen: St Machar's Cathedral
Aberdeen: St Ninian's	Aberdeen: Midstocket
Aberdeen: Trinity (C of S)	Aberdeen: Kirk of St Nicholas Uniting
Aberdeen: Trinity (FC)	Aberdeen: St Mark's
Aberuthven	The Stewartry of Strathearn
Abington	Glencaple
Addiewell	Breich Valley
Afton	New Cumnock
Airdrie: West	Airdrie: New Wellwynd
Airlie	The Isla Parishes
Aldbar	Aberlemno
Aldcambus	Dunglass
Alford	Howe Trinity
Alloa: Chalmers	Alloa: North
Alloa: Melville	Alloa: North
Alloa: St Andrew's	Alloa: North
Altries	charge dissolved: Presbytery of Kincardine and Deeside
Altyre	Rafford
Alvah	Banff
Ancrum	Ale and Teviot United
Annan: Erskine	Annan: St Andrew's
Annan: Greenknowe	Annan: St Andrew's
Anwoth	Gatehouse of Fleet
Arbroath: East	Arbroath: St Andrew's
Arbroath: Erskine	Arbroath: West Kirk
Arbroath: High Street	Arbroath: St Andrew's
Arbroath: Hopemount	Arbroath: St Andrew's
Arbroath: Ladyloan	Arbroath: West Kirk
Arbroath: Princes Street	Arbroath: West Kirk
Arbroath: St Columba's	Arbroath: West Kirk
Arbroath: St Margaret's	Arbroath: West Kirk
Arbroath: St Ninian's	Arbroath: St Andrew's

Name no longer used	Present name of parish
Arbroath: St Paul's	Arbroath: St Andrew's
Ardallie	Deer
Ardclach	charge dissolved: Presbytery of Inverness
Ardwell	Stoneykirk
Ascog	The United Church of Bute
Auchindoir	Upper Donside
Auchmithie	Arbroath: St Vigean's
Auldcathie	Dalmeny
Aultbea	Gairloch and Dundonnell
Ayr: Cathcart	Ayr: St Columba
Ayr: Darlington New	Ayr: Auld Kirk of Ayr
Ayr: Darlington Place	Ayr: Auld Kirk of Ayr
Ayr: Lochside	Ayr: St Quivox
Ayr: Martyrs'	Ayr: Auld Kirk of Ayr
Ayr: Sandgate	Ayr: St Columba
Ayr: St John's	Ayr: Auld Kirk of Ayr
Ayr: Trinity	Ayr: St Columba
Ayr: Wallacetown South	Ayr: Auld Kirk of Ayr
Back	charge dissolved: Presbytery of Lewis
Badcall	Eddrachillis
Balbeggie	Collace
Balfour	charge dissolved: Presbytery of Dundee
Balgedie	Orwell and Portmoak
Baliasta	Unst
Ballachulish	Nether Lochaber
Ballater	Glenmuick
Ballingry	Lochgelly and Benarty: St Serf's
Balmacolm	Howe of Fife
Balmullo	charge dissolved: Presbytery of St Andrews
Balnacross	Tarff and Twynholm
Baltasound	Unst
Banchory-Ternan: North	Banchory-Ternan: West
Banchory-Ternan: South	Banchory-Ternan: West
Bandry	Luss
Bara	Garvald and Morham
Bargrennan	Penninghame
Barnweil	Tarbolton
Barrhead: Westbourne	Barrhead: Arthurlie
Barrock	Dunnet
Bedrule	Ruberslaw
Beith: Hamilfield	Beith: Trinity
Beith: Head Street	Beith: Trinity
Beith: Mitchell Street	Beith: Trinity
Belkirk	Liddesdale
Benholm	Mearns Coastal
Benvie	Fowlis and Liff
Berriedale	The Parish of Latheron
Binny	Linlithgow: St Michael's
Blackburn	Fintray Kinellar Keithhall
Blackhill	Longside
Blairlogie	congregation seceded: Presbytery of Stirling
Blanefield	Strathblane
Blantyre: Anderson	Blantyre: St Andrew's
Blantyre: Burleigh Memorial	Blantyre: St Andrew's
Blantyre: Stonefield	Blantyre: St Andrew's
Blyth Bridge	Kirkurd and Newlands
Boddam	Peterhead: Trinity
Bonhill: North	Alexandria

Name no longer used	Present name of parish
Bothwell: Park	Uddingston: Viewpark
Bourtreebush	Newtonhill
Bow of Fife	Monimail
Bowmore	Kilarrow
Boyndie	Whitehills
Brachollie	Petty
Braco	Ardoch
Braehead	Forth
Brechin: East	Brechin: Gardner Memorial
Brechin: Maison Dieu	Brechin: Cathedral
Brechin: St Columba's	Brechin: Gardner Memorial
Brechin: West	Brechin: Gardner Memorial
Breich	Breich Valley
Bridge of Teith	Kilmadock
Brora	Clyne
Bruan	The Parish of Latheron
Buccleuch	Ettrick and Yarrow
Burnhead	Penpont, Keir and Tynron
Cairnryan	charge dissolved: Presbytery of Wigtown and Stranraer
Cambuslang: Rosebank	Cambuslang: St Andrew's
Cambuslang: West	Cambuslang: St Andrew's
Cambusmichael	St Martin's
Campbeltown: Longrow	Campbeltown: Lorne and Lowland
Campsail	Rosneath: St Modan's
Canna	Mallaig: St Columba and Knoydart
Carbuddo	Guthrie and Rescobie
Cardenden	Auchterderran: St Fothad's
Carlisle	The Border Kirk
Carmichael	Cairngryffe
Carnoch	Contin
Carnousie	Turriff: St Ninian's and Forglen
Carnoustie: St Stephen's	Carnoustie
Carrbridge	Duthil
Carruthers	Middlebie
Castle Kennedy	Inch
Castleton	Liddesdale
Caterline	Kinneff
Chapelknowe	congregation seceded: Presbytery of Annandale and Eskdale
Clatt	Noth
Clayshant	Stoneykirk
Climpy	charge dissolved: Presbytery of Lanark
Clola	Deer
Clousta	Sandsting and Aithsting
Clova	The Glens and Kirriemuir: Old
Clydebank: Bank Street	Clydebank: St Cuthbert's
Clydebank: Boquhanran	Clydebank: Kilbowie St Andrew's
Clydebank: Hamilton Memorial	Clydebank: St Cuthbert's
Clydebank: Linnvale	Clydebank: St Cuthbert's
Clydebank: St James'	Clydebank: Abbotsford
Clydebank: Union	Clydebank: Kilbowie St Andrew's
Clydebank: West	Clydebank: Abbotsford
Coatbridge: Cliftonhill	Coatbridge: Clifton
Coatbridge: Coatdyke	Coatbridge: Clifton
Coatbridge: Coats	Coatbridge: Clifton
Coatbridge: Dunbeth	Coatbridge: St Andrew's
Coatbridge: Gartsherrie	Coatbridge: St Andrew's
Coatbridge: Garturk	Coatbridge: Calder
Coatbridge: Maxwell	Coatbridge: St Andrew's

Name no longer used	Present name of parish
Coatbridge: Trinity	Coatbridge: Clifton
Coatbridge: Whifflet	Coatbridge: Calder
Cobbinshaw	charge dissolved: Presbytery of West Lothian
Cockburnspath	Dunglass
Coigach	charge dissolved: Presbytery of Lochcarron-Skye
Coldstone	Cromar
Collessie	Howe of Fife
Corgarff	Upper Donside
Cortachy	The Glens and Kirriemuir: Old
Coull	Cromar
Covington	Cairngryffe
Cowdenbeath: Cairns	Cowdenbeath: Trinity
Cowdenbeath: Guthrie Memorial	Beath and Cowdenbeath: North
Cowdenbeath: West	Cowdenbeath: Trinity
Craggan	Tomintoul, Glenlivet and Inveraven
Craig	Inchbrayock
Craigdam	Tarves
Craigend	Perth: Moncreiffe
Crailing	Ale and Teviot United
Cranshaws	Kirk of Lammermuir
Crawford	Glencaple
Crawfordjohn	Glencaple
Cray	Kirkmichael, Straloch and Glenshee
Creetown	Kirkmabreck
Crofthead	Fauldhouse St Andrew's
Crombie	Culross and Torryburn
Crossgates	Cowdenbeath: Trinity
Cruggleton	Sorbie
Cuikston	Farnell
Culbin	Dyke
Cullicudden	Resolis and Urquhart
Cults	Howe of Fife
Cumbernauld: Baird	Cumbernauld: Old
Cumbernauld: Bridgend	Cumbernauld: Old
Cumbernauld: St Andrew's	Cumbernauld: Old
Dalgarno	Closeburn
Dalguise	Dunkeld
Daliburgh	South Uist
Dalkeith: Buccleuch Street	Dalkeith: St Nicholas Buccleuch
Dalkeith: West (C of S)	Dalkeith: St Nicholas Buccleuch
Dalkeith: West (UP)	Dalkeith: St John's and King's Park
Dalmeath	Huntly Cairnie Glass
Dalreoch	charge dissolved: Presbytery of Perth
Dalry: Courthill	Dalry: Trinity
Dalry: St Andrew's	Dalry: Trinity
Dalry: West	Dalry: Trinity
Deerness	East Mainland
Denholm	Ruberslaw
Denny: Broompark	Denny: Westpark
Denny: West	Denny: Westpark
Dennyloanhead	charge dissolved: Presbytery of Falkirk
Dolphinton	Black Mount
Douglas	The Douglas Valley Church
Douglas Water	The Douglas Valley Church
Dowally	Dunkeld
Drainie	Lossiemouth St Gerardine's High
Drumdelgie	Huntly Cairnie Glass
Dumbarrow	charge dissolved: Presbytery of Angus

Name no longer used	Present name of parish
Dumbarton: Bridgend	Dumbarton: West
Dumbarton: Dalreoch	Dumbarton: West
Dumbarton: High	Dumbarton: Riverside
Dumbarton: Knoxland	Dumbarton: Riverside
Dumbarton: North	Dumbarton: Riverside
Dumbarton: Old	Dumbarton: Riverside
Dumfries: Maxwelltown Laurieknowe	Dumfries: Troqueer
Dumfries: Townhead	Dumfries: St Michael's and South
Dunbeath	The Parish of Latheron
Dunblane: East	Dunblane: St Blane's
Dunblane: Leighton	Dunblane: St Blane's
Dundee: Albert Square	Dundee: Meadowside St Paul's
Dundee: Baxter Park	Dundee: Trinity
Dundee: Broughty Ferry East	Dundee: Broughty Ferry New Kirk
Dundee: Broughty Ferry St Aidan's	Dundee: Broughty Ferry New Kirk
Dundee: Broughty Ferry Union	Dundee: Broughty Ferry St Stephen's and West
Dundee: Chapelshade (FC)	Dundee: Meadowside St Paul's
Dundee: Downfield North	Dundee: Strathmartine
Dundee: Hawkhill	Dundee: Meadowside St Paul's
Dundee: Lochee East	Dundee: Lochee Old and St Luke's
Dundee: Lochee St Ninian's	Dundee: Lochee Old and St Luke's
Dundee: Martyrs'	Dundee: Balgay
Dundee: Maryfield	Dundee: Stobswell
Dundee: McCheyne Memorial	Dundee: West
Dundee: Ogilvie	Dundee: Stobswell
Dundee: Park	Dundee: Stobswell
Dundee: Roseangle	Dundee: West
Dundee: Ryehill	Dundee: West
Dundee: St Andrew's (FC)	Dundee: Meadowside St Paul's
Dundee: St Clement's Steeple	Dundee: Steeple
Dundee: St David's (C of S)	Dundee: Steeple
Dundee: St Enoch's	Dundee: Steeple
Dundee: St George's	Dundee: Meadowside St Paul's
Dundee: St John's	Dundee: West
Dundee: St Mark's	Dundee: West
Dundee: St Matthew's	Dundee: Trinity
Dundee: St Paul's	Dundee: Steeple
Dundee: St Peter's	Dundee: West
Dundee: Tay Square	Dundee: Meadowside St Paul's
Dundee: Victoria Street	Dundee: Stobswell
Dundee: Wallacetown	Dundee: Trinity
Dundee: Wishart Memorial	Dundee: Steeple
Dundurcas	charge suppressed: Presbytery of Moray
Duneaton	Glencaple
Dunfermline: Chalmers Street	Dunfermline: St Andrew's Erskine
Dunfermline: Maygate	Dunfermline: Gillespie Memorial
Dunfermline: Queen Anne Street	Dunfermline: St Andrew's Erskine
Dungree	Kirkpatrick Juxta
Duninald	Inchbrayock
Dunlappie	Brechin: Cathedral
Dunning	The Stewartry of Strathearn
Dunoon: Gaelic	Dunoon: St John's
Dunoon: Old	Dunoon: The High Kirk
Dunoon: St Cuthbert's	Dunoon: The High Kirk
Dunrod	Kirkcudbright
Dunsyre	Black Mount
Dupplin	The Stewartry of Strathearn
Ecclefechan	Hoddam

Name no longer used	Present name of parish
Ecclesjohn	Dun and Hillside
Ecclesmachan	Strathbrock
Ecclesmoghriodan	Abernethy and Dron
Eckford	Ale and Teviot United
Edinburgh: Abbey	Edinburgh: Greenside
Edinburgh: Abbeyhill	Edinburgh: Holyrood Abbey
Edinburgh: Arthur Street	Edinburgh: Kirk o' Field
Edinburgh: Barony	Edinburgh: Greenside
Edinburgh: Belford	Edinburgh: Palmerston Place
Edinburgh: Braid	Edinburgh: Morningside
Edinburgh: Bruntsfield	Edinburgh: Barclay
Edinburgh: Buccleuch	Edinburgh: Kirk o' Field
Edinburgh: Cairns Memorial	Edinburgh: Gorgie
Edinburgh: Candlish	Edinburgh: Polwarth
Edinburgh: Canongate (FC,UP)	Edinburgh: Holy Trinity
Edinburgh: Chalmers	Edinburgh: Barclay
Edinburgh: Charteris Memorial	Edinburgh: Kirk o' Field
Edinburgh: Cluny	Edinburgh: Morningside
Edinburgh: College	Edinburgh: Muirhouse St Andrew's
Edinburgh: College Street	Edinburgh: Muirhouse St Andrew's
Edinburgh: Cowgate (FC)	Edinburgh: Muirhouse St Andrew's
Edinburgh: Cowgate (R)	Edinburgh: Barclay
Edinburgh: Cowgate (US)	Edinburgh: Mayfield Salisbury
Edinburgh: Dalry	Edinburgh: St Colm's
Edinburgh: Davidson	Edinburgh: Stockbridge
Edinburgh: Dean (FC)	Edinburgh: Palmerston Place
Edinburgh: Dean Street	Edinburgh: Stockbridge
Edinburgh: Fountainhall Road	Edinburgh: Mayfield Salisbury
Edinburgh: Grange (C of S)	Edinburgh: Marchmont St Giles
Edinburgh: Grange (FC)	Edinburgh: St Catherine's Argyle
Edinburgh: Guthrie Memorial	Edinburgh: Greenside
Edinburgh: Haymarket	Edinburgh: St Colm's
Edinburgh: Henderson (C of S)	Edinburgh: Craigmillar Park
Edinburgh: Henderson (UP)	Edinburgh: Richmond Craigmillar
Edinburgh: Hillside	Edinburgh: Greenside
Edinburgh: Holyrood	Edinburgh: Holyrood Abbey
Edinburgh: Hope Park	Edinburgh: Mayfield Salisbury
Edinburgh: Hopetoun	Edinburgh: Greenside
Edinburgh: John Ker Memorial	Edinburgh: Polwarth
Edinburgh: Knox's	Edinburgh: Holy Trinity
Edinburgh: Lady Glenorchy's North	Edinburgh: Greenside
Edinburgh: Lady Glenorchy's South	Edinburgh: Holy Trinity
Edinburgh: Lady Yester's	Edinburgh: Greyfriars Tolbooth and Highland
Edinburgh: Lauriston	Edinburgh: Barclay
Edinburgh: Lochend	Edinburgh: St Margaret's
Edinburgh: Lothian Road	Edinburgh: Palmerston Place
Edinburgh: Mayfield North	Edinburgh: Mayfield Salisbury
Edinburgh: Mayfield South	Edinburgh: Craigmillar Park
Edinburgh: McCrie	Edinburgh: Kirk o' Field
Edinburgh: McDonald Road	Edinburgh: Broughton St Mary's
Edinburgh: Moray	Edinburgh: Holy Trinity
Edinburgh: Morningside High	Edinburgh: Morningside
Edinburgh: New North (C of S)	Edinburgh: Marchmont St Giles
Edinburgh: New North (FC)	Edinburgh: Greyfriars Tolbooth and Highland
Edinburgh: Newington East	Edinburgh: Kirk o' Field
Edinburgh: Newington South	Edinburgh: Mayfield Salisbury
Edinburgh: Nicolson Street	Edinburgh: Kirk o' Field
Edinburgh: North Morningside	Edinburgh: Morningside United

Name no longer used	Present name of parish
Forfar: West	Forfar: St Margaret's
Forgan	Newport-on-Tay
Forgue	Auchaber United
Forres: Castlehill	Forres: St Leonard's
Forres: High	Forres: St Leonard's
Forteviot	The Stewartry of Strathearn
Forvie	Ellon
Foula	Walls and Sandness
Galashiels: East	Galashiels: Trinity
Galashiels: Ladhope	Galashiels: Trinity
Galashiels: South	Galashiels: Trinity
Galashiels: St Aidan's	Galashiels: Trinity
Galashiels: St Andrew's	Galashiels: Trinity
Galashiels: St Columba's	Galashiels: Trinity
Galashiels: St Cuthbert's	Galashiels: Trinity
Galashiels: St Mark's	Galashiels: Trinity
Galashiels: St Ninian's	Galashiels: Trinity
Galtway	Kirkcudbright
Gamrie	charge dissolved: Presbytery of Buchan
Garmouth	Speymouth
Gartly	Noth
Garvell	Kirkmichael, Tinwald and Torthorwald
Garvock	Mearns Coastal
Gauldry	Balmerino
Gelston	Buittle and Kelton
Giffnock: Orchard Park	Giffnock: The Park
Girthon	Gatehouse of Fleet
Girvan: Chalmers	Girvan: North (Old and St Andrew's)
Girvan: Trinity	Girvan: North (Old and St Andrew's)
Glasgow: Abbotsford	Glasgow: Gorbals
Glasgow: Albert Drive	Glasgow: Pollokshields
Glasgow: Auldfield	Glasgow: Pollokshaws
Glasgow: Baillieston Old	Glasgow: Baillieston St Andrew's
Glasgow: Baillieston Rhinsdale	Glasgow: Baillieston St Andrew's
Glasgow: Balornock North	Glasgow: Wallacewell
Glasgow: Barmulloch	Glasgow: Wallacewell
Glasgow: Barrowfield (C of S)	Glasgow: Bridgeton St Francis in the East
Glasgow: Barrowfield (RP)	Glasgow: St Luke's and St Andrew's
Glasgow: Bath Street	Glasgow: Renfield St Stephen's
Glasgow: Battlefield West	Glasgow: Langside
Glasgow: Bellahouston	Glasgow: Ibrox
Glasgow: Bellgrove	Glasgow: Dennistoun Blackfriars
Glasgow: Belmont	Glasgow: Kelvinside Hillhead
Glasgow: Berkeley Street	Glasgow: Renfield St Stephen's
Glasgow: Bluevale	Glasgow: Dennistoun Central
Glasgow: Blythswood	Glasgow: Renfield St Stephen's
Glasgow: Bridgeton East	Glasgow: Bridgeton St Francis in the East
Glasgow: Bridgeton West	Glasgow: St Luke's and St Andrew's
Glasgow: Buccleuch	Glasgow: Renfield St Stephen's
Glasgow: Burnbank	Glasgow: Lansdowne
Glasgow: Calton New	Glasgow: St Luke's and St Andrew's
Glasgow: Calton Old	Glasgow: Calton Parkhead
Glasgow: Calton Relief	Glasgow: St Luke's and St Andrew's
Glasgow: Cambridge Street	Bishopbriggs: Springfield Cambridge
Glasgow: Candlish Memorial	Glasgow: Govanhill Trinity
Glasgow: Cathcart South	Glasgow: Cathcart Trinity
Glasgow: Central	Glasgow: St Luke's and St Andrew's
Glasgow: Cessnock	Glasgow: Kinning Park

Name no longer used	Present name of parish
Glasgow: Chalmers (C of S)	Glasgow: St Luke's and St Andrew's
Glasgow: Chalmers (FC)	Glasgow: Gorbals
Glasgow: Claremont	Glasgow: Anderston Kelvingrove
Glasgow: College	Glasgow: Anderston Kelvingrove
Glasgow: Cowcaddens	Glasgow: Renfield St Stephen's
Glasgow: Cowlairs	Glasgow: Springburn
Glasgow: Crosshill	Glasgow: Queen's Park
Glasgow: Dalmarnock (C of S)	Glasgow: Calton Parkhead
Glasgow: Dalmarnock (UF)	Rutherglen: Old
Glasgow: Dean Park	Glasgow: New Govan
Glasgow: Dennistoun South	Glasgow: Dennistoun Blackfriars
Glasgow: Dowanhill	Glasgow: Partick Trinity
Glasgow: Dowanvale	Glasgow: Partick South
Glasgow: Drumchapel Old	Glasgow: Drumchapel St Andrew's
Glasgow: East Campbell Street	Glasgow: Dennistoun Central
Glasgow: East Park	Glasgow: Kelvin Stevenson Memorial
Glasgow: Edgar Memorial	Glasgow: St Luke's and St Andrew's
Glasgow: Eglinton Street	Glasgow: Govanhill Trinity
Glasgow: Elder Park	Glasgow: Govan Old
Glasgow: Elgin Street	Glasgow: Govanhill Trinity
Glasgow: Erskine	Glasgow: Langside
Glasgow: Fairbairn	Rutherglen: Old
Glasgow: Fairfield	Glasgow: New Govan
Glasgow: Finnieston	Glasgow: Anderston Kelvingrove
Glasgow: Garnethill	Glasgow: Renfield St Stephen's
Glasgow: Garscube Netherton	Glasgow: Knightswood St Margaret's
Glasgow: Gillespie	Glasgow: St Luke's and St Andrew's
Glasgow: Gordon Park	Glasgow: Whiteinch
Glasgow: Govan Copland Road	Glasgow: New Govan
Glasgow: Govan Trinity	Glasgow: New Govan
Glasgow: Grant Street	Glasgow: Renfield St Stephen's
Glasgow: Greenhead	Glasgow: St Luke's and St Andrew's
Glasgow: Hall Memorial	Rutherglen: Old
Glasgow: Hamilton Crescent	Glasgow: Partick South
Glasgow: Highlanders' Memorial	Glasgow: Knightswood St Margaret's
Glasgow: Hyndland (UF)	Glasgow: St John's Renfield
Glasgow: John Knox's	Glasgow: Gorbals
Glasgow: Johnston	Glasgow: Springburn
Glasgow: Jordanvale	Glasgow: Whiteinch
Glasgow: Kelvinhaugh	Glasgow: Anderston Kelvingrove
Glasgow: Kelvinside Botanic Gardens	Glasgow: Kelvinside Hillhead
Glasgow: Kelvinside Old	Glasgow: Kelvin Stevenson Memorial
Glasgow: Kingston	Glasgow: Carnwadric
Glasgow: Lancefield	Glasgow: Anderston Kelvingrove
Glasgow: Langside Avenue	Glasgow: Shawlands
Glasgow: Langside Hill	Glasgow: Battlefield East
Glasgow: Langside Old	Glasgow: Langside
Glasgow: Laurieston (C of S)	Glasgow: Gorbals
Glasgow: Laurieston (FC)	Glasgow: Carnwadric
Glasgow: London Road	Glasgow: Bridgeton St Francis in the East
Glasgow: Lyon Street	Glasgow: Renfield St Stephen's
Glasgow: Macgregor Memorial	Glasgow: Govan Old
Glasgow: Macmillan	Glasgow: St Luke's and St Andrew's
Glasgow: Milton	Glasgow: Renfield St Stephen's
Glasgow: Netherton St Matthew's	Glasgow: Knightswood St Margaret's
Glasgow: New Cathcart	Glasgow: Cathcart Trinity
Glasgow: Newhall	Glasgow: Bridgeton St Francis in the East
Glasgow: Newton Place	Glasgow: Partick South

Name no longer used	Present name of parish
Glasgow: Nithsdale	Glasgow: Queen's Park
Glasgow: Old Partick	Glasgow: Partick Trinity
Glasgow: Paisley Road	Glasgow: Kinning Park
Glasgow: Partick Anderson	Glasgow: Partick South
Glasgow: Partick East	Glasgow: Partick Trinity
Glasgow: Partick High	Glasgow: Partick South
Glasgow: Phoenix Park	Glasgow: Springburn
Glasgow: Plantation	Glasgow: Kinning Park
Glasgow: Pollok St Aidan's	Glasgow: St James' Pollok
Glasgow: Pollok Street	Glasgow: Kinning Park
Glasgow: Polmadie	Glasgow: Govanhill Trinity
Glasgow: Queen's Cross	Glasgow: Ruchill
Glasgow: Renfield (C of S)	Glasgow: Renfield St Stephen's
Glasgow: Renfield (FC)	Glasgow: St John's Renfield
Glasgow: Renfield Street	Glasgow: Renfield St Stephen's
Glasgow: Renwick	Glasgow: Gorbals
Glasgow: Robertson Memorial	Glasgow: The Martyrs'
Glasgow: Rockcliffe	Rutherglen: Old
Glasgow: Rockvilla	Glasgow: Possilpark
Glasgow: Rose Street	Glasgow: Langside
Glasgow: Rutherford	Glasgow: Dennistoun Central
Glasgow: Shamrock Street	Glasgow: Renfield St Stephen's
Glasgow: Shawholm	Glasgow: Pollokshaws
Glasgow: Shawlands Cross	Glasgow: Shawlands
Glasgow: Shawlands Old	Glasgow: Shawlands
Glasgow: Sighthill	Glasgow: Springburn
Glasgow: Somerville	Glasgow: Springburn
Glasgow: Springbank	Glasgow: Lansdowne
Glasgow: St Clement's	Glasgow: Bridgeton St Francis in the East
Glasgow: St Columba Gaelic	Glasgow: New Govan
Glasgow: St Cuthbert's	Glasgow: Ruchill
Glasgow: St Enoch's (C of S)	Glasgow: St Enoch's Hogganfield
Glasgow: St Enoch's (FC)	Glasgow: Anderston Kelvingrove
Glasgow: St George's (C of S)	Glasgow: St George's Tron
Glasgow: St George's (FC)	Glasgow: Anderston Kelvingrove
Glasgow: St George's Road	Glasgow: Renfield St Stephen's
Glasgow: St James' (C of S)	Glasgow: St James' Pollok
Glasgow: St James' (FC)	Glasgow: St Luke's and St Andrew's
Glasgow: St John's (C of S)	Glasgow: St Luke's and St Andrew's
Glasgow: St John's (FC)	Glasgow: St John's Renfield
Glasgow: St Kiaran's	Glasgow: New Govan
Glasgow: St Mark's	Glasgow: Anderston Kelvingrove
Glasgow: St Mary's Govan	Glasgow: New Govan
Glasgow: St Mary's Partick	Glasgow: Partick South
Glasgow: St Matthew's (C of S)	Glasgow: Renfield St Stephen's
Glasgow: St Matthew's (FC)	Glasgow: Knightswood St Margaret's
Glasgow: St Ninian's	Glasgow: Gorbals
Glasgow: St Peter's	Glasgow: Anderston Kelvingrove
Glasgow: Steven Memorial	Glasgow: Ibrox
Glasgow: Strathbungo	Glasgow: Queen's Park
Glasgow: Summerfield	Rutherglen: Old
Glasgow: Summertown	Glasgow: New Govan
Glasgow: Sydney Place	Glasgow: Dennistoun Cental
Glasgow: The Park	Giffnock: The Park
Glasgow: Titwood	Glasgow: Pollokshields
Glasgow: Tradeston	Glasgow: Gorbals
Glasgow: Trinity	Glasgow: St Luke's and St Andrew's
Glasgow: Trinity Duke Street	Glasgow: Dennistoun Central

Name no longer used	Present name of parish
Glasgow: Tron St Anne's	Glasgow: St George's Tron
Glasgow: Union	Glasgow: Carnwadric
Glasgow: Victoria	Glasgow: Queen's Park
Glasgow: Wellfield	Glasgow: Springburn
Glasgow: Wellpark	Glasgow: Dennistoun Cental
Glasgow: West Scotland Street	Glasgow: Kinning Park
Glasgow: White Memorial	Glasgow: Kinning Park
Glasgow: Whitehill	Glasgow: Dennistoun Blackfriars
Glasgow: Whitevale (FC)	Glasgow: St Thomas' Gallowgate
Glasgow: Whitevale (UP)	Glasgow: Dennistoun Central
Glasgow: Wilton	Glasgow: Kelvin Stevenson Memorial
Glasgow: Woodlands	Glasgow: Wellington
Glasgow: Woodside	Glasgow: Lansdowne
Glasgow: Wynd (C of S)	Glasgow: St Luke's and St Andrew's
Glasgow: Wynd (FC)	Glasgow: Gorbals
Glasgow: Young Street	Glasgow: Dennistoun Blackfriars
Glen Convinth	Kiltarlity
Glen Ussie	Fodderty and Strathpeffer
Glenapp	Ballantrae
Glenbervie	West Mearns
Glenbuchat	Upper Donside
Glenbuck	Muirkirk
Glencaple	Caerlaverock
Glendoick	St Madoes and Kinfauns
Glenfarg	Arngask
Glengairn	Glenmuick
Glengarnock	Kilbirnie: Auld Kirk
Glenisla	The Isla Parishes
Glenluce	Old Luce
Glenmoriston	Fort Augustus
Glenprosen	The Glens and Kirriemuir Old
Glenrinnes	Mortlach and Cabrach
Glenshiel	Glenelg and Kintail
Glentanar	Aboyne – Dinnet
Gogar	Edinburgh: Corstorphine Old
Gordon	Monquhitter and New Byth
Graemsay	Stromness
Grangemouth: Dundas	Grangemouth: Abbotsgrange
Grangemouth: Grange	Grangemouth: Zetland
Grangemouth: Kerse	Grangemouth: Abbotsgrange
Grangemouth: Old	Grangemouth: Zetland
Greenloaning	Ardoch
Greenock: Augustine	Greenock: East End
Greenock: Cartsburn	Greenock: East End
Greenock: Cartsdyke	Greenock: East End
Greenock: Crawfordsburn	Greenock: East End
Greenock: Gaelic	Greenock: St Luke's
Greenock: Greenbank	Greenock: St Luke's
Greenock: Martyrs'	Greenock: St George's North
Greenock: Middle	Greenock: St George's North
Greenock: Mount Park	Greenock: Mount Kirk
Greenock: Mount Pleasant	Greenock: Mount Kirk
Greenock: North (C of S)	Greenock: Old West Kirk
Greenock: North (FC)	Greenock: St George's North
Greenock: Sir Michael Street	Greenock: Ardgowan
Greenock: South	Greenock: Mount Kirk
Greenock: South Park	Greenock: Mount Kirk
Greenock: St Andrew's	Greenock: Ardgowan

Name no longer used	Present name of parish
Greenock: St Columba's Gaelic	Greenock: Old West Kirk
Greenock: St Mark's	Greenock: St Luke's
Greenock: St Thomas'	Greenock: St George's North
Greenock: The Old Kirk	Greenock: St Luke's
Greenock: The Union Church	Greenock: Ardgowan
Greenock: Trinity	Greenock: Ardgowan
Greenock: Union Street	Greenock: Ardgowan
Greenock: West	Greenock: St Luke's
Gress	Stornoway: St Columba
Guardbridge	Leuchars: St Athernase
Haddington: St John's	Haddington: West
Hamilton: Auchingramont North	Hamilton: North
Hamilton: Avon Street	Hamilton: St Andrew's
Hamilton: Brandon	Hamilton: St Andrew's
Hamilton: Saffronhall Assoc. Anti-Burgher	Hamilton: North
Hardgate	Urr
Hassendean	Ruberslaw
Hawick: East Bank	Hawick: Trinity
Hawick: Orrock	Hawick: St Mary's and Old
Hawick: St Andrew's	Hawick: Trinity
Hawick: St George's	Hawick: Teviot
Hawick: St George's West	Hawick: Teviot
Hawick: St John's	Hawick: Trinity
Hawick: St Margaret's	Hawick: Teviot
Hawick: West Port	Hawick: Teviot
Hawick: Wilton South	Hawick: Teviot
Haywood	Forth
Helensburgh: Old	Helensburgh: The West Kirk
Helensburgh: St Andrew's	Helensburgh: The West Kirk
Helensburgh: St Bride's	Helensburgh: The West Kirk
Heylipol	Tiree
Hillside	Unst
Hillswick	Northmavine
Hilton	Whitsome
Holm	East Mainland
Holywell	The Border Kirk
Hope Kailzie	charge suppressed: Presbytery of Melrose and Peebles
Horndean	Ladykirk
Howford	charge dissolved: Presbytery of Inverness
Howmore	South Uist
Hume	Kelso Country Churches
Huntly: Princes Street	Huntly: Strathbogie
Inchkenneth	Kilfinichen and Kilvickeon and the Ross of Mull
Inchmartin	Errol
Innerwick	Dunglass
Inverallan	Grantown-on-Spey
Inverchaolain	Toward
Inverkeithny	Auchaber United
Inverness: Merkinch St Mark's	Inverness: Trinity
Inverness: Queen Street	Inverness: Trinity
Inverness: St Mary's	Inverness: Dalneigh and Bona
Inverness: West	Inverness: Inshes
Irving	Gretna, Half Morton and Kirkpatrick Fleming
Jedburgh: Abbey	Jedburgh: Trinity
Jedburgh: Blackfriars	Jedburgh: Trinity
Jedburgh: Boston	Jedburgh: Trinity
Johnshaven	Mearns Coastal
Johnstone: East	Johnstone: St Paul's

Name no longer used	Present name of parish
Johnstone: West	Johnstone: St Paul's
Kames	Kyles
Kearn	Upper Donside
Keig	Howe Trinity
Keith Marischal	Humbie
Keith: South	Keith: North, Newmill, Boharm and Rothiemay
Kelso: East	Kelso: North and Ednam
Kelso: Edenside	Kelso: North and Ednam
Kelso: St John's	Kelso: North and Ednam
Kelso: Trinity	Kelso: North and Ednam
Kennethmont	Noth
Kettle	Howe of Fife
Kilbirnie: Barony	Kilbirnie: Auld Kirk
Kilbirnie: East	Kilbirnie: St Columba's
Kilbirnie: West	Kilbirnie: St Columba's
Kilblaan	Southend
Kilblane	Kirkmahoe
Kilbride (Cowal)	Kyles
Kilbride (Dumfries and Kirkcudbright)	Sanquhar
Kilbride (Lorn)	Kilmore and Oban
Kilbride (Stirling)	Dunblane: Cathedral
Kilchattan Bay	The United Church of Bute
Kilchousland	Campbeltown: Highland
Kilcolmkill (Kintyre)	Southend
Kilcolmkill (Lochaber)	Morvern
Kildrummy	Upper Donside
Kilkerran	Campbeltown: Highland
Kilkivan	Campbeltown: Highland
Killintag	Morvern
Kilmacolm: St James'	Kilmacolm: St Columba
Kilmahew	Cardross
Kilmahog	Callander
Kilmarnock: King Street	Kilmarnock: Howard St Andrew's
Kilmarnock: Portland Road	Kilmarnock: Howard St Andrew's
Kilmarrow	Killean and Kilchenzie
Kilmichael (Inverness)	Urquhart and Glenmoriston
Kilmichael (Kintyre)	Campbeltown: Highland
Kilmoir	Brechin: Cathedral
Kilmore	Urquhart and Glenmoriston
Kilmoveonaig	Blair Atholl and Struan
Kilmun: St Andrew's	Strone and Ardentinny
Kilpheder	South Uist
Kilry	The Isla Parishes
Kilwinning: Abbey	Kilwinning: Old
Kilwinning: Erskine	Kilwinning: Old
Kinairney	Midmar
Kincardine O'Neil	Mid Deeside
Kincraig	Alvie and Insh
Kinedar	Lossiemouth: St Gerardine's High
Kingarth	The United Church of Bute
Kingoldrum	The Isla Parishes
Kininmonth	charge dissolved: Presbytery of Buchan
Kinkell	Fintray Kinellar Keithhall
Kinloch	Caputh and Clunie
Kinlochewe	Applecross, Lochcarron and Torridon
Kinlochluichart	Contin
Kinlochrannoch	Foss and Rannoch
Kinneil	Bo'ness: Old

Name no longer used	Present name of parish
Kinnettas	Fodderty and Strathpeffer
Kinnoir	Huntly Cairnie Glass
Kinrossie	Collace
Kirkandrews	Borgue
Kirkapol	Tiree
Kirkcaldy: Abbotsrood	Kirkcaldy: St Andrew's
Kirkcaldy: Bethelfield	Kirkcaldy: Linktown
Kirkcaldy: Dunnikier	Kirkcaldy: St Andrew's
Kirkcaldy: Gallatown	Kirkcaldy: Viewforth
Kirkcaldy: Invertiel	Kirkcaldy: Linktown
Kirkcaldy: Old	Kirkcaldy: St Bryce Kirk
Kirkcaldy: Raith	Kirkcaldy: Abbotshall
Kirkcaldy: Sinclairtown	Kirkcaldy: Viewforth
Kirkcaldy: St Brycedale	Kirkcaldy: St Bryce Kirk
Kirkcaldy: Victoria Road	Kirkcaldy: St Andrew's
Kirkchrist	Tarff and Twynholm
Kirkconnel	Gretna, Half Morton and Kirkpatrick Fleming
Kirkcormick	Buittle and Kelton
Kirkdale	Kirkmabreck
Kirkforthar	Markinch
Kirkhope	Ettrick and Yarrow
Kirkintilloch: St Andrew's	Kirkintilloch: St Columba's
Kirkintilloch: St David's	Kirkintilloch: St Columba's
Kirkmadrine (Machars)	Sorbie
Kirkmadrine (Rhinns)	Stoneykirk
Kirkmaiden	Glasserton and Isle of Whithorn
Kirkmichael	Tomintoul, Glenlivet and Inveraven
Kirkpottie	Abernethy and Dron
Kirkwall: King Street	Kirkwall: East
Kirkwall: Paterson	Kirkwall: East
Kirriemuir: Bank Street	The Glens and Kirriemuir: Old
Kirriemuir: Barony	The Glens and Kirriemuir: Old
Kirriemuir: Livingstone	Kirriemuir: St Andrew's
Kirriemuir: South	Kirriemuir: St Andrew's
Kirriemuir: St Ninian's	The Glens and Kirriemuir: Old
Kirriemuir: West	The Glens and Kirriemuir: Old
Ladybank	Howe of Fife
Lagganallochie	Dunkeld
Lamberton	Foulden and Mordington
Lamington	Glencaple
Lanark: Broomgate	Lanark: Greyfriars
Lanark: Cairns	Lanark: Greyfriars
Lanark: St Kentigern's	Lanark: Greyfriars
Lanark: St Leonard's	Lanark: St Nicholas'
Largieside	Killean and Kilchenzie
Lassodie	Dunfermline: Townhill and Kingseat
Lathones	Largoward
Laurieston	Balmaghie
Laxavoe	Delting
Leadhills	Lowther
Leith: Bonnington	Edinburgh: Leith North
Leith: Claremont	Edinburgh: Leith St Andrew's
Leith: Dalmeny Street	Edinburgh: Pilrig St Paul's
Leith: Elder Memorial	Edinburgh: St John's Oxgangs
Leith: Harper Memorial	Edinburgh: Leith North
Leith: Kirkgate	Edinburgh: Leith South
Leith: South (FC)	Edinburgh: Leith St Andrew's
Leith: St Andrew's Place	Edinburgh: Leith St Andrew's

Name no longer used	Present name of parish
Leith: St John's	Edinburgh: St John's Oxgangs
Leith: St Nicholas	Edinburgh: Leith North
Leith: St Ninian's	Edinburgh: Leith North
Lemlair	Kiltearn
Lempitlaw	Kelso: Old and Sprouston
Leny	Callander
Leochel	Cushnie and Tough
Lesmahagow: Cordiner	Lesmahagow: Abbey Green
Lethendy	Caputh and Clunie
Lilliesleaf	Ale and Teviot United
Lindowan	Craigrownie
Linlithgow: East	Linlithgow: St Ninian's Craigmailen
Linlithgow: Trinity	Linlithgow: St Ninian's Craigmailen
Lintrathen	The Isla Parishes
Livingston: Tulloch	Livingston: Old
Livingston: West	Livingston: Old
Lochaline	Morvern
Lochcraig	Lochgelly and Benarty: St Serf's
Lochdonhead	Torosay and Kinlochspelvie
Lochearnhead	Balquhidder
Lochlee	Glenesk
Lochryan	Inch
Logie (Dundee)	Fowlis and Liff
Logie (St Andrews)	charge dissolved: Presbytery of St Andrews
Logie Buchan	Ellon
Logie Mar	Cromar
Logie Pert	charge dissolved: Presbytery of Angus
Logie Wester	Ferintosh
Logiebride	Auchtergaven and Moneydie
Longcastle	Kirkinner
Longformacus	Kirk of Lammermuir
Longnewton	Ale and Teviot United
Longridge	Breich Valley
Longtown	The Border Kirk
Luce	Hoddam
Lude	Blair Atholl and Struan
Lumphanan	Mid Deeside
Lumphinnans	Beath and Cowdenbeath: North
Lumsden	Upper Donside
Luncarty	Redgorton and Stanley
Lund	Unst
Lybster	The Parish of Latheron
Lynturk	Cushnie and Tough
Mailor	The Stewartry of Strathearn
Mainsriddle	Colvend, Southwick and Kirkbean
Makerstoun	Kelso Country Churches
Maryburgh	Ferintosh
Marykirk	Aberluthnott
Maryton	Inchbrayock
Meadowfield	Caldercruix and Longriggend
Meathie	Glamis, Inverarity and Kinnettles
Megget	Ettrick and Yarrow
Melville	charge suppressed: Presbytery of Lothian
Memus	The Glens and Kirriemuir: Old
Methil: East	Innerleven: East
Mid Calder: Bridgend	Kirk of Calder
Mid Calder: St John's	Kirk of Calder
Midholm	congregation seceded: Presbytery of Jedburgh

Name no longer used	Present name of parish
Migvie	Cromar
Millbrex	Fyvie
Millerston	charge dissolved: Presbytery of Glasgow
Millport	Cumbrae
Milnathort	Orwell and Portmoak
Minto	Ruberslaw
Monecht	charge dissolved: Presbytery of Gordon
Monifieth: North	Monikie and Newbigging
Montrose: Knox's	Montrose: Melville South
Montrose: St George's	Montrose: Old and St Andrew's
Montrose: St John's	Montrose: Old and St Andrew's
Montrose: St Luke's	Montrose: Old and St Andrew's
Montrose: St Paul's	Montrose: Melville South
Montrose: Trinity	Montrose: Old and St Andrew's
Monzievaird	Crieff
Moonzie	charge dissolved: Presbytery of St Andrews
Morton	Thornhill
Mossbank	Delting
Mossgreen	Cowdenbeath: Trinity
Motherwell: Brandon	Motherwell: Crosshill
Motherwell: Cairns	Motherwell: Crosshill
Moulin	Pitlochry
Mount Kedar	Ruthwell
Mow	Linton, Morebattle, Hownam and Yetholm
Moy	Dyke
Moyness	charge dissolved: Presbytery of Moray
Muckersie	The Stewartry of Strathearn
Muirton	Aberluthnott
Murthly	Caputh and Clunie
Musselburgh: Bridge Street	Musselburgh: St Andrew's High
Musselburgh: Millhill	Musselburgh: St Andrew's High
Nairn: High	Nairn: St Ninian's
Nairn: Rosebank	Nairn: St Ninian's
Navar	Edzell Lethnott
Nenthorn	Kelso Country Churches
New Leeds	charge dissolved: Presbytery of Buchan
New Liston	Edinburgh: Kirkliston
Newcastleton	Liddesdale
Newdosk	Edzell Lethnott
Newmills	Culross and Torryburn
Newseat	Rothienorman
Newton Stewart	Penninghame
Newtongrange	Newbattle
Nigg	charge dissolved: Presbytery of Aberdeen
Nisbet	Ale and Teviot United
North Bute	The United Church of Bute
Norwick	Unst
Ogston	Lossiemouth: St Gerardine's High
Old Cumnock: Crichton Memorial	Old Cumnock: Trinity
Old Cumnock: St Ninian's	Old Cumnock: Trinity
Old Cumnock: West	Old Cumnock: Trinity
Old Kilpatrick: Barclay	Dalmuir Barclay
Oldhamstocks	Dunglass
Ollaberry	Northmavine
Olnafirth	Delting
Ord	Ordiquhill and Cornhill
Paisley: Canal Street	Paisley: Castlehead
Paisley: George Street	Paisley: Glenburn

Name no longer used	Present name of parish
Paisley: High	Paisley: Oakshaw Trinity
Paisley: Merksworth	Paisley: Wallneuk North
Paisley: Middle	Paisley: Castlehead
Paisley: Mossvale	Paisley: Wallneuk North
Paisley: New Street	Paisley: Glenburn
Paisley: North	Paisley: Wallneuk North
Paisley: Oakshaw West	Paisley: St Luke's
Paisley: Orr Square	Paisley: Oakshaw Trinity
Paisley: South	Paisley: St Luke's
Paisley: St Andrew's	Paisley: Laigh
Paisley: St George's	Paisley: Laigh
Paisley: St John's	Paisley: Oakshaw Trinity
Papa Stour	Walls and Sandness
Park	Kinloch
Pathhead	Ormiston
Pathstruie	The Stewartry of Strathearn
Pearston	Dreghorn and Springside
Peebles: West	Peebles: St Andrew's Leckie
Pennersaughs	Middlebie
Pentland	Lasswade
Persie	Kirkmichael, Straloch and Glenshee
Perth: Bridgend	Perth: St Matthew's
Perth: East	Perth: St Leonard's-in-the-Fields and Trinity
Perth: Knox's	Perth: St Leonard's-in-the-Fields and Trinity
Perth: Middle	Perth: St Matthew's
Perth: St Andrew's	Perth: Riverside
Perth: St Columba's	Perth: North
Perth: St Leonard's	Perth: North
Perth: St Stephen's	Perth: Riverside
Perth: West	Perth: St Matthew's
Perth: Wilson	Perth: St Matthew's
Perth: York Place	Perth: St Leonard's-in-the-Fields and Trinity
Peterhead: Charlotte Street	Peterhead: Trinity
Peterhead: East	Peterhead: St Andrew's
Peterhead: South	Peterhead: St Andrew's
Peterhead: St Peter's	Peterhead: Trinity
Peterhead: West Associate	Peterhead: Trinity
Pettinain	Cairngryffe
Pitcairn (C of S)	Redgorton and Stanley
Pitcairn (UF)	Almondbank Tibbermore
Pitlessie	Howe of Fife
Pitroddie	St Madoes and Kinfauns
Plockton	Lochalsh
Polmont South	Brightons
Poolewe	Gairloch and Dundonnell
Port Bannatyne	The United Church of Bute
Port Ellen	Kildalton and Oa
Port Glasgow: Clune Park	Port Glasgow: St Andrew's
Port Glasgow: Newark	Port Glasgow: St Andrew's
Port Glasgow: Old	Port Glasgow: St Andrew's
Port Glasgow: Princes Street	Port Glasgow: St Andrew's
Port Glasgow: West	Port Glasgow: St Andrew's
Port Sonachan	Glenorchy and Inishail
Port William	Mochrum
Portobello: Regent Street	Edinburgh: Portobello Old
Portobello: Windsor Place	Edinburgh: Portobello Old
Portsoy	Fordyce
Prestonkirk	Traprain

Name no longer used	Present name of parish
Skerrols	Kilarrow
Skinnet	Halkirk and Westerdale
Slains	Ellon
Smailholm	Kelso Country Churches
South Ballachulish	charge dissolved: Presbytery of Lochaber
Spittal (Caithness)	Halkirk and Westerdale
Spittal (Duns)	charge dissolved: Presbytery of Duns
Springfield	Gretna, Half Morton and Kirkpatrick Fleming
St Andrew's (Orkney)	East Mainland
St Cyrus	Mearns Coastal
St Ola	Kirkwall: St Magnus Cathedral
Stenton	Traprain
Stewartfield	Deer
Stewarton: Cairns	Stewarton: St Columba's
Stewarton: Laigh	Stewarton: St Columba's
Stichill	Kelso Country Churches
Stirling: Craigs	Stirling: St Columba's
Stirling: North (FC)	Stirling: St Columba's
Stobhill	Gorebridge
Stockbridge	Dunglass
Stonehaven: North	Stonehaven: South
Stoneyburn	Breich Valley
Stornoway: James Street	Stornoway: Martin's Memorial
Stracathro	Brechin: Cathedral
Strachan	Birse and Feughside
Stranraer: Bellevilla	Stranraer: St Ninian's
Stranraer: Bridge Street	Stranraer: St Ninian's
Stranraer: Ivy Place	Stranraer: Town Kirk
Stranraer: Old	Stranraer: Town Kirk
Stranraer: St Andrew's	Stranraer: Town Kirk
Stranraer: St Margaret's	Stranraer: High
Stranraer: St Mark's	Stranraer: Town Kirk
Strathconon	Contin
Strathdeveron	Mortlach and Cabrach
Strathdon	Upper Donside
Stratherrick	Dores and Boleskine
Strathgarve	Contin
Strathglass	Kilmorack and Erchless
Strathmartine (C of S)	Dundee: Mains
Strathy	The North Coast Parish
Strowan	Comrie
Suddie	Knockbain
Tarfside	Glenesk
Tarland	Cromar
Tarvit	Cupar: Old and St Michael of Tarvit
Temple	Gorebridge
Thankerton	Cairngryffe
The Bass	North Berwick: St Andrew Blackadder
Tighnabruaich	Kyles
Tongland	Tarff and Twynholm
Torphins	Mid Deeside
Torrance	East Kilbride: Old
Towie	Upper Donside
Trailflat	Kirkmichael, Tinwald and Torthorwald
Trailtrow	Cummertrees
Trefontaine	Kirk of Lammermuir
Trossachs	Callander
Trumisgarry	Berneray and Lochmaddy

Name no longer used	Present name of parish
Tullibole	Fossoway: St Serf's and Devonside
Tullich	Glenmuick
Tullichetil	Comrie
Tullynessle	Howe Trinity
Tummel	Foss and Rannoch
Tushielaw	Ettrick and Yarrow
Uddingston: Aitkenhead	Uddingston: Viewpark
Uddingston: Chalmers	Uddingston: Old
Uddingston: Trinity	Uddingston: Old
Uig	Snizort
Uphall: North	Strathbrock
Uyeasound	Unst
Walston	Black Mount
Wandel	Glencaple
Wanlockhead	Lowther
Waternish	Bracadale and Duirinish
Wauchope	Langholm, Ewes and Westerkirk
Waulkmill	Insch-Leslie-Premnay-Oyne
Weisdale	Tingwall
West Kilbride: Barony	West Kilbride: St Andrew's
West Kilbride: St Bride's	West Kilbride: St Andrew's
Wheelkirk	Liddesdale
Whitehill	New Pitsligo
Whiteness	Tingwall
Whittingehame	Traprain
Wick: Central	Wick: Pulteneytown and Thrumster
Wick: Martyrs'	Wick: Pulteneytown and Thrumster
Wick: St Andrew's	Wick: Pulteneytown and Thrumster
Wilkieston	Edinburgh: Ratho
Wilsontown	Forth
Wishaw: Chalmers	Wishaw: South Wishaw
Wishaw: Thornlie	Wishaw: South Wishaw
Wiston	Glencaple
Wolfhill	Cargill Burrelton
Wolflee	Hobkirk and Southdean
Woomet	Newton
Ythan Wells	Auchaber United

INDEX OF SUBJECTS

INDEX OF ADVERTISERS

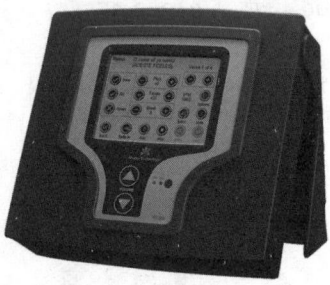